Understanding Physical Anthropology and Archeology

FOURTH EDITION

D0077874

FOURTH EDITION

Understanding Physical Anthropology and Archeology

Robert Jurmain
Department of Anthropology
San Jose State University
San Jose, California

Harry Nelson
Emeritus
Department of Anthropology
Foothill College
Los Altos, California

William A. Turnbaugh
Department of Sociology and Anthropology
University of Rhode Island
Kingston, Rhode Island

West Publishing Company
St. Paul   New York   Los Angeles   San Francisco

Library of Congress Cataloging-in-Publication Data

Jurmain, Robert.
 Understanding physical anthropology and archeology /
Robert Jurmain, Harry Nelson, William A. Turnbaugh.—
4th ed.
  p. cm.
 Includes bibliographical references.
 ISBN 0–314–66758–X
 1. Physical anthropology. 2. Archaeology.
 I. Nelson, Harry. II. Turnbaugh, William A.
 III. Title.
GN60.J84 1990
573—dc20   89–70420
                                CIP

ISBN 0–314–66758–X

Design: Janet Bollow
Copy editor: Stuart Kenter
Illustrations: Barbara Barnett, Brenda Booth, Sue Sellars,
Evanell Towne
Composition: Alphatype
Cover: Photo by Carol Howell

Credits
Chapter 1: 5 Public Relations, San Francisco State University.
H. Nelson. 6 H. Nelson. 7 H. Nelson. 8 Courtesy of Frank Spencer.
9 R. Jurmain. 13 Georg Gerster, Photo Researchers, Inc. 14 (top)
R. Jurmain; (bottom) John E. Hall, University of Miami. 16 Diana L.
Davis, University of Oklahoma.
Chapter 2: 23, 25, 27, 30, 31, 32 Courtesy of the American Museum
of Natural History. 34 Courtesy Library of the New York Academy of
Medicine. 39 M. W. F. Tweedie, Photo Researchers, Inc.
Chapter 3: 44 Dr. Linus Pauling, Institute of Orthomolecular
Medicine. 45 from J. D. Watson, *The Double Helix*, Atheneum, New
York, 1968, p. 215. © 1968 by J. D. Watson. 49 Prenatal Diagnosis and
Cytogenetics Laboratory, University of California, San Francisco.
Chapter 4: 67 Courtesy of the American Museum of Natural History.
69, 70 Malcolm Gutter. 83 Courtesy of *Annual Reviews of Genetics*.
Chapter 5: 111 Courtesy of R. Heglar, photo by H. Nelson. 113 (top)
Courtesy of New York Academy of Medicine; (bottom) H. Nelson. 115,

116 Courtesy of P. E. Schreiber, IBM Research Laboratory, San Jose,
California.
Chapter 6: 136 (bottom) Courtesy of Biological Sciences Curriculum
Study. Permission to use this figure does not constitute an endorsement.
137 Courtesy of the American Museum of Natural History. 143 Re-
printed by permission of *American Scientist*. 146 Courtesy of Biological
Sciences Curriculum Study. Permission to use this figure does not consti-
tute an endorsement. 147 (top) San Diego Zoo photo; (bottom) New
York Zoological Society photo. Drawing: From *Life: An Introduction to
Biology* by Simpson, Pittendrigh, and Tiffany. Copyright © 1957 by Har-
court Brace Jovanovich, Inc. Redrawn by permission of the publishers.
Redrawn from Romer, *The Vertebrate Body*, W. B. Saunders.
Chapter 7: 155 © National Geographic Society. Courtesy Dr. Dian
Fossey. 159 Redrawn with permission of Quadrangle/The New York
Times Book Co. from *The Antecedents of Man* by W. E. LeGros Clark.
Also redrawn by permission of Edinburgh University Press, Edinburgh,
Scotland. 162 San Diego Zoo photo. 164, 165 Courtesy Fred Jacobs.
166 (top) R. Jurmain; (bottom) R. D. Schmidt, San Diego Zoo photo.
167 San Diego Zoo photo. 169 H. Nelson. 172 (left) R. Jurmain;
(right) Courtesy of Phyllis Dolhinow. 173 H. Nelson. 175 (top) R. Jur-
main; (a) © Jill Matsumoto/Jim Anderson; (b) R. Jurmain. 176, 177 Jill
Matsumoto/Jim Anderson.
Chapter 8: 190, 192 (top) Courtesy of Phyllis Dolhinow. 192 (bottom) Courtesy of Jean DeRousseau. 193 Courtesy of Phyllis Dolhinow.
195 Courtesy of John Oates. 198 (a) Phyllis Dolhinow; (b), (c) H. Nelson; (d) Jill Matsumoto/Jim Anderson. 199 (a) Ron Garrison, San
Diego Zoo photo; (b) H. Nelson. 200 H. Nelson. 201 Harry Harlow,
University of Wisconsin Primate Laboratory. 203 Courtesy Hans Kummer. 205 Courtesy of Phyllis Dolhinow. 209 (top) H. Nelson; (bottom
left) Masao Kawaki; (bottom right) Gladys S. Porter Zoo, Brownsville,
Texas. 216 Wide World Photos.
Chapter 9: 221 David Bygott © National Geographic Society.
223 Photo courtesy of T. W. Ransom. 224 H. Nelson. 225, 230,
231 Courtesy of Phyllis Dolhinow. 232 Jill Matsumoto/Jim Anderson.
238 Baron Hugo van Lawick. © National Geographic Society.
239 Wide World. 240 Baron Hugo van Lawick. © National Geographic
Society. 245 (a) Geza Teleki; (b) Phyllis Dolhinow. 247, 248 Courtesy
of Phyllis Dolhinow. 249 From *In the Shadow of Man*, by Jan van Lawick-
Goodall. Copyright © 1971 by Hugo and Jane van Lawick-Goodall. Redrawn with permission of Houghton Mifflin Co. 250 Courtesy Beatrice
Gardner. 254, 257, 258 From George Schaller, *The Serengeti Lion*. Uni-
versity of Chicago Press, © 1972 by the University of Chicago. 261, 262,
263, 264 Courtesy Jon Yellen.
Chapter 10: 275 Redrawn with permission of Quadrangle/The New
York Times Book Co. from *The Antecedents of Man* by W. E. LeGros
Clark. Also redrawn by permission of Edinburgh University Press, Edin-
burgh, Scotland. 276 © 1959 by W. E. LeGros Clark. 280 Courtesy of
Dr. E. L. Simons. 285 (top) Courtesy the British Museum; (bottom)
R. Jurmain. 286 © 1959 W. E. LeGros Clark. 289 Courtesy David Pil-
beam. 292 Courtesy of Dr. David Pilbeam. 293 The Bettmann Archive.
294 R. Jurmain. 300 From *Populations, Species and Evolution* by Ernst
Mayr, Harvard University Press. © 1963, 1970 by the President and Fel-
lows of Harvard College.
Chapter 11: 308 R. Jurmain. 313 M. D. Leakey, *Olduvai Gorge*, Vol.
III. Cambridge University Press, 1971. 314 David Siddon, L. S. B.
Leakey Foundation. 315, 317, 318 R. Jurmain. 319 H. Nelson. 325,
328 R. Jurmain. 334 Tools manufactured by A. Leventhal; photographed by H. Nelson and R. Jurmain. Used by permission of A. Leventhal.

∞

(*continued following Index*)

Contents

Human Diversity   103

Evolutionary Record   127

CHAPTER 7
Issue: Can the Mountain Gorilla Be
Saved?   154

Living Primates   153

CHAPTER 8
Issue: Primates in the Laboratory   184

Primate Behavior   183

Models for Human Behavior   219

CHAPTER 9
Issue: Killer Apes   220

Plio-Pleistocene Hominids   339

Plio-Pleistocene Hominids: Organization and Interpretation   379

Post-Pleistocene Adaptations in the Old World 489

CHAPTER 17
Issue: In Pursuit of the Earliest
Americans 528

Prehistory of the Americas 527

Preface

Archeological material gives life to the fossil bones paleoanthropologists analyze. Bones, in turn, help the archeologist comprehend the artifacts found and the cultural processes under study. This textbook is designed for teaching a course that combines both archeology and physical anthropology, especially from a human evolutionary point of view. Since human evolution is best understood within the context of both organic and cultural evolution, archeology and paleoanthropology are integrated in the text with materials on fossil hominids.

The first six chapters discuss the discipline of paleoanthropology and the biological basis of evolution, as well as present a chronological overview of the evolutionary record itself. The next four chapters on primates lead up to the topic of hominids. They are titled Living Primates, Primate Behavior, Models for Human Behavior, and Primate Evolution.

Chapter 10 begins the section on hominid evolution with a discussion of paleoanthropology. Following in order are chapters on australopithecines, *H. erectus*, and *H. sapiens*. Included in these chapters is material on both physical and cultural evolution. The final two chapters, 16 and 17, are archeological approaches to the Post-Pleistocene Old World and the prehistory of the New World.

Because the backgrounds of students who take the course vary, we have restricted, as much as possible, the use of technical and professional jargon. However, when it becomes necessary to do so, we have provided a running glossary on the pages where such terms are used. This useful device is in addition to the extensive alphabetical glossary in place at the back of the book. We have also included a comprehensive index to facilitate locating desired subjects.

Maps, charts, diagrams, photographs, and other illustrations, we believe, are important learning aids for students; consequently, the text contains an abundance of these. Information that is not easily fitted into the text, but may be useful to the student, has been placed in boxes. Interesting sidelights, not necessarily vital to the course, are placed in tinted boxes.

The authors wish to express their appreciation to Clyde Perlee, Denise Simon and Melody Rotman of West Publishing Co.; Janet Bollow, text designer; Stuart Kenter, copy editor; Lynn Kilgore and Sandy Nelson for their proofing and other assistance, and to our reviewers and students, whose comments have been most useful. Thanks to you all.

Robert Jurmain
Harry Nelson
William Turnbaugh

Understanding
Physical Anthropology
and Archeology

FOURTH EDITION

Introduction

CONTENTS

Fact, Fantasy, and Anthropology

At the beginning of each chapter throughout this book you will find brief discussions of an assortment of contemporary issues. Some of these—for example, the existence and implications of such phenomena as Bigfoot, extraterrestrials, and frozen Neandertals—may seem too bizarre to be discussed in a scholarly textbook. However, scientists and scholars cannot make these issues disappear by ignoring them. Someone in the scientific community must deal with them, hopefully in a rational way. This task often falls to the physical anthropologist.

Since the public is concerned about these topics, we shall address them. You may not always agree with our conclusions (you may notice, by the way, that our own personal biases occasionally emerge), but to induce you to agree or disagree with us is not the point. What you should do is think seriously and rationally about these issues. In light of all the bizarre and ridiculous claims floating around today in pseudoscientific guise, you will do best by adopting the cautious "show me" approach attributed to inhabitants of Missouri. Without hard evidence, no distinction may be made between fiction, fantasy, and fact. Judge for yourself!

What Is Anthropology?

Anthropology is the study of human beings. As a scientific discipline, anthropology is concerned with all aspects of humankind: social behavior, language, attitudes, values, personality, government, kinship, history, prehistory, art, illness, healing, religion, economics, technology, and clothing, to name just a few. Furthermore, anthropology is concerned with such biological aspects of humans as body build, pigmentation, blood types and other biochemical traits, our ancestry and ancestors, and the evolutionary processes involved in our physical development.

Anthropology, therefore, is a **holistic** science, with the entire gamut of humankind as the focus of study. Other disciplines that deal with people—sociology, psychology, economics, political science, history, and others—tend to specialize in single aspects of human activity. Economists, for example, study the production, distribution, and consumption of goods; market systems, and other systems of exchange; but they would rarely consider the effect of religion or kinship on the economic system. Anthropology, however, takes a broader, holistic approach and considers the findings of all academic fields pertaining to humans; in fact, anything associated with humankind is considered within the scope of our discipline.

The wide scope of anthropology is reflected in the two broad categories of anthropology—cultural and physical—which are further divided into subdisciplines, as we see in Fig. 1-1.

The focus of cultural anthropology is **culture**, which has recently been defined as:

> . . . a set of rules or standards that, when acted upon by members of a society, produces behavior that falls within a range of variance the members consider proper and acceptable (Haviland, 1983, p. 31).

ANTHROPOLOGY
anthropos: man
logos: science study of

HOLISM
Viewing the whole in terms of an integrated system; cultural and ecological systems as wholes.

CULTURE
The set of rules, standards, and norms shared by members of a society; transmitted by learning, and responsible for the behavior of those members.

ANTHROPOLOGY	

Physical Anthropology
  Human evolution (macroevolution)*
  Paleoanthropology
    Comparative anatomy
    Primatology
  Human variation (microevolution)
    Human genetics
    Population genetics
      Human diversity (race)
    Human osteology
	Cultural Anthropology
	  Sociocultural anthropology
	  Archeology
	  Linguistics
	
	      or
	
	Behavior Anthropology
	  Cultural anthropology
	  Archeology
	  Linguistics

*See Box 1-1 for these and other terms used in the discussion of the subdivisions of anthropology.

Figure 1-1
The field of anthropology. This chart is a general guide to the field of anthropology and its many subdivisions. Other anthropologists may, according to their own views, add, subtract, or rearrange what is presented here.

SOCIOCULTURAL ANTHROPOLOGY
The study of the entire range of the behavior of a society.

ARCHEOLOGY
(ar-kee-ol'-o-jee)
arche: beginning, ancient
logos: discourse, science or study of
The study of material things (artifacts) of past human life and activities; reconstruction of culture of peoples no longer in existence.

ARTIFACT
artis: art
fact: make
Any object made or modified by humans.

LINGUISTICS
In anthropology, the description and study of the structure and history of language and its relationship to culture.

BIOCULTURAL
A combination of the biological, cultural, and ecological. An approach to the study of human evolution and behavior that stresses the influence of each of these three clusters and their reciprocating effects on one another.

Culture, as the term is used by anthropologists, embraces the totality of the behavior of a society (its physical behavior, social behavior, value systems, norms, mental sets of all kinds) which is organized into an integrated system that is learned and not biologically inherited.

Our cultural behavior cannot, of course, be separated from our biological structure. We are built to walk erect on two legs, which leaves our hands free for performing an infinite number of various tasks; our vocal apparatus enables us to communicate symbolically* through spoken language, which is capable of rapid and complex transmission of knowledge and skills; and we possess a large brain with capacity for abstract thought. Without these inherited characteristics, it is doubtful that human beings would have evolved.

Given this special biological inheritance, our ancestors developed a *way of life* we call culture, which enabled them to adapt to the environment and survive. We perceive our environment through a cultural screen and, unlike other animals whose behavior is more biologically oriented, we are completely dependent on culture for our survival.

The **sociocultural** anthropologist concentrates on the culture of existing peoples, traditionally focusing on the less technologically complex societies of the world. Studying, say, the Yurok, a California Indian society, the sociocultural anthropologist would not restrict investigation to clothing, food, and religious practices, but would include the entire range of Yurok behavior.

An **archeologist** would be concerned with the same society through attempting to reconstruct its ancient culture. Studying the **artifacts** obtained by excavation, the archeologist could learn the kinds of food the Yurok once gathered, hunted, and ate; what kinds of tools and weapons they made and used; what sort of housing they had erected and clothing they had worn; how they disposed of the dead and, perhaps, their attitudes toward death; what goods they traded with neighbors, etc. The archeologist would also study old documents, if available, to help understand the artifacts he finds. He would, in a sense, do what the sociocultural anthropologist does, but data would come mainly from artifacts rather than from informants and actual observation of the people.

As a focus of culture, the linguist would take the description and history of language. Anthropological **linguistics** may be considered a part of cultural anthropology because language is such an integral part of culture. Language is the basic means by which humans communicate, organize themselves, and transmit their culture from one generation to the next. In investigating the Yurok, the linguist would probably look at the entire culture, but could concentrate, perhaps, on the relationship of Yurok behavior and the Yurok language to those of neighboring societies, on analyzing the structure of the language itself, or on tracing the history of the language, or its relation to the culture.

Unlike anthropologists whose main concern is culture, the physical anthropologist, in a comprehensive study of the Yurok, would collect data on all aspects of inherited physical characteristics, such as body build, blood types, pigmentation, ability to tolerate cold, and susceptibility to various diseases. The physical anthropologist would also include notes on such cultural behavior as

---

*Apes—chimpanzees, gorillas, and orangutans—have been taught by humans to use symbols, and a few chimps have taught symbols to other chimps. This is done, of course, only in captivity. (See Chapter 11 for an extended discussion of apes and language.)

marriage and kinship, population patterns, migrations, dietary practices, and other cultural behavior that may affect Yurok biology.

In order to understand the human condition, anthropologists believe it necessary to investigate human biological *and* cultural behavior. Since we are both animal and human, such a broad perspective—what is known as a **biocultural approach**—makes sense. Examining only cultural behavior fails to consider our animal capabilities and limitations, and concentrating on our biology omits the single most important attribute of humans: culture.

This biocultural approach to the study of human beings makes anthropology a unique discipline. As a social science, cultural anthropology is the study of culture—that broad area of learned behavior that humans have developed as their basic strategy for survival. As a biological science, physical anthropology is the study of the biologically inherited aspects of humans. Combining the biological and social aspects, we are able to develop a comprehensive view of the animal *Homo sapiens*, which we call human.

What Is Physical Anthropology?

As already indicated, anthropology may be divided into cultural and physical approaches to the study of human beings. Whereas it is possible to emphasize one or the other, it is impossible to separate completely the subject matter of these two branches.

In order to understand the physical human being, we must of necessity consider the special way of life of this organism. Unlike all other creatures in the animal kingdom, we human beings have developed a strategy of adaptation—obtaining food, producing the next generation, protecting the group against enemies and the elements, developing concepts of life's meaning—that we call

Figure 1-2
Physical anthropologist in his lab.

culture, which serves as a mediator between society and the environment. In order to serve this function, culture must be learned by humans, as contrasted to the direct comprehension of the environment by other animals. All animals, especially mammals, are capable of learning, and nonhuman **primates** are very good at this. The learning ability of the great apes (gorillas, orangutans, chimpanzees) is now well recognized. In fact, primatologists have found much more learned behavior among some primates—especially the great apes—than was believed possible only a few years ago. It might even be said that great ape's ability to learn (and the amount learned) is merely quantitatively rather than qualitatively different from humans. Nevertheless, no other mammal is as dependent on learning as are humans. While possessing a biologically based capacity for culture, we humans must learn behavior anew every generation. We must learn what, when, where, and with whom to obtain food, eat, marry, associate, etc. We must learn what is right and wrong, what to wear and not wear, what weapons and utensils to use and when, and how to relate to parents, cousins, and friends. All of this learning process comes under the heading of culture.

Culture, then, is the accumulation of knowledge, rules, standards, skills, and mental sets that humans utilize in order to survive; that is to say, adapt to the environments in which they live. One cannot imagine humans today surviving without culture. Indeed, such a case is very likely impossible. Obtaining and preparing food, coping with severe climatic conditions, trying to understand the world around us, cooperating with others—all of these normal and daily activities require cultural solutions. Our bodies alone are not adequate for the task of living. We must have material items to help us acquire what we need and ideas to help us communicate with one another.

Cultural anthropology, as indicated, is the comprehensive study of what humans have learned to do, and are doing, in order to survive and adapt. What is the connection between these learned processes and our biological constitution? Was our evolutionary development dependent on culture? Was the development of culture dependent on our biological constitution?

In the biocultural view, culture and our biological structure are critically related. Had we not come from primate beginnings, culture would never have developed, and had our ancestors not developed culture, we would not have evolved our present physical form. The two are inextricably related, and if we wish to learn something of physical anthropology, we *must* understand the role culture has played in the process of human evolution. As one anthropologist has stated it:

> Our present biological makeup is a consequence among other things of cultural selection pressures. We are, therefore, biologically constituted to produce culture, not simply because by some accident we got a brain that could do cultural things, but because the cultural things themselves propelled us into getting a larger brain. We are not simply the *producers* of institutions like the family, science, language, religion, . . . we are the product of them (Fox, 1971, p. 59).

With this introduction, let us examine more closely the field of physical anthropology and then the field of archeology. Although physical anthropologists are not in complete agreement on precisely what is to be included within their field, they do generally agree that two areas are basic: **human evolution** and **human variation**.

Human evolution, the subject of much of this text, especially Chapters 13 through 17, may be divided into two areas: paleoanthropology and primatology.

Paleoanthropology is the study of the fossil remains of our ancestors. Physical anthropologists, together with archeologists, geologists, and other scientists, have unearthed fossil remains in many parts of the world. With their knowledge of **osteology**, paleoanthropologists examine, measure, and reconstruct these remains, often from mere fragments. This has enabled physical anthropologists to propose possible lines of descent from our ancient ancestors to our present form, *Homo sapiens.*

Primatology, as the word suggests, is the study of nonhuman primates, the group (*order* is the technical term) of the animal kingdom to which humans, apes, monkeys, and **prosimians** belong. The anatomy of nonhuman primates, especially monkeys and apes, has been studied to ascertain the similarities and differences between these primates and humans. This kind of study helps trace the evolutionary relationships of human and nonhuman primates. Because of the

PRIMATES
(pry'-mates)
The order of mammals to which humans, apes, monkeys, and prosimians belong. All life forms are arranged in a number of divisions. These divisions (e.g., *class, order, family, species*) include groups of animals or plants.

HUMAN EVOLUTION
Physical changes over time leading to anatomically modern human beings.

HUMAN VARIATION
Physical differences among humans.

OSTEOLOGY
(os-tee-ol'-o-jee)
osteon: bone
The study of bones.

PROSIMIANS
(pro-sim'-ee-ens)
pro: before
simian: ape or monkey
Common form of Prosimii, a suborder of primates, composed of small primates such as lemurs and tarsiers.

Figure 1-4
Early humans possessed a small and simple tool kit. At a modern hardware store, an overwhelming variety of tools, utensils, and weapons is available.

Figure 1-5
Primatologists. (a) Jane Goodall;
(b) Shirley Strum; (c) Biruté Galdikas;
(d) Dian Fossey; *(e) Phyllis Dolhinow.*
[(a), (b), (c), (d), © National Geographic
Society; (e) photograph by Phyllis
Dolhinow.]

Dian Fossey was murdered December 26,
1985, in her cabin in Rwanda's National
Volcanic Park. Her book, Gorillas in the
Mist, *has been made into a film.*

remarkable similarities among monkeys, apes, and humans, researchers have been able, through laboratory experiments with monkeys and apes, to learn what effects certain diseases, stresses, and other conditions might have on humans.

A fascinating area of primate investigation concerns observing primates in their natural habitat as a means of understanding the organism-environment interaction. This kind of investigation, often difficult and dangerous, has been practiced for many years; only recently, however, have primate field studies become so frequent. Perhaps the best-known program is Jane Goodall's work in East Africa, but a number of others bear mention: Phyllis Dolhinow's work with langurs in India; Dian Fossey's study of gorillas in Rwanda; Biruté Galdikas' work with orangutans in Borneo; the extensive research on baboons in Africa and macaques at the Japanese Monkey Centers (Fig. 1-5).

We have been discussing what might be termed *academic anthropology*. There are, however, physical anthropologists who pursue their work outside of (or in addition to) academe in a branch called *applied anthropology*. In this field, the principles and data of anthropology are related to practical situations. Many years ago, for example, physical anthropologists were already applying their knowledge by developing standard sizes for the clothing industry and the military, and more comfortable seats for automobiles and airplanes. Space requirements for industrial workers were also analyzed, and mechanical problems associated with the body, such as the placement of foot pedals and hand controls for machine operators, were studied.

Physical anthropologists sometimes also assist judicial and law enforcement agencies. Practitioners of **forensic anthropology**, as the field is called, may be asked to ascertain the age and sex of a corpse, and how long it has been buried; they may, in some cases, assist the coroner in determining the cause of death.

A final area of physical anthropology that has been a central focus since the beginnings of the discipline in this country might be termed *skeletal biology*. Over the years, archeologists have excavated thousands of human burials from sites all around the world. As the most durable parts of the human organism, the hard tissues (bones and teeth) may endure for centuries (and, if fossilized, perhaps for millions of years).

As experts in the anatomical structure of these hard tissues, physical anthropologists (here usually called osteologists) can, by using techniques similar to those of forensic anthropologists, often determine the sex and the age-at-death of the individual from which the specimen came. In addition, osteologists can, with the aid of specialized instruments, exactly measure hundreds of different dimensions regarding size and shape variation. Finally, osteologists carefully inspect the skeletal material for indications of such diseases as tuberculosis, healed fractures, arthritis, and rickets. This approach, called **paleopathology**, can inform us not only about the history of human disease, but can also occasionally help elucidate the causes of certain diseases as well.

Human variation (Chapters 4 and 5), the second focus of physical anthropology, examines the differences within and between human populations. Within a population such as the Eskimos* or San,† variation occurs in body

*Some Eskimos are now referred to as Inuit.
†San has replaced Bushman as the name of the hunters of the Kalahari Desert, South Africa. See p. 259.

See p. 259.

FORENSIC
(from forum)
Pertaining to courts of law. In anthropology, the use of anthropology in questions of law.

PALEOPATHOLOGY
(pay'-lee-o-path-ol'-o-jee)
pathos: suffering
The study of ancient diseases.

Figure 1-6
Paleopathology. The infectious reaction on the frontal part of this twelfth-century Pueblo Indian skull suggests syphilis. Other diseases are also a possibility.

MICROEVOLUTION
Pertains to minor, gradual changes that may not be observable except over time. (Macroevolution, on the other hand, pertains to great changes in evolutionary history, such as the origin and extinction of species.)

PHYLOGENY
(fy-loj'-en-ee)
phylon: tribe or race
The evolutionary history of a species; evolutionary relationships of organisms; a "family tree."

GEOCHEMISTRY
(jee-o)
ge: earth
The study of the chemical composition of the earth's crust.

CHRONOMETRIC DATING
Dating by methods that give time in years, also known as absolute dating (compared with relative dating). It includes radiometric techniques (carbon 14 and potassium-argon) and dendrochronology (tree-ring dating).

GEOLOGY
The study of the history and structure of the earth, as recorded in rocks.

HOMINID
The common term for Hominidae, the family to which humans belong.

AGONISTIC
agones: ancient Greek contests; therefore, combative
Used by primatologists to describe aggressive, hostile, or threatening behavior.

shapes and sizes; in anatomical structures, organs, and tissues; and in physiological responses to heat, cold, humidity, and exercise. Physical anthropologists are interested in the environmental and hereditary bases of this diversity and attempt to make evolutionary explanations of it.

While all human beings belong to the same genus and species (*Homo sapiens*) and can interbreed and produce fertile offspring, there is a wide variation within the species. Physical anthropologists study these variations to learn how humans have biologically and culturally adapted to the stressful conditions of heat, humidity, altitude, working conditions, and other human activities. As evolutionary biologists, anthropologists are interested in **microevolution**, small-scale evolutionary changes (see Microevolution, p. 93). More recently, anthropologists have considered the probability of rapid evolution that produces new species more quickly than small-scale modifications. Such rapid evolutionary change has been called *punctuated equilibrium* (see p. 92).

As comparative human geneticists, physical anthropologists have studied variations among humans and, in the past, have classified the world's population into physical types called races, a practice rarely followed in recent years.

Paleoanthropology and Other Disciplines

Searching for ancient human remains—organic and cultural—is the work of *paleoanthropologists* (see Chapter 10). Organic material, such as bones and teeth, is examined and analyzed by physical anthropologists; cultural material, such as tools, weapons, shelters, and so forth, by archeologists.

However, as our discussion suggests, paleoanthropology is quite closely associated with other disciplines. In fact, a paleoanthropologist could not function without cooperation from a host of other scientists. For example, in working out the **phylogeny** of our species, one must have the vital knowledge (as accurately as possible) concerning the dates of fossil remains. To obtain this crucial information, the paleoanthropologist consults the **geochemist** for a **chronometric dating** of the fossils themselves, or of the matrix containing the fossil material.

If these facts are unobtainable, then a **geologist** may be able to give some idea of the dating from an analysis of the rock strata holding the material, and may also be able to reconstruct the physical landscape of the period in which these ancient creatures were living. Thus, armed with such information, the physical anthropologist may justifiably speculate about the environment of the now-fossilized creatures, how they lived, how they obtained their food, how they used their bodies, and, to some extent, what kind of stone was available for tools.

For purposes of searching for fossils, the actual excavation is usually the responsibility of the archeologist, who studies the material remains—tools, indications of clothing, shelters, fire, etc.—and attempts to reconstruct the culture of that period.

Recently, primatologists have studied the same group of primates for years, and these longitudinal studies have given them insights into the way of life of **hominid** ancestors. Feeding practices, age and sex relationships, **agonistic** behavior, and other nonhuman primate behavior offer suggestive clues to the transitional period of prehominid to hominid. Paleoanthropologists utilize data from primatologists and archeologists in constructing models for hominid origins (see Chapter 13 for examples of one of these models).

Also of assistance to paleoanthropologists have been the increasing contributions of a fairly new science, **taphonomy**, defined as "the laws of burial" (Olson, 1980). Taphonomists analyze fossil assemblages and "hope to find the means for reconstructing animals in their community context" (Behrensmeyer, 1980, p. 2). Through their analysis of animal bones found at ancient sites, taphonomists can offer information on: the paleoecology of the early hominid period; the relationship of hominids to the animals they hunted (or scavenged); the possible dates of mammalian bones found in the fossil assemblages; the changes that occur to bones after death, and whether these changes are due to chemical, carnivore, or hominid activity. This information may give paleoanthropologists a better picture of the early hominid environment. It thus extends the ability of paleoanthropologists to understand the behavior, as well as the physical structure, of the hominid remains they discover.

In reconstructing the way of life of our ancient ancestors, one must have certain important knowledge concerning what other animals and plants were living at the same time. Such information would suggest clues to kinds of food eaten, the hunting and gathering techniques, the possible materials for clothing and shelter, and other anthropological data about how these ancient peoples adapted to their environment. For this, the physical anthropologist looks to the **paleontologist** and **palynologist** (who identifies plants by pollen samples taken from the soil) to identify the remains of these materials.

Much of physical anthropology deals with evolution, including physical changes within a species and the transmission of physical characteristics from one generation to the next. Scientists from all the biological sciences have contributed insights to evolutionary theory, and geneticists, in recent years, have greatly expanded their understanding of the processes of biological heredity. This knowledge has been of considerable theoretical assistance to physical anthropologists as they speculate about the processes of transition from prehuman to human.

Since cultural information would shed light on the evolution of the human form, physical anthropologists have currently become increasingly interested in how our early ancestors lived. Necessarily, then, we have come to rely on the findings of those cultural anthropologists who work with less technologically complex societies. Living patterns seen today, such as family structure, division of labor, and hunting techniques, suggest ideas and concepts to physical anthropologists in their reconstructions of the life of early humans and the evolution of physical form.

Similarly, primate anatomy and behavior studies done by zoologists, psychologists, psychiatrists, medical scientists, linguists, and others have contributed to the physical anthropologist's exploration of human evolutionary processes.

TAPHONOMY
(taf-on'-o-mee)
taphe: grave or burial
nomy: rules or laws of
The study of fossil assemblages—especially human and animal bones—to reconstruct human activity.

PALEONTOLOGY
(pay'-lee-on-tol'-o-jee)
onta: existing things
The study of ancient forms of life based on fossil bones.

PALYNOLOGY
Identifying ancient plants by examining pollen from archeological sites.

What Is Archeology?

Archeology is a set of methods applied to the study of past human cultures. Although most archeology deals with cultures that existed before the invention of writing, some archeologists specialize in the study of artifactual and structural evidence of later societies, including those which produced written records.

Archeologists are concerned with culture, yet they differ from sociocultural anthropologists in that their data sources are not living people but rather the artifacts and other material remains of earlier cultures.

Culture is uniquely human; it is learned behavior, patterned, and highly perishable. No one has ever excavated a language, a set of religious beliefs, or a political system. However, archeology assumes that the patterning observed in surviving human materials reflects the patterning of the culture that produced them. The remains of a given ancient society, therefore, serve to substantially inform the archeologist about the culture of that society.

Archeology has undergone considerable change over the past thirty years. It has become more methodical, theoretical, experimental, and rigorous. The earlier goals of establishing the chronology of a site, reconstructing the lifeways and history of the people who lived there, and fashioning evolutionary cultural sequences are still important. In recent years, though, more emphasis has been placed on the relationship of one society to another, on society to environment, and especially on the processes involved in ecological and cultural changes.

Archeologists have, in pursuit of their data, developed a variety of approaches that tend to allow them to be categorized into one of two groups: (a) those who work *exclusively* with material remains of prehistoric societies, and (b) those who use written records to supplement their material data. Of course, if written material happens to be available for a prehistoric society (such as Spanish records for Mesoamerica), archeologists will certainly use it.

Historic Archaeology

Classical archaeologists,* academically trained in departments of fine arts, classics, or Near Eastern studies rather than anthropology departments, are primarily interested in ancient history and fine arts. Thus they usually work in the Old World, especially around the Mediterranean, although areas in Southeast Asia, China, and other historic regions have also been excavated. While classical archaeologists use methods similar to those of other archeologists, they supplement their findings and interpretations from the historical records. (The excavation of King Tut's tomb is an example.) Also, they tend to place more emphasis on artifacts as art objects.

Some classical archaeologists, whose training may include divinity school, specialize in the study of Near East sites associated with events mentioned in the Old and New Testaments. This area of investigation may be called *Biblical Archaeology*.

Other historical archaeologists, often interested in the lives of ordinary people, work at sites dating from fairly recent times. Written documents associated with such sites, while consulted, are almost always incomplete. They often lack such basic information as descriptions of ordinary artifacts or other details of interest in analyzing the culture involved. For example, in the reconstruction of colonial Williamsburg in Virginia, historical archeologists were able to provide many details lacking in the written historical record of that period.

The word "archeology" is often spelled "archaeology." It is always spelled with the additional *a* when used in association with classical archaeology.

Figure 1-7
Classical archaeologists often excavate great architectural complexes, such as this temple at Aswan, Egypt.

In recent years, a number of archeologists have investigated contemporary activities of Americans, such as swap meets, drive-in movies, and one of the most interesting, the Garbage Project conducted by Professor William Rathje of the University of Arizona. Rathje's team collected garbage from over 7,000 households in Tucson, Arizona, in Milwaukee, Wisconsin, and in Marin County (California). It was found that the average household "discarded between 7 and 14 percent . . . of its purchased food, estimated . . . to come to about $11 billion a year nationally. This represents enough food to feed the entire population of Canada for one year" (Rathje and Schiffer, 1982, p. 35).

Another kind of historic archeology is *Underwater (Marine) Archeology.* Using diving equipment, underwater archeologists explore ancient shipwrecks and other submerged sites. They are able to recover numerous details of the structure of the ships and their respective cargoes. Some marine archeologists have attempted to excavate sites on the continental shelf, where ancient people might have camped during glacial times, when the oceans were much lower than they are today.

Prehistoric Archeology

Trained in anthropology, most American archeologists fall into this category and are often called *anthropological archeologists.* Since 99% of human history extends back beyond the invention of writing, prehistoric archeologists work with this vast period of over 2 million years. Without the assistance of historical records, prehistoric archeologists pursue several goals (Binford, 1968):

1. Reconstruction of culture history
2. Reconstruction of extinct lifeways
3. Delineation of culture process

Culture history is an account of the growth and development of culture in space and time, and considers such questions as: When and where were the first tools made? Were our early ancestors hunters or scavengers? Who were the first farmers? When was metal first used? Prehistoric archeologists, using material

Figure 1-8
The colonial town of Williamsburg, now a tourist attraction, was reconstructed with archeological assistance. (An example of historic archeology.)

Figure 1-9
An archeologist, using diving equipment, examines underwater artifacts.

data from their excavations, seek answers to these questions, and arrange their data into a spatial and temporal sequence of events.

Until recently, prehistoric archeologists spent much of their time trying to reconstruct the way of life of earlier people from the material remains they excavated: What animals were hunted? What techniques may have been used for hunting and for making tools and weapons? What foods were eaten? What was the architecture of their structures? In short, what lifeways did earlier people follow?

More recently, archeologists have come to feel that such description comprises only part of their work. Also important is understanding the processes of culture; that is, to *explain* what happened in the past. It is not enough to simply describe the lifeways of ancient peoples and compile a history of culture; it is also absolutely necessary to understand the how and the why of past cultural events. *How* did the domestication of plants and animals originate? *How* can the origin of the state be explained? *Why* did the Indians of North America fail to develop the sophisticated political, religious, and economic institutions of Mesoamerica? And that fundamental question always confronting prehistoric archeologists: Did definable patterns of culture growth and change even exist—or was it all accidental?

In addition to these goals, a movement toward developing a more rigorous methodology (led by Professor Binford of the University of New Mexico) began in the 1960s. "The archeologist," Binford stated (1968, p. 14),

> must make use of his data as documents of past conditions, proceed to formulate propositions about the past and devise means for testing them against archeological remains.

Thus, a problem such as the origins of agriculture should be stated in hypothetical terms. The fieldwork would then be planned to evaluate the hypothesis, and the data collected would be used to accept, reject, or modify the hypothesis. The conclusions could then be applied to theories concerning general cultural processes.

14   Chapter 1   Introduction

Ethnoarcheology In order to understand the behavior of the people whose remains they excavated, prehistoric archeologists referred to data collected by ethnographers for descriptions of analogous behavior that might be useful in interpreting the artifacts they had uncovered. Because the **ethnographic** material was not always helpful, archeologists began making their own studies of living societies. They are interested in such data as settlement patterns, population size, the relationship of population to subsistence systems, social organization, migrations, and environment. Many such studies have been made. Much of the description of the !Kung San in Chapter 9, for example, is taken from an ethnological study made by John Yellen.

Just as the finds made by physical anthropologists are studied by specialists in other fields, so there are specialists, working with archeologists, who study archeological material. *Archeometrists*, for example, may be experts in dating techniques, the physical and chemical analysis of artifacts, and human-bone biochemistry. *Archeozoologists* study faunal remains for data on diet, and *archeobotanists* study plant remains for similar reasons.

What Is Human?

Two terms already introduced—"human" and "hominid"—require some clarification. The word hominid comes from *homo*, the Latin word for man:

> From its use in Latin works on logic [and] scholastic language, in the sense "human being" (Oxford English Dictionary).

Whatever its origin, hominid is used by anthropologists as an abbreviated or popular form of **Hominidae**, the animal kingdom category we belong to. Hominid is a useful term since it is neutral, unaffiliated with gender, time, or superiority, and we shall use it extensively in this textbook. Hominidae includes the genus *Australopithecus* (the earliest hominids we know of), who emerged somewhere around 4 m.y.a.* Hominidae also includes the genus *Homo*, with several species (see chart on p. 134 for details). Because **australopithecines**, the early hominids, did not possess all the criteria we assign to humans, especially a complex brain, we are reluctant to place them in the category of humans.

The concept "human" is more difficult to clarify.† What makes human beings unique and thereby different from all other animals is a perplexing and age-old question that has been the subject of religious, philosophical, and sociological inquiry. Human uniqueness is based on two general classes of criteria: biological and behavioral.

From the biological view, the differences between humans and other animals are quantitative. The difficulty is not that we possess physical characteristics lacking in, or radically different from, other animals, but that we possess the same attributes to a greater or lesser degree. To mention only a few: we are larger

ETHNOGRAPHY
(eth-nog'-ra-fee)
ethnos: nation
graphy: a writing or description
The study and description of a culture through fieldwork done by a sociocultural anthropologist.

HOMINIDAE
From *homo* (man) and the suffix *dae*, indicating the group humans belong to.

AUSTRALOPITHECINES
(os-tray-lo-pith'-e-seens)
australo: southern
pithecus: ape
The earliest hominids known; located in South and East Africa.

---

*The abbreviation m.y.a. (also written mya) indicates "million years ago."
†For example, is a fetus human? An embryo? A just-fertilized egg? Such questions may not constitute anthropological problems (or do they?), but they certainly raise matters of serious concern for many people.

Bird Human Gorilla

Figure 1-6
Bipedal vertebrates. An upright (orthograde) posture with a striding gait evolved from an apelike structure. With striking similarities to humans in skeletal structures, apes (a gorilla in this illustration) are neither bipedal nor orthograde. Note the differences, especially in arms (length), legs (length), feet (arch and big toe), and pelvis (height and width).

Figure 1-11
Jesabel, a six-year-old chimp signing "drink."

than most animals, but have less hair; our brain is not the largest in relative or absolute size, but it is very large according to the standards of both these categories. We are not the only animal that is bipedal (birds are, too), but we are the only primates who are so structured—we have a skeleton adapted for standing upright and walking, which leaves the hands free for purposes other than locomotion. All these traits, elaborated and coordinated under the control of a brain capable of abstract thought, give us our remarkable physical uniqueness.

In the behavioral area, human uniqueness is even more noteworthy. Every species, in adapting to its **ecological niche** (econiche), has developed its own distinct behavior, but human uniqueness is revealed in behaviors absent in other animals. For example, our sexual behavior does not include a mating season or **estrus** for females. Or, as another example, most animals build shelters for themselves and eat in ways particular to their species; but among humans, activities like the building of shelters and preparing of food are learned, vary in each society, and can be successfully accomplished only with the assistance of **tools**. Without tools, it is unlikely that any culture could survive.

Our social relationships are not only learned but also vary from society to society. Cultural anthropologists have routinely observed societal differences in marriage, residence, and kinship patterns, in attitudes toward the elderly and the young, and in behavior between the sexes. This diversity is unlike other animal species, where relatively little flexibility occurs in the behavior of individuals. Within species, members of a particular category (such as sex or age) tend to behave similarly. Mammals exhibit more flexibility than other vertebrates, with primates displaying the most of all. Recent observations of the variety of behavior among chimpanzees in the wild, along with the apparent ability of captive chimpanzees to learn sign language in a number of experiments, have astonished scientists. Nevertheless, no troop of chimpanzees displays the degree of variety in behavior found in *any* human society.

One of the most important factors that differentiates humans from other species is our ability to communicate symbolically through language, an activity that, as far as we know, is specific to humans. Chimpanzee achievements with sign language (discussed in Chapter 8) are truly remarkable. Even when these intelligent apes do occasionally sign to other chimps, such a display in no way compares to the crucial reliance humans place on symbolic communication. Furthermore, what chimpanzees or any other animals achieve with *human assistance* is quite different from what humans, as a species, developed by themselves.

What then is "human"? There may well be as many definitions as there are human beings! We suggest, however, that a sound explanation of the term be based on the two criteria previously mentioned: first, a body structured for standing upright and walking on two legs (**bipedalism**), thus leaving the arms free for functions other than locomotion; second, a complex brain that provides the abilities for abstract thought, symbolic communication, and the development of culture as a way of life. With this dual emphasis on biology and culture, our definition once again underlines the biocultural view of human evolution.

ECOLOGICAL NICHE
(econiche)
Environment to which a species is totally adapted.

ESTRUS
(also oestrus)
oistros: sting, frenzy
Period of sexual heat of female mammals; receptive period.

TOOL
A natural object deliberately modified for utilitarian purposes.

BIPEDALISM (BIPEDALITY)
(by-pee'-dal-ism)
bi: two
ped: feet
Walking on two feet as among hominids and some other animals.

Summary

Anthropology is the study of human beings and their primate ancestors. It is a holistic science divided into two main branches: cultural and physical. Cultural anthropology is the study of what humans have learned to do in order to adapt to their environment; physical anthropology, the study of humans as animals, is mainly concerned with human variation and human evolution.

Specialized fields within physical anthropology include comparative human genetics, growth and development, human paleontology, human osteology, and primatology. Some physical anthropologists have specialized in applied anthropology, forensic anthropology, and human paleoepidemiology. For assistance in their research, physical anthropologists work closely with a variety of biological, social, and physical scientists.

Seeking cultural remains of ancient humans by digging for them is the task of archeologists. Archeologists may be divided into two groups: historical and prehistorical. Historical archaeologists include the classical scholars who work especially in the Near East and emphasize an interest in the fine arts. Other historical archeologists work in a more recent time period (the past several hundred years), at contemporary sites and underwater sites.

Prehistoric archeologists, on the other hand, work with sites ranging over a vast time period—from those of nonliterate societies of recent date to those of ancient hominids dating back several million years. A recent trend among prehistoric archeologists is the emphasis on a more rigid scientific methodology, as well as investigating contemporary societies in order to help interpret past events.

Archeologists, in the same way as physical anthropologists, are assisted in their work by specialists in such areas as the dating of artifacts and the analyzing of bones and plants.

Two terms of similar meaning—hominid and human—are discussed. "Human" is defined similarly to hominid, but its definition includes the phenomenon of a complex brain capable of abstract thought, symbolic communication, and culture.

Questions for Review

1. What is meant by "holistic," and why is anthropology a holistic science?
2. Explain the biocultural approach in anthropology.
3. What are the two main branches of anthropology?
4. What are the two main areas of physical anthropology?
5. Define archeology and explain how it differs from physical anthropology.
6. List various subfields of archeology and the approach of each.
7. How does the field of contemporary archeology seek a more rigorous scientific method?
8. How do other disciplines assist paleoanthropological and archeological research?
9. What are the fields of specialization within physical anthropology?
10. How does the concept "hominid" differ from the concept "human"?
11. In what ways are humans unique from other animals?
12. What role does culture play in human uniqueness?

CHAPTER 2

Darwin and the Principles of Evolution

CONTENTS

Evolution on Trial

That it shall be unlawful for any teacher in any of the universities, normals and all other public schools of the State . . . to teach any theory that denies the story of the Divine Creation of man as taught in the Bible, and to teach instead that man has descended from a lower order of animals (Section 1 of the Butler Act, March 21, 1925, State of Tennessee).

In May, 1925, several leading citizens from Dayton, Tennessee (population 1,800) were sitting around Doc Robinson's drug store, the town's social center, discussing various and sundry topics of great import. To settle an argument, they sent for John T. Scopes, a local high school coach and teacher of algebra, physics, and chemistry. Scopes came over from his tennis game not realizing that he was about to enter the most dramatic period of his life, one he would never forget.

One of the men, a local businessman, said, "John, we've been arguing, and I said that nobody could teach biology without teaching evolution."

"That's right," said Scopes, and showed them the biology textbook that had been adopted by the State of Tennessee.

"Then, you've been violating the law," Doc Robinson said.

Although he did not teach biology, Scopes had, one day in April, substituted for the principal, who did. Technically, therefore, it could be said that he had taught biology and had thus violated the newly passed law.

As the discussion continued, and it became clear that Scopes felt strongly on the matter of academic freedom, Robinson asked him whether he would stand for a test case. Scopes said he

would, whereupon Robinson called the *Chattanooga News* and reported, "This is F. E. Robinson in Dayton. I'm chairman of the school board here. We've just arrested a man for teaching evolution." The man who had been "arrested" finished his soft drink and returned to his tennis game. (Writing forty years later in 1967, Scopes suggested that the trial was deliberately planned by Dayton businessmen to put that town on the map and bring in business, which is precisely what happened.)

The "arrest" made front page news across the country. William Jennings Bryan—three times Democratic nominee for President, Secretary of State under Woodrow Wilson, famous for his Cross of Gold speech at the Democratic convention of 1896, and acknowledged leader of the crusade against Darwinism—offered his services to the prosecution as the representative of the World's Christian Fundamentals Association.

With Bryan's entry into the fray, Clarence Darrow, nationally known labor and criminal lawyer, offered his services to the defense without fee or expense. The American Civil Liberties Union was in charge of the case for the defense and provided other well-known lawyers: John Randolph Neal, Arthur Garfield Hayes, and Dudley Field Malone.

In the weeks before the trial, the town of Dayton took on the atmosphere of a circus. The trial was referred to as "the monkey business." Merchants used monkey motifs in their advertising: little cotton apes were featured in store windows; pins that read "Your Old Man's a Monkey" could be purchased; and at Doc Robinson's drug store, a monkey fizz was available for refreshment from the summer heat. Hot dog stands, lemonade peddlers, booths selling books on biology or religion, and Bryan's truck, equipped with a loudspeaker touting Florida real estate,

all added spice and noise to the carnival.

The trial began on Friday, July 10, 1925, with Judge John T. Raulston on the bench, and ended on Tuesday, July 21. It was clear from the start that Scopes would be convicted. The court, strongly religious, consistently favored the prosecution and forbade the testimony of expert defense witnesses—scientists—who were prepared to prove that evolution was a valid scientific concept. The prosecution insisted that the trial was not about the validity of evolution but that the real issue was simply whether or not Scopes had violated the law.

There were magnificent speeches. On Monday, July 13, in his support of the motion to squash the indictment against Scopes, Darrow displayed his famous forensic ability, and the crowded courthouse hung on every word. If the teaching of evolution is outlawed, he argued, then:

After a while, Your Honor, it is the setting of man against man and creed against creed until with flying banners and beating drums we are marching backward to the glorious age of the sixteenth century when bigots lighted faggots to burn the men who dared to bring any intelligence and enlightenment and culture to the human mind.

On Thursday, Bryan stood up to speak against the admissibility of scientific testimony. The crowd had been waiting for this moment, but they were to be disappointed. Bryan was an old man, not the man he once was; the fire was missing. H. L. Mencken, the acidulous reporter from the *Baltimore Sun*, attended the trial and wrote:

His . . . speech was a grotesque performance and downright touching in its imbecility. Its climax came when he launched into a furious denunciation of the doctrine that man is a mammal. It seemed a sheer impossibility that any literate man should stand up in public and discharge any such nonsense. Yet the poor old fellow did it. . . . To call man mammal, it appeared, was to flout the revelation of God (Tompkins, 1965, p. 48).

Malone replied to Bryan, his former superior officer at the State Department, and his eloquence carried the day even among the spectators who fully supported Bryan. Bryan himself recognized this when he told Malone afterwards, "Dudley, that was the greatest speech I have ever heard."

The climax of the trial came on Monday afternoon, July 20, when the defense called Bryan as an expert witness on the Bible. The prosecutors immediately jumped to their feet protesting, aware of the danger inherent in the questions that might be asked and the answers that might be given. However, Bryan himself insisted on testifying, perhaps because he felt compelled to defend the Bible and "show up" the evolutionists. It was an opportunity not to be missed.

Darrow's strategy was to question Bryan about his literal interpretation of the Bible. The Bible, Bryan held, was true, every word of it, every comma. Every miracle recorded in the Bible actually happened. And it was on these points that Darrow broke Bryan, made him appear foolish, unthinking, and even a "traitor" to the cause of fundamentalism. At one point Darrow asked, "Do you think the earth was made in six days?"

"Not in six days of twenty-four hours," Bryan replied.

The crowd gasped at this heresy. The Bible read six days, and a day was obviously twenty-four hours. What was Bryan thinking of? Toward the end of the afternoon Darrow brought up the Bible story of Adam and Eve and the serpent. Had God punished the serpent by making him crawl on his belly? Bryan said he believed that. Then, Darrow asked, "Have you any idea how the snake went before that time?"

"No, sir."

"Do you know whether he walked on his tail or not?"

"No, sir, I have no way to know."

The crowd laughed and Bryan's hands nervously trembled and his lips quivered. *

The trial ended the next day. The jury (excused for most of the trial) was called back and charged to decide whether Scopes had violated the law; no other question was to be considered. The jury took but a short time and returned with their verdict—guilty! Judge Raulston fined Scopes $100 and the trial closed.

The case was appealed to the Tennessee Supreme Court, which handed down its decision on January 15, 1927. The Court upheld the Butler Act and also recommended that the State drop the indictment against Scopes on the technicality that the judge had imposed the fine, instead of the jury, as Tennessee law required. The Court thus made it impossible to appeal the case before the United States Supreme Court.

Update

In the sixty years since the Scopes trial, religious fundamentalists have not ceased their attempts to remove the teaching of evolution from the public schools of the nation. Known as "creationists" because they explain the existence of the universe, energy, and life as a result of sudden creation, they are determined either to eliminate the teaching of evolution or to introduce anti-evolutionary subject matter. In a ploy developed in recent years, creationists have insisted that "creation-science" is just as much science as what they term "evolution science." Therefore, they claim, in the interest of fair play, a balanced view should be offered to students—if evolution is taught as science, then creationism should also be taught as science.

So-called "creation-science" is not science as we know it.† Far from the spirit of science, creationists, for instance, assert that their position is absolute and not subject to error. Therefore, it is impossible for any sort of evidence to alter their position, for anything that might modify creationism is automatically rejected.

Creationists have been active in state legislatures, promoting the passage of laws mandating the inclusion of creationism in school curricula wherever evolution is taught. To this effect, creationists successfully lobbied the legislature of the State of Arkansas, which passed Act 590 in March of 1981.

As used in the Act, "creation-science" means the scientific "evidence" for creation, as well as inferences based on such evidence, including the

1. sudden creation of the universe, energy, and life, from nothing
2. inadequacy of mutation and natural selection to explain how all living kinds developed from a single organism
3. changes of forms of life only within fixed limits of originally created kinds of plants and animals
4. idea of a separate ancestry for humans and apes
5. explanation of the earth's geology by catastrophism
6. concept of a relatively recent inception of the earth and living kinds

The American Civil Liberties Union (ACLU) challenged Act 590 (also known as the "Balanced Treatment for Creation-Science and Evolution-Science Act") in the case of *McLean* vs. *Arkansas State Board of Education*. The case came to trial in federal district court in December, 1981. The ACLU contended that Act 590 infringed on three separate rights

---

*A diabetic and in ill health, Bryan died on Sunday, July 26, five days after the trial ended.

†See Eldridge, Niles, "Creationism Isn't Science," *The New Republic*, Apr. 14, 1981, pp. 15–20.

guaranteed under the United States Constitution:

1. separation of church and state, guaranteed by the First Amendment
2. academic freedom, guaranteed by the First Amendment
3. the right to due process under the Fourteenth Amendment: The Act was vague, and teachers could be placed in jeopardy since it would be easy to misinterpret such phrases as "fixed limits" and "kinds of plants and animals," these being too unclear for identification

On January 5, 1982, Judge William Ray Overton ruled against the State of Arkansas. He found that "creation science has no scientific merit or education value," that "a theory that is by its own terms dogmatic, absolutist and never subject to revision is not a scientific theory," and that "since creation is not science, the conclusion is inescapable that the only real effect of Act 590 is the advancement of religion."

Judge Overton declared that the Act violated the Constitution's guarantees of separation of church and state, and he accompanied his decision with an injunction against the enforcement of the Act.

Further Update

A related contemporary event involving a textbook occurred in Louisiana. In 1981, the Louisiana state legislature passed a law stating that if the concept of evolution were included in the biology text used, then a school district could add the teaching of creationism to its curriculum. This law was challenged and, on appeal, reached the U.S. Supreme Court.

On June 19, 1987, declaring the Louisiana law unconstitutional, the U.S. Supreme Court ruled (seven to two in favor) that teaching creationist theory alongside evolution is not required, and that the purpose of the Louisiana legislature was clearly to ad-

vance the religious viewpoint that a supernatural being created humankind.

In August, 1987, another textbook case, Smith v. Wallace, was decided in Alabama by the 11th U.S. Circuit Court of Appeals. Judge W. Brevard Hand had ruled that 44 textbooks, used in Alabama public schools, promoted "secular humanism"—which may be defined as a "nonsupernaturally based ethical and moral philosophy"*—as a religion. Hand, well known to be sympathetic to the plaintiffs, ruled that the parents had a constitutional right to prevent their children from being exposed to books they found repugnant to their children.

In overturning Hand's decision, the appellate court said that the books did not violate the First Amendment and concluded there was no evidence that

omission of certain facts regarding religion from these textbooks of itself constituted an advancement of secular humanism or an active hostility towards theistic religion.

Still another textbook case originated in Hawkins County, Tennessee, about 150 miles northeast of Dayton, Tenn., where the Scopes trial, discussed above, was tried. This case, Mozert v. Hawkins County Public Schools, was also decided in August, 1987, by the 6th U.S. Circuit Court of Appeals. Several Fundamentalist families had sued the Hawkins County School Board claiming a number of books were anti-Christian and antagonistic toward their religion. These unsuitable books included such titles as *Wizard of Oz, Cinderella, Jack and Jill, the Diary of Anne Frank, Three Little*

*Contributed by Dr. Eugenie C. Scott, Executive Director, The National Center for Science Education, Inc., Box 9477, 1218 Milvia St., Berkeley, CA 94709, (415) 528-2521. As the name of the organization suggests, NCSE promotes the teaching of science and maintains continuing opposition to the introduction of creationism into the classroom.

Pigs, and many others traditionally used in the nation's public schools.

Overturning the lower court decision, appellate court Chief Judge Lively stated there was no proof

that any plaintiff student was ever called upon to say or do anything that required the student to affirm or deny a religious belief or to engage or refrain from engaging in any act either required or forbidden by the students' religious convictions.

Both of the two latter decisions are being appealed.

SOURCES FOR ISSUE:

Ginger, Ray. *Six Days or Forever?*, Boston: Beacon Press, 1958.

Scopes, John T. and James Presley. *Center of the Storm*, New York: Holt, Rinehart and Winston, 1967.

Tompkins, Jerry R. (ed.). *D-Days at Dayton*, Baton Rouge: Louisiana State University Press, 1965.

SOURCES FOR UPDATE:

City newspapers carry news of U.S. Supreme Court decisions, as do weekly news magazines. *Science*, *Science News*, and other science journals frequently include articles on creationists and their attempts to influence textbook adoption and assignment, especially in the area of science courses. *Creation/Evolution*, (7 Harwood Drive, P.O. Box 146, Amherst, NY 14226–0146) is a small journal published four times a year. It is "dedicated to promoting evolutionary science."

Introduction

Evolution—in the sense of the *origin of plant and animal species through a process of development from earlier forms*—was not a view seriously considered by medieval philosophers. Scholarly interpretations of the Bible, especially Genesis, had given European philosophers a *Weltanschauung* (world view) in which change had no place. Evolution, therefore, is an idea that would not only have been considered heretical, but "common sense" of the era would have labeled it ridiculous.

Nevertheless, scholars of the fifteenth, sixteenth, and seventeenth centuries demonstrated that the universe—planets (including the earth) and stars (including the sun)—was not rigidly fixed, and the belief that organic beings were similarly not fixed was being entertained. Attempts to explain how the process of evolution worked failed until Charles Darwin, in the nineteenth century, succeeded with his theory of natural selection.

How we understand evolution today is drawn directly from Darwin's work, as well as from contributions, mainly from the field of genetics, made during the twentieth century. Our focus throughout this text is *human evolution*, but, in this chapter, we discuss the general evolutionary principles applicable to all organisms. The evolutionary process is a unified one, and the principles are the same for all life forms, including humans. We will examine the changes in intellectual thought that led to the theory of natural selection, acclaimed as the most important scientific contribution of the nineteenth century. First, though, let's take a brief look at the man responsible for this theory: Charles Darwin.

Darwin's Life

Figure 2-1
Charles Darwin (at age 32).

Charles Darwin (1809–1882) was the son of Dr. Robert and Susannah Darwin and grandson of the eminent Dr. Erasmus Darwin. Charles, one of six children, was thought by his family and by himself to be a "very ordinary boy." As an ordinary boy, he did the usual things (collecting shells, stamps, coins) and, at school, he displayed no special inclination for scholarship.

Because he showed little interest in, or aptitude for, anything particular (with the possible exception of science), Dr. Darwin decided that Charles should study medicine at Edinburgh. After two years, Charles conceded medicine was not for him, and instead turned to hunting and fishing, which he thoroughly enjoyed. His father complained that Charles was only interested in "shooting, dogs and rat-catching."

For sons who had no discernible academic leanings, parents could, as a last refuge, turn them to the church. Although indifferent to religion, Charles dutifully took up residence at Christ's College, Cambridge, in 1828, at the age of 19. While ostensibly enrolled in theology, Charles became interested in what we today call natural science. He became a constant companion of the Reverend John Stevens Henslow, professor of botany, and often joined his classes in their botanical excursions.

Figure 2-2
Examples of some of Darwin's finches. Note the similarities and differences in beak structure.

Darwin was graduated in 1831, at the age of 22, not with a distinguished record, but one good enough to satisfy his family, and he could look forward to a serene future as a country cleric. However, that was not to be, for something happened that summer that Darwin referred to as "the most important event of my life."

He received a letter from his friend, Professor Henslow, informing him that he had recommended Darwin as the best-qualified person he knew for the position of naturalist on a scientific expedition that would circle the globe. (See Box 2-1.) Darwin was willing, even eager, for this opportunity to combine travel with the pursuit of botany, zoology, and geology, but his father objected and Charles regretfully declined. However, Charles found a champion in his uncle, Josiah Wedgewood, who persuaded Dr. Darwin that the voyage would be desirable. Dr. Darwin reluctantly gave his consent. With mixed feelings of elation and dismay, Charles set sail on board the H.M.S. *Beagle*, December 27, 1831, on a voyage where attacks of seasickness would place him in his hammock for days on end. Having begun the voyage as a clergyman (at least such had been his intent) with hobbies of zoology, botany, and geology, Darwin found, within a short time, that his true calling was natural science. Through his industrious and diligent work of collecting, arranging, and dissecting specimens, Darwin matured from an amateur observer into a professional naturalist.

Darwin went aboard the *Beagle* not as an evolutionist but as a believer in the fixity of species. His observations, however, quickly raised evolutionary suspicions in his mind. As early as 1832, for example, he noted in his diary that a snake with rudimentary hind limbs marked "the passage by which Nature joins the lizards to the snakes." He came across fossils of ancient giant animals that looked, except for size, very much like forms living in the same vicinity, and wondered whether the fossils were the ancestors of those forms. He observed that the Andean Mountain Range constituted a natural barrier to life and, as might be expected according to geologists, flora and fauna on opposite sides of the range differed.

The stopover at the Galápagos Islands profoundly impressed Darwin. He noted that the flora and fauna of South America were very similar—yet dissimilar—to those of the Galápagos. Even more surprising, the inhabitants of the various islands differed slightly. The thirteen kinds of finches resembled one another in the structure of their beaks, body forms, and plumage, and yet each constituted a separate species (but only one species existed on the mainland) despite the fact that few geographic differences existed among the islands. What, he asked himself, could cause this modification if the physical geography and climate were not responsible? These observations, and the questions they raised, caused Darwin to wonder whether the theory of fixity of species was a valid one after all.

This abbreviated account of Darwin and his research on the *Beagle* does not do justice to the significant role the voyage played in Darwin's intellectual growth. He returned to England on board the *Beagle* on October 2, 1836, just short of five years from the date he sailed, a more mature and serious scientist.

In 1842, Darwin wrote a short summary of his views on natural selection and revised it in 1844. The 1844 sketch was surprisingly similar to the argument he presented fifteen years later in *On the Origin of Species*, but Darwin did not feel he had sufficient data to support his views, and he continued to accumulate facts.

Time passed. In 1855, an article by Alfred Russel Wallace on the succession of species impressed Darwin because it supported his views on species' mutability.

BOX 2-1

Darwin: Naturalist or Companion?

Robert Fitzroy, Captain of the *Beagle*.

Was Darwin invited to sail aboard the H.M.S. *Beagle* as a naturalist or as a companion to **Captain Fitzroy**?* Since Darwin had been recommended as a naturalist, and had acted in that capacity throughout the *Beagle*'s five-year voyage (during which he developed ideas that ultimately led to his concept of natural selection), the answer has always seemed obvious.

However, Dr. Stephen Jay Gould (1976) has suggested that Darwin was invited to be Fitzroy's companion, and that the position of naturalist was an enticement to that

*The captain's name is spelled variously as Fitz-Roy, FitzRoy, and Fitzroy.

end. The reasons, says Gould, were that a captain in the British navy was not permitted to speak to members of his crew except on ship's business; that Fitzroy was aware of the awful loneliness of a captain who had to dine by himself in his own cabin; and that he, Fitzroy, was not too stable. Therefore, someone to share his cabin, meals, and conversation was absolutely mandatory. For this, Fitzroy required someone of the proper social rank—a gentleman—and in order to persuade such a person, the captain offered the position of naturalist.

The interesting and important aspect of this, according to Gould, is that Darwin's view of evolution may have grown out of the strained relationship that developed between the two men. They argued on several subjects: slavery, for one; God and nature, for another. Fitzroy's dogmatic assertions about the universe, suggests Gould, acted as the catalyst that drove Darwin to an opposite view, leading to "an evolutionary theory based on chance variation and natural selection by a largely external environment: a rigidly materialistic (and basically atheistic) version of evolution."

Today it is difficult to know why Fitzroy wanted a naturalist on board. He has been described as "a public spirited and zealous officer." Since the purpose of the *Beagle*'s voyage was entirely scientific, it is certainly possible that Fitzroy may have been serious in his search for a naturalist who might also—as a subordinate function— serve as companion.

Darwin's correspondence to his friend and professor Dr. Henslow (who first recommended him for the position), and to his father, seems to leave no doubt about why he thought he was sailing: to work as a naturalist. Darwin was aware that he was expected to be a companion to Captain Fitzroy (Henslow mentioned it in his letter to Darwin), but this function must have impressed him very little. He never referred to it in his correspondence.

Darwin was not disturbed at this time by the possibility that the publication of his own theory might be anticipated. Darwin had been encouraged by his close friends, especially Lyell (see p. 34) and Hooker (a well-known botanist) to publish his "theory," but he declined because he felt there was much more evidence to collect. His friends cautioned him that someone else might publish before he did, and, indeed, his friends' warning was realized in June, 1858, when Wallace sent him his paper on natural selection.

Alfred Russel Wallace (1823–1913) was born in a small English village into a family of modest means. He went to work at 14 and, without any special talent,

Figure 2-3a
The route of the H.M.S. Beagle.

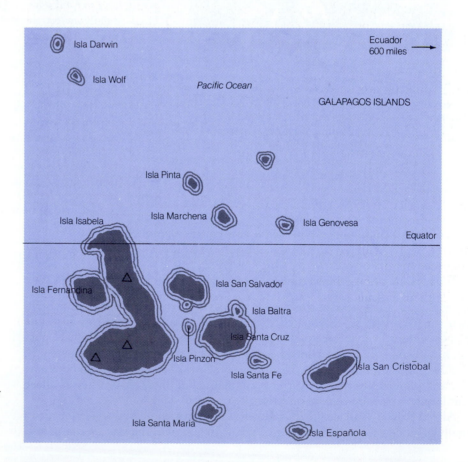

Figure 2-3b
The Galápagos Islands. Finches (because of their variety) and tortoises (because each island was inhabited by its own variety) influenced Darwin's thinking about evolution.

moved from one job to the next. He became interested in collecting, and joined an expedition to the Amazon Valley in 1848, at the age of 25. After four happy years of collecting specimens in South America, Wallace returned to England and two years later, in 1854, he sailed to the Malayan Archipelago to continue his study and collection of bird and insect specimens. He remained there eight years, collected 125,660 specimens, and often thought about the problem of the succession of species.

In 1858, on the island of Ternate, just off the coast of the Celebes Islands,* Wallace was in bed suffering from one of his periodic attacks of fever. Suddenly, the solution to the problem he had so long thought about flashed through his mind. Recalling the phrase, "the positive checks to increase," from Malthus' *Essay* (p. 35), he immediately realized that this phenomenon could apply to animals as well as to human beings. If there were no checks, the earth would quickly be overrun by the most prolific breeders. Why, then, did some species of plants or animals perish while others survived? The answer came at once: the best adapted survived; the less well adapted perished. Wallace at once set his thoughts down on paper and sent Darwin his essay, "On the Tendency of Varieties to Depart Indefinitely from the Original Type" (Löwenberg, 1959).

Figure 2-4
Alfred Russel Wallace.

When Darwin read Wallace's paper he was thoroughly depressed. He wrote Lyell, "Your words have come true with a vengeance—that I should be fore-stalled" (F. Darwin, 1950, p. 199). With the publication of Wallace's paper, Wallace would be given credit for a theory that Darwin felt belonged to him, since he had thought of it at least twenty years before. What to do? Darwin considered publishing a resume of his own work but wondered whether it would be honorable to do so. He told Lyell, "I would far rather burn my whole book, than that he [Wallace] or any other man should think I have behaved in a paltry spirit" (F. Darwin, 1950, p. 201). After much indecision, Darwin finally decided to let his close friends, Lyell and Joseph Hooker, devise a formula that would be fair to both Wallace and himself.

This difficult task was achieved by his friends, who decided that joint papers by Wallace and Darwin would be read before a meeting of the Linnaean Society. The Society agreed, and the papers were read on the evening of July 1, 1858, with Darwin ill in bed and Wallace in the Far East. What is remarkable is that the papers did not create a furor at the meeting, since most members of the Society disagreed with the concepts of natural selection.

The solution to the problem of Wallace's paper pleased Darwin, and Wallace was delighted that he had been so fairly treated. After the presentation of the two papers, the trustees of the Linnaean Society brought urgent pressure on Darwin to publish as speedily as possible a full account of his "theory." Darwin returned to his work with exemplary energy and, within a year, in 1859, had completed and published his great work, *On the Origin of Species.*†

With publication, the storm broke, and has not abated even to this day. While there was much praise for the book from many quarters, the gist of opinion was negative. Scientific opinion gradually came to Darwin's support, assisted especially by Darwin's able friend, Thomas Huxley (known as "Darwin's bulldog"), who for years wrote and spoke in favor of natural selection. The riddle of species was now explained: species were not fixed, but mutable; they evolved

*Now known as *Sulawesi.*

†The complete title of Darwin's book is *On the Origin of Species by Means of Natural Selection, or the Preservation of Favoured Races in the Struggle for Life.*

from other species through the mechanism of natural selection. Science was never to be the same again.

Darwin's Theory of Evolution

Darwin did not originate the idea of evolution, which had been suggested (or at least hinted at) 200 years previously—and much longer, if we include Greek thought of 2000 years ago. Darwin's grandfather, Erasmus Darwin, had written in defense of evolution before Charles was born, and Lamarck, a French scientist, had drawn up a schema trying to explain how new species were formed. However, his explanation met with unfavorable criticism and, in fact, did not accurately explain how the evolutionary process functioned.

Nor were the basic ideas used by Darwin completely of his own invention. Struggle for existence, extinction of species, variation, adaptation—these were all known and discussed for years by many European scientists. Darwin's great contribution was to bring these divergent ideas together and add the key: *natural selection*.

In his book, *On the Origin of Species*, published in 1859, Darwin explained his concept of evolution:

1. All species are capable of producing offspring faster than the food supply increases (see Malthus, p. 35)
2. All living things show variations; no two individuals of a species are exactly alike
3. Because there are more individuals than can possibly survive, there is a fierce struggle for existence and those with a favorable variation in size, strength, running ability, or whatever characteristics are necessary for survival, will possess an advantage over others (see Malthus, p. 35)
4. These favorable variations are inherited and passed on to the next generation
5. Over long periods of geologic time, these successful variations produce great differences that result in new species

Darwin called this process "natural selection." He did not believe in creation by design; that is, that life forms were placed on earth by creation, that variation in plants and animals was part of a grand divine design, or that the inorganic and the organic could be viewed as a progression from inferior to superior types, with humans at the top.

Darwin did not arrive at natural selection—his solution to the process of evolution—without assistance. When we look at the intellectual climate of Europe of the Middle Ages, we find that Christianity was associated with certain views of the universe. Since the time of Ptolemy, a Greco-Egyptian mathematician, geographer, and astronomer of the second century A.D., the earth was considered to be fixed at the center of a universe of spheres that revolved with perfect regularity around it. Not only was the inorganic world fixed and unchanging, but the organic world was believed to be equally static. It was believed that all species of the earth had been created (according to Genesis of the Old Testament) on a progression from the simplest living forms to the most complex—humans. This progression was not evolutionary; that is, one species did not lead to or evolve into the next. The forms and sequence were fixed, each creature forever linked to

BOX 2-2

The Great Chain of Being

Originating from ideas of Plato and Aristotle, the Chain of Being was a world view widespread in Europe especially during the seventeenth and eighteenth centuries. This philosophy held that the earth, even the universe, was "full"; that is, everything that was possible, existed. Also, the universe was composed of an infinite and continuous series of forms, each one *grading* into the next, arranged in an hierarchical sequence from the simplest kind of existence to the perfection of God.

Thus, there were superior and inferior beings, and perhaps more important (for evolutionary concepts), a being's step in this linear sequence was fixed, could not be altered and, since the earth was "full," i.e., complete, nothing new (like species) could be added. Gradation did not suggest that a superior being evolved from the next lower one; rather, a being was created forever set and unchangeable in its position in the chain of beings. Since God created the chain, change was inconceivable, for this would challenge God's perfection.

While such beliefs were prominently and widely believed, the concept of a closed and static system was under attack by various scientists and philosophers. It would only become a matter of time before outspoken supporters of evolution would make their ideas known.

the next in a great chain of beings. No new ones had appeared since creation, and none had disappeared.

This progression was, in fact, known as the Great Chain of Being (see Box 2-2), and the plan of the entire universe was seen as the Grand Design, that is, God's Design. The limbs of men and animals seemed designed to meet the purpose for which they are required. The wings of birds, eyes, etc., all of these structures were interpreted as neatly fitting the functions they performed. It was considered to be a deliberate plan, a design of the Grand Designer. Furthermore, it had all occurred in quite a short time, since creation was dated at 4004 B.C. by Archbishop James Ussher (1581–1656), an Irish prelate and scholar, who worked out the date by analyzing the "begat" chapter of Genesis.

Until these concepts of fixity and time were changed, it would be very unlikely that the idea of natural selection could even be conceived. What, then, upset the medieval belief in a rigid universe of planets, stars, plants, and animals? What scientific philosophy would, within the following 150 years, strike a death blow to the whole medieval system of thought? How would the scientific method as we know it today develop and, especially with Newton and Galileo in the seventeenth century, demonstrate a moving, not unchanging, universe?

The man who began this revolution was Copernicus (1473–1543), a Polish mathematician and astrologer, who simplified the Ptolemaic system by placing the sun at the center of the universe and the earth as one of the planets revolving around it. "The Copernican Revolution," as it is sometimes called, "is the supreme symbol of the passage from the medieval to the modern world, from an outlook which now seems like that of fairyland to the matter-of-fact outlook of the present day" (Dingle, 1959, p. 18).

Copernicus may not have realized the far-reaching effects of his new celestial system, but scientists of the seventeenth century—Bacon (inductive method), Harvey (circulation of the blood), Galileo (experimental science, central position of the sun, gravity, etc.), Newton (laws of motion and gravity)—gave the intellectual thought of their era a definite naturalistic basis. Although scientists

Figure 2-5
Linnaeus.

remained religiously oriented, their observations and experiments provoked notions of the universe that were new, exciting, and challenging, although sometimes condemned as heretical. Darwin, in the nineteenth century, was heir to the thinking and ideas of these seventeenth-century giants. At Cambridge, Darwin associated with professors (all churchmen) who were anti-evolutionists, but the radical change in intellectual thought of the seventeenth century enabled scientists of the eighteenth to think about the universe in a manner that made the idea of evolution possible, and paved the way for Darwin.

By the early decades of the 1700s, motion, not fixity, had become accepted for the physical universe, but most biological scientists held that change was unacceptable for living forms. Species had been fixed at creation, they still insisted, and since then there had been no new species formed or old species driven to extinction—there had simply been no change. Without change there cannot, of course, be evolution, and until it was recognized that species could alter, evolution and Darwin's natural selection could not be considered. This view of fixity of species was solidly held by one of the leading naturalists of his day, **Carolus Linnaeus**, who believed that "There are just as many species as there were created in the beginning," and again, "There is no such thing as a new species" (quoted in Singer, 1959, 379–380). He thought of nature as a system of unchangeable substances, "a continuum from algae to humans. He agreed with the notion of a "chain of being" (see Box 2-2), that all life forms were linked together in one great chain, and each species was fixed and unchangeable.

The son of a Lutheran pastor, Linnaeus (1707–1778) was born at Roeshult, Sweden. He is best known for developing a classification system for plants and animals, first published in 1735, which he called *Systema Naturae*. Linnaeus isolated those particular physical traits that best characterized a particular group of organisms. In plants, for instance, he used blossoms; in insects, wings; and in fish, scales. He even included humans in his classification of animals, thus defying the then-contemporary thought that humans, made in God's image, should be considered separately and outside the animal kingdom.

Linnaeus' scheme was well received throughout Europe, and, when applied to collections in museums and botanical gardens, it worked. He then proceeded to assign names to the animals and plants. Linnaeus used the simple but effective idea of assigning two Latin names to each organism. The first word would be the generic term—the genus—for the organism and the second word, the specific term—the species. Thus, the two words together would become a unit internationally recognized as the name for that particular form. This system of binomial (or binominal) nomenclature was widely accepted, and is still used today.

We are concerned not so much with the problems and solutions that resulted in Linnaeus' *Systema Naturae* as we are in his ideas about evolution, which reflected the scientific thought of his time. Linnaeus saw nature as a "rationally ordained system of means and ends"; that is, every living thing is created perfectly adapted to the environment in which it lives, making further change unnecessary. According to Linnaeus (and many other scientists as well as laymen), this natural relationship did not exist for its own sake, but for the glory of God. It is, they believed, the duty of humans to study nature diligently, so that God might be glorified. Although some scientists had abandoned the age-old notion that nature was fixed, Linnaeus still adhered to the idea that species, once divinely created, had never changed, and "to study nature diligently" meant assigning to every living thing its proper name. He is supposed to have said, "What is a botanist? Simply a person who can give the right names" (Lindroth, 1983, p. 24).

It was a fundamental belief of Linnaeus, as it was of his contemporaries, that species were immutable; therefore, there could be no new species, yet

> . . . with the years Linnaeus began to weaken in his belief that no new species could emerge . . . and in his old age worked out a theory, partly imaginary, according to which the multiplicity of organisms had arisen through hybridization among a limited number of original forms. But this did not mean turning his back on the past. The species, as much as ever, were fixed units, and in themselves just as sharply delimited as before (Lindroth, 1983, p. 24).

However, there were other voices, especially in France, raised loudly and clearly in favor of a universe based on change, and much more to the point, of the relationship between similar forms based on descent from a common ancestor.

The leading advocate of this point of view was Georges Louis Leclerc, who came from an old noble family in Burgundy and was later raised to the rank of Count, under the name of Buffon, by Louis XV. **Buffon** (1707–1788), as he is known, was born the same year as Linnaeus. He knew of his contemporary and disagreed with him on most points. Buffon's writings made natural science popular drawing-room conversation, in which he himself excelled with sly wit. Talking one day with his female visitors, he said, "Nothing stands still. Everything moves. Even the seed of man does so, otherwise it would never reach its goal. May I show it to you under the microscope?" (Wendt, 1963, p. 83).

Buffon believed neither in the perfection of nature nor in the idea that nature had purpose. He stressed again and again the importance of change in the universe, and he underlined the changing nature, or mutability, of species.

In contrast to Linnaeus' static "rationally ordained system of means and ends," Buffon emphasized the variety and minute gradations of nature, which he explained in terms of "a system of laws, elements and forces." Thus, nature could be seen as functioning by natural means rather than through a divine mind. Buffon considered it important to see life as a dynamic system of processes instead of a static pattern of structure. He felt that the true aim of natural history was to discover and understand these processes, not simply to classify their result. Buffon

> put the hypothesis of organic evolution . . . in clear and definite form. He called . . . attention to the facts of comparative anatomy which constitute one of the principal evidences for that hypothesis. . . . He, finally, did more than any one else to habituate the mind of his time to a vastly (though not yet sufficiently) enlarged time-scale in connection with the history of organic nature, a necessary prerequisite to the establishment of transformation (Lovejoy, 1959, pp. 111–112).

The contrast between the thinking of Linnaeus and that of Buffon reflects not merely the old and the new, but also the response of many scientists and clergymen to the publication of Darwin's *Origin.* Although Linnaeus appeared to have modified his views about new species late in life, the concept of immutability of species continued to be the dominant theme among most scientists. Darwin was familiar with the writings of Buffon, which helped to make a belief in evolution acceptable. With the voluminous publications of Buffon and others, it is not at all surprising that when we arrive at the latter portion of the eighteenth century, the ideas of mutability of species and the possibility of unlimited organic change were well known throughout Europe. This doctrine of organic change was not

Figure 2-6
Buffon.

Figure 2-7
Erasmus Darwin.

widely accepted, but at least it was being discussed at length in intellectual circles.

In this enlightened era of the popularization of science (which saw the beginnings of archeology and the recognition that fossil bones belonged to species of animals since perished), we must take notice of a most interesting figure who saw clearly the force of evolutionary ideas. Charles Darwin was well aware of the writings of this man, his grandfather, **Erasmus Darwin** (1731–1802), who was a country physician, poet, and versatile and eccentric scientist. More than fifty years before his grandson was to startle the world with his views on natural selection, Erasmus had expressed such ideas as "evolution by natural and sexual selection, protective adaptation, inheritance of acquired characteristics, and even the evolution of mankind" (Francoeur, 1965, p. 68). In fact, one biographer wrote of Erasmus Darwin, "the theory of natural selection was the only cardinal one in the evolution system on which Erasmus Darwin did not actually forestall his more famous and greater namesake" (Clodd, 1897, p. 114).

Although Charles Darwin had read his grandfather's writings, it is not possible to say what influence these had on his views. Erasmus had not solved the problem of the evolutionary process, but it is likely that his discussion of evolution made it easier for Charles to approach it. Erasmus Darwin had little influence on the scientific thought of his day, which is not difficult to understand, since he described his scientific ideas in ambiguous verse. For example, he expressed his thoughts on the struggle for existence thus:

Where milder skies protect the nascent brood
And earth's warm bosom yields salubrious food,
Each new descendant with superior powers
Of sense and motion speeds the transient hours;
Braves every season, tenants every clime,
And nature rises on the wings of Time.
(Wendt, 1955, p. 138)

During the eighteenth century, Erasmus Darwin wrote about and believed in evolution, but was never able to explain the process. He came close but, as Buffon before him and Lamarck afterwards, he relied on the concept of acquired characteristics to indicate how species were transformed: " 'All animals undergo perpetual transformations; which are in part produced by their own exertions . . . and many of these acquired forms or propensities are transmitted to their posterity' " (E. Darwin, quoted in Singer, 1959, p. 505). However, neither Buffon nor E. Darwin codified their beliefs into a comprehensive system. The first European scientist to do this was Jean Baptiste Pierre Antoine de Monet de **Lamarck** (1744–1829).

Like Erasmus Darwin and Buffon, Lamarck also developed most of the ingredients of the concept of evolution, but he went beyond these men by organizing his ideas. Ernst Heinrich Haeckel, the well-known scientist of the late nineteenth century, said that to Lamarck "will always belong the immortal glory of having for the first time worked out the Theory of Descent as an independent scientific theory of the first order, and as the philosophical foundation of the whole science of Biology" (Clodd, 1897, p. 115).

One of the points stressed by Lamarck was the interaction of organic forms with their environment. He believed the stability of organic forms was directly

Figure 2-8
Lamarck.

proportionate to the stability of the conditions of life, and, as the conditions of life changed, organic forms were altered.

The alterations were caused by the *effort* the form makes in using those parts of its body that are most adaptive under given environmental conditions. Little by little, as time goes on, these changes result in new organs that are passed on through heredity. What is the mechanism that induces change?

If a particular part of the body feels a certain need, "fluids and forces" would be directed toward that point and a new organ would be slowly produced to satisfy that need. That the environment affects and can eventually induce change in organic forms is commonplace knowledge today, but that felt needs are the mechanism, while an intriguing idea, is not true.

Lamarck also believed that a characteristic acquired in the manner described above for a new organ could be passed on through heredity to the next generation. This theory of acquired characteristics, or Lamarckism, had already been suggested by Erasmus Darwin, but was not really questioned until it was carefully scrutinized by one of the leading scientists of France, Georges Cuvier, whose ideas we shall discuss shortly.

It should be stressed, on the other hand, that many of Lamarck's views of nature and evolution are as valid today as they were 175 years ago. His emphasis on the dynamic interaction of organic forms with the environment and the consequent adaptation is well placed. He brought together vast quantities of materials to support his evolutionary ideas, carrying them beyond those of Buffon. The world of science, especially biology, owes him a great debt.

However, like E. Darwin, he failed to solve the riddle of "how it works." It is true enough that all living forms may acquire characteristics during their lifetime. We know, for example, that a man may develop large muscles simply through exercise, but we also know that the physical characteristics we acquire in our lifetime (with the possible exception of mutations(are not transmitted to our offspring. Our highly muscled man does not pass on his overdeveloped muscles to his children. It is interesting to note that Charles Darwin, while he used natural selection as the mechanism for evolution, also used, at times, the belief that acquired characteristics could be inherited.

Lamarck, we might say, popularized the idea of evolution, but there remained vehement opposition to the notion that species may change and develop into new species. The outstanding opponent of evolution at this time was one of the best known scientists of his day. He was not only a contemporary of Lamarck, but a man to whom Lamarck had given a position at the Jardin des Plantes, the institution where Buffon had worked for so many years. This was **Georges Cuvier** (1769–1832), who was to become famous as the "Pope of Bones," the father of zoology, paleontology, and comparative anatomy.

Our interest in Cuvier resides mainly in his unwavering, obstinate, and at times nasty criticism of Lamarck's views on evolution. Although not an especially religious person, Cuvier never grasped, as Lamarck did, the dynamic concept of nature. Cuvier insisted upon the fixity of species with almost religious fervor, refusing to believe that a new species could evolve from an old one. By this time, most scientists thought it quite obvious that new species of animals and plants had come into existence, and, if Cuvier was to successfully counteract the growing interest in evolution, he had to offer an alternative explanation about how new species could appear. He did so by proposing a theory of catastrophism.

This theory was based on the assumption of a series of violent and sudden

Figure 2-9
Cuvier.

catastrophes.* These catastrophes were produced by natural, not divine,† means, such as the formation of the Alps, and were responsible for ending each major stratigraphical sequence (see geologic table, p. 134). All creatures living in those parts of the world where "revolutions" or catastrophes took place were destroyed. Then, after things settled down, these areas were restocked with new forms, different from those previously living there. These new forms came from neighboring areas unaffected by the catastrophes. Cuvier's representation thus avoided the idea of evolution to explain the appearance of new forms.

Cuvier, one of the most brilliant scientists of his time, was an unwavering anti-evolutionist who believed, like Linnaeus, that "to name, to classify, and to describe was the beginning and end of science" (Greene, 1959, p. 174). Did his anti-evolutionist views retard the development of evolutionary ideas? As we have seen, they did not affect Lamarck, who developed his evolutionary scheme despite Cuvier. Oldroyd (1980) suggests that, on the contrary, Cuvier's work led to Darwin!

Cuvier divided the animal kingdom into four divisions or embranchments: vertebrates, molluscs, jointed or segmented animals, and zoophytes (no special nervous system or sense organs). Each of these major groupings was seen as a separate organizational type, and each one had its particular anatomical and physiological characteristics functionally adaptive for the conditions of its environment. Thus, each of these divisions, one separate from the other, was not rigidly set in an inseparable Chain of Being, as was the Linnaean arrangement. Although separate, Cuvier believed these divisions fixed and not subject to change. However, since Cuvier separated these four divisions, thus eliminating the Chain of Being concept, he also opened the way for someone else to explain the appearance and disappearance of forms by an evolutionary theory.

Changes necessary from Cuvier's representation had to suggest mutability instead of fixity and to link species with their environments. Darwin did this, and added natural selection to complete the scheme. Thus, as Oldroyd suggests (1980, p. 43), "the route from Linnaeus to Darwin lay through the anti-evolutionist Cuvier, as much as the evolutionist Lamarck."

Cuvier's influence on Darwin was indirect, since his ideas did not act specifically on matters discussed by Darwin. Still, it may have made it easier for Darwin to argue (and others to accept) the notion that the Chain of Being concept was inadequate. On the other hand, Cuvier's catastrophism was of no help to Darwin; it is quite likely that, early in his thinking, Darwin rejected catastrophism because of the influence of Lyell, the period's most influential opponent of Cuvier's view.

Charles Lyell (1797–1875) was a lawyer by training and geologist by choice. When Darwin returned to England in 1836, he became Lyell's close friend and confidant, a relationship that was to last a lifetime despite differences on a number of intellectual points.

Lyell's important contribution to science was his popular three-volume work, *Principles of Geology* (1830–1833), in which he rejected the catastrophism of

Figure 2-10
Lyell.

* A recent school of thought suggests that evolution can occur with sudden and rapid change. This idea (quite different from catastrophism) is known as "punctuated equilibrium" and is discussed on p. 106.

† Cuvier's catastrophism had no religious basis, and he was careful to separate his religious beliefs from his scientific work. Creationists mistakenly use Cuvier's views to support their position.

Cuvier. Lyell reaffirmed the principle of **uniformitarianism**; that is, no forces had been active in the past history of the earth that are not also working today—an idea introduced into European thought in 1785 by James Hutton. Lyell showed, through the process of uniformitarianism, that the earth's crust was formed via a series of slow and gradual changes. Mountains, rivers, valleys, lakes, deserts, and coastlines were not the sudden result of cataclysms, but rather the result of purely natural forces, such as erosion by land, water, frost, ice, and rain. These forces, which could be seen operating in the present, could (assuming sufficient time) have caused all geological events of the past.

When he embarked on the *Beagle*, Darwin was more interested in geology than in any other science. In 1832, while in South America, Darwin received the second volume of Lyell's *Principles* (Professor Henslow had presented Darwin with the first volume just before the *Beagle* sailed, but cautioned Darwin not to believe everything Lyell had written). Lyell's work immediately struck a responsive chord as Darwin observed the mountains, rocks, and coastline of South America. From Lyell, Darwin learned first of all about the development of the earth's crust, the environmental conditions that, through the struggle for existence, could modify living forms, and, secondly, about the immense age of the earth, far beyond Archbishop Ussher's 4004 B.C.

Two important points in Darwin's explanation of evolution are the struggle for existence and descent with modification. The principle of struggle for existence was basic to Darwin's evolutionary theory, and this he credits to Lyell, though the idea was not original with him. Descent with modification Darwin saw as a slow and gradual process and, for this to work, time would be necessary. Lyell believed the earth was extremely old, on the order of hundreds or thousands of million years (much older than Buffon had suggested in the previous century), thus giving to Darwin a notion of time that would have made the gradual process of evolution possible.

Shortly after his return to England, Darwin opened his first notebook in July, 1837. He planned to collect evidence on the subject of the gradual modification of species since, as he said ". . . the subject haunted me" (F. Darwin, 1950, p. 15). As he worked, he came to realize that "selection was the keystone of man's success in making useful races of animals and plants. But how selection could be applied to organisms living in a state of nature remained for some time a mystery to me" (F. Darwin, 1950, p. 53). The mystery was solved for Darwin in October, 1838, fifteen months after he had begun his systematic enquiry, when he happened "to read for amusement" Malthus' essay on the principle of population.

Thomas Robert Malthus (1766–1834) was an English clergyman, political economist, and devotee of the natural sciences. His work was to become a standard consulted by politicians dealing with population problems and a source of inspiration to both Charles Darwin and Alfred Wallace in their separate discoveries of the principle of natural selection.

In his *Essay*, Malthus pointed out that if human population growth is unrestrained by natural causes, it will double every twenty-five years, but that the capacity for food production increases only in a straight arithmetic progression. In nature, Malthus noted, this impulse to multiply was *checked by the struggle for existence*, but humans had to apply artificial restraints. Malthus emphasized two facts: the infinite fertility of humankind, and the limited size and resources of the earth.

UNIFORMITARIANISM
The thesis that geological processes have always been the same as they are today.

Upon reading this, Darwin wrote:

> . . . it at once struck me that under these circumstances favourable variations would tend to be preserved, and unfavourable ones to be destroyed. The result of this would be the formation of a new species. *Here then I had at last got a theory by which to work* (F. Darwin, 1950, pp. 53–54). (Emphasis added.)

While Darwin had already realized that selection was the key to evolution, it was due to Malthus that he saw how selection in nature could be explained. In the struggle for existence, those *individuals* with favorable variations would survive; those with unfavorable variations would not. The significance here is that Darwin was thinking in terms of individuals (not species) that interact with one another. This was quite different from the nineteenth-century philosophy prevalent in Europe since the time of Plato. It was the significance of individuals in the struggle for existence that led Darwin to his concept of natural selection.

Before Darwin, scientists (Linnaeus and Lyell, for example) thought of species as an entity that could not change, and, if species changed, they were not species. It was species that were at the basis of the discussions of plants and animals. Individuals within the species did not appear to be significant and, therefore, it was difficult for many scientists to imagine how change could occur. Darwin, as we have pointed out, saw that variation of individuals could explain how selection occurred. Favorable variations were selected by nature for survival; unfavorable ones eliminated (Malthus, of course, believed God did the selecting, not nature). Thus, "Population thinkers stress the uniqueness of everything in the organic world. What is important for them is the individual, not the type. They emphasize that every individual in sexually reproducing species is uniquely different from all others. . . . There is no 'typical' individual, . . ." (Mayr, 1982, p. 46).

This emphasis on the uniqueness of the individual (the variation that occurs in all populations—that a population is a group of interacting individuals and not a type) led Darwin to natural selection as the mechanism that made evolution work. Natural selection operates on individuals, favorably or unfavorably, but it is the population that evolves. As pointed out on p. 101, the unit of natural selection is the individual; the unit of evolution is the population.

Darwin's Evidence

By 1859, Darwin had accumulated a tremendous amount of data. In addition to the thousands of observations made during his five-year voyage on the *Beagle*, Darwin read voluminously in geology, paleontology, and related disciplines, and meticulously collected observations on domesticated plants and animals. Darwin had originally planned to detail all this information in a huge multivolume treatise. But when Wallace forced his hand, Darwin—in *Origin*—summarized his conclusions in what he modestly called an "abstract."

Domesticated Plants and Animals Through what Darwin called "unconscious selection" (what today is called "artificial selection"), animal and plant breeders had greatly modified varities of domestic species during historic times. Darwin believed such observations provided strong support for the process of natural selection, and was particularly impressed with pigeons (which he had studied and bred for years):

Altogether at least a score of pigeons might be chosen, which if shown to an ornithologist, and he were told that they were wild birds, would certainly, I think, be ranked by him as well-defined species. Moreover, I do not believe that any ornithologist would place the English carrier, the short-faced tumbler, the runt, the barb, pouter, and fantail in the same genus; more especially as in each of these breeds several truly-inherited sub-breeds, or species as he might have called them, could be shown him.

Great as the differences are between the breeds of pigeons, I am fully convinced that the common opinion of naturalists is correct, namely, that all have descended from the rock-pigeon (*Columbia livia*) including under this term several geographical races or sub-species, which differ from each other in the most trifling respects (Darwin, 1859, pp. 22–23).

Geographic Distribution of Life Forms   Darwin drew widely upon his experience from the *Beagle* voyage, as well as an intimate knowledge of the flora and fauna of his native England, to argue further for the role of natural selection:

Isolation, also, is an important element in the process of natural selection. In a continued or isolated area, if not very large, the organic and inorganic conditions of life will generally be in a great degree uniform; so that natural selection will tend to modify all the individuals of a varying species throughout the area in the same manner in relation to the same conditions. Intercrosses, also, with the individuals of the same species, which otherwise would have inhabited the surrounding and differently circumstanced districts, will be prevented (Darwin, 1859, p. 104).

The Geological and Paleontological Record   Darwin clearly understood that the major verification for his theory of slow and gradual evolutionary modification must come from fossil evidence embedded within the earth's strata. He also recognized that the paleontological record could never be complete (much less, of course, was known about this record at that time). Even given these limitations, Darwin's perceptive use of paleontological examples strengthened his argument and provided a great stimulus for future research:

We can understand how it is that all the forms of life, ancient and recent, make together one grand system; for all are connected by generation. We can understand, from the continued tendency to divergence of character, why the more ancient a form is, the more it generally differs from those now living. Why ancient and extinct forms often tend to fill up gaps between existing forms, sometimes blending two groups previously classed as distinct into one; but more commonly only bringing them a little closer together. The more ancient a form is, the more often, apparently, it displays characters in some degree intermediate between groups now distinct; for the more ancient a form is, the more nearly it will be related to, and consequently resemble, the common progenitor of groups since become widely divergent (Darwin, 1859, pp. 344–345).

Comparative Anatomy   A basic element of biological interpretation in Darwin's time (as well as our own) involves anatomical comparison. How do we know whether two living forms are really related to each other, or to whom a fossil form is related?

We have seen that the members of the same class, independently of their habits of life, resemble each other in the general plan of their organisation. This resemblance is often expressed by the term "unity of type," or by saying that the several parts and organs in the different species of the class are homologous. The whole subject is included under the general name of Morphology. This is the most interesting department of natural history, and may be said to be its very soul. What can be more curious than that the hand of a man, formed for grasping, that of a mole for digging, the leg of the horse, the paddle of the porpoise, and the wing of the bat, should all be constructed on the same pattern, and should include the same bones, in the same relative positions? (Darwin, 1859, p. 434).

Embryology   It has long been known that the immature stages organisms pass through during development can give important clues concerning evolutionary relationships—a fact that did not escape Darwin's attention.

> The embryos, also, of distinct animals within the same class are often strikingly similar; a better proof of this cannot be given, than a circumstance mentioned by Agassiz, namely, that having forgotten to ticket the embryo of some vertebrate animal he cannot now tell whether it be that of a mammal, bird, or reptile. The vermiform larvae of moths, flies, beetles, &c., resemble each other much more closely than do the mature insects (Darwin, 1859, p. 439).

Vestigial Organs   A final line of evidence presented by Darwin concerned those "rudimentary, atrophied, or aborted" organs that appeared to no longer perform any apparent function. If life had not evolved, what possible "Design" could explain their presence?

> Rudimentary organs may be compared with the letters in a word, still retained in the spelling, but become useless in the pronunciation, but which serve as a clue in seeking for its derivation. On the view of descent with modification, we may conclude that the existence of organs in a rudimentary, imperfect, and useless condition, or quite aborted, far from presenting a strange difficulty, as they assuredly do on the ordinary doctrine of creation, might even have been anticipated, and can be accounted for by the laws of inheritance (Darwin, 1859, pp. 455–456).

Natural Selection in Action

A modern example of natural selection can be shown through research on the process in operation. The best historically documented case of natural selection acting in modern populations deals with changes in pigmentation among peppered moths near Manchester, England. Before the nineteenth century, the common variety of moth was a mottled gray color that provided extremely effective camouflage against lichen-covered tree trunks. Also present, though in much lower frequency, was a dark variety of moth. While resting on such trees, the dark, uncamouflaged moths against the light tree trunks were more visible to birds and were therefore eaten more often. Thus, in the end, they produced fewer offspring than the light, camouflaged moths. Yet, in fifty years, by the end of the nineteenth century, the common gray, camouflaged form had been almost completely replaced by the black variety.

What had brought about this rapid change? The answer lies in the rapidly changing environment of industrialized nineteenth-century England. Pollutants released in the area settled on trees, killing the lichen and turning the bark a dark color. Moths living in the area continued to rest on trees, but the gray (or light) variety was increasingly conspicuous as the trees became darker. Consequently, they began to be preyed upon more frequently by birds and contributed fewer genes to the next generation.

In the twentieth century, increasing control of pollutants has allowed some forested areas to return to their lighter, preindustrial conditions with lichen growing again on the trees. As would be expected, in these areas the black variety is now being supplanted by the gray.

The substance that produces pigmentation is called *melanin*, and the evolutionary shift in the peppered moth, as well as in many other moth species, is termed *industrial melanism*. Such an evolutionary shift in response to environmental change is called **adaptation**.

This example provides numerous insights into the mechanism of evolutionary change by natural selection:

1. A trait must be inherited to have importance in natural selection. A characteristic that is not hereditary (such as a change in hair pigmentation brought about by dye) will not be passed on to succeeding generations. In moths, pigmentation is a demonstrated hereditary trait.

2. Natural selection cannot occur without variation in inherited characteristics. If all the moths had initially been gray (you will recall some dark forms were present) and the trees became darker, the survival and reproduction of all moths may have been so low that the population would have become extinct. Such an event is not unusual in evolution and, without variation, would nearly always occur. *Selection can only work with variation already present.*

3. "Fitness" is a relative measure that will change as the environment changes. Fitness is simply reproductive success. In the initial stage, the gray moth was the most-fit variety, but as the environment changed, the black moth became more fit, and a further change reversed the adaptive pattern. It should be obvious that statements regarding the "most-fit" life form mean nothing without reference to specific environments.

The example of peppered moths shows how different death rates influence natural selection, for moths that die early tend to leave fewer offspring. But mortality is not the entire picture. Another important aspect of natural selection is fertility, for an animal that gives birth to more young would pass its genes on at a faster rate than those who bear fewer offspring. However, fertility is not the whole picture either, for the crucial element is the number of young raised successfully to the point where they reproduce themselves. We may state this simply as *differential net reproductive success*. The way this mechanism works can be demonstrated through another example.

In a common variety of small birds called swifts, data show that giving birth to more offspring does not necessarily guarantee that more young will be successfully raised. The number of eggs hatched in a breeding season is a measure of fertility. The number of birds that mature and are eventually able to leave the nest is a measure of net reproductive success, or offspring successfully raised. The following tabulation shows the correlation between the number of eggs hatched (fertility) and the number of young that leave the nest (reproductive success) averaged over four breeding seasons (Lack, 1966).

Number of eggs hatched (fertility)	2 eggs	3 eggs	4 eggs
Average number of young raised (reproductive success)	1.92	2.54	1.76
Sample size	72	20	16

ADAPTATION
An evolutionary shift in a population in response to environmental change; the result of natural selection.

Figure 2-11
Variation in the peppered moth. In (a), the dark form is more visible to bird predators on the light (unpolluted) trees. In (b), the light form is more visible: trees are darker due to pollution.

(a)

(b)

As the tabulation shows, the most efficient fertility number is three eggs, for that yields the highest reproductive success. Raising two is less beneficial to the parents since the *end result* is not as successful as with three eggs. Trying to raise more than three young is actually detrimental, since the parents may not be able to provide adequate nourishment for any of the offspring. An offspring that dies before reaching reproductive age is, in evolutionary terms, an equivalent of never having been born in the first place. Actually, such a result may be an evolutionary minus to the parents, for this offspring will drain their resources and may inhibit their ability to raise other offspring, thereby lowering their reproductive success even further. Selection will favor those genetic traits that yield the maximum net reproductive success. If the number of eggs laid* is a genetic trait in birds (and it seems to be), natural selection in swifts should act to favor the laying of three eggs as opposed to two or four.

Darwin's Failures

Darwin argued eloquently for the notion of evolution in general and the role of natural selection in particular, but he did not entirely comprehend the exact mechanisms of evolutionary change.

As we have seen, natural selection acts on *variation* within species. Neither Darwin, nor anyone else in the nineteenth century, understood the source of all this variation. Consequently, Darwin speculated about variation arising from "use"—an idea similar to Lamarck's. Darwin, however, was not as dogmatic in his views as Lamarck, and most emphatically argued against inner "needs" or "effort." Darwin had to confess that when it came to explaining variation, he simply did not know.

> Our ignorance of the laws of variation is profound. Not in one case out of a hundred can we pretend to assign any reason why this or that part differs, more or less, from the same part in the parents. But whenever we have the means of instituting a comparison, the same laws appear to have acted in producing the lesser differences between varieties of the same species, and the greater differences between species of the same genus. The external conditions of life, as climate and food, &c., seem to have induced some slight modifications. Habit in producing constitutional differences, and use in strengthening, and disuse in weakening and diminishing organs, seem to have been more potent in their effects (Darwin, 1859, pp. 167–168).

In addition to his inability to explain the origins of variation, Darwin also did not completely understand the mechanism by which parents transmitted traits to offspring. Almost without exception, nineteenth-century scholars were confused about the laws of heredity, and the popular consensus was that inheritance was *blending* by nature. In other words, offspring were always expected to express intermediate traits as a result of a blending of their parents' contributions. Given this view, we can see why the actual nature of genes was thus unimaginable. Without any viable alternatives, Darwin accepted this popular misconception. As it turned out, a contemporary of Darwin had systematically worked out the rules of heredity. However, the work of this obscure Augustinian monk, Gregor Mendel (whom you shall meet in Chapter 4), was not recognized until the beginning of the twentieth century.

*The number of eggs hatched is directly related to the number of eggs laid.

Summary

The concept of evolution as we know it today is directly traceable to developments in intellectual thought in Western Europe over the last 300 years. In particular, the contributions of Linnaeus, Lamarck, Buffon, Lyell, and Malthus all had significant impact upon Darwin. The year 1859 marks a watershed in evolutionary theory for, in that year, the publication of Darwin's *On the Origin of Species* crystallized the evolutionary process (particularly the crucial role of natural selection) and, for the first time, thrust evolutionary theory into the consciousness of the common person. Debates both inside and outside the sciences continued for several decades (and in some corners persist today), but the theory of evolution irrevocably changed the tide of intellectual thought. Gradually Darwin's formulation of the evolutionary process became accepted almost universally by scientists as the very foundation of all the biological sciences, physical anthropology included. In this, the twentieth century, contributions from genetics allow us to demonstrate the mechanics of evolution in a way unknown to Darwin and his contemporaries.

Natural selection is the central determining factor influencing the long-term direction of evolutionary change. How natural selection works can best be explained as differential reproductive success, meaning, in other words, how successful individuals are in leaving offspring to succeeding generations.

Questions for Review

1. Trace the history of evolutionary ideas from Copernicus to the time of Darwin.
2. In what ways do Linnaeus and Buffon differ in their approach to the concept of evolution?
3. What are the bases of Lamarck's theory of acquired characteristics? Why is this theory unacceptable?
4. What was Lamarck's contribution to nineteenth-century evolutionary ideas?
5. Explain Cuvier's catastrophism.
6. What did Malthus and Lyell contribute to Darwin's thinking on evolution?
7. What is the difference between a population approach? Why is this significant to the concept of natural selection?
8. What major areas of evidence did Darwin use to strengthen his argument concerning evolution?
9. How did Darwin's explanation of the source of variation compare with that of Lamarck?
10. What hereditary mechanism did Darwin utilize to explain transmission of traits from parents to offspring?
11. What is meant by adaptation? Illustrate through the example of industrial melanism.

Biological Basis of Life

CONTENTS

The Race to Discover the Genetic Code

Linus Pauling.

At Cambridge University's Cavendish Laboratory, from 1951 to 1953, a brash young American scientist from Chicago, **James D. Watson**, and a garrulous Englishman from Northampton, **Francis H. C. Crick**, worked more or less together (with the assistance of English physicist Maurice Wilkins and others) to solve the puzzle of DNA structure.

Watson should have been hard at work in Copenhagen learning chemistry to help him in his postdoctoral biological research, and Crick, already at Cambridge, should have been busily engaged researching hemoglobin crystals for his Ph.D. Neither should have been involved in DNA research, but, as a matter of fact, both men were very much involved, and they hoped not only to discover the structure of DNA and win a Nobel Prize, but to beat **Linus Pauling** who, they were quite sure, was close to success on the same project at California Institute of Technology.

But Pauling was not as close to success as Crick and Watson believed. In November, 1951, Pauling started working on a triple helix and thought he succeeded, "although the structure was described as 'an extraordinarily tight one, with little opportunity for change in positions of the atoms'" (Pauling, 1974). A copy of the paper on his experiment was sent to Crick and Watson, who had themselves built an unsuccessful triple helix model a year earlier. They had considered their model a failure, and, after reading Pauling's paper (and catching an error in basic chemistry), knew his to be a failure also.

As Watson tells the story, he knew that Pauling was wrong, and that the earlier model he and Crick had constructed was also wrong, and now he was stumped. It was not until Wilkins showed him an X-ray diffraction photograph of DNA (taken by Cavendish scientist Rosalind Franklin) early in 1953, that Watson thought he saw a bit of light. The X-ray indicated that a helix was the correct structure, which he had been sure of anyway, and, further, that a 2-chain model—a double helix rather than a triple helix—might possibly be the answer. Watson and Crick deliberately kept the X-ray photograph from Pauling, since they feared that if he saw the X-ray, he would solve the problem before they did.

Watson designed a 2-chain metal helical model of DNA for experimental purposes to be built by the Cavendish Laboratory. The key to the mystery occurred abruptly to Watson while he was impatiently waiting for the Lab machine shop to complete the model. He had cut accurate representations of the four bases from stiff cardboard and was shifting them around trying out various pairing possibilities when:

> Suddenly I became aware that an adenine-thymine pair held together by two hydrogen bonds was identical in shape to a guanine-cytosine pair held together by at least two hydrogen bonds. All the hydrogen bonds

seemed to form naturally; no fudging was required to make the two types of base pairs identical in shape (Watson, 1968, p. 194).

The enigma of the basic DNA structure was solved and the race won. In 1962, the Nobel Prize for Medicine and Physiology was awarded to Crick, Watson, and Wilkins.

Actually, Watson and Crick need not have worried about Pauling's beating them to the DNA solution since Pauling did not consider this research a race (Pauling, personal communication); however, Pauling does believe there was a chance, had he seen the X-ray photograph,

> . . . that I would have thought of the Watson-Crick structure during the next few weeks. . . . Nevertheless, I myself think that the chance is rather small that I would have thought of the double helix in 1952, before Watson and Crick made their great discovery (Pauling, 1974, p. 771).

S O U R C E S :

Olby, Robert. *The Path to the Double Helix*, Seattle: University of Washington Press, 1974.

Pauling, Linus. "Molecular Basis of Biological Specificity," *Nature*, **248** (no. 5451):769, 771, April 26, 1974.

Watson, James D. *The Double Helix*, New York: Atheneum, 1968.

James Watson and Francis Crick.

SOMATIC CELLS
soma: body
Cells that do not divide by meiosis and
do not become gametes.

SEX CELLS
Cells that divide by meiosis and become
gametes.

NUCLEUS
A body, present in most types of cells,
containing chromosomes.

CHROMOSOME
chrome: color
soma: body
Threadlike, gene-containing body
found in the nucleus.

CENTROMERE
centro: central
mere: part
That part of the chromosome to which
spindle fibers are attached during
mitosis and meiosis.

Introduction

In the preceding chapter, evolution was discussed from a conceptual point of view, but the mechanics of evolution—how hereditary characteristics are actually passed on from one generation to the next—were not included in that generalized presentation. In the body, what physiological processes operate to produce and distribute variation and enable natural selection to function? In this chapter, we shall examine the specifics, beginning with the nature of the cell, since that is where, in a sense, the evolutionary process begins. The basic evolutionary process applies to all forms of life—to plants as well as to animals; however, our interest is mainly humankind, and cells and genetics will be discussed for the most part from the point of view of human beings. Nevertheless, we should keep in mind that the cell is basic to all forms of life, and that cellular characteristics (such as genes, chromosomes, and DNA) are found in the cells of all animals and plants. Finally, we should remember that the process of heredity is essentially similar in all species. Heredity, as we deal with it here, refers simply to the passage of genetic information from the cells of one generation to those of the next.

The Cell

Figure 3-1
Generalized diagram of a cell.

Vacuole
Lysosome
Nuclear membrane
Cell membrane
Ribosomes
Cytoplasm
Mitochondrion
Nucleolus
Golgi body
Nucleus
Centrosome
Endoplasmic reticulum

Somatic and Sex Cells

Basically, two kinds of cells are directly involved with heredity: **somatic cells** and **sex cells**. The body is composed of various kinds of specialized tissues (blood, liver, muscle, skin, nerve) consisting of billions of somatic cells continually being manufactured to replace those that have died. Indeed, one estimate has it that the cells of the human body are replaced every seven years.

Sex cells are similar to somatic cells but play no part in the structural composition of the body. They originate in the testes of males and ovaries of females, and their only function is to transmit life and hereditary information from parents to offspring.

In all organisms, except bacteria and blue-green algae, the focal point of heredity is the **nucleus**, usually located in the center of the cell and separated from the cytoplasm by a thin nuclear membrane. Within the nucleus are two nucleic acids central to understanding the hereditary process: ribonucleic acid (RNA) and deoxyribonucleic acid (DNA).

Chromosomes   In the higher-organism cells possessing nuclei, the genetic material (DNA) is usually found in a loose, unwound state called *chromatin*. This material, which consists of exceedingly long, thin molecules, is crammed into a very small space. Geneticists estimate that as much as six feet of DNA is packed into the nucleus of each of our somatic cells. This would be the equivalent of

BOX 3-1

Terms Used in Discussion of Chromosomes

AUTOSOMES In humans, the first 22 pairs of chromosomes; not sex chromosomes.

DIPLOID (*dipl*: double; *oid*: resembling, similar to). The full set of chromosomes, 46 in humans. Since there are 23 different chromosomes, doubling that makes 46, the diploid number. There are two (a pair) of each kind of chromosome.

HAPLOID (*hapl*: single, simple; *oid*: resembling, similar to). Simple here means uncomplicated, the basic number, referring to the 23 different chromosomes found in the gamete after the second division. There is a single representative, not a pair, of each kind of chromosome.

HOMOLOGOUS CHROMOSOMES A matched pair of chromosomes.

LOCUS (pl. *loci*, pronounced lo'-sigh, lo'-see, lo'-kee). The place of a gene on a chromosome.

OÖCYTE (oh-oh-site). Female sex cell; a cell that undergoes meiosis and produces an egg, or ovum.

OÖTID A haploid cell produced by meiosis and differentiating into an ovum.

OÖGENESIS Division process of the female sex cell that produces ova.

SPERMATOCYTE A cell that undergoes meiosis and produces a spermatid. A male sex cell.

SPERMATOGENESIS Division process of the male sex cell that produces sperm.

SPERMATID A haploid cell produced by meiosis and differentiating into a sperm cell.

---

stuffing several thousand feet of extremely fine thread into a thimble. This DNA material is normally active during the life cycle of the cell, most of which is spent in various metabolic activities and not in the process of dividing.

However, when the cell does begin to divide, a difficulty arises. All this somewhat jumbled genetic material is first replicated, making two versions of the DNA. As one (and only one) version is to be transmitted to each daughter cell, the problem, more specifically, is one of packaging and organization. In order to efficiently divide and transmit the genetic material, the DNA is condensed into much more compact packages called *chromosomes*.

Chromosomes—meaning "colored bodies"—were given their name in the last century because they took up certain vegetable dyes and were visible under a light microscope. It is important to remember that chromosomes are visible *only* when a cell is entering active division, and this condensed structure basically serves as a packaging vehicle to distribute the genetic material to the next generation of cells.

When chromosomes can be seen, their structure may be depicted as two arms joined by a **centromere** (Fig. 3-2). The number of chromosomes in different plant and animal species varies, but normally all the members of a single species possess the same number of chromosomes (46 for humans).

The 46 chromosomes normally found in the somatic cells of all human beings are more accurately considered as 23 pairs, since there are two sets of 23 different

Figure 3-2
A normal chromosome.

Double-stranded

Centromere

Figure 3-3
*When a chromosome replicates itself,
each unit is a separate DNA molecule,
joined together at the centromere.*

chromosomes (Fig. 3-4). One set comes from the father (P, for paternal) and one from the mother (M, for maternal). Thus, one-half of a person's heredity derives from each parent. The first 22 pairs of chromosomes are known as *autosomes*; the 23rd pair (or *sex chromosomes*) is known alphabetically as XX or XY. (A female carries two X chromosomes and a male one X and one Y.)

Chromosomes play their role during division of both somatic and sex cells. We can better understand these functions as we follow chromosome behavior during somatic cell division (*mitosis*) and sex cell division (*meiosis*) in the following sections.

Cell Division: Mitosis

The nature of most cells is to divide. Since division of the two kinds of cells differs, let us first take the less complex somatic cell division, called **mitosis**.

Somatic cell division serves several functions. As cells divide, they multiply, thus aiding in the growth of the organism. Cell division is also a means by which old cells are replaced by new ones. What is of interest to us is the part of this process of cell division resulting in the development of two daughter cells identical to the mother cell. In this way, as new body cells are produced they are exactly the same as those they replace, and the body, except for maturation and degeneration, remains essentially the same throughout life.

Mitosis operates in ingenious fashion in order to produce these two identical daughter cells (Fig. 3-5). A cell with 46 chromosomes divides into two daughter cells, each containing the exact number of chromosomes as the mother cell. This is accomplished in the following manner:

At the beginning of the division process, each chromosome duplicates itself, and now consists of two identical strands, or DNA molecules, joined by a common centromere. There are now 46 double-stranded chromosomes. (See Fig. 3-3.)

The double-stranded chromosomes position themselves along the equator of the nucleus and, as the cell divides, the centromere splits and the strands, or DNA molecules, separate.

As the cell continues to divide, the DNA molecules move away from each other to opposite ends of the cell. When the cell completes its division, there are two daughter cells, each with a complete set of 46 chromosomes (each with one DNA molecule).

The result of this division is the production of two daughter cells, each identical to the other and to the mother cell. Each daughter cell contains the same 46 chromosomes, exactly the same genetic material as the mother cell.

Cell Division: Meiosis

We have seen how mitosis produces two daughter cells with the same number of chromosomes and genetic material as the mother cell. Reproduction, however, is quite another matter, requiring a specialized division process called **meiosis**.

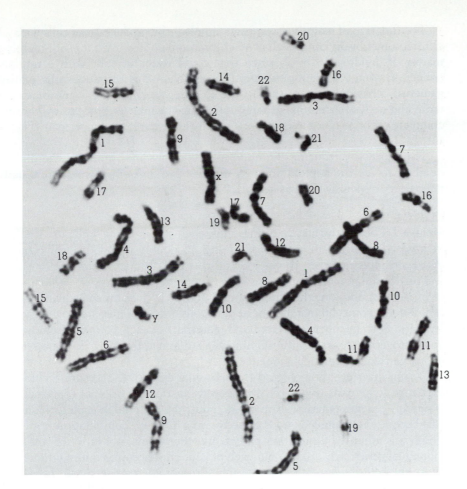

Figure 3-4
Human chromosomes; a male **karyotype**. *Upper portion: Chromosomes as they appear under a microscope. Lower portion: Each pair of chromosomes is identified by the size of the arms on each side of the centromere and arranged, by number, from large to small.*

Somatic cell with 46 chromosomes in nucleus

Cell divides; the nucleus of each daughter cell contains 46 chromosomes

Figure 3-5
An "ingenious" method of dividing a cell with 46 chromosomes and producing two daughter cells with 46 chromosomes identical to each other and to the mother cell.

A haploid cell (sperm or ovum) that may combine with a haploid cell of the other sex to form a fertilized cell.

The function of meiosis also appears simple—the production of cells with 23 chromosomes by dividing a cell of 46 chromosomes. However, it is not merely a matter of dividing 46 by 2, since that could result in cells with a random collection of any 23 chromosomes. The problem is to produce cells (called **gametes**) containing one of each of the 23 different kinds of chromosomes, no more and no less. A normal gamete, following the meiotic process, will have a complete set of 23 chromosomes, one member of each homologous pair (Fig. 3-6).

The process of reducing the number of chromosomes from 46, the diploid number, to 23, the haploid number, requires two divisions, which are usually referred to as Meiosis I and Meiosis II.

Meiosis I Before the first division begins, each chromosome replicates itself, as in mitosis, resulting in a cell containing 46 double-stranded chromosomes. However, unlike mitosis, the meiotic process will ultimately produce four cells and reduce the number of chromosomes in each from 46 to 23.

In the first division, the chromosomes line up in *pairs* on the equator of the cell. At this point, 46 matched or homologous chromosomes are now joined in 23 pairs. Both members (paternal and maternal) of each pair of chromosomes line up together; however, the alignment is random in that they do not assemble in any particular numerical sequence.

During this stage, homologous chromosomes cross-over or, more accurately, exchange some parts (Fig. 3-7). In this way, sections of original (paternal and maternal) chromosomes are exchanged. Thus, the material in each DNA molecule becomes rescrambled and is passed on as a different combination from that which was inherited from either parent. In other words, not only are you as an individual genetically unique, but each of your chromosomes is also unique.

As the cell divides, members of each chromosome pair separate, carrying a mix of maternal and paternal hereditary material into *separate* cells (Fig. 3-8). At this point, each of the two resulting daughter cells contains 23 double-stranded chromosomes. Please note that while the members of each pair have separated into different cells, the chromosomes remain double-stranded.

Meiosis II The second division completes the meiotic process as the two cells, resulting from Meiosis I, divide. This produces a total of four daughter cells (Fig. 3-8). In each cell, the 23 double-stranded chromosomes again line up at the cell's equator. As the cell divides, the double-stranded chromosomes separate at the centromere. With completion of the process, each new daughter cell receives one strand, or DNA molecule, from each of the 23 chromosomes. At this point, each strand is considered to be a chromosome consisting now of one DNA molecule.

The result of Meiosis I and Meiosis II is the division of one cell into four, each containing 23 single-stranded chromosomes. To reiterate, each daughter cell contains the haploid number (23) of chromosomes. This is one-half of the diploid number, or total complement of 46 chromosomes present in human somatic cells.

In males, the newly produced gametes are known as *spermatids* and the process of sperm cell formation is called *spermatogenesis*. Once meiosis is completed, the spermatids will develop tails and become mature sperm cells.

A   B

Chromosome pair number 1

Note that at the same loci on this pair of chromosomes, the genes match.

Figure 3-6
Idealized chromosome form. Each space represents a locus; 12 are shown here. Actually, there are thousands of loci on a chromosome. The figure is a diagrammatic representation of a pair of chromosomes with matching genes: a homologous pair.

Figure 3-7

Female cell division (oögenesis) differs somewhat from spermatogenesis, although the two processes are the same regarding the just-described mechanics of cell division. One difference is that, in females, the first meiotic division produces one relatively large cell (the *primary oöcyte*) and one very small cell called a *polar body*. It is the primary oöcyte that is destined to become the egg, although the polar body does receive chromosomes. In Meiosis II, both these cells divide, and the final result is one larger egg—the ovum—and three smaller polar bodies (Fig. 3-8). Normally, the polar bodies are not functional. It should be clear, however, that in spite of certain differences, the purpose of meiosis is the same in both sexes: to produce functional gametes ready for the fertilization process.

In sexually reproducing organisms, meiosis also plays a role in sex determination. As you already know, the 23rd pair of chromosomes comprises the sex chromosomes. You also know that, in mammals, females possess two X chromosomes whereas, in males, there is one X and one Y. The X and Y chromosomes are equally divided among the lavish supply of sperm in the male

SPERMATOGENESIS

1A 1B 2A 2B

OOGENESIS

1A 2B 1B 2A

DIPLOID NUMBER
Chromosomes
duplicate
crossing over

MEIOSIS I
Pairs separate:
Chromosomes remain
doubled

MEIOSIS II
Haploid number
(23 chromosomes.
1 each of the
23 chromosomes)

1A 2B

2A 1B

Polar body

1B 2A

1A 2B   1A 2b   2A 1B   2A 1B

1B 2A

Polar bodies
(not functional)

1B 2A

Fertilization of oötid
by spermatotid forms zygote

Figure 3-8
*Spermatogenesis and oögenesis. Be-
cause of limited space, 4 chromosomes
represent 46 here.)*

testes, but females can only transmit an X, since that is the only sex chromosome
they carry. Males, on the other hand, can pass on an X or a Y, and the chances of
either are fifty-fifty. If a man contributes a Y, the offspring is male; if X, a female.

Let us return to meiosis. What is the function of the doubling, singling,
dividing, and separating? Are these arithmetic performances critical for survival?
Do they affect natural selection and evolution? Or is nature playing genetic
games? Obviously, they are critical—let us see how.

As Charles Darwin noted, variation within species is important. It is clear
that, without genetic variation, natural selection would be impossible; without
natural selection, evolution would be impossible; and without evolution, life as
we know it on earth would not exist.

One of the advantages of sexual reproduction over asexual reproduction is
that, by combining genetic information from two individuals, it increases
genetic variability within a population. Meiosis, then, is important as a source of
variability because it is fundamental to sexual reproduction. Moreover, through
the mechanism of cross-overs between homologous chromosomes, the genetic
material of each parent is recombined so that individual chromosomes are *altered*
as they pass from one generation to the next. Consequently, no two children
(except monozygotic twins) of the same parents possess exactly the same genetic
material. As you will learn later, meiosis is not the only source of genetic
variation in sexually reproducing populations, but it is an important one.

The reason for two divisions in meiosis is simple. The first division separates
members of chromosome pairs; the second division reduces the double-stranded
chromosomes to single strands. The magic number of chromosomes for normal,
healthy humans is 46. More is bad and so is less. Except for some changes in sex
chromosome number, any change from 46 is invariably associated with problems
ranging from relatively serious to usually fatal diseases.

DNA: Structure

CROSSING-OVER
Exchange of genetic maaterial between chromatids of homologous chromosomes.

We have now seen how heredity is influenced through what might be called mechanical processes. Sex cells divide, chromosomes **cross-over**, and genes recombine. These mechanical processes do not, however, transmit actual characteristics; in fact, parents do not pass on physical traits, they pass on information. Cell division, crossing-over, and gene recombination do not explain how the information passes from parents to offspring. For that, we must turn to the chemical nature of the phenomena involved.

Heredity is transmitted through information chemically coded in deoxyribonucleic acid (DNA), which is usually referred to as the carrier of the genetic code. An examination of the structure and process of DNA will help us understand how the information carried in chemically coded form is transformed from a code to actual physical characteristics of the body.

DNA is a large molecule consisting of four (among other) chemical substances that are its building blocks, or *bases*: *adenine, guanine, cytosine,* and *thymine*. Each base is combined with a sugar (deoxyribose) and a phosphate residue which, all together, ties into a long chain (see Figs. 3-9 and 3-10). The sugar and phosphate alternate to form a backbone of the molecule, and the base may be any one of the four (A, G, C, T) mentioned above. Every base of this long chain is attached to another base (shown in Fig. 3-9), so that the DNA molecule is actually composed of two long chains, or strands, of nucleotides.

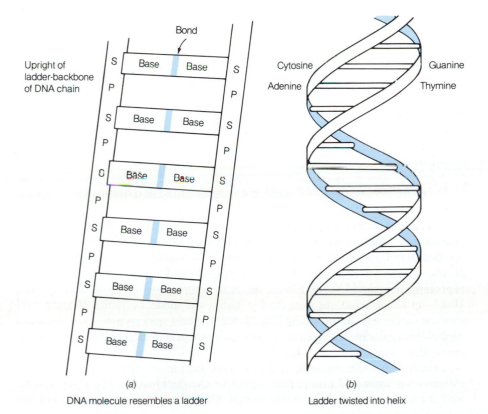

(a) DNA molecule resembles a ladder

(b) Ladder twisted into helix

Figure 3-9
(a) *DNA molecule resembles a ladder.*
(b) *Ladder twisted into a helix.*

Vocabulary: Terms Used in Discussion of DNA

BASE One of the four chemicals attached to a sugar molecule and a phosphate to make up a nucleotide; in DNA, a base is always paired with another base.

ADENINE
GUANINE
CYTOSINE
THYMINE } The four chemical bases. Adenine and thymine are paired; cytosine and guanine are paired.

URACIL A chemical base found in RNA in the same position as thymine in DNA.

AMINO ACIDS Small molecules that are the building blocks of protein.

CODON A triplet sequence of bases on DNA and mRNA.

ANTICODON A triplet sequence of bases on tRNA.

DNA Deoxyribonucleic acid; a large molecule composed of adenine, guanine, cytosine, and thymine plus phosphate and sugar; carries the genetic code.

RNA Ribonucleic acid; slightly different chemically from DNA; found in the nucleus and the cytoplasm.

mRNA Messenger RNA; carries genetic information from DNA in the nucleus to the ribosomes in the cytoplasm.

tRNA Transfer RNA; brings an amino acid to match the mRNA bases.

rRNA Ribosomal RNA; a major constituent of ribosomes.

MOLECULE Smallest portion of a substance (element or compound) that acts like that substance and is capable of existing independently. Several to many atoms constitute a molecule.

NUCLEOTIDE A base attached to a sugar and a phosphate group; a subunit of DNA and RNA.

PEPTIDE A compound of two or more amino acids joined by peptide bonds. Linked peptides form polypeptides which, in turn, join to form proteins.

POLYPEPTIDE A group of peptides joined together.

PROTEIN A macromolecule, composed of one or more polypeptide chains of amino acids, responsible for carrying out most of the cell's metabolic activities; also contributes to cell structure.

RIBOSOMES Small, minute bodies found in the cytoplasm of the cell; composed of rRNA and proteins; site of protein synthesis.

PROTEIN SYNTHESIS The manufacture of a protein. The process by which amino acids are linked (by a peptide bond) to form a polypeptide chain. The completed chain or chains form a protein.

In Figure 3-9(a), the DNA molecule is represented as a flat structure, which might be compared to a ladder. The alternating sugar and phosphates represent the sidepieces of the ladder and the bases represent the rungs. Actually, the two chains twist around each other to form a loose spiral called a **helix**. Since there are two strands, and each one forms a helix, DNA is referred to as a **double helix**. If the ladder in Figure 3-9(a) were twisted to form a double helix, the representation would be more accurate, as in Figure 3-9(b). The discovery of the DNA molecule structure as a double helix was made by James Watson and Francis Crick, an American and English team. Their work, which earned them a Nobel Prize, sparked a phenomenal period of research in molecular biology. (See Issue, this chapter.)

Figure 3-9 illustrates the double helix nature of the DNA molecule. Alternating sugar and phosphates represent the backbone of the DNA chain, and the bases are paired according to rule. (See the following section.) For our purposes, the significance of the DNA structure lies in the bases, especially in the sequence of the bases, because this arrangement is where the hereditary information is stored. In the following sections on DNA *process*, note carefully the role of the bases in transmitting the genetic message.

DOUBLE HELIX
The structure of DNA, composed of a pair of matching helices.

DNA: The Genetic Code

We have mentioned that the genetic information is contained within the DNA molecule, and it is this information that is passed on from parent to offspring. The first requirement of the genetic material (DNA) is, then, that it have some

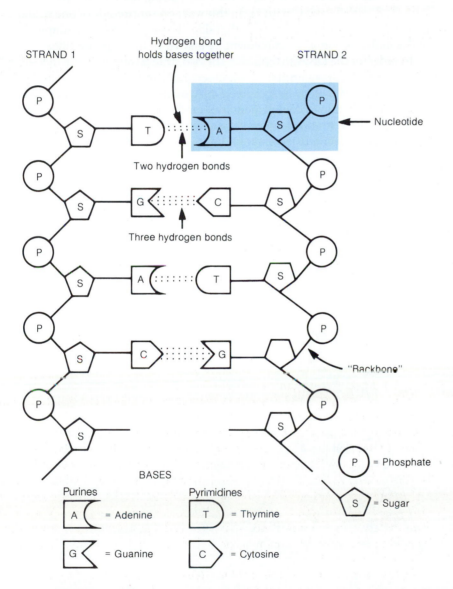

Figure 3-10
Part of a DNA molecule.

efficient means of *self-replication*, so that hereditary information can be accurately reproduced and passed on to succeeding generations of individuals (or, even more basically, to succeeding generations of cells). Replication is essential because it enables parents to retain the master copy, so to speak, of the genetic information and send the duplicate copy to offspring. Without replication, the only set parents possessed would be transmitted to offspring, and parents would then be left without genetic material for future transmissions.

The way replication is accomplished is revealed directly in the beautifully simple structure of the DNA molecule itself. Figure 3-10 shows the DNA molecule simplified as a ladderlike structure. As we can easily see, the molecule has two sides, with each base on one side paired with a specific base on the other side. In other words, according to the base-pairing rule, T only pairs with A; G with C; A with T; and C with G. In this way, one entire side of one strand of the molecule is *complementary* to the other side. To put it even more simply, one side of the molecule forms a complementary pairing of the opposite side.

In order for the DNA to replicate, the two strands must first unwind—much in the manner of a zipper unzipping—and separate, as indicated in Figure 3-11. The two single strands then attract free DNA nucleotides (bases, phosphates, and sugars), thus forming a complementary strand. The result is that where we started with one double-stranded molecule, we now have two identical double-stranded molecules. The genetic information has been completely replicated.

Figure 3-11
The replication of a DNA molecule. The double helix uncoils and then unzips, separating base pairs. Complementary base pairs are attracted and attach to the exposed nucleotides. When replication is completed, each daughter strand is composed of one strand of the parent DNA and one new strand.

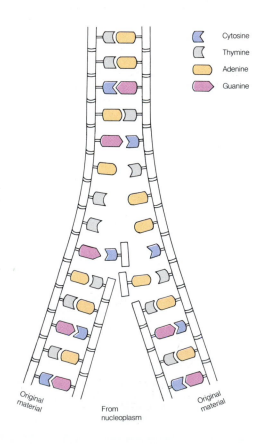

Cytosine
Thymine
Adenine
Guanine

Original material

From nucleoplasm

Original material

DNA: Process

Hereditary information, we know, is transmitted from parents to children through the process of meiosis. Once the father and mother contribute a sex cell each with 23 chromosomes, the result (if fertilization occurs) is a cell with 46 chromosomes called a zygote. The zygote acts as a body cell and passes through the stages of embryo, fetus, and birth. During this period of growth, and for the rest of the individual's life, the hereditary information (coded in the DNA of the nucleus) is taken from the DNA by another nucleic acid called RNA (ribonucleic acid) out into the cytoplasm, where the protein-synthesizing machinery is located. Here, it is converted into proteins, which build and maintain the body according to that hereditary information. The information is coded in the *sequence of bases*, and the student is again asked to bear in mind the significant role of the sequence.

Transcription   The two strands of DNA separate (unzip), and one of the strands, acting as a template, assembles a strand of messenger RNA (mRNA) by attracting mRNA nucleotides that match the DNA bases (Fig. 3-12a). A DNA nucleotide sequence of CGG, for example, will be complemented on the mRNA strand by a GCC **codon**. DNA AAA will transcribe as UUU, instead of TTT, because mRNA does not contain thymine but substitutes uracil instead.

When transcription is completed (Fig. 3-12b), the mRNA strand will be an exact copy of the DNA sequence but with corresponding bases. At this point mRNA, acting as a messenger, carries its coded message out of the nucleus into the cytoplasm of the cell.

Translation   Once in the cytoplasm, mRNA is chemically bonded to a ribosome. The ribosome then moves along, reading the mRNA codons and attracting transfer RNA (tRNA) molecules that match the sequence of mRNA codons. Each tRNA is attached to a specific amino acid. Since there are 20

Strands separate

Free nucleotides attracted to DNA bases

(a) Transcription

(b) Completed mRNA strand; mRNA will leave nucleus and migrate to cytoplasm

Figure 3-12
Formation of mRNA strand. (a) DNA has separated. One DNA strand attracts complementary RNA nucleotide (uracil in RNA replaces thymine), a basic step in the transmission of genetic information. (b) RNA strand completed. Note that RNA bases are exact complements of DNA bases. The sequence of the bases is important.

SICKLE-CELL ANEMIA
A disease caused by a mutant form of hemoglobin (when inherited in double dose).

POINT MUTATION
The change in a single base in the DNA molecule.

INTRON
Within a genetic locus, a section of DNA that is not coded.

different amino acids, there are 20 different tRNAs. As the tRNA moves away from the codon, the amino acid is detached from its tRNA and is bonded to the existing polypeptide chain. This process continues until the ribosome reaches a stop codon, and the synthesis of the polypeptide chain is complete. The complete chain of amino acids is a protein, or part of one, and the process of converting the DNA genetic code for this particular protein has ended.

Proteins are the basic structural and functional compounds of the cell; they are responsible for carrying out most of the metabolic functions of the cell, as well as making up most of the cell structure. The structural components of tissue, hormones, enzymes, hemoglobins, etc., are proteins. In turn, the kind of protein that is synthesized depends upon the information that comes from the DNA. Consequently, the body the proteins build (pigmentation, body build, blood type, etc.) is largely determined by the sequence of bases found in DNA.

Theory of the Gene

Point Mutation

Normal adult hemoglobin is made up of protein chains that are direct products of gene action. One of these chains, called the *beta chain*, is in turn made up of 146 amino acids. Individuals with **sickle-cell anemia** inherit from *both* their parents deleterious gene variants (alleles) that produce a different type of hemoglobin. As a result, these individuals usually have major circulatory disturbances, destruction of red blood cells, and severe anemia often resulting in early death. Individuals who inherit this gene from only one of their parents are much less severely affected and usually have a normal life span.

The cause of all these dramatic changes in the individual's health is a seemingly minute change in the gene that produces hemoglobin. Both normal adult hemoglobin and the sickle-cell variety have 146 amino acids and, of these, 145 are identical. A substitution of only one amino acid (at position #6—see Fig. 3-13) causes all the problems.

We know, of course, that it is the sequence of bases in the DNA that codes for the sequence of amino acids in the final protein product. We also know that 3 bases (1 codon) code for one amino acid. Therefore, it takes 438 bases (146 × 3) to produce the chain of 146 amino acids seen in the adult hemoglobin beta chain.

While DNA replication is highly efficient and accurate, it is not perfect— mistakes can and *do* occur. The difference between normal and sickling hemoglobin, however, concerns a change at only one point in the hemoglobin gene. The first 5 and the last 140 amino acids in the protein chains of both varieties of hemoglobin are identical. Only at position #6 (Fig. 3-13) is there an alteration.

Figure 3-13 shows a possible DNA base sequence and the resulting amino acid products for both normal and sickling hemoglobin. As can be seen, a single base substitution (from CTC to CAC) could result in an altered amino acid sequence (. . . proline—*glutamic acid*—glutamic acid . . . to . . . proline—*valine*— glutamic acid . . .). This, in turn, would alter the properties of the whole protein (hemoglobin), changing its three-dimension structure and resulting in differently shaped red blood cells, oxygen-bonding properties, etc. In other words, the

POINT MUTATION

				Figure 3-13

Figure 3-13
Substitution of one base at position #6 produces a sickling hemoglobin.

only difference between normal hemoglobin and sickling hemoglobin is a change in *one base* out of the 438 bases that make up the coded portion of this gene. Such an alteration is called a **point mutation** and, in evolution, is probably the most common and most important source of new variation.

Recent research has shown that, within the DNA, there are considerably more nucleotides than just those that are eventually translated into amino acid sequences. In fact, in human DNA (and other organisms with nucleated cells, but *not* bacteria) most genes are fragmented. Between those sections that are eventually coded there are often long intervening sequences called **introns**, which do not contribute information for protein synthesis. For example, for the hemoglobin beta locus we have seen there is a total of 438 nucleotides that codes for the eventual polypeptide chain. However, when one also counts those sections at the beginning and end of the locus (promoter and termination regions), as well as two long introns, the entire locus is 1,652 nucleotides long.

While all this genetic information is not utilized directly in protein synthesis, it may serve some function. The entire locus is transcribed onto mRNA. However, before the molecule leaves the nucleus, the intervening sequences are excised and the coded regions are spliced precisely back together. Such apparent DNA superfluity may provide an evolutionary basis for flexible recombination of genetic components. Another possible role in *direct* cell metabolism might operate through the excised sequences being used as "messages" sent to other genes—informing them that the synthesis of a particular polypeptide chain is taking place (Lewin, 1981).

With recent advances in recombinant DNA technology, it has become possible to sequence the nucleotides within the introns. As a result, a variety of *evolutionary* mechanisms have been brought into clearer focus. For example, comparisons of intron sequences in different populations has indicated that the sickle-cell mutation has probably occurred several different times (that is, mutated in slightly different ways in these groups).

Point mutations probably occur relatively frequently during cell division, but a new mutation will have evolutionary significance only if it is passed on to offspring through the gametes. Once such a new mutation has occurred, its fate in the population will depend on the other evolutionary forces, especially natural selection. Sickle-cell, in fact, is the best-demonstrated example of natural selection acting in human beings.

Definition of the Gene

Although not all biologists agree on the definition, we have defined the gene as that section of DNA—a sequence of codons on the DNA template—responsible for the ultimate synthesis of a specific polypeptide chain of amino acids. To put it another way, a gene is that portion of a DNA molecule that specifies the manufacture (synthesis) of a protein or part of a protein (hemoglobin, say) that will produce, or assist in the production of, one or more physical traits. A gene, then, is not a discrete unit operating in the nucleus or the cell; it is part of a large DNA molecule.

Heredity and Environment

For years scientists, debating societies, philosophers, writers, preachers, and others have debated, often acrimoniously, the question of what is more important: heredity or environment, nature or nurture. The question is whether human beings—physically, behaviorally, and psychically—are the result of their heredity or are fashioned and molded by their environment. Or, if both, which is more influential? Differences of opinion on this subject have been bitter.

The English philosopher John Locke (1632–1704) believed that, at birth, the mind of the human being is a blank slate (*tabula rasa*), and all differences are environmentally produced. On the other hand, the French writer Count Joseph Arthur de Gobineau (1816–1882), notorious for his belief in the inequality of races, held that differences in ability are inherited. The behavioral psychologist J. B. Watson left no doubt of his position:

> Give me a dozen healthy infants, well-formed, and my own specified world to bring them up, and I'll guarantee to take any one at random and train him to become any type of specialist I might select—doctor, lawyer, artist, merchant and yes, even beggar and thief, regardless of the talents, penchants, tendencies, abilities, vocations, and race . . . (Watson, 1924, p. 42).

To demonstrate whether heredity or environment is the primary factor responsible for human development is very difficult. Genetics teaches that it is not an either-or proposition, since both factors contribute to what we are physically and behaviorally. As biochemist Daniel Kosland succinctly states it, "In fact the neurobiological evidence indicates that part of the brain is 'hard-wired' in advance of birth and part is designed to be plastic and learn from experience" (1987, p. 1445). From our discussion of genes, we might infer that heredity determines exactly what the nature of a physical trait will be. This circumstance may be so with some genes, but probably not so with most. In the case of the ABO blood system mentioned above, the genes do determine blood type, and, as far as we know, the environment has no effect on the expression of the blood-group genes. If both parents are O, then all their children will be O, regardless of environmental conditions.

Genotypes and Phenotypes   The underlying basis of what we have called heredity in the preceding discussion is known as the **genotype**—"the sum total of the hereditary materials received by an individual from its parents and other ancestors" (Dobzhansky, 1979, p. 32).

An individual's genotype does not change during his or her lifetime—with the exception of some cells in aberrant tissue lines that arise from what are called *somatic mutations*. The consequences may be quite significant for the individual, since experimental work with animals suggests some cancers may well arise from somatic mutations. However, in no case are these somatic mutations passed to offspring. Moreover, for the vast majority of genes in the vast majority of one's cells, we could say the genotype is "fixed" at birth and does not change.

When we observe, probe, or measure people, what we see is their **phenotypes**; for example, a person's skin color, stature, blood type, etc. The phenotype is the *ascertainable* aspect of an organism. Phenotypes, as such, are partly products of the genotype, but, because of their plasticity, they *also* can be modified by the environment. However, other more complex traits, such as stature, weight, personality, or intelligence, are often modified dramatically by the environment. In these cases, a person's phenotype could be said to result from an interaction of the genotype with the environment.

Diet, good or poor, may affect stature and weight; sun exposure may affect skin pigmentation; phenotypes of monozygotic twins, genetically identical individuals, may vary if the twins are raised in different environments. Thus, it is obvious that an individual's phenotype changes continuously from birth to death as glandular and maturation effects occur.

What we are, then, for the most part, is the result of the interaction of hereditary material and environmental conditions. As the well-known geneticist Theodosius Dobzhansky wrote:

> Between the genes   and the adult phenotypes [observable characteristics] . . . there intervenes a set of developmental processes, which . . . may be exceedingly long and elaborate. This leaves ample opportunity for the uniform primary action of a gene to yield a variety of manifestations in the developing phenotypes. . . . Which potentialities will in fact be realized in a given individual at a certain stage of his development is decided by the sequence of the environments in which the development takes place (Dobzhansky, 1970, p. 33).

A gene may be perceived as potentiality. What potentiality will actually be realized, after an "exceedingly long and elaborate" developmental process, depends upon the environmental conditions. It is this interaction between biology and environment, nature and nurture, which makes us the kind of individuals we are—physically, behaviorally, and psychically. This interaction also emphasizes the point already made in the first chapter: That humans are biocultural beings.

With this introduction to the biological basis of life in mind, let us now, in the next chapter, examine how the genetic process can be applied to the process of evolution.

GENOTYPE
The actual physical makeup of an individual.

PHENOTYPE
(phee'-no-type)
phen: showing
The observable or measurable characteristics of an individual as determined by the genotype and the influence of the environment.

Summary

We have dealt with two kinds of cells in this chapter—somatic cells, of which our bodies are composed, and sex cells, which are used only in the transmission of hereditary information.

Somatic cells divide by mitosis, producing two daughter cells identical to each other and to the mother cell. Sex cells divide twice by meiosis and produce four gametes. Meiosis is known as reduction division because the diploid number of chromosomes (46) is reduced to the haploid number (a complete set of 23).

There are 23 pairs of chromosomes in a human cell. Two chromosomes with similar loci, of which there are 22 pairs, are called homologous. The 23rd pair is the sex chromosomes.

Genetic information is contained in the DNA double helix. Information is taken from nucleus to cytoplasm by mRNA. Ribosomes in the cell translate the mRNA message and attract tRNA molecules. The tRNA molecules transport amino acids to the ribosomes, forming a polypeptide chain. A polypeptide chain (or chains) of amino acids is a protein that makes up most of the cell structure and carries out most of the cell's metabolic functions.

A gene is not a discrete unit but is an orderly sequence of DNA codons that designates a specific chain of amino acids. The equation, one gene equals one polypeptide chain, is sometimes used as a definition of a gene.

Genes do not necessarily determine the precise nature of a physical characteristic. Genes are potentials modified by the environment, and it is the interaction of genes and environmental conditions that produces physical traits.

Questions for Review

1. Name the parts of a cell discussed in the chapter.
2. List the differences between mitosis and meiosis.
3. List the steps in mitosis; in meiosis.
4. Name two important functions of meiosis.
5. Why is a pair of homologous chromosomes homologous?
6. What is a locus?
7. What different kinds of RNA are there?
8. What is the function of mRNA?
9. What is the function of ribosomes?
10. What is a nucleotide?
11. Name the four DNA bases. Which bases complement each other in DNA?
12. What base is found in DNA but not in RNA?
13. What are the building blocks of a protein?
14. How is a chain of amino acids formed?
15. How are tRNA and mRNA matched?
16. What is the difference between codon and anticodon?
17. What is the difference between diploid and haploid?
18. Why do gametes contain the haploid instead of the diploid number?
19. What is the function of cross-over?
20. Why is variation important in the evolutionary process?
21. What is meant by recombination of genes?
22. How would you answer the question of nature versus nurture?
23. Give an example of how the effect of a gene may be modified by the environment.

Genetics and Evolution

CONTENTS

Biotechnology— For Better or for Worse?

When Stanley Cohen of Stanford University and Herbert Boyer of the University of California at San Francisco passed frog genes into the plasmids of *E. coli* bacteria in 1973, the bacteria were able to manufacture the frog RNA encoded in the genes. This was called *recombinant genetics* and was the first step for researchers in learning how to enable bacteria to produce animal protein.

Soon, visions of wondrous possibilities from the recombining of genes in the laboratory proliferated: the cure of incurable diseases; the production of bigger and better plants and larger crops from less acreage; disease-free plants; food products of almost interminable shelf life; and, of course, benefits of all sorts for the human body and brain.

Although most of these goals have not yet been reached, there have been noteworthy achievements. By 1982, the Food and Drug Administration (FDA) approved the first gene-cloned medical product: human insulin, which replaced the insulin formerly obtained from cow and pig pancreases. Within the past few years, FDA has approved recombinant human growth hormone for the treatment of growth-hormone-deficient children, alpha interferon to break down tumors in people with hairy cell leukemia, and a vaccine against hepatitis B (Murray, 1987).

Currently, medical researchers are energetically pursuing new forms of cancer-fighting enzymes, blood clot reducing-proteins, and hormones to reduce blood pressure and water retention.•

In plant research, the long-awaited field testing of Frostban occurred in April, 1987. Frostban consists of bacteria that have been genetically altered to prevent frost on strawberries. This was the very first field test of a genetically altered plant. It was carried out by Advanced Genetic Sciences, Inc., of Oakland, California. Many more such tests are planned for plants and animals.

However, in many of these applications, there are administrative, ethical, and moral issues to be considered. There are also risks involved. Biotechnology is a new science engineering products that many people think could be dangerous to plants and animals, humans, and the environment. Therefore, all concerned agree that regulations are necessary. Consequently, biotechnology cannot be confined unto itself but must be involved with many other areas (such as academe, business, agriculture, health, and religion).

The question is: Which federal agency (or combination of agencies) should be the regulator? There is the Federal Food and Drug Administration, the National Institutes of Health, the Department of Agriculture, the Office of Science and Technology Policy, and the Environmental Protection Agency (EPA), to name a few. Regulations of the various agencies differ, and this has occasioned delays in obtaining permission for testing and for bringing products to market. This, in turn, has resulted in confusion, frustration, and additional expense.

In the academic arena, there are serious ethical problems surrounding

•On November 13, 1987, the Food and Drug Administration gave permission to Genentech Inc., a biotech firm located in South San Francisco, to sell *tissue plasminogen activator* (TPA) designed to assist in dissolving blood clots that clog arteries and cause heart attacks.

Genentech cloned the gene that produces natural tpa and inserted it into mammal cells which became "factories" that manufacture large quantities of the drug.

recombinant technology. For example, to what extent can, or should, a university become a profit-making entity? (Stanford and the University of California have patented the Cohen-Boyer process). To what extent should university professors engage in research for private biotech corporations? The lure of high incomes has encouraged many scientists to leave the university and join biotech industry. How will this affect university education and research?

Business concerns operate on a profit basis and, in order to earn a profit, compete with other businesses to be the first to bring a new or improved product to market. If biotech companies maintain research secrecy to ensure or enhance their profits, to what extent will the traditional openness and cross-fertilization of scientific research be affected? If scientific journals are not given research findings, or are not permitted to publish them, will this hinder scientific progress? These are some of the important questions that have been discussed (see Kenny under Sources), and *Science* has published several articles on the subject in 1986 and 1987.

There is also the issue of morality. We noted above that Frostban, a genetically altered organism, was released during a field test in the spring of 1987. The organism, as demonstrated in lab tests, prevents plants from freezing. What works in the lab, however, does not always work in the field, so the field tests are necessary if the product is to be successfully marketed. For many people, the release of such an "artificial" organism into the environment is worrisome.

People raise such questions as: Should we be tampering with nature? If God didn't create it, shouldn't humans keep their hands off? If scientists can manufacture a new organism in the lab, admittedly a very small one, will they be able to design a big one—like a human! If an organism that did not evolve through natural selection is released into the environment, isn't it possible that it might be dangerous and pose a serious threat to the environment, to "natural" organisms and, more important, to human beings? (Ostensibly, if an organism evolved naturally, and if it were dangerous to other lifeforms, it would probably have been eliminated.) Religion also asks disturbing questions: Are biotechnology scientists replacing God's role as creator? Is it moral to change the natural order? Aren't scientists guilty of hubris (excessive pride, arrogance)?

Scientists reply that humans have been changing the natural order ever since the first plants and animals were domesticated, more than ten thousand years ago. Also, they believe that traditional scientific caution, so long practiced in the laboratory, is a safeguard against environmental and other kinds of hazards. Furthermore, scientists point out that they themselves are citizens with concerns about the environment. They are also aware of the possible risks, and so they have worked closely with government agencies to develop regulations for biotechnological activities.

Up until the present, biotechnology has not produced disasters or even unfortunate accidents in the lab or in the field. Biotechnologists and biotech companies, aware of the risks, nevertheless believe they have much to contribute to a richer and fuller life. This belief notwithstanding, a large number of people still worry.

SOURCES:

Judson, Horace Freeland. "Thumbprints in Our Clay," *The New Republic*, September 19 and 26, 1983:12–17. (Professor Judson discusses biotechnology and its relationship to religious and ethical questions.)

Kenny, Martin. *Biotechnology: the University-Industrial Complex*, New Haven: Yale University Press, 1986.

Murray, Mary. "Battling Illness with Body Proteins," *Science News*, January 17, 1987:131–143.

Introduction

In Chapter 3, we have seen in some detail how, within the cell, genetic material is organized, packaged, distributed, and passed on to succeeding generations of cells. But when we look at the world of organisms, we see individuals who are in most cases composed of billions of cells, and our focus of organization must be shifted to a different level. In this chapter, we shall investigate the processes that allow us not only to understand, but also to predict, how genes are passed from parent to offspring. This process is the basis of the science of genetics, and its modern beginnings date to Gregor Mendel's work in the 1850s and 1860s.

Early Theories of Inheritance

For ages humans have been interested in the rules of heredity. We can easily imagine the early farmers of 10,000 years ago wondering how tiny grains produced wheat. Already in the fourth century B.C., Theophrastus, a Greek, had carefully studied seed germination and written a book on the subject. Some early Greeks believed that heredity among humans was a question of which sex dominated in the sex act. In the eighteenth century, Linnaeus suggested a two-layer theory, which held that "the outer layer including the vascular system is derived from the father, the inner layer including the nervous system comes from the mother."

An interesting theory dating as far back as Aristotle was developed further in the seventeenth century (E. Gardner, 1965, p. 275). This theory was based on the belief, called *preformation*, that "the development of an organism is no more than the unfolding of that which is already present in miniature [Fig. 4-1]. Every organism must therefore contain in its reproductive organs an infinite series representing all of its future descendants." Ovists believed the female possessed this future of the series, and the spermists insisted it was the male.

While there were differences of opinion about the role of sex, and ignorance of the laws of animal heredity, plants were not generally discussed in these terms. That plants lacked sexuality was the conventional wisdom of the day. Not until the end of the seventeenth century was the presence of sex organs in plants demonstrated in the experiments performed in Germany by Rudolph Camerarius.

The notion that plants consisted of male and female parts came as a shock to many people. " 'What man,' exclaimed J. G. Siegesbeck, Professor of Botany at St. Petersburg, 'will ever believe that God Almighty should have introduced such confusion, or rather such shameful whoredom, for the propagation of the reign of plants. Who will instruct young students in such a voluptuous system without scandal?' " (Olby, 1985, pp. 18–19).

The discovery of sexual reproduction in plants was a notable achievement not simply because it added to our knowledge of plants, but also because it makes possible an experimental approach to plant hybridization. Once begun by Camerarius, crossing hybrids and observing what regularities might occur among

Figure 4-1
Some early investigators thought that they could see tiny human embryos within the sperm.

the offspring became one of the most popular methods of investigating the laws of heredity.

Hybridization experiments continued in the eighteenth and nineteenth centuries. Hybrids offered an opportunity, it was believed, to work out the rules of heredity. Purebred plants produced purebreds, and there was little to learn about heredity from that kind of experiment. Among the offspring of hybrids, on the other hand, some resembled the parents, but others were quite different. If, in this apparent confusion of offspring, there were regularities of such traits as form, color, or germination patterns, they would serve as clues to the principles of heredity.

Or so it seemed. Many investigators worked on plant hybrids, but the secrets of heredity eluded them. Experimenters demonstrated, for example, that neither sex was entirely responsible for offspring but both parents contributed equally. They also demonstrated that hybrids did not breed true (as Linneaus believed they did), yet the laws of heredity remained undiscovered.

There were several reasons for this failure. The plants used were not the proper ones for the study of heredity—they were genetically too complex for the kind of observations possible at that time. Experimenters did not work with enough plants, or through sufficient generations, to find regularities. And, finally, they did not count the offspring of hybrids; that is, they failed to examine the results of their experiments from a statistical point of view. What the early experimenters saw were offspring in a confusing variety of forms and colors, which they were unable to clarify. Their conclusion was that clarification was impossible, that there probably were no universal laws of heredity.

Thus matters stood, more or less at a standstill as far as the laws of heredity were concerned, until Gregor Mendel solved the riddle in the 1860s.

Figure 4-2
Gregor Mendel.

Mendel's Life

Gregor Mendel (1822–1884), shown in Figure 4-2, was born into a family of peasant farmers, in the small Silesian village of Heinzendorf in what we now call Czechoslovakia. At school, he did so well in his academic studies that his teachers recommended he be transferred to a high school in a nearby town. Within a year, he had moved on to the Gymnasium (an advanced high school) at Troppau where, in 1840, he received a certificate which recognized his "great industry and all-round ability."

To continue his studies, he enrolled in the University Philosophical Institute of Olmutz. Because of lack of funds, Mendel had a difficult time, and his attempts to earn money as a private tutor failed. He wrote of this period of his life (in the third person): "The sorrow over these disappointed hopes and the anxious, sad outlook which the future offered him, affected him so powerfully at that time that he fell sick and was compelled to spend a year with his parents to recover!" (in Olby, 1985, p. 106).

In 1841, Mendel returned to the university, and this time succeeded in finding part-time tutorial work, but he worked so hard his health failed again. In 1843, he discussed his future with one of his professors, Friedrich Franz, who suggested a monastery as a place that would provide the quiet kind of life Mendel required. He encouraged Mendel to apply to the monastery at Brünn and recommended him as "a young man of very solid character. In my own branch [physics] he is almost the best" (in Olby, 1985, p. 107). Mendel followed Franz' advice, was admitted as a novice on October 9, 1843, and took the name of Gregor.

Early on, it became clear that Mendel was not temperamentally suited to serve as a parish priest, since he could not witness suffering without falling ill himself. The understanding abbot of the monastery assigned him as a substitute teacher to a high school in a nearby town, and Mendel soon became known as an excellent teacher. He could not be given a permanent appointment because he lacked a teacher's certificate, and for him to obtain this document, he had to take courses at the University of Vienna.

It was at Vienna, where he came into contact with leading professors in botany, physics, and mathematics, that Mendel acquired his scientific education. His studies there helped him in his later experiments, especially in his mathematical approach, which was so different from that of other plant experimenters.

Upon completing his studies at Vienna, Mendel returned to the monastery and resumed his teaching career, as well as his work in the monastery garden. He

Figure 4-3
Central Europe during Mendel's lifetime.

had been experimenting for some time with the fertilization of flowers, attempting to develop new variations in colors. What impressed Mendel was the "striking regularity with which the same hybrid forms always reappeared when fertilization took place between the same species," which induced him "to follow up the development of the hybrids in their progeny."

Mendel's Experiments

Mendel was well aware that no laws governing the formation and development of hybrids had yet been formulated, and he was also aware that hybridization experiments were very difficult. Nevertheless, he decided to proceed with his experiments and had definite ideas of how to go about it. He pointed out that not one experiment

> had been carried out to such an extent and in such a way as to make it possible to determine the number of different forms under which the offspring of hybrids appear, or to arrange these forms with certainty according to their separate generations, or definitely to ascertain their statistical relation (Mendel, 1965, pp. 1–2).

What Mendel decided to do apparently even before he began his experiments on hybrids was: (a) to determine the number of different forms of hybrids produced; (b) to arrange the forms according to generations—F_2, F_3, etc.; and

Figure 4-4
The monastery at Brünn (as it looks today), where Mendel spent much of his life.

P₁   The parental generation in which homozygous dominants and recessives are crossed. Parents pure or homozygous for round seeds and parents homozygous for wrinkled represent such a parental cross.

F₁   First filial generation. The offspring resulting from a parental cross of homozygotes for different alleles.

F₂   Second filial generation. The offspring resulting from a cross of F₁ individuals (or self-fertilization of F₁ individuals, where this is possible).

(c) to attempt to evaluate the statistical relations (the proportions) of the various forms.

These three points, wrote the eminent geneticist of the early twentieth century, William Bateson, led to "the whole success of Mendel's work. . . . So far as I know this conception was absolutely new in his day" (Mendel, 1965, p. 2n) and is the basis of modern biological research.

Selection of Plants   Before discussing Mendel's actual experiments and his conclusions, one more point should be considered, for it illustrates Mendel's genius compared to other plant hybridizers. This point concerns the *kind* of plant to be used. "The value and utility of any experiment," Mendel noted in the paper he read at a meeting of the Natural History Society of Brünn in February, 1865, "are determined by the fitness of the material to the purpose for which it is used, and thus in the case before us it cannot be immaterial what plants are subjected to experiment and in what manner such experiments are conducted" (Mendel, 1965, p. 2). He went on to say that the selection of the plant "must be made with all possible care" and two qualifying conditions *must* be met: That the plant (1) possess constant differentiating characters and (2) the hybrids of such plants be protected from foreign pollen.

By constant differentiating characters—a most important point—Mendel meant that the plant must possess two contrasting characters of the same trait. If color were the trait, then the plant should possess two contrasting colors; if stature, then tall and short. These conditions led Mendel to devote his attention to legumes, and experiments with several members of this group led him to the genus *Pisum*, the common garden pea.

Clearly, Mendel knew what he was doing from the very beginning. Unlike those who preceded him, he concentrated on the underlying genetic factors,

Figure 4-5
Mendel's "plantation," where he conducted his genetic experiments. The garden is presently ornamental. Mendel's statue can be seen in the background.

what we today call genes. He proposed to follow the progress of the hybrids through a number of generations, counting the number of different types of hybrid progeny. He would carefully select the kind of plant that possessed the traits he considered necessary for the experiment, contrasting characters and fertility for a number of successive generations. Finally, he planned to use a large number of plants, so that the uniqueness of a small number of seeds would not bias the results.

From several nurserymen, Mendel obtained thirty-four varieties of peas, and, after checking them during a two-year trial, he selected twenty-two varieties for fertilization. Most of them belonged to the species *Pisum sativum*. As already noted, Mendel deliberately planned to use a plant that possessed at least one set of contrasting characters. With luck (insight, more probably), he selected the pea with *seven* characteristics (see Table 4-1), each of which occurred on a different pair of homologous chromosomes. Had this not been the case, it is doubtful his experiments would have succeeded.

The Pea Experiments—P₁ Generation

Mendel launched his experiment in the spring of 1856. He divided the garden into sections, one for each of the seven characters of the pea. He placed contrasting characters next to each other so they would be easier to compare. Round seeds went next to wrinkled; yellow next to green; tall next to dwarf.

When the plants were ready to blossom, Mendel opened the flower buds of each plant and performed the surgery necessary to prevent the peas from fertilizing themselves in the normal manner. He then proceeded to do the cross-fertilizing himself (Fig. 4-7). Altogether, Mendel made 287 cross-fertilizations on 70 plants and then waited for the plants to mature in what the other monks called "Mendel's pea plantation."

F₁ Generation   The offspring of the **P₁** cross (Fig. 4-8*a*) are designated as the **F₁** generation, and when the F₁ generation matured, Mendel observed the seeds. They were all round (as in Fig. 4-8*a*). He then grew plants from these F₁ round seeds and, when the plants matured, allowed them to self-fertilize (Fig. 4-8*b*). Mendel then examined the offspring of the F₁ generation of round peas and found that in this generation (F₂) there were both round seeds *and* wrinkled seeds (Fig. 4-8*c*). When he carefully counted the numbers of each, they added up to 5,474

Axial flowers
Terminal flowers

Round seed   Wrinkled seed

Figure 4-6
Contrasting characters.

Figure 4-7
Mendel cross-fertilizing his plants by hand.

Table 4-1   *The Seven Characteristics of the Garden Pea Mendel Selected*

| Characteristics | Contrasting | |
	Dominant Traits	Recessive Traits
1. form of the ripe seed	round	wrinkled
2. color of seed albumen	yellow	green
3. color of seed coat	gray	white
4. form of ripe pods	inflated	constricted
5. color of unripe pods	green	yellow
6. position of flowers	axial	terminal
7. length of stem	tall	dwarf

Figure 4-8

Gregor Mendel's logic. Mendel concluded: (1) the ½ of F₂ plants that produced a 3:1 ratio of round to wrinkled were the same as the F₁ rounds that produced a 3:1 ratio— therefore ½ of the F₂ plants must be hybrids (heterozygous); (2) the ¼ of the F₂ plants that produced only round seeds must be homozygous for round; (3) the ¼ of the F₂ plants that produced only wrinkled must be homozygous for wrinkled; (4) hybrid forms yield a genotypic ratio of 1:2:1 (that is, 1:homozygous dominant to 2:heterozygous dominant to 1:homozygous recessive).

P1 generation

(a)

Plant producing only round peas; homozygous

Plant producing only wrinkled peas; homozygous

F1 generation

(b)

All seeds are round

Plants allowed to self-fertilize and when mature seeds are counted

F2 generation

(c)

RESULT

5,474 Round to 1,850 wrinkled
A phenotypic ratio of 3:1

The round resembled P1 round
The wrinkled resembled P1 wrinkled

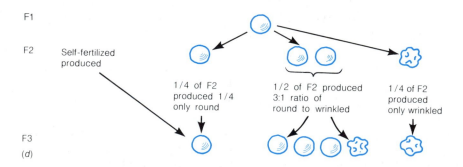

F1

F2

Self-fertilized produced

1/4 of F2 produced 1/4 only round

1/2 of F2 produced 3:1 ratio of round to wrinkled

1/4 of F2 produced only wrinkled

F3

(d)

round seeds and 1,850 wrinkled, a ratio of 2.96 to 1. Among the other traits, the ratios (Table 4-2) were slightly over or under 3:1, and the average ratio of all the seeds of all the traits in the F₂ generation was 3:1 (Fig. 4-8).

Mendel now saw clearly that when F₁ hybrids are bred, three offspring are produced that resemble one P₁ grandparent for every one offspring that resembles the other P₁ grandparent. The character that appeared three times, Mendel called **dominant**, and that which appeared once, **recessive**.

F₂ Generation The experiment continued through another (F₃) generation. The plants of the **F₂** generation were allowed to self-fertilize, and once more Mendel carefully counted the results. He found that one-half of the F₂ plants produced round and wrinkled seeds at a ratio of 3:1; one-fourth produced only round seeds; and one-fourth produced only wrinkled seeds. Since the one-half that produced a 3:1 ratio of round to wrinkled seeds behaved in exactly the same way as the F$_1$ hybrids, Mendel reasoned that these must also be **hybrids**, or **heterozygotes** (Fig. 4-8).

> . . . it is now clear [said Mendel] that the hybrids form seeds having one or the other of the two differentiating characters, and of these one-half develop again the hybrid form, while the other half yield plants which remain constant and receive the dominant or the recessive characters in equal numbers (Mendel, 1965, p. 13).

Experiment Results—The Riddle Solved

Using current terminology, we would say that one-half of the F$_2$ generation plants must be heterozygous, since they produced a 3:1 ratio just as the F$_1$ hybrids did. One-fourth of the F$_2$ plants produced only round seeds; therefore, they must be **homozygous** dominant. The remaining one-fourth produced only wrinkled seeds; therefore, they must be homozygous recessive. This led to Mendel's conclusion that the genotypic ratio is 1:2:1 for the F$_2$ generation:

¼ homozygous dominant
½ heterozygous dominant = 1 : 2 : 1
¼ homozygous recessive   RR : Rr : rr

Mendel continued his experiments through several succeeding generations, and the results reinforced conclusions already reached. He had succeeded brilliantly where others had failed. By carefully selecting the proper experimental plant, by using a large number of plants, and—perhaps, most importantly—by carefully counting the numbers and kinds of offspring, Mendel had accomplished two goals: (1) he clarified the confusion surrounding the reproduction of hybrids; and (2) he discovered the laws of heredity. For a modest, unknown amateur this achievement was indeed remarkable.

We should point out that this method of experimental breeding was simple, but original and unique. Moreover, the experiments were *deliberately designed to test a theory*, a new idea in biology (Dunn, 1965, p. 193).

Mendel's Report After eight years of constant work, Mendel was at long last prepared to report on his findings, and, at the February, 1865, meeting of the Natural History Society of Brünn, Mendel read his paper. Members of the society, familiar with the methodology of more traditional botanists, were confused

DOMINANT
A trait determined by a dominant allele. A trait that is visible or measurable and that prevents the appearance of the recessive. The allele for round seeds is dominant and when present "prevents" the appearance of wrinkled seeds.

RECESSIVE
A trait determined by the recessive allele. A trait is not visible or measurable when paired with the dominant allele. The heterozygote Rr possesses both the dominant and recessive allele, but the wrinkling is not expressed phenotypically. (R = uppercase of first letter of dominant trait; used as symbol for dominant trait. r = lowercase of dominant symbol, used as a symbol for recessive trait.)

HYBRID
The progeny resulting from a cross of different parental stock.

HETEROZYGOTE
A cell or individual that is heterozygous. (A hybrid is heterozygous for a particular trait.) A person who is AO is heterozygous for ABO blood system; an F$_1$ round pea (Rr) is heterozygous for form.

HETEROZYGOUS
Having different alleles at a given locus on a pair of homologous chromosomes.

HOMOZYGOUS
Having the same allele at a given locus on a pair of homologous chromosomes.

HOMOZYGOTE
A cell or individual that is homozygous. (A purebred is homozygous for a particular trait.) A pea that is RR or rr is a homozygote.

Table 4-2 *The Ratios of Mendel's Experiment*

Characteristics	Numbers of Peas		Ratio
1. form of ripe seed	5,474 round	1,850 wrinkled	2.96:1
2. color of seed	6,022 yellow	2,001 green	3.01:1
3. color of seed coat	705 gray	224 white	3.15:1
4. form of ripe pods	882 inflated	299 constricted	2.95:1
5. color of unripe pods	428 green	152 yellow	2.82:1
6. position of flowers	651 axial	207 terminal	3.14:1
7. length of stem	787 tall	277 dwarf	2.84:1

Figure 4-9
Dominance.

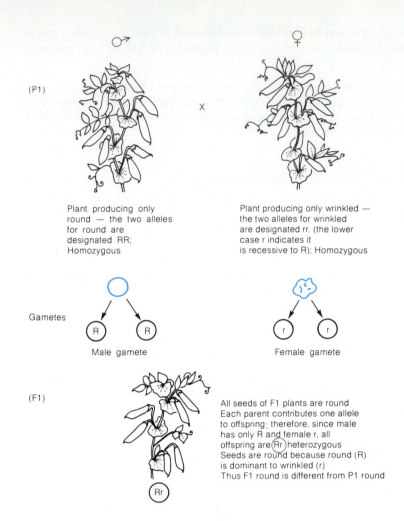

♂   ♀

(P1)

X

Plant producing only
round — the two alleles
for round are
designated RR;
Homozygous

Plant producing only wrinkled —
the two alleles for wrinkled
are designated rr. (the lower
case r indicates it
is recessive to R); Homozygous

Gametes

R   R

Male gamete

r   r

Female gamete

(F1)

All seeds of F1 plants are round
Each parent contributes one allele
to offspring; therefore, since male
has only R and female r, all
offspring are Rr heterozygous
Seeds are round because round (R)
is dominant to wrinkled (r)
Thus F1 round is different from P1 round

Rr

by his ideas. The next month, when Mendel presented his algebraic equations, the lack of understanding was even greater. The idea that "heredity was the giant shuffling and reshuffling of separate and invisible hereditary factors" was so different from what had been taught that it was probably incomprehensible. When Mendel finished his report, no one rose to ask a question, and the minutes of the society record no discussion.

The society published the monograph Mendel had prepared and copies were sent, as was the custom, to cities throughout Europe, but it attracted no attention. Mendel was disappointed. He was aware of the significance of his work and decided to send his report to one of Europe's outstanding botanists, Karl von Naegeli of Munich. Naegeli obviously failed to understand the experiment and replied in a condescending letter that Mendel's work was "far from being finished." Thus, a second opportunity for science to learn the rules of heredity was lost, not to be rediscovered until 1900.

In 1868, at the age of 46, Mendel was elected abbot of the monastery and, because of heavy administrative duties, he was unable to continue his scientific work. He died January 6, 1884, a beloved figure in the town of Brünn but unknown to the world of science.

Genes, Chromosomes, and Mendel

With this brief survey, let us now examine more systematically the rules of heredity Mendel discovered. First, it may be useful to summarize pertinent information regarding genes and chromosomes already presented in Chapter 3.

Sex cells carry two sets of chromosomes to make up a full complement (46 in humans), the diploid number. On a pair of homologous chromosomes there is a number of loci, and at each locus on the pair is genetic material (a segment of DNA—a gene) that affects a particular trait. Thus, in any individual there are two genes for each trait. There may be several loci, by the way, that affect the same trait (stature, say), but, for our purpose, it is sufficient to deal with only one locus at a time. These are called simple or Mendelian traits and follow Mendelian ratios. If at a locus there is genetically coded material, let us say, for round seeds or genetically coded material for wrinkled seeds, then these different forms of the gene are known as **alleles**. Alleles are similar, but slightly different, sequences of DNA that control the same trait. Normal hemoglobin and sickling hemoglobin discussed in the preceding chapter are examples of alleles for the same trait. With this review, we return to Mendel's rules.

Principle of Segregation

Dominant and Recessive Cross   In his experiment with peas, Mendel obtained seeds that were homozygous. He tested them by planting to make sure that those intended to produce round seeds did so, and those for wrinkled seeds produced only wrinkled. The second step was to cross the plants producing only round seeds with plants producing only wrinkled seeds. * The offspring of this cross were all round even though the sex cells of the plant contained an allele for wrinkled (Fig. 4-10). They were all round, as we know, because round is dominant to wrinkled. Please note that, phenotypically, the seeds are round, but, genotypically, both alleles are present, Rr, or heterozygous. The F_1 round (Rr) are genotypically different from their P_1 round (RR) parent (Fig. 4-10).

How is the difference between the F_1 and P_1 round seeds to be explained? Both seeds are phenotypically round, but the genotypes are different. Recalling the meiotic process, we know that after cell division a gamete contains one set of chromosomes, the haploid number. Therefore, the gamete contains only one of the alleles for a particular trait. To take Mendel's example, the parent plants each contained two genes for either roundness or wrinkledness. Because of meiotic division, each parent contributes only one. Since both parents are homozygous—one for round and the other for wrinkled—one parent would have to contribute an R allele and the other an r allele (Fig. 4-10).

The offspring in the F_1 generation possess both alleles, the big R from one parent and the small r from the other. Thus, the offspring are hybrid, or heterozygous.

Heterozygous Cross—3:1 Phenotypic Ratio   In the next step of the experiment, Mendel allowed these F_1 heterozygotes to fertilize themselves (pea plants

ALLELES
Alternative forms of the same gene. (In the ABO blood system, A, B, and O are alternative forms found at the same locus. In a population where alternative forms are available at a particular locus, they are called alleles. The gene for round seeds and the gene for wrinkled seeds are such alternative forms.)

*In our discussion, we shall use the round and wrinkled traits. Mendel, of course, experimented with all seven traits, and the results in every case were similar.

Figure 4-10
Segregation of gametes.

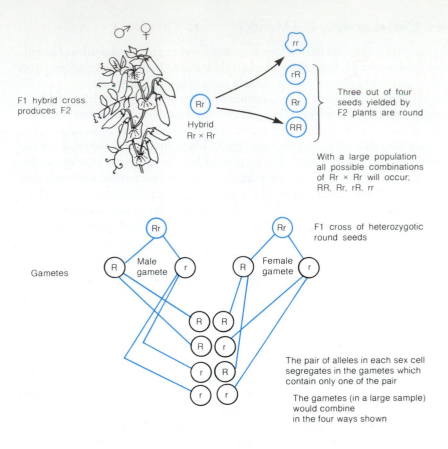

F1 hybrid cross produces F2

Hybrid
Rr × Rr

Three out of four seeds yielded by F2 plants are round

With a large population all possible combinations of Rr × Rr will occur: RR, Rr, rR, rr

F1 cross of heterozygotic round seeds

Gametes

Male gamete

Female gamete

The pair of alleles in each sex cell segregates in the gametes which contain only one of the pair

The gametes (in a large sample) would combine in the four ways shown

contain both male and female parts). Although fertilization occurs within one plant, the male and female sex cells may be diagrammed thus:

$$Rr \times Rr$$

The result of this self-fertilization, as we have seen, was the production of three round seeds for every wrinkled. What happened in the F_1 cross to produce a 3:1 ratio? Bearing in mind what we know of meiosis, homologous chromosomes, and alleles, it is only necessary to add one point, the element of chance.

We know that as a result of meiosis a parent can contribute, at any one time, only one of a pair of chromosomes and therefore only one of two alleles for a trait. In this case, each parent will contribute either R *or* r. There is an even chance that the male R will combine with the female R or with the female r. Similarly, the odds are even that the male r will combine with the female R or r. In other words, there are four, and only four, possible combinations. Each combination has an equal chance, a one out of four (or 25%) chance of occurring (Fig. 4-11).

Figure 4-11
Gametic combinations.

R R   Male gamete with R may fertilize female gamete with R   =   RR

R r   Male gamete with R may fertilize female gamete with r   =   Rr

r R   Male gamete with r may fertilize female gamete with R   =   rR

r r   Male gamete with r may fertilize female gamete with r   =   rr

Quarter | Dime

POSSIBLE COMBINATIONS

Heads | Heads | Heads | Tails

Tails | Heads | Tails | Tails

Figure 4-12
Possible combinations of coins. If any two coins are tossed many times, the probability is that each combination would come up the same number of times. Since there are four combinations, each combination will turn up 25% of the time. Or, in other words, there is a 25% chance of any one combination coming up. If you were betting on the toss, which combination would be your best bet? Heads/tails, of course, because there are two ways in which this combination could turn up. Therefore, there is a two out of four, or 50% chance of its success, whereas there is only a 25% chance of two heads or two tails coming up.

Since round, R, is dominant, a round seed must contain at least one gene for round, R. In the F_2 generation, Mendel counted three round seeds for every wrinkled, which means that three-fourths (or 75%) of the seeds contained at least one gene for round, R. A glance at Figure 4-10 indicates that this percentage is exactly correct. The fourth combination, rr, does not contain a big R; therefore, that seed cannot be round. A seed with two alleles for wrinkled—rr—must be phenotypically wrinkled.

An illustration using heads and tails of two coins might possibly let us see the situation more clearly. Let us say we have a dime and a quarter, both of which are tossed in the air simultaneously. What possible combinations will come up, and what are the chances of these combinations? The possibilities, as we see in Figure 4-12, are two heads, two tails, and one heads and one tails. The latter combination can occur in two ways: quarter heads and dime tails, or dime heads and quarter tails. Thus, there are four possible combinations.

What are the chances of any one of these combinations coming up? Well, if you were to wager on the toss of one coin, you would have a 50% chance of calling the right combination. You have as much chance of winning the bet as your partner. In our illustration, however, you are betting on the simultaneous toss of *two* coins, so the chances of calling the correct combination are cut to 25%, exactly half of the first. Since there are four possible combinations, you have one chance in four of any one combination turning up.

Statistically, that is precisely the situation with the round and wrinkled peas, and it was Mendel's insight that perceived this when none of his predecessors had done so. Perhaps it was Mendel's training in mathematics at the university that enabled him to approach his experiments from a statistical point of view.

Mendel could not have worked the statistics out had he used only a few plants. To flip a coin ten times and expect it to come up heads five times and tails five times is unreasonable. A thousand flips might average 500 heads and 500 tails. Similarly, Mendel was aware, as we have seen, that a large number of plants are required to achieve a complete random assortment. When Mendel counted all

Figure 4-13
Segregation of alleles during meiosis. This illustration represents an idealized division. If male, all gametes would be sperm; if female, one ovum and three polar bodies.

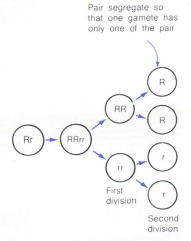

Pair segregate so that one gamete has only one of the pair

Rr — RRrr

RR — R — R

rr — r — r

First division | Second division

PHENOTYPIC RATIO
The ratio of phenotypes, especially from a hybrid cross. Mendel's famous F_1 hybrid cross of peas produced a 3:1 phenotypic ratio.

PRINCIPLE OF SEGREGATION
Genes occur in pairs. In the production of a gamete, the pair is separated so that each gamete contains only one of the pair.

PRINCIPLE OF INDEPENDENT ASSORTMENT
The separation of one pair of genes does not influence the separation of other pairs of genes.

the dominant and recessive characters of the seven traits, he found an average **phenotypic ratio** of 2.98 to 1, which he considered to be a 3:1 ratio.

Mendel's explanation for the 3:1 ratio solved the riddle of heredity. He suggested that the characters (alleles) are paired and *segregated* when they are passed on from one generation to the next. That is, the allele on one chromosome does not normally affect the allele at the same locus on the paired chromosome. We might say each allele goes its own way. Therefore, the capital R in the male influences inheritance separately from the influence of the lowercase r, and similarly with the female. (We have seen how this separation operated during meiosis.) This is Mendel's first law, called the **principle of segregation**, which states that alleles, the units of heredity, exist within individuals in pairs. The pairs are segregated during the production of gametes, so that a gamete has only one of each kind.

Interestingly, Mendel was not the first to observe this 3:1 ratio. In 1820, an Englishman named John Goss carried out an experiment very similar to Mendel's, even to the extent of using peas. When the hybrids produced a mixture of dominants and recessives, he merely pointed out the facts but did not count the numbers of each. He failed to see the significance of the ratio of dominants to recessives. Perhaps even more curious is Darwin's experience with snapdragons. Darwin crossed normal and irregular snapdragons and in the F_1 generation all the offspring were normal. When he bred the F_1 normal snapdragons, the offspring were normal to irregular at roughly a 3:1 ratio. Darwin noted the F_1 uniformity and the mixture of the F_2 generation, but the significance of the 3:1 proportion escaped him also (Iltis, 1966, pp. 118–127).

Principle of Independent Assortment

Having solved the problem of the 3:1 ratio, Mendel's next task was to determine whether what he called "the law of development" also applied to a cross of two different traits (a dihybrid cross). For this experiment he used the traits of form, round/wrinkled—Rr—and color, yellow/green—Yy. He crossed round and wrinkled peas with yellow and green peas, and he found the results were the same as in the first experiment. The proportions in the F_2 generation for color and form of seeds were:

9 round and yellow—both traits dominant

3 round and green—round dominant, green recessive

3 wrinkled and yellow—wrinkled recessive, yellow dominant

1 wrinkled and green—both traits recessive

When the numbers of round and wrinkled seeds are totaled, a proportion of 12 round to 4 wrinkled, or a 3:1 phenotypic ratio, emerges. When the number of yellow (dominant) and green seeds are totaled, we find 12 yellow to 4 green, also a 3:1 phenotypic ratio.

Conclusion: Gene pairs on one set of homologous chromosomes do not influence the distribution of gene pairs on other chromosomes; they separate independently from one another during meiosis, and are randomly assorted in the gametes. This phenomenon is known as Mendel's second law, the **principle of independent assortment** (Figs. 4-14, 4-16).

Figure 4-14
Mendel's principle of independent assortment.

Random Assortment   Mendel was not aware of the precise cellular mechanism that caused this random assortment of one trait with respect to another. However, a brief glance at our earlier discussion of meiosis (p. 54) quickly solves the mystery. As you will recall, when homologous pairs of chromosomes align along the equator of a cell, the relative positions of one homologous pair are independent of all other pairs.

Simply stated, this is the process of *random assortment*. The independent assortment of traits observed by Mendel is the direct result of the random assortment of chromosomes that respectively carry those traits.

Figure 4-16 shows two pairs of chromosomes in an F_1 (heterozygous) pea plant, each containing one of the two traits discussed above (color of seed, shape of seed). As can be seen, the way the chromosomes align during meiosis directly affects the combination of alleles in the resulting gametes, which, in turn, combine to produce individuals exhibiting the phenotypic ratios of observed traits (round and yellow, round and green, etc.).

Possible Alignments   There are four equally possible ways the chromosomes can align, and four different kinds of gametes that can be produced in this manner in each parent. This recombination of genes—by random assortment of chromosomes—leads to all the combinations of traits we observe in different individuals in the next generation.

If Mendel had used just *any* two traits for recombination, the phenotypic ratios would quite possibly not have conformed to those expected by independent assortment (9:3:3:1). The ratio came out as he predicted, because the traits Mendel chose to observe were carried on different chromosomes. Had the two traits *both* been carried on the *same* chromosome, the alleles for the two traits would not have assorted independently but would have been transmitted together.

An exception may be produced by the process of crossing-over (see p. 00). Even if carried on the same chromosome, genes can and usually do cross-over independently of each other *if* they are not located too closely together. In this

Figure 4-15
Crossing-over in chromosomes. Genes are more likely to cross-over and recombine when they are far apart (right) than when they are close together (left).

case, all four possible recombinations of alleles (CD, Cd, cD, cd) may be produced, and the expected ratios of independent assortment (9:3:3:1) may be approached (Fig. 4-15).

Genotypic Ratio   Going one step further, Mendel also demonstrated that the genotypic ratio for form and color remained the same as it did in his first experiment with the contrasting characters of only one trait. The ratio of homozygous dominant, RR, to heterozygous, Rr, to homozygous recessive, rr, is 1:2:1. (The entire process from the parental generation to the F_2 generation is shown schematically in Fig. 4-16.) The proportions for color, YY, Yy, yy, are of course the same, 1:2:1.

In summary, Mendel demonstrated, and cellular biology has confirmed, that there are regularities or laws of heredity. The laws may be explained in the following manner:

1. Each individual possesses two alleles for a particular trait.
2. During meiosis, the two alleles from each parent segregate into different gametes (principle of segregation). This means that a parent contributes only one of the two alleles to an offspring.
3. If each parent contributes a different allele for a particular trait (such as R or r), a hybrid (heterozygote) results.
4. When the two heterozygotes are crossed, or self-fertilized, there is an even chance that each of the two alleles from one parent will combine with each of the two alleless from the other parent. A male Rr and a female Rr can combine in four ways: RR, Rr, rR, rr. (In a large population, the result of such a hybrid cross would produce 25% RR, 25% Rr, 25% rR, and 25% rr. If we combine the two Rr, then the genotypic ratio would be 25% RR, 50% Rr, 25% rr, or 1:2:1.)
5. When two traits are crossed, each pair assorts independently of the other (principle of independent assortment).

The concept of two alleles for each trait—that the two alleles segregate independently of one another, that a parent contributes one of the two, that alleles from parents enter into all possible combinations with each other, that alleles during meiosis segregate into separate gametes—all of these made sense of what appeared to be unintelligible confusion in the process of heredity.

Professor L. C. Dunn has nicely summed up Mendel's contribution:

. . . his work has served as a kind of constructional keystone upon which subsequent developments of genetics have rested. The discovery of the statistical unit of heredity has turned out to be the spearhead of a changing conception of living matter which has penetrated and illuminated all of the major questions of biology (Dunn, 1965, p. 197).

It would be pleasing to report that Mendel's experiments and conclusions were swiftly accepted by an eager community of scientists that immediately applied his conclusions to the development of genetic research. Unfortunately, the case was otherwise. Mendel's methods were ahead of his time. It was not until 1900, thirty-five years after he read his paper before the Natural History Society of Brünn, that three geneticists—Hugo de Vries in Holland, Erich von Tschermak in Austria, and Carl Correns in Germany—working independently of one another, discovered for themselves the laws Mendel had already formulated. Genetics had lost thirty-five years.

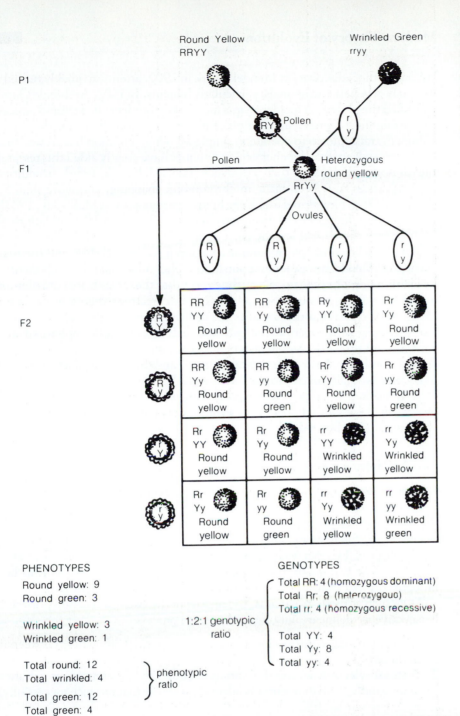

PHENOTYPES

Round yellow: 9
Round green: 3

Wrinkled yellow: 3
Wrinkled green: 1

Total round: 12
Total wrinkled: 4 } phenotypic ratio

Total green: 12
Total green: 4

1:2:1 genotypic ratio

GENOTYPES

Total RR: 4 (homozygous dominant)
Total Rr: 8 (heterozygous)
Total rr: 4 (homozygous recessive)

Total YY: 4
Total Yy: 8
Total yy: 4

VARIATION (genetic)
Inherited differences between individuals.
The basis of all evolutionary change.

NATURAL SELECTION
The evolutionary factor (first articulated by
Charles Darwin) that causes changes in allele
frequencies in populations due to differential
net reproductive success of individuals.

Modern Theory of Evolution

Following the rediscovery of Mendel's work in 1900, attention quickly turned to the study of genetics in animals, particularly humans. In 1902, Archibald Garrod identified the pattern of incidence in a metabolic disorder called *alkaptonuria* as a clear example of Mendelian inheritance in humans. Since that time the catalog of human traits known to operate in simple Mendelian fashion has grown steadily. Recent advances in biochemical techniques have greatly aided this research; the list now includes more than 3,300 such traits (McKusick, 1983). In addition, great advances have been made in chromosome mapping, and more than 500 genes have been pinpointed to specific human chromosomes (McKusick, 1983).

By the beginning of the twentieth century, the essential foundations for evolutionary theory had already been developed. Darwin and Wallace had articulated the key principle of natural selection forty years earlier, and the rediscovery of Mendelian genetics contributed the other major component—a mechanism for inheritance. We might expect that these two basic contributions would have been joined rather quickly into a consistent theory of evolution. However, such was not the case. For the first thirty years of this century, geneticists (working with experimental animals, such as fruit flies) emphasized sharp contrasts within particular characteristics of organisms. As such, evolution was seen as a process of fairly large radical "jumps," and this "mutationist" view came to be seen as an alternative to the "selectionist" tradition.

A *synthesis* of these two views was not achieved until the mid-1930s, and we owe much of our current view of the evolutionary process to this intellectual development. (See Box 4-1.)

The Modern Synthesis

Biologists working on mathematical models of evolutionary change in the late 1920s and early 1930s came to realize that genetic and selective processes were not opposing themes, but that a comprehensive explanation of organic evolution required *both*. Small new changes in the genetic material—transmitted from parent to offspring by strict Mendelian principles—are, in fact, the fuel for natural selection. The two major foundations of the biological sciences had thus been brought together in what Julian Huxley termed the "modern synthesis."

From such a "modern" (that is, the middle of the twentieth century onwards) perspective we define evolution as a two-stage process:

1. Production and redistribution of **variation** (inherited differences between individuals).
2. **Natural selection** acts on this variation (inherited differences, or variation, among individuals differentially affect their ability to reproduce successfully).

Definition of Evolution

Darwin saw evolution as the gradual unfolding of new varieties of life from previous forms over long periods of time. This depiction is what most of us think of as "evolution," and it is indeed the end result of the evolutionary process. But these long-term effects can only come about by the accumulation of many small evolutionary changes occurring every generation. In order to understand how

BOX 4-1

Development of Modern Evolutionary Theory

Theodosius Dobzhansky.

Our modern understanding of the evolutionary process came about through contributions of biologists in the United States, Great Britain, and the Soviet Union.

While "mutationists" were arguing with "selectionists" about the single primary mechanism in evolution, several population geneticists began to realize that both small genetic changes and natural selection were necessary ingredients in the evolutionary formula.

These population geneticists were largely concerned with mathematical reconstructions of evolution—in par-

ticular, measuring those small accumulations of genetic changes in populations over just a few generations. Central figures in these early theoretical developments included Ronald Fisher and J.B.S. Haldane in Great Britain, Sewall Wright in the United States, and Sergei Chetverikov in the Soviet Union.

While the work of these scientists often produced brilliant insights (see particularly Fisher's *The Genetical Theory of Natural Selection*, 1930) their conclusions were largely unknown to most evolutionary biologists, especially in North America. It remained, therefore, for an individual to transcend these two worlds: the mathematical jargon of the population geneticists and the general constructs of theoretical evolutionary biologists. The scientist who performed this task (and to whom we owe the most credit as the first true synthesizer) was Theodosius Dobzhansky. In his *Genetics and the Origin of Species* (1937), Dobzhansky skillfully integrated the mathematics of population genetics with overall evolutionary theory. His insights then became the basis for a period of tremendous activity in evolutionary thinking that directly led to major contributions by George Gaylord Simpson (who brought paleontology into the synthesis), Ernst Mayr,[*] and others. In fact, the "Modern Synthesis" produced by these scientists stood basically unchallenged for an entire generation as *the* explanation of the evolutionary process. In recent years, however, some aspects of this theory have been brought under serious question. (See the section "Recent Challenges to the Modern Synthesis," this chapter.)

[*] For an interesting discussion of the intellectual developments concerning the formulation of modern evolutionary theory, see Ernst Mayr and William B. Provine (eds.), *The Evolutionary Synthesis*, Cambridge, Mass.: Harvard University Press, 1980.

the process of evolution works, we must necessarily study these short-term events. Darwin attempted this kind of study in his breeding experiments, but because the science of genetics was still in its infancy, he was not able to comprehend fully the mechanics of evolutionary change. Today, we study in various organisms (including humans) evolutionary changes occurring between generations, and are able to demonstrate how evolution works. From such a modern genetics perspective, we define evolution as *a change in allele frequency from one generation to the next.*

Allele frequencies are numerical indicators of the genetic makeup of an interbreeding group of individuals known as a **population**. (We will return to this topic in more detail on page 94.) Here, let us illustrate the way allele frequencies change (that is, how evolution occurs) through a simplified example. First of all, we must look at a physical trait that is inherited, in this case human blood type. The best known of the human blood-type traits is ABO. There are, however, many similar blood-type systems controlled by different genes, which determine genetically transmitted properties of the red blood cells.

An inherited trait, such as human blood type, may be of slightly different form in different individuals. As mentioned, we call the variant genes that underlie these different forms of an inherited trait, alleles. The best-known blood-type alleles are A, B, and O. These different expressions of inherited traits constitute genetic variation within a population.

Let us assume that your present class represents a population, an interbreeding group of individuals, and that we have ascertained the blood type of each member for the ABO trait. To be a population, individuals in your class must choose mates more often from *within* the group than from outside it. Of course, the individuals in your class will not meet this requirement, but for this example's sake we will make the assumption that they do. The proportions of each of the A, B, and O alleles are the allele frequencies for this trait. For example, suppose we find that the proportion of alleles in your class (population) is as follows:* A = .50; B = .40; O = .10.

Since the frequencies for combinations of these genes represent only proportions of a total, it is obvious that allele frequencies can refer only to whole groups of individuals; that is, populations. Individuals do not have an allele frequency, they have either A, B, or O (or a combination of these). Nor can individuals change allele frequency. From conception onward, the genetic composition of an individual is fixed. If you start out with blood type A, you will remain type A. Therefore, an individual cannot evolve: Only a group of individuals—a population—can evolve over time.

What happens when a population evolves? Evolution is not an unusual or a mysterious process. In fact, it is incredibly commonplace, and may occur between every generation for every group of organisms in the world, including humans. Assume we measure the allele combination frequencies for the ABO blood trait twenty-five years later in the children of our classroom population and find the following: A = .30; B = .40; O = .30.

We can see that the relative proportions have changed: A has decreased, O has increased, while B has remained the same in frequency. Such a simple, apparently minor, change is what we call evolution. Over the short run of just a few

*This simplified example shows frequencies for the various gene combinations, what are called genotypes.

generations, such changes in inherited traits may be only very small, but if further continued and elaborated, the results can and do produce spectacular kinds of adaptation and whole new varieties of life.

Whether we are talking about such short-term effects as our classroom population from one generation to the next, which is sometimes called **microevolution**, or the long-term effects through fossil history, sometimes called **macroevolution**, the basic evolutionary mechanisms are similar. As we will discuss below, however, they are not necessarily identical.

The question may be asked: How do allele frequencies change? Or, to put it another way, what causes evolution? The modern theory of evolution isolates general factors that can produce alterations in allele frequencies. As we have noted, evolution is a two-stage process. Genetic variation must be first produced and distributed before it can be acted upon by natural selection.

Factors That Produce and Redistribute Variation

Mutation   An actual alteration in genetic material is called **mutation**. A genetic trait may take one of several alternative forms, which we have defined as alleles (A, B, or O, for example). If one allele changes to another—that is, if the gene itself is altered—a mutation has occurred. As we have seen, a mutation is a molecular alteration—a change in the base sequence of DNA. For such changes to have evolutionary significance, they must occur in the sex cells, which are passed between generations. Evolution is a change in allele frequencies *between* generations. If mutations do not occur in sex cells (either the egg or sperm), they will not be passed to the next generation, and no evolutionary change can result. If, however, a genetic change does occur in the sperm or egg of one of the individuals in our classroom (A mutates to X, for instance) the offspring's blood type also will be altered, causing a change in allele frequencies of that generation. Evolution would have occurred by mutation.

Actually, it would be rare to see evolution occurring by mutation *alone*. Mutation rates for any given trait are quite low, and, thus, their effects would rarely be seen in such a small population as our class. In larger populations mutations might be observed (one individual in 10,000, say), but would, by themselves, have very little impact on shifting allele frequencies. However, when mutation is coupled with natural selection, evolutionary changes are quite possible.

Mutation is the basic creative force in evolution, and in fact is the only way to produce "new" variation. Its key role in the production of variation represents the first stage of the evolutionary process. Darwin was not aware of the nature of mutation. Only in the twentieth century, with the spectacular development of molecular biology, have the secrets of genetic structure been revealed.

Migration   The movement of genes from one population to another is called **migration**. If all individuals in our classroom population do not choose their mates from within the group, significant changes in allele frequencies could occur. For example, if four of the people who were type A married and settled outside the population, and four new individuals who were type O moved in and interbred with classroom individuals, the allele frequencies would be altered. If a change in allele frequency does take place, evolution will have occurred, this time by migration.

POPULATION
Within a species, a community of individuals where mates are usually found.

MICROEVOLUTION
Small, short-term changes occurring over just a few generations.

MACROEVOLUTION
Large changes produced only after many generations.

MUTATION
An alteration in the genetic material (a change in the base sequence of DNA).

MIGRATION
Movement of genes between populations.

In humans, social rules, more than any other factor, determine mating patterns, and cultural anthropologists must work closely with physical anthropologists in order to isolate and measure this aspect of evolutionary change.

Genetic Drift   The random factor in evolution is called **genetic drift**, and is due primarily to sampling phenomenon (that is, the size of the population). Since evolution occurs in populations, it is directly tied not only to the nature of the initial allele freqencies of the population, but to the size of the group as well. If, in our parent population of, say, 100 individuals, two type O individuals had been killed in an auto accident before completing reproduction, their genes would have been removed from the population. The frequency of the O allele would have been reduced in the next generation, and evolution would have occurred. In this case, with only 100 individuals in the population, the change due to the accident would have altered the O frequency in a noticeable way. If, however, our initial population had been very large (10,000 people), then the effect of removing a few individuals would be very small indeed. In fact, in a population of large size, random effects, such as traffic accidents, would be balanced out by the equal probabilities of such events affecting all the other individuals with different genetic combinations (i.e., different genotypes). As you can see, evolutionary change due to genetic drift is directly related to population size.

When considering genetic drift, we must remember that the genetic makeup of individuals is in no way related to the chance happenings that affect their lives. When applied to our example, this fact means that the genetic makeup of individuals has absolutely nothing to do with their being involved in automobile accidents. This is what is meant by a random event and why this factor is usually called *random genetic drift*. If, for example, a person had died in an auto accident caused by hereditary poor eyesight, such an event would not be genetic drift. If the individual, because of some such hereditary trait, dies early and produces fewer offspring than other individuals, this is not random genetic drift, it is natural selection.

Recombination   Since in any sexually reproducing species both parents contribute genes to offspring, the genetic information is inevitably reshuffled every generation. Such recombination does not in itself change allele frequencies (i.e., cause evolution). However, it does produce the whole array of genetic combinations, which natural selection can then act upon. In fact, we have shown how the reshuffling of chromosomes during meiosis can produce literally trillions of gene combinations, making every human being genetically unique.

Natural Selection Acts on Variation

The evolutionary factors just discussed—mutation, migration, genetic drift, and recombination—act to produce variation and to distribute genes within and between populations. But there is no long-term *direction* to any of these factors. What then does enable populations to adapt to changing environments? The answer is, of course, natural selection—the process so well elucidated by Darwin more than 125 years ago. Given that there is genetic variation among individuals within a population, some of these variations *may* influence reproductive success (numbers of offspring successfully raised). If, as a result of genetic variation, some individuals contribute more offspring to succeeding generations, this is natural selection. In fact, we have defined natural selection as *differential net reproductive success* (see p. 39).

How then do populations adapt? A result of natural selection is a change in allele frequency relative to specific environmental factors. If the environment changes, then the selection pressures change as well. Such a functional shift in allele frequencies is what we mean by **adaptation**. If there are long-term environmental changes in a consistent direction, then allele frequencies should also shift gradually each generation. If sustained for many generations, the results may be quite dramatic. (See Box 4-2.)

The Unit of Selection Selection acts on the individual. It is individuals who reproduce or do not reproduce and who continually attempt to maximize their own reproductive success. Thus, statements such as "The group was undergoing selection in order to survive" have no meaning. *The individual, not the group, is the unit of selection.* If the total reproductive success of all members of a population continuously falls below replacement value (where more individuals die than are born in a generation), the population will become extinct. Individuals will attempt to maximize their own reproductive success even in the face of such impending extinction.

Overpopulation is the result of individuals maximizing their reproductive success. Even if such behavior means the whole group will perish, no special evolutionary mechanisms exist to keep individuals from reproducing at their greatest capacity. Of course, humans have the potential to manipulate their numbers, and the entire world now faces the problem of controlling an exploding population. Evolution, therefore, has no built-in mechanism to guard against extinction. Indeed, extinction is actually the rule—not the exception—in evolution. Of all the species that have ever lived on earth, less than .1% (one-tenth of one percent) are now currently living; the remaining 99.9% met their almost inevitable evolutionary fate.

The Unit of Evolution While selection acts on the individual, changes in allele frequency occur *between* generations for an entire population; that is, an interbreeding group of organisms. The net result of all individuals' reproductive success (natural selection)—in addition to the possible effects of mutation, migration, and genetic drift—will affect the entire population. *The population, then, is the unit of evolution*, and it is the population that changes (as measured by allele frequencies) from generation to generation.

Evolution at the Species Level

A species is defined as a group of interbreeding organisms that are *reproductively isolated* and, therefore, cannot successfully interbreed with other groups. The capacity to reproduce is the critical factor in defining species. Theoretically, one can test whether two kinds of organisms are members of different species by observing their reproductive behavior under natural conditions (who mates with whom), and by observing the results (are the offspring fertile?).

Actually, a species is composed of subunits that are the breeding communities we have called populations. All members of a species can potentially interbreed, and some degree of interbreeding (migration) is theoretically possible between all populations.

GENETIC DRIFT
Evolutionary changes produced by random factors.

ADAPTATION
Genetic changes in response to selection (environmental) factors.

Models of Natural Selection

Directional Selection As environmental pressures change gradually, selection pressures should also shift. If the environmental pressure is directional, selection should also be directional (see Fig. 1). For example, in the last one million years, there have been long periods of gradual cooling in the earth's climate. One means of coping with cold among mammals has been increase in body size. If we assume animals, such as mammoths, are descendants from smaller ancestors, how did they gradually get bigger? The answer lies in understanding natural selection. Those animals with genotypes for larger overall size perhaps resisted cold better, lived longer, mated more often, cared better for their young offspring, and so forth. In any case, the result was that they reproduced more successfully than other (smaller) individuals. Gradually, then, allele frequencies shifted. As the climate continued to grow progressively colder, allele frequencies also continued to shift, and average mammoth size gradually increased.

Stabilizing Selection If, on the other hand, environments remain relatively stable, there should be selection for those genotypes already established within an "adaptive plateau" (see Fig. 2). In other words, those phenotypes (which are influenced by genotypes) in the center of the populational distribution ("modal" varieties) should have higher reproductive success, and those at either extreme will be selected against (as long as the environment remains stable).

If we again choose size as a characteristic, we can note that some varieties of turtle have changed little in millions of years. In any given generation, the environment of turtles has not changed much from that of previous generations. Therefore, the "optimal" phenotype is probably an average-sized turtle, and those much larger or much smaller should be selected against.

Diversifying Selection In this type of selection, phenotypic variants at *both* extremes are favored, and those in the center of the distribution (closer to the mean) are selected against. For example, in the case of baboon size relative to predation pressure, it may be advantageous to be small (less conspicuous) or very large (for active defense).

Over time, such selection pressure would act to create a twin-peak (bimodal) phenotypic distribution as shown in Figure 3.

In fact, such a process would not have long-term effects in a *fully* reproductive population, since individuals of all sizes would be mating with each other, thus producing individuals of intermediate body size. In order for the diversifying selection pressures to be maintained, some degree of *reproductive isolation* between segments of the population would be required. Another possibility is that phenotypic

Figure 1
Directional selection.

Figure 2
Stabilizing selection.

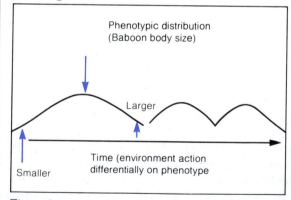

Figure 3
Diversifying selection.

variation can be partitioned and maintained by other genetic differences—sex, for example. In fact, baboons do differ markedly in size, with males averaging about twice the size of females.

The net result of all the forces of evolution (mutation, migration, genetic drift, recombination, and natural selection) acting on all populations determines the fate of the species as a whole. If sustained over a long period of time, gradual changes in allele frequencies between member populations can eventually lead to sufficient genetic differences, so that fertile reproduction is no longer possible. We then may recognize a new form of life having arisen from one species "splitting" and producing new species, a process called **speciation**. (See Box 4-3.) This level of evolutionary change was the one described by Darwin and Wallace. If, on the other hand, total reproductive success is so low that all, or even most, populations become extinct, the whole species will be doomed and will disappear from the earth forever. The gross interference of natural habitats by modern industrial society has pushed numerous "endangered species" to this crucial juncture.

SPECIATION
The evolutionary process that produces new species from previous ones.

Recent Challenges to the Modern Synthesis

In the last decade, serious reexamination has stimulated ongoing debate concerning some aspects of modern evolutionary theory.

Neutral Mutations

One of the premises postulated by traditional evolutionists is that natural selection is the major factor explaining most of the variation found in contemporary organisms. There is general agreement that significant aspects of variation are channeled by selection, thus leading to adaptation. But is all (or even most) of the "genetic baggage" that a species carries understandable strictly in terms of natural selection? Some scientists believe it is not. Pointing to the vast amount of variation seen in all organisms (28% of all human genes are estimated to exhibit significant population variation), these researchers argue that *much* of variation seen in natural populations is due to neutral mutations and chance factors (i.e., genetic drift).

A major aspect of this argument is that many mutations are neutral; in other words, they have no impact on reproductive success in any conceivable environment. We know, of course, that there is considerable redundancy in the DNA code, so that many point mutations will not alter the amino acid sequence whatsoever. In such a case, the phenotype is not affected at all, and selection cannot act on what it cannot see. Or as King and Jukes have put it, "Natural selection is the editor, rather than the composer of the genetic message" (King and Jukes, 1969, p. 788). These researchers, however, go far beyond postulating strictly synonymous mutations as neutral—they claim a large majority of other genetic changes are completely neutral to selective action, and are established in populations by random genetic drift.

This controversy has not yet been resolved. There is a vast store of genetic variation in all interbreeding populations. Certainly, both selection and drift have contributed, but what has been the primary architect? The consensus among most evolutionary biologists still is that natural selection is the most significant factor in explaining evolutionary change. Moreover, the action of selec-

BOX 4-3

Speciation

According to the biological species concept (Mayr, 1970), the way new species are first produced involves some form of isolation. Picture a single species of some organism (baboons, say) composed of several populations distributed over a wide geographic area. Gene exchange (migration) will be limited if a geographic barrier, such as a river, lake, ocean, or mountain range, separates these populations. This extremely important form of isolating mechanism is called *geographic isolation.*

Now, if one population (A) is separated from another population (B) by a mountain range, individual baboons of A will not be able to mate with baboons from B. As time passes (several generations), genetic differences will accumulate in both populations. If group size is small, we can predict that drift will cause allele frequency changes in both population A and population B. Since drift is *random* in nature, we would not expect the effects to be the same. Thus, the two populations would begin to diverge.

As long as gene exchange is limited, the populations can only become more divergent with time. Moreover, further genetic difference would be expected if the baboon groups are occupying somewhat different habitats. (Ecological conditions usually do vary from one area to another within a species' range.) These additional genetic differences would arise through the process of natural selection. Certain individuals in population A may be most reproductively fit in their own environment, but may be less fit in the environment occupied by population B. Consequently, allele frequencies will change, and the pattern will be dissimilar in the two populations.

Again, as time passes, and perhaps as environments change further, the populations will become still more divergent.

With the cumulative effects of drift and natural selection acting over many generations, the result will be two populations which—even if they were to come back into geographic contact—could no longer interbreed fertilely.

More than just geographic isolation would now apply; there may, for instance, be behavioral differences interfering with courtship—what we call *behavioral isolation.* There may even be sufficient differences in body size and proportions to make copulation physiologically impossible.

Using our *biological* definition of species, we now would recognize two distinct species, where initially only one existed.

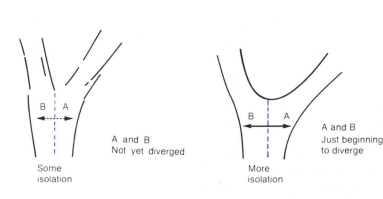

B | A

A and B
Not yet diverged

Some
isolation

B | A

A and B
Just beginning
to diverge

More
isolation

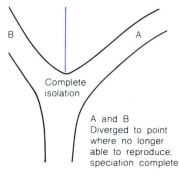

B   A

Complete
isolation

A and B
Diverged to point
where no longer
able to reproduce;
speciation complete

This model of speciation
is called branching evolution
or cladogenesis

tion is the explanation of the "fit" between an organism and its environment, a relationship that so intrigued Darwin. A recent review of genetic variation among humans concludes that "there is little doubt that many amino acid substitutions appear to be neutral or quasi-neutral, but neutral models do not seem to fit the distribution of most loci in the human species" (Livingstone, 1980, p. 39).

Modes of Evolutionary Change

The modern synthesis primarily explains those allele frequency changes seen over just a few generations—what is called *microevolution*. Until recently, the general consensus among evolutionary biologists was that these microevolutionary mechanisms could be translated directly into larger-scale evolutionary changes—what is called *macroevolution*, or transspecific evolution. These major evolutionary events involve the appearance of new species (i.e., speciation) as well as even broader more encompassing groups of organisms. A smooth gradation of changes was postulated to run directly from microevolution into macroevolution. A representative view was expressed by a leading synthesist, Ernst Mayr:

> The proponents of the synthetic theory maintain that all evolution is due to the accumulation of small genetic changes, guided by natural selection, and that transspecific evolution is nothing but an extrapolation and magnification of the events that take place within populations and species (Mayr, 1970, p. 351).

In the last decade, however, this view has been seriously challenged. Many theorists now believe that macroevolution cannot be explained *solely* in terms of accumulated microevolutionary changes. Many current researchers are now convinced that macroevolution is only partly understandable through microevolutionary models, as recently stated by two proponents of this revised view:

> We recognize that the within-population concept of adaptation via natural selection is a viable hypothesis accounting for the deterministic part of much genetic, behavioral, and morphological change in evolution. However, we strongly disagree that a smooth extrapolation of within-population (microevolutionary) processes is a logical or effective integration of such within-population mechanisms with among-species phenomena (macroevolution) (Eldredge and Cracraft, 1980).

Gradualism vs. Punctuationalism   The traditional view of evolution has emphasized that change accumulates gradually in evolving lineages—the idea of "phyletic gradualism." Accordingly, the complete fossil record of an evolving group (if it could be recovered) would display a series of forms with finely graded transitional differences between each ancestor and its descendant. The fact that such transitional forms are only rarely found is attributed to the incompleteness of the fossil record, or, as Darwin called it, "a history of the world, imperfectly kept, and written in changing dialect."

For more than a century, this perspective dominated evolutionary biology. Paleontologists searched diligently to find evidence of these gradual changes. So strong was this notion of gradualism that when little evidence was found to support it, researchers assumed there must be something wrong with their data—either their geological beds were inadequately dated or the paleontological record was yet too incomplete to allow a firm conclusion. Rarely did anyone suspect that the premise of gradualism itself might be flawed.

In the last decade, some evolutionary biologists have called this notion into serious question. The evolutionary mechanisms operating on species over the long run are often not continuously gradual. In a great many cases, species persist for thousands of generations basically unchanged. Then, rather suddenly—at least in evolutionary terms—a "spurt" of speciation occurs. This nongradual process of long stasis and quick spurts has been termed **punctuated equilibrium** (Gould and Eldredge, 1977).

From a comprehensive survey of well-documented and long-ranging fossil series (including especially marine invertebrates), paleontologists Stephen Gould and Niles Eldredge conclude that:

> Most species during their evolutionary history, either do not change in any appreciable way, or else they fluctuate mildly in morphology, with no apparent change in any direction. Phyletic gradualism is very rare and too slow, in any case, to produce the major events of evolution. Evolutionary trends are not the product of slow, directional transformation within lineages; they represent the differential success of certain species . . . speciation may be random with respect to the direction of a trend (Gould and Eldredge, 1977, p. 115).

What the punctuationalists are disputing concerns the "tempo" and "mode" of evolutionary change comonly understood since Darwin's time. Rather than a slow steady tempo, this new view postulates long periods of no change interspersed only occasionally by sudden bursts. From this observation, punctuationalists concluded that the mode of evolution, too, must be different from that suggested by classical Darwinists. Rather than gradual accumulation of small changes within a single lineage, advocates of punctuated equilibrium believe an additional evolutionary mechanism is required to push the process along. Accordingly, *speciation* (see Box 4-3) is seen to be the major influence in bringing about rapid evolutionary change. Given numerous small population isolates and corresponding opportunities for random genetic drift, speciation events could occur in a sudden flurry—a whole array of new, fairly isolated and small incipient species would then possess a great deal of evolutionary potential. Of these, probably only a small minority would survive—through a "higher" evolutionary process sometimes called *species selection*.

How well does the paleontological record agree with this new theory? Indeed, a tremendous amount of fossil data shows long periods of stasis punctuated by occasional quite rapid changes (the transformation taking perhaps on the order of 10,000 to 50,000 years). Intermediate forms are rare, not because the record is so poor, but because the speciation events and longevity of these transitional species were so short we should not expect to find them very often.

The best supporting evidence for punctuated equilibrium has come from the fossilized remains of a variety of invertebrates, the paleontological specialty of both Gould and Eldredge. How well, then, does the human fossil record fit a punctuationalist model? Gould and Eldredge (1977, p. 115) believe "the record of human evolution seems to provide a particularly good example." When it comes to the evolution of our family, other researchers, however, are still not as convinced. Many believe punctuationalism is not all that apparent in the human evolutionary record and, alternatively, that gradualism fits the facts better (Cronin et al., 1981). Others (e.g., Tobias, 1983) believe human evolution displays periods of both punctuated *and* gradualistic changes.

It would be unreasonable to expect a single mode of evolutionary change to characterize all lineages at all times. Clearly, the rigid Darwinian belief that evolutionary change must *always* be gradual in nature is improbable. Abundant evidence shows that, in many evolutionary lines, this has not been the case. Punctuated equilibrium with change brought about by rapid speciation is another mode that now must be considered. Regarding human evolution, it is still not clear which of the two models (gradualism or punctuationalism)—or a combination of the two—provides the best approximation. As we will be discussing in great detail later in this text (Chapters 12–15), speciation was probably never very common within our particular evolutionary line since the time we diverged from other primates. As such, our lineage may not be typical, and is thus not a good example on which to base general theories of evolutionary change.

Microevolution and Macroevolution   As we have seen, allele frequencies over the span of a few generations seem to change in gradual fashion. Thus, microevolution, as conceived within the modern synthesis, conforms to the gradualistic model.

We have also seen that long-term changes (i.e., macroevolution) are not always gradual in nature; in fact, in many evolutionary lineages, the rate of change is manifestly sporadic. Are, then, microevolution and macroevolution really quite different phenomena?

While the mechanisms of microevolution and macroevolution may be partially "decoupled," that is not to say that they are unrelated. In fact, speciation can be understood as the result of accumulated genetic changes, particularly when facilitated by geographic isolation. This does not imply that the process is always gradual. Indeed, since processes affecting isolating mechanisms (for instance, mountain building, formation of island chains, etc.) are themselves irregular, we should expect speciation rates to vary as well. Species, once they have formed, are real entities. Categories of higher rank (genera, families, and so on) are merely human abstractions; they do not exist in nature. Populations evolve; species may eventually diverge and, once distinct, can only become more genetically separate. All the rest of evolutionary change is basically an extension of this process.

Evolution in Modern Populations

The process of evolution acts on all species, including *Homo sapiens*. In modern populations, recombination and mutation continue to produce variation, the fuel for natural selection. Can we then see these ongoing evolutionary processes at work in human populations?

Today we find only one species of hominid represented by 5 billion individuals widely scattered over most of the earth. However, the distribution is by no means even, since both geographical and social factors influence where people live, how many individuals collect to form a group, and who mates with whom. Moreover, there are obvious visible physical differences as well as numerous biochemically detectable variations among groups of modern human beings. How do we explain these differences?

The branch of anthropology dealing with modern human variation is centrally concerned with answering such questions in *evolutionary* terms. As discussed throughout this text, anthropology is the study of human evolution, not just in the past but the present as well.

Human populations continue to be influenced by the forces of evolution, continue to adapt to their biocultural environments, and thus continue to evolve. Investigating the dynamic processes that mold our species is the domain of **microevolutionary** studies. From such work we not only develop a fuller understanding of why *Homo sapiens* varies from area to area (as well as from individual to individual), but we also can more fully comprehend how *Homo sapiens* came to be in the first place.

The following chapters tell the tale of a long succession of hominid fossils, but these are simply luckily preserved bits and pieces of earlier populations who were subject to the same dynamic evolutionary processes influencing humankind today. Over the space of several tens of thousands or millions of years small microevolutionary changes can be modified into **macroevolutionary** ones. Given the process of punctuated equilibrium, macroevolutionary changes do not necessarily translate *completely* from microevolutionary events.

The Population

The unit of evolutionary change is the *population*, which we have defined as a group of interbreeding individuals. More precisely, the population is the group within which one is most likely to find a mate. As such, a population is a genetic unit marked by a degree of genetic relatedness and sharing in a common **gene pool**. In theory, this concept is not particularly difficult. Picture a kind of giant blender into which every generation's genes are mixed (by recombination). What comes out in the next generation is a direct product of the genes going into the pool, which in turn is a direct result of who is mating with whom.

In practice, however, isolating and describing actual human populations is a sticky business. The largest population of *Homo sapiens* that could be described is the entire species, all of whose members are at least potentially capable of interbreeding (but are incapable of interbreeding, fertilely, with members of other species). Our species is thus a *genetically closed system* (human/nonhuman hybrids are not known). The problem arises not in describing who potentially can interbreed, but in isolating exactly the patterns of those individuals who are doing so.

Factors that determine mate choice are geographical, ecological, and social. If individuals are isolated into groups in an Alpine village or on an island in the middle of the Pacific, there is not much possibility of finding a mate outside the immediate vicinity. Such **breeding isolates** are fairly easily defined and are a favorite target of microevolutionary studies. Geography plays a dominant role within these isolates through influencing the range of available mates. But even within these limits cultural prescriptions can still play a powerful part in deciding who is most proper among those potentially available.

Since social factors usually play such a crucial role in human mating patterns, a cultural anthropologist is an invaluable aid to population studies in helping to decipher what is going on in the complex world of real human beings. Additional complexity (sometimes found in other cultures) is introduced when biological and social paternity are defined differently. Moreover, the physical anthropologist must always be aware of the possibility of illegitimacy; whereas marriage patterns are useful indicators, what we are ultimately after is the pattern of actual matings.

Smaller human population segments within the species are defined as groups with relative degrees of **endogamy** (marrying/mating within the group). They are not, however, totally closed systems. Migration often occurs between groups, and individuals may choose mates from distant localities. The advent of modern means of rapid transportation has greatly accelerated **exogamy** (marrying/mating outside the group), a process which always has characterized human society to some degree.

It is obvious that most humans today are not clearly members of specific breeding populations as they would be in breeding isolates. Inhabitants of large cities may seem to be members of a single population, but actually within the city borders social, ethnic, and religious boundaries crosscut in a complex fashion to form smaller population groupings. In addition to being members of these highly open local population segments, we are simultaneously members of overlapping gradations of larger populations—the immediate geographical region (a metropolitan area or perhaps a whole state), a region of the country, the whole nation, the Western world, and ultimately again, the whole species.

In all this confusion how do anthropologists locate a population? Since most humans today live in densely inhabited, socially complex areas, a population must be isolated arbitrarily. Usually the population is defined with a particular research goal in mind.

For example, the Jewish inhabitants of New York City form a *partially* closed population defined by socioreligious affiliation—an example of religious endogamy. Certainly, considerable migration occurs both in and out of this group, and degree of genetic relatedness is therefore probably not all that significant. However, for some purposes it is useful to treat this group as a population. The incidence of Tay-Sachs disease is known to be considerably higher in descendants of Eastern European Jewish populations than in other groups. In order to ascertain the frequency of this tragic disease in New York City and to target prevention programs, it is useful to contrast parents of Jewish and non-Jewish heritage. In addition, studies of changes in allele frequency (evolution) in this or any other population can be facilitated in the same manner. Of course, the definition of this population does not refer directly to the socioreligious makeup of this group, but only to a degree of shared relationship dating back to earlier generations in Eastern Europe. For that matter, the whole Jewish "population" could be broken down further into smaller populations, those with Eastern European ancestry and all others. In fact, this has been done, and Jewish descendants of non-Eastern European populations have about the same low incidence of Tay-Sachs disease as that of the overall United States population.

Several other social/ethnic subpopulations are treated in this manner for particular microevolutionary studies. Please remember that none of these populations is a completely closed system and, indeed, most of them are quite open.

Population Genetics

Once the microevolutionist has isolated a specific human population, the next step is to ascertain what evolutionary forces, if any, are operating on this group. In order to determine whether evolution is taking place, we measure allele frequencies for specific traits and compare the observed frequencies with a set predicted by a mathematical model: the **Hardy-Weinberg equilibrium** equation. This model provides us with a baseline set of evolutionary expectations under *known* conditions.

MICROEVOLUTIONARY
Small-scale evolutionary changes (shifts in allele frequency) that can occur over the span of just a few generations and can, therefore, be seen in living populations.

MACROEVOLUTIONARY
Large-scale evolutionary changes that require many hundreds of generations and can, therefore, usually only be seen paleontologically (that is, in the fossil record).

GENE POOL
The total complement of genes in a population.

BREEDING ISOLATES
Populations geographically (and/or socially) separate and, therefore, easy to define.

ENDOGAMY
Mating within a social unit.

EXOGAMY
Mating outside a social unit.

HARDY-WEINBERG EQUILIBRIUM
The mathematical relationship expressing—under ideal conditions—the predicted distribution of genes in populations; the central theorem of population genetics.

More precisely, Hardy-Weinberg equilibrium postulates a set of conditions where *no* evolution occurs. In other words, none of the forces of evolution is acting, and all genes have an equal chance of recombining in each generation (that is, random mating of individuals):

1. The *population* is assumed to be *very large* (therefore no sampling error—*no random genetic drift*)
2. *No mutation* (no new alleles are added by molecular alterations within gametes)
3. *No migration* (no new alleles added by influx from outside our target population)
4. *No selection* (alleles have no differential advantage relative to reproductive success)
5. *Random mating* (panmixia—no bias in who mates with whom; any female is assumed to have an equal chance of mating with any male)

If all these conditions are satisfied, allele frequencies will not change (that is, no evolution will take place) and a permanent equilibrium will be maintained as long as these conditions prevail. An evolutionary "barometer" is thus provided which may be used as a standard against which actual circumstances are compared. Similar to the way a typical barometer is standardized under known temperature and altitude conditions, the Hardy-Weinberg equilibrium is standardized under known evolutionary conditions.

The relationship of the allele frequencies in populations to Mendelian genotypic proportions is a straightforward extension of simple Mendelian genetics. In fact, in 1903, soon after the rediscovery of Mendel's work, the American geneticist and animal breeder W. E. Castle developed a model showing the relationship of genes to populations. However, Castle felt the results were so obvious that he did not take the trouble to state unequivocally the conditions for genetic equilibrium nor did he actively push for acceptance of his views.

However, within just five years the English mathematician G. H. Hardy (1877–1947) and the German physician W. Weinberg (1862–1937) independently reached the same conclusion, and their formulation eventually won wide acceptance. The mathematical relationship of allele and genotype frequencies in populations is therefore usually called the Hardy-Weinberg formula or "law."

Interestingly, we note once again that the science of genetics was advancing intellectually along a broad international front. At the turn of the century three scientists in three different countries discovered Mendel's initial contribution and realized its implications. Within just another eight years the application of these principles to populations was again independently reached in three separate countries, and the discipline of population genetics was born.

Under the idealized conditions of Hardy-Weinberg equilibrium no new alleles are added and no alleles removed from the population. Moreover, every allele for a given locus has an equal chance of combining with any other allele at that locus within the gene pool.

The simplest situation applicable to a microevolutionary study is a genetic trait that follows a simple Mendelian pattern and has only two alleles (A, a). As you recall from earlier discussions, there are then only three possible genotypes: AA, Aa, aa. Proportions of these genotypes (AA:Aa:aa) are a function of the allele frequencies themselves (percentage of A; percentage of a). In order to provide uniformity for all genetic loci, a standard notation is employed to refer to these frequencies:

Frequency of first allele (A) = p (p = dominant allele—if there is dominance)

Frequency of second allele (a) = q (q = recessive allele)

Since in this case there are only two alleles, their combined total frequency must represent all possibilities. In other words:

$$p + q = 1 \text{ (unity; that is, 100\% of alleles in the gene pool)}$$

(Proportion of A alleles) (Proportion of a alleles)

To ascertain the expected proportions of genotypes, we simply compute the chances of the alleles combining with one another into all possible combinations. Remember, they all have an equal chance of combining and no new alleles are being added.

These probabilities are a direct function of the frequency of the two alleles. The chances of all possible combinations occurring randomly can be simply shown as:

$$
\begin{array}{r}
p + q \\
\times \quad p + q \\
\hline
pq + q^2 \\
p^2 + pq \\
\hline
p^2 + 2pq + q^2
\end{array}
$$

(Mathematically, this is known as a binomial expansion)

What we have just calculated is simply:

Allele Combination	Genotype Produced	Expected Proportion in Population
Chances of:		
A combining with A	AA	$p \times p = p^2$
Chances of:		
A combining with a	Aa	$p \times q$
a combining with A	aA	$p \times q$ $= 2pq$
Chances of:		
a combining with a	aa	$q \times q = q^2$
Proportions of		
genotypes AA: Aa: aa		
p^2 2pq q^2		

where p=frequency of dominant allele and q=frequency of recessive allele in a population.

Calculating Allele Frequencies: An Example

How microevolutionists use the Hardy-Weinberg formula is best demonstrated through an example. Let us return to the classroom "population" we discussed on page 94 (and now assume it consists of 100 individuals). Now that you are aware of the precise definition of a breeding population you can see that a classroom group does not meet the key prerequisite of social and/or geographic isolation. But once again let us assume that it does and thus represents a good biological population.

In addition, we will use the MN blood group locus as the gene to be measured. This gene produces a blood group antigen—similar to ABO—located on red blood cells. We therefore can fairly quickly ascertain everyone's phenotype by taking blood samples and observing reactions with specially prepared antisera. From the phenotypes we can then directly calculate the allele frequencies. So let us proceed.

All 100 individuals are tested and the results are shown in Box 4-4. Although the match between observed and expected frequencies is not perfect, it is close enough statistically to satisfy equilibrium conditions. Since our population is not a large one, sampling may easily account for the small observed deviations. Our population is therefore probably in equilibrium (that is, it is not evolving). At the minimum, what we can say scientifically is that we cannot reject the *null hypothesis* (a statement of equilibrium in this case).

Review, Genetics and Evolutionary Factors

Starting in Chapter 2 with a discussion of natural selection, we proceeded in Chapter 3 to show the molecular and cellular bases of heredity, and to illustrate in this chapter how such genetic information is passed from individuals in one generation to those in the next. It may seem that these different levels, molecular, cellular, individual, and populational, are different aspects of evolution, but they are all related and highly integrated in a way that can eventually produce evolutionary change. A step-by-step example will make this clear.

In our earlier discussion of sickle-cell hemoglobin (see p. 58), you will recall that the actual genetic information was coded in the sequence of bases in the DNA molecule. We started out with a situation where everyone in the population has the same hemoglobin type; therefore, initially no variation for this trait exists, and without some source of new variation evolution is not possible. How does this gene change? We have seen that a substitution of a single base in the DNA sequence can alter the code significantly enough to alter the protein product and ultimately the whole phenotype of the individual. Imagine that, several generations ago, just such an "accident" occurred in a single individual. For this mutated gene to be passed on to succeeding offspring, the gametes must carry the alteration. Any new mutation, therefore, must be transmitted during sex cell formation.

Once the mutation has occurred in the DNA, it will be packaged into chromosomes, and these chromosomes in turn will assort during meiosis to be passed to offspring. The results of this process are seen by looking at phenotypes (traits) in individuals, and the mode of inheritance is described simply by Mendel's principle of segregation. In other words, if our initial individual has a mutation in only one paired allele on a set of homologous chromosomes, there will be a 50% chance of passing this chromosome (with the new mutation) to an offspring.

Thus far, we have seen what a gene is, how it can change, and how it is passed on to offspring. But what does all this activity have to do with *evolution*? To re-

BOX 4-4

Calculating Allele Frequencies in a Hypothetical Population

Observed Data:

Genotype	Number of Individuals*	Percentage	Number of Alleles M	N
MM	40	(40%)	80	
MN	40	(40%)	40	40
NN	20	(20%)		40
Totals	100	(100%)	120 + 80 = 200	
		Proportion:	.6 + .4 = 1	

Observed allele frequencies:

M = .6(p)   p + q should = 1 (and they do)
N = .4(q)

Expected Frequencies   What are the predicted genotype proportions if genetic equilibrium (no evolution) applies to our population? We simply apply the Hardy-Weinberg formula:

$p^2 + 2pq + q^2$

$$
\begin{aligned}
p^2 &= (.6) \times (.6) &&= .36 \\
2pq &= 2(.6)(.4) = 2(.24) &&= .48 \\
q^2 &= (.4) \times (.4) &&= .16
\end{aligned}
$$

Total   1.00

There are only three possible genotypes (MM:MN:NN) so the total of the relative proportions should equal 1.00; as you can see, they do.

How do these expected frequencies compare with the observed frequencies in our population?

	Expected Frequency	Observed Frequency
MM	.36	.40
MN	.48	.40
NN	.16	.20

*Each individual has two alleles; thus a person who is MM contributes two M alleles to the total gene pool. A person who is MN contributes one M and one N. One hundred individuals, then, have 200 alleles for the MN locus.

peat an earlier definition, evolution is a change in allele frequency in a *population* from one generation to the next. The key point here is that we are now looking at a whole group of individuals, a population, and it is the population that will or will not change over time.

We know whether allele frequencies have changed in a population where sickle-cell anemia is found by ascertaining the percentage of individuals with the sickling allele (Hb^S) versus those with the normal allele (Hb^A). If the relative proportions of these alleles alter with time, evolution has occurred. In addition to discovering that evolution has occurred, it is important to know why. Several possibilities arise. First, we know that the only way the new allele Hb^S could have arisen is by mutation, and we have shown how this process might happen in a single individual. This change, however, is not yet really an evolutionary one, for in a relatively large population the alteration of one individual's genes will not significantly alter allele frequencies of the entire population. Somehow, this new allele must spread in the population.

Table 4-3 *Levels of Organization in the Evolutionary Process*

Evolutionary Factor	Level	Evolutionary Process	Science	Technique of Study
Mutation	DNA	Storage of genetic information; ability to replicate; influences phenotype by production of proteins	Molecular biology	Theoretical: from evidence of spectrophotometry, biochemistry, electron microscopy
Mutation	Chromosomes	A vehicle for packaging and transmitting genetic material (DNA)	Cytogenetics	Light, electron microscope
Recombination (sex cells only)	Cell	The basic unit of life that contains the chromosomes and divides for growth and for production of sex cells	Cytogenetics	Light, electron microscope
Natural selection	Organism	The unit, composed of cells, which reproduces and which we observe for phenotypic traits	Genetics	Visual, biochemical
Drift, migration	Population	A group of interbreeding organisms. We look at changes in allele frequencies between generations; it is the population that evolves	Population genetics	Statistical

One way this could happen is in a small population where mutations in one of just a few individuals and their offspring may indeed alter the overall frequency quite quickly. This case would be representative of genetic drift. As discussed above, drift acts in small populations where random factors may cause significant changes in allele frequency. Due to small population size, there is not likely to be a balance of factors affecting individual survival, reproduction, etc. Consequently, some alleles may be completely removed from the population, while others may become established as the only allele present at that particular locus (and are said to be "fixed" in the population).

In the course of human evolution, drift may have played a significant role at times, but long-term evolutionary trends could only have been sustained by *natural selection*. The way this has worked in the past and still operates today (as in sickle-cell) is through differential reproduction. That is, individuals who carry a particular allele or combination of alleles produce more offspring. By producing more offspring than other individuals with alternative alleles, such individuals cause the frequency of the new allele in the population to increase slowly in proportion from generation to generation. When this process is compounded over hundreds of generations for numerous genes, the result is significant evolutionary change.

Summary

We have now come full circle. We started our discussions of evolution (Chapter 2) talking about populations and, indeed, this is where evolution occurs. But populations are made up of individual organisms, organisms are made up of cells,

cells contain chromosomes, and chromosomes are composed of DNA. Understanding the actual mechanics of the evolutionary process comes *only* from considering all these various levels of organization.

Questions for Review

1. Explain why botanists before Mendel failed to solve the problem of heredity.
2. How was Mendel's approach to the study of heredity different from those of his predecessors?
3. Why did the pea plant suit Mendel's experimental model?
4. What is the significance of contrasting characters?
5. What are the differences between P_1 and F_1 crosses?
6. Explain the principle of segregation.
7. Explain the principle of independent assortment.
8. How do these principles help us to understand evolution?
9. How is a mutation—a change in the DNA genetic code—transmitted into an actual physical change? Use sickle-cell hemoglobin as an example.
10. What are the major elements of the modern synthesis? What earlier dispute did the modern synthesis resolve?
11. Discuss two recent challenges to the modern synthetic theory of evolution.
12. Assume a mutation occurs in a small human population. What does this mutation have to do with evolution? In other words, how might allele frequencies be changed?
13. Why is it so important to study human *populations* in order to understand human evolution?
14. Why is it so difficult to isolate (for scientific study) actual populations?
15. Under what conditions does the Hardy-Weinberg equilibrium model hold true? If a deviation from expected frequencies is found, what does that suggest?

CHAPTER 5

Human Diversity

CONTENTS

ISSUE

Sir Cyril's Strange Stats

Note: Arthur R. Jensen is one of the leading proponents of the usefulness of IQ tests for measuring intelligence, a subject discussed in this chapter. To support his position, Jensen has cited evidence on twins gathered by British psychologist Sir Cyril Burt.

The issue for this chapter recounts the story of Burt and his statistics. (Jensen has stated he can no longer accept Burt's evidence, but he continues to believe that IQ tests reflect intelligence.)

Did Sir Cyril cook the figures?

One of the most influential educational psychologists of this century, especially in the field of intelligence testing, was Sir Cyril Burt, who died in 1971.

Burt believed that heredity could explain the high scores achieved in intelligence tests, that mental abilities were inborn, and that intelligence was concentrated in the higher social classes. When he found an unusually high IQ among orphans or adopted children, he explained, "We commonly learned later on that the child was the illegitimate offspring of a father belonging to a superior social class." The class system, he firmly believed, was an economic reflection of a genetically determined order of human merit.

It is not surprising to learn that Burt was influenced by eugenicists, and, as a matter of fact, was acquainted with Sir Francis Galton, the principal founder of eugenics, who believed that social controls could improve or impair the qualities of future generations. Burt's explanation of differences in intelligence was invariably associated with social class. In 1912, he coauthored a paper in which Liverpool slum boys were compared with Oxford preparatory boys. He claimed the results were consistent with investigations of savage and civilized races!

Burt also conducted studies of separated pairs of identical twins.* His results showed a high correlation in the IQs of the separated twins, thus effectively reducing the significance of the environment on intelligence scores.

Burt's work influenced educational legislation in England. The British Education Act of 1944 was based explicitly on his statistical reports, which established principles of educational selectivity and segregation: three types of schools established for different innate abilities—grammar schools, technical schools, and secondary schools.

---

*Monozygotic twins raised from birth in separate households.

In 1961, he published a major paper, "Intelligence and Social Mobility," which was a deadly attack against those who argued that the environment could affect scores achieved in intelligence tests. This paper also demonstrated a remarkable correlation between intelligence and social class.

This work has been widely quoted by geneticists and psychologists, especially those involved in IQ testing, since it appeared to be the most comprehensive study ever performed in the relation of intelligence to social class and social mobility. Burt's publications had great impact on such men as Jensen, Eyesenck, and Herrnstein, staunch supporters of the importance of heredity on intelligence and intelligence scores. Burt was knighted in 1946 for his work on intelligence and his recommendations for educational reform.

Doubts about the validity and accuracy (as well as the honesty) of Burt's work surfaced just a few years after his death. Professor Leon Kamin (1971) of Princeton questioned Burt's studies of twins. Kamin pointed out that Burt's number of separated identical twin pairs increased from 15 in 1943 to 21 in 1955, to 30 in 1957, to 42 in 1958, and in 1966 reached 53, probably the world's largest sample of an extremely rare phenomenon. Yet the correlation of intelligence of the separated twin pairs remained constant to three decimal places over this period of twenty-five years, even though the number of pairs had increased almost four times. Such a stable correlation is so unlikely that statisticians consider it impossible unless the figures were deliberately fixed.

An English journalist, Oliver Gillie (1978, 1979), tried to find the women who had collaborated with Burt in his research and publications in order to learn more of Burt's unlikely statistics. Gillie searched records at universities and psychological societies for traces of these three women associates, and he also talked to friends and employees of Burt who should have known the women and something of their whereabouts. However, he found no trace of them with the possible exception of one—a Miss Howard—who, said Gillie, if she did exist, was not the person Burt said she was. It is difficult to know why Burt would fabricate such associates, or what purpose this might have served.

The most damaging report on Burt's work is probably Professor D. D. Dorfman's examination of the statistics given in Burt's 1961 report. Burt claimed he had studied 40,000 people over a period of fifty years, comparing the intelligence of children and their fathers. He illustrated his findings in tables that showed the intelligence of fathers of six social classes and, in another table, the intelligence of their children.

In results so perfect (and too good to be true), Burt found an almost perfect normal curve of intelligence among fathers and children, and the statistics for each group were almost identical. The probability of a normal curve for intelligence is highly unlikely. The U.S. Army, for example, in the Alpha test scores for intelligence given to draftees in World War I, found a skewed, not a normal, curve. Other summaries of intelligence scores show similarly skewed results. That children's intelligence scores would be identical with their fathers', over a period of fifty years, is equally unlikely.

Dorfman concluded that Burt's results were precisely what they should have been according to a theoretical formula for such work, but, he added, such results do not occur in nature. "The almost perfect fit of Burt's adult and child distributions to the normal curve suggests that his 'actual' distributions are not actual distributions." Furthermore, "we may now say that, beyond a reasonable doubt, the frequency distributions of Burt's tables . . . were carefully constructed so as to [be] in agreement with the normal curve." And, finally, "these findings show, beyond any reasonable doubt, that Burt fixed the row and column totals of the tables in his highly acclaimed 1961 study."

We might ask, along with Gillie, "Why did psychologists, educationalists, and civil servants let him get away with it for so long?—for any reasonably careful inspection shows Burt's work to be careless, riddled with implausibilities, and inadequately documented? . . . Sir Cyril Burt, the supposed guardian of intellectual rigour, the hero of the educational conservatives, the defender of a future which was to be given over to the genetically pure, was one of the most formidable confidence tricksters British society has produced. . . . Sir Cyril takes his place alongside the manufacturers of the Piltdown Skull."

S O U R C E S :

Dorfman, D. D., "The Cyril Burt Questions: New Findings," Science, 201:1177, September 29, 1978.

Gillie, Oliver, "Sir Cyril Burt and the Great IQ Fraud," New Statesman, 24, November, 1978.

———, "Burt's Missing Ladies," Science, 204:1035, June 8, 1979.

Jensen, Arthur R., Bias in Mental Testing, New York: Free Press, 1980.

Kamin, Leon, The Science and Politics of IQ, New York: John Wiley & Sons, 1974.

Introduction

We examined human variation in Chapters 3 and 4 from an adaptive point of view, in which physical differences among populations were explained largely in terms of selection pressures leading to possible adaptive responses.

This emphasis on selection and adaptation is a recent approach to human variation. In the past, scholars busied themselves constructing racial typologies, seeking the origin of races, and attributing to races a variety of personality traits.

In this chapter, we shall briefly trace the history of the scholarly and scientific approaches to human diversity. We shall question the value of racial typologies and the concept of race itself. We shall also examine the relationship—if any—between human diversity and behavior. Do physical traits determine what people do? Does pigmentation, for example, limit or aid intelligence? Is intelligence, as reflected in IQ test achievements, the result of heredity or environment, or the interaction of both?

Racial Classification

As early as 1350 B.C., Egyptians recognized physical differences of populations by using four colors to distinguish various groups: red for Egyptians, yellow for those to the east, white for people from the north, and black for Africans to the south (Gossett, 1963, p. 4). In more recent times, classification of populations has been based mainly on such physical traits as pigmentation of skin, eyes, and hair; hair form, body build, and nose form. Three hundred years ago, in 1684, François Bernier, a French physician, divided the world's populations into what we call races: Europeans, Far Easterners, Blacks, and Lapps. It was "probably the first attempt in history to classify all the races of mankind" (Gossett, 1963, p. 33).

From that time until the present, scientists, including such luminaries as Linnaeus, Buffon, Huxley, and others have constructed racial classifications. In Box 7-1 are examples of racial classifications, which range from the simple fourfold division of Linnaeus to the complex schemes of Deniker and Hooton.

During the sixteenth and seventeenth centuries, explorers returning from their travels to newly discovered continents brought back information about people unknown to Europeans. Scholars, like Linnaeus, attempted to fit this knowledge into an orderly arrangement, basing their classifications mainly on skin color and geography. Johann Blumenbach, a professor of medicine at the University of Göttingen in Germany, made a thorough study of numerous skulls and developed an influential racial classification. His 1781 division of Caucasian,* Mongolian, Malay, Ethiopian, and American (which came to be popu-

---

*Blumenbach was the first to use the term Caucasian for Europeans. Thomas Huxley commented that "A Georgian woman's skull was the handsomest in his collection. Hence it became his model exemplar of human skulls, from which all others might be regarded as deviations; and out of this, by some strange hocus-pocus, grew up the notion that the Caucasian man is the prototypic 'Adamic' man, and his country the primitive centre of our kind" (cited in Count, 1950, p. 119).

larly known as white, yellow, brown, black, and red) still persists to this day as one of the most common racial divisions of humankind. Blumenbach used the same criteria of skin color and geography as earlier scholars had done and he added a number of others, such as shape of skull and face, hair color, nose and chin form.

Differences in races at this time were often explained by climate and environment. In the United States, the Reverend Mr. Samuel Stanhope Smith, a professor at the College of New Jersey (later Princeton) attributed color mainly to climate and believed dark skin could "be considered as a universal freckle" (Gossett, 1963, p. 39). He further believed that environment was "all that stood in the way of the advancement of Negroes and other non-white races . . ." (Gossett, 1963, p. 39).

In the latter half of the eighteenth century and during much of the nineteenth century, there was a continuing discussion of the origin of races: The **monogenists** believed all races were derived from a single pair, and credited Adam and Eve as the source. The multitudinous progeny of the original pair then spread over the world and assumed their present diversity in response to the climate and other conditions to which they were subjected. Monogenists also explained differences in human populations as deviant degeneration from the original stock.

Polygenists took the position of a multiple origin of races and ridiculed the idea that all people could have descended from Adam and Eve. In the nineteenth century, an American physician, Dr. Samuel George Morton (1799–1851), argued in favor of polygenism by pointing to his researches, which indicated that the offspring of a black and white cross, a mulatto, could bear children only with difficulty. If these women mated only with mulattoes, he maintained, their descendants would bear fewer and fewer children, and in time there would be no descendants at all! (Gossett, 1963).

In the latter part of the eighteenth century, researchers such as Blumenbach began what they considered a more scientific approach, and initiated the careful study and measurements of skulls. This practice was refined in the nineteenth century when Samuel Morton developed new ways of measuring crania by filling skulls with seed (and, later on, shot) and then weighing this material. This new science, called **anthropometry**, became the primary concern of physical anthropologists. In 1842, Anders Retzius, a Swedish anatomist, believed he had discovered a true scientific basis for racial classification: the shape of the head. This measurement, called the *cephalic index* and a refinement of Morton's technique, was a measure of the ratio of the breadth of the skull to its length. Retzius used the cephalic index to divide Europe into two types: a longheaded or **dolichocephalic** type and a roundheaded or **brachycephalic** type.

Anthropometry was enthusiastically promoted by Paul Broca, a French neurosurgeon and physical anthropologist, who, in 1859, founded The Anthropological Society of Paris, the first anthropological organization in Europe. He published statistical treatises with complicated diagrams and arranged his collection of 2,000 skulls into 60 different series (Gossett, 1963, p. 76). Broca was also a resourceful, ingenious inventor of measuring instruments and devised craniometers and other gadgetry in order to discover statistical relationships of the skull. Cranial measurements proceeded with enthusiastic zeal, and the peak of anthropometry was probably reached in 1900, when A. von Törok took 5,000 measurements on a single skull (Barzun, 1965, p. 117).

MONOGENISTS
Term applied to those who believe that all races derived from a single pair (Adam and Eve).

POLYGENISTS
Term applied to those who believe in a multiple origin of races.

ANTHROPOMETRY
anthropos: man
metric: measure
Measurement of the human body.

DOLICHOCEPHALIC
dolicho: narrow
cephal: head
Narrow or long-headed; a skull in which the width is less than 75 percent of the length.

BRACHYCEPHALIC
brachy: short, broad
Broad-headed; a skull in which the width is 80 percent or more of the length.

BOX 5-1

Racial Classifications

Linnaeus, 1758

Homo europaeus
Homo asiaticus
Homo afer
Homo americanus

Buffon, 1749

Lapland
Tartar
Southern Asiatic
European
American

Blumenbach, 1781

Caucasian
Mongolian
Malay
Ethiopian
American

Saint Hilaire, 1861

Caucasian	(Caucasian, Alleghenian)
Mongolian	(Hyperborean, Malay, American, Mongolian, Paraborean, Australian)
Ethiopian	(Kaffir, Ethiopian, Negro, Melanesian)
Hottentot	(Hottentot)

Thomas H. Huxley, 1870

Negroid	(Bushman, Negro, Papüan)
Australoid	(Australians, Dravidians, Ethiopian)
Mongoloid	(Mongol, Polynesian, American Eskimo, Malay)
Xanthochroid	(Xanthochroid of Northern Europe, Melanochroid of Southern Europe, Melanochroid of Asia—Arabs, Afghans, Hindus, etc.)

J. Deniker, 1900

TYPES	EXAMPLES
Wooly hair, broad nose:	Bushman, Negrito, Negro, Melanesian
Curly or wavy hair:	Ethiopian, Australian, Dravidian, Assyroid
Wavy brown or black hair, dark eyes:	Indo-Afghan, Arab or Semite, Berber, Littoral-European, Ibero-insular, Western European, Adriatic
Fair, wavy or straight hair, light eyes:	Northern European, Eastern European
Straight or wavy hair, dark, black eyes:	Ainu, Polynesian, Indonesian, South American
Straight hair:	Northern American, Central American, Patagonian, Eskimo, Lapp, Ugrian, Turkish, Mongol

E. A. Hooton, 1946

PRIMARY RACE	PRIMARY SUBRACE	COMPOSITE RACE[*]	COMPOSITE SUBRACE[*]	RESIDUAL MIXED TYPES[*]
White	Mediterranean	Australian	Armenoid	Nordic-Alpine
	Ainu	Indo-Dravidian	Dinaric	Nordic-Mediterranean
	Keltic	Polynesian		
	Nordic			
	Alpine			
	East Baltic			

[*]Example of categories, not to be read across.

PRIMARY RACE	PRIMARY SUBRACE	COMPOSITE RACE*	COMPOSITE SUBRACE*	RESIDUAL MIXED TYPES*
Negroid	African Negro Nilotic Negro Negrito	Bushman-Hottentot		
Mongoloid	Classic Mongoloid Arctic Mongoloid	Indonesian-Mongoloid American Indian		

SECONDARY SUBRACE

Malay-Mongoloid
Indonesian

Stanley M. Garn, 1965

GEOGRAPHICAL RACES: "A collection of race populations, separated from other such collections by major geographical barriers" (p. 14).

Amerindian
Polynesian
Micronesian
Melanesian-Papuan
Australian
Asiatic
Indian
European
African

LOCAL RACES: "A breeding population adapted to local selection pressures and maintained by either natural or social barriers to gene interchange" (p. 16).

Northwest European
Northeast European
Alpine
Mediterranean
East African   These are examples of local races; there are many, many more.
Bantu
Tibetan
North Chinese
Extreme Mongoloid
Hindu

MICRO-RACES: Not well defined but apparently refers to neighborhoods within a city or a city itself since "marriage or mating, is a mathematical function of distance. With millions of potential mates, the male ordinarily chooses one near at hand" (p. 19).

TYPOLOGY
The science of dividing humankind into discrete racial types.

MONGRELIZATION
Racial mixture.

Broca, as did many other anthropologists during this period, believed there was some connection between brain and race, and that measuring the shape of the skull was the best way to determine the content of the brain. He even believed it possible to identify the social class of the skulls he studied!

Despite the emphasis on anthropometry by these "scientific anthropologists," others were questioning the value of such measurements. Broca himself noted that two anthropologists rarely obtained the same figures when they measured the same skull. "The human head," he complained, "is too irregular . . . to allow accurate comparison on a statistical basis" (Gossett, 1963, p. 76), a conclusion which nevertheless did not deter his anthropometric research.

With the publication of Darwin's *Origin of Species* in 1859, there was some attempt to take evolutionary principles into consideration for racial classifications. But the emphasis on typology continued, as we see (Box 5-1), in the racial types suggested by Deniker in 1900 and Hooten as late as 1946.

However, concern with the division of the earth's human population into races was the goal of many physical anthropologists during the latter half of the nineteenth century. The assumption throughout this period was that pure races existed (some time in the past), and it was the responsibility of anthropologists to define them. To support such a position, it was necessary to believe that races had not basically changed from whatever they were at the time of origin. And if races were fixed—a conflict with evolutionary thought, which anthropologists accepted—then there must be physical traits that remain fixed. That is, those physical traits that did not adapt to environmental conditions could be used for racial classification; those that did adapt, could not. There was, therefore, constant effort to locate *nonadaptive* traits. It was believed that once races evolved, racial traits persisted even if the people moved to another environment. Since it was obvious that pure races did not exist, certainly not in Europe, physical differences in modern populations were said to be the result of a mixture of already formed races.

The search for nonadaptive traits to serve as a basis for the classification of racial types centered on the cephalic index, although hair form, eye form, and prominence of the nose were also considered nonadaptive. W. Z. Ripley, in a book published in 1899 and widely read in the United States, summarized much of the research of European scientists. Ripley relied heavily on headform as a basis for his racial classification of Europe into three types. Not everyone agreed with the emphasis on head measurements, and Franz Boas, early in this century, criticized Ripley for "treating the cephalic index as the 'primary principle of classification' " (Stocking, 1968, p. 181). As a result of his well-known study of head form and body form of immigrants and their children, first published in 1909, Boas (1940) recognized environmental influences on head length and width, stature, face width, and so forth. He even suggested the term "ecotype" might be used in place of race or subrace to emphasize these environmental or ecological factors (Boas, 1940, p. 77). Although it was clear that Boas understood that head length and other body forms were adaptive, he maintained his belief in racial types. It would not be until the middle 1950s that physical anthropologists, realizing that most nonadaptive traits vary with the environment, changed their approach to the study of race.

Typology presents problems not readily resolved. How many divisions are there? Estimates range from as few as 3 to more than 300. There are primary divisions, major subdivisions, minor subdivisions, composite subdivisions, and so on. What is the significance of these divisions of divisions, and what is their reality? Do they represent actual living populations, or merely ideal types? What criteria are used to separate one type from another, one subdivision from another? Is one trait more important than another? Skin pigmentation, for example, is the trait most people would consider as the basic classificatory criterion; should it carry more weight than, say, head shape, nose shape, body build, or stature? If so (or if not), why? For example, in his racial classification of 1900, Deniker typed northern Europeans as tall with wavy, reddish hair, reddish white skin, and dolichocephalic skulls. What, then, shall we do with a northern European answering this description whose brother is short, not tall, with straight rather than wavy hair, and a darkish rather than reddish white skin?

There is a basic assumption in typological classification (noted above) that races existed in a pure state at some time in the past, before migrations of recent times produced the mixtures of today. **Mongrelization** is the term often used by racists. But migration has always existed; with culture, humans are capable of taking a goodly portion of their environment with them, and as Hooten has succinctly aphorized, "when groups meet they may or may not bleed, but they always breed." As Mayr has said, "To speak of 'pure races' is sheer nonsense" (1970, p. 397).

Finally, typologies tell us little if anything of human evolution. Classification, as Washburn noted, is useful if we are concerned with anatomical, genetic, and structural differences between people, "but it is useful under no other circumstances, as far as I can see" (Washburn, 1963, p. 527).

For these and other reasons, many anthropologists no longer accept the assumption that races exist and have turned away from the racial concept as biologically unrealistic. Such studies are regarded as unrewarding. Those still concerned with classification have drawn upon population genetics and consider the breeding population "the basic unit of evolutionary change . . . the unit whose structure changes in response to the action of the mechanisms of evolution" (Kelso, 1974, p. 301).

It is difficult to escape the conclusion that as a concept, race, like quicksilver, is awkward to take hold of. Just when we think we have it in our grasp, it slips through our fingers. As French anthropologist Jean Hiernaux puts it:

> To dismember mankind into races as a convenient approximation requires such a distortion of the facts that any usefulness disappears; on the contrary, only the harm done by such practices remains (Hiernaux, 1964, p. 43).

Figure 5-1
Craniometer.

Definitions of Race

To understand the difficulties the concept of race presents, it may help to review briefly the process of speciation (p. 90). Species is defined as "a group of interbreeding organisms that are reproductively isolated from other such groups" (p. 87), and biologists are agreed that species is an evolutionary unit. The definition of race is more elusive, and race is not an evolutionary unit, but an arbitrary one. We see this more clearly with the process of speciation.

As the populations within a species diverge, especially between isolated groups, differences arise. When the differences become detectable, taxonomists may classify the populations as races, or subspecies. With continued isolation and divergence, the groups are known as *incipient species* (or biological races), on their way to becoming species. However, ". . . the decisions about what characteristics to emphasize in describing differences between the populations are relatively arbitrary ones" (Bodmer and Cavalli-Sforza, 1976, p. 561).

The division of the populations of any species into biological "races" tends to be arbitrary to some degree, but when it comes to human races, the situation is a quagmire. The populations of *H. sapiens* are not on their way to becoming separate species, and the reasons for this are quite clear. Human groups have been isolated in the past but never long enough to speciate. As mentioned, humans take their culture with them when they migrate, and are not entirely dependent on their environment. They can and do migrate to a considerable extent. Consequently, there has been gene exchange between groups that has kept them interfertile and, therefore, members of the same species. As communication and the means of transportation improved, and as more efficient technology developed, humans became even more independent of the environment, and the chance of speciation has become remote.

Perhaps the basic problem in defining race is to decide on the criteria. As we see from the examples on pages 108–109, these are arbitrary. A recent definition demonstrates the dilemma: A race is ". . . a division of a species which differs from other divisions by the frequency with which certain hereditary traits appear among its members" (Brues, 1977, p. 1). Which hereditary traits? How are they selected? On what basis? Do the same traits apply in all cases? There is no agreement on the answers. Besides, no group classified as a race differs in all its traits from another race. ". . . the boundaries between the races drawn on the basis of one trait will not coincide with boundaries drawn on the basis of another trait" (Bodmer and Cavalli-Sforza, 1976, p. 562). If we cannot agree on racial criteria, then defining race and classifying populations into racial groups appears impossible.

Although we question the value of the racial concept, it may be instructive to list definitions of race, which may delineate even further the reasons why anthropologists are dissatisfied with the concept.

Already, in 1749, Buffon (see p. 31) was aware that humankind did not consist of separate species, but were varieties of the same species. This is not, strictly speaking, a definition, but it does recognize the separation of our species into subdivisions based upon the environment and interbreeding.

> Upon the whole, every circumstance concurs in proving that mankind are [*sic*] not composed of species essentially different from each other; that, on the contrary, there was originally but one species, who, after multiplying and spreading over the whole surface of the earth, have undergone various changes by the influence of climate, food, mode of living, epidemic diseases, and the mixture of dissimilar individuals . . . . (Buffon, cited in Snyder, 1962, p. 102).

Rudolf Virchow (1896) also saw races as varieties originating from two factors, heredity and environment: ". . . there can be no doubt that *races are nothing* *more than hereditary variations . . .* we must derive races also from the influence of external causes, and we may define them as *acquired deviations from the original type*" (cited in Count, 1950, p. 193). Although not the first, Virchow's view of race as hereditary variations suggests an evolutionary orientation.

As time went on, anthropologists emphasized phenotypic traits as important in racial analysis. In 1926, Hooton offered the following definition:

> A race is a great division of mankind, the members of which, though individually vary-ing, are characterized as a group by a certain combination of morphological and metri-cal features, principally non-adaptive, which have been derived from their common descent.

In addition to emphasizing visible phenotypic traits (morphological features), Hooten included measurements of the body that had occupied so much of an-thropological research in the latter half of the nineteenth century. He also made an attempt to construct a more precise definition by restricting it to traits that were presumably nonadaptive—that is, unaffected by the environment—since he considered these the most objective racial markers. Implicit in this approach is the belief that races do not change over time, that if it were possible somehow to find traits unaffected by the environment, true or pure races could be deter-mined (see p. 111).

We now know the search for nonadaptive traits is a futile quest, that a phenotype is the result of the dynamic interaction of several genes *and* the envi-ronment.

As population genetics became important in biological research, the concept of population became part of the definition. In 1950, Boyd defined race "as a population which differs significantly from other human populations in regard to the frequency of one or more genes it possesses" (Boyd, 1950, p. 207).

Livingstone objects to the simplistic use of gene frequencies as a criterion for race, since such a position implies that each population—which probably differs in the frequency of some gene from other populations—would be a separate race (Livingstone, 1964, p. 49).

One of the most recent modifications of the definition of race adds the concept of a *breeding*, or Mendelian, population (Garn, 1969). Livingstone again objects since the concept of breeding population may be difficult to apply (see p. 111). Garn, however, views race "as a breeding population, neither more nor less" (1969, p. 6). One local race (see Box 5-1), ranging from Tangier to the Dar-danelles and including the Arabian Peninsula, Garn calls Mediterranean. How-ever, this is a very unlikely breeding population, containing, as it does, wide dif-ferences in such factors as social class, religion, economy, and philosophy. Very few Christians interbreed with Muslims, or Arab Beduins with, say, Italian farm-ers. And even if it were possible to identify a local race, "The actual fabric of human mating behavior today is made of such a complicated and continually changing weave that not only is a simple count impossible, but even an estimate is a deception" (Kelso, 1974, p. 304).

The foregoing definitions of race and comments are not intended to discour-age or confuse. The plain fact is that a great deal of confusion abounds among an-thropologists, geneticists, and other researchers concerned with the concept of race. That there are physical differences among human beings is an obvious fact requiring no discussion. No one will mistake an indigenous resident of China for a European or African. But the matter is not that simple.

Figure 5-2
Virchow.

Figure 5-3
E. A. Hooton.

Topinard, writing almost 100 years ago, already recognized the problems still being discussed today:

> Races exist; it is undeniable; our intelligence comprehends them; our minds see them; our labors separate them out. If in thought we suppress the intermixtures of peoples, their interbreedings, in a flash we see them stand forth—simple, inevitable, with their trait-patterns and physiological systems—a compulsive consequence of collective heredity. *But nowhere can we put our fingers upon them* (emphasis ours, cited by Scheidt, 1924, p. 389).

To confuse the matter of race definition even further, the term "race," as it is popularly used, is more a sociocultural than biological concept. That is, a group of people may be designated as a race regardless of their genetic traits. Thus, children of mixed black and white parents are considered black, though genetically they are as much "white" as "black." Often designated as races are ethnic groups (Germans, French, Russians, etc.), religious groups (Muslims, Buddhists, Jews, etc.), political groups (communists, fascists). This also adds to the confusion. In wartime, when emotions run high, all manner of vices, based on "racial" traits, are attributed to the enemy (e.g., the Germans and Japanese in World War II and the Vietnamese in the Vietnam War).

If we restrict the word "race," no matter how difficult it may be to define the term, to genetic traits, it may be possible to eliminate some of the misunderstanding associated with the concept of race. However, the prognosis is not optimistic.

What, then, are we to do about the concept of race? Is race a reality? Is a breeding population a race? Are races geographic isolates? Is it even possible to study races? Is the word "race" so loaded with misconception, misunderstanding, fallacy, prejudice, and bigotry that the term itself should be changed and its study limited? Or is Dunn more perceptive when he suggests, "It seems better to define and explain its use, and to free it from its bad and false meaning, than to give up the problem by excluding the word" (Dunn, 1951, p. 12).

The validity and utility of race, as a concept, are still debated by anthropologists. Typological divisions of humankind, however, which once occupied so much anthropological effort, appear to be a phenomenon of the past. As we have indicated, there are too many problems in the construction of racial typologies, and, once a typology is developed, the nagging question remains: So what?

Instead of placing an entire population in, as it were, a racial straightjacket, many anthropologists consider the study of the distribution of single traits to be more rewarding from the point of view of evolutionary theory. This is the clinal approach to human diversity.

Clinal Distribution: One Genetic Trait

A relatively recent approach* to human variation is *clinal distribution*. Just as temperatures are plotted on a weather map by means of isotherms that join points with the same temperature, so also may gene frequencies be plotted. Thus, the distribution of a particular trait is indicated on a map by zones, known as clines (Fig. 5-4). This description simply reveals the variation of that trait over a geo-

*J. S. Huxley introduced the clinal concept, as it applied to plants, in 1938.

▨ Greater than 0.160	▤ From 0.100 to 0.120	⬚ From 0.040 to 0.060
▨ From 0.140 to 0.160	▨ From 0.080 to 0.100	
‖ From 0.120 to 0.140	‖ From 0.060 to 0.080	

Figure 5-4
A cline frequency of the B allele. This computer-generated map shows the frequency of the B allele of the ABO blood-group system. Note the higher frequencies in Asia and the gradual decreasing frequencies as the clines move into Europe. (Courtesy of P. E. Schreiber, IBM Research Laboratory, San Jose, California.)

graphic area, and by itself implies no explanation, racial or otherwise. Nor does such a distribution lead to racial typologies. A clinal distribution calls for an *evolutionary explanation* of the variation: Why does the frequency of allele B, in our figure, vary as we move from east to west across Europe? Evolutionary theory—mutation, genetic drift, natural selection, migration—is one way in which clinal variation may be explained.

Human variation is perceived quite differently when approached from a clinal point of view. No attempt is made to construct a typology of traits, but rather to apply the principles of evolution. Is the variation of gene frequency due to the advantage of one gene over another? Has there been migration to or from the clinal area that may have altered the gene frequency, or perhaps an accident known genetically as drift? An advantage of a clinal study is that gene and trait frequencies can be graphically represented as they are in Figures 5-4 and 5-5. They suggest "migratory patterns and other aspects of population history" and "observed clinal variation in a trait is particularly amenable to explanation by mathematical methods of population genetics. In this sense, there is probably no superior method by which the evolutionary mechanisms responsible for interpopulation variation in single traits can be identified" (Bennett, 1979, pp. 357–358).

An example of an evolutionary clinal approach may be seen in Dr. Joseph Birdsell's discussion of the distribution of tawny hair he found in his fieldwork among Australian aborigines. The heaviest distribution of this blond hair is among several tribal groups in the Australian western desert (see Fig. 5-5), and

Figure 5-5
Gene distribution, tawny hair in Australia. Note the concentration of tawny hair in the center of distribution which can be traced by clines in a decreasing gradient. This pattern can thus be viewed on an evolutionary and genetic basis.

Observed Phenotypic Frequencies for Tawny Hair

0		30–39.9		70–79.9	
0–9.9		40–49.9		80–89.9	
10–19.9		50–59.9		90–99.9	
20–29.9		60–69.9		100	

the frequency then declines on a gradient outward from this center, although not uniformly in all directions. Professor Birdsell writes (1981, pp. 352–353):

> The evolutionary significance of this clinal distribution seems apparent, even though the exact genetic basis for its inheritance has not yet been unraveled. The trait acts as though it was determined by a single codominant gene. It would appear that somewhere in the central region of high frequency, mutations, and probably repeated mutations, occurred from normal dark brown hair to this depigmented variety. The pattern of distribution indicates that it was favored by selection in some totally unknown fashion. Over considerable periods of time, through gene exchange between adjacent tribes, the new mutant gene prospered and spread outward. It seems unlikely that lightly pigmented hair in childhood should in itself have any selective advantage. Rather, it is much more probable that certain effects of this mutant gene have somehow biochemically heightened the fitness of these Aborigines in their generally desert environment. Presumably the new gene mixed well with the other genes in their pools and so *new coadaptive equilibria were produced*. The equilibria seem to have attained a plateau in the region where frequencies exceed 90 percent. [See p. 142 for a discussion of coadaptation.]

Professor Birdsell goes on to point out that one character cannot define a subspecies or race, and that "this example illustrates why races are scientifically undefinable." (Birdsell, p. 352). However, while this example does nothing for the definition of race, it is a good example of microevolution. "This pattern of blondness is a spectacular case of *transient polymorphism*, that is, a polymorphic character changing in time, here reflected as changes in space" (Birdsell, 1981, p. 352). And Birdsell wonders whether, if British colonization had not cut the process short, all Australian aborigines might have become blond-haired.

Multivariate Population Genetics

MULTIVARIATE
Pattern for several traits.

Whereas clinal studies isolate patterns of genetic variation one trait at a time, **multivariate** studies seek to describe the pattern for several traits simultaneously. Because the statistical manipulations of such analyses are exceedingly complex, high-speed computers have proven an invaluable tool.

An excellent example of this kind of approach to human diversity was undertaken by Harvard population geneticist R. D. Lewontin (1972), and his results are most informative. Lewontin measured the degree of population differences in gene frequencies for seventeen polymorphic traits, including many of those discussed in Chapter 4. In his analysis, Lewontin immediately faced the dilemma: Which groups (populations) should he contrast and how should they be weighted (all equally, or bigger groups like Arabs weighted differently than smaller ones like residents of the island, Tristan da Cunha)? After considerable deliberation, Lewontin decided to break down his sample into seven geographical areas (corresponding to the traditional concept of "major race") and included several (all equally weighted) populations within each. He then calculated how much of the total genetic variability within our species could be accounted for by these population subdivisions. (See Table 5-1.)

Surprisingly, only 6.3% of all variation can be accounted for at the level of major (geographic) race. In other words, close to 94% of human genetic diversity occurs *within* these gigantic groups. The large population units within races (generally corresponding to Garn's local races) account for an average of an additional 8.3%. Amazingly, the traditional concept of race (which isolates large human groups) explains about 15% of human genetic variation, leaving the remaining 85% unaccounted for.

The vast majority of genetic differences among human beings is thus explicable in terms of differences from one village to another, from one family to another, and to a very significant degree, from one person to another—even within the same family. Of course, when you recall the vast amount of human polymorphism (discussed in Chapter 4) and the ways this genetic variability is rescrambled during meiosis/sexual reproduction (discussed in Chapter 3), all this individual variation should not be that amazing.

Our superficial visual perceptions tell us race does exist. But the visible phenotypic traits usually used to make racial distinctions (skin color, hair shape, nose shape, etc.) may very well be a highly biased sample, not giving an accurate picture of the actual patterns of *genetic variation*. The polymorphic traits used by Lewontin are a more objective basis for accurate biological comparisons of human groups, and they indicate that the traditional concept of race tells us very little about human variation. Indeed, Lewontin concludes with a ringing condemnation:

> Human racial classification is of no social value and is positively destructive of social and human relations. Since such racial classification is now seen to be of virtually no

Table 5-1 *Inclusive List of All Populations Used in Lewontin's Population Genetics Study (1972)*

Caucasians

Arabs, Armenians, Austrians, Basques, Belgians, Bulgarians, Czechs, Danes, Dutch, Egyptians, English, Estonians, Finns, French, Georgians, Germans, Greeks, Gypsies, Hungarians, Icelanders, Indians (Hindi-speaking), Italians, Irani, Norwegians, Oriental Jews, Pakistani (Urduspeakers), Poles, Portuguese, Russians, Spaniards, Swedes, Swiss, Syrians, Tristan da Cunhans, Welsh

Black Africans

Abyssinians (Amharas), Bantu, Barundi, Batutsi, Bushmen, Congolese, Ewe, Fulani, Gambians, Ghanaians, Hobe, Hottentot, Hututu, Ibo, Iraqi, Kenyans, Kikuyu, Liberians, Luo, Madagascans, Mozambiquans, Msutu, Nigerians, Pygmies, Senegalese, Shona, Somalis, Sudanese, Tanganyikans, Tutsi, Ugandans, U.S. Blacks, "West Africans," Xosa, Zulu

Mongoloids

Ainu, Bhutanese, Bogobos, Bruneians, Buriats, Chinese, Dyaks, Filipinos, Ghashgai, Indonesians, Japanese, Javanese, Kirghiz, Koreans, Lapps, Malayans, Senoy, Siamese, Taiwanese, Tatars, Thais, Turks

South Asian Aborigines

Andamanese, Badagas, Chenchu, Irula, Marathas, Naiars, Oraons, Onge, Tamils, Todas

Amerinds

Alacaluf, Aleuts, Apache, Atacameños, "Athabascans," Aymara, Bororo, Blackfeet, Bloods, "Brazilian Indians," Chippewa, Caingang, Choco, Coushatta, Cuna, Diegueños, Eskimo, Flathead, Huasteco, Huichol, Ica, Kwakiutl, Labradors, Lacandon, Mapuche, Maya, "Mexican Indians," Navaho, Nez Percé, Paez, Pehuenches, Pueblo, Quechua, Seminole, Shoshone, Toba, Utes, "Venezuelan Indians," Xavante, Yanomama

Oceanians

Admiralty Islanders, Caroline Islanders, Easter Islanders, Ellice Islanders, Fijians, Gilbertese, Guamians, Hawaiians, Kapingas, Maori, Marshallese, Melanuans, "Melanesians," "Micronesians," New Britons, New Caledonians, New Hebrideans, Palauans, Papuans, "Polynesians," Saipanese, Samoans, Solomon Islanders, Tongans, Trukese, Yapese

Austrialian Aborigines

Source: Evolutionary Biology, Volume 6, ed. by Dobzhansky et al. (article by R. Lewontin), p. 387. Reprinted with permission of Plenum Publishing Corporation.

genetic or taxonomic significance either, no justification can be offered for its continuance (Lewontin, 1972, p. 397).

Not all population geneticists, however, are quite this critical. After all, Lewontin did find that slightly more than 6% of human variation is accounted for in the large geographic segments traditionally called major races. Whereas this is certainly a minority of all variation within *Homo sapiens*, it is not necessarily biologically insignificant. If one feels compelled to continue classifying humankind into large geographic segments, population genetics offers some aid in isolating consistent patterns of geographic variation. One such classification suggests our species can be partitioned into three major geographic groups: Africans, Caucasians, and a heterogeneous group of Easterners, including all aboriginal populations of the Pacific area (Bodmer and Cavalli-Sforza, 1976).

Whereas, to some degree, these three groups form contrasting genetic units, we must remember that the total amount of genetic variation *within* them (from one person to another, one village to another, one tribe to another, etc.) is far more than exists *between* them.

We have thus far discussed race in the abstract, as a concept, but there is a very practical aspect of race that must be considered in our modern world: the association of race and behavior, which we take up in the following section.

Race and Behavior

The fact that people differ has, as we remarked at the beginning of this chapter, long been recognized, at least as far back in recorded history as the ancient Egyptians. Association of personality traits and race has also long been suggested. In his famous taxonomic scheme, Linnaeus (see p. 30), in 1758, classified humans into four groups (Box 5-1). He also assigned behavioral traits to each group: American Indians are choleric; Europeans, sanguine; Asiatics, melancholy; and Africans, phlegmatic.

One hundred years later, personality traits were still being attributed to race by, among others, Count de Gobineau, sometimes called the "Father of Racist Ideology" (Biddiss, 1970). We must point out that a *racial* classification differs from a *racist* one. The former attempts—usually unsuccessfully—to categorize humans into meaningful groups without making distinctions concerning the superiority of one versus another. Racist typologies, on the other hand, explicitly attempt—always unsuccessfully—to impute "superior" behavioral characteristics to some races and "inferior" attributes to others. Not surprisingly, whoever is doing the classifying invariably places himself or herself in the most "superior" group. Anthropologists, for the most part, have avoided the inevitable pitfalls of racist thinking. This, however, has not prevented those who exploit racist ideology from using anthropological classifications.

Gobineau claimed undesirable traits for Africans, more desirable for Asiatics, and most desirable, of course, for Europeans. Needless to say, neither psychologists nor anthropologists find any validity to the correlation of personality and race. As Professor Alexander Alland, Columbia University anthropologist, points out (1971, p. 35):

> For those who have done fieldwork in Africa, there can be little doubt that behavioral and cognitive patterns in the black community in the United States bear little resemblance to those in Africa, and that, in fact, such patterns are highly variable in Africa and dependent more upon cultural differences than shared gene pools.

Race and Intelligence

Belief in the relationship between race and personality is popular even today, but there is no evidence that personality or any cultural trait, or any aspect of culture, such as religion or language, is in any way racial. Very likely, most scholars today would agree with this last statement, but there is an area of disagreement still being debated with a vehemence and emotion usually uncharacteristic of the academic community. That area is the question of whether race and intelligence are associated. The overwhelming majority of academic opinion (in anthropology, biology, genetics, psychology, and sociology) cannot find valid evidence that relates the two phenomena. There are, however, scientists who *do* believe in the relationship, and perhaps the best-known advocate of the proposition that race (i.e., heritability) is the *causal* factor in intelligence is Professor Arthur R. Jensen. He estimates the heritability of intelligence at about 75% (Jensen, 1980, p. 244).

Jensen, professor of educational psychology at the University of California, Berkeley, believes that intelligence is a correlate of race, that intelligence is inherited, that IQ tests measure intelligence, that racial intelligence differences can be researched from a heritability point of view, that the uncertainty of the heredity-environment problem can be reduced, and that the lower average IQ scores of blacks (about 15 points) are a function of race (Jensen, 1969a).

Jensen's views have been criticized by scientists from various disciplines. In his review and analysis of the literature on testing intelligence, Eckberg (1979, p. 55) is led to seriously question the degree to which the idea of a general intelligence can have usefulness in real-world pursuits. Instead, all the various lines of evidence indicate that behavior is too multiform to be encapsulated under the label of *intelligence*, unless what we intend by intelligence is something quite a bit different from that which is usually intended.

Much of the criticism of Jensen's (and other similar) views may be grouped under two headings: (1) inadequacy of the IQ test as a measure of intelligence; and (2) the failure to consider the influence of environment (in a broad sense) on ability and performance.

The IQ Test: Unitary Character of Intelligence

IQ tests, such as the Stanford-Binet, purport to give a single *general* rating of mental ability, known as "g," but many scientists have questioned whether intelligence is, in fact, a single variable. Geneticists refer to intelligence as polygenic, that is, a number of genes are involved in producing a phenotype (see p. 61). As Bodmer, a geneticist, says, "intelligence must be a complex characteristic under the control of many genes" (Bodmer, 1972, p. 91). William Howells, an anthropologist, echoes this view:

> First of all, intelligence is hardly a unitary character, even if forced into a single scale by IQ tests. Much work in human and animal psychology indicates that intelligence consists of differing faculties combined or substituted for one another in different ways for which the test situation may not provide an adequate measure (Howells, 1971, p. 7).

If intelligence is a complex, not unitary, characteristic and consists of a combination of differing faculties, as Bodmer and Howells suggest, then it is questionable whether intelligence consists of a single large general factor, as Jensen claims. And it is, therefore, questionable whether an intelligence test can be constructed to test the differing mental faculties.

Environment and Intelligence

Those who believe that intelligence is largely genetic and can be measured by IQ tests have probably been criticized most sharply because they have failed to consider the significance of environment in the development of intelligence. The controversy over which factor is more important, nature *or* nurture, no longer applies. Both nature *and* nurture contribute, and it is probably impossible, at this point, to separate out the percentage of each contribution.

There have been attempts to sort out environmental and genetic factors, one of the best known being the study of *monozygotic* (MZ) *twins*. MZ twins share identical genotypes, and a comparison of those who have been reared together and reared apart (that is, in different environments) should prove instructive. While such studies have been done, their reliability and applicability from one population to another (often living in very different environments) are very hotly disputed. For example, Kamin (1974) analyzed studies of separated monozygotic twin pairs. In these studies, especially those performed by Sir Cyril Burt (see Issue, p. 104)—used by Jensen to support his heritability arguments— Kamin found methodological problems serious enough to throw doubt on the validity of their conclusions. After examining Kamin's analysis of Burt's figures, Jensen conceded that Burt's studies of twins were not usable for hypothesis testing (Jensen, 1974).

That average performance on IQ exams varies among groups of schoolage children is not disputed. What causes all the furor is how to *explain* these differences. If results of twin studies, etc., do not conclusively support the Jensen, et al. argument for heredity as the clearly most dominant factor, what does that leave us with? Obviously, some form of explanation that views environmental influence as significant must be considered. The following three studies reflect the view that environment must be considered as a crucial factor in IQ test results.

In 1981, Scarr reported a study, conducted by Scarr and Barker, of the cognitive differences among black and white children in Philadelphia (Scarr, 1981). These researchers found that black children performed relatively better on less culturally loaded material once the instructions were made more comprehensible to them, and also that the black environment failed to develop the skills sampled by the tests. They also noted that twins' scores were more highly correlated in the black group because family membership was more important in determining the degree to which children were exposed to the intellectual skills sampled in the tests. Their conclusion:

> The results of this study support the view that black children are being reared in circumstances that give them only marginal acquaintance with the skills and the knowledge being sampled by the tests we administered. Some families in the black community encourage the development of these skills and knowledge, whereas others do not. In general, black children do not have the same access to these skills and knowledge as white children, which explains the lower performance of black children as a group. *The hypothesis that most of the differences among the cognitive scores of black and white children are due to genetic differences between the races cannot, in our view, account for this pattern of results* (Scarr, 1981, p. 288). (Emphasis added.)

In an earlier study of genetic and environmental influences on IQ test scores, Scarr and Weinberg (1976) examined 130 black and interracial children who were adopted by advantaged white families. The authors found that the average IQ scores of these children was 106 (scores of early-adopted children were even higher). This was about 12 points higher than the score of black children with two black parents living in the same area, and compared favorably with white children's scores. The authors concluded that:

The major findings of the study support the view that the social environment plays a dominant role in determining the average IQ level of black children and that both social and genetic variables contribute to individual variation among them (Scarr and Weinberg, 1976, p. 133).

Willerman, et al. (1970) conducted a somewhat similar test with 4-year-old black children of mixed parents—white mother and black father and black mother and white father. The results of this study indicate a difference in IQ scores if the mother is white, or if she is black. The mean score for black children with a white mother was 100.9; with a black mother, 93.7. Marital status of the mother also made a difference. The mean score of children of a white married mother was 102.3; of an unmarried mother, 98.5. Children of a black married mother, 97.6; unmarried mother, 82.6.

It seems quite clear from these studies that environment must be seriously considered as a significant influence on IQ scores. A number of environmental factors have been noted by researchers.

Scarr, in her 1981 report, suggests that many black families fail to provide the skills and knowledge sampled by the tests. Where these skills are provided in the home (black children adopted by advantaged white parents and black children of white mothers), black children scored significantly higher than black children of black parents. *

Poor nutrition may be another factor that makes for lower IQ scores. Passamanick and his associates found that a deficient maternal diet associated with low income can produce pregnancy and parturition complications followed by intellectual retardation and behavioral disorders in the children (cited in Rose, 1972, p. 139). Rose also refers to a study in which nutritional supplements were added to the deficient diets of pregnant women. This resulted in significantly raised IQs in their children at the ages of 2, 3, and 4 compared with children whose mothers did not receive the supplements.

Still other factors are the attitude toward education in some socioeconomic groups, attitude toward tests, social and economic goals, and a general **weltanschauung** (world view). All of these may combine to reduce the IQ scores of blacks; it is, therefore, difficult to reconcile the glib assertions of those who promote the genetic basis of intelligence with the environmental conditions we have just reviewed.

The core of the dispute between Jensen and the majority of scientists is whether differences in black and white IQ scores are due mainly to heredity or to environment. Most scholars are agreed that it is difficult, if not impossible, to separate the two, because (as we have just discussed), the evidence is not so clearly objective that it can be easily interpreted. IQ tests, especially, are difficult to interpret because, as many investigators have emphasized, it is not possible to construct a culture-free IQ test; that is, an IQ test that eliminates completely environmental factors.

Professor Liam Hudson, professor of educational sciences at Edinburgh University, concludes a discussion of the IQ test with the observation that:

> At the moment, and probably in principle, it is impossible to design an experiment that separates out in any neat and tidy way, the influence of hereditary and environmental factors on a human being's ability to do IQ tests (Hudson, 1972, p. 15).

*It is important to point out that Scarr did *not* attribute lower scores of disadvantaged blacks to inferior intelligence.

A similar comment is made by Professor Paul Baker, a physical anthropologist from Penn State, who has for years researched the adaptability of phenotypic traits to environmental conditions:

> Finally, I must note that popular questions such as whether race differences in intelligence exist, and if so, are they cultural or genetic in origin, are not meaningful questions at the present state of adaptational theory or evidence. At this time, we cannot even state with certainty the degree of genetic versus environmental patterning involved in the presumably adaptive variation in hand temperature: therefore, to debate seriously the genetic versus environmental patterning involved in man's total adaptive behavioral capacity (a common definition of intelligence) is inappropriate at this time as a scientific endeavor (Baker, 1966, p. 37).

Anthropologists Brace and Livingstone (1971, p. 67) suggest that *all* measured differences among major groups of humans may be explained primarily by environmental factors.

With the bulk of scientific opinion opposed to heritability as the explanation for racial intelligence, troublesome questions arise regarding the validity of IQ tests as well as the reliability of the monozygotic twin studies. We agree with Professor William Howells (1971, p. 8): "In all honesty, therefore, scientists must decline to see the existence of racial variation in mental ability at this stage."

Racism

As a subject of inquiry, racism is not usually pursued by physical anthropologists. It may be surprising, therefore, that a discussion of racism is included in a physical anthropology textbook. Although racism, from a holistic and biosocial point of view, is a cultural phenomenon (based on attitudes, values, philosophies, economics, etc.), we believe it is not possible to divorce biological from cultural aspects in the study of humans.

Racism is the belief that one race is superior to another, and is associated with discriminatory acts and attitudes toward the "inferior" race(s). Belief in racism is usually based on the alleged inferior mental abilities of a people, and is often extended to the moral and ethical character of the "inferior" race. It is also assumed that mental abilities, ethics, and morals are hereditary.

The belief that a people is genetically inferior may be due to a number of factors, such as conquest, religion, family practices, moral and ethical systems, economic practices, and technology. Economic exploitation by imperialistic powers and competition for jobs, for example, have been suggested as reasons (or justification) for racist attitudes. European and American whites have frequently been singled out as practitioners of racism. However, there is evidence of racism in Japanese behavior toward the Eta (a lower social class in Japan) and the Ainu; in the historic attitude of the Chinese toward Mongols; and among the Bantu of South Africa toward the San (Bushmen).

From a physical anthropological point of view, racism is a cultural phenomenon that has no genetic basis. That one race is mentally or morally superior or inferior to another has yet to be demonstrated. Realistically, it is more likely that the basis of racism is rooted in economic, political, social, and psychological factors. Because it is cultural rather than genetic in character, it is difficult for physical anthropologists to address the problem. No matter what we say about the lack of evidence for mental inferiority and raise doubts about the validity of IQ scores, racism continues in many areas of the world. People point to the "strange," "immoral," and "odious" behavior of other people, and assign this to genetic factors of the "inferior" race.

We end our discussion of race and racism with a comment from the geneticist Dobzhansky:

> The contention of racists is that cultural achievements of different races are so obviously unlike, their genetic capacities for achievement are just as different. It is, however, a matter of elementary genetics that the capacities of individuals, populations, or races cannot be discovered until they are given an equality of opportunity to demonstrate these capacities . . . (Dobzhansky, 1961, p. 31).

Summary

This chapter is essentially divided in two parts: (1) racial classification; and (2) race and behavior.

In the past 300 years, the trend in the study of race has moved from developing typologies based on climate and geography to the use of anthropometry to the application of evolutionary and genetic principles. At the present time, many anthropologists and other scientists believe the concept of race as a research tool is futile.

Race and behavior are discussed from the point of view of IQ tests and intelligence. Jensen and others, in recent years, have emphasized the notion that race and intelligence are correlated and support their position with IQ test results. The value of IQ tests as a measure of intelligence, without considering environmental factors, is questioned. The preponderant scientific view is that the IQ test is inadequate as a measuring instrument for intelligence, and the environment is so considerable a factor, that heredity cannot be accepted as the primary reason for racial variation in intelligence.

This controversy again serves to emphasize the dual nature of humans. Human heredity/evolution is meaningless without consideration of the relevant environmental factors, and human environments have for a long time been *cultural* ones.

Racism is discussed as a cultural phenomenon, allegedly rooted in genetics, a concept for which there is no scientific evidence.

Questions for Review

1. What various criteria have been used for racial classification?
2. Why is racial typology no longer considered a useful concept in the study of human diversity?
3. Why are anthropologists dissatisfied with the concept of race?
4. Trace the definition of race from Virchow to Garn. What are the objections to the criteria used in the definitions?
5. What is a cline? What is the utility of a clinal distribution?
6. What is the value of multivariate population genetics?
7. What are the problems in correlating personality with race?

8. What are the objections to the use of IQ tests as measures of intelligence?
9. How may the environment affect IQ scores?
10. Discuss intelligence in terms of "nature or nurture."

Evolutionary Record

CONTENTS

A Cosmic Calendar

How can we possibly conceive of the awesome stretch of time that has been flowing since, scientists inform us, our universe was first formed by the cosmic explosion called the Big Bang 15 billion years ago? In *Dragons of Eden*, Carl Sagan (1977) has condensed this pro-digious period into one year he calls "The Cosmic Calendar." There are three parts to the calendar.

1. A pre-December calendar. A list of a few of the significant events in the history of the universe and earth in the first 14 billion years, represented by the 334 days from January 1 through November 30

2. A month of December calendar. Events of the last 1.25 billion years represented by the month of December

3. An evening of December 31 calendar. From 10:30 P.M. (the first humans) until midnight (now), which represents the last 2.5 million years

Examine the calendar and the place of *Homo sapiens* in a time perspective. Modern humans appeared a bit more than a minute before 12:00 midnight. You may feel humble before the immensity of time of our universe, or you may feel proud of the human achievements accomplished in such a brief speck of time.

Pre-December Dates

Big Bang	January 1
Origin of the Milky Way Galaxy	May 1
Origin of the solar system	September 9
Formation of the Earth	September 14
Origin of life on Earth	≈September 25
Formation of the oldest rocks known on Earth	October 2
Date of oldest fossils (bacteria and blue-green algae)	October 9
Invention of sex (by microorganisms)	≈November 1
Oldest fossil photosynthetic plants	November 12
Eukaryotes (first cells with nuclei) flourish	November 15

December 31

Origin of *Proconsul* and *Ramapithecus*, probable ancestors of apes and men[?]	≈ 1:30 P.M.
First humans	≈10:30 P.M.
Widespread use of stone tools	11:00 P.M.
Domestication of fire by Peking Man*	11:46 P.M.
Beginning of most recent glacial period	11:56 P.M.
Seafarers settle Australia	11:58 P.M.
Extensive cave painting in Europe	11:59 P.M.
Invention of agriculture	11:59:20 P.M.
Neolithic civilization; first cities	11:59:35 P.M.
First dynasties in Sumer, Ebla and Egypt; development of astronomy	11:59:50 P.M.

*See page 417 for comment on Peking Man's association with fire.

Invention of the alphabet; Akkadian Empire	11:59:51 P.M.
Hammurabic legal codes in Babylon; Middle Kingdom in Egypt	11:59:52 P.M.
Bronze metallurgy; Mycenaean culture; Trojan War; Olmec culture; invention of the compass	11:59:53 P.M.
Iron metallurgy; first Assyrian Empire; Kingdom of Israel; founding of Carthage by Phoenicia	11:59:54 P.M.
Asokan India; Ch'in Dynasty China; Periclean Athens; birth of Buddha	11:59:55 P.M.
Euclidean geometry; Archimedean physics; Ptolemaic astronomy; Roman Empire; birth of Christ	11:59:56 P.M.
Zero and decimals invented in Indian arithmetic; Rome falls; Moslem conquests	11:59:57 P.M.
Mayan civilization; Sung Dynasty China; Byzantine Empire; Mongol invasion; Crusades	11:59:58 P.M.
Renaissance in Europe; voyages of discovery from Europe and from Ming Dynasty China; emergence of the experimental method in science	11:59:59 P.M.
Widespread development of science and technology; emergence of a global culture; acquisition of the means for self-destruction of the human species; first steps in spacecraft planetary exploration and the search for extraterrestrial intelligence	Now: The first second of New Year's Day

1 year	=	15,000,000,000 years				
1 month	=	1,250,000,000 years				
1 day	=	41,000,000 years				
1 minute	=	29,000 years				
1 second	=	475 years				
1 billion years	=	24 days				

DECEMBER   COSMIC CALENDAR

SUNDAY	MONDAY	TUESDAY	WEDNESDAY	THURSDAY	FRIDAY	SATURDAY
	1 Significant oxygen atmosphere begins to develop on Earth.	2	3	4	5 Extensive vulcanism and channel formation on Mars.	6
7	8	9	10	11	12	13
14	15	16	17 Precambrian ends. Paleozoic Era and Cambrian Period begin. Invertebrates flourish.	18 First Oceanic plankton. Trilobites flourish.	19 Ordovician Period. First fish; first vertebrates	20 Silurian Period. First vascular plants. Plants begin colonization of land.
21 Devonian Period begins. First insects. Animals begin colonization of land.	22 First amphibians. First winged insects.	23 Carboniferous Period. First trees. First reptiles	24 Permian Period begins. First dinosaurs.	25 Paleozoic Era ends. Mesozoic Era begins.	26 Triassic Period. First mammals.	27 Jurassic Period. First birds.
28 Cretaceous Period. First flowers. Dinosaurs become extinct.	29 Mesozoic Era ends. Cenozoic Era and Tertiary Period begins. First cetaceans. First primates.	30 Early evolution of frontal lobes in the brains of primates. First hominids. Giant mammals flourish.	31 End of the Pliocene epoch. Quaternary (Pleistocene and Holocene Period. First humans.			

SOURCE:

Sagan, Carl, *Dragons of Eden*, New York: Random House, Inc., 1977.

Calendar reprinted by permission of the author and the author's agents, Scott Meredith Literary Agency, Inc., 845 Third Avenue, New York, New York 10022.

Introduction

In preceding chapters, we have discussed the mechanics of the evolutionary processes—adaptation and change through natural selection—according to concepts developed by Charles Darwin. We have also discussed the mechanisms of genetics that explain evolutionary changes between generations.

Having already dealt with the *process* of evolution, we shall now consider the *result* of that process. What actually occurred in the evolutionary record of life on earth? What were the adaptations made by living forms, and what physical changes took place in the various organisms that inhabit our globe? What evolutionary changes led to hominids, what other groups do hominids belong to, and what are the origins of these groups? We shall briefly trace invertebrate and vertebrate evolutionary history which, we believe, will help answer these questions, provide a deeper insight into evolutionary processes, and place humankind in a zoological and chronological perspective. (See Box 6-2, p. 138, Box 6-3, p. 139, and Box 6-5, p. 149, for additional views of the evolutionary processes.)

Since this book is about *Homo sapiens*, we can present only in outline the infinite number of events that occurred over the vast period of 3 billion years (and probably more) (Gurin, 1980), the time of life on earth. Let us then begin with the place of humans in evolutionary history.

The Human Place in the Animal Kingdom

The first chapter emphasized that we are both animals and human beings. We intend, throughout the text, to discuss the relationship between both these aspects of humankind, but since we wish to trace our antecedents, we will concern ourselves first with *Homo sapiens*, the organic being.

Humans are zoologically classified as animals because they possess animal characteristics, such as:

1. Obtaining food from other organisms, not through photosynthesis
2. Mobility; most animals are mobile and can move about in one way or another at some stage of life
3. Structure and organization; tissue and organ differentiation in animals is usually more complex than in plants. Individual plant cells usually have rigid walls; animal cells usually do not
4. Nerves and muscles; most animals have nerves and muscles, which are absent in plants

This list, although incomplete, places humans in the Animal Kingdom. As multicelled animals within the Animal Kingdom, we belong to the Metazoa, a subdivision classified into more than twenty major groups called *phyla* (sing., *phylum*).

Figure 6-1
Homologies. The similarities in the bones of these air-breathing animals can be most easily explained by descent from a common ancestor.

FROG
(amphibian)

LIZARD
(reptile)

BIRD

HUMAN

Taxonomy

Before going further it may be useful to discuss the basis of animal classification.

Organisms are classified on the basis of evolutionary relationships; that is, the degree one group is related to another through descent from a common ancestor. The extent of the relationship is determined mainly by structural similarities based on common descent, called *homologies*. Thus, the bones of the forelimb of air-breathing vertebrates are so similar (Fig. 6-1) in arrangement and number that the simplest and best explanation for the remarkable resemblances—homologies—is that all four kinds of air-breathing vertebrates ultimately derived their forelimb from a common ancestor.

Structures that are *functionally* similar, but without genetic affinity—not derived from a common ancestor—are *analogous*. The wing of a butterfly and the wing of a bird are analogous; they perform a similar function but are without genetic affinity (Fig. 6-2).

Hominids (the group to which humans belong), prosimians, monkeys, and apes are all classified as primates. Why? When the nervous system, (especially the brain), teeth, limbs, digits, and other physical traits of these animals are examined, it becomes clear they share an ancestor in common. Their homologies bring these animals into one group just as the homologies of lions, tigers, leopards, and the domestic cat bring these together into one group that evolved from a common ancestor.

The system of classification based on homologies is usually attributed to Linnaeus, although there were classificatory schemes before his. Linnaeus, it will be recalled, successfully instituted the binomial system of naming animals using two terms, genus and species. Thus, we are known as *Homo sapiens*, the domestic cat as *Felis domesticus*, the lion as *Panthera leo*, and the gorilla as *Gorilla gorilla*.

All people in the world today belong to one species, *Homo sapiens*, a form that has existed for at least the past 100,000 years.

Figure 6-3 is a classification chart arranged according to evolutionary relationships. Observe in both Fig. 6-3 and the adjoining chart, Fig. 6-3a, that the

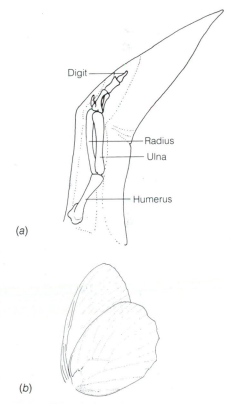

(a)

(b)

Figure 6-2
Analogies. The wings of these animals perform the same function, but their structure is quite different. Similar structure may be traced to a common ancestor; similar function represents a similar adaptive response, not necessarily a common ancestor.
(a) Structure of bird wing; (b) butterfly wing.

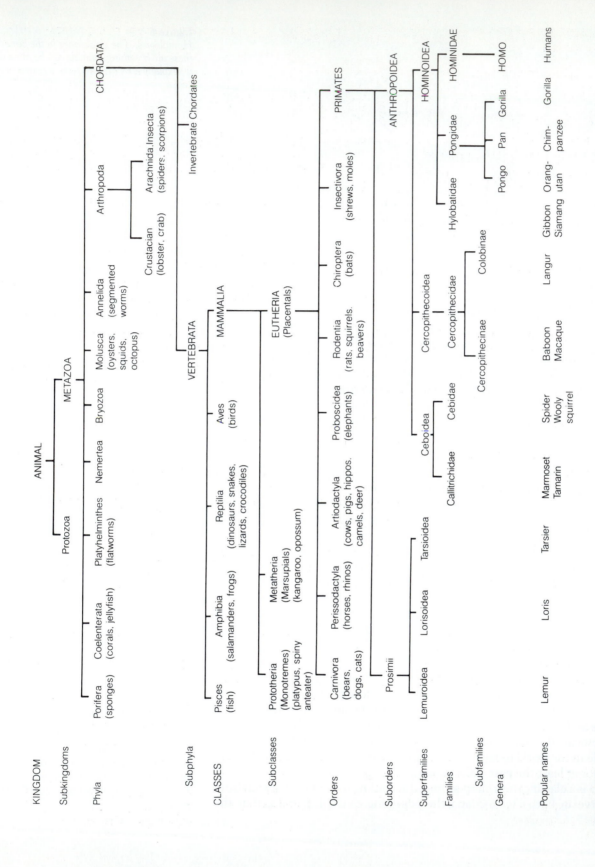

Figure 6-3
Classification chart. Modified from Linnaeus. All animals are placed in certain categories based on structural similarities. Those categories connected by a horizontal line share a common ancestor (Pongo, Pan, and Gorilla, for example).

BOX 6-1

Vocabulary

ANALOGOUS (ah-nal'-o-gus) Similar in function or appearance but not in origin or development.

HOMOLOGOUS (hom-ol'-o-gus) Structures that are similar in form (or function) in two or more groups of organisms related through descent from a common ancestor.

PHYLUM (fy'-lum; pl. phyla) A primary division of the Animal (or Plant) Kingdom. We belong to Phylum Chordata.

SUBPHYLUM A major division of a phylum, such as Vertebrata.

CLASS A subdivision of subphylum.

SUPERFAMILY A group of closely related families.

FAMILY Members of a family usually inhabit a similar environment; a category which includes genera and species.

GENUS (jee'-nus; pl. genera) A category that groups together closely related species usually inhabiting similar ecological niches.

SPECIES (spee'shies; sing. and pl.) A reproductive community; an interbreeding population (or populations) reproductively isolated from other interbreeding populations.

DORSAL (dor'-sull) Back, pertaining to the back of an animal.

VENTRAL (ven'-trull) Toward the belly; the front of an organism (as in humans) or the undersurface of an animal that does not stand erect (as a dog).

ENDOSKELETON (en'-doe-skeleton) An internal bony skeleton, characteristic of vertebrates.

EXOSKELETON (ex'-o-skeleton) A hard, supporting external covering, characteristic of many invertebrates such as ants and lobsters.

TAXONOMY The theoretical study of classification, including its bases, principles, procedures, and rules (Simpson, 1961, p. 11).

---

closer the animals resemble one another (the more homologies they share), the smaller the group to which they are assigned. The two species (in Fig. 6-3a), *H. sapiens* and *H. erectus*, belong to the genus *Homo* because they resemble each other more than either of them resembles the other three hominid species, *A. afarensis*, *A. africanus*, and *A. robustus*, which are assigned to the genus *Australopithecus*. *Homo* and *Australopithecus* resemble each other more than either one resembles apes and are, therefore, placed in the family Hominidae, and apes in Pongidae. Apes and humans resemble each other more than either resembles monkeys and are, therefore, placed in the superfamily Hominoidea, and so forth.

In summary, the more homologies two groups share, usually the more recent their descent from a common ancestor, the closer their evolutionary relationship, and the closer their position on the taxonomic chart.

To place hominids in their proper perspective in nature and to help understand human evolution, we shall glance very briefly at the evolutionary history of the Metazoa.

Metazoa

Metazoa are composed of a number of phyla, most of which are invertebrates, animals lacking a bony backbone. Invertebrates range in organization from relatively simple structures, such as sponges, to relatively complex structures, such as chordates. Chordates are important to humans because our subphylum, Vertebrata, belongs to this category.

METAZOA
meta: beyond
zoion: animal
Multicellular animals. A major division of the Animal Kingdom.

Kingdom
  Phylum
    Class
      Order
        Family
          Genus
            Species

The Linnaean hierarchy of zoological classification. Indentation indicates decreasing inclusiveness of the various levels (Simpson, 1961).

Figure 6-3a
Classification of Hominoidea.

Vertebrates, the most numerous of the chordates, are different in certain ways from all other Metazoa. Their primary structural feature, a vertebral column, distinguishes them from invertebrates and has given them their name. Since we belong to this group, we shall discuss vertebrates later in the chapter.

With this short discussion of the human place in nature concluded, we shall return our attention to the time dimension of evolution.

Early Evolutionary History

We reviewed earlier in the chapter the place of humans in nature. We now turn to their place in the time dimension of evolution. To do this, we shall briefly review the chronology of life on earth with special reference to vertebrates. Our review will follow the outline in the Geologic Time Scale (Figs. 6-4 and 6-13). The

Figure 6-4
The Periods of the Time Scale reflect systems of rock strata (layers) and the fossil remains that were prevalent in those systems as shown under "Events." Boundaries between systems reflect those points where rocks and fossil assemblages were in great contrast to those in the strata above and below.

ERA	PERIOD SYSTEMS	Time m.y.a.*	EVENTS
MESOZOIC (Middle Life)	Cretaceous (chalk)	65 / 136	Appearance of placental and marsupial mammals. Dinosaurs peak and become extinct. First modern birds.
	Jurassic (Jura Mts., France)	190	Great age of dinosaurs — flying and swimming dinosaurs. First toothed birds.
	Triassic (from tripartite division of strata of Germany)	225	Reptiles dominant. First dinosaurs. Egg-laying mammals.
PALEOZOIC (Ancient Life)	Permian	280	Reptilian radiation. Mammal-like reptiles. Many forms die out.
	Carboniferous (abundance of coal)	345	First reptiles. Radiation of amphibia. Modern insects evolve.
	Devonian (Devonshire in England)	395	Age of fish. Amphibians — first air-breathing vertebrates. First forests.
	Silurian (the Silures, an ancient British tribe)	430	Jawed fishes appear. First air-breathing animal — scorpion-like aurypterid. Definite land plants.
	Ordovician (the Ordovices, an ancient British tribe)	500	First fishes. Trilobites still abundant. Graptolites and corals becoming plentiful. Possible land plants.
	Cambrian (Roman name for Wales)	570	Trilobites abundant, also brachiopods, jellyfish, worms, and other invertebrates.
PRECAMBRIAN			

*Million years ago.

student is encouraged to refer frequently to the Time Scale as we follow the evolutionary sequence of life on earth.

The earliest evidence of life comes from Greenland sedimentary rock, perhaps 3.8 billion years old (Gurin, 1980). The earliest known structurally preserved organisms are stromatolites found near the old mining town of North Pole, Australia. Also found in the North Pole area are "fossils—a diverse collection of long, filamentous chains of cells—[that] resemble some modern bacteria, including species that are capable of performing photosynthesis" (Gurin, 1980, p. 45). This material from North Pole has been reliably dated at 3.5 billion years. This fossil material belongs to the immense segment of geologic time called the Precambrian, which goes back to the beginning of life and ends about 600 m.y.a., with the beginning of the Paleozoic era.

Abundant fossil evidence for the Precambrian is lacking, and what does exist points to different kinds of algae as the dominant life form. Toward the end of the Precambrian, there is evidence of plants, most of which are of unknown affinity, and burrows and trails of wormlike animals. It is not until the Cambrian (the first period of the Paleozoic) is reached that the rocks contain enough fossils to give a fuller view of the life forms in existence at that time.

Paleozoic Era (570–225 m.y.a.)

Beginning with the Paleozoic era, fossils become more abundant and a much fuller account of life is available. During the 345 million years of the Paleozoic, evidence for members of every phylum of animals is present. Evolution continues primarily in water, but land plants appear toward the middle, and land animals toward the end, of the era. Invertebrate fossil evidence appears in the very first period and becomes a dominant form. Vertebrates evolve fairly early to become very successful aquatic animals and, toward the end of the Paleozoic, invade land habitats as well in the form of amphibians and reptiles.

The southern continents—South America, Africa, Antarctica, Australia, and India—were all closely associated into one mass known as *Gondwanaland*. The northern continents—North America, Greenland, Europe, and Asia— were known as *Laurasia*. As the Paleozoic continued, these two great land masses united during the Carboniferous and Permian periods to form an enormous land mass known as *Pangea*. (See Fig. 6-8.)

Fish

Seventy million years after the beginning of the Paleozoic, during the Ordovician, jawless fishes—**Ostracoderms**—appeared (Romer, 1959). By the Devonian (395–345 m.y.a.) fish had multiplied so rapidly in numbers and species that they became the dominant marine animal; thus, we give the name *Age of Fish* to this period.

Not as numerous or successful as the main branch of bony fish (ray-fins) were the lobe-fins, which had diverged from the others by the middle Devonian and went (or swam) their own way. Of importance to vertebrate evolution is the structure of their fins, which have a fleshy lobe containing bones remarkably similar to those of land vertebrates. They also possess internal nostrils (absent in ray-fins) probably useful for breathing air.

OSTRACODERM
ostraco: hard shell
derm: skin
Shell-skin or armored.

Figure 6-5
(a) *Lobe-fin. The fin is fleshy and contains a bone structure similar to vertebrates.*
(b) *Ray-fin. The fin is composed of a web of skin supported by hornlike rays.*

Figure 6-6
Crossopterygian. The fish that made the transition to amphibians. Long thought to be extinct. A modern survivor is the coelacanth.

Figure 6-7
Early amphibian and lobe-finned fish. These drawings of an early amphibian and a lobe-fin illustrate the similarities of the two forms. Not a great deal of change was required to transform the fish to the air-breathing amphibian.

With fins containing a bony structure, nostrils, and lungs for air breathing, the lobe-finned **crossopterygians** were able to adapt to the drought conditions of the Devonian. As pools of water dried up, these fish could move across land—on their fleshy, bony fins—and, breathing air, seek a pool of water that had not yet become parched (Romer, 1959, p. 94). From this group of fish thus arose the amphibians.

Amphibians

The explosive radiation of fish in the Devonian coupled with drought conditions of that period led crossopterygians toward an amphibian body plan allowing them, as it were, to have their cake and eat it. On the one hand, they are able to spend much of their time in water; in fact, the early stages of growth have to be aquatic. On the other hand, they are able to adapt, to a certain extent, to life on land. They are, so to speak, neither fish nor land animals, but a "compromise" of both.

In terms of numbers of individuals and species, the amphibians cannot be considered as successful as other vertebrate classes. Typical amphibians are still chained to water, to which they must periodically return. As paleontologist Romer (1959, p. 101) has said: "It is, in many respects, little more than a peculiar type of fish which is capable of walking on land."

As vertebrate evolution continued, amphibians diverged into many different forms. From one of these amphibian forms another milestone in vertebrate evolution was reached with the rise of reptiles, the first true land vertebrates. These are known as *stem reptiles*, ancestors of the huge ruling reptiles of the Mesozoic and of the line leading to mammals.

Figure 6-8
Pangea. Continents at the end of the Paleozoic (a) and during much of the Mesozoic (b).

LAURASIA

GONDWANA

(a)

ASIA

NORTH AMERICA

EUROPE

Tethys Sea

AFRICA

SOUTH AMERICA

INDIA

AUSTRALIA

ANTARCTICA

(b)

Reptiles

The reptilian strategy of adaptation was more successful than the amphibian. Developing a more efficient limb structure, an improved heart, and (perhaps most important) a self-contained, self-protected, and self-feeding egg—the *amniote* egg (Fig. 6-9)—reptiles filled many of the terrestrial econiches.

One of the results of reptilian radiation was a reptilelike mammalian form (or a mammal-like reptilian form) called *therapsids*. With a bony palate separating the oral and nasal cavities, teeth differentiated into **incisors**, **canines**, and **cheek teeth** (the latter cusped instead of cone-shaped) and limbs arranged in a fore-and-aft position under the body (see Fig. 6-10), therapsids were "on their way" to becoming mammals and are, in fact, considered to be the ancestors of mammals.

Therapsids appeared toward the end of the Paleozoic, and in the next era, the Mesozoic, reptiles and mammals continued to evolve.

Mesozoic Era (225–65 m.y.a.)

Climatic conditions of the Mesozoic were not as extreme as they had been during the late Paleozoic. The great glaciers of the Permian Ice Age had disappeared, erosion had reduced many mountain ranges, and mountain-building produced others. The continents, which had been joined at the end of the Permian, began to drift apart and when the Mesozoic ended, the continents had approached their present locations.

In the early Mesozoic, reptiles became the dominant land animal and reigned supreme for the remainder of the era, known as the *Age of Reptiles*. Reptilian radiation (see Box 6-2) proceeded at a tremendous rate and the most well-known of all reptiles—the dinosaurs—appeared in the Triassic. Not only did dinosaurs cover much of the earth, they also took to the air and water.

Dinosaurs reached their peak in the Cretaceous, but the days of these dominant beasts were numbered, and when the Cretaceous (and Mesozoic) came to a close, the enormous creatures that ruled the earth for about 150 million years ended their reign. Changing geographic and climatic conditions, competition from the newly evolving mammals, possible extraterrestrial events, plus perhaps

CROSSOPTERYGIANS
krosso: fringe
pteryg: fin

INCISORS
Front teeth used for cutting and nipping.

CANINES
Usually long and pointed teeth used for piercing and grasping.

CHEEK TEETH
Premolars and molars used for chewing and grinding.

Amniote Egg

Figure 6-9
Amniote egg. Generalized diagram of the amniote egg. The embryo is surrounded by the liquid-filled amniotic chamber. The yolk sac contains food, and within the allantois enclosure (which also serves as a waste receptacle), oxygen-carbon dioxide exchange takes place.

Figure 6-10
Therapsid. Mammal-like reptiles or reptilelike mammals. Mammalian characteristics include heterodont teeth, at least some chewing instead of swallowing whole, probably a coat of hair, and perhaps incipient milk glands. The limbs are more mammalian than reptilian. (Artist's rendition.)

Evolutionary Processes

Adaptive Radiation The potential capacity of an organism to multiply is practically unlimited; its ability to increase its numbers, however, is regulated largely by the available resources of food, shelter, and space. As the size of a population increases, its food, shelter, and space decrease, and the environment will ultimately prove inadequate. Depleted resources engender pressures that will very likely drive some members of the population to seek an environment where competition is considerably reduced and the opportunity for survival and reproductive success increased. This evolutionary tendency to exploit unoccupied habitats may eventually produce an abundance of diverse species.

An instructive example of the evolutionary process known as *adaptive radiation* may be seen in the divergence of the stem reptiles to the profusion of different forms of the late Paleozoic, and especially the Mesozoic. It is a process that has taken place many times in evolutionary history when a new form of life rapidly takes advantage, so to speak, of the many now available ecological niches.

The principle of evolution illustrated by adaptive radiation is fairly simple, but important. It may be stated thus: *When a new form arises, it will diverge into as many variations as two factors allow—(1) its adaptive potential and (2) the adaptive opportunities of the available zones.*

In the case of reptiles, there was little divergence in the very early stages of evolution, when the ancestral type was little more than one among a variety of amphibian water-dwellers. A more efficient kind of egg had already developed and, although it had great adaptive potential, there were few zones to invade. However, once reptiles became fully terrestrial, there was a sudden opening of available zones—ecological niches—accessible to the adaptive potential of the reptilian evolutionary grade.

This new kind of egg provided the primary adaptive ingredient of the reptilian form that freed reptiles from attachment to water; strengthened limbs and skeleton for locomotion on land followed. The adaptive zones for reptiles were not limitless; nevertheless, continents were now open to them with no serious competition from any other animal. The reptiles moved into the many different econiches on land (and to some extent in the air and sea), and as they adapted to these areas, diversified into a large number of species. This spectacular radiation burst with such evolutionary rapidity, it may well be termed an adaptive explosion.

Generalized and Specialized Another aspect of evolution closely related to that of adaptive radiation involves the transition from *generalized* to *specialized characteristics*. These two terms refer to the adaptive potential of a particular trait: one that is adapted for many functions is termed generalized whereas a trait that is limited to a narrow set of ecological functions is called specialized.

For example, a generalized mammalian limb has five fairly flexible digits adapted for many possible functions (grasping, weight support, digging). In this respect, our hands are still quite generalized. On the other hand (or foot), there have been many structural modifications in our feet suited for the ecologically specialized function of stable weight support.

These terms are also sometimes used when speaking of the adaptive potential of whole organisms. For example, the aye-aye (a curious primate living in Madagascar) is a highly specialized animal structurally adapted in its dentition for an ecologically narrow rodent/woodpecker-like niche—digging out insect larvae with prominent incisors.

The notion of adaptive potential is a relative judgment and can estimate only crudely the likelihood of one form evolving into another form or forms. Adaptive radiation is a related concept, for only a generalized ancestor can provide the flexible evolutionary basis for such rapid diversification. Only a generalized organism with potential for adaptation into varied ecological niches can lead to all the later diversification and specialization of forms into particular ecological niches.

Superior/Inferior, Primitive/Derived

Arthropods (see p. 132) illustrate an important point in understanding the process of evolution. It is not possible to rank organisms as better or worse. Or, if we do, our criteria must be stated. One criterion is biological success, which may be said to depend on the number of species, the number of individuals, the number of adaptations to different kinds of environments and habitats and duration of the phylum. On all these counts, arthropods are superior to vertebrates. Arthropods are

> from ten to a hundred times more numerous than vertebrates in species, incomparably more abundant in individuals, and divergently adapted to an even wider range of environments and habits. They easily hold their own against all the attacks of man and of other animals (Simpson et al., 1957, p. 570).

Evolution is not the process of superior animals triumphing over inferior ones but is, rather, a series of alternative adaptive strategies that have arisen in response to inconstant environments.

In this connection it may be well to add two more terms often used in discussing evolution: *primitive* and *derived*. The same point made with the terms superior/inferior may be applied here if primitive is interpreted as somehow inferior to derived. There are no backward or advanced animals, only animals that have adapted, or extinct forms that have not. Nor can modern forms be considered advanced over fossil forms. Living species have adapted to present environmental conditions; fossil species to the environments of their day.

Sometimes the word "primitive" is used for an early form from which later (called "derived") forms have arisen. Even when terms are carefully defined in this way, their use can be misleading and confusing.

other unknown factors (either singly or in combination) may have caused their demise. No one really knows. (See Box 6-4.)

ARBOREAL
Tree living.

Mammals

Mesozoic mammals were small animals, about the size of mice, which they resembled in appearance. Since they were so small, and many of the dinosaurs so large, the primitive mammals remained inconspicuous by dwelling in wooded or bushy areas and may have been **arboreal**. They are not what we would consider to be very noble creatures to have as ancestors. Romer (1959) suggests the Mesozoic

Figure 6-11
Evolution of body support in land vertebrates. The figures illustrate changes in land vertebrate limbs: (a) amphibian limbs project laterally from the body; (b) reptiles, with stronger pectoral and pelvic girdles, are more upright in an intermediate position; (c) in mammals, the legs project straight down.

(a)   (b)   (c)

TERTIARY
Third part.

QUATERNARY
Fourth.

may be seen as a training period during which mammalian characters were being perfected and wits sharpened. The mammalian radiation of the Cenozoic (65 m.y.a. to present) saw the rise of the ancestors of all modern mammals. Mammals replaced reptiles as the dominant terrestrial vertebrate, a position they still retain.

Cenozoic Era (65 m.y.a. to present)

The modern world as we know it—geologically and geographically—assumed its present configuration during the Cenozoic era. Major continental drifting slowed considerably, and interior seas on most continents were reduced. This alteration of the topography may explain the diversity of climates, patterns of seasons, water and wind currents, and the eventual onset of the Pleistocene Ice Ages. We may view life in the Cenozoic as a process of adaptation to the climatic extremes and topographic diversity, a situation for which mammals are well equipped.

The Cenozoic is divided into two periods, the **Tertiary** (about 63 million years' duration) and the **Quaternary**, from about 1.8 m.y.a. up to and including the present. Because so much evidence of living forms is available from the Cenozoic, the two periods are further subdivided into epochs. The five epochs of the Tertiary are: Paleocene, Eocene, Oligocene, Miocene, and Pliocene. The Quaternary, the final period of the Cenozoic, is divided into two epochs: the Pleistocene, well known for its *ice ages*, and the present epoch, the Holocene, which begins with the melting of the last glaciation.

Mammals

Conditions in the Cenozoic were nearly ideal for mammals. They radiated so rapidly and filled the available econiches so well that the Cenozoic is known as the *Age of Mammals*.

Figure 6-12
Mesozoic mammal. A speculative reconstruction of what a Mesozoic mammal might have looked like. Probably no bigger than a kitten, but with mammalian teeth, these animals were capable of attacking small lizards.

Figure 6-13
Geologic Time Scale: Cenozoic.

Era	Period	Epoch	Time	Glacial Sequence
			Years ago	Alpine
CENOZOIC	QUATERNARY	HOLOCENE		
			10,000	
		UPPER PLEISTOCENE	40,000	WÜRM
			75,000	
			100,000	RISS WÜRM
			125,000	
			175,000	RISS
			225,000	
			265,000	
		MIDDLE PLEISTOCENE	300,000	MINDEL RISS
				MINDEL
			380,000	
			400,000	
			430,000	
			500,000	GUNZ- MINDEL
			750,000	GÜNZ
		LOWER PLEISTOCENE		Uncertain Geological Sequences
			1.8 million	
	TERTIARY	Pliocene	5 million	Hominids (Australopithecines) present
		Miocene	25 million	Hominoidea (apelike creatures) Dryopithecines flourish . . . Probable appearance of hominids
		Oligocene	35 million	Anthropoidea and appearance of Hominoidea
		Eocene	53 million	Prosimians flourish; possible appearance of Anthropoidea
		Paleocene	65 million	Appearance of Prosimii

Figure 6-14
The Cenozoic. The most recent era. The two epochs, Tertiary and Quaternary, and their divisions are shown. (The Precambrian, Paleozoic, and Mesozoic are shown on p. 134.)

Placental Mammalian Characters   Campbell (1974, p. 39ff) has proposed that mammalian evolution was based on a single adaptive development: The ability for constant lively activity; that is, "the maintenance of a steady level of activity in the face of basic changes in the external environment." The constant and lively activity, Campbell further points out, was made possible by "the evolution of only four great complexes, all of a homeostatic nature": homoiothermy, mas-

HOMOIOTHERMY
Homo: same
therm: heat
Same temperature.

HOMODONTISM
homo: same
dont: teeth

HETERODONTISM
hetero: different
dont: teeth

OVIPARITY
ovum: egg
parere: to bear

VIVIPARITY
vivus: alive
parere: to bear

tication, improved reproductive efficiency, and new ways of determining behavior. (The following discussion of these complexes is summarized from Campbell, 1974.)

Homoiothermy   A constant and appropriate body temperature regardless of external conditions is a decided advantage for an active animal. **Homoiothermy** may have evolved among mammallike reptiles as early as the Permian and very probably was found later among at least some dinosaurs. It is difficult to know from fossil bones whether the warm-bloodedness of these forms was the same as that of mammals today. It would appear, however, that homoiothermy, as a basic characteristic, gave mammals the constant energy necessary for animals adapting to a highly active way of life. In addition, for the first time, vast forests of the temperate zone became available for exploitation by a vertebrate form.

Homoiothermy is so basic to the mammalian way of life that a number of physiological and behavioral adjustments have been developed to maintain a constant body temperature. To lower body temperature, mammals may perform one or more of the following activities: spread their limbs, lay their hair or fur flat against the skin, increase their respiration rate, dilate their capillaries, or sweat. To raise body temperature, they may curl into a ball, raise their hair/fur layer, constrict their capillaries, eat (metabolic action generates body heat), or shiver.

Mastication and Heterodontism   Except for extinct herbivorous forms, reptile teeth all have the same (**homodont**) structure. They curve inward with the jaw serving as a trap. Prey once caught cannot escape and is eaten whole without chewing. On the other hand, the mammalian jaw and **heterodont** dentition exploit various kinds of food more effectively. Different kinds of teeth—incisors, canines, premolars, and molars—evolved especially for trapping, nipping, chewing, cutting, crushing, and grinding, and the jaw was modified to make this dental activity possible. Mastication enables mammals to obtain more nutritive value from a wider variety of food by breaking up nuts, seeds, plant material, and meat, among other edibles. This is important to active homoiothermic animals, since they require more food intake.

Reproductive Efficiency   Reptiles changed the external method of amphibian fertilization by introducing internal fertilization. They lay eggs—**oviparity**—which, although not as vulnerable as amphibian eggs, are still easy prey for small carnivores.

Mammals evolved a new reproductive system. They retain copulation and internal fertilization, but the egg is kept within the mother, where it is protected and nourished until it achieves quite an advanced stage of growth. Birth is live—**viviparity**—and, because of the newborn's advanced stage, young mammals suffer fewer casualties than young reptiles.

Nevertheless, most mammalian young are born helpless although some, such as horses, cattle, and hares, are active within minutes or hours of birth. All newborn mammals, however, are unable to feed themselves and must be fed by special milk glands (mammae—modified sweat glands) of the mother. Suckling requires the young to remain close to the mother, a practice serving several functions. The young are fed, protected, and, through imitation, learn the behavior adaptive for their species.

Table 6-1 *Mammalian Innovations (Distinguishing Mammals from Reptiles)**

Innovations	Complexes
Warm blood	
Hair/fur	Homoiothermy
Sweat glands	
Heterodontism	
Strong jaw	Mastication and heterodontism
Viviparity	
Suckling	Reproductive efficiency
Mammalian play	Effectance motivation

*There is some evidence that homoiothermy, fur, and viviparity are more common than once believed.

streams and in burrows along the banks. Instead of teeth, it has developed a ducklike bill used for burrowing in the mud in search of worms and grubs. The anteater is protected by a coat of sharp spines (recalling the porcupine), a spur on the hind legs, and the jaws—also without teeth—are formed into a long, tubular snout used for probing anthills.

Monotremes are classified as mammals since the young are nursed from teatless mammary glands. However, they are very primitive mammals and retain a number of reptilian characters. They lay eggs, have but one opening for elimination, mating, and birth (hence the term **monotreme**) and display various other reptilian traits in the shoulder girdle, skull, and vertebral column. Some authorities consider monotremes as surviving mammallike reptiles.

Marsupials (Metatheria)   At the present time, **marsupials** are found only in Australia and the New World (opossums) although they were once more widely distributed in North America, South America, and Europe. Their extermination can be laid at the hands (or claws and teeth) of the brainier placental mammals

MONOTREME
mono: one
treme: a hole

MARSUPIUM
Pouch; pouched animals such as the kangeroo, koala, opossum.

Figure 6-16
Human brain. In humans the gray matter (cerebral cortex) is highly convoluted, which provides a greater surface for nerve connections and for eight billion brain cells. The cerebral cortex has also greatly expanded to cover most of the brain.

Cerebral hemisphere
Neocortex
Frontal lobe
Cerebellum
Medulla
Depth of cortex

MAMMALIA

Prototheria   Metatheria   Eutheria
(monotremes)   (pouched)   (placental)

Figure 6-17
Mammalian classification chart.

Figure 6-18
*The duck-billed platypus. Offspring licking
milk from mother's fur.*

whenever these two mammals have competed. Pouched animals survived in Australia because placental mammals never reached that continent before its separation from other land masses. Marsupials entered Australia before its sep-aration and remained isolated, except for bats, which probably flew in early, and rodents, which island-hopped in. The marsupials, therefore, were protected from the onslaught of the more developed Cenozoic placental mammals.

Most South American marsupials were destroyed by placentals invading that continent at the end of the Tertiary when North and South America were joined. Only the opossums survive today.

Marsupials bear their young alive as a tiny embryo after a short gestation period. These tiny infants work their way into their mother's pouch by a swim-ming motion of the forelimbs over a pathway of dampened mother's hair. Once in the pouch they remain attached to nipples that line the pouch and are fed by the mother literally pumping milk into them. When they are old enough to move around, they live in and out of the pouch until they are surprisingly large.

Aside from the method of reproduction, marsupials differ from placentals in brain size and other details of the skull. Teeth are also somewhat different from those of placental mammals, but the post-cranial skeleton is generally com-parable.

Placental Mammals (Eutheria)   One of the outstanding features of placental mammals (**Eutheria**) is the placenta, which gives the subclass its name. This disclike organ furnishes oxygen and nutrients from mother to developing embryo and gets rid of waste products as well. Young are born alive, as are marsupials, but in a much more advanced stage of development.

Among the many other differences distinguishing marsupials and placentals, two stand out. First, placentals possess an expanded brain, which has been suggested as the most important reason for their superiority over the pouched mammals. It may be of interest to briefly review this development.

The evolutionary history of the brain, center of the nervous system, reflects a steady growth in size and complexity as we move from fish to mammals (Fig.

6-21). The diversification of vertebrates depends largely upon the operation of the central nervous system, and the relative success of mammals over reptiles (and perhaps reptiles over amphibians) may be largely due to greater brain efficiency.

Fish reflect the basic vertebrate brain, which is composed of three sections: forebrain, midbrain, and hindbrain. The forebrain includes the **olfactory** lobes and the cerebrum; the midbrain, the largest section in fish and the center of control and coordination, is associated mainly with the optic lobe; the hindbrain combines the **cerebellum** and medulla oblongata, which act as message center and source of some autonomic and reflex actions.

The trend in brain evolution has been toward an increase in the forebrain and decrease in mid- and hindbrain. The amphibian brain is not much modified from the fish; the olfactory lobe is somewhat smaller and the cerebrum slightly larger.

Significant changes appeared in the reptile brain. The **cerebrum** is greatly enlarged but much of the forebrain is still devoted to smell. A striking innovation developed in the reptilian cerebrum. The cerebral hemispheres are coated by a pallium of neurons; in the reptile a small portion of the front part of the cerebrum is covered with a new sort of nervous tract called the **neopallium** or **neocortex**. This covering in general is what we know as "gray matter," and while the reptilian neopallium was a feeble beginning, it was a most important one.

In mammals, the neopallium dramatically expanded and spread over the cerebral hemispheres. Central control, formerly in the midbrain, passed almost entirely to the neopallium of the forebrain. The cerebrum increased in size to compose most of the brain and developed convolutions making for an even greater surface area without increasing brain size.

In humans, the growth of this section of the brain reaches its ultimate development, a fact which has made the human brain, in proportion to body weight, one of the largest and most complex of any animal (Passingham, 1982).

The second important difference between placentals and marsupials is *teeth*. These clearly distinguish the two forms and have been used as a basis for classification as well as the reconstruction of mammalian evolutionary history.

The structure of teeth often informs us of their use so that it is fairly easy, for example, to distinguish between the specializations of predator and herbivore teeth. Of all the teeth, it is probably the molars that are the most specialized.

Figure 6-19
Spiny anteater, a monotreme.

Figure 6-20
Wallaby with infant in pouch, marsupials.

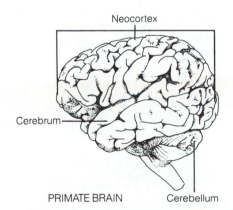

Figure 6-21
Lateral view of brain. The illustration shows the increase in the cerebral cortex of the brain. The cerebral cortex integrates sensory information and selects responses.

CARNIVORE
carni: meat
A flesh-eating animal.

HERBIVORE
herba: grass
A plant-eating animal.

OMNIVORE
omnis: all
Plant and meat eating.

ARTIODACTYL
(are-tee-o-dak′-til)
artios: even
daktylos: finger, toe
Even-toed hoof.

PERISSODACTYL
perissos: odd
Odd-toed hoof.

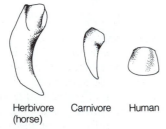

Herbivore   Carnivore   Human
(horse)

Figure 6-22
Canines.

Figure 6-23
Examples of specialization in herbivorous and carnivorous teeth. There is great variation in the size and shape of the canine in herbivorous animals, and canines are entirely lacking in many species.

They perform the powerful grinding, chewing, and crushing functions, and their structure is closely associated with diet. It is difficult to exaggerate the role of teeth in studying mammalian (and especially for our purposes, primate) evolution. The student is asked to keep this in mind when we look at primate evolution, since in many cases identification, classification, relationships, and chronological placement may be based on the structure of fossil teeth. This is particularly the case for hominids because, quite often, teeth are the only fossil evidence available.

Appearing in placentals of Cretaceous age and still persisting in many modern animals, the basic pattern of placental mammalian teeth is (on each side and in both upper and lower jaws) three incisors, one canine, four premolars, and three molars (see Box 7-2, p. 168). Incisors tend to be pegs or blades—adapted for nipping or cutting food, as can be seen when biting into an apple.

Canines come in a variety of forms. **Carnivore** canines are spikelike and used for stabbing, piercing, and holding. In **herbivores** canines tend to be molarlike with a grinding surface, and among humans, **omnivores**, canines are spatulate, similar to incisors and utilized in a similar manner.

Premolars (called "bicuspids" by dentists) are generally complex and used for crushing and/or grinding (as are molars, which are even more complex).

Placental mammals today are found almost everywhere on earth. With sea mammals such as dolphins and seals, we find them in water, and some placentals, the bats, have taken to the air. But placentals are essentially terrestrial animals and land is where they are found in abundant numbers and species. For example, there are the even-toed ungulates (**artiodactyls**), such as cows, deer, camels, and pigs; odd-toed ungulates (**perissodactyls**), such as the horse and rhino; carnivores, such as the bear, dog, and cat; proboscids, such as elephants; insectivores, such as shrews, moles, and hedgehogs; the incredibly successful rodents, including rats, squirrels, beavers, and gophers; and, of course, the primates, including prosimians, monkeys, apes, and humans.

Of all these groups the rodents are clearly the most successful of all mammals if number of species and individuals is our criterion. In fact, they outnumber all other species of mammals combined (Romer, 1959, p. 228). Their enormous

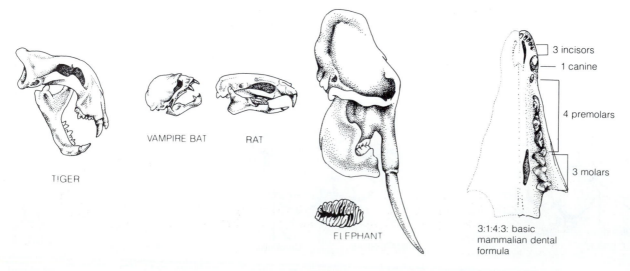

TIGER   VAMPIRE BAT   RAT   ELEPHANT

3 incisors
1 canine
4 premolars
3 molars

3:1:4:3: basic mammalian dental formula

BOX 6-5

Convergent and Parallel Evolution

Convergent Evolution   The discussion of marsupials offers an opportunity to present another evolutionary process, *convergent evolution*. We pointed out (in Box 6-2, Evolutionary Processes) that in the early stages of development, there is a tendency for newly evolved forms to become highly diversified when they invade varied environments. The diversification results from the modification of the ancestral type in adapting to new ecological niches.

Convergent evolution—a variation of adaptive radiation—is the process in which two *unrelated* groups of organisms, living in similar but separate environmental conditions, develop a similar appearance and life style. That is, similar environmental demands make for similar phenotypic responses (Mayr, 1970, p. 365). This should not be surprising since the requirements of adapting to a particular environment would require modifications of physical traits. Two similar environments would, therefore, result in similar adaptive characters.

Striking examples of convergence are the pouched mammals of Australia and placental mammals. As we have seen, Australia was isolated from South America before the great placental mammalian radiation of the Cenozoic, and marsupials survived because they were free from the competition of the more efficient placentals. When placental mammals became prominent in the Cenozoic, only a few were able to invade Australia (via island-hopping from Southeast Asia).

Without competition, the pouched mammals spread into the varied environments of the isolated continent. There were marsupials that resembled, to a lesser or greater degree, a wolf, cat, flying squirrel, groundhog, anteater, mole, and mouse. And they occupied ecological niches similar to the placental mammals they resembled (Simpson et al., 1957, p. 470).

The variety of marsupials illustrates adaptive radiation; the resemblance in form due to similarity of econiches illustrates convergent evolution.

Parallel Evolution   A variation of both adaptive radiation and convergent evolution is *parallel evolution*. This process may be illustrated as a kind of tailed U. *Related* forms diverge as in adaptive radiation, responding to different ecological niches. Then, because of the similarity of econiches, the two or more forms respond to similar selection pressures and evolve somewhat similar phenotypes, for example, the New World and Old World monkeys (see further discussion in Chapter 7).

Figure 1

(a) Divergent evolution

Converge

Different forms

Convergent evolution

(b)

Original form

Figure 2

Similar phenotypes

X   X

Similar econiches

Initial divergence

Parallel evolution

Original form

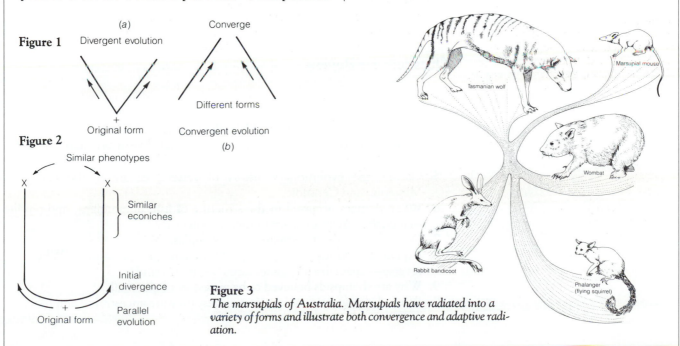

Figure 3

The marsupials of Australia. Marsupials have radiated into a variety of forms and illustrate both convergence and adaptive radiation.

Tasmanian wolf

Marsupial mouse

Wombat

Rabbit bandicoot

Phalanger (flying squirrel)

Figure 6-24
Ungulates.

adaptive flexibility is clearly demonstrated by their ability to cope successfully with humanmade environments.

We have traced the evolution of vertebrates from fish to mammals. Mammals, as we have seen, had come a long way from the small, insignificant, insectivorelike animals of the Mesozoic to the highly diversified and very successful vertebrates of the present. We are now prepared to take up the discussion of our own order, Primates, which, like other mammals, most likely originated as shrewlike animals in the Paleocene (or possibly the late Cretaceous). Very early, they adapted to an arboreal way of life that emphasized vision, an expanded brain, and prehensile digits, as we shall see in the next three chapters.

Summary

In this chapter, we have placed humans in their natural perspective by tracing the development of evolutionary changes of invertebrates and vertebrates. We also placed humans in a temporal perspective by tracing the evolutionary development of life forms, especially vertebrates, over the immense time period of Precambrian through Tertiary.

Structural modifications of the evolutionary sequence of vertebrates—from fish to amphibians to reptiles to mammals—were included to give the very long developmental background of the hominid form. This will be continued in the chapter on primate evolution.

The basis for taxonomic classification (why animal X is placed in category Y) and several evolutionary concepts (adaptive radiation, generalized and specialized, and convergent and parallel evolution) were discussed to give a deeper understanding of "how evolution works."

Questions for Review

1. What characteristics place humans in the Animal Kingdom?
2. Distinguish between homologies and analogies.
3. To what groups of the Animal Kingdom do hominids belong?
4. Explain the basis for the arrangement of the classification chart. Give several examples.
5. Outline the evolutionary history of vertebrates during the Paleozoic, Mesozoic, and Cenozoic.
6. What changes occurred in the structure of fish, amphibians, and reptiles that enables them to adapt to their econiches?
7. Define adaptive radiation and give examples.
8. Explain the evolutionary principle "generalized to specialized." Why is the reverse—"specialized to generalized"—rarely found?
9. Why are therapsids believed to be ancestors of mammals?
10. What characteristics of lobe-fins suggest they are ancestral to amphibia?

11. What "four great complexes" distinguish mammals from reptiles and contributed to mammalian success?
12. Explain the differences between convergent and parallel evolution.
13. Why are placental mammals so much more successful than marsupials?

CHAPTER 7

Living Primates

CONTENTS

Can the Mountain Gorilla Be Saved?

Today, one species of primate, *Homo sapiens*, dominates our planet. Numbering now 5 billion, we use, alter, and ultimately destroy huge hunks of the world's surface.

In the face of such an onslaught, many of the other species that share our planet are being driven to the brink of extinction. As primates ourselves, we have a special interest in the problem of preserving our primate relatives.

Even before the advent of modern technological society, primates (compared to such groups as rodents or even-toed ungulates) were not abundant. Largely restricted to forested areas in South America, Africa, and South Asia, the primates had—despite their comparative numerical inferiority—achieved a successful adaptation.

Such is no longer the case. In addition to being diminished by the dangers stemming from reduced or completely obliterated habitats, nonhuman primates are also easy prey for local peoples looking for food, hunters looking for scientific (mostly medical) specimens, or for poachers strictly after financial gain.

What does the future hold for these animals? The prospects are not hopeful. The Convention on International Trade in Endangered Species (ratified by the United States in 1973) already lists *all* non-human primates as endangered or facing the prospects of soon becoming so. All of the apes—gibbons, orangutans, gorillas, and chimpanzees—are now in the convention's "most endangered" category. (All are also on the United States' endangered species list, with chimps just "upgraded" to endangered status in 1989.)

Among the most imminently endangered of all primates is the mountain gorilla—a subspecies of the largest primate form—now restricted to an exceedingly small area of East Africa (where the borders of Rwanda, Uganda, and Zaire converge).

Mountain gorillas once ranged widely through the densely forested mountain regions bordering the great lakes of East Africa. Foraging in rough terrain, gorilla groups survived for centuries, impervious to any potential predator. In fact, the mountain gorilla was not even known to the Western world until 1903, when it was first reported by a German military expedition.

The mountain gorilla's comparative isolation from humans has been dramatically altered in recent years. It is estimated that today there are only about 360 mountain gorillas left in the wild. In the last twenty years alone, their numbers have been reduced by one-half.

Most of the deaths (perhaps as many as two-thirds) are at the hands of poachers. Gorillas are prized specimens for trophy hunters; consequently, they are often shot with high-powered rifles, after which they are decapitated, their hands cut off, and these grisly remains sold for trophies.

Gorillas also are victims of poachers in a more accidental fashion. Traps and snares are set by poachers primarily to capture antelope and buffalo, which can be sold as meat. Mountain gorillas who live in the same area step into these traps and, even if they manage to escape, usually die later from infected wounds.

Why is such reckless exploitation allowed? The answer is that, legally, it is not. Throughout the world illegal poaching of endangered species is banned, and most countries prohibit imports of products derived from such animals. Enforcement, however, is another matter. Due to political instability and periodic warfare in East Africa, central governments have been at a loss to stop the killing. In Zaire and Uganda most of the mountain gorillas are now gone. Rwanda continues to struggle with the problem, but the choices are not always easy. Among the most overcrowded and undernourished populations in Africa, Rwandans are hard-pressed to find adequate sources of animal protein. Local populations consequently feel compelled to trap antelope and buffalo and, in the process, gorillas as well.

Despite wide publicity of the gorilla's plight in the Western world and a large influx of money from concerned conservationists, the slaughter goes on. Is there then any hope for saving the mountain gorilla? Perhaps— but time is growing dangerously short. As Dian Fossey, the late leading field researcher of these primates, ominously warned, "The mountain gorilla may become an animal which was discovered and driven extinct—in the same century."

The tragic story of Dian Fossey's work with the mountain gorilla

Digit, an adult male gorilla; found after poachers had decapitated him and cut off his hands.

reached a terrible climax when, on Christmas Eve 1985, she was brutally murdered at her research station in Rwanda. Following her wishes, she was buried next to her beloved Digit and the other gorillas for whom she had given so much.

S O U R C E S :

Fossey, Dian. "The Imperiled Mountain Gorilla," *National Geographic,* **159**:501–523, April, 1981.

Fossey, Dian. *Gorillas in the Mist,* Boston: Houghton-Mifflin Co., 1983.

Introduction

We have seen in Chapter 6 that we are a certain kind of placental mammal, a primate. This order of rather diverse animals is characterized by a set of evolutionary trends that sets it apart from other mammals. In this chapter, we will discuss what characteristics link us to our primate cousins, and we will explore some of the fascinating and unique adaptations that the nonhuman primates display.

Primate Evolutionary Trends

Structurally, primates are not easily distinguished as a group chiefly because of the fact that, as an order, we and our close relatives have remained quite *generalized*. Unlike the specialized dentition of rodents or the specialized limbs with great reduction of digits found in artiodactyls (cows, deer, camels, pigs), primates are characterized by their *lack* of extreme structural specializations.

For this reason, we cannot point to a single anatomical feature that can be applied exclusively and universally to the primates. On the other hand, there is a group of **evolutionary trends** (Clark, 1971) which, to a greater or lesser degree, characterize the entire order. Keep in mind, these are a set of *general* tendencies and are not equally expressed in all primates. Indeed, this situation is one that we would expect in such a diverse group of generalized animals. In addition, trends are not synonymous with *progress*. In evolutionary terms, we are using "trend" only to reflect a series of shared common characteristics (i.e., general homologies).

Following is a list of those evolutionary trends that tend to set the primates apart from other mammals. A common evolutionary history with similar adaptations to common environmental challenges is reflected in the limbs and locomotion; teeth and diet; and in the senses, brain, and behavior of the animals that make up the order.

A. LIMBS AND LOCOMOTION

1. *Retention of five digits* in the hands and feet—*pentadactyly*. As in primitive mammals, this characteristic is found in all primates, though some show marked reduction of the thumb (e.g., spider monkeys, langurs) or the second digit (e.g, lorises). In no case is reduction as extreme as that seen in such animals as cows or horses.

2. *Nails instead of claws.* A consistent characteristic on at least some digits of all contemporary primates. Unlike rodents or cats, primates must climb by wrapping their hands and feet around branches and holding on by grasping. This grasping function is further aided by the presence of tactile pads at the ends of digits.

3. *Flexible hands and feet* with a good deal of **prehensility** (grasping ability). This feature is associated directly with the lack of claws and retention of five digits.

Figure 7-1
Primate (macaque) hand.

Figure 7-2
Position of the clavicle in the human skeleton.

4. *A tendency toward erectness* (particularly in the upper body). Shown to some degree in all primates, this tendency is variously associated with sitting, leaping, standing, and, occasionally, walking.

5. *Retention of the clavicle* (collarbone). Seen in all primates. The clavicle has been lost in many other quadrupedal mammals. In primates, the clavicle allows for more flexibility of the shoulder joint.

B. TEETH AND DIET

6. *A generalized dental pattern*, particularly in the back teeth (molars). Characteristic of primates, such a pattern contrasts with the highly specialized molars seen in herbivores.

7. *A lack of specialization in diet.* This attribute is usually correlated with a lack of specialization in teeth. In other words, primates can generally be described as *omnivorous*.

C. SENSES, BRAIN, AND BEHAVIOR

8. *A reduction of the snout* and the proportionate reduction of the smell (olfactory) areas of the brain. Seen in all contemporary primates, but baboons show a secondary (coming later) increase of a *dental* muzzle.

9. *An increased emphasis on vision* with elaboration of visual areas of the brain. A trend related to the decreased dependence on smell. Binocular and stereoscopic vision is a further elaboration wherein visual fields of the two eyes overlap, transmitting both images to the brain, thus allowing depth perception. Except for some specialized nocturnal forms, color vision is most likely present in all primates.

10. *Expansion and increasing complexity of the brain.* A general trend among placental mammals and one especially true of primates. This expansion is most evident in the visual and association areas of the neopallium and to some degree in the motor cortex and cerebellum. (See p. 145.)

11. *A more efficient means of fetal nourishment*, as well as *longer periods of gestation (with single births the norm), infancy*, and extension of the whole life span.

12. *A greater dependency on highly flexible learned behavior* is correlated with longer periods of infant and child dependency. As a result of both these trends, parental investment in each offspring is increased so that although fewer young are born, they receive more efficient rearing.

13. *Adult males often associate permanently with the group.* A behavioral trait rarely seen in other mammals, but widespread among the primates.

The Arboreal Adaptation

The single most important factor influencing the evolutionary divergence of primates (with elaboration of all the trends just noted) was the adaptation to **arboreal** living. While other placental mammals were going about their business adapting to grasslands, subterranean or even marine environments, primates found their **adaptive niche** in the trees. Indeed, some other mammals also were adapting to arboreal living, but primates found their home (and food) mainly in

EVOLUTIONARY TRENDS
General structural and behavioral traits that are commonly shared by a related group of organisms.

PREHENSILITY
Adapted for grasping.

ARBOREAL
Anatomy is adapted to life in the trees.

ADAPTIVE NICHE
The whole way of life of an organism: where it lives, what it eats, how it gets food, and so forth.

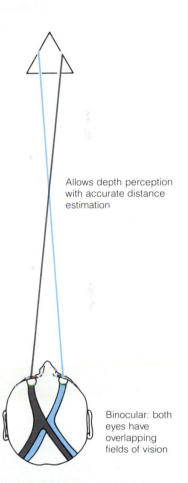

Allows depth perception with accurate distance estimation

Binocular: both eyes have overlapping fields of vision

Stereoscopic: optic nerve transmissions from each eye are relayed to *both* sides of the brain

Figure 7-3
Binocular, stereoscopic vision. Fields of vision overlap and sensory information from each eye is relayed to both sides of the brain.

SUBSTRATE
The surface on which an animal moves or rests.

NOCTURNAL
Active at night.

DIURNAL
Active during daylight hours.

POSTORBITAL BAR
The bony element that closes in the outside of the eye orbit—a characteristic of primates.

the tree tops and at the ends of terminal branches. This environment—with its myriad challenges and opportunities—was the one in which our ancestors established themselves as a unique kind of animal.

Primates became primates *because* of their adaptation to arboreal living. We can see this process at work in their reliance upon vision for survival (as opposed to their depending chiefly on a sense of smell). In a complex environment with uncertain footholds, acute vision with depth perception is a necessity. Climbing can be accomplished by either digging in with claws or grasping around branches with prehensile hands and feet. Primates adopted the latter strategy, which allowed a means of progressing on the narrowest and most tenuous of **substrates**. Thus, we also see in primates pentadactyly, prehensility, and flattened nails. In addition, the varied foods found in an arboreal environment (such as fruits, leaves, berries, insects, small mammals) led to the primate omnivorous adaptation and, hence, to retention of a generalized dentition.

Finally, the long life span, increased intelligence, and more elaborated social system are primate solutions to coping with the manifold complexities of their arboreal habitat (that is, such factors as varied and seasonal food resources; and potential predators from above, below, and in the trees). This crucial development of increased behavioral flexibility may have been further stimulated by a shift from **noctural** (nighttime) to **diurnal** (daytime) activity patterns (Jerison, 1973).

A recent critique of the traditional arboreal explanation for the origin of primate structure has been proposed by Matt Cartmill (1972, 1974) of Duke University. Cartmill points out that the most significant primate trends—close-set eyes, grasping extremities, and reduced claws—may *not* have arisen from adaptive advantages in an arboreal environment.

According to this alternative theory, ancient primates may have first adapted to living in bushy forest undergrowth and only the lowest branches of the forest canopy. All these traits would have been well-suited for an animal that foraged for fruits and insects. Particularly in searching for insects, early primates are thought to have relied heavily on vision, and this theory is hence called the *visual predation hypothesis*.

The close-set eyes would have allowed these primates to judge accurately the distance from their prey without moving their heads, similar to the hunting manner of cats and owls. The regression of the olfactory sense is then viewed as a necessary result of the eye orbits coming closer together. Grasping extremities may have initially been an adaptation for pursuing insects along very narrow supports (like twigs) in the forest undergrowth. Feet, as well as hands, would be prehensile to allow the animal to maintain support while snaring its prey with both hands.

The visual predation hypothesis is as internally consistent and as likely an explanation for the early evolution of primates as the arboreal theory. In fact—given the fossil record and the morphology typical of many contemporary prosimians—it may be a better explanation for the functional developments among the *earliest* primates. In particular, the small body size and insectivorous diet seen in several living prosimians and a similar adaptation inferred from the fossilized remains of many very early primates are consistent with the visual predation hypothesis.

The visual predation ("bug snatching") hypothesis and the arboreal theory are not mutually exclusive explanations. The complex of primate characteristics

Primate Cranial Anatomy

Several significant anatomical features of primate skulls help us distinguish primates from other mammals. Continuing the mammalian trend of increasing brain development, primates go even further as shown by their well-expanded brain boxes. In addition, the primate trend of increased dependence on vision is shown by the generally large eye sockets; less emphasis on smell is shown in the reduced snout; the shift to using hands for grasping (instead of using the front teeth for this purpose) is revealed in the dentition; and the tendency towards more upright posture is indicated by the relationship of the head to the spinal column.

Some of the specific anatomic details seen in all modern and most fossil primate crania are:

1. Eye sockets are enclosed circumferentially by a complete ring of bone, compared to other placental mammals where the ring is incomplete (no **postorbital bar**). This bony arrangement provides protection for the eyes.

2. The entrance into the skull for the spinal column, the *foramen magnum* (Latin: "big hole") on the base of the skull, faces more downwards instead of backwards as it does in other completely quadrupedal mammals. The position of the *foramen magnum* indicates the direction of the spinal column and is related to the posturing and balancing of the head on the trunk.

3. The face of primates is reduced (snout shortened) with the axis at the base of the skull bending, thus pulling the face more underneath the brain box. This arrangement now provides a greater vertical distance in the movable lower jaw from the point of pivot (P) to the plane of the teeth (T) allowing more biomechanical action for up-and-down crushing, grinding, etc., instead of just simple back-and-forth tearing and gnashing.

4. The ear region containing the middle ear ossicles is completely encircled by a bony encasement (bulla) whose floor is derived from a particular segment of the temporal bone. Most primate paleontologists consider this feature and the formation of a postorbital bar as the structurally best diagnostic characteristics of the primate order.

(a) Cat   (b) Lemur

Figure 1
Postorbital bar. A characteristic of primates.

(a) Dog

(b) Lemur

Figure 2
Basi-cranial flexion relative to tooth row. In primates, the skull base is more flexed, elevating the point of pivot (P) further above the tooth row and thereby increasing the force of chewing. (© 1959 by W. E. Le Gros Clark.)

could have begun in nonarboreal settings, but would have become even more adaptive once the bug snatching was done *in the trees*.

At some point, in fact, the primates did take to the trees in earnest, and that is where the vast majority still live today. Whereas the basic primate structural complexes may have been initially adapted for visual predation, they became ideally suited for the arboreal adaptation that followed. We would say then that primates were "preadapted" for arboreal living.

The Living Primates

When we apply the set of evolutionary trends under discussion here, we are able to classify a remarkable array of living forms as members of the same mammalian order, the Primates. We and our primate cousins, you will recall, share these characteristics due to **homology**. In other words, primates are part of a single evolutionary radiation, and the traits we all share derive from a common evolutionary descent.

Primate Classification

While controversy on some minor points still exists, the living primates are traditionally categorized into subgroupings (based on increasingly similar evolutionary relationships) in the following manner:

ORDER   Primates
  SUBORDER   Prosimii
    SUPERFAMILY   Lemuroidea (lemurs of Madagascar)
    SUPERFAMILY   Lorisoidea (loris, bushbaby)
    SUPERFAMILY   Tarsiioidea (tarsier)
  SUBORDER   Anthropoidea
    SUPERFAMILY   Ceboidea (New World monkeys; e.g., spider monkey, howler monkey, capuchin)
    SUPERFAMILY   Cercopithecoidea (Old World monkeys; e.g., baboon, macaque, langur)
    SUPERFAMILY   Hominoidea
      FAMILY   Hylobatidae (gibbons)
      FAMILY   Pongidae
        GENUS   *Pan* (chimp)
        GENUS   *Gorilla*
        GENUS   *Pongo* (orangutan)
      FAMILY   Hominidae
        GENUS   *Homo* (human)

Table 7-1 shows an alternative primate classification.

Table 7-1 *Alternative Classification of Living Primates—Based upon Biochemical Data (after Dene et al., 1976)*

Order Primates
  Semiorder Strepsirhini
    Suborder Lemuriformes
      Superfamily Lemuroidea
        Family Lemuridae
          Genus *Lemur*   common lemur
        Family Lepilemuridae
          Genus *Lepilemur*   sportive lemur
        Family Indriidae
          Genus *Propithecus*   sifaka
      Superfamily Cheirogaleoidea
        Family Cheirogaleidae
          Genus *Microcebus*   mouse lemur
          Cheirogaleus   dwarf lemur
      Superfamily Daubentonioidea
        Family Daubentoniidae
          Genus *Daubentonia*   aye-aye
    Suborder Lorisiformes
      Superfamily Lorisoidea
        Family Galagidae
          Subfamily Galaginae
            Genus *Galago*   bushbaby
        Family Lorisidae
          Genus *Nycticebus*   slow loris
          Loris   slender loris
        Family Perodicticidae
          Subfamily Perodicticinae
          Genus *Perodicticus*   potto
          Arctocebus   angwantibo
  Semiorder Haplorhini
    Suborder Tarsioiidea
      Family Tarsiidae
        Genus *Tarsius*   tarsier

    Suborder Anthropoidea
      Infraorder Platyrrhini   New World monkeys
        Superfamily Ceboidea
          Genus *Ateles*   spider monkey
          Logothrix   woolly monkey
          Alouatta   howler monkey
          Saguinus   tamarin
          Aotus   night monkey
          Callicebus   titi
          Chiropotes   saki
          Cebus   capuchin
          Saimiri   squirrel monkey
      Infraorder Catarrhini
        Superfamily Cercopithecoidea
          Family Cercopithecidae
            Subfamily Colobinae
              Genus *Colobus*   guereza
              Presbytis   langur
              Pygathrix   douc langur
              Nasalis   proboscis monkey
           Subfamily Cercopithecinae
              Genus *Macaca*   macaque
              Papio   baboon
              Theropithecus   gelada
              Mandrillus   drill
              Cercocebus   mangabey
              Erythrocebus   patas
              Cercopithecus   guenon
        Superfamily Hominoidea
          Family Hylobatidae
            Subfamily Hylobatinae
              Genus *Hylobates*   gibbon
              Symphalangus   siamang
          Family Hominidae
           Subfamily Ponginae
             Genus *Pongo*   orangutan
           Subfamily Homininae
             Genus *Gorilla*   gorilla
              Pan   chimpanzee
              Homo

Grades of Primate Evolution

In terms of size, structure, and behavior, contemporary primates certainly represent a varied group of animals. What is even more remarkable about the living primates is that they still display in some form all the major grades of evolution that primates have passed through over the last 70 million years.

An evolutionary grade is, in Mayr's terms, "A group of animals similar in level of organization" (Mayr, 1970). We do not use the term, as some evolutionary biologists have done, to imply a strict commonality of evolutionary descent and/ or an equivalent adaptive response (suggesting selection above the species level).

In evolutionary terms, an organism that is closer to an evolutionary divergence than a later (more derived) one.

In fact, such processes are not now believed to be accurate depictions of macroevolution (Eldredge and Cracraft, 1980). (See p. 93.)

You should also note that the concept of grade does not imply any inferiority or superiority. Grades only reflect different stages of organizational levels seen during primate evolution—from more primitive to more derived. (See p. 139.)

Grade I: Tree Shrews (Primitive Mammalian Grade)

Tree shrews are an enigma to the taxonomist. In classifying the natural world into the higher taxonomic categories of family, order, etc., we are attempting to simplify and hopefully make sense out of the complex organic continuum that evolution has produced. Indeed, the categories are *created by us* for us. They are symbolic devices typical of the human mind's capacity to "impose arbitrary form on the environment." A tree shrew could care less whether it is classified as a primate, an insectivore (another order of placental mammals), or a whale.

It is often readily apparent that similar structural and behavioral characteristics of contemporary life forms reflect their shared evolutionary ancestry (for example, lemurs and lorises both as prosimians; humans and apes both as hominoids). There are, however, many organisms that do not fit neatly into *any* of our categories.

The tree shrew is such an animal. Some investigators, impressed by several structural similarities, regard tree shrews as primates (Simpson, 1945; Clark, 1971). However, most current researchers (Simons, 1972; Buettner-Janusch, 1973) view the primatelike characteristics of tree shrews as merely reflections of their primitive mammalian heritage. As another popular alternative, tree shrews have often been placed among the insectivores, where they do not really fit either. As a final act of taxonomic desperation, then, most experts now place tree shrews within their own order of placental mammals (Luckett, 1980a).

Given that tree shrews are an order unto themselves, what are their closest relatives among the placentals? Morphological and some biochemical data suggest that tree shrews, flying lemurs, and primates form an evolutionary "cluster" and could be included together within a common superorder (Cronin and Sarich, 1980; Luckett, 1980). However, other biochemical techniques suggest the tree shrew/flying lemur/primate cluster is not a natural grouping, and that tree shrews, in fact, find their nearest mammalian affinities with bats (Dene, et al., 1980) or even rabbits (Goodman, et al., 1983). What makes tree shrews intriguing and relevant to a discussion of primate evolution is that their overall anatomical structure and level of adaptation are probably very similar to the earliest primates of 70 million years ago.

Today, tree shrews live in Southeast Asia, extending from India to the islands of Indonesia. They are all generally small, squirrellike animals and may not be recognized initially as primatelike in appearance. First, they have long, projecting snouts, and their eyes do not face forward (see Fig. 7-4). Second—even more unprimatelike—they have claws (not nails) on *all* their digits. Finally, their social behavior is most unlike primates in their "absentee" system of mothering. (On the other hand, their tendency toward grasping definitely parallels the well-developed grasping features of the primates.) It is no wonder that the tree shrews look **primitive**, since they are not much altered from the probable general appearance and adaptive level of very early placental mammals. Since the primate adaptive radiation goes back to the roots of the placental mammal radiation at

Figure 7-4
Tree shrew.

Figure 7-5
The grades of primate evolution.

Hominoid

Monkey

Tarsier

Lemur/loris

Tree shrew

the beginning of the Cenozoic (*circa* 65 m.y.a.), living tree shrews provide an excellent structural model for the earliest primates as well as for generalized placental mammals.

Grade II: Lemurs and Lorises

Lemurs are found today only on the island of Madagascar off the east coast of Africa. They probably reached their island sanctuary several million years ago and were able to diversify into the many ecological niches offered on this large island of 227,000 square miles. As the *only* primates on the island, lemurs were able to survive. In continental areas, most of their prosimian cousins perished. Thus, these surviving forms represent a kind of "living fossil," preserving an evolutionary grade that has long since vanished elsewhere.

Lemurs, however, are not uniform. Some are nocturnal, others diurnal; some are completely arboreal, others are more terrestrial. In fact, the range of forms and habitats occupied before recent human interference (in the last few hundred years) reveals a remarkable evolutionary display. One unusual lemur (called the aye-aye), still living in Madagascar, suggests a rodentlike adaptation; another (indri) resembles a small monkey; and, finally, an incredible beast with extremely short hind limbs (*Megaladapis*, now extinct) weighed more than 100 pounds (Szalay and Delson, 1979).

Some forms like the aye-aye are socially solitary, whereas others primarily associate in large permanent groups (the ring-tailed lemur). All these forms evolved in the relative sanctuary that Madagascar provided. This kind of evolution, characterized by rapid diversification and expansion into varied ecological niches, is another beautiful example of **adaptive radiation**.

Lorises, very similar to lemurs, were able to survive in *continental* areas by adopting a nocturnal activity pattern at a time when most other prosimians became extinct. In this way, they were (and are) able to avoid competition with their primate descendants, the monkeys, as well as another group—including many highly successful arboreal, diurnal forms—the rodents.

Today, the geographic range of lorises is confined to tropical areas in Africa and Southeast Asia. Their nocturnal adaptation is immediately revealed structurally by their greatly enlarged eyes. Usually quite small animals, they have elongated hindlimbs, providing an adaptation for leaping and hopping. Socially, most lorises are solitary and only occasionally form sleeping pairs.

Both lemurs and lorises represent the same general adaptive level. They both have good grasping and climbing abilities and have fairly well-developed vision that is not completely stereoscopic. They all have nails on at least one of their digits (the aye-aye has a nail only on the big toe). Most of the other varieties have only one clawed digit (on the second toe). This digit is used for grooming and is called the toilet digit. Lemurs and lorises also have prolonged life spans as compared to other small mammals, averaging about fourteen years for the lorises and nineteen years for the lemurs.

However, lorises and lemurs still show many characteristics suggesting their relatively closer relationship to early placental mammals than is true for the anthropoids (monkeys, apes, and humans). For example, their faces for the most part are still quite snouty, with a markedly projecting nose. As this feature would suggest, they still rely a great deal on the olfactory sense, and some lemurs have developed specialized scent glands for the purpose of leaving "smell" messages. Dependence on olfactory cues is also shown by the naked area of moist skin—*rhinarium*—on the nose. This area is used to conduct scent efficiently. Suggestive also of their early primate ancestry are their expressionless faces, large mobile ears, and a generally unelaborated pattern of social behavior. Finally, there are some unusual specialized aspects in their dentition, particularly the projecting lower incisors and canines forming a structure used for grooming and hence called a dental comb.

Figure 7-6
Distribution of modern lemurs.

Figure 7-7
Ring-tailed lemur.

Grade III: The Tarsier

A once widespread prosimian form, the living tarsier is today limited to one genus (*Tarsius*) and is confined to island areas in Southeast Asia. This tiny animal (about the size of a small kitten) has avoided competition in much the same

Figure 7-8
Sifakas in native habitat in Madagascar.

way as the lorises—by adapting to a nocturnal niche. The large forward-placed eyes which dominate the face strikingly reveal this adaptation. Another unusual feature shown by the tarsier is a greatly elongated ankle joint (tarsus), which gives the animal its name and allows it to leap great distances.

Like lemurs and lorises, tarsiers are traditionally classified as prosimians, as revealed by their small body size, large ears, "primitive" dental pattern, and unelaborated social behavior. However, they exhibit several physical characteristics similar to anthropoids, placing them at a different organizational level than lemurs and lorises. Indeed, like the tree shrew, tarsiers present somewhat of a taxonomic dilemma. Today, most primatologists, pointing to the numerous

Figure 7-9
Distribution of modern lorises.

STREPSIRHINI
strepsi: twisted   rhini: nose
The classificatory term used to group lemurs
and lorises (either suborder or semiorder).

HAPLORHINI
haplo: simple   rhini: nose
The classificatory term used to group tarsiers
with monkeys, apes, and humans (either suborder or semiorder).

Figure 7-10
Galgo or "bushbaby."

Figure 7-11
Distribution of modern tarsiers.

Figure 7-12
Tarsier. Note the huge eyes.

physical characteristics that tarsiers share with anthropoids (which are seen as derived states), classify tarsiers closer to anthropoids than to prosimians. Moreover, biochemically, tarsiers are more closely related to anthropoids than to lemurs or lorises (Dene et al., 1976). However, chromosomally tarsiers are unique among primates. In order to accommodate this revised view, classification schemes and classificatory labels have been changed. For example, the suborder that includes lemurs and lorises is termed the **Strepsirhini**, while tarsiers, monkeys, apes, and humans are included within another suborder, the **Haplorhini** (Szalay and Delson, 1979). Another means of accomplishing the same goal is to retain the traditional subordinal nomenclature but to distinguish lemurs and lorises from tarsiers, monkeys, apes, and humans at a level above suborder (i.e., semiorder—see Table 7-1) (Dene et al., 1976).

As we indicated above, tarsiers show many similarities to anthropoids. Contrasted to those of other prosimians, tarsier eye orbits are completely closed *in back* by bone in the manner of the anthropoids. (Lorises and lemurs are "primitive" in this respect, having an opening between the orbit and the cranial vault, or brainbox.) You will recall that all primates have orbits that are completely encircled by bone *on the outside*. In addition, tarsier skulls are more rounded and their snouts less projecting than those of other prosimians, a situation partially explained by their small size and huge eyes. Another anthropoidlike feature is their lack of a rhinarium and a more flexible upper lip, a structure allowing for more facial expression. Finally, the bony ear canal of the tarsier is also more like anthropoids than that of prosimians.

In addition to those features already pointed out, several other characteristics exist that tend to distinguish monkeys, apes, and humans from the "lower" primates. These are:

1. Generally larger body size
2. Larger brain size (in absolute terms and relative to body weight)
3. More rounded skull (seen to some degree in tarsiers also)
4. Eyes completely in front of skull, full stereoscopic vision
5. Complete back wall to eye orbit (also seen in tarsiers)
6. No rhinarium (also seen in tarsiers)
7. Only two incisors (on each side) in both jaws
8. More complex social systems
9. More parental care; often by males as well as females
10. More mutual grooming

Grade IV: Monkeys

The monkey grade of evolution is today the most varied group of primates (see Table 7-2). Of the 185 or so living species of primates, approximately 70% (about 130 species) are classified as monkeys. These are divided into two groups separated by geographical area (New World and Old World), as well as several million years of separate evolutionary history.

New World Monkeys   The New World monkeys (Ceboidea) exhibit a wide range of size, diet, and ecological adaptation. In size, they vary from the tiny (about twelve ounces) marmosets (family: Callitrichidae) to the twenty-pound howler monkey, a member of the family Cebidae (see Table 7-3). New World monkeys are almost exclusively arboreal and will usually come to the ground only

Table 7-2 *Numbers of Groups of Living Primates*

	Genera	Species
Lemur	12	28
Loris	5	11
Tarsier	1	3
New World monkey	16	52
Old World monkey	16	78
Hominoids	6	14
Total	56	186

Source: Data abstracted from A. Jolly, 1985, pp. 6–11.

Table 7-3 *New World Monkey Classification*

SUPERFAMILY	Ceboidea
FAMILY	Callitrichidae (marmosets and tamarins)
FAMILY	Cebidae (howler monkey, spider monkey, woolly monkey, capuchin, night monkey, squirrel monkey)

to cross spaces in order to gain access to other trees. Although confined to tree environments, New World monkeys can be found in a wide range of arboreal habitats throughout most forested areas in southern Mexico, Central America, and South America.

Nose shape is one of the characteristics distinguishing New World monkeys from those found in the Old World. New World forms have broad, widely flaring noses with a thick nasal septum, with nostrils facing outward. Conversely, Old World monkeys have narrower noses with a thinner nasal septum, and the nostrils face downward. This difference in nose form has given rise to the terms *platyrrhine* (flat-nosed) and *catarrhine* (down-nosed), the latter referring to *all* Old World anthropoids (Old World monkeys, apes, and humans). Another characteristic of New World monkeys is seen in their dentition, which has retained three premolars. All Old World anthropoids have only two (see Box 7-2). Another feature found only in the New World, though not in all forms, is the development of a prehensile (grasping) tail that can be used like a fifth limb.

Figure 7-13
Distribution of modern New World monkeys.

Figure 7-14
A pair of golden marmosets.

Figure 7-15
Howler monkey with infant.

BOX 7-2

Tale of the Teeth

Extremely important for interpreting the relationships of *both* living and fossil forms are the number and kinds of teeth present. There are four different kinds of teeth found in a generalized placental mammal, and primates have almost universally retained all four types: incisors, canines, premolars, and molars. A shorthand device for showing the number of each kind of tooth is called a **dental formula**. This formula indicates the teeth in one-quarter of the mouth (since the arrangement of teeth is symmetrical and usually the same in upper and lower jaws). For example, the dental formula in New World monkeys for cebids is 2-1-3-3 (2 incisors, 1 canine, 3 premolars, and 3 molars in each quarter of the mouth—a total of 36 teeth); and 2-1-3-2 in marmosets, which typically lose their third molars, a situation perhaps analogous to the loss of third molars, or wisdom teeth, in modern humans. The formula in *all* Old World monkeys, apes, and humans is normally 2-1-2-3—a total of 32 teeth. Most lemur and loris dental formulae are 2-1-3-3 (total of 36), but the highly specialized aye-aye shows (for a primate) remarkable reduction in numbers of teeth

$$\frac{1\text{-}0\text{-}1\text{-}3}{1\text{-}0\text{-}0\text{-}3}{}^{*}$$

for a total of only 18 teeth.

Relative dental formulae are extremely useful indicators of phyletic relationships because they are normally under

*When the formula differs in the lower jaw from that of the upper jaw, both are shown. For example, the tarsier has one less incisor in each half of its lower jaw than it does in its upper jaw:

$$\frac{2\text{-}1\text{-}3\text{-}3}{1\text{-}1\text{-}3\text{-}3}.$$

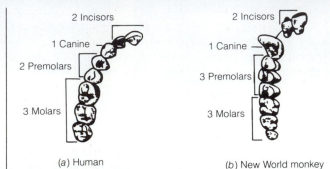

(a) Human   (b) New World monkey

Figure 1
Dental formulae. The number of each kind of tooth is given for one-quarter of the mouth.

tight genotypic control. In other words, environmental influence will usually not alter the tooth formula. In making studies of primate dental phenotypes, we are quite certain, therefore, that our comparisons are based on structural homologies. Thus, similarities in structure (relative numbers of teeth) can be used as indicators of evolutionary similarity.

Dental evidence is extremely important in the interpretation of fossils, since teeth—the hardest component of the body—are the most commonly fossilized part and comprise the vast majority of fossil primate discoveries. In addition, cusp pattern and functional wear can be used to help reconstruct dietary behavior in fossil animals. The identification of diet is of central importance in any attempt to reconstruct the nature of the ecological niche, and ultimately the whole way of life of a fossil form.

In locomotion, all New World forms are basically **quadrupedal**, but some forms (for example, the spider monkey, or the howler monkey) are able to perform considerable arm-swinging suspensory locomotion (see Box 7-3).

Old World Monkeys   After humans, Old World monkeys (Cercopithecoidea) are the most widely distributed of all living primates. They are seen throughout subsaharan Africa and southern Asia, ranging from tropical jungle habitats to semiarid desert and even to seasonally snow-covered areas in northern Japan.

The classification of Old World monkeys reveals how the same root with different endings designates the various levels (taxonomic categories) in a formal classification:

		Ending Indicates Level of Classification
SUPERFAMILY	Cercopithecoidea (sur-ko-pith-e-koid'-ee-uh)	oidea = superfamily
FAMILY	Cercopithecidae (sur-ko-pith-ee'-si-dee)	idae = family
SUBFAMILY	Cercopithecinae (sur-ko-pith-ee'-si-nee)	inae = subfamily
	Colobinae (kol-o-bine'-ee)	
GENUS	Colobus (kol'-o-bus)	genus endings are variable, but -us is common

Figure 7-16
A New World monkey prehensile tail. Shown here in a spider monkey.

Figure 7-17
Distribution of modern Old World monkeys.

BOX 7-3

Tale of the Limbs

Besides teeth (and diet), the other major functional complex most useful in describing both extant (living) and extinct primates relates to the structure of the limbs and the form of locomotion.

A meaningful functional description of locomotion among contemporary primates should include position of the body, which limbs are used, the manner and frequency they are employed, and the nature of the substrate (such as wide tree branch, narrow branch, flat ground). By under-

standing the locomotory behavior of contemporary primates we can analyze their respective limb structures and form meaningful *structural-functional correlations*. With such a perspective, we can then interpret fossil primates and reconstruct their probable locomotory behavior.

A common locomotory classification of contemporary primates with their typical structural correlations is shown below (after Napier and Napier, 1967):

Category	Description of Behavior	Structural Correlates	Examples
A. Vertical clinging and leaping	leaping in trees with propulsion from hindlimbs, clinging with forelimbs for vertical support	elongated hindlimbs, particularly ankle area, upper body held semi-erect	tarsier, galago
B. Quadrupedalism	using all limbs relatively equally; body horizontal	front- and hindlimbs relatively equal length; spine flexible	
1. Slow climbing	slow, cautious climbing; often associated with capturing insects	widely abducted (spread) thumb, reduction of 2nd digit	potto, slow loris
2. Branch running and walking	walking or running on tops of branches, also leaping	generalized quadruped; limbs equal sized; spine flexible	ringtailed lemur, all marmosets, squirrel monkey, guenons
3. Ground running and walking	quadrupedal walking and running on ground, also tree climbing	all limbs elongated, body size usually larger than strictly arboreal species	baboons, most macaques, patas monkey
4. New World "semibrachiation"	usually quadrupedal, some arm-swinging beneath branches with use of prehensile tail; little or no leaping	forelimbs elongated; fingers often curved, thumb reduced	howler monkey, spider monkey
5. Old World "semibrachiation"	usually quadrupedal with arm-swinging and often considerable acrobatic leaping from branch to branch	forelimbs elongated; fingers often curved, thumb reduced	colobines (colobus, langurs)
C. Ape locomotion			
1. True brachiation	acrobatic swinging arm-over-arm along (under) same branch, associated with feeding on small terminal branches	small body size, greatly elongated forelimb, curved fingers, shoulder joint oriented upward, upper body held fairly erect; spine not flexible	gibbon, siamang

Category	Description of Behavior	Structural Correlates	Examples
2. Quadrumanual climbing	slow deliberate climbing using all four limbs for grasping	large body size, hip joint flexible like shoulder, upper body held erect, spine not flexible	orang
3. Knuckle-walking	on ground semiquadrupedal, but hands supported on knuckles; while in trees considerable arm-swinging (gorillas only as subadults)	large body size, elongated fore-limbs; stable wrist joint; upper body held erect; spine shortened and inflexible	chimp, gorilla
D. Bipedalism	strictly terrestrial, standing, strid-ing, running upright; weight al-ternately on single hindlimb	medium-large body size; hind-limb elongated; pelvis altered for support and muscular lever-age; feet altered for stable sup-port with little flexibility, toes shortened; upper body com-pletely erect; head balanced on spine; spine shortened and inflexible	human*

*True bipedalism among the primates is an adaptation *only* of modern humans and our hominid ancestors. Thus, the structural correlates as-sociated with this functional complex are crucial in determining the status of our possible ancestors.

It is important to remember that the above classification is a *simple* one, intended to give a sense of the range of locomotory behaviors among the primates. However, if not viewed care-fully, it can obscure the diversity of locomotory behavior within a species; indeed, that displayed by a single animal.

Some species are, of course, less varied than others in terms of their typical locomotory repertoire. For example, baboons are easily classified as "quadrupeds," as this is mostly what they do. Likewise, humans are "bipeds," since this is pretty much exclusively what we do. Nevertheless, many primate species are quite diverse in how (and where) they move about. David Pilbeam (1986, p. 298) has summarized some of the most sa-lient features of the locomotory behavior of several species, three examples of which are listed below:

	Terrestrial				Arboreal					
	Terrestrial/ arboreal	Biped	Quadruped walk/run	Knuckle walk	Knuckle walk	Quadruped walk/run	Leap sway	Quadruped climb	Arm-swing brachiate	Biped
Baboon	50/50	2	48	—	—	25	20	5	—	—
Orang	—/100	—	—	—	—	13	15	51	21	—
Chimp	50/50	2	—	48	3	11	6	15	10	5

(Figures are relative percentage of behavior. Note especially the marked behavioral diversity of the chimp.)

The same tooth formula, 2-1-2-3 (2 incisors, 1 canine, 2 premolars, 3 molars) found in apes and humans also characterizes Old World monkeys. They are all quadrupedal and mainly arboreal, although some (baboons, for example) are adapted primarily to life on the ground. Whether in trees or on the ground, these monkeys spend a good deal of time sleeping, feeding, and grooming while sitting with their upper bodies held erect. Associated with this universal sitting posture are usually areas of hardened skin on their rear ends called *ischial callosities* that serve as sitting pads. Old World monkeys have a good deal of manual dexterity and most have well-developed tails that are never prehensile (in adults), as is true of many New World forms; the tail, however, does serve a purpose in such functions as communication and balance.

Within the entire group of Old World monkeys (superfamily: Cercopithecoidea), there is only one taxonomically recognized family, Cercopithecidae. Within this family there are in turn two subfamilies, the cercopithecines and the colobines. The former are found mainly in Africa, but some forms (the macaques) are widely distributed in southern Asia. The colobines are found mainly in Asia, but the colobus (kol'-o-bus) monkey (from which the group is named) is widely distributed in tropical Africa.

The cercopithecines are the more generalized of the two subfamilies, showing a more omnivorous dietary adaptation. The colobines, on the other hand, are more limited dietarily, specializing more on mature leaves, a behavior that has led to their designation as "leaf-eating monkeys." As a result of this behavior, structural adaptations for digestion of cellulose (a usually indigestible plant substance) have arisen. These adaptations are reflected in the high crowned molars, sacculated (divided) stomachs, and elongated intestines.

The most common forms of cercopithecines include the highly diversified arboreal guenons (genus: *Cercopithecus*); the slightly larger but still arboreal mangabeys (genus: *Cercocebus*); and the more terrestrial macaques (genus: *Macaca*), baboons—both savanna and hamadryas (genus: *Papio*), forest baboon (genus:

Figure 7-18
A patas monkey *with infant.*

Figure 7-19
A toque macaque *with infant (nursing).*

Figure 7-20
Black-and-white colobus monkeys.

Mandrillus), and the gelada baboon (genus: *Theropithecus*)—as well as the patas monkey (genus: *Erythrocebus*).

The colobus monkey of Africa (genus: *Colobus*) and the various forms of Asian langurs (genus: *Presbytis, Rhinopithecus*, etc.) and the proboscis monkey of Borneo (genus: *Nasalis*) make up the colobine subfamily.

Locomotory behavior among Old World monkeys includes arboreal quadrupedalism in the guenons and mangabeys, arm-swinging and acrobatic leaping in many of the colobines, and terrestrial quadrupedalism in the baboons, macaques, and patas monkey. In the baboons particularly, adaptation to ground living has given rise to larger body size, especially in males. Such a marked difference in body form between males and females of a species is called *sexual dimorphism*. Another striking difference in baboons is canine size, which is much larger in males.

In addition, many Old World monkey females (especially baboons and many macaques) exhibit pronounced external changes, such as swelling and coloration of the genitalia, associated with the **estrous cycle**—a hormonally initiated period of sexual receptivity in female mammals correlated with ovulation.

Because of their general hardiness even under extremely trying circumstances, Old World monkeys (particularly the versatile macaques) have been the preferred laboratory subjects for both biomedical and behavioral experiments. Indeed, much of what we know about the effect of infant and child deprivation has been learned from the Harlows' well-known experiments with rhesus macaques at the University of Wisconsin (Harlow, 1959). (See p. 201.)

However, recent stronger enforcement limiting monkey exportation by the Indian government has made acquisition of rhesus macaques much more difficult and more expensive. Consequently, laboratory researchers routinely use smaller (and also very hardy) New World varieties, especially squirrel monkeys and

Figure 7-21
A female mandrill in estrus. Note the sexual swelling of the genitals.

Figure 7-22
Monkey origins. Model I.

Figure 7-23
Monkey origins. Model II.

Figure 7-24
Distribution of modern Asian apes.

cebus monkeys. Despite what would now appear as large free-ranging populations, many conservationists are concerned for their future given the huge demands (thousands of animals per year) that such exploitation places upon the species.

Monkeys, Old and New World: A Striking Case of Parallel Evolution   We have mentioned several differences between monkeys in the Old World compared to those in the New World. However, the striking fact remains that they are *all* monkeys. By this statement, we mean that they all are adapted to a similar (primarily arboreal) way of life. With the exception of the South American night monkey (*Aotus*), they are diurnal and all are social, usually fairly omnivorous, and quadrupedal, though with variations of this general locomotory pattern (see Box 7-3).

These similarities are all the more striking when we consider that Old and New World monkeys have gone their separate evolutionary paths for tens of millions of years. In fact, a noted primatologist, Dr. E. L. Simons (1969), suggests the split may have occurred more than 50 m.y.a. Both forms of monkey would then have evolved independently from separate prosimian ancestors. The current consensus among researchers, however, disputes this claim (Hoffstetter, 1972; Ciochon and Chiarelli, 1980) and postulates both Old and New World monkeys arose in Africa from a common monkey ancestor and later reached South America by rafting over. (Note: South America and Africa were considerably closer together earlier in the Cenozoic. In addition, migration over water barriers may have been facilitated by "island hopping" over a chain of volcanic islands.)

In either case, what is most remarkable is that the two forms of monkey have not diverged more than they have—given the time depth of separate evolutionary history in the two hemispheres. What we see today in the diverse arboreal adaptations of monkeys is then a result of **parallel evolution** (see p. 149). Similar ecological selective forces, mainly in tropical arboreal environments, led to structural evolution in different but parallel directions. The result is that the same grade of primate we today recognize as "monkey" evolved in both New and Old Worlds.

Grade V: Hominoids

The superfamily Hominoidea includes "lesser" apes (gibbons and siamangs), great apes (orangutans, gorillas, chimpanzees), and humans. Classifying humans with the apes is not an arbitrary device, for it indicates our close structural similarities, as well as shared evolutionary history. This close similarity was noted by Tyson at the end of the seventeenth century and was forcefully restated by Huxley and Darwin in the nineteenth century. As this classification indicates, we and the apes are more closely related to each other than *either* is to an Old World monkey. In fact, many primatologists feel that the relationship between humans and great apes is so close that they are often grouped within a single family (Dene et al., 1976; Szalay and Delson, 1979). (See Table 7-1.)

The structural similarities we share with the apes are numerous but most importantly include absence of a tail, generally large body size, shortened deep trunk, stable spine, and the position and musculature of the shoulder joint (the latter adapted particularly for suspensory locomotion).

The Gibbon and Siamang The gibbon and closely related siamang (Hylobatidae) are today found in the southeastern tropical areas of Asia. These animals are the smallest of the apes, with a long, slender body weighing only about thirteen pounds in the gibbon and about twenty-five pounds in the larger siamang.

The most distinctive structural feature of the hylobatids is related to their functional adaptation for **brachiation**. Consequently, they have extremely long arms, long, permanently curved fingers, and powerful shoulder muscles. This highly specialized locomotory adaptation may be related to feeding behavior while hanging beneath branches.

The Orangutan The orang (genus: *Pongo*) is found today only in heavily forested areas on the Indonesian islands of Borneo and Sumatra. Due to poaching by humans in the past and the continuing commercial encroachment on its habitats, the orang faces imminent extinction. Such a loss would be tragic on several counts, especially because little is currently known of these mysterious red giants of the forest. Orangs are slow, cautious climbers whose whole locomotory behavior can best be described as a **quadrumanual** adaptation—a tendency to use all four limbs for grasping and support. They are large animals with pronounced sexual dimorphism (males weigh about 150 pounds and females about half that). Orangs were thought to be exclusively arboreal, but recent evidence (Galdikas, 1979) suggests they (especially males) occasionally come to the ground to traverse fairly long distances.

The Gorilla The largest of all living primates, the gorilla (family: Pongidae; genus: *Gorilla*) today is confined to forested areas in West Africa and the great

HYLOBATIDAE
(Hy-lo-bat'-i-dee)

BRACHIATION
Arm-over-arm suspensory locomotion beneath branches.

QUADRUMANUAL
quadru: four
manual: hand
Using all four limbs for grasping during locomotion.

Figure 7-25
Siamang.

Figure 7-26
(a) *Male orangutan;* (b) *orangutan climbing quadrumanously.*

Chimpanzees: any area in color

||||| Gorillas: only in hatched areas

Figure 7-27
Distribution of modern African apes.

Figure 7-28
A male lowland gorilla.

lakes area of East Africa. This species exhibits marked sexual dimorphism, with males weighing up to 400 pounds in the wild and females around 200 pounds. Due to their very large adult weight, gorillas are almost completely terrestrial, adopting a semiquadrupedal (knuckle-walking) posture on the ground. Their forelimbs are elongated, though not so much as in gibbons, their upper bodies are normally held semierect, and their arms possess considerable mobility. Consequently, there are numerous structural modifications: a flattened (front-to-back) and broadened (side-to-side) chest; a shortened, more stable spine (compared to quadrupedal monkeys); longer clavicles; and flexible, powerful shoulders. The wrist joint is also modified to support the considerable weight of the upper body during knuckle-walking. In addition, gorillas have brains more complexly organized than monkeys or gibbons, thus allowing for more learned behavior. Once considered a wild and savage beast, the gorilla has been shown by field studies to be a shy, usually gentle vegetarian (Schaller, 1963; Fossey, 1970). Recent reports, however, have shown that—like many other primates—gorillas fairly frequently attack and kill other members of their species, particularly infants (Fossey, 1981).

The Chimpanzee Probably the best known and most loved of all the nonhuman primates is the chimpanzee (family: Pongidae; genus: *Pan*). Often misunderstood because of their displays within zoos and carnival sideshows, the chimps' true nature did not come to light until long hours of fieldwork in their natural environments provided a reliable picture. Chimps are found today in

equatorial Africa stretching in a broad belt from the Atlantic Ocean in the west to Lake Tanganyika in the east.

There are actually two species of chimpanzee: the "common" chimpanzee (*Pan troglodytes*) and the bonobo or pygmy chimp (*Pan paniscus*). The bonobo is smaller than most common chimps (though some *P. troglodytes* are almost as small as the bonobo) with several intriguing differences in social behavior as well. Today, the bonobo's range is extremely restricted. It is found only in Central Zaire, where it is greatly in danger of extinction.

Chimpanzees are in many ways structurally quite similar to gorillas, with corresponding limb proportions and thorax (chest) shape as well as specific features of the upper limb and wrist joint. This similarity is due to the likeness in their mode of locomotion (knuckle-walking) while on the ground. Indeed, many authorities (for example, Buettner-Janusch, 1973) consider chimps and gorillas as members of a single genus (*Pan gorilla* for the gorilla; *Pan troglodytes* for the common chimp). However, the ecological adaptations of the chimp and gorilla differ, since chimps spend a great deal of time arm-swinging in the trees and feeding primarily on fruit. Conversely, gorillas are almost exclusively terrestrial vegetarians, consuming such vegetative matter as roots, shoots, and bark.

Like the brain of the gorilla, the chimpanzee brain is highly developed, and the learning capabilities of these animals are well known to visitors to animal shows as well as to scientific investigators.

Humans Humans (family: Hominidae; genus: *Homo*) belong to the one remaining genus of the superfamily Hominoidea, a genus that today consists of only one species, *Homo sapiens*. Our primate heritage is shown again and again in the structure of our body: our dependence on vision; our lack of reliance on olfactory (smell) cues; and our flexible limbs and grasping hands are all long rooted in our primate, arboreal past. Indeed, among the primates, we show in many ways the most developed set of primate characteristics. For example, the development of our cerebral cortex and reliance on learned behavior with resulting complexity in social behavior are but elaborations of long-established primate trends.

As we will discuss in the next chapter, there are several features of humans and our most immediate ancestors that distinguish us from other primates. However, probably the most distinctive, and certainly that most clearly observable in our earliest (hominid) ancestors is our unique manner of locomotion. The striding, bipedal gait with alternating support placed on a single hindlimb has required significant structural modifications in the pelvis and leg. By isolating similar structural modifications in the remains of fossil animals, we are able to distinguish our closely related or direct ancestors.

KARYOTYPE
The characteristic number, size, and pattern of the chromosomes that are distinctive for particular species.

(a)

(b)

Figure 7-29
Chimpanzees. (a) male; (b) female.

Primate Chromosomes, Proteins, and DNA

The classification of primates used thus far in this chapter has employed the traditional approach of looking for homologies in morphological traits. However, another relatively new perspective with enormous potential for helping to clarify taxonomic problems compares **karyotypes** (chromosome numbers, shapes, banding patterns), proteins, and even roughly correlates the DNA code itself.

Figure 7-30
Fusion of two small chromosomes. This fusion produces one large chromosome (human chromosome number 2?).

The usefulness of this approach is immediately obvious. When we compare outward morphology, such as limb proportions and dental formulae, we are comparing phenotypes, usually far removed from their underlying genetic basis. However, what we are really after in the construction of classification schemes are homologies, traits based on common evolutionary descent. In other words, we want to compare traits that are inherited—those coded directly in the genotype.

Direct protein products of DNA, such as hemoglobin and serum proteins (found in the blood), are excellent indicators of homologies. If two species of primates are systematically similar in their protein structure, we can infer their DNA sequences are also similar. When two species share similar DNA, that means both inherited the same blueprint (with minor revisions) from a common ancestor. Thus, we have *direct* indicators of real homologies. Two primates that superficially resemble one another (some New World and Old World monkeys, for example) may in fact not be closely related at all. Using outward morphology alone may be confusing due to unknown effects from parallel evolution. But such evidence as biochemical data and karyotype comparisons avoids these pitfalls, and indeed shows Old and New World monkeys as genetically (and evolutionarily) quite distinct.

Primatologists utilizing these techniques have, in conjunction with biochemists, in the last few years added considerable insight into our classifications of the primate order. A point worthy of mention: In most cases, biochemical evidence has reaffirmed the taxonomies constructed from comparative morphological studies (thereby supplying an extremely important independent source of data). When contradictions with traditional taxonomies have cropped up, much needed new knowledge has been gained. For example, classifying the orang with the African great apes superficially makes good sense since their outward body structures appear similar. Biochemical evidence, however, shows that both Asian apes (orangs and gibbons) are quite distinct from chimps and gorillas. Since our classifications are designed to reflect evolutionary relationships, they will have to be revised in the future to accord with this new information. (See Table 7-1.)

The way the various chromosomal and biochemical techniques are performed requires considerable technological sophistication, but their applications are straightforward. For example, two species can be compared for karyotype. The more closely two species are related, the closer their karyotypes should be. When one looks at the chromosomes of the hominoids, it is readily apparent that humans and the great apes are all quite similar, with gibbons and siamangs having the most distinctive (i.e., derived) pattern (Stanyon and Chiarelli, 1982; Mai, 1983).

Among the large-bodied hominoids, the orang karyotype is the most conservative, with humans and the African apes displaying more derived features. It is interesting to note that the fossil data (which we'll take up in Chapter 10) also now suggests that orangs are probably the most conservative (i.e., primitive) of the large hominoids.

Within the human/gorilla/chimp group there are a tremendous number of similarities of the structural arrangement and banding patterns of almost all the chromosomes. A relatively small number of alterations are required to transform all three living species from a theoretical ancestor (Yunis and Prakash, 1982).

The exact sequence of evolutionary relationships among humans and the African great apes is still in some dispute. Some tentative chromosomal data have suggested that humans and chimps share a more recent ancestry after separating from gorillas (Yunis and Prakash, 1982). A more controlled study, however, with consideration of within-species variation of karyotype (Stanyon and Chiarelli, 1982), has supported the more traditional branching order, where humans and *both* African apes diverge first—followed later by a separation of chimps and gorillas.

Detailed protein structures can be compared, as between chimp and human hemoglobin, by isolating the amino acid sequences. Comparisons between humans and the African great apes for the approximately half dozen proteins analyzed in this manner show striking similarities; they are either identical or show a difference of only one or two amino acids in the entire sequence (as you will recall, the hemoglobin beta chain is 146 amino acids long).

Another method used to contrast proteins in different species is not as precise as a detailed protein analysis but is less time consuming and less costly. By measuring the strength of reaction to specially prepared antisera, similarities in proteins are calibrated on a relative scale, indicating *antigenic distance*. This approach, developed by Vincent Sarich and Allan Wilson at the University of California, Berkeley, has enabled many more proteins to be compared among a wide variety of different primate species. The results again generally tally favorably with traditional classifications (see Table 7-4).

Moreover, differences in DNA strands themselves can be compared using an elaborate technique called DNA hybridization. Scientists have recently performed some remarkable experiments in which double strands of DNA are artificially separated in two different species and then recombined into a new molecule, a hybrid DNA unlike anything nature ever concocted. The genetic (and evolutionary) similarity of the two species is then calculated by measuring

Table 7-4 *Biochemically Determined Distances between Humans and Other Animals*

	Amino Acid Distance	Antigenic Distance	DNA Distance
Human—chimp	0.27	1.0	1.8
Human—gorilla	0.65	0.8	2.3
Human—orang	2.78	2.0	4.9
Human—gibbon	2.38	2.6	4.9
Human—macaque	3.89	3.6	—
Human—spider monkey	8.69	7.6	—
Human—tarsier	—*	8.8	—
Human—loris	11.36	11.2	42.0
Human—tree shrew	—	12.6	—
Primates—other placentals	—	12.11–14.91	—
Placentals—marsupials	—	15.83	—

All these figures are averages drawn from numerous individual comparisons. Each scale should be interpreted not as absolute measures, but only as *relative* ones. In addition, the scalings for each of the three sets of comparisons are independent of one another.

*Line (—) indicates data undetermined.

Source: Data abstracted from Goodman and Lasker, 1975.

the number of mismatched base pairs along the hybrid sequence (in other words, places where the two sides of the molecule are not complementary: A with T, G with C, etc.).

As in the other techniques discussed above, DNA hybridization has reaffirmed the basic tenets of primate classification. Indeed, better than any of the other approaches, DNA hybridization has shown *how* close genetically we and the African great apes are. A recent systematic application of this relatively new and fascinating technique (Sibley and Ahiquist, 1984) has shown that humans and chimps are closer genetically than two similar species of gibbons. Or, for that matter, humans and chimps are more similar than zebra and horse or goat and sheep. On the basis of these results, it would be entirely consistent to classify human and chimps (perhaps, gorillas as well) within the *same* genus. In other words, we would continue to be called, *Homo sapiens*, while the chimp would be classed as *Homo troglodytes*. Certainly, not everyone is prepared to accept this terminology; nevertheless, it underlines the basic genetic/evolutionary facts.

Finally, the revolution in molecular biology brought about by recombinant DNA research has now made it possible to directly sequence the nucleotides of humans and other organisms (Goodman, et al., 1983). As a result—when this new technique has been more widely applied—we should be able to ascertain even more unambiguously the precise genetic/evolutionary relationships among the primates.

In addition, these nucleotide sequence data will inform us concerning the frequency of "neutral" mutations and (when calibrated with fossil data) may elucidate whether primate evolution has been more characterized by gradual or punctuated modes of change (see pp. 91–93).

Summary

Primates are an order of placental mammals characterized by their generalized limb structure, dependence on vision, lack of reliance on smell, developed brain (particularly cerebral cortex), and complex social organizations. All these evolutionary trends have developed, or at least have been elaborated, as a direct result of adaptation to an arboreal environment.

In addition to the primitive placental mammal—tree shrew grade (Grade I, not a true primate)—living primates today represent four major grades of evolution that correspond to various stages of primate evolution over the last several million years. These grades are:

I. Lemurs and lorises
II. Tarsiers
III. Monkeys (New World and Old World)
IV. Hominoids (apes and humans)

We are a primate and our ancestors have been primates for at least 70 million years. Only by looking at humans *as a primate* can we hope to understand the kind of animal we are and how we came to be this way.

Questions for Review

1. How are primates similar to other placental mammals?
2. Discuss how binocular vision, prehensility, and an expanded cerebral cortex are adaptations for an arboreal niche.
3. What are the various superfamilies of the primate order? To which one do humans belong?
4. Discuss the geographic distribution and ecological adaptations of contemporary prosimians.
5. What are the most important differences between prosimians and anthropoids?
6. How do monkeys in the Old and New Worlds exhibit parallel evolution?
7. How do teeth reflect evolutionary relationships?
8. What are some important relationships between limb structure and locomotion in contemporary primates?
9. In what ways are humans typical primates?
10. How does biochemical evidence give indication of homologies? Why are effects due to parallel evolution more likely to cloud the picture for morphological traits than for biochemical traits?

Primate Behavior

CONTENTS

Primates in the Laboratory

In the Issue for Chapter 7 (p. 154), we discussed the critical problems of continued survival faced by primates in the wild. We will return to this crucial issue later in this chapter. Indeed, the conservation of primates in their natural habitats could be regarded as *the* issue in contemporary primate field studies. As anthropologists have chiefly been the researchers who study primates in the field (see p. 191), it is of central importance to ponder whether, in the next century, any primates will be left to study.

A major drain on wild populations has been their capture for use in medical research laboratories. In the recent past, the numbers have been staggering. In the late 1960s and 1970s, an estimated 60,000 to 80,000 primates were trapped *annually* in the wild to supply labs in the United States alone. Indeed, in the development and testing of polio vaccines, more than one million rhesus monkeys were used!

As a result of this huge drain on their indigenous rhesus monkey populations (coupled with concern for humane treatment), the Indian government has recently moved to severely restrict export. Even though species such as macaques are no longer as readily available, capture of nonhuman primates for laboratories still continues at a rapid level. Now, however, varieties of New World species are the chosen targets (including squirrel monkeys, cebus monkeys, and a variety of marmosets). No accurate estimates of numbers captured are available, but for the labs in the United States, Europe, and Japan there are surely tens of thousands of animals seized every year.

Given this steady loss of wild animals—in addition to the other problems faced by free-ranging nonhuman primates (especially habitat destruction; see p. 214)—it is obvious that continued use of *any* species cannot be long sustained. Recognizing this fact, federal research agencies in the United States have sought to establish breeding colonies in North America. However, up to now, the annual supply of captive-born animals falls far short of the numbers required (less than 10% of the primates needed).

A more basic ethical question remains: Even if we could supply all the nonhuman primates sought by laboratories, is all the proposed research really necessary? And, if so, how should the animals be treated in these facilities?

Much of the use of animals (primates and other species as well) is not within state-of-the-art or life-saving contexts. Indeed, the pharmaceutical industry has used many primates to test a host of "elective" therapies and even a variety of cosmetic products.

The answers are not easy, and we do not wish to advocate an overly strident position. *Some* research is obviously essential for human well-being. But we do ask that what is considered "essential" be appraised more critically than has been done in the past.

Those primates who find their way

into most research facilities face a very unhappy future. Because they are easier to capture and maintain, young animals have frequently been used. We know that immature primates (human and nonhuman) require intimate physical contact and care from their mothers. For monkeys, this period of crucial dependency lasts two to four years, and, in great apes, it can extend for eight years. In addition, as highly social animals, primates grow up in an environment rich in social stimuli from age-mates and other members of the social group (a situation also demonstrated as essential for normal psychological development—see p. 201).

Nevertheless, young primates are frequently removed from their mothers and peers, and are maintained in complete isolation. Often in painfully small cages, in darkness and solitude, these animals live out their lives. Sometimes imprisonment is for a short term. For other experiments, though, particularly those involving infectious diseases, such as hepatitis or AIDS, confinement may extend for years, or even decades. In such a deprived environment, captive primates display a variety of abnormal behaviors, such as pacing constantly about their cage, pulling out their hair, biting themselves, or incessantly rocking back-and-forth. Humans in similar circumstances who display quite similar behavioral abnormalities are usually termed "severely disturbed" or "insane."

In response to these conditions, a variety of legislative measures have been considered by the U.S. Congress and by numerous state legislatures as well. In Congress, several bills have included language specifying "procedures to insure that animal pain and distress is minimized" and, in the case of primates, to consider "the psychological well-being of the animals."

In the United States, the leading financial sponsor of research utilizing nonhuman primates is the National Institutes of Health (NIH). In the past year they have more intensively consulted with those primatologists (most notably, Jane Goodall) who can provide them with better information regarding the social needs of primates.

Assuming some research will continue, what can be done? First of all, the issue of minimal cage size can be addressed. A research lab outside Washington, D.C., recently was found to house two young chimpanzees together in a cage 24 inches by 24 inches by 22 inches. Here, there was not even enough room to stand up, much less move about! Secondly, except where isolation is absolutely necessary for experimental purposes, primates should be kept in a *social* environment. For example, a lab in Europe has instituted measures so that the primate lab subjects are daily brought together in a common area, allowed to interact and play. And, finally, those individuals charged with the responsibility for care of captive animals can be recruited partly on the basis of awareness and compassion. Moreover, their training can be much more specifically oriented toward learning about the psychosocial requirements of their charges.

All of this will not be done easily. In addition, it will cost more money than current funds provide. Most importantly, however, public awareness must first be heightened.

Introduction

How can we better understand human behavior? Observing an urbanized industrialized society such as ours will not tell us very much of our hominid heritage. After all, we have been urbanized for only a few thousand years, and the industrial revolution is merely a few centuries old, barely a flicker in evolutionary time. Consequently, to understand what behavioral components may have shaped our evolution, we need a perspective broader than that which our own culture supplies. Since little is known about early hominid behavior, we study the behavior of contemporary animals adapted to environments similar to those of early hominids in the hope of gaining insight into early hominid evolution.

In this chapter, we place nonhuman primate behavior in the context of its possible relationship to human behavior; that is, we address the question: Does the study of nonhuman primates serve as a window on (or model for) human behavior? Or are nonhuman primates so different in behavior from hominids that the uniqueness of the latter derives little from the former?

Behavior and Human Origins

What does it mean to be human? There are several *physical* characteristics, such as adaptations for bipedal locomotion and enlarged brain, that characterize humans and—to varying extents—our hominid ancestors. But from a strictly structural point of view, we are not really that unique compared to other primates, especially when compared with the great apes. In patterns of dentition, bone development, muscle structure, and so forth, we and the other hominoids are very similar, reflecting a fairly recent shared ancestry. (Probably no more than 7 or 8 m.y. at most separate us from the African great apes.) Indeed, in the nonrepeated portions of DNA, humans and chimpanzees are 98% identical. So what, precisely, is it that distinguishes the human animal?*

Quite clearly, it is behavioral attributes that most dramatically set humans apart. Human culture is our strategy for coping with life's challenges. No other primate even comes close to the human ability to modify environments. Communication through symbolic language is yet another uniquely human characteristic (see pp. 249–254 for a discussion of "language" in great apes). In addition, several other features differentiate humans from the majority of other primates. These are summarized below, but keep in mind that any one of the following may be found in one or another primate species. While all of these are part of human behavior, there is no other primate species of which this may be said. For example, humans are bipedal; however, apes occasionally walk bipedally, but not regularly. All primates learn, as do all mammals, but none learn nearly as much as humans, and so forth.

*"Our species is unique because, in only 35,000 years or so, we have revolutionized the face of the Earth. We have created entirely new environments for ourselves, have changed the lives of animals, and have the power to threaten the existence of life on our planet" (Passingham, 1982, p. 21).

Humans are bipedal.

Humans live in permanent bisexual social groups with males often bonded to females.

Humans have large brains relative to body weight and are capable of *complex* learning.

Partly as a consequence of neurological reorganization, humans make *highly advanced* use of symbolic language.

Also related to neurological developments and bipedality, *cultural* response has become the *central* hominid adaptive strategy.

Humans obtain food through some male/female division of labor; moreover, food is actively transported back to a base camp (home) for purposes of sharing.

There is a relaxation of the estrous cycle and concealed ovulation in humans, so that females can be sexually receptive throughout the year.

These traits are fairly characteristic of all modern humans. Moreover, much of this behavioral complex is thought to be a good *baseline* for the early stages of hominid emergence. In fact, behavioral reconstructions are often central to theories explaining how hominids came to be hominids in the first place.

A recent comprehensive reconstruction of the factors influencing human origins has been proposed by C. Owen Lovejoy (1981).* The Lovejoy model attempts to integrate the behavioral and structural modifications that prevailed during the earliest stages of hominid emergence (10–5 m.y.a.). A "prime mover," according to Lovejoy, was the selective advantage of increased male parental investment.

Lovejoy sees ecological strategies of early hominids based on some *division of labor*, where males and females exploited slightly different resources. This pattern was elaborated further as males ranged farther away (particularly in search of game), while females remained closer to a central rendezvous point, which eventually became a base camp. With females staying closer to a fixed base, they would avoid carrying their infants long distances, thus reducing infant mortality. While females are thought to have ranged closer to camp, gathering wild plant foods and perhaps small mammals, they alone presumably could not provide sufficient subsistence for themselves and several young. The solution, Lovejoy believes, lay in male provisioning—bringing food back to the base camp for purposes of sharing. This key aspect concerning active transport of food to a central point in order to be shared is not seen in any other primate. The same idea had also been put forth by Glynn Isaac (1976, 1978) as a significant influence on early human emergence.

With males investing more, females could raise more young than would otherwise be the case. Thus, birth spacing could be reduced, and hominid males and females behaving in this way would consequently increase their reproductive success.

Several males returning to the females at the base camp might encourage male-male competition, but this could possibly be diffused by the development of

---

*Lovejoy's model is given simply as one of a number of scholarly suggestions of human origins. Many anthropologists disagree with this interpretation and organization of the data. The authors do not necessarily agree with Lovejoy's point of view.

SOCIAL BEHAVIOR
Exhibiting gregariousness, sociability. The
behavior of animals that live together in, and
interact as, a group consisting of adults and
young of both sexes.

POLYGYNY
(po-lyj'-y-nee)
poly: much, many
gyn: female
One male and two or more females in a mating relationship.

one-to-one male/female bonding; i.e., a monogamous relationship (an idea championed by Desmond Morris, 1967).

Bipedality* (probably the first major distinction of hominids) would have evolved because the male carrying food to his female would have to do so bipedally. Bipedality in the female would be adaptive because she could carry an infant in one arm, and provision herself with the other.

For this system to work, it would be necessary for the male to carry food to his female throughout the year. He would have to be permanently attracted to her, not just at the time of estrus. This could be arranged through the development of permanent features on the female's body, such as hair, skin, shape, and prominent breasts, which would permanently attract the male and keep him interested the year-round (also proposed by Morris). According to Lovejoy's model, distinctive human traits, such as bipedality, pair bonding, food sharing, and sexual and reproductive behavior, are thus explained.

The Lovejoy model proposes a comprehensive and internally consistent explanation of human origins. However, it is not a scientific theory, since it cannot be framed into testable hypotheses. More appropriately, Lovejoy's assertions (just as those of others before him—Desmond Morris, Robert Ardrey, and so forth) could be termed a *scenario*, a speculative reconstruction. Since **social behavior** does not fossilize (except for some tantalizing hints—see Chapter 11), it is unlikely that we will be able to fully reconstruct the details of early hominid biosocial evolution. If anything, the physical evidence of the early hominids themselves (Chapter 12) suggests that some of the central premises in Lovejoy's scenario are probably wrong.

However, the Lovejoy model is extremely useful in highlighting some of the major differences between humans and other primates. Sometime during the course of human evolution, the complex of features discussed in this scenario did emerge. We mainly disagree with Lovejoy, though, concerning the *sequence* and *timing* of these behavioral modifications. Unlike Lovejoy, we do not believe it likely (or even probable) that very early hominids were paired monogamously. The other developments—bipedalism, increased meat exploitation, food sharing, and greater parental investment (by males, too, but indirectly)—could very well all have proceeded in a **polygynously** mating early hominid society similar to the vast majority of living primates.

Nonhuman Primates

Modern apes and humans last shared an ancestor in common somewhere between 14–8 m.y.a., according to some specialists, or 8–4 m.y.a., according to others. Researchers believe that ape behavior has changed since then, but not nearly as much as the behavior of hominids, who developed culture as their strategy of adaptation. Therefore, if we are interested in what hominid behavior might have been like before culture became a significant factor, and if we wish to know what behaviors may have led hominids to become dependent on culture,

*There are other explanations for the origin of bipedality. Tanner, for example, suggests that bipedality may have been the result of sexual selection, a theme developed by Darwin. Females may have been attracted to males who exhibited bipedalism. Obvious visual cues, such as male genitalia, "could have attracted female attention and action" (1981, pp. 165–166).

we may find clues in the behavior of our closest relatives, the nonhuman primates.

The social behavior of nonhuman primates may be viewed as a simplified model of human behavior. The shorter life span of nonhuman primates allows us to follow their behavior through developmental stages with more ease than a similar study of human behavior would provide. As intimated, nonhuman primate behavior provides clues to, or suggests ideas about, what early hominid behavior may have been like. This approach emphasizes correlating particular social structures of given animals with attributes of their habitats, since all living organisms must adapt to their environment (Figs. 8-1 and 8-2). Such observations may offer hints to the environmental pressures involved and may ultimately lead to comprehending the factors that led to human emergence (see pp. 193–197).

Studies of nonhuman primates also assist with present human behavioral problems. Humans are *not* monkeys or apes, of course, but similarities do exist. For example, the way human infants learn to love and bond to mother and then family is reflected in the infant behavior patterns of monkeys and apes. It is, after all, possible that "The more we can learn about the evolutionary history and adaptations of other primate forms, the more we will know about the processes which shaped our own species" (Lancaster, 1975, p. 5).

Species of primates are numerous, and their behavior varies a good deal. Nevertheless, there are characteristics common to most, if not all, primates. Most primates live in tropical or semitropical regions, but a few, such as the Japanese macaque and some langurs, have adapted to cold weather. Although

Figure 8-1
These baboons have adapted quadrupedally to a terrestrial savanna life.

DIURNAL
Active during the day.

CREPUSCULAR
(kre-pus'-kew-ler)
creper: dark, dusty
Active at twilight or dawn.

NOCTURNAL
Active at night.

FREE-RANGING
Applied to animals living in their natural habitat.

they vary, primates are mainly **diurnal**, some are **crepuscular** and others, especially among prosimians, are **nocturnal**. Relatively few nonhuman primates are terrestrial—savanna baboons and gorillas are the best known; most others are arboreal. Intelligence, a difficult concept to define, is another characteristic common to primates, and it is generally conceded that all primates are more intelligent than most, if not all, other mammals.

Living in social groups (see Box 8-1) is one of the major characteristics of primates, who solve their major adaptive problems within this social context. For other animals, "mating, feeding, sleeping, growth of the individual, and protection from predators are usually matters for the solitary individual to solve, but for . . . primates they are most often performed in a social context" (Lancaster, 1975, p. 12).

Many different patterns of social groupings exist among the primates. Typically, the primate social group includes members of all ages and of both sexes, a composition that does not vary significantly during the annual cycle. This situation differs from that of most mammals, whose adult males and females associate only during the breeding season, and whose young do not remain with the adults after reaching puberty.

Because they remain together over a long period of time, members of the specific primate group learn to know each other. They learn—as they must—how to respond to a variety of actions that may be threatening, cooperative, or indifferent. In such social groups, individuals must be able to evaluate a situation before acting. Evolutionarily speaking, this would have placed selective pressure on social intelligence which, in turn, would select for brains that could assess such situations and store the information. One of the results of such selection would be the evolution of proportionately larger and more complex brains, especially in the higher primates.

Figure 8-2
Chimpanzee family, a long-term cohesive unit. These individuals associate often throughout their lives (see Chapter 9).

BOX 8-1

Types of Nonhuman Primate Social Groups*

1. *One-male.* A single adult male, several adult females, and their offspring. This is the commonest primate mating structure, in which only one male actively breeds (Jolly, 1985). Usually formed by a male or males joining a kin group of females. Females usually form the permanent nucleus of the group. Examples: guenons, orangs, gorillas, some pottos, some spider monkeys, patas.

*These are called breeding groups by Jolly and permanent groupings by Napier and Napier. There are also other groupings, such as foraging groups, hunting groups, all female or male groups, and so on. Like humans, nonhuman primates do not always maintain one kind of group; single male groups may sometimes form multimale groups and vice versa. The gelada and hamadryas baboons, for example, are listed here as one-male groups but "form herds of 100 or more at night when they move towards the safety of the steep cliffs where they sleep" (Napier and Napier, 1985, p. 61). Also variability is seen in other forms, for example, red colobus monkeys (see p. 196).

2. *Multimale.* Several adult males, several adult females, and their young. Several of the males reproduce. The presence of several males in the group may lead to tension and to a dominance hierarchy. Examples: some lemurs, macaques, mangabeys, savanna baboons, vervets, squirrel monkeys, spider monkeys, chimpanzees.

3. *Family,* or *monogamous.* A mated pair and their young. Usually arboreal, minimal sexual dimorphism, frequently territorial. Adults usually do not tolerate other adults of the same sex. Not found among great apes, and least common of the breeding structures among nonhuman primates. Examples: gibbons, indris, tarsiers, titis, owl monkeys, pottos, some marmosets.

SOURCE:
Jolly, 1985; Napier and Napier, 1985.

Primate Field Studies

While other disciplines, such as psychology and zoology, have long been concerned with nonhuman primates, the study of these animals in their *natural* habitats has primarily become a focus of anthropology. Early work—that done before World War II—was especially stimulated through the influence of the American psychologist Robert Yerkes, who in the late 1920s and 1930s sent students out to the field to study gorillas, chimpanzees, and howler monkeys. It was the last of these studies by Clarence Ray Carpenter (along with his work on gibbons) that stands out particularly as a hallmark of early primate field investigations.

American anthropologists became vitally involved somewhat later—the 1950s—following the lead established by Sherwood Washburn who, with his colleague, Irven DeVote, carried out a pioneering study of savanna baboons in the late 1950s. At about the same time, Phyllis Dolhinow was researching langurs in India and George Schaller was collecting data on mountain gorillas in Africa. And, of course, there is the famous research that Jane Goodall began with chimpanzees in 1960 (see p. 239). In addition, primate studies were also being pursued in the 1950s by Japanese anthropologists, who actively began their long-term study of Japanese macaques in 1952 (see p. 246). They have since extended their fieldwork to include numerous other species elsewhere in Asia and in Africa.

The key aspect of these field studies is that they attempt to collect and synthesize information on **free-ranging** animals. That is, the animals are in their "nat-

Figure 8-3
Black-and-white colubus monkeys high up in the forest canopy. Can you spot the animals? Imagine trying to recognize them as individuals!

Figure 8-4
Rhesus monkeys. Part of the large colony on Cayo Santiago Island.

ural" settings in which they travel, feed, mate, and so forth without severe constraints imposed by humans.

Several points, however, must be kept in mind. Free-ranging does not necessarily imply that these animals remain uninfluenced by human activities. It is highly unlikely that there is a single group of nonhuman primates anywhere in the world that has not experienced some human interference. Indeed, the incredibly rapid destruction of tropical rainforests (see pp. 214–217) now threatens the very existence of most primates. Moreover, while "free-ranging" implies that animals move about on their own volition to find food, in several cases (Japanese macaque studies, Jane Goodall's work at Gombe Stream) the animals have been **artificially provisioned** by the observers. This means, of course, that some of their food comes from other than normal or natural sources. We would also expect that the different levels of provisioning employed would affect the free-ranging behavior of the animals in foraging and other activities.

Why, then, is artificial provisioning practiced? The answer relates to the difficulties involved in following free-ranging primates. As discussed in Chapter 7, most species of nonhuman primates live in the tropical rainforests of the Americas, Africa, and Asia. Dense foliage and ground cover severely inhibit the movement of observers as they attempt to follow their study animals. Perhaps even worse, these animals are usually high up in the forest canopy, obscured from vision, and are often moving rapidly. Then there are almost invariably numerous individuals in a social group who can be expected to exhibit highly individualistic behaviors. The problem: How does one recognize individuals under such field conditions? In fact, individuals frequently cannot be recognized accurately, so that the best that can be accomplished is to record the sex and age of the animals. Some provisioning of the study animals draws them into the open, where they can be observed and recognized.

Because of these problems, the most systematic information thus far collected on free-ranging animals comes from species that spend considerable time on the ground (including langurs, gorillas, chimps) and most especially those species that travel and feed frequently in open (i.e., mostly treeless) country (for example, macaques, baboons, vervet monkeys, patas monkeys). Note that the selection and emphasis on certain species in this and the next chapter reflect this research bias.

Another research tack pursued by some anthropologists involves studying primates not in their natural habitats but rather in large provisioned colonies, where at least some movement, group dynamics, etc. are possible. Probably the best example of this type of research is the long-term study of rhesus macaques conducted on Cayo Santiago Island off the coast of Puerto Rico. First established in 1938, the island population now totals close to 1,000 individuals (Richard, 1985).

Despite significant gaps in our knowledge about many aspects of primate behavior, we nevertheless presently have field data on more than 100 nonhuman primate species. The information from this fascinating and rapidly advancing discipline of primatology forms the remainder of this chapter.

The Ecology of Nonhuman Primates

For those anthropologists who study free-ranging primates, the key considerations have always been (1) to characterize the nature of the animals' environments and (2) to hypothesize how these environments shape primate social behavior.

Early on, researchers routinely recorded the types of food eaten, the distances traveled to get to food/water/sleeping sites, the size of groups, the composition of groups, and so on. In the 1970s, an emerging perspective called *socioecology* grew out of this approach and looked at such factors as the following regarding the possible effects on primate social groups:

1. Quantity and quality of different kinds of food (caloric value, digestive energy required, net value to the animals)
2. Activity patterns: Are the animals nocturnal or diurnal?
3. Distribution of food resources (widely spread or tightly packed?)
4. Distribution of water
5. Distribution of predators
6. Distribution of sleeping sites

A great deal of enthusiasm resulted from this approach and led to new research directions as well as attempts to synthesize the information in order to discern broad patterns for the entire order. Initially, schemes were relatively simple and attempted to show very broad aspects of ecological/behavioral correlations (Crook and Gartlan, 1966; Crook, 1970; Eisenberg, et al., 1972). Rather quickly, as more data accumulated, it became obvious that primates in the wild displayed considerably more variability of social behavior than these simple schemes could accommodate.

As a result, more sophisticated approaches have evolved (Clutton-Brock and Harvey, 1977; Richard, 1985). Primatologists now view ecology, behavior, and

ARTIFICIALLY PROVISIONED
Food is made available to primates by humans.

Figure 8-5
Rhesus monkeys in India. These "urban" monkeys have adapted well to new environmental challenges—reflecting the behavioral flexibility characteristic of many primates.

biology as complexly interdependent. In addition to the general ecological factors listed above, primatologists must also consider an animal's body size, relative brain size, metabolism, reproductive physiology, the distribution of food resources into "food patches," and the nutritional value of foods and how they are selected and processed. Moreover, the variability exhibited between closely related species (and even *within* the same species) in ecological adaptations must be understood. Also, the way primates relate to their overall surrounding biological communities, especially to other species of primates, must be described. Indeed, it is a common phenomenon among many prosimian and monkey species to travel, and to socially relate over long periods, with other primate species. Do they eat different foods? How do they efficiently subdivide their habitat? These questions, too, must be addressed. Lastly, it is of interest to study why primates select certain foods and avoid others. What is the nutritional value of insects, fruits, leaves, nuts, gums, small mammals, etc., that are available to them? What toxins exist in certain plant foods that could do harm? Thus, as a central focus of ecology, let us turn to the diets of nonhuman primates.

What Do Primates Eat?

Certainly a basic way any animal relates to its environment concerns the foods it finds and eats. We mentioned in Chapter 7 that primates are omnivorous, implying they eat many plant and animal foods. But as Alison Richard has pointed out (1985, p. 167), omnivory is rarely carefully defined—and, as such, does not constitute a particularly useful concept.

It is more productive, then, to describe in some detail what primates actually eat. Of course, most primate species do in fact have quite diversified diets. For example, macaques (e.g., Japanese macaques, rhesus macaques), like most primates, are primarily vegetarians. Yet, when we consider ground cover accumulation of snow (which is an important seasonal factor for some macaques), we can see that very different foods may be exploited. Consequently, in the winter, rhesus macaques in highland Pakistan eat tough plant leaves (oak), pine needles, pine gum, and herb roots. At other times of the year, they eat flower blossoms, fruits, grasses, and seeds (Richard, 1985). This is perhaps an extreme case (for most primates do not live in such seasonal environments, and foods are thus more consistently available). And, in fact, most species do concentrate on a particular combination of food sources. Special terminology has been devised to describe the type of diet as characterized by the most predominant type of food:

1. Insectivore—primarily eats insects
2. Folivore—primarily eats leaves
3. Frugivore—primarily eats fruits
4. Gramnivore—primarily eats seeds
5. Gumnivore—primarily eats gums

Characterizing particular primate species according to this scheme is difficult; however, some species are easier to classify than others. Chimps in all parts of their range where they have been observed eat primarily fruits (i.e., they are primarily frugivorous). On the other hand, olive baboons (one variety of savanna baboons) show dietary diversity in different areas of their range. In one area of Kenya, they eat primarily grass blades and seeds, but little fruit. In Ethiopia, however, they spend almost half their time eating fruit. Although there are certainly differences in the environment between the two regions, it has been suggested that the dietary differences may also relate to differences in food-harvesting techniques (Richard, 1985). Indeed, such differences in local *traditions* can dramatically influence primate behavior, a point to which we will return in the next chapter.

Environment and Social Behavior

In the remainder of this chapter and in the chapter following, we will discuss various aspects of nonhuman primate social behavior. An ecological focus can, in many ways, be utilized to illuminate much of primate behavior (see Jolly, 1985, and Richard, 1985, for excellent discussions of this perspective). Here, we cannot adequately discuss all the ways primatologists use ecological, behavioral, and biological data. Nor can we completely summarize the huge amount of information that has accumulated in recent years. What is important, however, is to get a sense of how this approach is used currently by primatologists; hence, we will discuss a comprehensive example of such primate ecological research.

Five Monkey Species in the Kibale Forest, Uganda   One of the most detailed and controlled studies of primate socioecology has been undertaken in the Kibale Forest of western Uganda (Struhsaker and Leyland, 1979). The five species studied are all varieties of Old World monkeys and include black-and-white colobus (*Colobus guereza*), red colobus (*Colobus badius*), mangabey (*Cercocebus albigena*), blue monkey (*Cercopithecus mitus*), and the redtail monkey (*Cercopithecus ascanius*). Thus, three different genera and both subfamilies of Old

Figure 8-6
Kibale Forest habitat, Uganda.

SYMPATRIC
sym: at the same time
patra: fatherland
Two or more species living in the same area.

GROOMING, SOCIAL
Cleaning through the hair and fur.

World monkeys all live in the same general area and are consequently said to be **sympatric**. In addition, three other anthropoid species live in Kibale (another *Cercopithecus* species, baboons, and chimps. (See Ghiglieri, 1984.) Comparisons are facilitated in this study because all species were sampled using similar methodologies. This avoids the pitfall of making comparisons between highly variable research strategies, a problem usually unavoidable in making cross-species comparisons. Moreover, the research at Kibale is important because this region is probably the least disturbed habitat where primates have been studied long-term.

While sympatric, numerous fascinating differences exist among the five species. Body weights vary considerably (3–4 kg for redtails and up to 7–10 kg for the mangabey and colobus species). Diet also differs at a gross level, with the two colobus species eating primarily leaves (i.e., they are folivorous) and the other three species showing more dietary diversity: concentration on fruits supplemented by insects.

At the same time, several aspects of social organization varied among the five species. For example, the red colobus and mangabey had several adult males in the group, while only one fully adult male was typically present in the other species. Furthermore, all five species occasionally had solitary males moving independently of the bisexual groups, but bachelor groups (consisting solely of adult and subadult males) did not typically form (as has been observed in other primates, such as langurs and gelada baboons). Even among the multimale bisexual groups there is a marked difference. In mangabeys, the females are the permanent core of the group (with males transferring out), while in red colobus, it is the females who transfer (with the males remaining the long-term residents). Indeed, there is so much variability that Struhsaker and Leyland could find little correlation between social organization and gross feeding ecology.

More detailed analysis of feeding patterns showed even further differences. For instance, while both colobus species eat mostly leaves, they still exploit different resources (black-and-white colobus eat considerably mature leaf blades, some high in protein; red colobus, on the other hand, eat a wider variety of leaves, but usually not mature ones). Perhaps correlated with these dietary differences are the observations that black-and-white colobus spend less time feeding but more time resting and, in contrast, red colobus range further and live in higher density (i.e., higher biomass). In addition, some species show dramatic variability from month to month. Among redtail monkeys, the proportion of fruit in the monthly diet varies from as low as 13% to as much as 81% (Richard, 1985).

Ecological patterns and social ramifications are unquestionably most complicated. In the same forest at Kibale, the closely related species black-and-white colobus and red colobus show marked differences in social organization. Yet in another area (the Tana River Forest of Kenya), red colobus have only one-male groups (like black-and-white at Kibale) and *both* males and females transfer (unlike either colobus species at Kibale) (Richard, 1985). The distinct impression one gathers from attempts to find correlations is that most primate species are exceedingly flexible, a fact that makes generalizing an extremely tentative undertaking at best.

Still, the highly controlled nature of the Kibale study makes some comparisons and provisional generalizations such as the following possible:

1. The omnivores (mangabeys, redtails, blues) locomoted more than the folivores (the two colobus)
2. Among the omnivores there is an inverse relationship of body size and group size; also among the omnivores, there is a direct relationship of body size with home range (area exploited, see p. 222)
3. Omnivores were spatially more spread than folivores
4. Female sexual swelling (see p. 173) was obvious only in those species (red colobus and mangabeys) that lived in multimale groups
5. Feeding, spacing, group residency, dispersal, and reproductive strategies may be very different for males and females of the same species. These considerations have become a central focus of ecological and sociobiological research (see p. 204).

Because of the complexity of the social relationships among primates, long-term studies are absolutely necessary. As Struhsaker and Leyland conclude from their studies at Kibale, "Meaningful data on group dynamics and probable degree of genetic relatedness among the members can only be collected by observing groups for at least half the adult life span, which for most Old World monkeys means a period of five to six years" (1979, p. 222). Alison Richard (1985) is even more conservative in generalizing about long-term ecological patterns. She suggests such patterns should be observed at least as long as the periodicity of cycles of critical resources. For Old World monkeys, then, as much as ten generations might be required—a total of up to eighty years of study!

Clearly, the kinds of data now emerging from primate ecological research (and its manifold social and biological connections) pose tremendous interest and opportunities for primatologists. However, the challenges involved in collecting such data are equally great.

Social Behavior

Since primates solve their major adaptive problems in a social context, we might expect that they participate in a number of activities to reinforce the integrity of the group for purposes of holding it together. The better known of these activities are described in the sections that follow.

Aspects of Social Behavior

Grooming Almost all primates groom one another. **Grooming** occurs in other animal species, but social grooming is a unique primate activity and plays an important role in the life of most primates. It is hygienic since it removes ectoparasites, dead skin, and debris from the skin and fur, but it is much more than that. It has been called a social lubricant because it eases the interaction between male/female and higher/lower rank, where there is a possibility of friction. It has also been called "the social cement of primates from lemur to chimpanzee" (Jolly, 1984, p. 207) since it helps in maintaining the organization of the group. Grooming is often reciprocal with roles interchanged—the groomer may become the groomee, a process resulting in the establishment of friendly social relations among the animals in the group.

(a)

(b)

(c)

(d)

Figure 8-7
Grooming Primates. (a) vervet monkeys;
(b) patas monkeys; (c) black-and-white
colobus monkeys; (d) chimpanzees.

Displays A wide variety of body movements, vocalizations, olfactory signals (scent-marking, for example), and facial gestures communicate to other members of the species such emotional signals as fear, threats, greeting, danger, pain, hunger, courtship, and many other messages as well.

Animals often **display** when they are excited, a state that may be brought about by such situations as the presence of an outsider, a response to the display of another member of the group, or a need for reinforcing status relationships. The gorilla is known for its magnificent display involving such activities as hooting, throwing vegetation, and chest beating.

Displays of other primates include grunting, yawning, ground slapping, branch-shaking, head bobbing and bouncing, screams, hoots, strutting, scratching, barks, scent-marking (among prosimians), and facial gestures, such as smiling and grimacing. A display primarily communicates information that "is advantageous to the individual of the species, to the social group to which he belongs, to others of the same species, and to other species" (Buettner-Janusch, 1973, p. 307).

Dominance[*]   Dominance rank, or status rank, may be measured by priority access to a desired object, such as food or sex, and also by the result of threat situations. A dominant individual is given priority, and in a confrontation is the one that usually does not give way. It is believed, although not all primatologists agree, that because dominant males compete more successfully for fertile females than do subordinate males, they have greater reproductive success. Also, dominant females, because they compete for food more successfully than subordinate females, are thus provided with more energy for offspring production and have greater reproductive success than subordinate females (Fedigan, 1983).

In many primate societies males are generally dominant over females of the same age, older or stronger individuals supplant weaker ones, and each group member must learn its rank in the hierarchy, at least within its own sex and age class. "Further, the length of time spent in the group, called 'residence' or male

[*]See Fedigan, 1983, for a review of dominance theory.

Figure 8-8
(a) A gorilla display; (b) a chimp display. The old male rocks side-to-side, swings his arms, often takes a running start, and throws objects at zoo spectators.

(a)

(b)

Figure 8-9
Primate mothers and their infants.

'tenure,' also correlates significantly with rank, positively in the case of macaques . . . and negatively with the case of baboons" (Fedigan, 1983, pp. 111–112). Dominant males are sometimes responsible for protecting the troop from predators as well as for defense against other troops if that situation should arise. They may also, as in savanna baboons, act as "policemen" to break up fights among juveniles, females, and other adult males within their troop.

Dominance is adaptive because it operates to avoid conflict. When two individuals compete for the same scarce item, the dominant one assumes priority by threat behavior. Thus dominance serves to organize social interactions; individuals know where they belong and act accordingly, avoiding chaotic, unorganized social relations. The result is a more or less smoothly functioning order of priority, which reduces endless quarrels for scarce resources.

Mother-Infant Relationship   The basic social unit among primates is the female and her infants. Adult males **consort** with females for mating purposes, but they may or may not participate as members of the social unit. Observations both in the field and in captivity suggest that this mother-offspring core provides the group with its stability.

The **mother-infant attachment**, one of the most basic themes running throughout primate social relations, begins at birth. A primate infant's first bond (in the anthropoids especially) is to its mother. After birth, the infant clings to its mother while she performs her daily activities, often without seeming regard for her offspring's success in holding on. Quite often, however, as she leaves for some activity, a mother will gather her infant protectively to her body. Unlike other social animals, in which the newborn are left in a nest or den, the clinging primate infant develops a closeness with the mother that does not end with weaning. This closeness is often maintained throughout life and is reflected in grooming behavior that continues between mother and offspring even after the children reach adulthood.

The crucial role played by primate mothers was clearly demonstrated by the Harlows, (1959), who raised some infant monkeys with surrogate mothers fashioned from cloth and other monkeys with no mothers at all. In one experiment, infants raised with surrogate mothers retained an attachment to their cloth mother, but those raised without a mother were incapable of forming a lasting affectional tie.

In another experiment (Harlow and Harlow, 1961), monkeys raised without a mother sat passively in their cages and stared vacantly into space. Some punished themselves by seizing one of their arms with the mouth and tearing the flesh until blood flowed. Those raised with a surrogate mother acted similarly, but somewhat less dramatically. None of the males or females raised without real or surrogate mothers ever achieved any semblance of normal sexual behavior. No motherless male ever successfully copulated, and he often violently assaulted the female with whom he was paired. Females (those raised without mothers as well as those raised with cloth mothers) that were successfully impregnated and bore young, paid very little attention to their infants. A mother often brushed away her baby "as if she were brushing off flies" or crushed her infant to the floor, and these mothers rarely held their infants or protected them as normal mothers do.

The Harlows conclude: "We only know that these monkeys without normal mothering and without peer affectional relationships have behaved toward their infants in a manner completely outside the range of even the least adequate of normal mothers" (1961, p. 55).

In more recent studies, Professor Suomi of the University of Wisconsin Primate Laboratory and a student of Harlow, has confirmed the importance of the mother-infant relationship. Even brief separations from the mother have lasting effects. He further points out that peer relationships suffer if the individual does not have a good relationship with its mother (Greenberg, 1977). His review of isolation studies has led Suomi to emphasize that social isolation initiated early in life can have devastating effects on subsequent development and behavior for

Figure 8-10
Wire mother and cloth mother.

ALLO
Combining form indicating different or
other.

NULLIPAROUS
null: none, not any
parous: birth
Never having given birth.

many species of primates. The primate deprivation syndrome that results from early isolation is characterized by displays of abnormal self-directed and stereotypic behavior and by gross deficits in all aspects of social behavior (Suomi, 1982, p. 190).

Infants are mainly cared for by the mother, of course, but adult males are also known to take more than a casual interest. This phenomenon has frequently been noted among male hamadryas baboons, who sometimes "adopt" an infant. "He then carries it en route, allows it to sleep huddled against his belly at night, and prevents it from moving too far away" (Kummer, 1971, pp. 81–82).

What may be an extension of the mother-infant relationship has been called **allo**parent, or "aunt" behavior. This type of behavior occurs among many animal species but is most richly expressed in primates, and some researchers believe it is found among all social primates. Usually, the alloparents crowd around the newborn infant and attempt to carry, cuddle, groom, hold, or just touch it. Some species, like the common langur, are well known for their aunts, and as many as eight females may hold the infant during its first day of life. Among patas monkeys, the mother may threaten a female that touches her baby, so the interested female resorts to a subtle maneuver. "A patas female may begin to groom a mother's arm and then slowly and cautiously transfer her grooming to the infant within it" (Kummer, 1971, p. 80).

Several functions are suggested for alloparenting. If the mother dies, the infant stands a chance of being adopted by an alloparent or other individual of the group. The practice may bind together the adults of the group, since it may be more convenient for the mother to leave her infant occasionally with another female. It may also assist the training of **nulliparous** females for motherhood.

Male-Female Sexual Bond   A close sexual bond between adult males and females is not common among the higher primates, although it does occur. In the one-male group, the adult male keeps his females close to him and maintains a very alert eye for any wandering adult male. Some researchers suggest that the one-male group is adaptive in arid regions where food is scarce and widely scattered, and attack by predators a constant peril. An adult male is protection for the females and offspring, and the structure of only one male to a group diminishes the consumption of scarce food resources.

Forest monkey groups, such as the black-and-white colobus, are also often composed of one-male groups. Here, food is no great problem and predators hunt by stealth. The best defense is constant vigilance by all concerned. The adult male's role, therefore, is minimal, and one male is adequate for protective and reproductive functions. And, as we shall see shortly, with only one male present, there is less competition for food, leaving more for females with dependent young.

The one-male/one-female "monogamous" or family group is characteristic of gibbons (but not great apes) and some monkeys, and can be understood in terms of adaptation to their environment. A gibbon family—one adult male, one adult female, and their offspring—controls a small patch of tropical forest, which provides enough food for a small group. Gibbons jealously protect this territory from neighbors. When a young gibbon reaches maturity, it is driven out by the adult of the same sex, thus maintaining the small size of the group and its limited food supply.

Figure 8-11
Hamadryas one-male groups.

Role Separation between Adults and Young   Among primates, especially the higher primates, there is a relatively long growth period spent in the protected environment of the social group. It is during this learning stage, when the young play and learn the skills needed in adulthood, that the brain develops the special intelligence characteristic of primates. This learning period is spent in physical and psychological safety because of the behavioral and psychological separation of roles between adults and young. The young play for many hours every day, learning many of the skills required by adults, free from anxiety because alert adults are always present. The separation of roles between adults and young enable the young to learn and practice the social, intellectual, and physical skills they will need as adults.

Role Separation by Sex   Perhaps one of the most interesting points to be made about the separation of sex roles is that there is often very little separation. Except for the protective role played by males and the childbearing and nursing role of the mother, in many primate species both sexes perform similar functions. Females are expected to obtain their food, as are juveniles after they are weaned, and there is little sharing of food.

Among terrestrial primates, there is very often a sexual dimorphism in body size, weight, muscularity, distribution of hair on the body, and size of canines. Usually associated with separate roles, the larger size (as in baboons and gorillas) enables the male to play a dominant and protective role. In those species without sexual dimorphism, the females may be highly aggressive, as in gibbons, and join the males in defense of their territory.

The sociobiological perspective has recently become widely used in primatology. In the last decade, this approach has been applied to a wide variety of animals, including nonhuman primates (see Barash, 1982, for a good general review of sociobiology). Indeed, for primatological interpretations, sociobiology holds a central position as a theoretical framework for a majority of current researchers (for example, Richard, 1985; Richard and Schulman, 1982; Smuts, 1985; Small, 1984; Hausfater and Hrdy, 1984; and, to a moderate degree, Goodall, 1986). Beyond the suppositions concerning nonhuman primates, some contemporary scholars even go so far as to extend this field to the interpretation of *human* primates as well.* Naturally, not all primatologists, and certainly not all anthropologists, are sociobiologists. Indeed, sociobiology has created and continues to generate a great deal of controversy.

First brought to popular attention in 1975 by Harvard zoologist E. O. Wilson, this approach can be traced to the pioneering works of R. A. Fisher (1930), J. B. S. Haldane (1932), W. D. Hamilton (1964), G. C. Williams (1966), and Robert Trivers (1971, 1972). Following publication of Wilson's monumental synthesis, vehement arguments exploded both inside and outside academia. What has caused all this furor, and what relevance does sociobiology have to understanding primates, particularly human primates?

Sociobiologists are basically classical Darwinists, postulating the evolution of behavior through operation of natural selection. Sociobiologists assume that, if any behavior has a genetic basis, its evolutionary impact will be directly measured by its effect on reproductive success. In other words, with behavioral phenotypes (just as with physical morphology), the success of genes underlying the phenotypes will be determined by their influence on reproduction. Individuals with genotypes coding for behaviors leading to higher reproductive success than other individuals will, by definition, be more fit. Consequently, they should pass on their genes at a faster rate. Sociobiologists believe genotypes have evolved in this way, producing such phenomena as sterile worker castes in bees, courtship dances in birds, and scent-marking in dogs. As a speculative model, this reasoning is all well and good. In fact, much of the theoretical way natural selection is discussed in Chapter 2 of this text utilizes terminology and concepts developed by sociobiologists.

When applied to relatively simple organisms—social insects, for example— sociobiological theory has proven of tremendous explanatory value. In fact, recent sophisticated molecular biological research with the DNA of marine snails has identified a family of genes that produce specific proteins whose combined action in turn governs the animal's egg-laying behavior (Scheller and Axel, 1984). This is of note because, for the first time, something that could be termed "complex" behavior has been traced to a specific genetic mechanism (i.e., DNA sequences that have been decoded).

Of course, neither insects nor snails are mammals (to say nothing of primates). The major dispute arises, then, when trying to postulate the actual

---

*Some recent publications reflect this trend. See *Child Abuse and Neglect*, Gelles and Lancaster, 1987; *Parenting Across the Life Span*, Lancaster, et al., 1987; *The Biology of Moral Systems*, Alexander, 1987; *Homicide*, Daly and Wilson, 1987; *Despotism and Differential Reproduction*, Betzig, 1987.

mechanics of behavioral evolution in complex social animals like primates. Which specific behaviors among primates have a genetic basis, and how do these behaviors influence reproductive success?

In order to answer the first question, we will have to learn considerably more about genotype/phenotype interactions in complex traits. Such an understanding is probably decades away. To answer the second question, we will need accurate data on reproductive success in primate groups similar to that shown for birds in Chapter 2 (p. 39). As of yet, such data are almost completely lacking, but it is hoped this situation will be remedied in the near future. Thus, sociobiology as an *explanation* of primate behavior remains almost entirely a matter of open speculation. Application of evolutionary models specifically to explain human behavior are presently even more hypothetical.

Obtaining conclusive data for primates and other mammals, we will see, is no easy matter. A good starting point, however, is framing hypotheses concerning behavioral evolution on the basis of the evidence that does exist. A good example of such a perspective is Sarah Blaffer Hrdy's (1977) explanation of infanticide among langur monkeys of India.

Langurs typically live in social groups composed of one adult male, several females, and their offspring (sometimes called a "harem"). Other males without mates associate in bachelor groups. These peripheral males occasionally attack a harem, violently overthrow the previous reproductive male, and take over the group. Often following this admittedly bloody contest, even more gruesome behavior ensues. The infants, fathered by the previous male, are attacked and killed. The adult females in the group usually try to interfere with the males' infanticidal intentions, but to little avail. In the end, most or all the infants are killed.

Figure 8-12
Langur group in India.

Why should langurs behave so? Are they not dooming their species to ultimate extinction by such destructive actions? The answer, according to sociobiologists, is *not* in terms of the species. Male langurs do not know they are members of so-and-so species, nor, if they did, would they care what its future would be. Natural selection theory, as clarified by sociobiology, teaches us that individuals act to maximize their *own* reproductive success, no matter what its ultimate effect on the species.

Ostensibly, that is exactly what the male langur is doing. By killing the infants, he avoids a two to three year wait before the females come back into estrus. Once the infants are dead, the females stop lactating and become reproductively accessible to the newly arrived male. He can then inseminate them much earlier than would have been the case had he waited while the young (in which he had no genetic interest) were reared.

We might reasonably ask why the females should allow their infants to be slaughtered. Actually, females do attempt to resist infanticide, but their efforts in the face of large, aggressive, and determined males usually fail. Interestingly, it is not the infant's mother who assaults the attacking male, but other females in the group. Some writers suggest that these females are closely related (sisters of the mother, for example) and, if so, sociobiological theory provides an explanation for such seemingly **altruistic** behavior. Since individuals share genes with close relatives, they can contribute to their *own* reproductive success by aiding their relatives' offspring.

In diploid species (like langurs, humans, and all vertebrates), individuals share, on the average, ½ their genes with parents and, likewise, ½ with full siblings. For example, when a langur defends her sister's offspring, she is helping contribute genes to the next generation; genes she shares in common with her nieces and nephews (on the average she shares ¼ her genes in common with them). In this way, genes that underlie such cooperative behavior may spread in populations.

Of course, there are many possible strategies. Aiding a relative does not always completely inhibit one's own reproduction. The success of an individual's genes (that is, one's fitness in natural selection terms) is then measured as the sum of one's own offspring *plus* those of close relatives ("discounted" according to how closely they are related: ¼ for her nieces and nephews, half-siblings, or grandchildren, ⅛ for first cousins, etc.).

Langurs are, of course, not doing this consciously. As is true of the cooperative female defense efforts noted above, females are not making conscious choices as if they *knew* the alternatives. What occurs is simply that individuals who behave one way will have higher reproductive success than those individuals behaving in another way. Consequently, their genes (including any that underlie this behavior) are differentially passed onto the next generation, theoretically just another example of natural selection acting on variation.

The social pattern among common (hanuman) langurs is not extremely clearcut, and controversy thus exists regarding the observations and interpretations of infanticide in this species. Geographically, infanticide has been seen (or logically deduced) at three field sites, but has not been seen at two others. As a result, some experts (most notably, Boggess, 1984) have argued that infanticide is *not* that common, is not adaptive, and could better be described as a "social pathology." As we will see shortly in our discussion of the limitations of sociobiological research (p. 211), controversies such as this are not easy to resolve.

Beyond langurs, however, it must be considered that infanticide is, after all, not that uncommon among primates. Infanticidal episodes have been observed (or surmised) in redtail monkeys, red colobus, blue monkeys (these three from studies at Kibale, see p. 195), chimpanzees, and gorillas. Such episodes have also been documented in at least eighty-four human societies. Interestingly, in the majority of these cases (chimps and humans are exceptions), infanticide occurred in conjunction with a male transfer into a group or a change in the status (and reproductive access?) of an adult male. Moreover, in no case has it been thought that a male was attacking one of his own offspring. In both these patterns, the circumstances under which infanticide is seen conform to the expectations of the Hrdy model (what could be termed "sexual selection").

Sociobiological interpretations have also been applied to a wide range of other behaviors seen in primates. For example, the extremely large testes of male chimpanzees have been explained as an adaptation to a fairly promiscuous mating pattern—where several males successfully copulate with an estrous female (a kind of "sperm competition") (Popp and DeVore, 1979). Also, the differential ranging patterns of male and female orangutans have been viewed as the result of differing reproductive strategies between sexes and maximization of food resources (Galdikas, 1979).

Male and Female Reproductive Strategies

The reproductive strategies of primates, especially how they differ between the sexes, has been a primary focus of sociobiological research. When we consider the tremendous degree of care required by young, growing primate offspring, it is clear that tremendous investment by at least one parent is necessary. Indeed, primates are among the most K-selected (i.e., high parental investment in but a few young) of all mammals (see Box 8-2). And, most especially, it is usually the mother who carries most of the burden (before, of course, as well as after birth). Primate offspring are born extremely dependent. They develop slowly (particularly constrained by brain growth), and in so doing, are exposed to expanded learning opportunities within a social environment.

Such an interplay between behavior and biology has promoted a feedback relationship that has led to larger brains, even slower development, and yet more chances for learning. Particularly in the large-bodied hominoids (great apes and humans) and most dramatically of all in the hominid line, this trend has been further emphasized, eventually producing the distinctively human primate. Thus, what we see in ourselves and our closest primate kin (and presumably in our more recent ancestors as well) is a strategy wherein a few "high quality," slowly maturing offspring are produced through extraordinary investment by the parent(s), usually the mother. Taken to an extreme, birth spacing (the time between live births following successful rearing or death of the previous offspring) is pushed to the limits in the great apes, with chimps giving birth only every five to six years and gorillas and orangs even more slowly than this. Consequently, a female chimp may only have opportunities for about five live births in her entire reproductive life span, and certainly not all of these are likely to survive into adulthood (a female chimp with three grown children is doing very well indeed). You will recall that Owen Lovejoy's model of early human origins (see p. 187) greatly emphasizes the reproductive limitations imposed on the highly K-selected

r- and K-Selection

Differing reproductive strategies are found in various organisms, and can influence numerous aspects of biology and behavior.

r-selection   A strategy in which numerous offspring are born (or hatched), and usually mature rapidly. There is little parental investment in each. Moderate–high mortality is shown. Such strategies are seen in insects and most fish.

K-selection   A strategy in which only a few young are born (or hatched), and take longer to mature (*in utero*, incubation, and afterward), thus considerable parental investment is involved in each. Consequently, mortality is fairly low. Such strategies are common to birds and mammals.

Note: Neither strategy is necessarily advantageous over the other. r-selection may work well in diverse and fairly rapidly changing environments, in which young disperse widely. K-selection, conversely, may work better in fairly stable environments.

You should realize, however, that insects are by far the fastest reproducers (r-selectionists *par excellence*) among animals, and are probably the most successful animal form, if number of species, number of individuals, or biomass are taken as criteria. Even among the primarily K-selected mammals, the rodents (the most r-selected of the group) are probably the most successful.

great apes. Certainly, in most contemporary primate species, males and females face different challenges.

As a result of the heavy cost of carrying and caring for offspring, females especially are put under physiological stress. For the majority of nonhuman primates, females spend most of their adult lives either pregnant or lactating. Accordingly, the metabolic demands are quite high. A pregnant or lactating female primate, although perhaps only half the size of her male counterpart, may require about the same amount of calories per day. Even then, her physical resources may be drained over the long-run. For example, analysis of chimpanzee skeletons from Jane Goodall's population at Gombe shows significant loss of bone and bone mineral in older females (Sumner, et al., 1987).

It is not surprising, then, that considerable attention in current primatological research has been directed to the biological and social role of females. Sociobiological perspectives (with concentration on reproductive issues) has contributed to this trend (see Small, 1984). Early in the development of modern primate field studies, notably in discussions of savanna baboons, a definite male bias emerged. Workers seemed especially fascinated by the dominance interactions of the adult males, and consequently paid little attention to what the females were doing. Since 1970, however, the situation has been corrected, not the least reason being that much of the crucial research was done by female primatologists.

Male-male relationships are thus now only one aspect of what is considered important in defining nonhuman primate social behavior. As Alison Richard (1985, pp. 206–207) has suggested in describing primate reproductive behavior, "The following discussion focuses upon the reproductive life of female primates, therefore, and we shall simply assume that males provide willing and able partners when called upon."

Further, as mentioned in our discussion of primate ecology (see p. 193), there may be real differences in the ways male and female primates exploit their environments. Perhaps due to the higher energy/metabolic needs of females, it has been argued (Wrangham, 1980) that they must concentrate their efforts around high-yielding food patches (e.g., particular fruiting trees). Since there is a limited number of such resources, females would tend to defend these areas against other females. However, in order to mount an effective defense, it may take more than one adult female. With whom, however, should an adult female associate? Here, too, sociobiology predicts a likely answer. In sharing resources, it would be most advantageous for an individual to bond with a close relative (e.g., a sister). In so doing, not only her own offspring, but other young in the group (potentially her nieces, nephews, etc.) are related to her and share genes. As a result, a female's inclusive fitness (see Box 8-3) is increased.

Carrying this model further, the pattern of female-female kin-based social bonding may also help explain dispersal patterns among many primates. In most species of Old World monkeys, it is the male who transfers (usually as a young adult). The long-term social core of the group is thus composed of females, who likely share some degree of genetic relatedness. Conversely, males who transfer *into* new groups are unlikely to share much genetic relatedness with other adults.

As we noted in Box 8-1, in several primate groups only one adult male is found socially bonded to a group of females. In these cases (e.g., hamadryas baboons, patas monkeys, most groups of red colobus) at least one breeding male is required, of course, for reproductive purposes and possibly to aid in defense against predators. But why should females tolerate more than one adult male in their group? Again, sociobiological/socioecological perspectives can possibly explain the evolution of multimale societies among primates. Some resources are

Figure 8-13
Primate mothers with nursing infants.

BOX 8-3

Sociobiological Concepts and Terminology

ALTRUISM   Self-sacrificing behavior (technically, costing in Darwinian fitness). On the surface, it may appear harmful to the individual as, for example, in the case of sterile worker castes in social insects, such as bees. However, through behaviors that contribute to *inclusive fitness* (see below), genotypes might actually spread (through relatives), even though some individuals may have no offspring themselves.

COST/BENEFIT ANALYSIS   Borrowed from economic theory, this approach attempts to measure potential costs and benefits to individual reproductive success (or inclusive fitness) of certain behaviors. Though theoretically intriguing, in practice this is most difficult to apply.

DARWINIAN FITNESS   The proportional contribution of genes (compared to other individuals) as a measure of one's *individual* reproductive success (i.e., number of successful offspring). (See p. 39.)

FITNESS   Generally, a measure of reproductive success, relative to others in the group, taken as the lifetime contribution of genes to successive generations.

INCLUSIVE FITNESS   The *total* contribution of genes through offspring *and* other relatives. Relatives are devalued on the basis of closeness of genetic relatedness, which prompted the British biologist J.B.S. Haldane's famous quip, "I would gladly lay down my life for two sibs or eight cousins." This phenomenon, first clearly elucidated in social insects, may provide a clue to some forms of altruism.

KIN SELECTION   The process in which genes are contributed to successive generations through relatives other than offspring. In this way, *inclusive fitness* is improved.

NATURAL SELECTION   The process in which some genotypes (individuals) contribute genes disproportionately to successive generations as a result of differential net reproductive success (see p. 39).

PARENTAL INVESTMENT   Any behavior or contribution of a parent (gametes, energy, time, risk) to an offspring at the cost of investing in other offspring.

PROXIMATE EXPLANATION   A way to explain a behavior on the basis of immediate social/ecological/physiological factors. For example, an individual baboon may leave his natal group following a dominance encounter to avoid future encounters with particular older, larger, and more dominant males.

REPRODUCTIVE VALUE   The *potential* remaining reproductive output of an individual. This can be assessed at different stages of the life cycle, so that a 15-year-old baboon female has less reproductive value than an 8-year-old baboon female.

SEXUAL SELECTION   The process by which certain physical traits or behavior evolve to facilitate success in competition among one sex for access to matings with the other sex. This notion was championed by Darwin. The large horns of the male mule deer or the large size and aggressive behavior in the male walrus are examples.

---

harder to defend, so females may, in a sense, "use" males to help aid in defense of food patches. In addition, for some animals like savanna baboons, concerted action by numerous adult males apparently is crucial in predator defense (at least, out in the open—see p. 226).

We do not wish to convey an opposite bias to the early period of modern primatology by suggesting that *males* are doing next to nothing. In all primate societies, the interplay of behavior is extremely complex for *all* individuals. We see a marked degree of variability among different species in male parental care, male dispersal, and ecological constraints.

We have observed that, in langurs, male and female reproductive interest may be quite different. Indeed, it has been argued that, in the long run, neither the reproduction of females *nor* males is really helped by infanticide. But in the short run the presence of one infanticidal male in a group, potentially acting to serve his own reproductive interest, sets a whole chain of events in motion, so that other males are induced to behave similarly. Here, it is apparently the case that immediate, individual reproductive success can act to shape social determinants—even at the cost of the whole group, and perhaps even to the detriment of the *individuals* within the group as well. Glenn Hausfater, one of the leading researchers concerned with ascertaining reproductive success in primates, especially as related to infanticide, has put this relationship nicely:

> Thus, infanticide is an excellent example of a behavioral strategy that produces a short-term increase in reproductive success for some individuals of one sex but that thereby also locks adults of both sexes into patterns of behavior that ultimately result in a decreased rate of reproduction for themselves and for their population as a whole. As with so many other examples in modern behavioral ecology, the present analysis of langur infanticide supports the prevailing notion that evolution does not favor behavior that is "good for the species," but rather behavior that is good for the individual and, moreover, "good" only in the short-run. (Hausfater, 1984, p. 281)

Numerous other examples of variability of male/female strategies are known among primates. For example, in most callitrichids (tamarins and marmosets) and some cebids (titis and owl monkeys), it is thought that the typical social group is *monogamous*. Moreover, in these animals, typically, it is the male who is more responsible for parental care. In chimps yet another pattern is seen. Males are the ones who are tightly bonded (presumably for organized defense against other potentially aggressive males—see p. 236), and it is the females who disperse by transferring to a new group, usually when they are young adults.

Thus, as we have said before, there is no simple relationship of biology, ecology, and behavior among primates. Nor, obviously, can simplistic evolutionary scenarios adequately account for the diversity of behavior among primates. What makes sociobiology (and its ecological correlates) so important, however, is that it provides a framework to ask *relevant* questions, thus helping shape future research. Nevertheless, sociobiological interpretation has been subject to considerable criticism by other biologists and social scientists.

Primate Sociobiology—Limitations and Critiques

As we have seen, sociobiological interpretation has had dramatic impact on directions of current research—on reproductive strategies, male/female behavioral differences, ecological patterning, and much more.

However, sociobiologists have not been without their critics. Indeed, most primatologists who use theoretical models from sociobiology readily admit some of the current shortcomings. For example, Richards and Schulman (1982, pp. 243–244) in a review of primate sociobiological research list the following central problems:

1. The lack of long-term data on the demography and social behavior of large groups of individually known animals
2. The lack of long-term, fine-grained data on the distribution of resources in time and space
3. The nearly complete absence of information on genetic relatedness through the male line
4. The difficulty in assigning reproductive and other costs and benefits to particular behaviors
5. Our almost total ignorance of the genetics of primate social behavior
6. The untestable nature, even under the best of conditions, of many sociobiological models

Some critics have gone even further to question the basic validity of sociobiology as a perspective. Eminent Harvard biologists Stephen Jay Gould and Richard Lewontin (1979) have portrayed sociobiology as a teological (circular-reasoned) pursuit. In making this point, Gould and Lewontin compare sociobiological adaptive "stories" to the wistful, naive renderings of Candide's sidekick, Dr. Pangloss (from Voltaire's classic satire *Candide*). Even in the most humiliating of circumstances, Pangloss would philosophize that, "All is for the best in the best of all possible worlds." In similar fashion, Gould and Lewontin see sociobiologists devising their scenarios to create perfectly adaptive situations.

Is natural selection indeed such a clearly self-perfecting process? Of course, no one can say for certain, since we see only a small slice of possible evolutionary strategies among living animals; but evidence does suggest that natural selection often works simply "to get by." In this way, a whole host of marginal traits and behaviors could endure for substantial periods of time. The recent lemurs of Madagascar (see p. 163) are a case in point.

Just a few hundred years ago, the island was inhabited by a host of different lemur species, but human intervention caused rapid extinction of many forms. Consequently, the survivors (like the indri) have probably moved into a variety of habitats from which competitors had once excluded them. Without such competition they now make do, but probably could not be described as particularly well-adapted.

> The lemurs alive today inhabit forests from which many species, some of them probably competitors, have vanished. It is not difficult to imagine that the surviving lemurs have expanded their life-style to include foods and perhaps whole habitats from which they were once excluded by competitors. It does not matter that they do not make very good use of these new resources, so long as they do not have to compete with more efficient animals. In short, there is no reason to suppose that the distribution, feeding habits, and social organization of lemurs today are the results of long, slow evolutionary process, each species finely tuned to make the best of its environment. More likely, what we see are animals getting by and making ecological experiments after two thousand years of rapid evolutionary change (Richard, 1985, pp. 356–358).

Of course, this is not an evolutionary situation that has had much time to reach equilibrium. But when we look at *any* modern primate, can we be assured that they are not changing (perhaps rapidly)? Are they then showing particularly functional adaptations, and if so, to which circumstances? Are they in equilibrium? Have they ever been in equilibrium? Beyond these thorny theoretical difficulties, sociobiologists must address the type of information needed to test at least limited hypotheses. Presently, however, it is the lack of long-term precise data that most bedevils attempts to make sociobiology more scientific. As Sarah Blaffer Hrdy has noted:

> In order to evolve, strategies must on average increase the reproductive fitness of those animals who enact them. Nevertheless, small sample sizes and the near-total absence of lifetime reproductive output means that at this stage it is rarely possible either to confirm or exclude most of the hypothetical strategies being proposed. Furthermore, limited funds, limited hours, and most especially the rapid destruction of tropical forests together with their primate inhabitants make it unlikely that we will ever have such data for more than a few selected groups belonging to a handful of wild species.

Hence a few long term studies, such as those carried out among the Amboseli baboons will loom large in interpretation of primate evolution (1984a, p. 106).

Indeed, among wild primates, the longest-term studies concern Old World monkeys (baboons at Amboseli or Gilgil in Kenya) or chimpanzees in Tanzania (Gombe and Mahale), but still encompass less than two complete generations. Data from captive (e.g., Cayo Santiago) or heavily provisioned populations (e.g., Japanese macaques) are more complete, but are difficult to interpret, given the potentially large disruption of behavior these animals have experienced.

Since primates (especially anthropoids) are so long-lived, as Hrdy notes, it may be difficult to *ever* get the kinds of data we really need to test sociobiological models adequately. For other animals (who reproduce faster) the situation is considerably better. Most notably is a population of red deer on an island off the coast of Scotland for which detailed records were kept on reproductive success of all individuals (over 200) for 12 years (Clutton-Brock, et al., 1984).

Behavioral Data and Objectivity in Science   Perhaps an even more nagging problem than lack of long-term data is the very nature of the information itself. Primates are highly complex animals. Their behavior does not reduce down to simple discrete categories that can readily be described. Indeed, for behavioral studies it is often the case that the kinds of data collected and conclusions reached are often the product of the kinds of questions asked, the methodologies employed, and perhaps most importantly (and underlying everything else), the particular training and orientation of the observer.

We do want to make it clear that most scientists attempt to be objective and, in fact, often recognize that they have biases that must be controlled. Moreover, the great majority of scientists are honest in the presentation of research findings. In those few cases where human failings have overwhelmed scientific objectivity, the perpetrators are usually culled out by other researchers, who constantly challenge ideas and in so doing try to advance the field.

Nevertheless, when dealing with mostly subjective data—such as that on primate behavior—it is often exceedingly difficult to resolve differences of opinion without years of data accumulation and at least some agreement on basic methodologies.

As Sarah Blaffer Hrdy has courageously acknowledged concerning challenges to her interpretation of langur infanticide:

It has struck me more than once that critics of the sexual selection model sometimes apply a double standard: The criteria for accepting negative evidence appear to be far less stringent than the criteria applied to support the sexual selection model. . . . My own writing errs in the opposite direction, a consequence of the evolutionary bias of my own world view (1984b, p. 317).

When researchers noted for integrity differ so profoundly not only over interpretation of the evidence but even on the point of what is admissible as evidence, we must look for underlying causes. Inevitably, what researchers see is affected by expectations about their natural world and the way that biological and social systems "ought" to work; the resulting disagreement will not be easily resolved. Often frustrating, invariably time-consuming and inefficient, such debates remain, nevertheless, the best antidote we possess against the biases implicit in every researcher's world view (1984b, p. 319).

Probably the greatest challenge facing primatologists of the next generation is the urgent need to find ways to preserve in the wild what is left of primate species. It cannot be overstated how imminent the danger is. Without massive changes in public opinion and in the economics of countries with surviving rainforests, it will not be long before there are few primates left in the wild.

Indeed, the problem ranges far beyond primates. Habitat destruction in rainforests rushes ahead at a startling rate, swallowing huge tracts of forests and annihilating *all* those populations within them. Tragically, these very areas are among the richest biological communities known, and include more than one-half of all mammalian and bird species. Literally thousands of different life forms are threatened.

Perhaps it would be best to outline the dimensions of the crisis. Tropical rainforests once spanned vast areas of Central and South America, Central Africa (and Madagascar), and Southeast Asia (see Fig. 8-14). More than 90% of living primates live in what is left of these tropical forests, and they are vanishing rapidly. No precise estimates exist, as so many countries are involved, and national governments are, understandably, reluctant to reveal such details. In any case, researchers place the current rate of destruction at 25 to 50 million acres per year (or an area the size of New York devastated every year!) (Mittermeier,

Figure 8-14
Tropical rainforests of the world (modern distribution before recent, massive destruction).

Primates in Danger*

About one-third of all living primate species live on the African continent; that is, 50 to 60 of the world total of approximately 180 species. Although Africa is a large continent, primates inhabit a relatively small area of it, and much of it is greatly threatened from expanding agriculture and commercial lumbering.

The basic problem in Africa can easily be seen from the following:

1. Forest land is diminishing; e.g., of the 49,900 km² of forests in southern Ivory Coast in 1966, only 33,000 km² remained in 1974, a loss of 31% in only 8 years.
2. The human population rate will have increased over 3% for the 1980–1990 decade.
3. The food supply is decreasing because of environmental factors, inefficient agricultural techniques, and lack of capital resources. From 1970 to 1980, the annual increase in food production was −1.1% per capita.

As a result of the increase in population and lack of a similar increase in the rate of food production, there is agricultural pressure on forests. Where pressures on forest land are not great, monkeys and apes are often hunted for food. It is possible that by the end of the century, 13 species of very distinct local populations could be extinct if significant action is not taken to reverse the forces currently acting against them.

In 25 years another 10 species will be in danger if current trends continue. An informed guess is that in 50 years time, in the absence of major conservation action, about *half the African primate fauna* could be extinct or verging on extinction.

What can be done? Some suggestions: identify the most urgent conservation priorities; educate all involved as to the meaning, value, and practice of primate (and other resource) conservation; establish more effective wildlife reserves in forest areas; work in close collaboration with African countries; demonstrate to Africans, especially residents of rural Africa, that conservation *can* provide them with tangible benefits.

*Adapted from John Oates.

African Primates in Danger of Extinction

Species/Subspecies Common Name	Location	Estimated Size of Remaining Population	Species/Subspecies Common Name	Location	Estimated Size of Remaining Population
Barbary macaque	North Africa	23,000	Bouvier's red colobus	Congo Republic	?
Tana River mangabey	Tana R., Kenya	800–1100	Tana River red colobus	Tana R., Kenya	200–300
Sanje mangabey	Uzungwa Mts., Tanzania	1800–3000	Uhehe red colobus	Uzungwa Mts., Tanzania	10,000
Drill	Cameroon, Fernando Po	?	Zanzibar red colobus	Zanzibar	1500
Preuss's guenon	Cameroon, Fernando Po	?	Mountain gorilla	Virunga Volcanoes, and Bwindi Forest	360–370
White-throated guenon	Southwest Nigeria	?			
Pennant's red colobus	Fernando Po	?			
Preuss's red colobus	Cameroon	8000			

Dian Fossey—A Hero for the Twentieth Century

Despite her articles, a well-received book, and her eighteen years of dedicated work with the wild mountain gorillas, Dian Fossey, ironically, came into the full glare of media attention only after her death on December 26, 1985. She was brutally murdered in her cabin at the Karisoke Research Center, Rwanda, Africa, which she established and directed.

Dian was born in San Francisco in 1932. As a child, she loved animals, but was only allowed to keep goldfish. She later said that the first trauma of her life was the death of her pet goldfish, a trauma that foreshadowed the later tragic and brutal death of her favorite gorilla (named Digit), in 1977.

Interrupting her career as an occupational therapist, Dian borrowed $8,000 in 1963 to go on a seven-week African safari. Her purpose was to observe animals, especially gorillas. There, she met renowned anthropologist Dr. Louis Leakey, who later sponsored her long-term study of mountain gorillas in the Virunga Volcanos, first in Zaire and then in the Parc National des Volcans in Rwanda.

Beginning in 1967, Dian achieved great success, and she came to understand gorilla behavior better than anyone else in the world. Living alone in her cabin, mostly isolated from her staff and occasional students, she became disillusioned with people who failed to share her concern for gorillas. Shortly before her death she told a reporter, "I have no friends. The more you learn about the dignity of the gorilla, the more you want to avoid people."

Increasingly over the years, Dian's concerns turned to what she termed "active conservation." She vigorously led and directed antipoaching patrols against native poachers who, with their snares for other game, posed the most severe threat to gorilla survival in the Virunga Volcanos.

While teaching briefly at Cornell University, Dian completed the book *Gorillas in the Mist*, which appeared in 1983. With this work, and *National Geographic* articles,

Dian Fossey.

public lectures, and television appearances, Dian tirelessly and effectively campaigned to educate the public to a better understanding of gorillas and their endangered plight in Africa.

For eighteen years Dian lived and worked heroically with mountain gorillas. Hopefully, she did not die in vain. The Rwandan government has indicated that not only will the research center she established be maintained, but it will be strengthened and enlarged. Perhaps in death Dian Fossey will achieve what eluded her in life: absolute protection for the mountain gorillas. In her devotion to these animals, Dian will be remembered for generations as one of the heroes of the Twentieth Century. Without her work, it is doubtful that mountain gorillas would have survived to the twenty-first.

Biruté M. F. Galdikas

1982). Another way to look at it is to consider that anywhere between 12.5 and 100 acres are lost every minute (Lovejoy, 1982).

Much of the motivation behind the devastation of the rainforests is, of course, economic—the short-term gains from use of trees for lumber and paper products, or from large-scale mining operations (with their necessary roads, digging, etc., all of which cause habitat destruction). Regionally, the loss of rainforest ranks as a national disaster for some countries. For example, the West African nation

Sierra Leone had an estimated 15,000 square miles of rainforest earlier in this century. Today, only 535 square miles remain. At least 70% of this destruction has occurred since World War II (Teleki, 1986).

While habitat destruction is far-and-away the leading danger to contemporary nonhuman primates, assaults against them from other directions are happening as well. Primates in many areas are hunted for food, particularly in the Americas and western and central Africa. "Thousands are killed every year for the pot" (Mittermeier, 1982). Primates are also hunted for their pelts as, for example, the skins of black-and-white colobus monkeys. It is estimated that 2 million skins of this species alone were taken just in the last decade of the nineteenth century (Mittermeier, 1982).

Insofar as the food question is concerned, the choices for local human inhabitants are far from easy. Most tropical rainforests are located in third world countries that face current massive overpopulation and continued high growth rates. Malnutrition and undernutrition are thus major problems, and are worsening. It is sobering to consider that the horrible starvation so well-publicized in Ethiopia in the last few years is probably just the tip of the iceberg. Starvation on a massive scale will almost certainly become commonplace in Africa (and elsewhere) before the end of this century.

Faced with overwhelming economic hardship, cash-poor nations seek foreign investment and an influx of capital. But what do they have to offer that will produce ready cash? Their natural resources are their most immediately available commodity, so in reality their very landscapes are being chopped, packaged, and exported. This—as Sierra Leone illustrates—is only a stopgap for in barely an instant, resources will all be gone. In the face of such an onslaught, nonhuman primates are merely pawns in a worldwide catastrophe-in-the-making.

What, then, is the status of free-ranging primates today? Of the approximately 180 to 190 species, 67 (one out of three) are already considered endangered, and another 26 (one out of seven) are listed as *highly* endangered. These latter could be extinct by the end of the century (Mittermeier, 1982). "And, I must emphasize that these are minimum estimates . . . Almost every time a researcher goes out to study a poorly known species, we find that it is necessary to add yet another primate to the endangered list" (Mittermeier, 1982, p. 14).

There are no simple solutions. The world's booming population, the uneven distribution of wealth among the world's peoples, and the understandable, but short-sighted, attempts by nations to maximize income all would seem to offer little hope for turning the situation around. It is obviously already too late for many species. What will the next few decades bring, and what will our descendants say of us?

Summary

We have seen in Chapter 7 that, structurally, the primate order is a most diverse group. In this chapter, we have seen that *socially* as well primates are both complex and diverse. Indeed, the myriad demands of primate existence have produced these living forms through an integrated process of *biosocial* evolution.

While the scope of this book does not allow us to touch upon all the fascinating aspects of primatological research, we have introduced some of the more dynamic areas. In particular, we have shown that ecological challenges and how they act to influence primate social relationships is a central concern of current primatology. Another main focus of many contemporary researchers involves evolutionary explanations (through natural selection) of primate behavior. This approach, called sociobiology, is not without its drawbacks and its detractors, both within and outside primatology. Nevertheless, along with ecological considerations, such a perspective has allowed researchers to frame a whole array of new questions concerning primate behavior. We may never have complete answers to these questions, but we can gain useful information only by *attempting* to answer what we consider relevant questions. Such is the nature of science, particularly the science of behavior.

Beyond these methodological considerations, there are specific avenues of research that have been used to provide information on the evolution of human behavior. It is to this information that we turn in the next chapter.

Questions for Review

1. Discuss several reasons for studying nonhuman primates.
2. What features are unique to humans (or at least tend to distinguish humans from other primates)?
3. Why should primates be studied in free-ranging circumstances?
4. What are the primary methodological obstacles to studying free-ranging primates?
5. Given the methodological constraints, which primates are known best in free-ranging circumstances?
6. What major aspects of the environment are thought to influence social behavior of nonhuman primates?
7. Discuss how the study of the five species of primates in the Kibale Forest contributes to our understanding of primate socioecology.
8. What behavioral traits are common to all nonhuman primates?
9. What are the functions of grooming? Displays? Dominance?
10. Why is the mother-infant bond so crucial for primates?
11. What experimental evidence is there to argue for this strong mother-infant attachment?
12. What is the basis of sociobiology?
13. Discuss the sociobiological explanation for infanticide in langurs.
14. Give examples of how male and female nonhuman primates differ in their adaptive strategies.
15. Discuss some of the major limitations of sociobiological research.
16. Try to develop your own scenario of hominid evolution. Take into account the various sociobiological and ecological factors mentioned in this chapter.
17. What problems does artificial provisioning create?
18. Why have primatologists placed so much emphasis on socioecology in recent years?
19. Three types of nonhuman primate groups are given in Box 8-1. Can you give reasons for this variation in social organization in nonhuman primates?

Models for Human Behavior

CONTENTS

ISSUE

Killer Apes

For years, scholars and popular writers have discussed human aggression. One of the very basic questions has been (and still is, for that matter) whether human aggression is instinctive or learned, or a combination of both. This issue is significant because, if aggression is learned, it can be unlearned; or, the learning of aggression can be modified or replaced by other attitudes. If it is instinctive, then it may be necessary to develop quite different techniques in dealing with it. Many believe that a clue to the source of human aggression might be found in nonhuman primate behavior, especially that of the apes. Field studies have shown monkeys—especially baboons and macaques—to be quite aggressive, but since humans are more closely related to apes, the question of ape aggression is more relevant.

Until recently, field studies of apes have been infrequent, and those that were done were not nearly as thorough as those that are contemporary. While much evidence remains to be obtained, the number of field studies since 1960 has increased manyfold, and data are accumulating in great quantities on chimpanzees, gorillas, and orangutans.

Dian Fossey's early reports on gorillas did not mention aggression, but in her recent account, Fossey writes of two kinds of gorilla aggression. One, witnessed by a student of Fossey—Peter Veit—was a violent attack by a male on a female that resulted in the female's death. The female was ill and probably would have soon perished in any event, but the male literally stomped her to death.

Fossey also reported that infanticide accounted for the deaths of 6 out of 38 infants born over a 13-year period. The killing of the infants was perpetrated by males. Fossey believes that infanticide "is the means by which a male instinctively seeks to perpetuate his own lineage by killing another male's progeny in order to breed with the victim's mother" (Fossey, 1981, p. 512). (See Sociobiology for a discussion of this theory, p. 204).

In contrast to gorillas, abundant field studies of chimpanzees show evidence of frequent aggression—including killing—among these primates. Are there killer apes—apes guilty of calculated, premeditated "murder"? The case of the male gorillas mentioned above is evidence there are. More evidence comes from chimpanzees.

For more than twenty-five years, beginning with Jane Goodall's study of chimpanzees in Tanzania's Gombe Stream National Park, intensive research on chimpanzees, gorillas, and orangutans has been conducted in Africa and Borneo. Early reports from these studies led us to believe that apes were "gentle folk," kind to their children and playing out a more or less "live and let live" existence. The only animal that murdered its own kind, it seemed, was the human animal.

Beginning in 1974, Goodall and her colleagues at Gombe Stream observed a series of at least five unprovoked (or so it seemed to the observers) brutal, savage gang attacks by males of one group against the males of another group that had splintered off several years earlier. All seven males of the splinter group were wiped out by 1977. One attack even involved an elderly female who died as a consequence of the beating. The attackers were usually young males, using their teeth, hands, and feet, although on one occasion an older male was seen throwing a rock at a prostrate victim.

Even more disturbing, perhaps, is the cannibalism that Goodall has witnessed. She reports on a mother-daughter pair of chimps that had killed and eaten possibly up to ten newborns. Another case of cannibalism in East Africa was recently reported for the chimpanzees of the Mahale Mountains. We do not know how widespread the practice is, or what its adaptive value might be.

Because of the biochemical and genetic similarity between chimpanzees and humans, chimpanzee behavior may hold clues to human origins and even present-day human behavior. The significance of the killings and the cannibalism observed among chimpanzees remains to be worked out. Meanwhile, it is distressing to find that our image of the playful, friendly chimpanzee may well be illusion rather than reality.

As Goodall observed, "It is sobering that our new awareness of chimpanzee violence compels us to acknowledge that these ape cousins of ours are even more similar to humans than we thought before."

SOURCES:

Fossey, Dian. "Imperiled Giants of the Forest," *National Geographic*, **4**: 501–522, April, 1981.

Goodall, Jane. "Chimp Killings: Is it the 'Man' in them?" *Science News*, **17**: 276, April 29, 1978.

———. *National Geographic*, **5**: 592–620, May, 1979.

Hamburg, David A., and E. R. McCown. *The Great Apes*, Menlo Park, Calif.: The Benjamin/Cummings Publishing Co., 1979.

Norikashi, Kohshi. "One Observed Case of Cannibalism among Wild Chimpanzees of the Mahale Mountains," *Primates*, **23** (1):66–74, January, 1982.

Introduction

In Chapter 10, we discussed sociobiology and socioecology as theories that help explain nonhuman behavior. In this chapter, we look at the social behavior of two primate societies: a monkey group—savanna baboons—and an ape group—the common chimpanzees. We proceed on the assumption that when we study nonhuman primates, we gain insights into the evolution of our early ancestors who, we believe, lived in a similar savanna environment.

We also consider as possible models for this purpose the social carnivores of the savanna—lions, wolves,* and wild dogs. Finally, we examine a modern hunting-gathering society as a possible model for early hominid adaptation, specifically deriving detailed information from the !Kung San† people of the Kalahari Desert of South Africa.

Examples of Primate Social Behavior

Baboon Social Behavior‡   Baboons are diurnal and (with some exceptions) open-country monkeys. There are several kinds of baboons, including the common or savanna hamadryas, drill and mandrill, and gelada. The social behavior of each type varies. We shall describe the savanna baboon (*Papio cynocephalus*, which includes olive, yellow, and chacma varieties), the most widespread baboon in Africa.

Group size among savanna baboons ranges from under 10 to as many as 200 individuals, with a mean somewhere around 40. The reason for this wide range is not clear; although the reproductive rate, death rate, emigrations and immigrations, and perhaps environmental conditions are likely factors. Food abundance does not seem to influence group size (Altmann and Altmann, 1970). Usually, the sex ratio in a troop is about even, although among adults, females outnumber males from about 2:1 to 4:1.

Home range varies from 1.5 to 15 square miles, with the difference in area probably associated with proximity of neighbors, concentration of food and water resources, group size, and other factors. Within the home range, the group makes its daily round in the **core area**, which contains the crucial elements in the baboon world: sleeping trees, resting places, water holes, and food sources. There may be several core areas within one home range, and a troop may occasionally shift from one to the other.

Home ranges of neighboring groups overlap, which may or may not lead to hostility, but even where there is intergroup hostility, convincing evidence for **territoriality** is lacking.

---

*Wolves, of course, are not savanna animals, but their environment—except for temperature—resembles the savanna.

†The diacritical mark "!" indicates the proper way to sound this name. Please see footnote, p. 259.

‡Much of the description of baboon life and behavior is taken from Altmann and Altmann (1970) at Amboseli, and from Smuts (1984) at Eburru Cliffs.

Baboons sleep in trees. In the morning, they descend from their trees and move off to forage. They walk in a long file (not necessarily a single file) until they reach the foraging area, where they spread out into a long, horizontal line. They continue to feed, moving forward slowly in this horizontal line and covering a total distance of roughly 3½ miles a day. By late afternoon they have reached the "sleeping" trees for that night. Some baboon troops return to the same sleeping trees on successive nights.

Baboons eat a wide variety of food. Their excellent vision, ability to climb, dig, and to cover a large area enable them to exploit many varieties of food and survive in many kinds of habitats. In the Amboseli Game Reserve in Kenya, baboon diet—grasses and acacia trees—is especially important. These baboons eat leaves, sap, cambium, blooms, seeds, seed pods, and even rotten wood. Both grass seeds and grass blades are commonly eaten. During the dry season, their special food is the rhizome and base of grass blades.

In addition to plant food, baboons eat a variety of animal food. They prey on earthworms and insects (grasshoppers, butterflies, and termites), eat bird chicks, eggs, small frogs, lizards, and mammals (hares, young gazelles), several species of rodents, and primates (vervet monkeys and bushbabies).

The baboons at Amboseli did not share their food, although there was fighting among adult males for the meat on an infant gazelle. After the fighting ended, other baboons waited quietly, watching the one who was eating. When he finished, they walked over and picked up the scraps.

Harding and Strum (1976), observing a savanna (olive) baboon group at Kekopey, Kenya, found that, over a period of several years, the group developed rather sophisticated hunting techniques. At first their hunting was fortuitous,

HOME RANGE
The area utilized by an animal; the living area in which an animal performs its normal activities; the area the group is most familiar with, and which provides the group with food.

CORE AREA
An area within the home range where the group habitually sleeps, feeds, and performs routine activities. The area within the home range of greatest regular use.

TERRITORY
The area a group defends. That part of the home range used exclusively by one group. Neighbors of the same species do not enter or else enter only on a brief foray.

Figure 9-1
Baboon eating a Thomson's gazelle.

occasionally capturing a Thomson gazelle they happened to come across. Later, they developed systematic cooperative efforts, even to the extent of pursuing the gazelles in relays. Females also began to capture prey (hares) in significant numbers. In one two-year period, 14% of all prey was caught by females and 16% by juveniles.

Adult males, females, and juveniles participated in the pursuit and capture of prey animals, but complex hunting (stalking and extended pursuit) was restricted to adult males (Strum, 1981; Hausfater, 1976).

Baboons at Kekopey also developed a form of meat-sharing and thus differed from the baboons of Amboseli. Males shared with other males and females with their young. Hausfater (1976) noted several kinds of sharing at Kekopey. Adult and juvenile baboons of both sexes all fed from a prey item, but adult males did so most frequently. Animals feeding on a carcass usually fed sequentially, but only rarely were two individuals observed to feed simultaneously from the same carcass.

While meat eating is not uncommon among baboons, and sharing of a sort occurs, it is doubtful that meat—vertebrate meat—is an important part of the diet of most baboons. As Hausfater states, ". . . vertebrates are probably a negligible protein source in the diet of all classes of baboons with the possible exception of adult males" (Hausfater, 1976, p. 64).

A savanna baboon troop is composed of a core of females and young males who have not yet transferred to another group, and adult males most, perhaps all, of whom have migrated into the troop. Young, fully grown (or not quite fully grown) males normally transfer out of their natal group and emigrate to a neighboring troop. It is difficult to say why these young males leave their natal group, but there is evidence that both male and female baboons are attracted to opposite-sexed individuals from other groups. Before transferring, males often

Figure 9-2
Primate grooming. A male patas monkey grooms a female.

(a)

(b)

(c)

Figure 9-3
Baboon troop. Note grooming, feeding, infant play, and threat display. (a) Dominant male, foreground, faces possible threat at the left (from a source that is out of the photograph). (b) Male reacts to the threat with threat display—the "yawn"; other troop members appear to pay no attention. (c) Threat behavior ended, members continue their activities undisturbed as gazelle wanders through.

AGONISTIC
agonia: contend, struggle
Aggressive behavior.

MATRILINE
matri: mother
Individuals related through the mother.

monitor other groups during intergroup encounters, and they sometimes succeed in copulating with other-group females. Also, females sometimes act in a "flirtatious" manner to attract males from another group. These actions seem to encourage male transfer. The ultimate result is to promote outbreeding, and thus avoid the negative effects of inbreeding (see p. 229). Interestingly, most vertebrates have some type of mechanism to avoid inbreeding (usually through the dispersal of at least one sex).

Packer (1979) points out that males transferring into a group increase the number of males, add to the competition among males, and thus, from a sociobiological point of view, fathers may be the fittest of the troop.

Adult males are organized around a dominance hierarchy (which is one method of structuring a group), with an *alpha male* as the most dominant individual. In some cases, there may be several males in the central hierarchy. These codominants support each other in stress situations and cooperate in turning aside a threat to any one of them. The dominance hierarchy is lineal, that is, A ranks above B, B above C, and so on; however, competition is so keen among the males that rank positions change quite frequently. Adult males are dominant to all adult females, and immature males dominate females among their own-age and younger-age cohorts (Richard, 1985).

Dominant males enjoy certain perquisites. They often have prior access to estrous females at the time the females are most likely to conceive; however, it is also likely that female choice is a factor. Dominant males often have prior access to richer food sites, they are less harassed during mating, and they are assured of social space. Other, less dominant animals make submissive gestures toward them, or avoid them altogether.

Males are very aggressive and participate in many **agonistic** encounters,* especially when females are in estrus. They also frequently attack females, whom they sometimes wound severely. "With rare exceptions, males come together only to greet, fight, form alliances against other males, or compete over the same resources" (Smuts, 1984, p. 14).

Females form the core of the social system among savanna baboons. Whereas young adult male baboons do migrate to other groups, females remain in their own and rarely transfer. Thus, females in one group are related to one another through common ancestors. Furthermore, closely related females—mothers and daughters, sisters, and at times even grandmothers and grandaughters, aunts and nieces—tend to form subgroups within the larger unit. Members of the **matriline** frequently exchange friendly behaviors, such as grooming and sitting closely together. They also support one another during aggressive encounters with other troop members (Smuts, 1984).

Females are also organized in a lineal dominance hierarchy, which, more stable than the males', may remain unchanged for years. Dominance affects a wide variety of female social behavior. Baboon mothers with new infants are very attractive to other females (see allomothering, p. 229), and mothers are often harassed by other females at this time, especially high-ranking ones. A baboon female infant, by observing her mother's behavior as she reacts to other females, has ample opportunities to learn her mother's rank. Within a few months after birth, female infants seem to respond selectively to other individuals (Altmann, 1980). A daughter's rank, when she reaches maturity, is generally a rank immediately beneath her mother's (Richard, 1985).

*Strum denies the occurrence of significant male baboon aggression at Kekopey (lecture at San Francisco Academy of Science, November 18, 1987).

High-ranking females also enjoy certain advantages. A high-ranking female can displace a low-ranking female and take over resources, such as partially dug grass corms. High-ranking females are subject to less distress interactions, have more access to newly born infants, and, except for new mothers, are groomed more often by other females. Like less dominant males, low-status females make submissive gestures when approached by a high-ranking female.

We have already remarked on the social significance of primate grooming, which "is the most obvious and time-consuming form of primate social behavior" (Altmann, 1980, p. 89). New mothers are groomed more often than other females, and the grooming is initiated by others, not solicited by mothers. Mothers spend most of their grooming time on their infants, juvenile offspring, and one or two associated males. However, all combinations of sex-age classes groom together, except males, who do not form grooming pairs. The most common pairs are relatives, juvenile or adult females and lactating mothers, and adult males and females. Females groomed males more often than vice versa, except during estrus, when males became the more frequent groomers. Generally, the amount of grooming individuals receive reflects their rank.

Grooming episodes may be as brief as a few seconds or as long as an hour, but usually last from five to ten minutes. Grooming appears to be a pleasurable experience for all participants. The groomer lip-smacks (a friendly gesture) and "grunts softly while parting the partner's fur and gently removing dirt and ectoparasites, and the groomee tends to adopt a relaxed posture, sometimes sprawling on the ground with limbs splayed and eyes closed" (Smuts, 1984, p. 38).

Grooming, performed by both adults and young of both sexes, is an important mechanism for maintaining peaceful social relationships and bonding within the baboon troup. Another way is *friendship*.[*] In her study of the Eburru Cliff baboons, Smuts (1984) observed a special kind of friendship occurring in a very close male/female relationship. Males do not have male friends; they rarely associate with members of their own sex, nor are they ever in close proximity (except in agonistic encounters), and they almost never groom each other. For a male, only a female can be a "best" friend.

This special friendship is apparently initiated by females, probably because of their extreme vulnerability to males. A female is surrounded by males who are twice her size and who could easily injure or even kill her and/or her offspring. Males often attacked females, and although the injuries were not always serious, a female could expect a serious injury at least once a year. Smuts observed such an attack (1984, p. 93), which could serve as a plot for a television soap opera:

> Phaedra is feeding on grass, surrounded by other baboons doing the same. Adonis, in consort with Andromeda, feeds 20 meters [65 ft.] away. He looks up at Phaedra and stares at her for a few seconds; she is unaware of his attention. Suddenly he rushes over and, with his canines, tears an 8 cm [3 in.] gash in her arm. Phaedra screams in pain and collapses on the ground. Adonis saunters back to Andromeda. (Phaedra's wound took two months to heal fully, and she did not use her arm for over 1 week.) (Smuts, 1984, p. 93).

Smuts believes the reason for the aggression was Phaedra's attacks on Andromeda, Adonis' Friend. Phaedra was also a Friend of Adonis and seemed annoyed by this relationship with Andromeda, who had been in consort with Adonis for over a week. Phaedra had chased Andromeda away from Adonis several times, and Adonis ran after her, which was the only way to avoid losing her

[*]Strum notes (1987:686) that this special friendship is a restraint against male aggression.

to another male. On those occasions he was too busy to display aggression toward Phaedra. This time was different, and he took advantage of the situation by punishing Phaedra for her harassment of his consort partner. It worked—Phaedra was severely wounded and ceased to show aggression toward Andromeda.

The Friend relationship benefits a female. By becoming a special Friend of a male, a female can rely on the possibility that her Friend will risk injury and come to her aid. Also, her Friend may protect her offspring from other males. To obtain these benefits, a female establishes a long-term bond with one or two males who become her Friends and allies. However, there are also costs, since this relationship does not protect her from her Friend's aggression.

Another form of social bonding is consortship, which differs from friendships since consortship is usually defined as the exclusive *mating* relationship of a male and an *estrous* female. About ten days after the estrous cycle begins, the female's **perineal** area begins to swell, reaching its maximum (*tumescence*) within a week or two. It remains fully swollen for a week or so and then begins to decrease (detumescence) and disappear. A female ovulates about one to four days before detumescence, and it is during these few days when conception occurs.

Once swelling begins, females are sexually receptive and solicit copulations from males. However, adult males are most interested during the peak of sexual swelling, and this is when consortships are formed. While a consortship often consists of one male and one female, Smuts reports seeing two males in consort and sometimes even three (1984, p. 124). During peak estrus, male baboons compete intensely over access to estrous females, who often change consort partners several times in one day. Peak estrus is also the time when high-status males are most successful.

It is not, by the way, entirely the male's choice that determines the partnership. A female may use several techniques to discourage a male. She may run away from him, hide, or in one way or another, refuse to be mounted. Smuts tells the story of Zizi who was in estrus and being courted by Virgil, who was very attentive and probably her current and exclusive mate.

> Zizi, however, apparently had something else in mind. She broke away from Virgil, moved rapidly through the troop, and **presented** her alluring sexual swelling to one male after another. Before Virgil caught up with her, she had managed to announce her receptive condition to several of his rivals. When Virgil tried to grab her, Zizi screamed and dashed into the bushes with Virgil in hot pursuit. I heard sounds of chasing and fighting coming from the thicket. Moments later Zizi emerged from the bushes with an older male named Cyclops. They remained together for several days, . . . [and] in Cyclop's presence, Zizi no longer approached or even glanced at other males (Smuts, 1987, p. 36).

Still another interesting bond often develops—between a male and an infant. A male (sometimes referred to as "godfather") may take a keen interest in an infant, especially if the infant's mother is friendly with the male. He may fulfill several paternal functions, such as baby-sitting, grooming, and carrying the infant, and provide reassuring contact. By overt behavior or merely his presence, the male can often serve as a buffer between mother/infant and other group members. If the male is nearby, others will approach apprehensively, cast "anxious" glances toward the adult male, and approach the mother/infant from the side opposite the male. The male sometimes threatens anyone who approaches the pair, especially if he or she pulls at the infant (Altmann, 1980, p. 114). This relation-ship often persists through the infant's third or fourth year.

A mother's male Friend is not the only baboon attracted to infants. Other male adults, but especially females, attempt to take hold of a new infant. This is known as alloparenting or allomothering (see p. 202), and occurs in a number of primate groups. Ransom describes the strategy of a potential alloparent:

> An adult baboon may slowly approach the mother, showing various indications of friendly intent such as lip-smacking, narrowing of the eyes, and flattening of the ears, and embrace her in a variety of ways depending on the mother's posture and the sex of the other adult. During this embrace the adult will touch the infant with hand or nose several times and eventually may attempt to pull it out of the mother's arms. Such attempts for the most part appear to be intended to facilitate further investigation of the infant, but others are obviously motivated by a desire to carry it off (Ransom, 1981, p. 222).

Quite frequently, the most eager allomothers are nulliparous females, but because they are inexperienced, they may harm the baby. Pregnant and lactating mothers are also eager to borrow newborns, but they soon lose interest, and their careless attention may again harm the infant. Still, allomothering is useful to nulliparous females since it provides them with the opportunity to learn mothering.

Does this brief overview of baboon behavior support Lovejoy's hominization scenario (p. 187)? Baboons differ from Lovejoy's scheme in three significant areas:

1. *Division of labor.* Division of labor usually refers to economic activities, such as food-getting. In the case of baboons, there is no such division. Males provide food for themselves, and females forage for their own, as well as their infant's, food.
2. *Monogamy.* Permanent pair bonding is another aspect of Lovejoy's scenario, and again this does not apply to savanna baboons. Consort pairs bond, as we have seen, but only when the female is in estrus. Furthermore, such bonding is of short duration and is certainly not a permanent monogamous relation-ship. Smut's special friendship is the bonding of a male and an *anestrous* female. While the relationship sometimes lasts through the female's preg-nancy and lactation, even for years, it is not Lovejoy's permanent, food-shar-ing pair bond.
3. *Base camp.* There is no base camp (home base) among baboons. A base camp is a more or less permanent site where females remain, or at least remain in that vicinity. The male leaves the site in his search for food and returns to the base to share it with his female bond partner. It is true that baboons live in a territory and especially its core area(s). However, females move along with the males to another core area, or wherever the males move within the territory.

Then, too, the ecology of savanna baboons has been compared to early hominids, also considered to have been savanna primates. However, as Fedigan notes (1982, p. 312), much of African savanna may be relatively recent, formed by humans who burned and cleared forests for farming purposes. Savanna baboon behavior, therefore, may not even be specially adapted to savanna life.

Would baboon society serve as a model for the hunting-gathering society of

PERINEUM
peri: near, about
inaion: empty out, defecate
The area between the anus and genitalia.

PRESENTING
A behavior, often indicating subordination or appeasement, in which an animal places itself on all fours and elevates its rear end to-ward another. During estrus, a female may present for purposes of copulation.

Figure 9-4
Females and offspring—a closely knit group.
The female sitting at left is Flo, one of Jane
Goodall's favorite chimps.

today and the recent past? Not very well. The agonistic behavior of baboon males —among themselves as well as toward females—contrasts with the more cooperative and peaceful activities of many (probably most) hunting-gathering cultures, for example, the !Kung San (p. 259). Also, the baboon dominance hierarchies of males and females is lacking, or is much more subtle among hunter-gatherers. Food distribution, an important economic activity among hunter-gatherers, is very restricted among baboons. It appears, then, that savanna baboons do not serve well as a model for hominization or for hunter-gatherers.

Does savanna baboon behavior help to resolve the question of hunting versus scavenging as the food source for early hominids? Strum believes nonhuman primate practices may help clarify the issue:

> The question left open for consideration is whether it is easier to develop technical and social innovations within a scavenging context, to gain a competitive edge on other predators, or within a hunting context, to allow the exploitation of larger prey. In either case non-human primate predatory behavior once again considerably clarifies the question we should ask about human evolution and the answers that will be acceptable. It also illustrates a complexity that predates the human experiment (Strum, 1983, p. 334).

Chimpanzees (*Pan troglodytes*)*—apes that live in the forest and on the forest-savanna border—offer another possible model for early hominid behavior.

Chimpanzee Social Behavior   Although chimpanzee communities vary, observers are pretty well agreed that chimpanzees are a *fusion-fission* society. Goodall describes such an organization this way:

---

*Pan troglodytes, the common chimpanzee, is the most studied, and is the species described here. The pygmy chimp, *Pan paniscus*, is similar in some respects, different in others.

> Fusion and fission in chimpanzee society are carried to the limits of flexibility; individuals of either sex have almost complete freedom to come and go as they wish. The membership of temporary parties is constantly changing. Adults and adolescents can and do forage, travel, and sleep quite on their own, sometimes for days at a time. This unique organization means, for one thing, that the day-to-day social experiences of a chimpanzee are far more variable than those of almost any other primate (1986, p. 147).

It is rare, adds Goodall, for a chimpanzee to see *all* the members of his or her community on the same day, and probably never two days in succession.

> He may travel one day in a large, noisy, excitable gathering; the next day, completely by himself. He may feed peacefully with a small, compatible party in the morning, then join fifteen other chimpanzees, after a successful hunt, in the late afternoon. He may be one of six males competing for the same female one week, and associate with one female, far from any other males, the next. He may spend one day at the very center of his core area and move out to a far-flung boundary on a patrol the next (p. 147).

It is a social group whose members frequently subdivide into smaller units for feeding and other purposes, and then join up again.

Ghiglieri (1984), who studied chimpanzees of the Kibale Forest in Uganda, found a very similar situation there, but he cautions that chimpanzee sociality is far from random. "Instead it is a highly evolved system that allows the individual the best of both worlds: rich sociality combined with low competition between individuals for scarce resources" (p. 23).

Unlike baboons, chimpanzees may be called a male-bonded society, since they remain in their natal community while females transfer in and out. However, except for male siblings, male bonds are not very tight. On the other hand, the matrilineal family, especially the mother-daughter relationship, is very strong.

Figure 9-6
Chimpanzee gallery. (a) Profile of female chimp; note especially facial prognathism and supraorbital torus. (b) Low vault is noticeably visible in three-quarter view. (c) Prehensile dexterity is seen in the chimp's grip. (d) Chimpanzees have long fingers (but cannot straighten digits). (e) Another view of fingers; note thumb, which is not as proportionately long to fingers as ours is. (f) Chimp and (g) Gorilla; note the differences in face and head of these two apes (chimp is female; gorilla is male).

A chimpanzee community varies in size from group to group and from year to year, apparently depending on habitat—thinly forested, rain forest—female birth rate, disease, available food, etc. At Ngogo in the Kibale Forest, Ghiglieri estimated the community size at 55 members; at Gombe, Goodall's records show a range between 36 and 48 over a period of almost 20 years. In a study at Kisoge, at the foot of the Mahale Mountains in East Africa, the researcher Nishida (1979) found that during a 7 year study, the size of groups varied from 21 to 34 individuals. Estimates from various other chimpanzee study sites show a range from 15 to 80.

The geographic area each adult male visits in a year (combined) is called the *community range*, and its size varies with the number of individuals in the community. The more chimps, the more food is required, and therefore the larger area is required.

> The community range must be large enough to support the males and their females and young. It is not sharply delineated from that of neighboring communities. . . . The chimpanzees sometimes cross these boundaries into the range of an adjacent community, but usually show signs of apprehension when they do so (Goodall, 1986, p. 228).

Goodall estimated the early 1960s community range at Gombe, with 14 adult males, to be not less than 15 square miles, but in 1981, when there were only 6 adult males, the community range was 6 square miles. Ghiglieri estimated that the 55 chimps at Ngogo lived in a range of from 14 to 23 square miles. *

In their search for food, chimpanzees, unlike most primates, do not follow a regular route. Nor do they return to the same sleeping sites each night, but construct their sleeping nests close to where they ate their last meal. Within their home range, each chimp is free to go wherever he or she pleases and to take any route to get there.

There is no overall leader; any chimp—dominant male, female, even adolescent male—can lead a small party and determine the direction it travels. It need not be the alpha male. In a consortship situation, once the male leads the female to his preferred location, the female determines the pace thereafter.

Within the community, chimpanzees travel, feed, and sleep in groups called *parties* (see Box 9-1), which range in size from a solitary individual to quite large groupings. Usually, the number is small, probably between 5 and 10. However, size varies with season, sex, and destination. Feeding parties, for example, tend to be larger than traveling parties, and gathering parties are the largest of all.

Composition of travel parties also varies a good deal. Male chimps tend to travel with other males; adult females without infants prefer other females without infants and then males; females with infants travel most with juvenile females and adult females, with or without infants.

Four key variables that influence size and composition of parties are: nature of the food supply; demographic, e.g., number of infants, number of males; danger—presence of a predator; and availability of females in estrus (Goodall, 1986, p. 155). "The presence or absence of cycling females is without doubt the single most significant factor in the overall patterning of the chimpanzee community from year to year" (Goodall, 1986, p. 158).

Grooming, as we have seen, is a widespread practice among primates, and is as significant in the chimpanzee society as it is in baboons. Aside from its hygienic function, it also serves, perhaps even more importantly, social functions.

> Social grooming permeates virtually every aspect of chimpanzee social life, serving many functions above and beyond skin care. . . . [and] plays a vital role in regulating relationships, especially in restoring harmony in the wake of aggression (Goodall, 1986, p. 387).

---

* In the Senegal, on the west coast of Africa's bulge, the Mount Asserik chimpanzees occupy a total area of between 173 and 207 square miles. This large range is apparently due to the region's ecology—the hottest, driest, and most open habitat known for chimps (MacGrew, Baldwin, and Tutin, 1981, cited in Goodall, 1986, p. 230).

BOX 9-1

Kinds of Parties

ALL-MALE PARTY   Two or more adult and/or adolescent males.

FAMILY UNIT   A mother and her dependents, with or without older offspring.

NURSERY UNIT   Two or more family units.

MIXED PARTY   One or more adult or adolescent males with one or more adult or adolescent females, with or without dependents.

SEXUAL PARTY   Mixed party in which one or more of the females is in estrus.

CONSORTSHIP   The exclusive mating relationship of a male and an estrous female.

GATHERING   Group comprising at least half of the members of the community, including at least half of the mature males (an extra-large, mixed, usually sexual, party).

LONE INDIVIDUAL   An animal who is completely alone.

Grooming often takes place when partners are in a relaxed and peaceful mood, and it is quite obvious that the groomee, as well as the groomer, enjoy the experience. Goodall recounts the story of a groomer coming across a tick or a louse:

> With a quick lunge that may almost knock his client off balance, he seizes the affected part and, tooth clacking loudly, picks off the prize—which he then chews with exaggerated movements of his jaw. His companion watches the whole operation with fascination (1986, p. 388).

Grooming also occurs in tense and anxious situations. A frightened subordinate may approach a superior and groom him (or her). A female, frustrated because she has been unsuccessfully begging a male for food, may groom him perfunctorily. Grooming may be a dominant individual's response to a subordinate seeking reassurance. Two adult males in a tense situation are likely to groom each other although, if they are bitterly hostile to one another, they may not groom each other at all.

An adult female spends a great deal of time grooming her infant and other members of her family; they supply her with companionship and support. She does not, however, spend much time grooming females who are not kin. Adult males tend to groom other males more than females, and are groomed by females more than vice versa (except during estrus, when males become the groomers).

Reciprocal or mutual grooming is characteristic of chimpanzees, but groomers do not always spend equal time at their work. After grooming for a bit, the groomer stops and waits to be groomed. Usually the groomee takes his turn, but a dominant male would groom an individual of lower-rank for a shorter period of time. So would a mother groom her young offspring longer than the reverse, and nonrelated females might not reciprocate at all.

Like baboons, chimpanzee males are also organized in a dominance hierarchy, and, also like baboons, the hierarchy is not static. Changes occur when young males challenge females and then, one by one, senior males; when immigrant females compete for food with resident females; and when males compete for females in estrus.

During a stable period of status interactions—once established by aggression, observation, or threat—each individual is aware of his/her place in the hierarchy, and aggression levels are low. A threat, instead of an attack, may be adequate to "keep the peace." For example, after Figan (a Gombe male) lost his clear-cut alpha status in 1976, there was one attack per 103.5 hours by a male on any victim. In 1978, when Figan regained his alpha position, the number of attacks dropped to one per 261.5 hours (Goodall, 1986).

However, the chimpanzee male hierarchy is not a simple linear arrangement. Bygott (1974) (cited in Goodall, 1986) suggested instead a hierarchy of levels: alpha, high ranking, middle ranking, and low ranking, with several males in each level except alpha.

The flexibility of the male dominance hierarchy may be seen in the following account from Kisoge, at the foot of the Mahale Mountains, south of Gombe (see map, p. 239). We can see that coalitions also play an important part in the chimp hierarchical system:

> Kasonta . . . had been an alpha male for a number of years when rivalry developed between him and Sobongo, the beta male. In this ongoing conflict, the gamma male, Kamemanfu, was pivotal. At times the gamma male joined alpha against beta; at other times he reversed his position and joined beta against alpha. When the latter occurred, Kasonta, the alpha male, lost confidence and the beta male, Sobonga, became the alpha male.
>
> In 1976, Sobongo, with the help of the gamma male, was threatening Kasonta and succeeded in becoming the alpha male in June. One of the rewards of the alpha male is more frequent access to estrous females. During the months February-April, while he was still alpha, Kasonta was responsible for 85.6% of the copulations. But in months June-July, Sobongo—now the alpha male—was responsible for 87%. In May, the alpha status was unstable because gamma male Kamemanfu had switched his support to Sobongo and assisted him in attacking Kasonta. Taking advantage of the unstable situation, Kamemanfu showed the highest copulation rate.
>
> In January, 1978, Kamemanfu threw his support back to Kasonta who reassumed his alpha status. (Nishida, 1983, p. 332).

A male's ability to dominate is related to age. As a male grows through adolescence, he becomes dominant to adolescents and then adult females. As a young adult he begins to dominante the older males, and by middle age he reaches his highest rank. At this time he can dominate most, if not all, younger and older males. As he ages and his physique deteriorates, younger individuals may begin to dominate him (Bygott, 1979).

A top-ranking male is not merely an alpha male that excels all other males of the community. In the Kisoge study (Nishida, 1979), Kasonta, the top-ranking male of his group, was the most prominent in frequency of both aggressive behavior and threat display. Among adult males, he groomed and was groomed most frequently. Perhaps the most conspicuous characteristic of a top-ranker is the frequency with which he is followed by other adult males, and Kasonta's subgroup was usually the largest. In his role as the top-ranking male, Kasonta assumed leadership in scouting and chasing, and he was the only male to defeat the male of an adjoining group without help from others.

As we noted at Kisoge, a male's access to estrous females is directly related to his dominance rank. At Gombe, however, Goodall has not observed such a close

AFFILIATE
Associate, join.

relationship between status rank and reproductive success (personal communication). What seems to be important here are the tactics used by a male. These may enable a low-ranking or younger male to gain access to an estrous female, or even to lure a female away from a high-ranking male (Goodall, 1986).

Dominance and structural relationships are not as clearly defined among adult chimpanzee females. This is because some females rarely associate (their ranking is thus difficult to ascertain), and because the presence or absence of family members, such as a young or adult male or a high-ranking mother, may affect relative rank. In a hostile encounter between two females, the presence of offspring who could support her, especially young adults, would almost guarantee her success. A high-ranking mother would invariably come to a daughter's defense, if the daughter had attacked females older than herself.

When a female comes into estrus, her dominance rank rises remarkably. Young adult females have been observed threatening high-ranking females, and may even snatch food from some nonconsorting adult males. Rise in dominance rank is also related to the fact that highest ranking males often monopolize estrous females. However, this high rank among estrous females is only temporary. Linear rank hierarchy may also be present, although dominance is difficult to determine because "physiological conditions of females make female relationships very complicated and unstable" (Nishida, 1979, p. 104). Generally speaking, older females are superior in rank to younger females. At Kisoge, for example, a past-prime female, Wantangwa, completely dominated all other females for the seven years of the group study (Nishida, 1979).

Chimpanzee males are territorial, * maintaining an exclusive home range by excluding alien males. This ensures the males exclusive access to their territory's breeding females, and reserves its forage resources for themselves and their offspring. Thus, "males benefit through increased individual and inclusive fitness" (Ghiglieri, 1984, p. 4). On the other hand, an estrous female maximizes her reproductive success by leaving her natal community and mating with an unrelated male. This would avoid "inbreeding depression," that is, *reduced* reproductive success.

The above paragraph is an example of how the concept of sociobiology (see discussion, p. 284) is used to explain primate behavior. **Affiliative** behavior is more frequent, and social interaction greater, among males than females. Adult males groom males much more often than adult females groom females.

The relationship between a chimpanzee mother and daughter is a very close one until the daughter is at least 7 years old. A newborn infant clings to the mother, holding on to her belly as she moves, and, for the first six months, the mother supports the newborn with her hand. During this time, the mother provides food, protection, transportation, and hygiene. At the end of six months, the infant begins to explore the environment without straying out of the mother's sight, and eats solid food while continuing to suckle. Weaning may begin at 1 year of age and continue until 4 or 5. For the first four years, an infant is almost completely dependent on its mother. As a juvenile (ages 5–7), a daughter is still heavily dependent on her mother, but this dependency is significantly

---

*Goodall concludes that chimpanzees should be considered territorial, but their form of territoriality differs from the relatively peaceful and ritualized maintenance of territory characteristic of many animals. The chimpanzee form is more aggressive, repelling intruders and sometimes injuring or eliminating them. They not only defend their home range, but aggressively attempt to enlarge it (Goodall, 1986, p. 528).

BOX 9-2

Stages of the Chimpanzee Life Cycle*

Infancy (0–5 years)

Birth to almost complete dependence on solid foods, usually weaned.

Childhood (5–7 years; juvenile)

Continuing close association with mother, but independent of her for transport and milk.

Early Adolescence (Ghiglieri, 1984, uses juveniles, 5–9 years)

MALES (8–12 YEARS)
Gradually increasing independence, more time spent with males, more and more aggression, beginning to try to dominate females.
FEMALES (8–10 YEARS)
Continuing closeness to mother, adolescent swellings of sex skin.

Late Adolescence (Ghiglieri uses subadult, 10–15 years)

MALES (13–15 YEARS)
Majority of time spent with adult males and estrous females; dominates adult females by end of period.
FEMALES (11–13 OR 14 YEARS)
Adolescent sterility, starting with menarche and ending when female is capable of carrying fetus to term; has regular sexual swellings, travels with males and mates, some consortships; occasional transfers (usually temporary); close ties with mother (not at all sites).

Maturity (Adult)

MALES
Young Adult (16–20 years)
Increasing integration with older males; patrols periphery of home range; attempts to raise social status.
Prime (21–26 years)
Continued vigorous attempts to raise social status.
Middle Age (27–about 33 years)
Glossy black of coat begins to change to brown; individuals still vigorous.
FEMALES (14 OR 15–ABOUT 33 YEARS)
Raising family. Female may be described as *young adult* when raising first child, *prime* for second, and *middle-aged* after third.

Old Age (about 33 years to death)

Gradual slowing down; tendency to withdraw from intensive social interaction; teeth severely worn or broken, hair thinning, back of old male scattered with gray hairs.

*Adapted from Goodall, 1985, p. 81.

reduced during adolescence (8–10) and disappears almost completely during the daughter's subadult stage (11–13, 14).

A similar change occurs in the close relationship between a mother and her son when he reaches about the age of 10. The young male at this time is attracted to adult males and cycling females and, again, inbreeding with female maternal kin is avoided.

Adult or adolescent females tend to disperse and form small subgroups within the home range. They travel within small areas inside the larger home range, and, where home ranges overlap, they move back and forth between the two communities. Nevertheless, the closest bonds in a chimpanzee society are family bonds—between a mother and her offspring and between siblings. These last a lifetime, and even an adult male, after a tense event, may seek his mother's "reassurance" touch.

XENOPHOBIC
(zeeno)
xeno: foreign
phobia: fear
Fear of foreigners, strangers, outsiders, other
races, etc.

Sexual attraction serves as a bond among chimpanzees, but mating with an estrous female is a competitive affair, since there are always a number of males in the vicinity who are eager and willing. In addition, (at Mahale) the alpha male has prior access. A more reliable strategy is forming a consortship which, however, may take some skill, since the female must be led away from other males (but in consorting may actually mate less!).

One way of achieving his end is for the male to keep close to the female and groom her frequently. When an opportune moment arises, he may succeed in taking her away in consort. A female who, for some reason, lags behind the others may be a strategic target. However, a female who is not interested can avoid consortship by showing her reluctance and making the association difficult for the male. There are courtship signals: gazing at the female, branch shaking, rocking, and arm stretching. If the female fails to follow after repetitions of this behavior, the male may display, and even attack.

Not all consortships are necessarily with an estrous female. A consort may be a female between fertile swellings, who is pregnant, or during adolescent sterility when the female is not ovulating.

Chimpanzee males live in what Ghiglieri (1984) has called a **xenophobic** community. Adult males patrol the periphery of their home range, traveling silently in close compact groups. They frequently stop to look and listen, often standing bipedally to look over the tall grass, and sometimes climb a tree to scan the area for signs of chimpanzees in the adjoining home range. When the chimpanzees return to familiar areas, they often break their remarkable silence by "an outburst of loud calling, drumming displays, and even some chasing and mild aggressive contact between individuals" (Goodall, 1986).

In their patrols, chimpanzees respond to the sight or sound of neighbors with reassurance contact behavior among themselves (Fig. 9-4), such as touching, grinning, erect hair, embracing, and mounting. If the two parties are approximately of equal size, they may approach and display until one or both groups retreat. Kawanaka (1982) relates the account of an inter-unit-group encounter in which two mixed groups (adult males and females) approached each other at their territorial boundary. Although hooting from both groups could be heard, they did not meet, nor was there any agonistic behavior on either side. However, there was a good deal of stress present, evidenced by the frequent defecation of the females. If one group is outnumbered or faced with more formidable opponents, it will probably approach and then retreat. Members of different communities seldom engage in agonistic behavior because only occasionally do they come close enough for face-to-face interaction. Should a patrol party encounter a single male, however, they might attack him.

While chimpanzee males rarely cross into the home range of another community, such "trespassing" can occur. Goodall (1979) relates the account of a community at Gombe that separated, a number of adult males moving to the southern part of their home range. Over a period of three years the original group ferociously attacked and killed most of the members of the southern community by forays into their home range. Goodall could not explain this behavior except for the possibility that the northern group had been prevented from using the southern part of what had once been their home range. By eliminating the southern group, this area once more became accessible to them.

Agonistic behavior occurs between adult males, reflecting a dominance-subordinance relationship, but is also directed by males against females and immature chimps. There is little agonistic behavior between adult males and infants,

Figure 9-7
Flo and Flint. Flint, at the age of eight, died of "loneliness" (depression) three weeks after the death of Flo, his mother. (Baron Hugo van Lawick, © National Geographic Society.)

BOX 9-3

Jane Goodall—Pioneer of Chimpanzee Research

Jane Goodall

It began in 1960 when a young Englishwoman, invited to visit a friend at a farm in Kenya, gave up her job and flew to Nairobi. Jane Goodall, who, at the early age of 8, had already decided to go to Africa and live with animals "when I grew up," could hardly pass up this opportunity to fulfill her childhood dream.

In Africa, a friend suggested to her that she get in touch with Louis Leakey, well-known anthropologist and, at that time, curator of what is now the National Museum of Natural History (back then, Jane had never heard of Dr. Leakey!). She sought him out and introduced herself. After they conversed, Leakey offered her a job at the museum. She accepted, and ultimately joined the Leakeys on their annual paleontological expeditions to Olduvai Gorge in Tanzania. Leakey was impressed with Jane's ability and dedication, and asked if she would like to study wild chimps in the Kigoma area on the shores of Lake Tanganyika (see map). Lacking what she felt to be the necessary academic background, Jane was surprised at the offer. Leakey himself, however, believed that university training might be a disadvantage in this case. What he wanted, he said, was someone "with a mind uncluttered and unbiased by theory," someone who had a sympathetic understanding of animals and a real desire for knowledge.

Jane happily accepted the position, and waited for the funding that Dr. Leakey set out to find. With monies eventually provided by the Wilkie Foundation (of the United States), Jane prepared to leave for Kigoma. She then learned that local officials objected to a young woman living alone in a jungle uninhabited by humans. Jane arranged for her mother to join her, which satisfied the government officials, and the two Englishwomen, along with a few African assistants, went on to undertake the now-famous research effort at the Gombe Stream Chimpanzee Reserve, today known as Gombe National Park.

Jane Goodall's pioneering research—now in its twenty-ninth year—is the longest continuous study of the behavior of any animal species. As a result of her work, we have come to a better understanding of humans as primates, an understanding substantially broadened by anthropologists, zoologists, and other researchers from around the world who have followed in her historic footsteps.

Figure 1 (at right)
Three chimpanzee research sites in East Africa. Kigoma is Jane Goodall's area; the Mahale Mountains have been the center of research for Japanese primatologists for more than 20 years. The Kibale site, in Uganda, was studied by M. Ghiglieri.

probably because infants are protected by the mother, although females with infants are sometimes attacked. Adult females are dominant to juveniles, but do not attack unless provoked. Adolescent males can generally intimidate young adult and adolescent females, but might be attacked by older adult females. In the rare agonistic interaction among females, the older of the two females is usually dominant.

Among males, agonistic behavior appears to occur among four groups: alpha males, high-ranking males, middle-ranking males, and low-ranking males. Agonistic interaction among these groups is frequent, and dominance-subordinance relationships are clearly defined (Bygott, 1979).

Estrous females may be subject to attacks from resident males when they refuse to follow a male or even show reluctance. Moreover, anestrous mothers and infants may be in serious danger in meetings with strange males. In several such encounters the mothers were severely beaten, and on two occasions the infants were eaten or partially eaten (Goodall, 1986). Similar behavior is reported from Mahale. Anestrous mother Wantendele and Masudi, her son (40 months old), encountered a party of four males and several females from another community in the overlapping area of the two home ranges. When found by the observers, the mother was suffering from a bleeding head and other wounds, and Masudi had also been attacked but not seriously. The encounter lasted two hours—20 attacks directed at the mother and 3 at the son—when observers intervened to prevent the mother's death (Nishida and Hiraiwa-Hasegawa, 1985).

Unlike anestrous mothers, young nulliparous females are usually well tolerated by neighboring males. These young females move freely between their natal and neighboring communities, but the nulliparous females may be in danger from the resident females.

In recent years, another form of agonistic behavior has been observed. Between 1971 and 1984, six infant chimpanzees of both sexes were killed and/or eaten at Gombe. Three of these were infants of stranger females and were eaten by males; the other three were infants of resident females and were eaten by a resident female, Passion, and her daughter. Cannibalism has also been reported from Uganda (Goodall, 1986). At Mahale, in 1982, Norikashi (1982) reported that a male killed an infant and consumed the flesh. Alpha or beta males, also at Mahale, killed and sometimes shared the meat of infants of mothers who had transferred in. The infants were all males; at Mahale, infants of resident mothers were never killed (Nishida and Kawanaka, 1985). It should be noted that among chimpanzees "cannibalism is not an exceptional accident, but is deeply rooted in the chimpanzee species society . . ." (Nishida, et al., 1979, p. 19).

It is difficult to understand this practice unless perhaps it is to change an existing mother into a reproductive-ready female. That is, when a mother loses an infant, she shortly comes into estrus and is available for conception. (See Sociobiology, p. 204, for a further discussion of infanticide.) However, this does not appear to be the case among chimpanzees, as it is among gorillas. In male attacks on strange females, it is the female who is the focus of the attack, not the infant, and the infant is not always killed. Further, after the attack, the males do not mate with the female, who is often seriously wounded. "Probably, we do not need to search for any causal explanation beyond the fact that the victims were all members of neighboring communities" (Goodall, 1986, p. 523). Chimpanzee males, it seems, just don't like outsiders.

Rape, as a form of agonistic behavior, is rare among chimpanzees* and appears to occur in an incest situation between maternal siblings—mother's offspring. The only rape cases Goodall reports were brother-sister encounters, which were infrequent and restricted to a few males, and one case of mother-son. In the latter case, the mother objected, and it was only after a number of attempts and many threats and even attacks, that the male succeeded. In the sibling cases, sisters usually discouraged or strenuously objected to their brother's approaches.

Chimpanzees are almost entirely herbivorous, consuming more than 50 different kinds of plants. For most chimpanzees, more than half their food comes from fruit, which is why they are considered frugivorous (see p. 194). It is interesting that chimpanzees at different locations eat different kinds of food, which Goodall refers to as "cultural differences." Of course, chimps cannot eat what grows elsewhere but not in their own foraging area. But chimpanzees in one region may eat food ignored in another. At Gombe, chimps feed on just about the entire oil-nut palm; Mahale chimps have never been seen eating any part of this palm. And in the Tai National Park, Ivory Coast, only the pith of the nut is eaten.

In addition to foraging for fruit and plant material, chimpanzees engage in predatory behavior. More than twenty years ago, Goodall observed chimpanzees eating animals they had killed, either by fortuitous capture or deliberate hunting (van Lawick-Goodall, 1971; Goodall, 1986). The chimpanzee animal diet, which supplements their predominant feeding pattern of fruits and leaves, consists mainly of the red colobus monkey and the anubis baboon, but they hunt other small mammals as well, such as bushpigs, red-tailed monkeys, and blue monkeys. In addition, chimps may gather various insects, fledgling birds, and birds' eggs. Their prey are medium to small-sized mammals and birds, always smaller than themselves. In the Mahale Mountains, chimpanzees have also been observed to kill mammals, carry away the carcasses, and eat the meat.

There is some question whether chimpanzees are cooperative hunters. Busse

*Galdikas reports witnessing cases of rape among orangutans.

DIVISION OF LABOR
Activities, especially food-getting, performed only by members of a particular status, such as age or sex.

(1978, p. 769) has pointed out that cooperative hunting might not be as efficient for chimpanzees as solitary hunting:

> The high level of observed competition for small kills supports the contention that over time individuals would obtain more meat by hunting alone than by hunting in groups. That chimpanzees do sometimes hunt in groups appears to be an incidental result of fortuitous encounters between chimpanzee groups and potential prey animals.

Nevertheless, chimpanzees on occasion hunt in groups of two or more. Goodall points out that baboons, one of the chimps' favorite hunting food, was rarely hunted by one individual. Colobus monkeys have also been hunted cooperatively, according to Goodall (1986).

Like the baboons observed at Kekopey (p. 223), chimpanzees also share meat, but sharing is always solicited. Unsolicited meat sharing does not seem to be on the chimpanzee menu. Goodall observed male chimps occasionally sharing meat with other chimpanzees who begged with outstretched hands (van Lawick-Goodall, 1971). Scraps of meat left by eaters were quickly picked up by others. Some chimps attempted to take away pieces of carcass while it was being eaten by the "owner," sometimes successfully and sometimes not. Meat requesting, or begging, has several forms: by hand; peering (placing the face close to the face or meat of the meat eater); touching the meat itself, or touching the chin and lips of the meat eater; extending the hand palm up; making "soft whimper or hoo sounds while doing any of the above" (Teleki, 1973, p. 148). Adult females, with the exception of mother-daughter pairs, rarely share meat with other females. Males are more likely to share (Goodall, 1986). Unlike meat, plant food is rarely shared by adult chimpanzees, although when sharing does occur, again it is males who do it, not females. Mothers, without solicitation, regularly share plant food with their infants, and one young adult female was observed bringing fruit to her sick mother, also unsolicited.

Attempts to share in the meat are not always successful, and males may threaten or display when they are annoyed by the solicitations. However, rarely is anyone severely injured in these instances.

Chimpanzee predatory behavior has been much discussed, and indeed it is an important chimpanzee behavior. However, meat does not make up a significant portion of the chimpanzee diet, even though they appear to enjoy the taste of it. "During the many tens of thousands of hours that field researchers have observed [all] nonhuman primates, fewer than 450 sightings of vertebrate hunting and/or feeding have been reported . . ." (Butynski, 1982, p. 423). Most of these sightings have been of chimpanzees, and although they may stalk their prey, hunt cooperatively, and share meat, these behaviors are infrequent and not well developed (Butynski, 1982).

Associated with food is an interesting aspect that might be considered a sexual **division of labor**. Hunting by males and gathering by females have, in the past, led students of hominid evolution to assign the sexual division of labor as a uniquely hominid characteristic. However, McGrew (1979) found that male and female chimpanzees do not ingest the same kind of food. An analysis of a ten-month collection of fecal samples of chimpanzees at Gombe showed "a marked sex difference in insect eating: 45 of 81 (56%) female fecal samples contained at least one type of insect remains. Only 31 of 113 (27%) male fecal samples did so" (McGrew, 1979, p. 448). Fecal remains also showed that, in thirteen out of fourteen cases, it was the males who had eaten birds and mammals. It would appear

BOX 9-4

A Day in the Life of an Observer* 14 October 1982

It was a clear day with a light breeze. I began to follow Melissa and her adult daughter, Gremlin, with their two infants, Gimble and Getty. At 0905 Melissa led her family (Gimble walking, Getty riding) toward the loud calls that for some time had been heard to the east.

At 0930 the Melissa family joined two other females, Fifi and Little Bee, and their families. Gremlin displayed, running along the ground, stamping her feet, hair bristling, then pant-grunted (see Box 9-5) submissively as she approached and briefly groomed Fifi. Then began a boisterous play session with the youngsters Frodo and Tubi.

At 0957 Melissa and her party joined forces with the males and the other females. There was an eruption of pant-hoots, barks, and pant-grunts before things finally calmed down.

At 1021 the aggressive Satan charged past Melissa (who rushed out of the way, screaming) in a magnificent display. Followed by Jomeo, the two field assistants, and (presently) Goblin, Satan vanished down the slope through the tall grass.

Melissa stayed with Gremlin and adult female Miff, who was in estrus (and who became my second target). Athena, also partially swollen, was nearby. Seven adolescent males stayed back with these females. From time to time one of the young males copulated with one of the females; each time one or more of the infants interfered, running up and touching or pushing at the male concerned.

Infant Mo, age three and a half, was being weaned. Each time she tried to suckle, Miff miffed her (at least initially). Mo whimpered and then screamed loudly and insistently for minutes on end, adding to the tension in the group.

There were occasional outbursts of calling from Jomeo's direction; each time, the females and youngsters gazed intently toward the big males, often responding with pant-hoots or waa-barks.

At 1230 Jomeo moved slightly apart from the others and fed quietly; soon he rejoined the gathering as all moved on, calling and displaying. During a rest period, Miff lay stretched out on a rock while other adults groomed.

Soon the males moved again, following Satan. Miff and the females followed along in the rear. Ahead of us Jomeo and the males climbed into tall trees. Some of the females joined them; others, including Miff, moved higher still and began feeding on delicious *muhandehande* fruits. Soon the whole gathering, widely spread out, was feeding on these fruits, moving leisurely from tree to tree.

At 1318 I changed targets again and began following the two orphans, Skosha and Kristal. Pant-grunting as Satan climbed into their tree, they moved to greet him. I saw Jomeo and the young male Atlas heading north. Satan climbed down and wandered after them, and one by one the others followed. An adolescent male, Beethoven, out of sight of his superiors, performed a spectacular, hair-bristling, charging display (directed at no one, as though "practicing"), then moved on after the others.

By 1415 the only chimpanzees visible, other than my targets, were Pom and her young siblings. Pax, age four and a half, tried to get Kristal to play, but she refused. Gradually the two families drifted apart.

Later in the day (we learn from the reports of the field assistants) other females dropped out as the main party headed farther and farther north. Only two females, both of whom were in estrus and both of whom had core areas to the north of the community range, stayed with the males after 1615.

One of the things that was so striking that day was the sheer exuberance of the chimpanzees. If they had been humans, we would not hesitate to say that they were having tremendous fun. There was a good deal of noise and much play, mating, and grooming. There were wild displays with a lot of screaming, but no serious fighting. It was a carnival atmosphere.

*Adapted, with permission, from Goodall, 1986, pp. 150–151.

BOX 9-5

Calls*

PANT-GRUNT   Made by a subordinate to a higher-ranking individual; token of respect; maintains friendly relations within community.

WAA-BARK   Loud, sharp sound, given in variety of agonistic contexts.

LIP SMACKING, TOOTH CLACKING   Frequently accompanies social grooming.

PANT-HOOTS   Most commonly heard call of adult individuals; serves to identify caller; given upon arrival at a new food source, when two parties meet, after return from patrol, during social excitement, during feeding, and during nesting in the evening.

*Adapted after Goodall, 1986.

from these data that, although males eat insects (especially termites), the bulk of insects are sought and eaten by females, but vertebrates are the domain of males.

Behavior associated with food seems especially pertinent in this discussion. We have seen that males share meat with friends and relatives (when solicited), and males also, on occasion, share plant food with both sexes. Mothers often share food (unsolicited) with their infants, and daughters have been seen sharing, again unsolicited, with mothers.

As mentioned, male chimps are occasional predators, and although much of their meat is obtained fortuitously, they deliberately pursue prey, perhaps even cooperatively. What is more significant is that obtaining meat

> often involves primarily male groups roaming relatively great distances and acting cooperatively when the appropriate situation fortuitously arises—in short, *hunting*. On the other hand, female chimpanzees (predominantly) obtain ants and termites by prolonged, systematic, and repetitive manipulative sequences . . . accumulating a meal of many small units that are usually concentrated at a few known permanent sources—in short, gathering (McGrew, 1979, p. 450).

This sex difference might be considered as the basis for the hominid division of labor of female-gatherer and male-hunter that at some point developed in hominid evolution.

Chimpanzees seem to be a somewhat better model for hominid evolution than baboons. A chimpanzee community is flexible (fusion-fission), not as highly structured as the baboon, and the close mother-daughter ties suggest a matrifocal emphasis found in many human societies.

Another chimpanzee activity resembling behavior once believed to be unique to hominids is the manufacturing of tools. No one knows when early hominids first made tools. The earliest evidence—stone tools—is about 2½ million years old. Although at present no evidence exists to show it, it is reasonable to assume that there were tools made of organic materials earlier than this.

In additon to making simple tools, chimpanzees manipulate objects for many purposes. They throw such objects as stones, vegetation, sticks, and feces (as visitors to zoos have learned to their sorrow and their dry cleaners' profit). They also play extensively with objects, and they use leaves for cleaning the body. Chimpanzee tool making and object manipulation suggests that the *potential* for tool-making is primate in origin.

There are, of course, important differences between chimpanzee and hominid behavior. The chimpanzee consort relationship is temporary, the home-range is not the human home base, the mother-daughter bond is not a complete family, chimpanzee hunting is mainly fortuitous (questions have been raised whether it is really cooperative), and meat sharing may be called sharing only by stretching the meaning of the word; "distribution" is a better term (Teleki, 1973). That is, meat is rarely given, but it is taken, and if it is given, it is done so grudgingly and reluctantly.

The chimpanzee behavior we have described—object manipulation, food sharing, hunting, division of labor—does not mean that hominids evolved from chimpanzees. First of all, chimpanzees today evolved from an earlier form, and it is very doubtful that present-day chimp behavior is the same as that of their ancestors. Furthermore, humans developed different strategies in adapting as hunters to a savanna environment. Possibly, however, the striking morphological, biochemical, and behavioral similarities of chimpanzees and humans may point to the *kind* of ancestor that led to the hominid line.

Cultural Behavior

At one time, anthropologists defined humans as toolmaking animals, and then modified the definition to read, "animals that make tools regularly." However, the observations of chimpanzees making and using tools by Goodall (1965) more than 20 years ago, brought such definitions into question. Many observers of chimpanzees, gorillas, orangutans, and some monkeys have verified the practice of tool manufacturing by apes and tool use by monkeys.

Probably the best-known example of nonhuman primate tool manufacture is termite fishing (Fig. 9-5). The chimpanzee inserts and probes in subterranean mounds or nests of termites with pieces of bark, vine, grass blades, or twigs. When the termites seize the probe, the chimp then withdraws the tool and eats the attached termites with its lips and teeth. Chimpanzees modify some of these objects, such as twigs, by removing the leaves—in effect manufacturing a stick from the natural material, a twig. Indeed, chimpanzees show the greatest frequency and diversity of tool-using behavior of any nonhuman animal. They drag or roll branches, fallen trees, stones, cans, and camp furniture while displaying. They have been observed throwing rocks at a bushpig during predation, throwing objects "overhead," "sidearm," and "underhand" (Beck, 1980), and even using a twig as a toothpick. They can, to some extent, modify objects to a "regular and set pattern," and have been observed preparing objects for later use at an out-of-sight location (Goodall, 1986). For example, a chimp will select a piece of vine, bark, twig, or palm frond and modify it by removing leaves or any extraneous material. She then modifies it further by reducing it to a certain length—not too long or too short—and may make several of these for future use. Chimps have also been seen making these tools even before the termite or ant mounds are in sight. The tools have thus been made to "a regular and set pattern," an ability once believed to be unique to humans.

(b)

Figure 9-9
(a) *Chimp termiting.* (b) *Closeup of chimp hands while termiting. Dexterity of chimp can be seen in ability to manipulate stem.*

Chimps also make sponges from a handful of leaves, chew them for a moment, and then push them into the hollow of a tree where water has accumulated. The liquid is then sucked from this homemade sponge. Leaves are also used to dab at wounds on their bottoms, and sometimes, when a chimp has diarrhea, leaves serve as toilet paper.

At Bossou, Guinea (Africa), observers Sugiyama and Koman (1979) watched chimpanzees crack nuts with what they call a pebble tool. The striking stone weighed from 17 to 30 lb., and the platform stone on which the nut was placed weighed about 35 lb.:

> A chimpanzee who crouched in front of the platform stone chose a dry palm-seed, placed it in the cavity of the platform stone, gripped the handle side of the pebble tool, lifted it up to a height of 5-20 cm, and then struck the palm-seed. . . . When a palm-seed was broken, the chimpanzee removed the white ovule with his fingers and ate it in about 1 minute (Sugiyama and Koman, 1979, p. 515).

The authors believe this nut-cracking behavior "is highly suggestive of early man's stone-tool culture," and perhaps it is. However, it is important to note that neither the hammer stone nor the platform stone was deliberately manufactured.* Beck (1980) points out that many animals use unmodified objects as tools, but only apes—mainly chimpanzees—deliberately manufacture tools for specific purposes. However, we should be aware of the significant differences in toolmaking between chimps and humans. Chimpanzees *usually* select their material for a tool from a nearby item, and use it with little delay; humans collect material from a wide area, and may store it for a long time before using it. Although chimpanzees use and make tools, they do so comparatively rarely, whereas humans are utterly dependent on tools for their survival. Also, humans use tools to make other tools; other primates do not (Chalmers, 1980).

Like chimpanzees, Japanese macaques (a variety of Old World monkey) have also demonstrated a capacity for "cultural" behavior. In 1952, Japanese scientists embarked upon a provisioning procedure in which they supplied food at various places in Japan for groups of monkeys living in those areas. This method has proved eminently successful for purposes of observation, and the Japanese researchers have added significantly to our understanding of macaques.

Japanese monkeys have not been observed making tools, but one of them "invented" at least two methods of preparing food for eating. In 1952, sweet potatoes, a food new to the monkeys, were made available by scattering on the beach. The following year Imo, a young female, was observed using one hand to brush the sand off the sweet potatoes and the other hand to dip the potatoes in the water of a brook. The invention was picked up by juveniles through playmate relationships and was passed from juveniles to mothers, who then passed it on to their children. Within ten years, 90% of all troop members were washing sweet potatoes, except adults older than twelve years and infants less than one year.

Another invention, again by the "genius" Imo, was wheat washing. Wheat was distributed to the Koshima Island troop by scattering it on the sand, from which the monkeys could pick out single grains. Imo introduced the practice of scooping up sand and wheat, carrying a handful to the edge of the sea, and tossing the mixture onto the water. The sand sank, and Imo then skimmed the wheat grains off the surface and ate them! This practice also spread through the troop

---

*Observers of nonhuman primates rarely distinguish *natural objects used as tools* from *modified objects deliberately manufactured* for specific purposes. The term tool is usually employed in both cases.

(a)

(b)   (c)

Figure 9-10
Japanese macaques. Japanese scientists established feeding centers and studied macaques as they came into the centers to feed. (a) In a tree nest; (b) at the feeding center; (c) eating at an old shrine.

much as the sweet-potato washing habit: first juveniles, then adults—especially mothers—along family lines (Kawamura, 1959).

What does all of this have to do with culture? Culture is learned behavior, and we have discussed the characteristics of culture early in the first chapter. We have already pointed out that mammals, and especially primates, are capable of learning. We have also described toolmaking and object manipulation and what have been called "cultural differences" in the kinds of foods eaten and in the making and using of tools. Chimpanzees do some similar things differently at different places. This kind of behavior may be called *cultural*, but that is not the same as saying that chimpanzees have *a culture*.

Since primates (like all mammals) learn part of their behavior, then certainly primates are capable of cultural behavior. Chimpanzees, it appears, learn more, perhaps, than any other nonhuman primate, but the extent to which chimpanzees depend on culture for survival is another matter. Among chimpanzees, there is a good deal of genetically based behavior, as we have seen. Triggered by estrus, male responses are genetic, not learned. It is highly probable that dominance

Figure 9-11
Centers for Japanese macaque studies.

HOKKAIDŌ

Sapporo

Sea of Japan

Sendai

HONSHU

KITAKYŪSHŪ

Tokyo

Hiroshima

Yokohama

Fukuoka

Ōsaka

SHIKOKU

Pacific Ocean

KYŪSHŪ

Figure 9-12
Macaque washing potatoes.

(that is, structuring social relationships based on rank) is also genetically based. Admittedly, though, it is difficult to know the extent of genetic influence upon chimpanzee behavior (and, sociobiologists might add, in human behavior as well). Nevertheless, the degree of human dependence on culture—for the human way of life—is total, or as total as we can determine. This is not the case with chimpanzees.

For one thing, cultural behavior is transmitted symbolically, and wild nonhuman primates do not transmit culture, or any kind of learned behavior as far as we can tell, symbolically. Chalmers points out that nonhuman primates can only learn from one another by direct observation; human beings suffer no such limitation. Freed from this restriction, humans can make use of experience accumulated over many generations, collected over many areas, and can develop rich and complicated traditions and cultures (Chalmers, 1980, p. 224). If culture is to have meaning as the human strategy for survival, then to refer to chimpanzee life style as "a culture" is to blur the concept of culture. Nor do we believe that a term such as "incipient culture" is useful in explaining their behavior. This suggests that chimpanzees are on their way to developing culture, a premise which is extremely doubtful. Still, the information we gain about chimpanzees and other primates is valuable, not only because we learn more about nonhuman primates, but because we gain a fuller understanding of the possible mechanisms of early hominid evolution.

This troublesome question of culture and whether or not it can be attributed to primates must take into account language, a core component in the definition of culture.

Language

Communication is common behavior among animals, from the smell and antenna signals of insects to the symbols of humans. Gestural and vocal signals have been observed among primates by a variety of investigators. Jane Goodall (1968a, 1971, 1986) documented numerous such signals among chimpanzees. She notes facial expressions, such as play-face and several grins, and vocal signals, including various kinds of hoots and grunts (Fig. 9-8). Expressions such as these are communication, of course, but can they be considered language?

Language, as distinct from communication, has been considered a uniquely human achievement, but work with apes has raised doubts about that position. Language has been defined in ways that would include insect communication on the one hand, or exclude everything except human speech on the other. While we prefer defining language in terms of symbolic communication, there is much disagreement on this subject. The assumption that *Homo sapiens* is the only organism capable of handling language has been brought into question by the success psychologists have achieved in teaching apes to communicate with symbols. Without attempting to settle the question of whether or not such ape ability should be called language, we shall briefly describe several successful experiments.

Washoe In 1966, Beatrice and Allen Gardner, psychologists at the University of Nevada, decided to teach a two-way communication system to an eleven-

Figure 9-13
Chimpanzee facial gestures. Chimpanzees are the most facially expressive of all nonhuman primates. (From In the Shadow of Man, *by Jane van Lawick-Goodall. Copyright © 1971 by Hugo and Jane van Lawick-Goodall. Redrawn with permission of Houghton Mifflin Company.)*

month-old chimpanzee named Washoe. The gestures they selected were those of American Sign Language (ASL), a means of communication long used by the deaf.

Washoe's progress was slow at the beginning, but by the tenth month she possessed a vocabulary of a dozen words. At about this time, she began to combine signs such as "go in," "go out," and, later, produced combinations of three to five signs in sequence. At the end of four years, the Gardners claimed she had a vocabulary of over 130 signs, and it was possible for her and her trainer to engage in short, simple dialogues.

Washoe learned syntax—the proper order of words—as she demonstrated in phrases like, "Roger you tickle." She occasionally signed to herself when alone and was seen signing "quiet" to herself before sneaking to a forbidden place, and "hurry" on the way to the potty chair.

The Gardners caution against evaluating chimpanzee linguistic ability on the basis of the Washoe data. If Washoe had been a preschool child, then her responses to the questions who? what? where? would place her at a relatively advanced level of linguistic competence. On the other hand, she would have been "a linguistically disadvantaged child." She was not exposed to American Sign Language until she was about one year old, and her trainers, learning ASL as a second language, were not fluent.

In a sequel to Project Washoe, the Gardners instituted major improvements in teaching language to chimpanzees. Among the improvements were exposing chimpanzee subjects to sign language from birth and using research assistants fluent in ASL, being deaf themselves or raised by deaf parents (B. T. and R. A. Gardner, 1975).

Figure 9-14
Washoe signing "hat" when being questioned about a woolen hat.

When Washoe was pregnant in 1976, researchers were interested in whether she would transmit her ASL signs to her baby. Unfortuntely, the infant died a few hours after birth. Washoe was again "expecting" in January, 1979, when Dr. Roger Fouts, a former student of the Gardners, began research at the University of Oklahoma into the ability of chimpanzees to transmit their signs to other chimps. Washoe's second baby also died a few months later.

Dr. Fouts, who had moved to Central Washington University and taken Washoe with him, decided to present Washoe with a ten-month-old male chimp named Loulis. Washoe accepted the infant male and, after observing their interaction, D. H. Fouts (wife of Roger Fouts and co-worker with him at their primate lab) stated (1985) that by the age of five years and three months, Loulis had acquired 55 signs from Washoe and other chimps. R. Fouts (1982, 1983) claims that his experiments demonstrate that chimps can communicate with each other using ASL, and they invent signs for objects that had no signs. Furthermore, not only do young chimpanzees learn signs from older ones, but older chimps learn from younger ones.

Loulis also *initiates* conversation with his fellow chimpanzees. In a study, videotaped (three times a day for 15 days) with no humans present, Loulis initiated conversation 54 times mainly in social and play contexts (D. H. Fouts, 1985).

Sarah   Another chimpanzee language, specially devised by Professor David Premack (1971), was taught to his six-year-old simian student, Sarah, in an experiment initiated at the University of California at Santa Barbara in 1967. The symbols in this language system consisted of differently shaped and colored plastic pieces with a bit of metal on the back that adhered to a magnetized board.

Sarah was taught to recognize the plastic chips as symbols for various objects. The chips did not resemble the objects they represented; for example, the plastic chip for "apple" was not round and red. Sarah soon learned to correctly identify fruit, and was able to place two chips together in the proper sequence. Verbs were then introduced, and Sarah was able to place the chips properly to form a sentence, such as, "Mary give apple Sarah."

Sarah also learned to indicate which objects were the same and which different by removing the chip for question mark and replacing it with the correct chip for "same" or "different." After eighteen months, Premack believed Sarah had acquired a language competence comparable in many respects to a child of two or two and a half years. The Premacks (1983) also believe chimpanzees possess the potential for abstract representation; however, intensive language training is necessary for the chimp to demonstrate this capacity.

Lana   There have been other experiments teaching language to chimpanzees, such as Rumbaugh's (1977) work with Lana at the Yerkes Regional Primate Center in Atlanta, Georgia. Lana worked with chips attached to keys on a specially built typewriter connected to a computer. After six months, Lana recognized symbols for thirty words, and was able to ask for food and answer questions through the machine.

In 1975, two young male chimps, Sherman and Austin, were added to the experiment. Because the experimenters were not certain Lana understood all the words she used, Sherman's and Austin's training emphasized the meaning of each word they encountered. This change in language training has led Rumbaugh and his colleagues to believe that Sherman and Austin (and, by extension, chimps in general) are capable of functional symbolic communication; that is, to these two chimps, words were representational, real symbols, understood and used by them. Sherman's and Austin's data demonstrate that chimpanzees can master referential use of learned symbols, the meanings of which have been arbitrarily assigned to lexigrams (words). In other words, apes are capable of mastering semantics! (Rumbaugh, et al., 1982, p. 379)

Koko   The first gorilla to be taught American Sign Language is Koko, a female, who is in her sixteenth year of instruction. Dr. Francine Patterson, in charge of the program, states that Koko knows and uses more than 500 signs. Michael, a slightly younger male, who has been in the program a few years less than Koko, also has a considerable ASL vocabulary. Patterson also maintains that Koko and Michael communicate with each other.

Not everyone, however, agrees that apes actually learn language. Sebeok (1980) compared the ape responses to their trainers' signals to those of a German horse named Clever Hans. Hans, it seemed, could count by tapping with his hoof, and his owner believed he had taught Hans to solve problems. Actually, it turned out that the owner involuntarily jerked when Hans reached the correct number. Given this unconscious cue, Hans stopped tapping at the correct answer.

Nim   Dr. Herbert Terrace, who raised a chimp (named Nim Chimpsky after the well-known linguist, Noam Chomsky) almost from birth, trained him to sign using ASL. Just like Washoe, Sarah, and other chimps, Nim was able to place the signs in sequence, but Terrace wondered whether Nim was actually fashioning proper sentences or reacting in the manner of Clever Hans to the trainer's signals.

After almost four years of working with Nim, Terrace analyzed videotapes of the training sessions. His conclusion:

> . . . it would be premature to conclude that a chimpanzee's combination [of words] shows the same structure evident in the sentences of a child. The fact that Nim's utterances were less spontaneous and less original than those of a child, and that his utterances did not become longer, both as he learned new signs and as he acquired more experience in using sign language, suggests that much of the structure and meaning of his combinations was determined, or at least suggested, by the utterances of his teachers (Terrace, 1979, p. 221).

Terrace believes there is a tendency among the experiments to project human meaning into

> the imitative utterances of an ape who was simply trying to manipulate its teachers to feed it or engage in some kind of social activity (Terrace, 1982, p. 9).

Criticizing some experiments, Terrace writes that the use of signs in certain instances

> suggest a type of interaction between an ape and its trainer that has little to do with human language. In each instance the sole function of the ape's signing appears to be to request various rewards that can be obtained only by signing. Little, if any, evidence is available that an ape signs in order to exchange information with its trainer, as opposed to simply demanding some object or activity (Terrace, 1983, p. 38).

Terrace's views are supported by Dr. Richard Sanders, one of Nim's trainers, who notes that Nim produced signs that made sense to the trainer, but did not learn the semantic relations in order to do so. Questioning whether chimps understand the signs they learn, Sanders writes, ". . . using reinforcement to coerce a subject into using signs on demand can cause the learner to adopt simple instrumental responses to please the trainer and gain reward but have no other meaning to the signer" (1986, p. 209).

Chantek   Taking a somewhat different approach, Dr. Lyn Miles worked with a three-year-old male orangutan at the University of Tennessee. She raised Chantek in a comfortable environment, arranged at least a partially aboreal environment for him, and planned his life to develop as normally as possible under the circumstances.

Dr. Miles was not so concerned that Chantek learn the conditions of true language use; her purpose was "to investigate the communicative, cognitive, and semantic processes that underlie the emergence of symbolic behavior" (1983, p. 47). Her method was not to use pressure to teach Chantek particular signs, but to teach signs in meaningful situations; for example, when Chantek showed interest in a cat that wandered nearby, he was taught the sign for cat. Signing was "introduced as a primary means of communication within the social relationships rather than presented as lessons in a classroom" (1983, p. 58).

Comparing him with Nim, Dr. Miles believed Chantek was much more successful. He imitated the trainers' signs much less; he had a higher level of spontaneous utterances, and he signed even when his trainer did not (Nim did very little of this). Miles concluded that "Chantek's slower, more deliberate, and spontaneous signing and the distinctive 'insightful' cognitive style of orangutans may indicate superior linguistic and cognitive abilities" (1983, p. 58).

R. Fouts criticizes Premack, Terrace, and Rumbaugh because they emphasized too much the structural aspects of language. Grammar, he writes, is not congenial to chimps. Fouts believes language is primarily a social activity, and the environment in which the teaching is performed should be a social environment. This was lacking in the work of the three psychologists noted (but it is crucial in the ongoing experiment with Washoe and her colleagues).

However, other scholars besides Terrace have raised questions about apes and their ability to learn language. Savage-Rumbaugh, who trained Lana and other chimps, asks, "Does a chimpanzee learn that a symbol is indeed a name for an object or is it learning that the execution of that symbol produces that object?" (1983, p. 454). If the latter, then apple means apple only as long as the execution of apple is followed by receipt of an apple. Atherton and Schwartz (1983) believe more emphasis should be placed on whether apes understand what they are talking about. Whether apes learn language or whether what they do *is* language, these experiments are significant for the study of human evolution in that they demonstrate that ape capability is greater than once believed. Such demonstrations may possibly suggest clues to the origins of human language. One practical result from these experiments has been the development of successful techniques to help mentally disadvantaged children to express themselves (Rumbaugh, et al., 1982).

It is clear that captive apes, in a learning situation, acquire signs and perhaps symbols as well. It is not clear, as several of the trainers mentioned above indicate, whether apes understand the signs *as symbols*. Nor is it clear whether apes are capable of creating grammatically correct English sentences. It is not even clear whether apes should be taught grammar as a means of learning language. These matters are still being sorted out by the scholars involved in teaching language to apes.

Apes have shown considerable skill and intelligence in learning and using signs, and perhaps symbols, under human direction. In their natural habitat, nonhuman primates are also capable, of course, of communicating via signals, as many animals are.

> Chimpanzees have a rich repertoire of sounds, postures, and facial expressions which function as signals during interactions between individuals . . . indicating physiological state, emotional mood, social rank and so on, [which] facilitate the exchange of information among community members (Goodall, 1986, pp. 114–115).

It has also been reported that vervets, an African monkey, communicate in a *semantic* manner; that is, they use "signals to refer to objects in the external world" (Seyfarth et al., 1980a, p. 801, and 1980b). Vervets, for example, have calls that communicate danger separately for eagles, leopards, and snakes. Monkeys, hearing the calls, respond in different ways. For an eagle call, they look up and run into dense bush; if on the ground, they respond to a leopard call by running up into the trees; and snake alarms cause them to look down at the ground around them.

While these activities are, of course, a form of communication and apparently a more sophisticated form than that of other animals (except humans), calls cannot be considered language. As for captive apes—chimps, gorillas, and orangs—whether their use of signs is language is still being debated by their teachers, as we have discussed.

What, then, can we say about apes, language, and culture? Captive apes, with human instruction, have shown potential for a number of activities, which some scholars have suggested are preadaptations for hominization. However, we are concerned with free-ranging, not captive, apes. In their natural state, chimps (even monkeys) use a complex system of calls for communication. Again, we emphasize that these are calls, and not language. We can only conclude that language is not part of the ape lifestyle. What about culture?

Among humans, instinctual strategy for survival has been replaced by a cultural strategy, and human problems—so we believe—can or must be resolved by cultural means. The ape situation is different. Certainly, apes are intelligent, much more so than was believed even 25 or 30 years ago. Certainly, apes are capable of learning and have unambiguously demonstrated this in the wild and in captivity. In free-ranging chimps, the evidence is overwhelming that learning has influenced certain areas of their lives to some extent. However, culture is not the main survival strategy for chimps or other apes, nor is it ever likely to be so.

Social Carnivores

Our closest relatives, the apes, are forest animals and are mainly vegetarians. Unlike apes, our early ancestors were most likely savanna dwellers and meat eaters (actually, of course, omnivorous). Early on, they probably hunted mostly small

Figure 9-15
Lioness and cub at play.

game and scavenged* larger animals; however, when they did hunt, it probably
was mostly in groups. To learn more about the origins of human social systems, it
may be useful to look at other savanna dwellers and group hunters, the social carnivores: lions, wolves, and wild dogs. It should be noted that social carnivores
and early hominids adapted in somewhat analogous ways to a similar ecological
situation. Phylogenetically, hominids are more homologous, of course, with primates, not with social carnivores.

Lions   Like chimps, a pride of lions is loosely organized. The core of the pride
consists of adult females and their young. A definite hierarchical system appears
to be lacking among lions who do, however, show dominance and rank. That
males are definitely dominant to females can easily be seen, especially at feeding
time. There is also dominance among females (Rudnai, 1973).

Moving across the savanna, a female leads the pride, and the adult males attach themselves to the pride or tag behind. Most of the hunting is the females'
task, either singly or communally. Once the prey is killed, males move in and eat
their fill before allowing lionesses to feed, one of the few expressions of male
dominance.

The close mother-infant relationship so typical of primates is not found
among lions. Mothering ranges between care and neglect. Female lions do nurse
and protect their young and snarl at males that roam too close to their cubs. On
the other hand, lionesses enjoy the conviviality of other females, and if taking
care of cubs means separation from the pride, the mother may abandon them.
Mothers do not bring meat from a kill to their cubs. If the cubs are at a kill, they

*There is some disagreement among anthropologists, paleontologists, and primatologists whether
hunting, scavenging, or both were the way of life of the earliest hominids. (See Binford, 1981, and
Shipman, 1985, for the scavenging point of view.)

usually obtain some meat; if they are not there, then the mother must fetch them—but only after she herself has fed. However, by the time she returns with the cubs, there may be no meat left.

When the cubs are almost two years old (about the time the mother has another litter), contact with the mother decreases and she ceases to care for them. The continuing relationship between mother and offspring so marked among chimpanzees is not present in lions. The lack of a close relationship between mother and cubs, as well as the frequent neglect of cubs by the mothers, may account for the high mortality rate of cubs, estimated to be over 60% by Schaller (1972).

The social structure of the lion pride, although loosely organized, nevertheless provides them with superior hunting techniques enabling them to catch large herbivores in open terrain. Operating as a group, lions are much more successful in hunting than solitary lions.

Lack of parental care and male participation in the group structure are not a good model for what we believe early hominid behavior to be; however, the lion pride has been a successful form of adaptation to a savanna environment. In this environment, lions have developed a strategy different from early hominids. Females are the hunters, and, as mentioned, a close mother-offspring relationship is lacking. Lion adaptations, however, help delineate early hominid strategies. Like lions, hominids also lived in social groups and most likely were social rather than solitary hunters. Like other primates, however, early hominid females were probably very closely associated with their offspring, which may help explain why males were most likely the primary hunters.

Wolves Social carnivore behavior more similar to hominid adaptations may be seen in wolves. A wolf pack and a human hunter-gatherer band maintain an optimal size of the group in relation to the availability of food in regions with similar ecological characteristics. Both groups tend to control births socially, both live well below the carrying capacity of the environment, and both groups hunt cooperatively.

Food sharing exists between young and old, and rituals control much aggression within both the pack and band. In both groups, allegiance appears to be maintained through rituals involving "dancing" and "music." During food scarcity, both groups tend to split up and rejoin during abundance (Fox, 1978).

A pack of wolves is formed when a mated pair leaves its parental group to produce a litter of its own. Occasionally, several families may combine to form a large pack of 7 to 10 adults of both sexes. Wolves are territorial and avoid using an area through which another pack has recently traveled—probably indicated by urine-marking.

Care of young pups is basically a function of the mother who suckles them; however, there is great interest in the pups shown by all adult pack members. Weaning takes place at six to eight weeks, and pups eat food regurgitated by the mother or other members of the pack. When the pack hunts, the mother, or another adult, remains with the pups, and pack members bring back food for all.

Wild Dogs Wild dogs of Africa form very amiable and closely interacting groups, which average 9 to 10 members. Schaller (1972) reports that since the young tend to remain with the adults even after the birth of a new litter, it is very likely that a pack is composed of related individuals. Most observers do not be-

Figure 9-16
Wolves attacking moose.

lieve a dominance hierarchy exists among wild dogs, but van Lawick (1970) is certain he observed dominance and submissive behavior. Unlike wolves, no territoriality exists among wild dogs. Ranges, which average around 240 square miles and may reach over 1,000 square miles, overlap considerably without agonistic behavior between the packs. It is not uncommon, however, for a pack that is otherwise nonterritorial to defend the area immediately around its den.

As among wolves, care of pups is a function of all pack members, but the mother retains certain prerogatives. She suckles the young, and when the den is moved, it is her task to move the pups.

Both males and females hunt, but if there are small pups, usually the mother and possibly one or two others remain at the den as guards. When they return, the hunters share the kill by regurgitating meat to all who remained in the den. When pups accompany adults, they take almost complete precedence at a kill, and are permitted to monopolize the carcass. Wild dogs hunt more successfully than lions or wolves and Schaller estimates a remarkable 89% success rate. For this reason, as well as their fierceness when attacking, they have been called "the super beasts of prey" (Wilson, 1975).

Studying social carnivores is instructive because they inhabit an ecological niche similar to that occupied by early hominids. And, like social carnivores, early hominids also probably hunted. It is possible, as Schaller suggests, "that some of the same selective forces which had an influence on the social [carnivores] also had an effect on hominid societies" (1972, p. 378). Since the carnivore group, as we have seen, is superior to the solitary hunter in its success rate, there may, at some point, have been selection pressures in hominids for such cooperative methods as group hunting and encircling the prey. Living in groups makes division of labor possible as seen in the case of wild dogs, where the mother guards the den while others hunt. We can conjecture that fairly early on hominids also divided their labor, shared food, and occupied a home base.

Figure 9-17
Pack of wild dogs attacking zebra.

Kortlandt makes the interesting suggestion that wolves (we would include wild dogs, also) developed their cooperative hunting techniques as a result of hunting animals larger than themselves. Early hominids, he goes on, evolved similar cooperative hunting techniques since they, too, hunted game larger than themselves. Furthermore, the teamwork techniques of wolves required considerable extension of their social communication system. Kortlandt believes a similar evolutionary trend must have occurred among early hominids, but because the largely "instinctive social communication system" in hominids is poorer, they achieved an alternative evolutionary solution by extending their primarily "*noninstinctive* communication patterns," that is, speech (Kortlandt, 1965, p. 321).

Hunting and Gathering Societies

We have reviewed two kinds of social animals, nonhuman primates and social carnivores, in order to gain some understanding of ourselves and our origins. Contemporary humans in an industrialized or agricultural community live far removed from ancient humans and, from an adaptive viewpoint, cannot easily be compared to nonhuman social mammals. However, there are peoples living at the present time in remote areas of the world who have maintained a way of life, to some extent at least, similar to that of early hominids. A review of these people, whom anthropologists classify as hunter-gatherers (or, as some prefer, gatherer-hunters), may give some idea of how hominids lived 1 or 2 million years ago. We cannot claim that contemporary hunter-gatherers live identically to those ancient ones, but since adaptive problems are somewhat similar, it will be worthwhile to see what adaptive strategies they developed that enabled them to survive.

A hunting and gathering pattern (that is, hunting wild game and gathering wild plant foods) is fundamental to human behavior. More than just characteristic of early hominids, a hunting and gathering way of life has been *the* strategy used by our ancestors throughout the vast majority of human evolution.* The time span of our genus, *Homo*, has extended for about 2 million years. Of that time, our ancestors were scavenger-hunter-gatherers for all but the last 10,000 years. In other words, 99.5% of the history of the genus *Homo* was spent as a scavenger-hunter-gatherer.

Hunter-gatherers live today in widely divergent environments we would consider to be forbidding regions of the earth: rain forests, deserts, and the arctic and subarctic. Such was not always the case. Before the invention of farming, hunters traversed the plains in search of food. However, with domestication, farmers pushed the hunters out of this desirable land to less hospitable areas.

Typically, hunter-gatherers live in small nomadic or seminomadic bands composed of loosely integrated families. They usually lack the more organized forms of kinship, such as clans and lineages. There are no specialized economic, religious, or political groups since the family itself is the organization that undertakes all these roles. Depending on the season and availability of food, the size of the band expands and contracts. Bands move from one area to another within their home range according to the availability of resources in different places at different times. The food resources used by the band are communal property, and all families have equal rights to them. To protect their resources, band members may defend their territory against encroachment by strangers (Service, 1966, p. 22).

A band is not a closed group; people constantly come and go, separating when food is scarce and regrouping for collective hunts, sharing a water hole, or participating in an important ceremony. Should a conflict arise, an individual may leave his band and seek to join another.

Men do most of the hunting and women the gathering, usually in small groups, but all share their food with other members of the band. Since hunter-gatherers exercise little or no control over the plants and animals upon which they depend, they have to accommodate themselves to seasonal and annual fluctuations in resources spread over wide areas.

As an example of a hunting-gathering society, let us take a brief look at the !Kung San of the Kalahari Desert in South Africa.

!Kung San†

During the past twenty years, San culture has altered dramatically as outside influences have introduced new ideas, new material things, new values, etc. (See Yellen, 1985, for a brief report on Dobe San culture change.) The following description of the !Kung San, as a hunting-gathering society, is written in the present tense, as is customary in anthropology, even though they no longer live this way.

The !Kung San of the Dobe live on the border of Namibia and Botswana on the northern fringe of the Kalahari Desert of southwest Africa. This area of hot, wet summers (October to May) and cool, dry winters (May to October) is a

---

*Some anthropologists believe scavenging preceded hunting and may have been the primary source of meat even for *H. erectus*. (See Shipman, 1985.)

†The diacritical mark "!" indicates a click (something like the clucking sound made to a horse), which is part of the San phonetic system. Anthropologists have discarded the term "Bushmen" for these foragers living in the Kalahari and now refer to them as San, of which the !Kung are one group. Material on the !Kung is derived from Yellen (1977) and especially Lee (1984).

Figure 9-18
Map of San area.

sparsely populated sand plain across which the hunting-gathering !Kung San occupy approximately 7,000 square miles. Within this area are 10 permanent water holes occupied by approximately 500 San. Some non-San people live here, also.

At the water holes, the !Kung live in camps or villages* of from 10 to 30 individuals. The type of village varies with the season. In the dry (summer) season, the village is fairly large. It is comprised of from 8 to 15 huts and 20 to 50 people, is located near a permanent water source, and is occupied for 3 to 6 months. In the rainy season, the village, from 3 to 20 huts, is located near a seasonal water and food source and is occupied for 3 weeks to 3 months. In the spring and fall the camp is temporary, rarely occupied for more than 2 or 3 weeks, and no huts are built.

Until recently, each !Kung group moved every season, building and abandoning 3 to 6 villages each year. Eventually, these abandoned villages become buried in sand, and were converted into archeological sites. ". . . !Kung village sites of the 1960s strongly resemble the village sites of prehistoric foragers 100 to 500 or

*Lee uses the words "camp" and "village" interchangeably.

more years old . . ." (Lee, 1984, p. 33). A !Kung camp consists of kinspeople and affines (inlaws) who have found that they can live and work well together. Brothers, for example, may live together or apart, as may fathers and sons. The composition of the camp changes from day to day and month to month because the !Kung enjoy visiting. Each year about 30% of the population makes a permanent residential shift from one camp to another. There is a visiting network among camps, and during a given lifetime an individual may live for varying amounts of time at many different water holes. However, establishing residence with a camp does not require relinquishing a claim to any other camp.

This constant circulation might appear to cause residential instability. However, an entire camp may move together for at least part of the year. What gives the camp its stability is its core, which is composed of related older people, usually siblings and cousins. Generally, the core is considered to be the water hole owners. Surrounding each water hole is land that contains food resources. This forms the basic subsistence area for the residing group. The water hole and the land immediately around it is "owned" by the *k'ausi*, the core of related people, and the ownership is passed from generation to generation as long as the descendants continue to live there.

The core group is also recognized as the hosts, and anyone wishing to visit at the water hole is expected to approach the hosts for permission. The *k'ausi* are not owners in the sense that they can sell the land if they wish; they are simply the people who have lived there longer than any other. Both male and female kin and their spouses are included in the *k'ausi*. After a time the name of one member of the group becomes the name of the camp, but this leader is in no sense a headman.

A camp is built up over time by the addition of in-marrying spouses of the core siblings. A brother brings in his wife, and a sister may bring in her husband. These in-laws then bring in *their* siblings so that the camp has a relative—parent, child, sibling, or spouse—with links to the core group.

Settling at a water hole, the !Kung arrange their huts in a circle, with the entrances facing center. The huts are generally occupied by nuclear families, with

Figure 9-19
A !Kung San camp.

Figure 9-20
A !Kung family works at home.

husband, wife, and immature children sharing a single hut and hearth. Young, unmarried adults of the same sex usually live together in a separate hut, whereas widowers and co-wives have huts of their own.

People living at a water hole—residents and visitors—all share the available resources. Members of a camp, of course, have access to the resources, and, if the sharing breaks down, it ceases to be a camp. Visitors also share, and it is understood that the residents at some future time will pay a return visit to their visitors' camp and share the resources there. A fairly complex system of obligations apply between hosts and visitors.

!Kung men are excellent hunters and devote a great deal of time and effort to their pursuit of game. While snaring game is practiced, most of the hunting consists of pursuing game either singly or in twos or threes. Known to the !Kung are some 262 species of animals, of which about 80 are eaten. Several varieties of antelopes and game birds are eagerly sought, but the species that provide the most meat are warthogs, wildebeests, gemsboks, kudus, elands, roan antelopes, and hartebeests. Although women do not hunt, men may gather when meat is scarce, and the food thus obtained accounted for 22% of all gathered food.

When a large animal is killed, it is feasting time, and great cauldrons of meat are cooked round-the-clock. People gather from far and wide, and meat is distributed to all. The sharing is made according to a set of rules, with great care, and the arranging and rearranging of the pieces may continue for an hour to ensure that each recipient is given the right proportion. Improper meat distribution can cause bitter wrangling among close relatives. Excellent distribution will be fondly recalled for months.

As in most foraging societies, women do the gathering (see p. 259). As a matter of fact, the foundation of !Kung subsistence depends on the 105 species of edible wild plants found in their area, especially the remarkable mongongo nut, which provides up to half the !Kung vegetable diet. The wide variety of vegetable food available to the !Kung provides a cushion against changing environmental conditions.

When the !Kung establish a campsite, they eat the more desirable plant food first. When that is consumed, young members range farther afield for less desirable species, and older members collect the food closer to home. The day's foods are pooled within families and shared with other families, so that a variety of food is available to every camp member and no one goes hungry.

In his fieldwork, Dr. Lee investigated the question of how hard the !Kung San worked. He found that over a four-week period, the overall work week was 2.4 days of work per adult. During the month of this study, at least, the people appeared to spend less than half their days in obtaining food. They enjoyed more leisure time than members of many agricultural and industrial societies. And this was during the dry season of a year of serious drought!

On the days the Dobe people were not hunting or gathering, they were either at the water hole entertaining visitors, or themselves visiting other camps.

It is interesting to note that the men worked longer hours obtaining food than the women. Men worked an average of 12 out of 28 days (providing about 45% of the food), while women worked about 9 (providing about 55% of the food), a work schedule that contradicts the view that women are the workhorses of a foraging society. A day of gathering by the women produced about 68% more calories on the average than a day of hunting. Women, it seems, work fewer days, but produce more calories than the men.

At one time, it was believed that hunter-gatherers lived a hand-to-mouth existence, ever on the brink of starvation. The !Kung, with a modest subsistence effort of 2.4 workdays per week, produced an adequate diet *and* a surplus. What makes this way of life possible, Lee believes, is sharing:

> If I had to point to one single feature that makes this way of life possible, I would focus on *sharing*. Each !Kung is not an island unto himself or herself; each is part of a collective. It is a small, rudimentary collective, and at times a fragile one, but it is a collective nonetheless. What I mean is that the living group pools the resources that are brought into camp so that everyone receives an equitable share. The !Kung and people like them don't do this out of nobility of soul or because they are made of better stuff than we are. In fact, they often gripe about sharing. They do it because it works for them and it enhances their survival. Without this core of sharing, life for the !Kung would be harder and infinitely less pleasant (Lee, 1984, p. 55).

In summary, the !Kung San possess what is central to a foraging economy: sexual division of labor; simple technology; collective, nonexclusive ownership of land and resources; and widespread food sharing within and among local groups according to the principle of generalized reciprocity.

Attempting to reconstruct the situation in which early hominids evolved is speculative since so little evidence is available, especially for specific events. Evidence from social carnivores, especially wild dogs and wolves, points up the utility of cooperative hunting, which may be at least one of the reasons for their success. Additionally, reproductive success is enhanced by their home base, where the young are guarded from intruders and fed by returning hunters. Whether cooperative hunting is found among baboons and chimpanzees is presently not entirely certain, but, in any case, it is not the prevalent mode of obtaining meat. Furthermore, meat is not as important in their diet as is vegetable matter.

!Kung San are cooperative hunters, share both meat and vegetables according to an organized and formal plan, use a home base, pair bond, and the sexes divide their labor. A few of these characteristics, such as sharing and division of labor

Figure 9-21
!Kung hunter returns to camp.

Figure 9-22
Carrying her child, a !Kung woman gathers.

(and perhaps cooperative hunting) may be practiced by nonhuman primates, but to a very limited degree.

On the other hand—like all contemporary *Homo sapiens*—San people have a fully modern human brain. As such, they have highly elaborated capabilities for abstract thought, symbolic language, complex tool making, and so forth. They thus are not strictly comparable to early hominids, whose brain sizes were much smaller, and who probably did not possess full language.

Moreover, the !Kung San were "disrupted" by outside civilization well before the first systematic anthropological studies were carried out (in the early 1950s). As a result, they use metal knives and arrowheads (the bow and arrow itself is probably a fairly recent import), wear cotton clothing, and employ many other introduced items. How much all of this has influenced their culture (from our point of view, specifically their ecological strategies) is difficult to say. Certainly the !Kung San (or, for that matter, any contemporary hunting-gathering group) do not have the same relationship with their environments that would have been true even a few generations ago.

Sadly, the degree of outside influence disrupting the traditional !Kung San culture has recently become overwhelming. Much of the wild game on which they had depended is either decimated or partially off-limits on protected game preserves. Pressure by governments (in South Africa and Botswana), as well as economic pressures to obtain cash resources, have led many San to settle on reservations. Here, many have become exposed for the first time to alcohol, to-bacco, transistor radios, infant formula, and other modern items (Kolata, 1981).

Southern Africa today is a tinderbox of conflicting political and racial groups. The !Kung San have not been able to avoid these powerful forces and, in many cases, have been swept directly into the conflict. Since about 1970, the South African government has actively recruited !Kung San into the army, where they are used to fight insurgent groups in Namibia and also in neighboring Angola (Kolata, 1981).

Conclusion: Fact and Fiction
of Human Behavioral Evolution

As we have seen, no single behavioral model is adequate for reconstructing early hominid beginnings. They are all flawed in one way or another. What we must do, consequently, is to *select* those aspects from each model we think are most useful.

Certainly, early hominids were social. Moreover, we know that by at least 4 m.y.a. they were exploiting open environments and were adapted for bipedalism (although perhaps not completely—we'll discuss this in further detail in Chapter 13). By at least 2 m.y.a., some hominids were using stone tools, regularly exploiting meat resources, and carrying these and other items back to a central place (i.e., a base camp). As we will see in Chapter 10, this meat exploitation initially was limited mostly to small animals and probably the scavenging of larger kills brought down by other predators. Probably, by 1 m.y.a., our ancestors were at least occasionally going after very large animals.

Thus, the models provided by social carnivores, savanna baboons, and modern hunter-gatherers have something to tell us about how socially organized animals cope in a savanna environment. Moreover, from social carnivores (analogously) and from hunter-gatherers (homologously), we can glean some clues regarding the advantages of group hunting, food sharing, and base camps.

In addition, chimpanzees offer further insight concerning incipient tool use, concerning parental strategies for raising slowly developing offspring, and concerning complex communication (this especially from captive chimps who have been taught American Sign Language).

Beyond these generalizations, the record allows little in the way of more specific statements. Lovejoy points out that early hominids were bipedal *before* they began to systematically use stone implements. From this, he assumes that the earliest hominids were adapted for carrying something else other than tools—and suggests it was food. Moreover, the food was carried by males back to central places and shared with females to whom they were monogamously paired.

As we have indicated, hominids certainly were bipedal early on, and at a stage where as yet no definite stone tools have been recovered. It is quite possible—even probable—that these hominids did have tools made of perishable materials (wood, bone, fiber) perhaps even before bipedalism evolved. It is also possible that early hominids did have marked sexual division of labor, monogamous pairs, concealed ovulation, and increased male parental investment. However, there is no way to know for certain.

In reading accounts of human behavioral evolution, particularly those aimed at the general public,[*] we caution you to keep these concerns in mind. In so doing, it will be more possible to separate the hard evidence from speculation, and you can then draw your own conclusions.

Summary

Since humans are primates and evolved from primates, anthropologists believe that the study of nonhuman primate behavior may offer insights into hominid origins and further the understanding of human behavior.

[*]For example, Morris (1967); Ardrey (1966, 1976); Tiger and Fox (1974); and Morgan (1972).

As an interpretive and organizational aid, we have presented the model of human behavioral origins proposed by Owen Lovejoy. In his model, Lovejoy emphasizes several key differences between human and nonhuman primates. These are helpful in highlighting how our primate cousins can be used to better understand human evolution. In addition, Lovejoy speculates about the sequence of certain behavioral innovations among our earliest hominid ancestors. We disagree with the implications of this, but controversies of this nature are helpful in demonstrating how various models can be used to illuminate our evolutionary history.

Baboon and chimpanzee social behavior, as a specific example of nonhuman primates, are described in some detail. Savanna baboons are organized around a core of related females. Adult males transfer out of their natal troop and, in their new troop, form consortships and friendships with adult females. Both males and females are organized around a lineal dominance hierarchy. Baboons hunt and share meat (to a limited extent), but meat is not an important part of their diet.

The organization of the common chimpanzees differs from baboons, since it is the male chimpanzees who remain in their natal community and the females who transfer out. Chimpanzees are a fusion-fission society, subdivided into smaller groups whose membership frequently changes. Although males are dominant to females, dominance is not as firmly structured as it is in baboon society. Chimpanzee males are territorial and maintain an exclusive home range. Almost entirely herbivorous (frugivorous), chimpanzees, like baboons, also hunt and share meat to a limited extent. Chimpanzees practice what might be considered a sexual division of labor—hunting by males and gathering by females.

The ability of apes—especially chimpanzees—to handle language raises interesting theoretical questions about the origin of language and the role language played in the evolution of early hominids. Whether chimpanzees who have been taught to sign can actually form sentences is also discussed.

Cultural behavior of chimpanzees (i.e., tool manufacturing) and Japanese macaques (i.e., inventing methods of food preparation) are discussed. With their more flexible social structure, ability to make tools, unsolicited food sharing, and matrifocal emphasis, chimpanzees, rather than baboons, serve as a better model of human evolution.

Social carnivores—lions, wolves, and wild dogs—are introduced to see whether we can find similar adaptive strategies in savanna- (or savannalike) living carnivores. Lions do not tell us very much, but wolves and wild dogs show several similarities. Cooperative hunting, hunting animals larger than the hunters, division of labor (wild dogs), and an extended communication system are found in wolves, wild dogs, and in hominids (and presumably early hominids).

Finally, we describe the social life of a recent hunting-gathering society, the !Kung San, as a reflection of the kind of adaptation that may have characterized early hominids. (There is no intention of classifying the !Kung San as early hominids. Obviously, they are anatomically modern humans with a culture far, far removed from hominid life three and more million years ago.)

Questions for Review

1. List several reasons for studying nonhuman primate behavior.
2. What behavioral traits are common to all nonhuman primates?
3. Describe the primate social group.
4. What are the functions of grooming? displays? dominance?

5. Why is the mother-infant relationship an important one for primates?
6. Compare baboon and chimpanzee social behavior. What is the relationship between the social behavior and group structure of these primates?
7. Are baboons or chimpanzees better models for hominid behavior? Why?
8. Discuss the learning achievements of chimpanzees. Why do the authors believe the concept of culture should not be applied to this behavior?
9. Chimpanzees have been taught to communicate symbolically; why is this significant?
10. What is the argument opposing the idea that chimpanzees are capable of learning language?
11. What is the basis for the sociobiological approach to animal behavior?
12. How does sociobiology explain altruistic behavior?
13. Describe the different adaptations of lions and wild dogs to a savanna ecological niche.
14. How does the study of social carnivores contribute to our understanding of hominid evolution?
15. What are the similarities in the adaptations of social carnivores and !Kung San?

Primate Evolution

C O N T E N T S

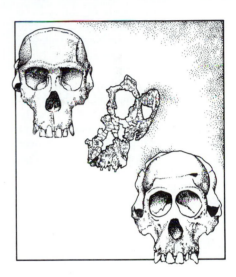

Is There a Bigfoot?

Ancient legends tell of Sasquatch, a strange, hairy, bipedal creature prowling the wilds of North America. In fact, Sasquatches, abominable snowmen, and other such creatures have been reported from at least 100 separate areas of the world. In North America, they have been reported most often from British Columbia, Washington, Oregon, and northern California. Various unexplained beasts, however, have also been "seen" from Alaska to Mexico and from the Pacific Coast to northern Michigan. Tales of these creatures, which are usually called *Bigfoot*, are today even further embellished as sightings, footprints, hair fragments, feces, and even photographs have been collected. Are we dealing with fact or fiction?

If Bigfoot lives, what could it be? Reports are consistent, detailing a very large (eight to twelve foot), upright animal. Its size, hair, and location (in the cold Northwest) all imply a mammal. Its body shape and locomotion further limit the possibilities. Possibly it is a bear, but the gait and footprints are not right. What is left then? A hominoid of some sort?

Is this possible? In any objective pursuit of knowledge we must admit that *anything* is possible, but some things are highly improbable. What kinds of hominoids are native to the New World? The only definite remains of indigenous hominoids in North, Central, or South America are those of *Homo sapiens* (and these are relatively recent—in the last 20,000 years or so).

If Bigfoot is a hominoid, where did it come from? The closest fossil primate matching the dimensions of the fleeting Sasquatches is *Gigantopithecus*. Remains of this extinct hominoid are well known from the Old World during the Pleistocene, but none has ever been found in the New World. Such a big animal has exceedingly large teeth, which generally have a fairly good chance of being preserved. From China alone there are more than 1,000 *Gigantopithecus* teeth, and this giant hominoid has not roamed the forests of China for half a million years. It seems very strange, indeed. If *Gigantopithecus* (or one of its supposed descendants) is still living, why have we not found any bones or teeth of this form? If such a large animal has existed for tens of thousands of years, where is the hard evidence?

What about the hundreds of sightings? Could they all have been faked? Probably not. Many of these people, no doubt, saw *something*. Perhaps often they were bears; the imagination can greatly influence our objectivity when primed with romantic tales of mythical beasts. What about footprints, photos, hairs, and fecal material? The prints (at least many of them) could have been faked, and so too with the photos (the primary evidence—a 16-mm film taken in northern California in 1967). Such a circumstance would suggest an elaborate, deliberate hoax, not a happy conclusion, but entirely possible (as you will see with Piltdown). The hairs and fecal material are from some animal, perhaps one already known, perhaps one yet to be discovered. The possibility exists that there are large terrestrial mammals in remote areas of North America unknown to science. Bigfoot may be such an animal. However, of all the possibilities, the suggestion that this creature is a hominoid is about the least likely imaginable.

The conclusion that Bigfoot is an archaic hominoid is therefore both unlikely and far from conclusively established. But it is not *completely* impossible. Perhaps descendant populations of gigantopithecines migrated from China (through thousands of miles of environments exceedingly inhospitable to such a forest-adapted form), ending up in the American Northwest. In so doing, perhaps they left nary a trace all along the way. Furthering our improbable conjectures, perhaps they have existed in North America for at least 500,000 years, without leaving a single fossil remnant. Finally, perhaps they still exist today, but deliberately conceal themselves and meticulously dispose of their dead.

SOURCES:

Napier, John. *Bigfoot; the Yeti and Sasquatch in Myth and Reality*, London: Jonathan Cape, 1972.

Sanderson, Ivan T. *Abominable Snowmen: Legend Come to Life*, New York: Chilton Co., 1961.

Shuman, James B. "Is There an American Abominable Snowman?," *Reader's Digest*, January 1969, pp. 179–186.

Introduction

In Chapters 6, 7, 8, and 9, you were introduced to the time scale of evolution, placental mammals, and particularly the primate order. We now turn to the fossil history of primates over the last 70 million years. With what you now know of primate anatomy (teeth, limbs, etc.) and social behavior, you will be able to "flesh out" the bones and teeth that comprise the evolutionary record of primate origins. In this way, the ecological adaptations and evolutionary relationships of these fossil forms to each other (and to contemporary primates) will become more meaningful. Please note that when we look at primate evolution, we are looking at our own evolution as well.

Time Scale

A brief review of the geological time scale will be helpful in understanding primate evolution during the Cenozoic.

Before discussing the fossil primates, we should caution that the formal taxonomic names for the various families and genera are horrendous to pronounce and even harder to remember. Unfortunately, there is no other adequate way to discuss the material. We must make reference to the standard nomenclature. As an aid, we suggest you refer to the marginal notes, pronunciation guide, and glossary for those names considered most significant.

Era	Epoch	Approximate Beginning (m.y.a.)
Cenozoic	Pleistocene	1.8
	Pliocene	5
	Miocene	25
	Oligocene	37
	Eocene	53
	Paleocene	65
Mesozoic	Cretaceous	135

Earliest Primates

The first radiation of the primate order has its roots in the beginnings of the explosive adaptive radiation of placental mammals in general. Therefore, it is not surprising that the earliest suggestions of primates in the fossil record are difficult to discern from early members of other placental mammal groups, particularly the insectivores.

The earliest discovered traces suggesting the beginnings of our order come from the late Cretaceous and early Paleocene in the Dakota area of North America. Known only from a few teeth, this fossil form, called **Purgatorius,**

Figure 10-1
Pleisiadapis *cranium.*

exhibits the primate tendency towards a bulbous cusp pattern in the molar teeth compared to the sharper cusps seen in insectivores. Such a dental pattern apparently indicates that early primates were adapting to fruit and leaf-eating diets (Szalay, 1968), or perhaps a diet also including insects exploited in an arboreal niche (Van Valen and Sloan, 1965). Reconstructions indicate that the dental formula is still that of a generalized primitive mammal: 3-1-4-3 (Szalay and Delson, 1979). All that can be said now of this still fragmentary and mysterious animal, *Purgatorius*, is that if it was a primate, it was quite "primitive," which is not surprising considering its early date and still close ties with primitive placental mammals.

Paleocene Primates (65 m.y.–53 m.y.)

During the Paleocene, the first clearly recognizable primates begin to diversify. In fact, we are able to isolate several different (at least four) families widely scattered in North America and Europe during this epoch.

One of the most widely distributed and best represented of these early primates is **Plesiadapis**, found in both North America and Europe. First known from the late Paleocene, the time range of *Plesiadapis* extends up into the early Eocene. This animal, known from a nearly complete skull plus several parts of the limb skeleton, has an estimated size range varying widely between that of a squirrel and a house cat. While these animals show definite primate tendencies, such as dependence on vision (though not completely binocular) and flexible wrists and ankles (though still probably with claws), they retain numerous primitive characteristics, such as lack of a postorbital bar, which serves to form a bony division between the orbit and the braincase. In addition, *Plesiadapis* and the majority of other Paleocene primates display unusual (compared to modern primates) specializations of their front teeth, which are large and procumbent (angled forward) and, in some respects, reminiscent of the specialized aye-aye.

Given these dental specializations, the possibility that any of the Paleocene forms thus far discovered are direct ancestors of later primates seems unlikely. This poses no insurmountable theoretical problem, for we must keep in mind that our meager discoveries represent only a tiny sample of the already diverse kinds of primates living at this time.

The overall anatomical plan of all these early forms could be described as prosimian or even "protoprosimian," for they are certainly more primitive than any living primate. In fact, they are more similar in evolutionary grade to the living tree shrews, which give a fairly good model of Paleocene primates (see p. 162).

Ancient Landscapes and Early Primate Evolution

The distribution and the eventual fate of early primate forms is understandable only within the context of the environments in which these animals lived. First and foremost, we must remember that 60 m.y.a. land masses were not arranged as they are today. As we discussed on p. 135, the continents have "drifted" to their present position, carried along on the shifting plates of the earth's surface.

In the late Paleozoic (*circa* 250 m.y.a.), the huge conglomerate land mass

Figure 10-2
Postorbital bar.

called Pangea began to break up into northern and southern continents. To the north, North America, Europe, and Asia were joined into Laurasia; to the south, Africa, South America, Australia, India, and Antarctica formed Gondwanaland (see Fig. 10-3a). Throughout the Mesozoic, the two basic land masses continued to move, with Gondwanaland breaking up into the southern continents. In the north, the continents also were separating, but North America and Europe continued to be connected through Greenland and would remain attached in this manner for several millions of years.

As we will see, this "northern connection" had a very significant influence on the geographic distribution of early primates. In fact, North America and Europe remained joined until mid-Eocene times (*circa* 45 m.y.a.) (see Fig. 10-3b). Though welded to North America, Europe was separated from Asia by a channel called the Turgai Strait. Not until the later Eocene (about 40 m.y.a.) does Europe disjoin from North America to the west and finally make contact with Asia to the east (forming an area that we today call Eurasia).

What makes all this geologic activity relevant to primate (and other paleontological) studies is that land-living animals could cross over land bridges, but were effectively cut off by water barriers. Thus, we see species of *Plesiadapis* in *both* North America and Europe. On the other hand, primates are scarcely known in Asia until the late Eocene, when presumably they could walk in from Europe once the Turgai Straight had been closed. As far as primates go, then, from their earliest beginnings (65 m.y.a. +) up until 40 m.y.a. they were mostly limited to North America and Europe (between which free migration was still possible). With further continental movements, the "New World" and "Old World" became completely separated and thereby influenced the evolutionary histories of primates still living today (see p. 277).

As the continents moved, climatic conditions changed dramatically. In the Mesozoic and into the Paleocene, the continental masses were clustered closer to the equator, and as Laurasia in particular moved north, its climate cooled. Moreover, the fragmenting of the land masses and the consequent altering of marine flow patterns (less exchange between northern and southern seas) caused the climate to cool even further.

PLESIADAPIS
(Please-ee-a-dap'-iss)

Figure 10-3
Continental drift. Changes in position of the continental plates from Late Paleozoic to Late Eocene. (a) The position of the continents at the end of the Paleozoic (c. 250 m.y.a.). Pangea is breaking up into a northern land mass (Laurasia) and a southern land mass (Gondwanaland). (b) The position of the continents during much of the Paleocene and Eocene (up to c. 45 m.y.a.). Note that North America and Europe are still joined but are separate from Asia.

(a)

(b)

Finally, these climatic shifts also heavily affected plant communities. Rather than the primitive, mostly tropical flora characteristic of the Mesozoic (ferns, cycads, etc.), what we see emerging in the Cenozoic is the rapid radiation of the seed plants (including flowering plants, deciduous trees, grasses, etc.). Indeed, many of these plants are frequently pollinated by insects. As insects thus became more abundant, so did the animals who fed on them—including early primates. The world was never to be the same again.

Clearly, then, it is extremely important to interpret primate evolution within the context of the earth's changing environments.

Eocene Primates (53 m.y.–37 m.y.)

The first primates of modern aspect appear during the Eocene. These can now clearly be called prosimians and closely resemble the loris/lemur evolutionary grade. Primate diversification accelerates during this epoch, with four new families and as many as thirty-seven genera represented during the 16-million-year span of the Eocene.

The Eocene may be characterized as the heyday of prosimians, who attained their widest geographic distribution and broadest adaptive radiation during this period. Indeed, more than twice as many genera are found in the Eocene than are known for the whole world today (sixteen living genera, with ten of these confined to Madagascar).

The most diversified and best-known Eocene primates are members of the lemurlike Adapidae, which includes some ten genera. The four best known of these are:

Cantius	North America and Europe
Adapis (Ad'-a-piss)	Europe
Notharctus (Noth-ark'-tus)	North America
Smilodectes (Smi-lo-dek'-teese)	North America

Some of these animals have been known from fossil evidence for a remarkably long time. In fact, the initial discovery of *Adapis* was made in France in 1821 and first described by Cuvier himself.

As mentioned, all these animals are fairly lemurlike in general adaptive level and show distinctive primate tendencies not seen in the Paleocene forms. For example, they all now have a complete postorbital bar, nails instead of claws, and the eyes are rotated forward, allowing overlapping fields of perception and thus binocular vision. In the limb skeleton, further developments in prehensility are suggested, and some evidence points to the presence of an opposable large toe. In all these respects, we see the typical primate adaptive strategies allowing exploitation of an arboreal environment. Whereas these forms resemble lemurs in overall anatomical plan, they do not show the same specializations seen in contemporary lorises and lemurs, such as development of the dental comb (see p. 164).

The separate evolution of the Malagasy lemurs may date to late Eocene times, but since this island was already isolated by a deep channel from mainland Africa, they apparently reached their island sanctuary by unintentionally floating over on drifting debris.

The evolutionary origins of the tarsiers are also indicated during the Eocene by the large-eyed and apparently noctural genus, **Necrolemur** ("dead lemur," actually a misnomer; "dead tarsier" would be more appropriate). In addition to the large size of its eyes, *Necrolemur*'s orbits are rotated completely forward, the *foramen magnum* is well forward (indicating the head was held upright over the spine), and there is some flexion in the angle at the base of the skull. All these traits reveal striking similarities with the modern tarsier. In addition, some limb bones, which may well be associated with *Necrolemur* skulls, display the distinctive tarsioid specialization of fused bones in the lower leg.

While *Necrolemur* almost certainly lies very close to the ancestral origins of the tarsioid line, it may not itself represent the actual ancestors. Specialization in the dental apparatus, shown by loss of some front teeth, indicates that this form could not have evolved into modern tarsiers. Such a circumstance would necessitate an **evolutionary reversal**, which would involve the reacquisition of a structure already lost—an incredibly unlikely event.

The last group of Eocene primates we will discuss is the family Omomyidae (which primatologists suggest show general affinities with the tarsiers; they include *Necrolemur* within this group) (Szalay and Delson, 1979). Although

NECROLEMUR
(Nek-roe-lee'-mur)

EVOLUTIONARY REVERSAL
The reacquisition of a structure previously lost in the evolution of a life form.

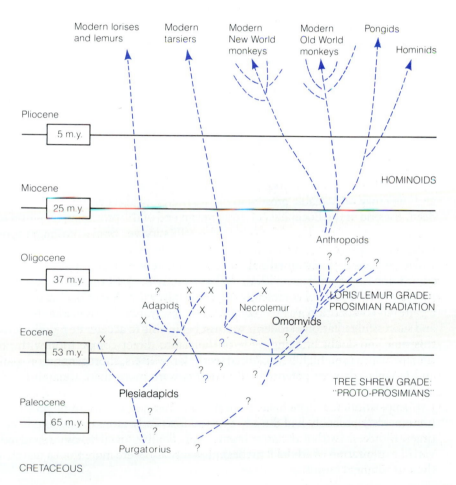

Figure 10-4
Summary, early primate evolution.

Figure 10-5
Tibio-fibula. (a) *Necrolemur;* (b) *modern tarsier. Note the two fused lower leg bones— a characteristic feature of tarsiers. (© 1959 by W. E. Le Gros Clark.)*

known mainly from bits of jaws and teeth, omomyids are the most widely distributed of known Eocene prosimians discovered in North America, Europe, and Asia. Indeed, they are the most widely distributed prosimian group ever! As we have just seen, primate migration into Asia was blocked until the late Eocene, when the straits separating it from Europe were closed.

The earlier members of this family are somewhat more generalized than the later ones, and may form the ancestral basis for all later anthropoids: New World monkeys, Old World monkeys, apes, and hominids. The affinities of these fossil omomyids with tarsiers (and inferentially with the anthropoids) have led many researchers to classify the entire group as one evolutionary unit—the Haplorhini—as opposed to the *true* prosimians (i.e., lemurs and lorises)—the Strepsirhini (see p. 166). The later forms are seemingly quite specialized, showing the highly unusual trait of incisor teeth in the upper and lower jaws to be larger than their canines.

Other evidence also argues for the emergence of anthropoids during the late Eocene. Fragmentary remains from Burma dating to about 40 m.y.a. suggest anthropoid affinities. In particular, a form referred to as *Pondaungia* shows several features of the dentition similar to that of Old World anthropoids (Maw et al, 1979). Another Burmese Eocene fossil known as *Amphipithecus* has also been proposed as a possible early anthropoid (Simons, 1972), but detailed consideration of dental anatomy suggests a more likely affinity with the prosimian adapids (Szalay and Delson, 1979).

Eocene Prosimians: Summary

During the Eocene epoch, a wide and highly successful adaptive radiation of prosimian forms occurred. Some, resembling modern lorises and lemurs (adapids), may have given rise to direct ancestors of these modern animals by late Eocene times. Others (omomyids) resemble modern tarsiers, and still others (other omomyids?) may have been the ancestral stock for all anthropoids.

By the end of the Eocene—as the continents drifted away from the equator and caused the climate to cool—tropical areas in the northern latitudes shrank, and the range of available prosimian niches therefore also began to contract. Indeed, the end of the Eocene seems to signal an end of the prosimian radiation except for small isolated areas, where some still survive. Some prosimian forms (adapids) did manage to survive for several million years in southern Asia— where perhaps they remained isolated from the "center-stage" of primate evolution (Gingerich and Sahni, 1979). What exactly brought on this evolutionary turn of events is still not completely clear. Certainly the change in climate played a part, but competition was also coming from new fronts. The remarkably diverse and successful radiation of rodents was just beginning to accelerate rapidly during this time, no doubt bringing some of them into direct competition with prosimians. With their highly specialized teeth, large litters, short generation spans, and flexible adaptive potential, the rodents were more than a match for the prosimians.

Competition may have come from still another quarter, for some prosimians (omomyids?) probably had already evolved into early monkeys by late Eocene times. Monkeys (with their larger brains, more flexible social behavior, and more varied exploitation of arboreal niches) probably also were more than a match for their prosimian cousins.

It is possible that many of these early forms were still nocturnal, and thus not in direct competition with most rodents or monkeys. A new competitor for foods in the trees at night might have been the bats—another highly successful group radiating at this time (Richard, 1985).

New World Monkeys

The center of action for primate evolution after the close of the Eocene is confined largely to the Old World, for only on the continents of Africa and Eurasia can we trace the evolutionary development of apes and hominids.

However, the New World, while geographically separated from the Old World, was not completely devoid of anthropoid stock, for here the ceboids evolved in their own right.

Any discussion of ceboid evolution and its relation to Old World anthropoid developments must consider crucial geological events, particularly continental drift (see pp. 272–273). By late Eocene times, Europe and North America had separated, and South America and Africa, though closer together than at present, were also drifting apart.

In such a geological context, the introduction of monkeys into South America poses a certain problem. Some authorities have postulated that, because the distance between South America and Africa was still not very great, monkeys, originating in Africa, could then have rafted to the New World (Gavan, 1977; Ciochon and Chiarelli, 1980).

In any case, that Old and New World primates shared any evolutionary history since at least the late Eocene (some 40 m.y.a) is unlikely. There is no trace of any ancestor of our lineage anywhere in the New World following this time until fully modern *Homo sapiens* walked in during the late Pleistocene.

While primate fossils abound in the Western Hemisphere (particularly North America) during the early Cenozoic, the record is extremely sparse later on. For the entire span of Oligocene to late Pleistocene, we have only a few bits and pieces, a jaw fragment from Bolivia, a nearly complete skull from Texas, another quite complete cranium from Argentina, and a few other small fragments from Colombia and Jamaica. Together, all the evidence comprises less than a dozen individuals. Thus, tracing the evolutionary heritage of New World monkeys with any degree of certainty is a difficult task.

Old World Anthropoids

The focus of our attention will henceforth exclusively be the Old World (Europe, Asia, Africa), for this area is where our ancestors have lived for the past 40 million years. This evolutionary and geographic fact is reflected in the grouping of Old World anthropoids (Old World monkeys, apes, and humans) into a common infraorder (Catarrhini) as opposed to the infraorder for New World monkeys (Platyrrhini).

Figure 10-6
Location of the Fayum, an Oligocene primate site in Egypt.

It is apparent that during this epoch a great deal of evolutionary action was taking place; by the end of the Oligocene, Old World monkeys and hominoids were probably evolving along their separate evolutionary pathways. No doubt, diverse species of anthropoids were adapting to varied ecological niches in Africa and probably Asia and Europe as well. Unfortunately, the fossil record for the entire period is limited to only one locality in Egypt, sixty miles southwest of Cairo. This site, called the *Fayum*, is today an extremely arid region 100 miles inland, but, in Oligocene times, it was located close to the Mediterranean shore and was traversed by meandering streams crisscrossing through areas of tropical rain forest. The upper fossil beds have been dated by potassium/argon at approximately 33 m.y.a., and a series of lower beds were probably deposited 35 m.y.a.

Much of the Fayum fossil material is quite fragmentary. Consequently, evolutionary interpretations are not as unambiguous as we would like. Given the nature of the material, the classification of the fossils into recognized genera and species (always a difficult task; see p. 298) is somewhat disputed. The leading researcher of the Fayum fossil primates, E. L. Simons of Duke University, has recognized seven different genera from the Fayum, six anthropoids and one prosimian (Simons, 1985). Altogether, an estimated 1,000 specimens have been recovered from the remarkably productive Fayum area. The three best known of these genera are discussed below.

Apidium (Two Species)

A well-known 30-million-year-old fossil animal from the Fayum is **Apidium**, represented by about 80 jaws or partial dentitions and over 100 postcranial elements. This animal, about the size of a squirrel, had several anthropoid-like features, but also shows quite unusual aspects in its teeth. *Apidium*'s dental formula (see p. 168) is 2-1-3-3 which, as you can easily see, reveals an extra premolar not found in any contemporary Old World anthropoid. For that matter, extremely few fossil anthropoids in the Old World have this extra premolar. As noted, *Apidium* is represented by a large array of specimens, both dental and from the limb skeleton. The teeth suggest a diet composed of fruits and leaves. In addition, preserved remains of the limbs indicate that this creature was a small arboreal quadruped, adept at leaping and springing.

Propliopithecus (Two Species)*

Among the first fossils found at the Fayum, an incomplete *Propliopithecus* mandible was recovered in 1907. Unfortunately, since detailed geological and paleontological methods were not yet developed, the precise geological position of this form is not known.

Morphologically, this fossil is a quite generalized Old World anthropoid, displaying a 2-1-2-3 dental formula. In most every relevant respect, this early *Propliopithecus* form is quite primitive, not showing particular derived tendencies in

---

*Some primatologists have suggested a third species of *Propliopithecus* (*P. markrafi*) at the Fayum (Fleagle and Kay, 1983). This species, however, is also known from only a single specimen.

any direction. To date, only this one specimen represents this *Propliopithecus (haeckeli)* species.

The second *Propliopithecus* species is considerably better known, with several new specimens discovered at the Fayum between 1977 and 1979. Geologically, this species (*P. chirobates*) comes from the upper beds (*circa* 33 m.y.a.) and is, therefore, probably later in time than the isolated *haeckeli* specimen. Consequently, it is not surprising that *chirobates* is more derived in several anatomical features. Still, this form is a remarkably primitive Old World anthropoid. Considerably more evolutionary change would be required to transform this animal into anything distinctively recognizable as either an ape or a monkey.

Earlier interpretations of fragmentary remains of this fossil suggested affinities with gibbons (Simons initially proposed a separate genus rank, "Aeolopithecus"). However, more complete recent discoveries have shown that such an evolutionary relationship is not likely (Kay et al, 1981).

Aegyptopithecus

The most complete and probably evolutionarily most significant fossil from the Fayum is *Aegyptopithecus* (*circa* 33 m.y.a.), which is known from a nearly complete skull found in 1966, as well as numerous jaw fragments and several limb bones (most of which have been found quite recently). The largest of the Fayum anthropoids, *Aegyptopithecus* is roughly the size of a modern howler monkey, 13 to 18 pounds (Fleagle, 1983). *Aegyptopithecus* is important because, better than any other fossil, it bridges the gap between the Eocene prosimians on the one hand and the Miocene hominoids on the other.

With a dental formula of 2-1-2-3, *Aegyptopithecus* shows the familiar Old World anthropoid pattern. More detailed aspects of the dentition possibly align this Oligocene form with the Miocene hominoids (which we shall discuss shortly), but the evolutionary affinities are not presently well established. In most respects, the dentition is primitive for an Old World anthropoid, without specifically derived features in either the hominoid or Old World monkey direction. Recently, there has been a change in interpreting Old World monkey dental evolution. It was previously believed that the dental patterns (particularly, the molar cusp pattern) seen in Old World monkeys were the more **primitive** and, conversely, those seen in hominoids were more **derived** from the ancestral **catarrhine** condition. Reevaluation of the fossil materials now suggests that, if anything, the Old World monkey pattern is more derived, and the hominoid cusp arrangement is the more primitive. (See Fig. 10-7.)

The establishment of the "polarities" of primitive/derived characteristics is crucial to making sound evolutionary interpretations. However, the trajectories of evolutionary change are not always easy to ascertain. The determination of the ancestral catarrhine molar cusp pattern is only one example. In the subsequent section on Miocene hominoids, we will encounter several further dilemmas in sorting out such issues.

Even more primitive than the teeth of *Aegyptopithecus* is the skull, which is small and resembles the skull of a monkey in some details. Brain size and relative proportions can be reconstructed from internal casts of the one well-preserved cranium thus far discovered (see Fig. 10-8). It appears that the brain was somewhat intermediate between that of prosimians and anthropoids. The visual cortex was large compared to prosimians, with concomitant reduction of the olfac-

APIDIUM
(A-pid'-ee-um)

PRIMITIVE
A character state of an organism that is inherited from an ancestor (before a divergence) when comparing with another lineage.

DERIVED
Character state found only in particular lineages—and thus indicative of forms **after** a divergence.

CATARRHINE
The group (infraorder) comprising all Old World anthropoids, living and extinct.

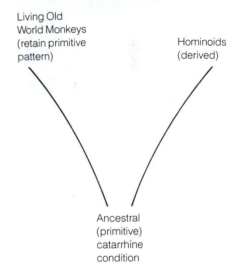

(a) Previous view—polarities of molar cusp pattern.

(b) Revised view.

Figure 10-7
Establishing polarities in character states among Old world anthropoids, an example.

(a)

(b)

Figure 10-8
Aegyptopithecus *skull from the Fayum,*
Egypt. Oligocene, circa 33 m.y.a., discov-
ered in 1966. (a) Front view; (b) side view.

tory lobes, but the frontal lobes were not especially expanded. Even considering the relative small size of this animal, the brain—estimated at only 30 to 40 cm³ (Radinsky, 1973)—was by no means large.

Evidence from the limb skeleton also revealed nothing particularly distinctive. From analysis of limb proportions and muscle insertions, primatologist John Fleagle (1983) has concluded that *Aegyptopithecus* was a short-limbed, heavily muscled, slowly moving, arboreal quadruped.

Further detailed study of *Aegyptopithecus'* anatomy has even allowed primatologists to speculate about the social behavior of this ancient primate. For instance, dental remains from different individuals vary greatly in canine size. This fact implies male/female differences (sexual dimorphism), which apparently were quite marked. Comparisons with living primates further suggest that males may have been competing for females and that the mating pattern was probably polygynous.

All in all, *Aegyptopithecus* presents somewhat of a paleontological enigma. In most respects, it is quite primitive as an Old World anthropoid, and could thus be potentially an ancestor for *both* Old World monkeys and hominoids. There are some slight yet suggestive clues in the teeth that have led some researchers (most notably, E. L. Simons) to already place *Aegyptopithecus* on the hominoid line. Primarily because of the primitive aspects of this creature, other researchers (e.g., Fleagle and Kay, 1983) are not as convinced.

There remains, then, the problem of how to classify *Aegyptopithecus*. Even though they recognize that this fossil may well have lived before the major evolutionary split between Old World monkeys and hominoids (see Fig. 10-4), John Fleagle and Richard Kay still opt to call *Aegyptopithecus* a hominoid. Accordingly, they recognize that the superfamily Hominoidea then becomes what they term a "wastebasket" category (i.e., it is used for convenience, but does not reflect phylogenetic reality). This is one solution, although it will not satisfy all researchers. Perhaps, for the moment, it would be best to regard *Aegyptopithecus* (as well as the other Fayum anthropoids) as "primitive catarrhines," without referring them to particular superfamilies.

Oligocene Fossil Anthropoids: Summary

The spectacular array of fossils from the Fayum in the period between 35 m.y. and 33 m.y. demonstrates that anthropoids were radiating along several evolutionary lines. As with the earlier primate fossil material from the Paleocene and Eocene,

Table 10-1   *Inferred General Paleobiological Aspects of Oligocene Primates*

	Weight Range	Substratum	Locomotion	Diet
Apidium	900–1,600 gm (2-3 lb.)	arboreal	quadruped	hardnut/ fruiteating
Propliopithecus	3,700–4,000 gm (8½–9 lb.)	arboreal	quadruped	fruiteating
Aegyptopithecus	5,900 gm (13.5 lb.)	arboreal	quadruped	fruiteating

(After Fleagle and Kay, 1985, p. 25)

the fragmentary nature of the Oligocene fossil assemblage makes precise reconstruction of these evolutionary lines risky.

Given the primitive nature of these fossil forms, it is wise, for the present, not to conclude specifically how these animals relate to later primates. In earlier primatological studies (as well as earlier editions of this book), such conclusions were indeed made, but reanalysis of the fossil material from the perspective of primitive/derived evolutionary modifications has cast serious doubt on many of these interpretations. The new interpretations, however, are still far from certain. As we have mentioned, untangling the polarity of primitive versus derived evolutionary states is a most difficult task. What many paleontologists would dearly like to establish is a clear link between these Oligocene fossils (particularly *Propliopithecus* and *Aegyptopithecus*) and the unambiguously hominoid forms of the Miocene. Unfortunately, as the following quote argues, this is not yet possible:

> In light of current knowledge about the very primitive dental, cranial, and skeletal morphology of the *Oligocene* hominoids, *Propliopithecus* and *Aegyptopithecus*, there is no reason to believe that any single group of extant hominoids (either hylobatids, hominids, or pongids) can be traced back to an Oligocene divergence (Fleagle and Kay, 1983, p. 190).

Miocene (25 m.y.–5 m.y.)—Hominoids Aplenty

If the Eocene was the age of prosimians and the Oligocene the time of great diversity for early anthropoids, the Miocene was certainly the epoch of hominoids.

A great abundance of hominoid fossil material has been found in the Old World from the time period 23 m.y.—7 m.y. The remarkable evolutionary success represented by this adaptive radiation is shown in the geographic range already established for hominoids during this period. Miocene hominoid fossils

Figure 10-9
Miocene hominoid distribution—fossils thus far discovered.

have been discovered in France, Germany, Spain, Czechoslovakia, Greece, Hungary, China, India, Pakistan, Turkey, Saudia Arabia, Egypt, Uganda, and Kenya.

Interpretations of this vast array of fossil material (now including more than 500 individuals, and perhaps as many as 1,000) were greatly complicated for several decades due to inadequate appreciation of the range of biological variation that a single genus or species could represent. As a result, the taxonomic naming of the various fossil finds became a terrible muddle, with more than 20 genera and over 100 species proposed. The biological implications of such taxonomic enthusiasm were unfortunately not seriously considered. In such an atmosphere, it was possible for two genera to be named—one with only upper jaws represented, the other with only lower jaws, each matching the other!

It is not difficult to understand why such confusion arose if we consider that discoveries of these fossils spanned more than 100 years (the earliest find came from France in 1856) and took place on three continents. Not until the early 1960s did scientists systematically study *all* the material, the result being a considerable simplification of the earlier confusion. As a result of this research, E. L. Simons and David Pilbeam "lumped" the vast majority of Miocene forms into only two genera: one presumably quite "pongidlike" and the other "hominidlike." In just the last few years, however, a tremendous amount of new data has come to light from both new field discoveries and finds in museum collections of previously unrecognized material. Consequently, it is now apparent that the Simons-Pilbeam simplification went too far. Hominoid evolutionary radiation during the Miocene produced a whole array of diverse organisms, many of which have no living descendants (and thus no clear analog among living higher primates).

As these new discoveries are analyzed, many of the perplexing problems concerning Miocene hominoids should be solved. For the moment, it is possible to make only general interpretive statements regarding Miocene hominoid adaptive patterns.

Paleogeography and Miocene Hominoid Evolution

As they were to early primate evolution (see p. 272), the factors of changing geography and climates (at work as well in the Miocene) are also crucial to interpretations of the later stages of primate evolution. The Oligocene revealed a proliferation of early Old World anthropoid forms from one area in North Africa. In the Early Miocene, the evidence is also restricted to Africa, with fossils coming from rich sites in the eastern part of the continent (Kenya and Uganda). It would thus appear, on the basis of current evidence, that hominoids originated in Africa and experienced a successful adaptive radiation there before dispersing to other parts of the Old World.

The hominoids would maintain this exclusive African foothold for some time. The earliest of these East African hominoid fossils is slightly more than 20 m.y. old, and later fossil finds extend the time range up to about 14 m.y.a. For most of this period, East Africa is thought to have been more heavily forested, with much less woodlands and grasslands (savannas) than exist today (Pickford, 1983).

As in the earlier Cenozoic, the shifting of the earth's plates during the Miocene played a vital role in primate evolution. Before about 16 m.y.a., Africa was cut off from Eurasia; consequently, once hominoids had originated there in the Early Miocene, they were isolated. However, around 16 m.y.a. the African plate "docked" with Eurasia (Bernor, 1983) through the Arabian Peninsula, a contact that was to revolutionize mammalian faunas of the later Miocene. Many forms, such as proboscideans, giraffoids, and pigs, that had originated in Africa now migrated into Eurasia (van Couvering and van Couvering, 1976). Apparently, included among these mid-Miocene intercontinental pioneers were some hominoids. Since they had evolved in the mainly tropical setting of equatorial Africa, most of the earlier hominoids probably remained primarily arboreal. Accordingly, it has been suggested that a relatively continuous forest would have been necessary across the Afro-Arabian-Eurasian land bridge.

Ecological changes were, however, already afoot in Africa. By 16 m.y.a., the environment was getting drier, with less tropical rainforest and, conversely, more open woodland/bushland and savanna areas emerging (Bernor, 1983; Pickford, 1983). In other words, the environments in East Africa were being transformed more into their contemporary form. With the opportunities thus presented, some African hominoids were almost certainly radiating into these more open niches about 16 to 17 m.y.a. Part of this adaptation probably involved exploitation of different foods and more ground-living than practiced by the arboreal ancestors of these hominoids. Some partly terrestrial, more open-country adapted hominoids were probably thus on the scene and fully capable of migrating into Eurasia, even through areas that were not continuosly forested.

The environments throughout the Old World were, of course, to alter even more. Later in the Miocene, some of these environmental shifts would further influence hominoid evolution and may have played a part in the origin of our particular evolutionary lineage, the hominids. More on this later.

Miocene Hominoids—Changing Views and Terminology

So, throughout the Miocene, environmental and geographic factors imposed constraints on hominoids as well as opened new opportunities to them. Over a time span of close to 15 m.y., hominoids in the middle two-thirds of the Miocene were successful indeed. Once they migrated into Eurasia, they dispersed rapidly and diversified into a variety of species. After 14 m.y.a., we have evidence of widely distributed hominoids from Pakistan, India, Turkey, Greece, Hungary, China, and Western Europe. Much of this material has only recently been uncovered and is incredibly abundant. For example, from Lufeng in southern China alone, 5 partial skulls and more than 1,000 teeth have been found in the past decade (Wu and Oxnard, 1983). The other areas have also yielded many paleontological treasures in the last ten years. Moreover, recent searches of museum collections in East Africa, as well as resurveys of fossil sites, have uncovered yet more fossils.

Given this quantity of new information, it is not surprising that heretofore existing theories of early hominoid evolution have been reevaluated. In fact, it would not be unfair to describe the last ten years as a "revolution" in paleontological views of Miocene hominoid evolution. With a great deal of this recent fossil material still unanalyzed, all the answers are not presently at hand. In fact, the more fossils found, the more complicated the situation seems to become. However, two major subgroups of Miocene hominoids have been described. These correlate nicely with the relevant ecology and geology:

Figure 10-10
The dryopith Y-5 pattern. A characteristic feature of hominoid molars.

1. A forest-living, primarily arboreal set of species, which early on are limited to Africa but later are found in Europe. This group we will call, "dryopiths," a simple descriptive term and nontaxonomic (so as to avoid the pitfalls of making hasty evolutionary judgments).*

2. A more open-country (woodland or woodland/bushland/savanna mosaic) and probably more ground-living set of species. This group, mostly Eurasian in distribution, we will call "ramapiths."

Dryopiths

These fossil forms are best known during the earlier Miocene from East Africa, where a diverse array of species has been recognized. Some researchers also believe some dryopiths may have lived in southern Asia during the Middle-Late Miocene, but this has not been conclusively demonstrated. Certainly, in the later Miocene, there are some fragmentary dryopithlike hominoids in Western Europe, but their relationship to the earlier forms in Africa is, presently, still unclear. Our discussion will thus emphasize the more complete and better-known East African varieties.

In East Africa, the first dryopiths are the earliest hominoids we have evidence of during the Miocene. Indeed, except by broadly expanding the definition of the hominoids (see p. 280), these are the first *definite* hominoids we have from anywhere.

No doubt, these forms occupied a wide range of niches. It is therefore not surprising that they also exhibit a great deal of morphological variation, with overall sizes ranging from that of a medium-sized monkey to that of a good-sized chimp. Accurate reconstructions of overall body size are, however, quite difficult, since most of the fossil material consists only of jaws and teeth. Interpretations of this important series of fossil animals must therefore be based almost exclusively on dental criteria.

When we look at the teeth of the dryopiths, we see in all of them a definite hominoid pattern, but with a great deal of variation in specific traits. Dryopith teeth are characterized first of all by the Y-5 pattern, an arrangement of cusps in the lower molars also seen in modern hominoids (see Fig. 10-10). Most of the Miocene forms also have fairly large canines that overlap, the upper one occluding with a sectorial (cutting) first lower premolar. However, we must keep in mind that, while the features of canine size and shape of the first lower premolar are diagnostic in separating later hominids from pongids, they do not apply consistently in the Miocene; the fossil sample is too variable for the uniform application of such simplistic criteria. We also must remember that it is crucial to distinguish those characteristics that are found in a *primitive* state in an evolutionary lineage (and, therefore, potentially representative of common ancestral stock of forms that diverge later) from *derived* characteristics found only in particular

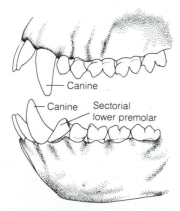

Figure 10-11
Overlapping canines and sectorial lower first premolar. (Shown here in a macaque.)

*What to call the Miocene hominoids? A proliferation of names has been suggested for group 1: Dryopithecidae, Dryopithecinae, Dryopitheci, dryopithecines, dryomorphs, and dryopiths; and, for group 2: Sivapithecinae, Sivapithecini, sivapithecines, Ramapithecidae, Ramapithecinae, Ramapithecini, ramapithecines, ramamorphs, and ramapiths. In two earlier editions of this book, in fact, we have used two different sets of terms. Not everyone at this point is going to be completely satisfied with any of these terms. Here we follow the suggestion of Russell Ciochon (1983) and use "dryopith" and "ramapith" as descriptive, short, and taxonomically unloaded referents.

offshoots (and, therefore, representative of forms that have already diverged). (See p. 139.)

Many of the presumed distinguishing features argued as evidence of "pongid" or "hominid" affinities for Miocene fossils are, in fact, primitive characteristics of hominoids in general. Whereas dryopith cranial remains are known from only a few discoveries, there is fortunately one splendidly preserved skull found in 1948 by Mary Leakey on an island in Lake Victoria, Kenya. Quite generalized in structure, it displays a mixture of primitive and derived features (Pilbeam, 1986). In any case, this skull does not exhibit any of the structural specializations (such as large jaws, face, and muscle attachment areas) found in modern pongids.

A few pieces of dryopith limb skeleton have also been found, including several parts of the postcranial skeleton of an individual found in Kenya (Walker and Pickford, 1983). Including most of the limb bones, several cranial and jaw fragments, and a few vertebrae and ribs, these remains from Rusinga Island are the most complete of any Miocene hominoid individual (and among the most complete for the entire primate fossil record until fairly recent times). From that well-preserved skeleton, it is possible to accurately estimate the body size of the animal, which turns out to be about that of a male colobus monkey (i.e., around 24 pounds). Detailed analysis of the forelimb and preliminary study of other skeletal parts suggest this was a fairly generalized quadruped. Earlier interpretations have indicated that this dryopith was a brachiator, potential knuckle-walker, a ceboidlike quadruped, or a cercopithecoidlike quadruped (Greenfield, 1980). The most reasonable inference is that this small hominoid was probably an arboreal quadruped (Morbeck, 1975) with some suspensory abilities (Fleagle, 1983), but with a more varied positional repertoire than any living Old World monkey (Pilbeam, 1986).

Such attempts to reconstruct the feeding or locomotory behavior of fossil animals like the dryopiths are made through comparisons with modern primates and their observed structural/functional relationships (see p. 170). However, we must be extremely cautious in applying such models too grossly to fossil animals, for they may not closely resemble the behavior of *any* contemporary primate. In our attempts to reconstruct the behavior of earlier primates, therefore, we must be careful not to obscure the uniqueness of the very animals we seek to understand.

A lack of appreciation of the structural (and presumably ecological) uniqueness found in many fossil primates has characterized recent interpretations of Miocene hominoids. It was once thought that dryopiths were clearly pongid and therefore in a direct evolutionary line leading to modern great apes and separate from that leading to hominids. While dryopiths resemble pongids in a few dental traits, they are all in all a quite varied lot, in most characteristics unlike *any* living hominoid (hominid or pongid). We should remember that using modern hominoids as models for those in the Miocene does not really provide a broad basis for comparison—only three genera of great apes (with perhaps only four species) and only one genus and one species of hominid now exist. It might well be that none of these provide a valid model for the behavior of the whole array of ecologically diverse hominoids of the Miocene. To look at these fossil animals and expect to assign them into neat categories, such as hominid and pongid, is much too simplistic. Our fossil sample almost certainly includes members of several evolving **lineages**; some of these are probably closely related to ancestors of living primates, but most of them are probably on extinct sidebranches of

LINEAGE
An evolutionary line of phylogenetically related forms.

(a)

(b)

Figure 10-12
(a) Proconsul africanus *skull. Discovered by Mary Leakey in 1948. (From early Miocene deposits on Rusinga Island, Kenya.) (b) A modern gorilla skull. By way of contrast, note the more projecting face, larger teeth, and more robust muscle attachments in the modern pongid.*

Figure 10-13
Reconstructed upper limb of Proconsul africanus compared to modern chimpanzee.
(a) Chimpanzee; (b) P. africanus.
(© 1959 by W. E. Le Gros Clark).

(a) Chimpanzee   (b) P. africanus

hominoid evolution. The complexity of the evolutionary process demands that we not think in overly simple terms, and we should thus conceive of our evolutionary history as an intricate "bush" instead of a simple "ladder" (Gould, 1976b).

Only in terms of this more complex framework can we understand the Miocene dryopiths. For example, anthropologists once postulated that dryopiths were pongids on the basis of shape of their **dental arcade.** Unlike hominids, and resembling modern great apes, they presumably possess *parallel* tooth rows, and, in fact, some dryopiths do seem to have such a dental arcade. But most of them have tooth rows that diverge in back, unlike the parallel rows of modern great apes or the parabolic row of modern humans. The shape of the dental arcade in modern chimps and gorillas is an obvious derived characteristic seen primarily in relatively recent pongids. The same can be said of the *parabolic* row for hominids. Therefore, neither kind of tooth row tells us much about dryopith relationships.

Much of the variation seen in dryopiths can be accounted for by time (15 million years of evolution) as well as geography. The earliest and most generalized dryopiths are found in East Africa. Many primatologists, recognizing that these East African forms lack many of the derived characteristics seen in later dryopiths, have referred them to a separate genus (*Proconsul* for the early East African forms, contrasted to *Dryopithecus* for the later, more derived ones from Europe). In fact *Proconsul* is so primitive *as a hominoid* that some authorities (Andrews, 1985) place it before the likely split of any of the major branches of hominoid evolution (see Fig. 10-22, p. 297). *Dryopithecus* from the middle Miocene of Europe, however, appears to be more derived as a large-bodied hominoid.

One general set of ecological adaptations does appear, however, to tie the dryopiths together: all are forest-adapted, primarily arboreal, and probably mostly fruit-eating (frugivorous) (Pilbeam, 1979). Given this type of adaptation, migration from area to area would require a relatively continuous forest. Ecological reconstructions of the Miocene world prior to 17 m.y.a. suggest that forests were quite widespread, thus providing the opporunity for migration within East Africa. How dryopiths were able to cross the Afro-Eurasian land bridge once climatic cooling began is still a mystery.

During the Middle Miocene, with this climatic cooling, considerable shrinkage of forested areas occurred. Consequently, further isolation of regional

Figure 10-14
Dental rows: Ape parallel arcade compared to human parabolic pattern. (a) Gorilla; (b) human.

(a) Gorilla   (b) Human

dryopith populations would have been promoted. The next time we pick up the threads of dryopith evolution is in Western Europe (Germany, Austria, France, Spain) several million years later (after 15 m.y.a.). We still do not know how these later, as-yet-fragmentary fossils are linked to the earlier, primitive dryopiths from East Africa.

On the other hand, as we have pointed out, with the shrinkage of forests, more open kinds of environments expanded, particularly woodland/forest fringe niches. Those hominoids already preadapted for exploitation of these environments would then have had considerably more evolutionary opportunities than was true previously.

Interestingly, it is at about this time (14–10 m.y.a.) that varieties of more ground-living hominoids began to diversify in several parts of the Old World. It is to this group, the ramapiths, that we now turn.

Ramapiths

The other major subgrouping of Miocene hominoids is the ramapiths, a highly successful and widely distributed group of species. In fact, except for later species of the genus *Homo* (in the last million years only), ramapiths were the most widely distributed hominoids that ever existed. The time range for these forms goes back at least 14 m.y. in East Africa, and they probably are also that old in Pakistan and Turkey.

The evidence for the earliest ramapith may go even further back. A newly discovered 16–18 m.y. old fossil, including pieces of the jaws and face, was uncovered in 1983 at Buluk in northern Kenya by Richard Leakey and Alan Walker (Leakey and Walker, 1985). Both large and small hominoids have been recovered at Buluk, and the larger species is thought by Leakey and Walker to be closely aligned with the Asian varieties of ramapiths we are about to discuss. If so, this would be the earliest representative of this group. Somewhat later (around 14 m.y.a.), again from Kenya, is another site (possibly there is a third as well) that also has some fragmentary pieces similar to ramapiths. In any case, these do not conform to the dryopith pattern we have described. The precise relationship of these African hominoids to those known in Asia, however, remains a matter of debate (Pilbeam, 1986). (See below.)

The prime evidence for the ramapith group, however, comes from Eurasia. Geographically, then, we have an interesting dichotomy: While dryopiths are mostly known from Africa, ramapiths are better known from Eurasia.

In recent years, these Eurasian ramapiths have been uncovered in several areas in remarkable abundance. As we noted on page 282, Lufeng in southern China (*circa* 8 m.y.a.) has yielded over 1,000 teeth as well as 5 partial crania. In addition, upwards of 50 individuals have been recovered from the Potwar Plateau (7–13.5 m.y.a.) in the Siwalik Hills of Pakistan (plus several more individuals recovered over several years from the Indian side of the Siwaliks). Included in the superb Pakistani collection is a multitude of mandibles (15 in all, some of which are nearly intact) many postcranial remains, and a recently discovered partial cranium, including most of the face (Pilbeam et al., 1977; Pilbeam, 1982). While not as productive as those in China and Pakistan, other sites in Western Asia and Europe have also recently added to the harvest. More than 20 individuals have been recovered from 3 sites in Turkey (12–13+? m.y.a.), and a similar yield has been excavated from the Rudabánya Mountains of Hungary (less than

DENTAL ARCADE
The shape of the tooth row.

Ladder   Bush

Figure 10-15
Two phylogenetic models: A simple ladder versus a complex bush.

11 m.y.a.?) (Morbeck, 1983). Finally, at least 12 or possibly 13 individuals have been found in northern Greece near Salonika (10–12 m.y.a.).

The earliest firmly dated ramapiths in Eurasia are from the lower beds at the Potwar Plateau, estimated minimumly at 13 m.y.a. (Raza, et al., 1983). The earliest sites in Turkey *may* also be this old, or even older (Kay and Simons, 1983). In any case, it is quite clear that no ramapiths (or any hominoid) are found anywhere in Eurasia until after the docking of the African plate with the Eurasian land mass around 16 m.y.a. (see p. 282). Once established, the ramapiths apparently lasted quite a long time, surviving in Pakistan up until about 7 m.y.a.

Dispersed over thousands of miles and over at least 7 million years of time, it is no wonder that ramapiths are quite variable. Indeed, several different species have been suggested, some in just the last few years. As we'll see later in this chapter, such interpretations can be a biological minefield. Here, then, we will primarily concentrate on the more general morphological and ecological characteristics and limit our taxonomic conclusions to some genus-level considerations.

The ramapiths differ morphologically from the dryopiths in their dentition and facial anatomy. The front teeth, especially the central incisors, are often quite large, while the canine is fairly good-sized (low-crowned and robust) (Andrews, 1983). In general, the canines are large compared to what we see in humans (and earlier hominids) but are not as big as they are in the large (male) extant apes (Kay and Simons, 1983). There are, however, large discrepancies in canine size among different ramapith individuals, partly because some species were bigger overall, but also because there was apparently considerable variation (sexual dimorphism) within the same species. In fact, in body size, some ramapiths were apparently as dimorphic as modern gorillas and orangs (Andrews, 1983).

The first lower premolar is also quite variable in shape. Usually, it is fairly sectorial; that is, it shows the shearing surface typical in most catarrhines (consequently, this is most likely to be the primitive condition). In some cases, however, an accessory cusp displays enlargement, perhaps either as a precursor to the derived condition seen in hominids (Kay and Simons, 1983) or as a separate evolutionary parallelism between these ramapiths and our line (Ciochon, 1983).

The most distinctive part of the dentition of ramapiths may be seen in the back tooth row, where the molars are large, flat-wearing, and thick-enameled (in some species, the enamel is heavily wrinkled as well). The thickness of the enamel cap has played a most significant role in recent interpretations of Miocene hominoid evolution. Among living hominoids, relative to body size, humans have by far the thickest molar caps. Gorillas and chimps have thin enamel, *but* orang molars could be described as moderately thick (Ward and Pilbeam, 1983). Thick (in fact, very thick) enamel is also seen in early hominids (in the period 1–4 m.y.a.).

As a characteristic, thick enamel in the ramapiths could then be seen as a derived feature linking them specifically with either orangs or hominids. A third possibility is that thick enamel is the *primitive* condition in large-bodied hominoids, with orangs and humans maintaining a more primitive expression, while chimps and gorillas are more derived.

Again, we have a thorny problem in attempting to establish the direction (polarity) of primitive-derived character transformation. Since our evolutionary reconstructions are ultimately based on such interpretations, the conclusions are less than clearcut. More on this presently.

Probably, the most characteristic anatomical aspects in at least some of the ramapiths are seen in the face, especially the area immediately below the nose (Ward and Kimbel, 1983). Facial remains of *Sivapithecus* from Pakistan and Turkey have concave profiles and projecting incisors (and, overall, remarkably resemble the modern orang). In particular, the partial cranium discovered in 1980 at the Potwar Plateau (Pakistan, *circa* 8 m.y.a.) and published two years later (Pilbeam, 1982) bears striking similarities to the orangutan (see Fig. 10-16). The published description of this specimen, with illustrations similar to those shown here, had a tremendous impact on paleoanthropology. As we have seen (p. 179), biochemical evidence demonstrates the distinctiveness of the orang from the African apes and humans; here, then, was fossil evidence suggesting some ancient Asian traces of the orang lineage. As a result, the views of biochemists and paleoanthropologists agree more closely (pp. 295–296).

It must be noted, however, that, except for the lower face, *Sivapithecus* is *not* like an orangutan. In fact, especially in the post-cranium (i.e., all skeletal parts except the head) *Sivapithecus* is distinctively *unlike* an orang, or any other known hominoid, for that matter. In most respects, then, *Sivapithecus* could be described as *highly derived* (Pilbeam, 1986).

Many earlier fossil-based interpretations of ramapith evolutionary affinities had, of course, to be reevaluated. As we hinted at the beginning of our discussion of Miocene hominoids (p. 282), in the 1960s E. L. Simons and David Pilbeam suggested a Middle Miocene ramapith hominoid as the first hominid (i.e., clearly diverged on our particular line and separate from that leading to any extant ape).

(a)

Figure 10-16

Comparison of Sivapithecus *cranium (center) with modern chimpanzee (left) and orangutan (right). The* Sivapithecus *fossil is specimen, GSP 15000 from the Potwar Plateau, Pakistan, c. 8 m.y.a. (a) lateral view; (b) frontal view.*

(b)

According to this view, this early hominid was *Ramapithecus*—known at that time mostly from India, with some bits from East Africa.

We have already illustrated some of the dramatic new discoveries of the 1970s and early 1980s. As a consequence of these new discoveries, the earlier suggestion that *Ramapithecus* was a definite hominid was seriously questioned, if not rejected altogether. One primary advocate of this revised view is David Pilbeam (1977; 1982; 1986), an initial architect of the earlier widely accepted theory. Pilbeam, who has led the highly successful paleoanthropological project at the Potwar Plateau, has been swayed by the new fossils recovered there and elsewhere. These more complete specimens (like that shown in Fig. 10-16) have been placed in the genus **Sivapithecus**.

A variety of other generic terms have also been put forward for other ramapiths (see Table 10-2). Some of these other generic designations may eventually stick. What does seem likely, at present, is that the ramapith material from Hungary, Greece, China, and East Africa is all different from *Sivapithecus*—as it is defined especially in Pakistan (Pilbeam, 1986). These other fossils do not display the same orang-like features seen in Pakistan (also suggested in India and Turkey—see Fig. 10-16). Consequently, they are probably not in the same evolutionary group (clade), and may only be distantly related to the orang and *Sivapithecus*. What about *Ramapithecus*? The strong consensus among primatologists is that this genus is also really part of *Sivapithecus*, although most probably a separate species (Greenfield, 1979; Ward and Pilbeam, 1983; Kay and Simons, 1983; Corruccini and Ciochon, 1983).

If *Sivapithecus* can be placed in—or at least close to—the lineage of modern orangs, what becomes of the assertion that "Ramapithecus" (now part of the same evolutionary group, or "clade") is an early hominid? Many researchers, seeing distinctive oranglike derived features in these Miocene fossils, would now reject this claim (Ward and Pilbeam, 1983; Cronin, 1983; Andrews, 1983).

Paleontologists are far from unanimous in this determination. The other primary exponent of the "Ramapithecus as hominid" hypothesis, E. L. Simons (with his colleague Richard Kay), believes that *Sivapithecus*—into which they have "sunk" *Ramapithecus*—shows many derived hominid features. They point particularly to aspects of the dentition they consider hominidlike and argue that other dental/facial similarities with orangs resulted from evolutionary parallelisms. They conclude that *Sivapithecus* is already a hominid (basically, this is

Table 10-2 *Some Suggested Names for Miocene Ramapith Forms*

Name	Locality
Ramapithecus	India/Pakistan
Sivapithecus	India/Pakistan
Kenyapithecus (usually sunk into *Ramapithecus*)	Kenya
Bodvapithecus	Hungary
Rudapithecus	Hungary
Ouranopithecus	Greece
Gigantopithecus	India/Pakistan (Pleistocene species from China)

the same theory proposed much earlier; however, where before we had *Ramapithecus*, we now read *Sivapithecus*).

A third alternative also exists: *Sivapithecus* may not already have diverged in the orang *or* the hominid direction. Perhaps it was a common ancestor for all later large-bodied hominoids—the Asian forms (orang) and the African ones (gorilla, chimp, and human). This view would then emphasize that many features of ramapith (and probably also orang) morphology, such as enamel thickness, lower face morphology, etc., are simply primitive expressions of the ancestral hominoid condition. The African hominoids would then be seen as the more derived forms (Wolpoff, 1983; Greenfield, 1983).

We have, then, three possible alternatives for interpreting the evolutionary relationships of some key Miocene ramapiths (i.e., *Sivapithecus*):

1. *Sivapithecus* is already on the orang line, not specifically related to any of the other hominoids. This suggests that the Asian/African hominoid divergence occurred close to 12 m.y.a. From this assertion, no direct claim is made on when hominids originated from African hominoid stock, but the implication is considerably after 12 m.y.a. (quite comfortably, after 10 m.y.a., in fact).
2. *Sivapithecus* is specifically on the hominid line. This suggests that orangs must have diverged considerably earlier than 12 m.y.a., while hominids and African apes (gorillas and chimps) must have been diverging at about that time (or a little earlier).
3. *Sivapithecus* is a possible common ancestor of all large-bodied hominoids—orangs, chimps, gorillas, and humans. The split leading to orangs is thus seen as occurring within the ramapith 'complex," somewhere between 10–12 m.y.a. The hominid/African ape split, then, is later yet (5–6 m.y.a.?).

Among knowledgeable primate paleontologists familiar with the original fossil material, one can find support for each of these three interpretations. It is thus easy to say, "more fossil material is needed to decide." However, one can *always* say that. Thanks to the spectacular successes of the last decade, we now have a wealth of hominoid fossils, including hundreds of teeth, several partial crania, dozens of jaws, etc. More fossil evidence is not likely to add substantially to the picture already emerging. In fact, more concrete interpretations of the Miocene hominoids have not come solely from additional fossils; sophistication of analysis, especially the sorting out of primitive/derived character states, has also contributed. We still have a way to go, though, in order to establish precisely which are the primitive, and which the derived, characteristics of hominoids.

For now, the first alternative on our list seems to us to be the best-supported interpretation, with the third somewhat less likely. New fossil material (especially facial remains), along with biochemical findings, indicate the second alternative to be the least probable.

Paleoecology of Sivapithecus   Of course, what *everyone* would like to know about *Sivapithecus* is: To whom is it related? We have just taken our best shot at that difficult question. Another fascinating research effort involves reconstructing the way of life of this early hominoid and speculating upon factors that influenced its evolution.

For example, what were these ramapiths eating? By referring to certain structural/functional analogs seen in modern primates, investigators have postulated a diet that correlates with ramapith dental structure. This diet is thought to chiefly

SIVAPITHECUS
(Shiv'-ah-pith-eh-kus)

Figure 10-17
Ramapith distribution during the Miocene,
14–7 m.y.a.—fossils thus far discovered.

include tough hard morsels, such as seeds, which some believe were exploited primarily on the ground (Jolly, 1970).

A more comprehensive comparison of a wide variety of living primates, however, reveals ramapith dental parallels (especially larger, flat-wearing, more thickly enameled molars) among several arboreal species eating nuts, seeds, and hard fruits found in the trees (Kay, 1981). Thus, ramapith dental features quite possibly could have originated in an arboreal setting. Most researchers attempting to reconstruct the paleoecology of the ramapiths, however, assume that, eventually, ramapiths did take greater advantage of terrestrial environments than their dryopith cousins. Evidence from Eurasian sites (Potwar Plateau, Lufeng, Rudabánya) suggests that ramapiths lived in environments exhibiting greater seasonality than the tropics (where most dryopiths lived). Consequently, fruits would not have been available all year long, and ramapiths could not have been primarily frugivorous (i.e., fruit-eaters) (Andrews, 1983).

Figure 10-18
Two ramapith mandibles from the Potwar
Plateau, Pakistan. Discovered in 1976 and
1977. Approximate age, 9 m.y.

Moreover, within these environments, there was less continuous forest vegetation, with more woodland/bushland mosaic niches. These changes were further stimulated by a general cooling of the earth's climate, after about 16 m.y.a. (see p. 283). Such a niche, being ecologically poor, is no place to find a primate. It is hypothesized, therefore, that ramapiths may have been environmental "opportunists," analogous to bears and pigs, exploiting below-ground resources, such as roots and tubers.

Utilization of nonarboreal resources would, of course, require some ground-living. Ramapiths are generally larger-bodied than dryopiths, a fact which could argue for greater terrestriality. Of course, body size varied greatly (some individuals may have exceeded 150 pounds) largely as a result of marked sexual dimorphism (Andrews, 1983). Postcranial evidence, however, does not suggest to David Pilbeam (1986) that *Sivapithecus* spent much time on the ground. We have noted above that *Sivapithecus* is quite unique in its postural anatomy, and it is thus difficult to interpret how and *where* it typically locomoted. Pilbeam argues that its behavior "would probably have involved quadrupedalism, palm and fist walking, quadrumanous scrambling, arm-swinging, bipedalism, leaping and diving. No obvious terrestrial component is present. If orangs are indeed derived from *Sivapithecus*, they have changed substantially." (Pilbeam, 1986, p. 306).

Some fairly diverse environmental adaptation did, indeed, prove successful for the ramapiths—witness their longevity and geographic dispersal. If ramapiths were such successful opportunists, what spelled their doom? No single answer suffices. Perhaps heightened competition from the extremely successful Old World monkeys (some of these were definitely becoming partly terrestrial) played a part. Also, in the later Miocene, recall that the environment continued to change. Further cooling and drying probably isolated some groups and may often have critically reduced effective breeding population size. As a part of this ongoing dessication process, the Mediterranean and Black Seas dried up (very late Miocene—approximately 6.5 m.y.a.) and there was further cooling in adjacent seas. To the north, in Eurasia, the challenges must have been harsh. With the exception of pockets in the more tropical areas of southern Asia, no hominoids (except *Gigantopithecus*—see the following section) apparently survived here beyond the Miocene.

To the south, in Africa, things were to be different. The African apes and hominids had diverged (or were about to), and within the still-changing (and probably more seasonal) environments of Africa, our family—the hominids—originated. The story that followed comprises the remainder of this book.

Gigantopithecus   Evidence exists for another and very distinctive ramapith that can trace its origins back into the Miocene. This highly unusual primate, called **Gigantopithecus**, came to the attention of scientists in a most unusual way. For centuries, Chinese folk medicine has prescribed the use of ground "dragon bones" in the concoction of various potions. The source of many of these bones was fossil sites and, from there, these dragon bones often found their way into Chinese apothecaries (drugstores). It was in such an establishment that the first *Gigantopithecus* teeth were recognized in 1935 by Ralph von Koenigswald, a young German paleontologist on the lookout for important fossil remains.

Since the 1930s, more than 1,000 individual teeth have been collected (largely from apothecaries). Three lower jaws were archeologically excavated in China in the 1950s, and one was recovered in northern India in 1968. The In-

Figure 10-19
A Chinese apothecary, or drugstore.

ALLOMETRIC GROWTH
The process of differential growth whereby some parts of the body grow proportionately more than others.

dian specimen is clearly the oldest of the lot, falling in the late Miocene (5 m.y.–9 m.y.), while the Chinese material belongs to the Middle Pleistocene (500,000 y.a.–1 m.y.a.).

Truly an animal to titillate the imagination, *Gigantopithecus* was apparently a huge hominoid. It was named for the enormous proportions of its teeth and jaws (all that is preserved of the animal), and estimates place its weight in excess of 600 pounds and its stature somewhere between 6 and 9 feet! (Simons and Ettel, 1970). Such estimates may, however, be somewhat exaggerated. Differential patterns of growth (called **allometric growth**) probably produced different body proportions in this extinct animal from those seen in living hominoids (Johnson, 1979). Some postcranial bones found in the Potwar Plateau (Miocene), which may belong to a *Gigantopithecus* form, support a smaller size estimate. From these data, it has been suggested that *Gigantopithecus* weighed about the same as a small female gorilla (equivalent to 150 pounds) (Pilbeam, 1979).

Numerous dental characteristics clearly establish *Gigantopithecus* as a ramapith hominoid, and some superficial features even appear hominidlike. However, these similarities are apparently functional analogies associated with heavy back tooth grinding and do not represent particularly close evolutionary relationships (that is, homologies). In fact, *Gigantopithecus* exhibits some rather unusual features, such as flat-worn canines, apparently heavily used as grinding teeth. Such a situation is unusual among primates (a similar pattern may also be present in *Sivapithecus*), and even the peglike incisors may have been used in mastication of heavy vegetation. Although some investigators have speculated that *Gigantopithecus* may be closely related to our particular evolutionary line (Weidenreich, 1946; Frayer, 1973; Gelvin, 1980), sophisticated statistical analysis has confirmed the unique status of this fossil form (Corruccini, 1975a).

Despite these findings, rather bizarre notions concerning this fossil still abound. Indeed, Soviet scientists have gone so far as to speculate the unsubstantiated "abominable snowman" as a descendant, and newspaper accounts tell of Soviet-led expeditions into the frozen heights of the Himalayas to find proof!

More conservative research has centered on reconstructions of what *Gigantopithecus* ecologically was "doing for a living." Apparently, its niche was a mixed one in China, probably consisting primarily of forest-type environments, while the earlier species lived in a more open environment in India (Simons and Ettel, 1970). Just what *Gigantopithecus* was chewing in its huge jaws is still a mystery,

Figure 10-21
Gigantopithecus mandible, occlusal view. Note that the canines (circled) are worn flat.

Timing the Hominid-Pongid Split

One of the most fundamental of all questions in human evolution is: When did the hominid line originate? Or, to put it another way: When did we last share a common ancestry with our closest living relatives, the pongids?

Scientists have taken different perspectives in attempting to answer this question. The traditional approach of paleontology is still the most common. Recent years have produced considerably more paleontological sophistication through a vast new array of fossil material, more precise chronometric dating, and more rigorous interpretation of primitive-derived characteristics. Still, the fossil record remains incomplete, and significant gaps exist for some of the most crucial intervals. So the question still persists: How old is the hominid line?

Data drawn from a completely different perspective have also been applied to this problem. Popularized by Vincent Sarich and Allan Wilson of the University of California, Berkeley (1967), this perspective utilizes comparisons of living animals. By calibrating the overall immunological reactions of proteins from different species, by sequencing the amino acids within proteins, or by doing DNA hybridization (see pp. 179–180), living species can be compared to each other.

Certainly, such data are immensely valuable in demonstrating *relative* genetic distances among contemporary organisms (as we discussed in Chapter 7. However, proponents of this view go considerably further and postulate that biochemical distance can be used directly to calculate evolutionary distance. In other words, a "molecular clock" is thought to provide unambiguous divergence dates for a host of evolutionary lineages, including hominids/pongids (Sarich, 1971).

Several hotly disputed assumptions are required, however, to perform this feat. Most importantly, the rate of molecular evolution must be constant over time. Such regularity could be accomplished if mutations were strictly *neutral* (see p. 89) or if selection pressures remained constant. Since environmental changes are decidedly not constant through time, the latter assumption is not valid. As for the first point, while neutral mutations certainly do occur (and perhaps do so quite frequently), many researchers are not convinced that most mutations are neutral (e.g., see Livingstone, 1980). Moreover, even if mutation was mostly neutral, major evolutionary shifts may still be quite nongradual in tempo—given the suggested punctuated mode of change (see p. 91).

Another possible complicating factor concerns genera-

tion length. Those species that reproduce in shorter periods of time should (according to strict application of the molecular clock) show, for the same period of time, greater amounts of molecular evolution than more slowly reproducing forms (Vogel, et al., 1976). Given the variation in generation lengths, it is not justifiable to make strict linear reconstruction for divergence times among prosimians, monkeys, and hominoids.

In fact, recently collected molecular data (in which DNA sequences are *directly* compared) indicate that the molecular clock does not run constantly with time. Rather, there is a marked *slowdown* in molecular divergence rate among primates, and most especially among the hominoids. Such a phenomenon is thought to be a function of greater generation length among higher primates when compared to other mammals (Li and Tanimura, 1987).

Another problem is that there is no certain indicator of molecular evolutionary rates; different proteins yield significantly different rates of evolution and thus greatly influence inferences about divergence times (Corruccini et al., 1980). In fact, the *greatest* margin of error would occur in attempting to calculate relatively recent evolutionary events—for example, the hominid-pongid split.

Analysis of amino acid sequences of proteins by another group of biochemists (at Wayne State University in Detroit) has confirmed that, indeed, rates of molecular evolution are not constant, but are rather characterized by periods of acceleration and deacceleration (the latter being particularly true in the last few million years). Thus, these researchers conclude: "For proteins demonstrating striking shifts in rates of amino acid substitutions over time, it is not possible to calculate accurate divergence dates within Anthropoidea using the molecular clock approach. Our analysis of amino acid sequence data of several proteins by the clock model yields divergence dates, particularly within the Hominoidea, that are far too recent in view of well-established fossil evidence" (Goodman et al., 1983, p. 68).

As a result of such criticisms of the "clock," some paleontologists have been skeptical of its claimed applications. For example, Milford Wolpoff (of the University of Michigan) argues that, "Probably the best way to summarize the very disparate points raised is that the 'clock' simply *should not* work" (Wolpoff, 1983a, p. 661).

Naturally, not everyone takes so negative a view of the

(continued on next page)

Timing the Hominid-Pongid Split, continued

clock approach. Vincent Sarich continues to believe firmly in its basic accuracy (when applied correctly) and, justifiably, feels vindicated by recent recalibrations of theories derived from fossil evidence, which bring them closer to the biochemically derived hypotheses.

The fossils themselves are not going to provide the whole answer. The paleontological record is usually too incomplete to provide clearcut ancestor-descendant associations. More fossils will always help, of course, but the way we think about them (i.e., the questions we raise about them) is also crucial in framing workable theories.

The biochemical perspective has been important in that it has articulated key issues for evolutionary consideration (for example, the place of the orang in relation to other large-bodied hominoids). The interplay between the paleontological and biochemical perspectives has thus been most productive. In fact, these viewpoints agree more now on several aspects of hominoid evolution than they did just a few years ago. The greatest furor has been raised from overly strong claims for the unique validity of either approach. We have shown in this chapter that more fossil evidence *and* more controlled analyses have forced previous views to be reconsidered. Moreover, it is equally unfair to portray the clock approach as a complete answer. As one of the leading advocates of this method has stated, "The clock is one of an approximate, not metronomically perfect nature" (Cronin, 1983, p. 116).

but apparently it consisted of enormous amounts of vegetable foods. There are many structural analogies between the teeth of *Gigantopithecus* and that of the bamboo-shoot-eating giant panda. An animal having the bulk of *Gigantopithecus* would have required a huge masticatory apparatus with large, grinding teeth and heavy jaws. And this picture is exactly the one that we envision, even to the extreme point of including the front teeth in this functional complex.

In addition to the apparent specialization of this animal, *Gigantopithecus* would seem an unlikely close relative of hominids, for it survived so late—up to the Middle Pleistocene in China. Long before this time, definite hominids had been diverging, and by the Middle Plesitocene they were already closely approximating modern humans in such features as body size and teeth.

Therefore, it seems likely that *Gigantopithecus* diverged from other hominoids in the middle-late Miocene, set out on a specialized evolutionary path, and eventually became extinct in the Middle Pleistocene.

Miocene Hominoids: Summary

Firm judgments concerning the diverse array of Miocene hominoids cannot yet be made, but it is apparent that the evolutionary picture is a good deal more complex than previously thought. In this regard, it is interesting to note that David Pilbeam, a proponent of the earlier simplistic view, has recently altered his opinions. Many of his current views are reflected in the interpretations given here.

There are probably at least three distinct genera of hominoids by mid-Miocene times, with a multitude of species. Most, if not all, of these forms are filling niches not strictly analogous to any living hominoid, and our interpretation must not obscure the evolutionary uniqueness these animals no doubt possessed.

Ideally, we would like to draw conclusions concerning how these Miocene hominoids are related to extant apes and to ourselves. The earlier, quite uncomplicated suggestions just have not worked out, as Pilbeam has noted: "We know enough now to realize that our earlier and simple scenarios were too simple, though not enough yet to choose among a variety of more complex ones" (Pilbeam, 1977, p. 3).

Presently, we cannot trace with any certainty the hominid lineage or that of the African apes back to any of these Miocene forms. The orang, however, may well share close relationship with some of the Asian ramapiths.

It would thus be fair to say, on the basis of current evidence, that not all possible evolutionary scenarios are equally probable. The placement and frequency of question marks in Figure 10-22 reflect this fact.

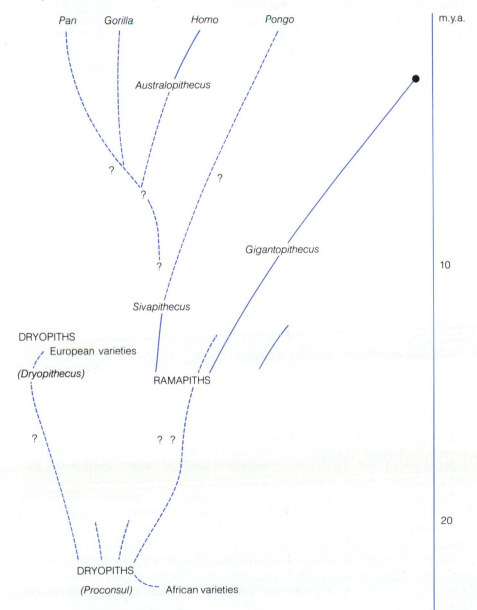

Figure 10-22
A provisional model showing possible relationships of Miocene and later hominoids.

The Meaning of Genus and Species

Our discussion of fossil primates has introduced a multitude of cumbersome taxonomic names. We should pause at this point and reasonably ask: Why use so many names like *Sivapithecus*, *Ramapithecus*, and *Gigantopithecus*? What does such naming mean in evolutionary terms?

Our goal when applying genus, species, or other taxonomic labels to groups of organisms is to make meaningful biological statements about the variation that is present. When looking at populations of living or long extinct animals, we are assuredly going to see the presence of variation. This situation is true of *any* sexually reproducing organism due to the factors of recombination (as independent assortment and crossing-over—see Chapter 3). As a result of recombination, each individual organism is a unique combination of genetic material, and this uniqueness is usually reflected to some extent in the phenotype. In addition to such *individual variation*, we see other kinds of systematic variation in all biological populations. *Age changes* certainly act to alter overall body size, as well as shape, in many animals. One pertinent example for fossil hominoid studies is the great change in number, size, and shape of teeth from deciduous (milk) teeth (only twenty present) to the permanent dentition (thirty-two present). It obviously would be a great error to assign two different fossil hominoids to different species *solely* on the basis of age-dependent dental criteria. If one were represented only by milk teeth and the other only by permanent teeth, they easily could be differently aged individuals of the *same* population.

Variation due to sex also plays an important role in influencing differences among individuals observed in biological populations. Differences in structural traits between males and females of the same population are called *sexual dimorphism*, and we have seen that great variation does exist between the sexes in some primates (for example, gorillas and baboons) in such elements as overall body size and canine size.

As we have seen when looking at body size differences, as well as differences in tooth size, among the ramapiths, a reasonable assumption is that what we are really viewing is simply the variations between males and females of the same species.

Keeping in mind all the types of variation present within interbreeding groups of organisms, the minimum biological category we would like to define in fossil primate samples is the *species*. As previously defined in Chapter 4, the species is biologically described as a group of interbreeding or potentially interbreeding organisms that are reproductively isolated from other such groups. In modern organisms, this concept is theoretically testable by observations of reproductive behavior. In animals long dead, such testing is obviously impossible. Therefore, in order to get a handle on the interpretation of variation seen in fossil groups like the ramapiths we must refer to living animals.

We know without doubt that variation is present. The question is: What is its biological significance? Two immediate choices occur: Either the variation is accounted for by individual, age, and sex differences seen within every biological species—**intraspecific**—or the variation present represents differences between reproductively isolated groups—**interspecific**. How do we judge between the alterntives intra- or interspecific? We clearly must refer to already defined groups where we can observe reproductive behavior; in other words, contemporary species.

If the amount of morphological variation observed in fossil samples is comparable with that seen today *within species of closely related forms*, then we should not "split" our sample into more than one species. We must, however, be careful in choosing our modern analogs, for rates of morphological evolution vary widely among different groups of mammals. In interpreting past primates, we do best when comparing them with well-known species of modern primates.

Our evolutionary interpretations of the vast array of variable Miocene hominoids is greatly simplified by adhering to relevant biological criteria:

1. First we must look at *all* relevant material. We are not justified in splitting fossil groups into several species on the basis of only presumed differences in the sample (Simons' and Pilbeam's contribution was a major step in rectifying this situation for Miocene hominoids).
2. We must statistically reconstruct the variation observed in our often very small fossil *samples* to realistic dimensions of actual biological *populations*. Every piece of every bone found is part of an individual, who in turn was part of a variable interbreeding population of organisms.
3. We then refer to known dimensions of variation in closely related groups of living primates, keeping in mind expected effects of age, sexual dimorphism, and individual variation.
4. Our next step is to extrapolate the results to the fossil sample and make the judgment: How many species are represented?
5. Since fossil forms are widely scattered in time, we also must place the different species within a firm chronology.
6. Finally, we would like to make interpretations (at least, educated guesses) concerning which forms are related to other forms. To do this, we must pay strict attention to primitive as opposed to derived characteristics.

Following the above steps will greatly reduce the kind of useless confusion that has characterized hominoid studies for so long. We do not, however, wish to convey the impression that the biological interpretation of fossils into taxonomic categories is simple and unambiguous. Far from it! Many complexities must be recognized. Even in living groups, sharp lines between populations representing only one species and populations representing two or more species are difficult to draw. For example, a chain of integrating subspecies in gulls exchange genes at overlapping boundaries. However, at the terminal ends of the chain, two subspecies (species?) live side-by-side along the coasts of Europe with little or no hybridization. In practice, isolating exactly where species boundaries begin and end is exceptionally difficult, especially in a dynamic situation like that represented by gulls (Fig. 10-23).

In contexts dealing with extinct species, the uncertainties are even greater. In addition to the overlapping patterns of variation *over space*, variation also occurs *through time*. In other words, even more variation will be seen in such **paleospecies**, since individuals may be separated by thousands or even millions of years. Applying strict Linnaean taxonomy to such a situation presents an unavoidable dilemma. Standard Linnaean classification, designed to take account of the variation present at any given time, describes a static situation. However, when dealing with paleospecies we are often involved in great spans of time and thus with much additional variation.

Where do we establish meaningful species boundaries in such a dynamic situation? Often, our task is made easier because of the incompleteness of the fossil

INTRASPECIFIC
Within one species.

INTERSPECIFIC
Between two or more species.

PALEOSPECIES
A group of organisms from different periods classified within the same species.

Figure 10-23
Circular overlap in gulls. A, B, C are sub-species of Larus argentatus. *D
(L. glaucoides) is a separate species. All
along the chain subspecies interbreed (C1
with C2; C3 with C4, etc.) but at the terminal ends A2 lives side-by-side with B3 and
B4 and does not interbreed. Where does one
then draw species designations?*

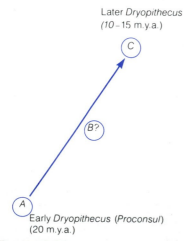

Later *Dryopithecus*
(10 – 15 m.y.a.)

Early *Dryopithecus (Proconsul)*
(20 m.y.a.)

Figure 10-24
*Evolution in a continuing evolving lineage.
Where does one designate the different
species?*

record. Quite frequently, fossil samples are separated by great gaps of time (as between A and C in Figure 10-24) and the morphological differences may therefore
also be clearcut. In such a case, we feel quite comfortable calling these different
species. But what about fossil populations (B, for example) that are intermediate
in both time and morphology? This question has no easy answer. Any taxonomic
designation in such a continuously evolving lineage is by necessity going to be
arbitrary.

Such a line, which has no speciation events (see p. 90), is referred to as
monophyletic. For such a lineage, many evolutionary biologists see no point in
making separate species designations—that is, the entire line is seen as a single
paleospecies (Eldredge and Cracraft, 1980). Many biologists believe, in fact,
that long, gradual transformations of this type are not the rule, but that branching (i.e., speciation) is much more typical of evolutionary change. (Once again,
the view of the punctuationalists—see p. 91).

Moreover, it is imperative in evolutionary interpretation to understand ancestor-descendant relationships. Most paleontologists have traditionally made
anatomical comparisons and then immediately constructed evolutionary trees
(also called *phylogenies*). Recently, another perspective has been advanced. In
this approach, a detailed interpretation of primitive versus derived states must
first be explicitly stated. Only then can patterns of relationships be shown.

These are best interpreted in the form of a *cladogram* (a set of relationships
shown as a hypothesis). In fact, usually several cladograms can be constructed

from the same set of data. Those that are seen as most economically explaining the patterns of derived characteristics are then provisionally accepted, while less adequate ones are rejected. Such a perspective has been termed **cladistics**, and has injected a good deal more objectivity into paleontology (Eldredge and Cracraft, 1980). It must be pointed out, however, that not all paleontologists have accepted this approach. A basic assumption of cladistic analysis is that trait *patterns* are developed as the result of ancestor-descendant relationships and, conversely, that parallelism and convergence (see p. 149) have little import. In primate evolution, this assumption may not hold true; an analysis of morphological features in lemurs and lorises showed that 80% of the traits studied displayed some parallelism (Walker et al., 1981).

The next level of formal taxonomic classification, the *genus*, presents another problem. In order to have more than one genus, we obviously must have at least two species (reproductively isolated groups), and, in addition, the species must differ in a basic way. A genus is therefore defined as a group of species composed of members more closely related to each other than they are to species from another genus.

Grouping contemporary species together into genera is largely a subjective procedure wherein degree of relatedness becomes a strictly relative judgment. One possible test for contemporary animals is to check for results of hybridization between individuals of different species—rare in nature but quite common in captivity. If two normally separate species interbreed and produce live, though not necessarily fertile, offspring, this process shows genetically that they are not too distant and that they probably should be classified into a single genus. Well-known examples of such interspecific crosses within one genus are horses with donkeys (*Equus caballus* × *Equus asinus*) or lions with tigers (*Panthera leo* × *Panthera tigris*). In both these cases, the close morphological and evolutionary similarities between these species are confirmed by their occasional ability to produce live hybrids.

As mentioned, we cannot perform breeding experiments with animals that are extinct, but another definition of genus becomes highly relevant. Species that are members of one genus share the same broad adaptive zone or, in Sewall Wright's terminology (Mayr, 1962), a similar "adaptive plateau." What this represents is a general ecological life style more basic than the particular ecological niches characteristic of species. This ecological definition of genus can be an immense aid in interpreting fossil primates. Teeth are the most often preserved parts, and they are usually excellent general ecological indicators.

Therefore, if among the Miocene hominoids some animals appear to inhabit different adaptive/ecological zones (for example *Proconsul* vs. *Sivapithecus* vs. *Gigantopithecus*), we are justified in postulating more than one genus present.

Operationally, then, categorization at the genus level becomes the most practical biological interpretation of fragmentary extinct forms. While species differences necessarily were also present (probably in great complexity), these are usually too intricate to recognize in incomplete material.

As a final comment, we should point out that classification by genus is also not always a clearcut business. Indeed, the argument among primate biologists over whether the chimp and gorilla represent one genus (*Pan troglodytes*, *Pan gorilla*) or two different genera (*Pan troglodytes*, *Gorilla gorilla*) demonstrate that even with living, breathing animals the choices are not always clear. Or, for that matter, some researchers—pointing to the very close *genetic* similarities between humans

MONOPHYLETIC
mono: one
phyletic: line of evolutionary descent

CLADISTICS
The school of evolutionary biology that seeks to make ancestral-descendant hypotheses through interpreting patterns of primitive/ derived characteristics.

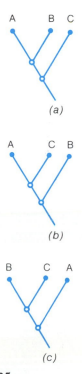

Figure 10-25
Cladograms. Three alternative statements representing ancestral-descendant relationships among three taxa. (a) C diverges earliest, with A and B sharing a more recent common ancestor; (b) B diverges earliest, with A and C sharing a more recent common ancestor; (c) A diverges earliest, with B and C sharing a more recent common ancestor.

and chimps—would place these in the same genus (*Homo sapiens*, *Homo troglodytes*). When it gets this close to home, it gets even more difficult to be objective!

Summary

In this chapter, we have traced the evolutionary history of our primate origins between 70 and 10 m.y.a. Beginning in the late Cretaceous, the earliest primate ancestors are probably little more than arboreally adapted insectivores. In the Paleocene, we begin to see more definite primate trends in such animals as *Plesiadapis*, but there are still numerous "primitive" characteristics present in these forms. In the following epoch, the Eocene, we begin to see an abundant diversification of primates of modern aspect. During this epoch, the lemurlike adapids and early ancestors of tarsiers begin their evolutionary radiation. Early anthropoid origins probably also date to sometime in the late Eocene. In addition, Old and New World primates apparently shared their last common ancestry in the Eocene or early Oligocene and have gone their separate ways ever since.

In the Old World, the Oligocene reveals a large number of possible early anthropoid ancestors at the Fayum. By and large, all these are primtive Old World anthropoids, and none of the modern lineages (Old World monkeys, gibbons, large-bodied hominoids) can definitely be traced into the Oligocene.

The Miocene reveals an abundant and complex array of hominoid forms that sort into an early African group (the dryopiths) and a later, mostly Asian group (the ramapiths). The best known of these Miocene hominoids—at least through abundance of recent discoveries—is the ramapith *Sivapithecus*. While again there is little firm evidence tying these fossil forms to extant apes or ourselves, some tentative evidence suggests that *Sivapithecus* is closely related to the ancestors of the orang. Where, then, are the ancestors of the African apes or, even more relevantly, of ourselves? In the next five chapters, we will seek to answer this question.

Questions for Review

1. Why is it difficult to distinguish the earliest members of the primate order from other placental mammals? If you found a nearly complete skeleton of an early Paleocene mammal, what structural traits might lead you to believe it was a primate?
2. Compare the fossil primates of the Paleocene and Eocene with living members of the primate order.
3. Why did so many prosimians become extinct at the end of the Eocene? Discuss the alternative explanations critically.
4. If you (as an expert physical anthropologist) were brought remains of a purported 30 m.y. fossil hominoid from South America, why might you be skeptical?
5. What kinds of primates were evolving at the Fayum in Oligocene times? What is meant by saying they are primitive catarrhines?
6. Compare and contrast the anatomical features of dryopiths and ramapiths.
7. Discuss the three alternative interpretations of the evolutionary affinities of *Sivapithecus*.

8. How did the shifting of the earth's plates, as well as climatic changes, affect hominoid evolution in the Miocene?

9. What kind of primate was *Gigantopithecus*, and why is it an unlikely hominid ancestor?

10. If two fossil groups are classified as *Sivapithecus indicus* and *Sivapithecus sivalensis*, at what taxonomic level is the distinction being made? What are the biological implications of such a classification?

11. If two fossil groups are classified as *Dryopithecus* and *Sivapithecus*, at what taxonomic level is this distinction? What are the biological implications?

Paleoanthropology

CONTENTS

ISSUE

Archeology and Science Fiction

Has our evolution, both cultural and biological, been systematically and deliberately tampered with by beings from other worlds? Popularized by Erich von Däniken in a series of fantastically successful books (1968, 1970, 1973), this bizarre theory has been further promulgated in movies and television. Is it possible?

Scientific inquiry cannot "prove" *anything* impossible, but it can attempt to demonstrate what is probable. Von Däniken is correct in asserting that, given the vast number of stars (and planets) in the universe, there is a high probability of intelligent life out there *somewhere*. Of all these life forms, however, how many are capable of efficient interstellar travel (necessitating speeds approaching that of light)? Furthermore, even if some life forms possessed this technology, where would they look for other intelligent life? If they randomly sampled all "inhabitable" planets in the universe, their probability of finding us would be low indeed. Perhaps, however, they are watching or listening for signs. They might assume, as we have, that an intelligent life form with even a modest degree of technological sophistication could produce radio waves. In the hopes of hearing such an intergalactic message, we have recently turned our own ears to the heavens.

If creatures "out there" have done likewise, they may *eventually* hear our radio signals. However, we have been producing such communications for only the last fifty years or so (and these radio waves have only traveled about fifty light years). Special frequency signals aimed specifically at distant worlds have only been initiated in the last few years. Consequently, on the basis of simple logical deduction, it would seem unlikely that we have even been detected, to say nothing of actually playing host to extraterrestrial travelers.

Remember, however, that whereas such a postulation is exceedingly improbable, it is not completely impossible. What, then, of evidence?

Von Däniken has audaciously postulated that extraterrestrial beings have visited earth dozens of times. Nor did they *just* visit; they helped construct huge monuments (presumably to themselves—what a being capable of building spaceships would see in a stone edifice is a mystery). They even assisted with the writing of tablets and making of maps, and let themselves become deified by the masses of humble *H. sapiens* in the bargain.

Surely mysteries abound in the archeological record, which is incomplete and, thus, far from perfect. However, that fact does not justify postulating the unlikely, the bizarre, or the ridiculous when a much more probable (but admittedly, less exciting) explanation is easily found. Indeed, much of von Däniken's primary "hard" evidence has been debunked. The huge pyramids of Egypt and Mesoamerica, the mysterious geometric designs of Nazca, Peru, and the formidable stone monu-

ments of Easter Island have all been demonstrated as *human* achievements using relatively simple technological principles and good old-fashioned human labor.

If, in 100,000 years, future generations of archeologists were to excavate some of the "wonders" of our world, they would (in the absence of written records) be struck by the seeming incongruities and mysteries. The incredible Gothic cathedrals of Europe, built during a period of economic and intellectual disorganization, would appear a giant paradox. Did space beings build them? Or, even closer to home, the massive vaults excavated into the Rockies housing the genealogical records of the Mormon Church might also confuse and befuddle our descendants. Yet, the architects and engineers in Utah clearly did not require or receive extraterrestrial assistance in constructing this marvel.

Human beings routinely achieve the incredible, the fantastic, the inexplicable, and they do it on their own. After all, the New York Mets did win the World Series back in 1969!

SOURCES:

von Däniken, Erich. *Chariots of the Gods?*, New York: G. P. Putnam's Sons, 1968.

———. *Gods from Outer Space*, New York: G. P. Putnam's Sons, 1970.

———. *Gold of the Gods*, New York: G. P. Putnam's Sons, 1973.

Introduction

In the last four chapters, we have seen how humans are classed as primates, both structurally and behaviorally, and how our evolutionary history coincides with that of other primates. However, we are a unique kind of primate, and our ancestors have been adapted to a particular kind of life style for several million years. Some kind of ramapith may have begun this process more than 10 m.y.a., but, beginning about 5 m.y.a., evidence from Africa reveals much more definite hominid relationships. The hominid nature of these remains is revealed by more than the morphological structure of teeth and bones; we know these animals are hominids also because of the way they behaved—emphasizing once again the *biocultural* nature of human evolution. In this chapter, we will discuss the methods scientists use to explore the secrets of early hominid behavior. We will then demonstrate these through the example of the best-known early hominid site in the world: Olduvai Gorge in East Africa.

Definition of Hominid

If any ramapith fossils represent the earliest stages of hominid diversification, our definition of them as hominid must then primarily be a *dental* one. Teeth and jaws are most of what we have of these Miocene forms. However, dentition is not the only way to describe the special attributes of our particular evolutionary radiation and is certainly not the most distinctive of its later stages. Modern humans and our hominid ancestors are distinguished from our closest living relatives (the great apes) by more obvious features than proportionate tooth and jaw size. For example, various scientists have pointed to other hominid characteristics, such as large brain size, bipedal locomotion, and toolmaking behavior, as being most significant in defining what makes a hominid a hominid (as opposed to a pongid, a cercopithecoid, or anything else for that matter). This last definition—humans as toolmakers—is the one that we wish to discuss in this chapter. The important structural attributes of the hominid brain, teeth, and locomotory apparatus will be discussed in the next chapter, where we investigate early hominid anatomical adaptations in greater detail.

Biocultural Evolution: Humans As Toolmakers

Although other primates do occasionally make tools (see Chapter 9), only hominids depend on culture for their survival. We and our close hominid ancestors alone have the ability to "impose arbitrary form on the environment" (Holloway, 1969). For example, chimps who use termite sticks have a direct and immediate relationship with the raw material and purpose of the tool. Such is not the case in most human cultural behavior, which usually involves several steps often quite arbitrarily removed from a direct environmental context.

We are defining culture primarily as a mental process. The human mind—presumably the minds of our hominid ancestors as well—has the unique capacity to *create* symbols. When a chimp sees water, it probably sees only the immediate environmental setting plus any learned experiences that are directly associated. Humans, however, can introduce all kinds of additional meanings, such as "holy water," physically identical to all other water but with symbolic value. A chimp can see water and know from experience it is wet, drinkable, etc. However, the chimp will never be capable of grasping the superimposed, arbitrary ideas invented and understood only by humans.

Obviously, we cannot "get inside the head" of a chimpanzee to know exactly what it is or is not thinking. The assumptions we have made are derived from behavioral observations in natural habitats, as well as results of learning experiments. However, as discussed in Chapter 9, among scientists there is still considerable dispute concerning the behavioral capacities of chimpanzees; the assumptions expressed here reflect the views of the authors. Humans, of course, also have the capacity to manipulate their environments in infinitely more complex ways than other animals. The simple human invention of a watertight container, such as a hollowed-out gourd or an ostrich egg, is several orders of magnitude more complex than chimp or macaque "cultural" behavior.

Culture as a complex adaptive strategy has become central to human evolution and has acted as a potent selective force to mold our anatomical form over the last several million years. In the archeological record, early cultural behavior is seen in the preserved remains of stone implements, traces of a uniquely human activity. "The shaping of stone according to even the simplest plan is beyond the behavior of any ape or monkey" (Washburn, 1971, p. 105).

Thus, when we find stone tools made to a standardized pattern, we know we have found a behavior indicator of a hominid, and *only* homind, adaptation. We are justified, then, in defining hominids as habitual toolmakers, *culturally dependent* animals, distinct in this respect from all other primates.

The Strategy of Paleoanthropology

In order to understand human evolution adequately, we obviously need a broad base of information. The task of recovering and interpreting all the clues left by early hominids is the work of the paleoanthropologist. Paleoanthropology is defined as "the science of the study of ancient humans." As such, it is a diverse *multidisciplinary* pursuit seeking to reconstruct every possible bit of information concerning the dating, structure, behavior, and ecology of our hominid ancestors. In just the last few years, the study of early humans has marshalled the specialized skills of many diverse kinds of scientists. Included primarily in this growing and exciting adventure are the geologist, archeologist, physical anthropologist, and paleoecologist (see Table 11-1).

The geologist, usually working with an anthropologist (often an archeologist) does the initial survey work in order to locate potential early hominid sites. Many sophisticated techniques can aid in this search, including aerial and satellite photography. Paleontologists may also be involved in this early search, for they can help find fossil beds containing faunal remains; where conditions are favorable for the bone preservation of such specimens as ancient pigs and elephants, conditions may also be favorable for the preservation of hominid remains. In addition, paleontologists can (through comparison with known faunal areas) give fairly quick estimates of approximate age of fossil sites without having to wait for

Figure 11-1
Early stone tools. Traces of hominid behavior, from Olduvai Gorge, East Africa, about 1.6 m.y.a.

Table 11-1 *Subdisciplines of Paleoanthropology*

Physical Sciences	Biological Sciences	Social Sciences
Geology	Physical Anthropology	Archeology
Stratigraphy	Ecology	Cultural Anthropology
Petrology	Paleontology	Ethnography
(rocks, minerals)	(fossil animals)	Psychology
Pedology	Palynology	
(soils)	(fossil pollen)	
Geophysics	Primatology	Ethnoarcheology
Chemistry		
Geomorphology		
Taphonomy*		

*Taphonomy (taphos: dead) is the study of how bones and other materials come to be buried in the earth and preserved as fossils. A taphonomist studies such phenomena as the processes of sedimentation, action of streams, preservation properties of bone, and carnivore disturbance factors.

the more expensive and time-consuming chronometric analyses. In this way, fossil beds of the "right" geologic ages (that is, where hominid finds are most likely) can be isolated.

Once potential areas of early hominid sites have been located, much more extensive surveying begins. At this point, the archeologist takes over in the search for hominid "traces." We do not necessarily have to find remains of early hominids themselves to know they consistently occupied a particular area. Behavioral clues, or **artifacts**, also inform us directly and unambiguously about early hominid occupation. Modifying rocks according to a consistent plan, or simply carrying them around from one place to another (over fairly long distances), are behaviors characteristic of no other animal but a hominid. Therefore, when we see such behavioral evidence at a site, we know absolutely that hominids were present.

No doubt, early hominids sometimes utilized implements of wood or bone, and probably began doing so several million years ago (6–4 m.y.a.?). It is not altogether clear, however, just how many of these potential tools were available without *first* processing them with stone. Naturally pointed pieces of wood could probably have been utilized as digging sticks or perhaps for puncturing an ostrich egg (to make a watertight container). Beyond this, it probably would have been quite difficult to make much use of wood resources without some modification; yet, how could this have been done without something harder with which to cut, scrape, or sharpen (i.e., stone tools)? Bone is even more intractable and would seem also to have been "off-limits" to hominids without some stone implement to crush, cut, etc. Probably the only bone sources available were splinters left behind at kills by large carnivores. This all remains, of course, speculative, since *direct* evidence is not available. Unfortunately, these organic materials usually are not preserved, and we thus know little about such early tool-using behavior.

On the other hand, our ancestors at some point showed a veritable fascination with stones, for these provided not only easily accessible and transportable weights (to hold down objects, such as skins and windbreaks) but also the most durable and sharpest cutting edges available at that time. Luckily for us, stone is almost indestructible, and early hominid sites are virtually strewn with thousands

PALEOECOLOGICAL
paleo: old
ecological: environmental setting
The study of ancient environments.

PEDOLOGIST
pedon: ground, soil

PETROLOGIST
petr: rock

of stone artifacts. The earliest artifact site now documented is from the Omo region of Ethiopia, dating from at least 2.4 m.y.a. Another contender for the "earliest" stone assemblage is from the Hadar area, farther to the north in Ethiopia—dated 2.0–2.5 m.y.a.

If an area is clearly demonstrated as a hominid site, much more concentrated research will then begin. We should point out that a more mundane but very significant aspect of paleoanthroplogy not shown in Table 11-1 is the financial one. Just the initial survey work in usually remote areas takes many thousands of dollars, and mounting a concentrated research project takes several hundred thousand dollars. Therefore, for such work to go on, massive financial support is required from governmental agencies and/or private donations. A significant amount of the paleoanthropologist's efforts and time are necessarily devoted to writing grant proposals or to speaking on the lecture circuit to raise the required funds for this work.

Once the financial hurdle has been cleared, a coordinated research project can commence. Usually headed by an archeologist or physical anthropologist, the field crew will continue to survey and map the target area in great detail. In addition, they will begin to search carefully for bones and artifacts eroding out of the soil, take pollen and soil samples for ecological analysis, and carefully recover rock samples for chronometric dating. If, in this early stage of exploration, the field crew finds a fossil hominid, they will feel very lucky indeed. The international press usually considers human fossils the most exciting kind of discovery, a situation that produces wide publicity, often working to assure future financial support. More likely, the crew will accumulate much information on geological setting, ecological data, particularly faunal remains, and, with some luck, archeological traces (hominid artifacts).

After long and arduous research in the field, even more time-consuming and detailed analysis is required back in the laboratory. The archeologist must clean, sort, label, and identify all the artifacts, and the paleontologist must do the same for all faunal remains. The kinds of animals present, whether forest browsers, woodland species, or open-country forms, will greatly help in reconstructing the local **paleoecological** settings in which early hominids lived. In addition, analysis of pollen remains by a palynologist will further aid in a detailed environmental reconstruction. All of these paleoecological analyses can assist in reconstructing the diet of early humans (see p. 335). Many complex kinds of contributions go into assembling and interpreting the relevant data in such analyses (see Table 11-2).

More information will be provided by analysis of soil samples by a **pedologist**, and rock and mineral samples by a **petrologist**. A geomorphologist may also be asked to reconstruct the sequence of past geologic events, including volcanics, mountain building, earth movements, such as faulting, and changes in the orientation of the earth's magnetic pole.

As work progresses in later field seasons with more laboratory analyses, even more experts from other scientific specialties may be consulted. If a hominid bone or tooth is eventually recovered, a physical anthropologist will clean it, reconstruct it if necessary, describe it in minute anatomical detail, and attempt to relate it to other fossil hominid finds. The archeologist may decide that a particularly well-preserved location or the site of a hominid discovery calls for precise archeological excavation. In order to recover and record all relevant information in such an undertaking, thousands of work-hours are required to excavate even a

Table 11-2 *Elements of Hominid Paleoecology*

Physical Environment:

Altitude	Mean wind speed
Temperature	Degree of wind gusting
Rainfall	Mean cloud cover
Relative humidity	Surface water availability
Insolation	Surface water salinity
Soil:	
Development	
Physical composition	
Chemical composition	
Tree and shrub density	Habitat selectivity
Shade cover	Herbaceous basal cover
Degree of clumping of woody plants	Grass and forb height

Diet:

Content:	Metabolic energy requirements
Animal	Energy intake
Vegetable	Digestibility
Soil (geophagy)	Time of feeding
Manner obtained	Season of feeding
Manner eaten	
Drinking	

Population:

Numbers	Mortality
Weights	Birth spacing
Growth	Sexual maturity
Natality	

Intraspecific Relations:

Grouping	Division of labor
Group interaction	Distances between group sleeping sites
Sexual relations	Grooming
Dominance interactions	

Interspecific Relations:

Cooperation with other species	Prey
Competition with other species	Predators
Tolerance of other species	

Other Behavior:

Extent of daily movement	Group activity at various times of the day:
Tool use and manufacture:	Feeding intensively and/or moving rapidly
material, source, use	Feeding leisurely and/or resting
Sleeping place	Resting
Vocalizations	
Diurnality/nocturnality	

Source: Reprinted by permission of the Kroeber Anthropological Society from Kroeber Anthropological Society Papers No. 50, ed., Noel T. Boaz and John E. Cronin (Berkeley: Kroeber Anthropological Society, 1977), p. 56, © 1977 by the Kroeber Anthropological Society.

relatively small area (a few dozen square feet). An extensively detailed *micro-stratigraphic analysis* may also be useful in re-creating the precise conditions of sedimentation, thus calling for the specialized skills of a taphonomist (see Table 11-1).

In the concluding stages of interpretation, the paleoanthropologist will draw together the following essentials:

1. *Dating*
   geological
   paleontological
   geophysical
2. *Paleoecology*
   paleontology
   palynology
   geomorphology
3. *Archeological traces of behavior*
4. *Anatomical evidence from hominid remains*

From all this information, the paleoanthropologist will try to "flesh out" the kind of animal that may have been our direct ancestor, or at least a very close relative. In this final analysis, still further comparative scientific information may be needed. Primatologists may assist here by showing the detailed relationships between the structure and behavior of humans and that of contemporary nonhuman primates (see Chaps. 7 through 9). Cultural anthropologists may contribute ethnographic information concerning the varied nature of human behavior, particularly ecological adaptation of those groups exploiting roughly similar environmental settings as those found at our hominid site (for example, the San or Australian aborigines—see p. 259). Ethnoarcheologists can assist further by demonstrating how observed behavioral patterns (as implement manufacture and meat eating) actually end up in the ground as artifacts. Finally, neuroanatomists, psychologists, and linguists may aid physical anthropologists in the reconstruction of physiological/behavioral information suggested by the fossil hominid remains, such as brain dimensions and their relationship to language capacities.

The end result of years of research by dozens of scientists will (we hope) produce a more complete and accurate understanding of human evolution—how we came to be the way we are. Both biological and cultural aspects of our ancestors pertain to this investigation, each process developing in relation to the other.

Paleoanthropology in Action—Olduvai Gorge

Several paleoanthropological projects of the scope discussed above are now in progress in diverse places around the globe. The most important of these include: David Pilbeam's work in the Miocene beds of the Potwar Plateau of western Pakistan (*circa* 13–7 m.y.a.); Don Johanson's project in the Hadar area of Ethiopia (*circa* 3.7–1.6 m.y.a.); a now completed research project along the Omo River of southern Ethiopia (*circa* 4–1.5 m.y.a.) directed by F. Clark Howell (both the Howell and Johanson projects have sometimes been forced to cease work due to warfare in Ethiopia); Richard Leakey's fantastically successful research near Lake Turkana (formerly Rudolf) in northern Kenya (*circa* 2.0–1.5 m.y.a.); and Mary Leakey's famous investigations at Olduvai Gorge in northern

Tanzania (*circa* 1.85 m.y.a.–present), now being continued by Don Johanson and Tim White.

Of all these early hominid localities, the one that has yielded the finest quality and greatest abundance of paleoanthropological information concerning the behavior of early hominids has been Olduvai Gorge.

First "discovered" in the early twentieth century by a German butterfly collector, Olduvai was soon thereafter scientifically surveyed and its wealth of paleontological evidence recognized. In 1931, Louis Leakey made his first trip to Olduvai Gorge and almost immediately realized its significance for studying early humans. Since 1935, when she first worked there, until she retired in 1984, Mary Leakey directed the archeological excavations at Olduvai.

Located in the Serengeti Plain of northern Tanzania, Olduvai is a steep-sided valley resembling a miniature version of the Grand Canyon. Indeed, the geological processes that formed the gorge are similar to what happened in the formation of the Grand Canyon. Following millions of years of steady accumulation of several hundred feet of geological strata (including volcanic, lake, and river deposits), faulting occurred 70,000 years ago to the east of Olduvai. As a result, a gradient was established, causing a rapidly flowing river to cut through the previously laid strata, eventually forming a gorge 300 feet deep—similar to the way the Colorado River cut the Grand Canyon.

Olduvai today is a deep ravine cut into an almost mile high grassland plateau of East Africa, and extends more than twenty-five miles in total length. In fact, if one were to include all the side gulleys and ravines, the area of exposures would total more than seventy miles with potentially hundreds of early hominid sites. Climatically, the semiarid pattern of present day Olduvai is believed to be similar to most of the past environments preserved there over the last 2 million years. The surrounding countryside is a grassland savanna broken occasionally by scrub bushes and acacia trees. It is a noteworthy fact that this environment presently

Figure 11-2
Major paleoanthropological projects.

Figure 11-3
Olduvai Gorge. A sketch map showing positions of the major sites and geologic localities.

Louis S. B. Leakey 1903–1972

Louis Leakey. Shown displaying casts of fossil hominid discoveries from East Africa. To the right is the skull of a male gorilla.

Called the "Charles Darwin of prehistory," Louis Leakey was truly a man for all seasons. Blessed with a superior intellect and an almost insatiable curiosity, Leakey untiringly quested after knowledge, which to him included everything there was to know about everything. His interests encompassed not just prehistory, archeology, and paleontology but modern African wildlife, African peoples, languages, and customs. He once stalked, killed, and butchered a gazelle with just his bare hands and stone tools he had fashioned himself. He had previously attempted to use only his teeth and hands to dismember dead animals, but found it impossible, leading him to the conclusion that early hominids also *must* have used stone tools for butchering. Leakey also was a leading authority on handwriting, a skill he put to good use as the chief of British military intelligence for Africa during World War II.

The child of British missionary parents, Louis was born in a Kikuyu village in 1903—probably one of the first white children born in East Africa. His upbringing was to be as much African as European, and he was actually initiated into the Kikuyu tribe. Sworn to a sacred oath of silence, Louis never revealed the secret rites of initiation, even to his wife Mary.

Following his early training in the African bush, Louis was dispatched to England for a more formal education, eventually receiving his degree from Cambridge. His consuming interest, however, was focused on Africa, where he returned to begin exploration of prehistoric sites—leading his first expedition in 1926 at the age of 23! In 1931, Leakey made his first trip to Olduvai Gorge with the German paleontologist Hans Reck. Louis liked to relate years later how he found the first stone tool in context at Olduvai within an hour of his arrival there!

In the next forty years, the fantastic discoveries at Olduvai by Louis and his archeologist wife, Mary, as well as their extensive work at other sites all around the Rift Valley, were to make them famous to professional and layman alike.

However, perhaps Louis' greatest contribution was not the many discoveries he made himself, but his ability to stimulate and involve others. The definitive research on all the great apes was initiated by Louis Leakey, who personally recruited Jane Goodall to work with chimpanzees, Dian Fossey to investigate the mountain gorilla, and Biruté Galdikas to learn the secrets of the orang. Louis' greatest legacy is probably that all these projects continue today,* and, of course, Mary continues analysis of data from Olduvai and their son Richard works on at Turkana in northern Kenya.

*The research goes forward on the mountain gorillas, despite the tragic death of Dian Fossey in 1985.

Figure 11-4
Aerial view of Olduvai Gorge. Volcanic highlands are visible to the south.

(as well as in the past) supports a vast number of large mammals (as zebra, wildebeest, and gazelle), representing an enormous supply of "meat on the hoof."

Geographically, Olduvai is located on the western edge of the eastern branch of the Great Rift Valley of Africa. The geological processes associated with the formation of the Rift Valley make Olduvai (and the other East African sites) extremely important to paleoanthropological investigation. Three results of geological rifting are most significant:

1. Faulting, or earth movement, exposes geological beds near the surface that are normally hidden by hundreds of feet of accumulated overburden
2. Active volcanic processes cause rapid sedimentation and thus often yield excellent preservation of bone and artifacts that normally would be scattered by carnivore activity and erosion forces
3. Volcanic activity provides a wealth of radiometrically datable material

The results of these geological factors at Olduvai are the superb preservation of ancient hominids and their behavioral patterns in datable contexts, all of which are readily accessible.

The greatest contribution Olduvai has made to paleoanthropological research is the establishment of an extremely well-documented and correlated *sequence* of geological, paleontological, archeological, and hominid remains over the last 2 million years. At the very foundation of all paleoanthropological research is a well-established geological picture. At Olduvai, the geological and paleogeographic situation is known in minute detail. Olduvai is today a geologist's delight, containing sediments in some places 350 feet thick accumulated from lava flows (basalts), tuffs (windblown or waterlain fine deposits from nearby volcanoes), sandstones, claystones, and limestone conglomerates, all neatly stratified. A hominid site can therefore be accurately dated relative to other sites in the Olduvai Gorge by cross-correlating known marker beds. The stratigraphic sequence at Olduvai is broken down into four major beds (Beds I–IV), with other, more recent, beds usually referred to by specific local place names (Masek, Ndutu, Naisiusiu). Moreover, careful recording of the precise context of geological samples also provides the basis for accurate radiometric dating.

Figure 11-5
The East African Rift Valley system.

Paleontological evidence of fossilized animal bones also has come from Olduvai in great abundance. More than 150 species of extinct animals have been recognized, including fish, turtle, crocodile, pig, giraffe, horse, and many birds, rodents, and antelopes. Careful analysis of such remains has yielded voluminous information concerning the ecological conditions of early human habitats. In addition, precise analysis of bones directly associated with artifacts can sometimes tell us about the diets and hunting capabilities of early hominids. (There are some reservations, however—see Box 11-1, p. 327.)

The archeological sequence is also well documented over the last 2 million years. Beginning at the earliest hominid site in Bed I (1.85 m.y.a.), there is already a well-developed stone tool kit, including chopping tools as well as some small flake tools (Leakey, 1971). Such a tool industry is called *Oldowan* (after Olduvai) and continues into Bed II with some small modifications, after which it is called *Developed Oldowan*. In addition, around 1.6 m.y.a., the first appearance of a new tool kit, the *Acheulian*, occurs in the Olduvai archeological record. This industry is characterized by large bifacial (that is, flaked on both sides) tools commonly known as hand-axes and cleavers. For several hundred thousand years, Acheulian and Developed Oldowan are *both* found side-by-side at Olduvai, and the relationship between these parallel tool kits remains to be determined.

Finally, remains of several fossilized hominids have been found at Olduvai, ranging in time from the earliest occupation levels (*circa* 1.85 m.y.a.) to fairly recent *Homo sapiens*. Of the more than forty individuals represented, many are quite fragmentary, but a few (including four skulls and a nearly complete foot) are excellently preserved. While the center of hominid discoveries has now shifted to other areas of East Africa, it was the initial discovery by Mary Leakey of the *Zinjanthropus* skull at Olduvai in July, 1959, that focused the world's attention on this remarkably rich area. "Zinj" provides an excellent example of how financial ramifications directly result from hominid bone discoveries. Prior to 1959, the Leakeys had worked sporadically at Olduvai on a financial shoestring, making marvelous paleontological and archeological discoveries. Yet, there was little support available for much needed large-scale excavations. However, following the discovery of "Zinj," the National Geographic Society funded the Leakeys' research, and within the next year, more than twice as much dirt was excavated than during the previous thirty!

Dating Methods

As we have discussed, one of the key essentials of paleoanthropology is putting sites and fossils into a chronological framework. In other words, we want to know how old they are. How, then, do we date sites—or, more precisely, the geological strata in which sites are found? The question is both reasonable and important, so let us examine the dating techniques used by paleontologists, geologists, paleoanthropologists, and archeologists.

Scientists use two kinds of dating for this purpose—relative and **chronometric** (also known as *absolute dating*). Relative dating methods tell you that something is older, or younger, than something else, but not how much. If, for example, a skull were found at a depth of fifty feet, and another skull at seventy feet at the same site, we usually assume the skull discovered at seventy feet is older. We may not know the date (in years) of either one, but we would know that one is older

CHRONOMETRIC
chrono: time
metric: measure
A dating technique that gives an estimate in actual numbers of years.

Figure 11-6
View of the Main Gorge at Olduvai. Note the clear sequence of geological beds. The discontinuity to the left is a major fault line.

Mary Leakey 1913–

Mary Leakey. At the site of the "Zinj" find on the thirteenth anniversary of its discovery.

Mary Leakey, one of the leading prehistorians of this century, spent most of her professional life living in the shadow of her famous husband. But to a considerable degree, Louis' fame is directly attributable to Mary. Justly known for his extensive fieldwork in Miocene sites along the shores of Lake Victoria in Kenya, Louis is quite often associated with important hominoid discoveries. However, it was Mary who, in 1948, found the best-preserved dryopith skull ever discovered.

The names Louis Leakey and Olduvai Gorge are almost synonymous, but here, too, it was Mary who made the most significant single discovery—the "Zinj" skull in 1959. Mary has always been the supervisor of archeological work at Olduvai while Louis was busily engaged in traveling, lecturing, or tending to the National Museum in Nairobi.

Mary Leakey did not come upon her archeological career by chance. A direct descendant of John Frere (who, because of his discoveries in 1797, is called the father of Paleolithic archeology), Mary always had a compelling interest in prehistory. Her talent to illustrate stone tools provided her entry into African prehistory, and was the reason for her introduction to Louis in 1933. Throughout her career, she has done all the tool illustrations for her publications, and has set an extremely high standard of excellence for all would-be illustrators of Paleolithic implements.

A committed, hard-driving woman of almost inexhaustible energy, Mary conducted work at Olduvai, where she spent most of the year. Busily engaged seven days a week, she supervised ongoing excavations, as well as working on the monumental publications detailing the fieldwork already done.

Since Louis' death in 1972, Mary, to some degree, has had to assume the role of traveling lecturer and fund raiser. Today, she lives outside Nairobi, where she energetically continues her research and writing.

(or younger) than the other. Whereas this may not satisfy our curiosity about the actual number of years involved, it would give some idea of the evolutionary changes in skull morphology (structure), especially if a number of skulls at different levels were found and compared.

This method of relative dating is called **stratigraphy** and was one of the first techniques to be used by scholars working with the vast period of geologic time. Stratigraphy is based upon the law of superposition, which states that a lower stratum (layer) is older than a higher stratum. Given the fact that much of the earth's crust has been laid down by layer after layer of sedimentary rock, like the layers of a cake, stratigraphy has been a valuable aid in reconstructing the history of earth and life on it.

Stratigraphic dating does, however, have a number of problems connected with it. Earth disturbances, such as volcanic activity, river activity, and mountain building, among others, may shift about strata of rock or the objects in them, and the chronology of the material may be difficult or even impossible to reconstruct. Furthermore, the time period of a particular stratum is not possible to determine with much accuracy.

Another method of relative dating is *fluorine analysis*, which applies only to bones (Oakley, 1963). Bones in the earth are exposed to the seepage of groundwater, usually containing fluorine. The longer bones lie in the earth, the more fluorine they incorporate during the fossilization process. Therefore, bones deposited at the same time in the same location should contain the same amount of fluorine. The use of this technique by Professor Oakley of the British Museum in the early 1950s exposed the Piltdown (England) hoax by demonstrating that the human skull was considerably older than the jaw found with it (Weiner, 1955). Lying in the same location, the jaw and skull should have absorbed approximately the same quantity of fluorine. But the skull contained significantly more than the jaw, which meant that it (the skull) had lain in the ground a good deal longer than the jaw. It was unlikely that the skull had met an untimely demise while the jaw lingered on for thousands of years. The discrepancy of fluorine content led Oakley and others to a closer examination of the bones, and they found that the jaw was not that of a hominid at all but of a young adult orangutan! (See p. 340.)

Unfortunately, fluorine is useful only with bones found at the same location. Because the amount of fluorine in groundwater is based upon the local river system and local conditions, it varies from place to place. Also, some groundwater may not contain any fluorine. For these reasons, comparing bones from different localities by fluorine analysis is impossible.

In both these methods—stratigraphy and fluorine analysis—the age of the rock stratum and the objects in it is difficult to calculate. To determine the absolute number of years of age, scientists have developed a variety of chronometric techniques based on the phenomenon of radioactive decay. The theory is quite simple: Certain radioactive isotopes of elements are unstable, disintegrate, and form an isotopic variation of another element. Since the rate of disintegration follows a definite mathematical pattern, the radioactive material forms an accurate geological time clock. By measuring the amount of disintegration in a particular sample, the number of years it took for the amount of decay is then known. Chronometric techniques have been used for dating the immense age of the earth as well as artifacts less than a thousand years old. Several techniques have been employed for a number of years and are now quite well known.

Uranium 238 (^{238}U) decays to form lead with a half-life of 4.5 billion years. That is, one-half of the original amount of ^{238}U is lost in 4.5 billion years and through various processes becomes lead. Therefore, if a chunk of rock is measured and one-half of the uranium has been converted to lead, the age of that piece of rock is 4.5 billion years. In another 4.5 billion years, half the remaining ^{238}U would have decayed. The isotope ^{238}U has proven a useful tool in dating the age of the formation of the earth.

Another chronometric technique involves potassium 40 (^{40}K)—which produces argon 40 (^{40}Ar)—with a half-life of 1.3 billion years. Known as the K/Ar, or potassium-argon method, this procedure has been extensively used by paleoanthropologists in dating materials in the 1 to 5 million year range, especially in East Africa. Organic material, such as bone, cannot be measured, but the rock matrix in which the bone is found can be. K/Ar was used to date the de-

Figure 11-7
Zinjanthropus *skull. Discovered by Mary Leakey at Olduvai Gorge in 1959. The skull and reconstructed jaw depicted here are casts at the National Museum of Kenya, Nairobi.*

Discovery of Zinjanthropus, July 17, 1959

That morning I woke with a headache and a slight fever. Reluctantly I agreed to spend the day in camp.

With one of us out of commission, it was even more vital for the other to continue the work, for our precious seven-week season was running out. So Mary departed for the diggings with Sally and Toots [two of their dalmatians] in the Land-Rover, and I settled back to a restless day off.

Some time later—perhaps I dozed off—I heard the Land-Rover coming up fast to camp. I had a momentary vision of Mary stung by one of our hundreds of resident scorpions or bitten by a snake that had slipped past the dogs.

The Land-Rover rattled to a stop, and I heard Mary's voice calling over and over: "I've got him! I've got him! I've got him!"

Still groggy from the headache, I couldn't make her out.

"Got what? Are you hurt?" I asked.

"Him, the man! *Our* man," Mary said. "The one we've been looking for [for 23 years]. Come quick, I've found his teeth!"

Magically, the headache departed. I somehow fumbled into my work clothes while Mary waited.

As we bounced down the trail in the car, she described the dramatic moment of discovery. She had been searching the slope where I had found the first Oldowan tools in 1931, when suddenly her eye caught a piece of bone lodged in a rock slide. Instantly, she recognized it as part of a skull—almost certainly not that of an animal.

Her glance wandered higher, and there in the rock were two immense teeth, side by side. This time there was no question: They were undeniably human. Carefully, she marked the spot with a cairn of stones, rushed to the Land-Rover, and sped back to camp with the news.

The gorge trail ended half a mile from the site, and we left the car at a dead run. Mary led the way to the cairn, and we knelt to examine the treasure.

I saw at once that she was right. The teeth were premolars, and they had belonged to a human. I was sure they were larger than anything similar ever found, nearly twice the width of modern man's.

I turned to look at Mary, and we almost cried with sheer joy, each seized by that terrific emotion that comes rarely in life. After all our hoping and hardship and sacrifice, at last we had reached our goal—we had discovered the world's earliest known human.

From: "Finding the World's Earliest Man," by L.S.B. Leakey, *National Geographic Magazine,* **118**:431, September 1960. Reprinted with permission of the publisher.

posit containing the Zinjanthropus skull (it actually dated a volcanic layer above the fossil).

Rocks that provide the best samples for K/Ar are those heated to an extremely high temperature, such as that generated by volcanic activity. When the rock is in a molten state, argon 40, a gas, is driven off. As the rock cools and solidifies, potassium (^{40}K) continues to break down to ^{40}Ar, but now the gas is physically trapped in the cooled rock. In order to obtain the date of the rock, it is reheated and the escaping gas measured. Potassium-argon has been used for dating very old events, such as the age of the earth, as well as those less than 100,000 years old (Dalrymple, 1972).

A well-known chronometric method popular with archeologists is carbon 14 (^{14}C), with a half-life of 5730 years. It has been used to date material from less than 1,000 years to as much as 75,000 years,[*] although the probability of error

[*]Grootes' studies (1978) suggest 75,000 years. A new technique using ^{14}C is being worked out at the University of California's Lawrence Berkeley Lab and at the University of Rochester. Scientists involved in the project believe it will extend the dating to 100,000 years with "no trouble" (Thomsen, 1978). This technique using a cyclotron ("atom smasher") requires a much smaller sample—"as little as one thousandth of a gram"—than the conventional method.

rises rapidly after 40,000 years. The ¹⁴C technique is based upon the following natural processes: Cosmic radiation enters the earth's atmosphere, producing neutrons, which react with nitrogen to produce a radioactive isotope of carbon, ¹⁴C. As the ¹⁴C is diffused around the earth, with the earth's rotation, it mixes with carbon 12 and is absorbed by plants in their life processes. It is then transferred to herbivorous animals that feed on plants and to carnivores that feed on herbivores. Thus, ¹⁴C and ¹²C are found in all living forms at a fixed ratio. When an organism dies, it no longer absorbs ¹⁴C, which then decays at a constant rate to ¹⁴N (and a beta particle). It takes 5370 years for half the amount of ¹⁴C to become ¹⁴N.

Let us say that charcoal, the remains of a campfire, is found at an archeological site and measured for the ¹⁴C/¹²C proportions. Suppose the findings are that the proportion of the ¹⁴C to ¹²C shows only 25% of the original ¹⁴C remaining. Since it takes 5730 years for half the ¹⁴C atoms to become ¹⁴N, and another 5730 years for half the remaining ¹⁴C to become ¹⁴N, the sample must be about 11,460 years old. Half the remaining ¹⁴C will become ¹⁴N in the next 5730 years, leaving 12.5% of the original amount. This process continues, and as you can see, there would be very little ¹⁴C left after 40,000 years, when measuring becomes difficult.

Other absolute dating techniques that do not involve radioactive elements are *dendrochronology*, or dating by tree rings, especially developed for the American Southwest, and *varve chronology* (annual glacial deposit), particularly useful for the late Pleistocene and the post-Pleistocene in northern Europe. Although neither of the techniques has a direct bearing on dating early human fossils, they are both ingenious dating methods with important regional applications.

We should stress that none of these methods is precise, and that each method is beset with problems that must be carefully considered during laboratory mea-

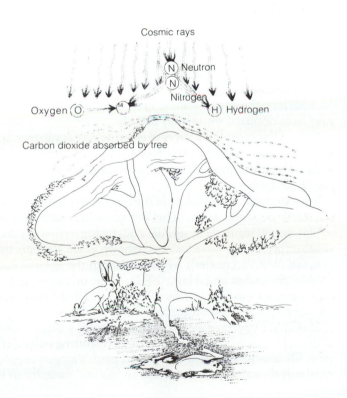

Cosmic rays
(N) Neutron
(N)
Nitrogen
Oxygen (O) →(14)
(H) Hydrogen

Carbon dioxide absorbed by tree

Figure 11-8
Carbon-14 dating. Cosmic rays bombard the upper atmosphere, producing neutrons. When these collide with nitrogen, small amounts of ¹⁴C are produced. The ¹⁴C combines with oxygen to form carbon dioxide. The carbon dioxide containing ¹⁴C is absorbed by plants, and eventually animals feeding on the plants add ¹⁴C to their bodies. When the plant or animal dies, it ceases to absorb ¹⁴C and the ¹⁴C changes back to nitrogen at a regular rate.

surement and in the collection of material to be measured. Because the methods are imprecise, approximate dates are given as probability statements with a plus or minus factor. For example, a date given as $1.75 \pm .2$ million years should be read as a 67% chance that the actual date lies somewhere between 1.55 and 1.95 million years.

There are, then, two ways in which the question of age may be answered. We can say that a particular fossil is x number of years old, a date determined usually either by K/Ar or ^{14}C chronometric dating techniques. Or, we can say that fossil X lived before or after fossil Y, a relative dating technique.

Dating Methods at Olduvai

Olduvai has proven a rich and varied source for numerous dating techniques, and as a result it has some of the best-documented chronology for any hominid site in the Lower or Middle Pleistocene.

Potassium-argon dating had its birth as a paleoanthropological tool in the early 1960s with its application to the dating of the "Zinj" site at Olduvai. To everyone's amazement, including Louis Leakey's, the chronometric age was determined at more than 1.75 million years—more than twice the age depth previously assumed for the *whole* Pleistocene. As a result of this one monumental date (Leakey, et al., 1961), the entire history of the Pleistocene and our corresponding interpretations of hominid evolution had to be rewritten.

Potassium-argon (K/Ar) is an extremely valuable tool for dating early hominid sites and has been widely used in areas containing suitable volcanic deposits (mainly in East Africa). At Olduvai, K/Ar has given several reliable dates of the underlying basalt and several tuffs in Bed I, including the one associated with the "Zinj" find (now dated at $1.79 \pm .03$ m.y.a.). When dating relatively recent samples (from the perspective of a half-life of 1.3 billion years for K/Ar, *all* paleoanthropological material is relatively recent), the amount of radiogenic argon is going to be exceedingly small. Experimental errors in measurement can therefore occur as well as the thorny problem of distinguishing the atmospheric argon normally clinging to the outside of the sample from the radiogenic argon. In addition, the initial sample may have been contaminated or argon leakage may have occurred while it lay buried.

Due to the potential sources of error, K/Ar dating must be cross-checked using other independent methods. Once again, the sediments at Olduvai (particularly in Bed I) provide some of the best examples of the use of many of these other dating techniques.

Fission-track dating is one of the most important techniques for cross-checking K/Ar determinations. The key to fission-track dating is that ^{238}Uranium (^{238}U) decays regularly by spontaneous fission so that, by counting the fraction of uranium atoms that have fissioned (shown as microscopic tracks caused by explosive fission of ^{238}U nuclei), we can ascertain the age of a mineral or natural glass sample (Fleischer and Hart, 1972). One of the earliest applications of this technique was on volcanic pumice from Bed I at Olduvai, giving a date of 2.30 ($\pm .28$ m.y.a.)—in good accord with K/Ar dates.

Another important means of cross-checking dates is called **paleomagnetism**. This technique is based on the constantly shifting nature of the earth's magnetic pole. Of course, as anyone knows, the earth's magnetic pole is now oriented in a northerly direction, but this situation has not always been so. In fact, the orien-

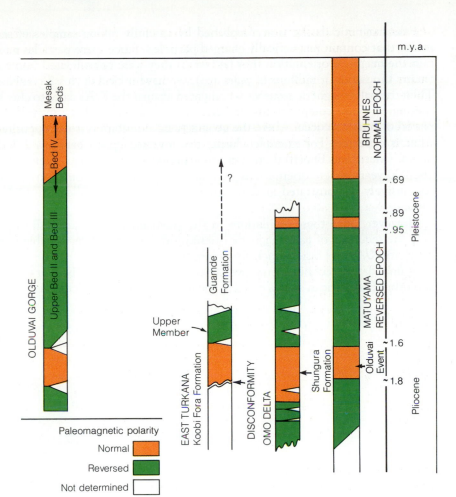

Figure 11-9
Paleomagnetic sequences. Correlated for major East African sites—Olduvai, East Turkana, Omo. (After Isaac, 1975.)

Paleomagnetic polarity

Normal

Reversed

Not determined

tation and intensity of the geomagnetic field have undergone numerous documented changes in the last few million years. From our present ethnocentric point of view, we call a northern orientation "normal" and a southern one "reversed." Major epochs of geomagnetic time are:

Normal

0.7 m.y.a.

Reversed

2.5 m.y.a.

Normal

3.4 m.y.a.

Reversed

'

'

'

'

?

BIOSTRATIGRAPHY
Dating method based on evolutionary
changes within an evolving lineage.

Paleomagnetic dating is accomplished by carefully taking samples of sediments that contain magnetically charged particles. Since these particles maintain the magnetic orientation they had when they were consolidated into rock (many thousands or millions of years ago), we have a kind of "fossil compass." Then the paleomagnetic *sequence* is compared against the K/Ar dates to check if they agree. Some complications can arise, for during an epoch a relatively long period of time can occur where the geomagnetic orientation is the opposite of what is expected. For example, during the reversed epoch between 2.5–0.7 m.y.a. (Matuyama Epoch) there was a time period called an *event*, lasting about 160,000 years, where orientations were normal. As this phenomenon was first conclusively demonstrated at Olduvai, it is appropriately called the *Olduvai Event*.

However, once these oscillations in the geomagnetic pole are well worked out, the sequence of paleomagnetic orientations can provide a valuable cross-check for K/Ar and fission-track age determinations.

A final dating technique employed in the Lower Pleistocene beds at Olduvai and other East African sites is based in the regular evolutionary changes in well-

Figure 11-10
Partial biostratigraphic sequence of pigs. Used to correlate East African sites. (After White and Harris, 1977.)

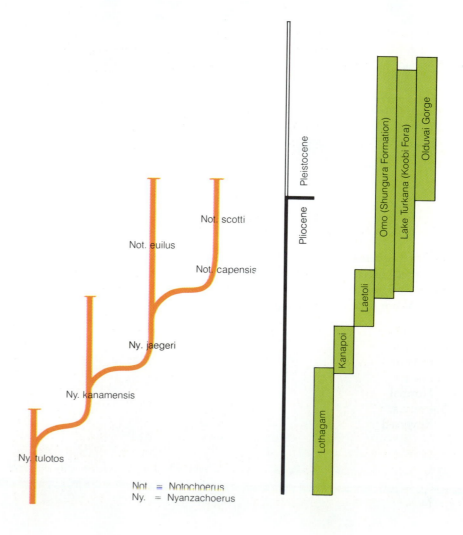

known groups of mammals. This technique, called *faunal correlation* or **biostratigraphy**, provides yet another means of cross-checking the other methods. Animals that have been widely used in biostratigraphical analysis in East Africa and South Africa are fossil pigs (suids), elephants (proboscids), antelope (bovids), rodents, and carnivores. From areas where dates are known (by K/Ar, for instance) approximate ages can be extrapolated to other less well-known areas by noting which genera and species are present.

All these methods, potassium-argon, fission-track, paleomagnetism, and biostratigraphy have been used in dating Beds I and II at Olduvai. So many different dating techniques are necessary because no single one is perfectly reliable by itself. Sampling error, contamination, and experimental errors can all introduce ambiguities into our so-called "absolute" dates. However, the sources of error are different for each technique, and therefore cross-checking between several independent methods is the most certain way of authenticating the chronology for early hominid sites.

Excavations at Olduvai

Because the vertical cut of the Olduvai Gorge provides a ready cross-section of 2 million years of earth history, sites can be excavated by digging "straight-in" rather than finding them by having first to remove tons of overlying dirt. In fact, sites are usually discovered by merely walking the exposures and observing what bones, stones, etc. are eroding out.

Several dozen hominid sites (at a minimum, they are bone and tool scatters) have been surveyed at Olduvai, and Mary Leakey has extensively excavated close to twenty of these. An incredible amount of paleoanthropological information

Figure 11-11
Excavations in progress at Olduvai. This site is more than one million years old. It was located when a hominid ulna (arm bone) was found eroding out of the side of the gorge.

CONTEXT
The environmental setting where an archeological trace is found.

ASSOCIATION
What an archeological trace is found with.

LIVING FLOOR
A narrow horizon of archeological remains;
corresponds to brief period of occupation.

has come from these excavated areas, data which can be generally grouped into three broad categories depending on implied function:

1. *Butchering sites.* Areas containing one or only a few individuals of a single species of large mammal associated with a scatter of archeological traces. An elephant butchering site and another containing a *Deinotherium* (a large extinct relative of the elephant) have been found at levels approximately 1.7 m.y.a. Both sites contain only a single animal, and it is impossible to ascertain whether the hominids actually killed these animals or exploited them (presumably for meat resources) after they were already dead. A third butchering site dated at approximately 1.2 m.y.a. shows much more consistent and efficient hunting of large mammals by this time. Remains of 24 *Pelorovis* (a giant extinct relative of the buffalo, with horn spans more than ten feet across!), have been found here, and Louis Leakey suggested they were driven into a swamp by a band of hominids and then systematically slaughtered (Leakey, 1971).

2. *Quarry sites.* Areas where early hominids extracted their stone resources and initially fashioned their tools. At such sites, thousands of small stone fragments are found of only one type of rock usually associated with no or very little bone refuse. At Olduvai, a 1.6 m.y.–1.7 m.y. old area was apparently a chert factory site, where hominids came repeatedly to quarry this material.

3. *Living sites.* Also called campsites. General purpose areas where hominids ate, slept, and put the finishing touches on their tools. The accumulation of living debris, including broken bones of many animals of several different species and many broken stones (some complete tools, some waste flakes) is a basic human pattern. As the late Glynn Isaac noted, "The fact that discarded artifacts tend to be concentrated in restricted areas is itself highly suggestive. It seems likely that such patches of material reflect the organization of movement around a camp or home base, with recurrent dispersal and reuniting of the group at the chosen locality. Among living primates this pattern in its full expression is distinctive of man. The coincidence of bone and food refuse with the artifacts strongly implies that meat was carried back—presumably for sharing" (Isaac, 1976, pp. 27–28). (See Box 11-1 for a different interpretation.)

Several campsites have been excavated at Olduvai, including one that is over 1.8 m.y. old (DKI—see Box 11-2). This site has a circle of large stones forming what may have been the base for a windbreak or, as Mary Leakey, who dug the site, has suggested, may have been the foundation for a primitive structure. Without the meticulous excavation and recording of modern archeological techniques, the presence of such an archeological feature would never have been recognized. This point requires further emphasis. Many people assume archeologists derive their information simply from analysis of objects (stone tools, gold statues, or whatever). However, it is the **context** and **association** of objects (that is, precisely where the objects are found and what is found associated with them) that give the archeologist the data he requires to understand the behavioral patterns of ancient human populations. Once pot hunters or looters pilfer a site, proper archeological interpretation is never again possible.

Other living sites at Olduvai include the large occupation area at the "Zinj" site (FLK = 1.75 m.y.a.) and a very thin (perhaps occupied just a few days) **living floor** (HWK East = 1.7 m.y.a.). Preservation of occupational debris along one

BOX 11-1

Are the Sites at Olduvai Really "Sites"?

The generally agreed-upon interpretation of the bone refuse and stone tools discovered at Olduvai has been that most, if not all, of these materials are the result of hominid activities. Recently, however, a comprehensive reanalysis of the bone remains from Olduvai localities has challenged this view (Binford, 1981; 1983). Archeologist Lewis Binford criticizes those drawn too quickly to the conclusion that these bone scatters are the remnants of hominid behavior patterns while simultaneously ignoring the possibility of other explanations. For example, he forcefully states:

> All the facts gleaned from the deposits interpreted as living sites have served as the basis for making up "just-so stories" about our hominid past. No attention has been given to the possibility that many of the facts may well be referable to the behavior of nonhominids (Binford, 1981, p. 251).

From specifics concerning the kinds of animals present, which body parts were found, and the differences in preservation among these skeletal elements, Binford concluded that much of what is preserved could be explained by carnivore activity. This conclusion was reinforced by certain details observed by Binford himself in Alaska—details on animal kills, scavenging, the transportation of elements, and preservation as the result of wolf and dog behaviors. Binford describes his approach thus:

> I took as 'known,' then, the structure of bone assemblages produced in various settings by animal predators and scavengers; and as 'unknown' the bone deposits excavated by the Leakeys at Olduvai Gorge. Using mathematical and statistical techniques I considered to what degree the finds from Olduvai Gorge could be accounted for in terms of the results of predator behavior and how much was 'left over' (Binford, 1983, pp. 56–57).

In using this uniquely explicit approach, Binford arrived at quite different conclusions than those previously suggested by other archeologists:

> For instance, the very idea of a site or living floor assumes conditions in the past for which there is no demonstration. In fact, it assumes the very "knowledge" we would like to obtain from the archeological remains. Site and living floor identifications presuppose that concentrations and aggregations of archeological and other materials are only produced by man. Are there not other conditions of deposition that could result in aggregations of considerable density found on old land surfaces? The answer must be a resounding yes.

And, later, he concludes:

> It seems to me that one major conclusion is justified from the foregoing analysis: The large, highly publicized sites as currently analyzed carry little specific information about hominid behavior . . . arguments about base camps, hominid hunting, sharing of food, and so forth are certainly premature and most likely wildly inaccurate (Binford, 1981, pp. 281–282).

Binford is not arguing that *all* of the remains found at Olduvai have resulted from nonhominid activity. In fact, he recognized that "residual material" was consistently found on surfaces with high tool concentrations "which could *not* be explained by what we know about African animals" (Binford, 1983).

Support for the idea that at least some of the bone refuse was utilized by early hominids has come from a totally different tact. Recently, researchers have analyzed (both macroscopically and microscopically) the cutmarks left on fossilized bones. By experimenting with modern materials, they have further been able to delineate clearly the differences between marks left by stone tools as opposed to those left by animal teeth (or other factors) (Bunn, 1981; Potts and Shipman, 1981). Analysis of bones from several early localities at Olduvai showed unambiguously that these specimens were utilized by hominids, who left telltale cutmarks from stone tool usage. The sites thus far investigated reveal a somewhat haphazard cutting and chopping, apparently unrelated to deliberate disarticulation. It has thus been concluded (Shipman, 1983) that hominids scavenged carcasses (probably of carnivore kills) and did *not* hunt large animals themselves. Materials found at later sites (postdating 1 m.y.a.), on the other hand, do show deliberate disarticulation, indicating a more systematic hunting pattern, with presumably meat transport and food-sharing as well (Shipman, 1983).

If early hominids (close to 2 m.y.a.) were not hunting consistently, what did they obtain from scavenging the kills of other animals? One obvious answer is, whatever meat was left behind. However, the positioning of the cutmarks suggests that early hominids were often hacking at nonmeat-bearing portions of the skeletons. Perhaps they were simply after bone marrow, a substance not really being exploited by other predators (Binford, 1981).

The picture that emerges, then, of what hominids were doing at Olduvai around 1.8 m.y.a. hardly suggests consistent big game hunting. In Binford's words:

> . . . this is evidence of man eating a little bit of bone marrow, a food source that must have represented an infinitesimally small component of his total diet. The signs seem clear. Earliest man, far from appearing as a mighty hunter of beasts, seems to have been the most marginal of scavengers (Binford, 1983, p. 59).

relatively narrow horizon is what is meant by a living floor, and the extraordinary conditions at Olduvai have preserved probably some of the bones and stones almost exactly as the hominids left them more than 1 m.y.a.

Another kind of living site is MNK (Lower Middle Bed II = 1.6 m.y.a.) where occupational debris is scattered through more than six feet of earth, suggesting hominids periodically reoccupied this area—perhaps seasonally.

The detailed excavations of all these different hominid occupation areas are of tremendous importance, since the dispersal pattern of the remains of ancient human behavior can yield great insight into the biocultural evolution of humankind.

Artifacts

While context, association, and ecological information are of paramount interest to the prehistoric archeologist, detailed analysis of the stone artifacts themselves can yield much additional information about the behavior of early hominids. Mary Leakey has been the pioneer in the study of Plio-Pleistocene African artifacts, and her classification system and description of some of the artifacts found at Olduvai are discussed in Box 11-3.

Experimental Archeology

Classifying artifacts into categories and types is scientifically insufficient. We can learn considerably more about our ancestors by understanding how they made and used their tools. It is, after all, the artifactual traces of prehistoric tools of stone (and to a lesser degree, bone) that comprise our primary information concerning early human behavior. Millions of tons of stone debris litter archeologi-

Olduvai Site Names

The naming of sites at Olduvai is a marvelous wonder concocted from fascinating combinations of the English alphabet. Sites are designated with such shorthand abbreviations as FLK, MNK, LLK, etc. The 'K' stands for Korongo, Swahili for gully (Olduvai is made up of dozens of side gullies). The first initial(s) is usually, though not always, that of the individual who made an important discovery at that locality. For example, FLK stands for Frida Leakey Korongo (Louis' first wife), MNK is Mary Nicol Korongo (Mary Leakey's maiden name), and LLK is Louis Leakey Korongo (where Louis found a hominid cranium in 1961). When more than one site is found in the same gully, those discovered later are given directional orientations relative to the initial site. For example, FLK is the main site name where "Zinj" was found in 1959. FLK N (that is, "FLK North," where the elephant and *Deinotherium* butchering sites occur at slightly different levels) is just north of the main site, and FLK NN ("FLK North North," the location of yet another important hominid discovery) is just a bit farther north up the gully.

cal sites worldwide. A casual walk along the bottom of Olduvai Gorge will be interrupted every few seconds by prehistoric tools that could be easily tripped over!

Archeologists are thus presented with a wealth of information revealing at least *one* part of human material culture. What do these artifacts tell us about our ancestors? How were these tools made? In which ways were they used? To answer these questions, contemporary archeologists have attempted to reconstruct prehistoric techniques of stone toolmaking, butchering, and so forth. In this way, experimental archeologists are, in a sense, trying to recreate the past.

LITHIC
lith: stone

FLAKE
Thin-edged fragment removed from a core.

CORE
Stone reduced by flake removal.

KNAPPING
Flaking stone tools.

Stone Tool (Lithic) Technology

Since stone is by far the most common residue of prehistoric cultural behavior, archeologists have long been keenly interested in this material.

When struck properly, certain types of stone will fracture in a controlled way. The smaller piece struck off is called a **flake**, while the larger remaining chunk is called a **core**. The obvious useful result is that both core and flake now possess sharp edges useful for cutting, sawing, or scraping. The earliest hominid cultural inventions probably employed nondurable materials that did not survive archeologically (such as a digging stick or an ostrich egg shell used as a watertight container). Still, a basic human invention was the recognition that stone can be fractured to produce sharp edges. In fact, the earliest stone tools (over 2 m.y.a.) show that both flake and core implements were already being fashioned.

Breaking rocks by bashing them together is one thing. Producing consistent results is quite another. It takes years of practice before stone **knappers** learn the intricacies of the type of rock to choose, the kind of hammer to employ, the angle and velocity with which to strike, etc. Such experience allows us to appreciate how skilled in stoneworking our ancestors truly were.

Flakes can be removed from cores in a great variety of ways. The object in making a tool, however, is to produce a usable surface. By reproducing results similar to those of earlier stoneworkers, experimental archeologists can infer which kinds of techniques *might* have been employed.

Classification of Artifacts

Stone artifacts, depending on context, shape, flake scars, and inferred function, fall into four broad categories:

1. *Manuports.* Rocks that are not modified but are found out of their natural context; that is, rocks that have been manually carried, a definite hominid behavior. The stone circle at DK I perhaps consisted of manuports, and much of the occupational debris at MNK is made up of unmodified manuports. Their functions remain unknown.

2. *Utilized material.* Stones used to modify other stones but not used as tools themselves. Under this category, Mary Leakey includes hammerstones and anvils.

3. *Debitage.* Very small flakes, either waste material struck off while making tools or perhaps used themselves as very small cutting implements.

4. *Tools.* A broad category of intentionally modified stones that have been shaped according to a preset, consistent pattern. Mary Leakey classifies the stone tools found at Olduvai primarily on the basis of shape and size. As yet no definite conclusions on their functions have been reached. Tools are thus classed as spheroids, discoids, polyhedrons, bifaces, etc. Occasionally, function is inferred with such terms as chopper, scraper, burin, and awl.

Debitage

Manuports

Figure 1
Stone artifacts.

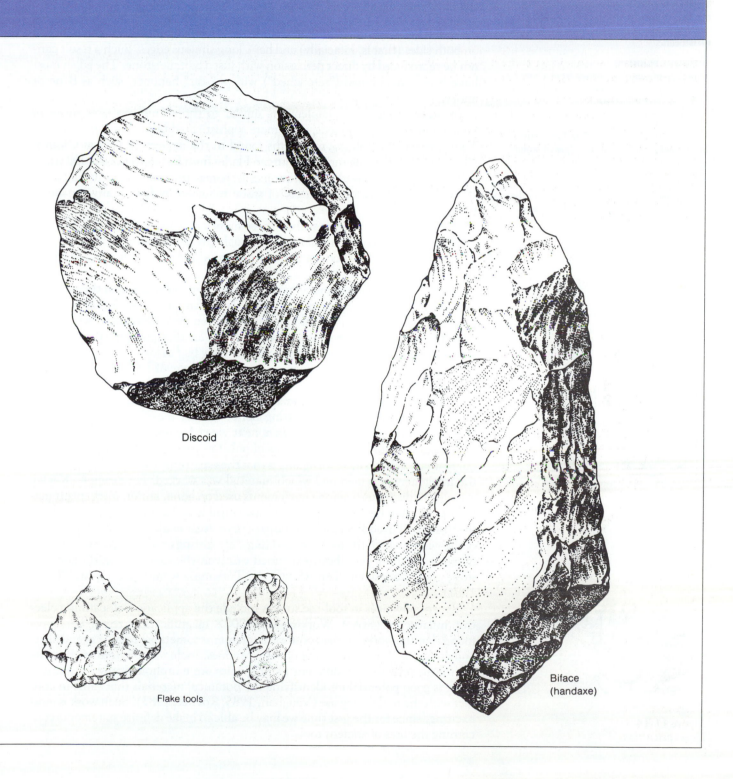

Discoid

Flake tools

Biface
(handaxe)

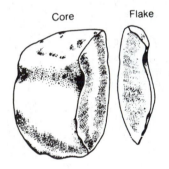

Core   Flake

Figure 11-13
Flake and core.

Figure 11-14
Direct percussion.

For example, the choppers found in sites in Beds I and II at Olduvai (*circa* 1.85–1.2 m.y.a.) are flaked on one side only (that is, unifacially). It is possible, although by no means easy, to produce such implements by hitting one stone—the hammerstone—against another—the core—in a method called **direct percussion** (see Fig. 11-14).

In Bed IV sites (*circa* 400,000 y.a.), however, the majority of tools are flaked on both sides (that is, bifacially) and have long sinuous edges. Such a result cannot be reproduced by direct percussion with just a hammerstone. The edges must have been straightened ("retouched") with a "soft" hammer, such as bone or antler.

In order to reproduce implements similar to those found in later stages of human cultural development, even more sophisticated techniques are required. Tools such as the delicate **microliths** found in the uppermost beds at Olduvai (*circa* 17,000 y.a.), the superb Solutrean blades from Europe (*circa* 20,000 y.a.), and the expertly crafted Folsom projectile points from the New World (*circa* 10,000 y.a.) all require a mastery of stone matched by few, if any, knappers today.

Reproducing implements such as those mentioned above requires removal of extremely thin flakes, possible only through **pressure flaking**—for example, using a pointed piece of bone, antler, or hard wood and pressing firmly against the stone (see Fig. 11-15).

Once the tools were manufactured, the ways our ancestors used them can be inferred through further experimentation. For example, archeologists from the Smithsonian Institution successfully butchered an entire elephant (which had died in a zoo) using stone tools they had made for that purpose (Park, 1978). Others have cut down trees using stone axes they had made.

Ancient tools themselves may carry tell-tale signs of how they were used. Lawrence Keeley, in his graduate work at Oxford University, performed a series of experiments in which he manufactured flint tools and then used them in diverse ways—whittling wood, cutting bone, cutting meat, and scraping skins (Keeley, 1980). The implements were next viewed under a microscope at fairly high magnification to reveal patterns of polishes, striations, and other kinds of **microwear**. What is most intriguing is that these patterns vary depending on how the implement was used and which material was worked. For example, Keeley was able to distinguish among implements used on bone, antler, meat, plant materials, or hides. In the latter case, he was even able to determine if the hides were fresh or dried! In addition, orientations of microwear markings are also indicative of the way in which the tool was used (e.g., for cutting or scraping). Evidences of microwear polish have been examined on even the extremely early hominid stone tools from Koobi Fora (East Lake Turkana), Kenya (Keeley and Toth, 1981).

Recent advances in tool-use studies include the application of scanning electron microscopy (SEM). Working at 10,000× magnification, researchers have found that the working edges of stone implements sometimes retain vegetal fibers and amino acids, as well as nonorganic residues, including **phytoliths**. Because phytoliths produced by different plant species are morphologically distinctive, there is good potential for identifying the botanical materials that came in contact with the tool during use (Vaughan, 1985; Rovner, 1983). Such work is most exciting, since for the first time we may be able to make definite statements concerning the uses of ancient tools.

Analysis of Bone

Experimental archeologists are also interested in the ways bone is altered by human and natural forces. We saw previously how ethnoarcheologists are able to trace the events that lead from human use of animal resources to archeological deposition of bony material.

Other scientists are also vitally concerned with this process; in fact, an entire new branch of paleoecology—taphonomy—has emerged (see p. 309). In recent years taphonomists have carried out comprehensive research on how natural factors influence bone deposition and preservation. In South Africa, C. K. Brain has collected data on Hottentot butchering practices, carnivore (dog) disturbances, and so forth, and has correlated these factors with the kinds and numbers of elements usually found in bone accumulations (Brain, 1981). In this way, he has been able to account for the accumulation of most (if not all) of the bones in South African cave sites. Likewise, in East African game parks, observations have been made on decaying animals to measure the effects of weathering, predator chewing, and trampling (Behrensmeyer et al., 1979).

Further insight into the many ways bone is altered by natural factors has come from experimental work in the laboratory by N. T. Boaz and A. K. Behrensmeyer (1976). In an experiment conducted at the University of California, Berkeley, human bones were put into a running-water trough. Researchers observed how far different pieces were transported and how much damage was done. Application of such information is extremely useful in interpreting early hominid sites. For example, the distribution of hominid fossils at Olduvai suggests that less active water transport was prevalent there than in the Omo River Valley.

Detailed examination of bones may also provide evidence of butchering by hominids, including cutmarks left by stone tools. Great care must be taken to distinguish scars left on bone by carnivore or rodent gnawing, weathering processes, or even normal growth. High magnification of a cut made by a stone tool may reveal a minutely striated and roughened groove scored into the bone's surface. Many such finds have been recognized at early hominid sites, including Olduvai Gorge (Potts and Shipman, 1981). (See p. 327.)

Reconstructing Behavior from Garbage

Since most of what we find littering archeological sites is the debris of earlier societies, an understanding of the ways behavior may be indicated via study of material refuse is essential. Since 1972 a major study of exactly this nature has been carried out in Tucson by William Rathje of the University of Arizona (Rathje and McCarthy, 1977). Rathje maintains that, by demonstrating the archeologist's ability to learn something about our present culture through the study of modern refuse, his project has helped to reinforce the claim that the past can be revealed through archeology (Rathje, 1979).

Over a three-year period more than 1,000 households were sampled and more than 70,000 items were collected, weighed, and classified into 200 categories of food and other household goods. In addition, census data were used to select representative samples in order to correlate information about garbage with family size, income, and ethnicity.

Figure 11-15
Pressure flaking.

Figure 11-16
Microwear: The polish left on an experimental flint implement by scraping wood for ten minutes. Bright, smooth areas are the microwear polish; dark, grainy areas are the unworn flint surface. Arrows indicate implement edge. (Magnification, 200×)

(a) Knapper, Alan Leventhal, starts with hammerstone and nodule of obsidian.

(b) Manufacturing technique: hard hammer direct percussion—applied force on striking platform.

(c) Removal of a large primary flake.

(d) Ventral side of flake (removed above) and striking platform for removal of next flake.

(e) Removal of second large flake (to be used as primary flake blank).

(f) Platform preparation on primary flake blank.

(g) Manufacturing technique: soft hammer percussion. Bifacial shaping and thinning.

(h) Removal of thinning flake.

(i) Further straightening of edge by soft hammer percussion.

(j) Manufacturing technique: pressure flaking with sharpened antler tip.

(k) Removal of pressure flakes for final straightening and sharpening of edge.

(l) Finished product. A bifacial knife.

Figure 11-17
Stone tool technology. Reduction sequences of an obsidian core to a finished product.

CONTEMPORARY INFLUENCES
OF NONHUMAN FACTORS:

Predation
Weathering
Active transport

CONTEMPORARY HUMAN
BEHAVIOR:

Lithic analysis (knapping
techniques, microwear, etc.)
Butchering techniques
Dietary patterns
(ethnoarcheology—
see Chapter 9)

Materials preserved
as artifacts

Reconstructing
contemporary behavior
through material remains
("Garbage Project")

Figure 11-18
Experimental archeology: reconstructing the past from the present.

The project has encouraged some rethinking about the assumed relationships between artifacts and the people and cultures who produce, use, and discard them. In the Tucson study, for instance, the correlations between demographic factors and discard behavior were not always the expected ones. Evidence from garbage provided substantially different (and, no doubt, more accurate) information concerning alcohol consumption than people admitted in questionnaire surveys. Moreover, since the data have been carefully sampled and quantified, we can get a far better idea of exactly how many usable items are thrown away. The middle-class households in the survey accounted for a higher percentage of wasted food (nearly 10% of the food purchased) than either the poor or the wealthy. But such patterns did not extend to nonfood waste. Despite the popular image of Americans as "conspicuous consumers," the archeologists encountered few usable household items in garbage or trash dumps. There seemed to be a widespread practice of recycling furniture and appliances through yard sales and charities. Higher-income households tended to replace items at a somewhat higher rate, thus replenishing the supply of goods entering the system (Schiffer, Downing, and McCarthy, 1981).

Diet of Early Hominids

Paleoanthropological research is concerned with more than the recovery and recording of bones and artifacts. What we are trying to obtain is a reconstruction of the kind of animal our ancestor was. Paleoanthropology must therefore be centrally concerned with interpretation of the behavioral patterns of early hominid populations.

One of the most important questions we would like to answer about early hominid behavior is: What did they eat? Scattered broken bone debris associated with artifacts *may* provide direct evidence concerning one important aspect of early human dietary behavior. However, we must not forget that modern analogs like the San of South Africa clearly show us that vegetable foods, which usually leave little trace in the archeological record, probably made up a large part (even a majority) of the caloric intake of early hominids. As Glynn Isaac noted, reconstructing dietary behavior is like navigating around an iceberg—four-fifths of what is of interest is not visible (Isaac, 1971, p. 280).

Postulated diets available to hominids 1–2 m.y.a. with use of only a simple digging stick as a tool include: berries, fruits, nuts, buds, shoots, shallow-growing roots and tubers, most terrestrial and smaller aquatic reptiles, eggs and nesting birds, some fish, molluscs, insects, and all smaller mammals (Bartholomew and Birdsell, 1953).

Olduvai has shown that the range of postulated meat resources was indeed exploited in Beds I and II (1.85–1.0 m.y.a.). Fossils of turtles, rodents, fish, birds, pigs, horses, and small antelopes are all fairly common at many Olduvai sites. Of course, exactly how much of these remains were eaten—as opposed to having just "dropped dead" there or having been preyed upon by other animals— is still undetermined (see Box 11-1). Evidence for fish eating has also come from a comparably aged site in southern Ethiopia (the Omo), where fish bones have been found in human coprolites (fossilized feces).

Moreover, as the elephant and *Deinotherium* butchering sites indicate, occasional exploitation of large mammals also occurred more than 1.5 m.y.a. By 1 m.y.a., systematic hunting of large mammals apparently provided important meat resources, as shown by the *Pelorovis* butchering site.

Thanks to the extraordinary dedication of Louis and Mary Leakey, just one relatively small area of northern Tanzania has provided a continuous record of the development of hominids and their behavior for almost 2 million years. Without Olduvai we would know much less than we do about the emergence of human culture prior to 1 m.y.a.

Summary

The biocultural nature of human evolution requires that any meaningful study of human origins examine both biological and cultural information. The multidisciplinary approach of paleoanthropology is designed to bring together varied scientific specializations in order to reconstruct the anatomy, behavior, and environments of early hominids. Such a task is centered around the skills of the geologist, paleontologist, paleoecologist, archeologist, and physical anthropologist.

Much of what we know about the origins of human culture between 1 and 2 m.y.a. comes from archeological excavations by Mary Leakey at Olduvai Gorge in East Africa. Olduvai's well-documented stratigraphic sequence, its superior preservation of remains (often as living floors), and the varied dating techniques possible there have made it an information bonanza for paleoanthropologists. Excavated sites have yielded a wealth of bones of fossil animals, as well as artifact traces of hominid behavior. Ecological reconstructions of habitat and dietary preferences are thereby possible and inform us in great detail concerning crucial evolutionary processes affecting early hominid populations.

Archeologists are better able to interpret the "bones and stones" of earlier populations through experimentation. In recent years much new light has been shed on the techniques of making stone tools as well as the factors affecting preservation of bone. In addition, anthropologists are using archeological techniques to help illuminate our understanding of contemporary behavior through systematic analysis of garbage.

In the next two chapters, we will survey the fossil hominid evidence in South and East Africa that inform us directly about human origins during the Plio-Pleistocene.

Questions for Review

1. Why are cultural remains so important in the interpretation of human evolution?
2. How are early hominid sites found, and what kind of specialist is involved in the excavation and analysis of paleoanthropological data?
3. What kinds of paleoanthropological information have been found at Olduvai Gorge? Why is this particular locality so rich in material?
4. What kinds of dating techniques have been used to date early hominid sites at Olduvai? Why is more than one technique necessary for accurate dating?
5. Why are context and association so important in the interpretation of archeological remains?
6. What different activities can be inferred from the different kinds of sites at Olduvai? Discuss alternative views in the interpretation of these "sites."
7. How do archeologists determine the functions of ancient stone tools?
8. How do archeological techniques contribute to understanding contemporary behavior?
9. How do we infer what early hominids were eating? Give a brief list of the kinds of food that were probably exploited.

Plio-Pleistocene Hominids

CHAPTER 12

CONTENTS

The Piltdown Caper: Who Dunnit?

When first announced to the world in 1912, *Eoanthropus dawsoni* ("Dawson's Dawn Man") created an anthropological sensation. Found during 1911 in Sussex in the south of England by Charles Dawson, a lawyer and amateur geologist/antiquarian, this "fossil" was to confuse, bewilder, and befuddle two generations of anthropologists. "Piltdown man," as he popularly came to be called, was comprised of a fragmented skull and parts of a lower jaw. The enigma of the fossil from the very beginning was the combination of a large *sapiens*-like skull (initially estimated at 1,070 cm³, but later shown to be more like 1,400 cm³) with an apelike lower jaw.

Most tantalizing of all, Piltdown was apparently extremely ancient, associated with long extinct fauna, such as mastodon, hippo, and rhino, all suggesting a date of early Pleistocene. A puzzling feature was the presence of these early fossils mixed in with clearly late Pleistocene fauna. The prevailing consensus, however, was that Piltdown was indeed ancient, "the earliest known representative of man in Western Europe."

Despite its seeming incongruities, Piltdown was eagerly accepted by British scientists, including Keith, Elliot Smith, and Smith Woodward (all later knighted). What made the fossil such a delectable treat was that it confirmed just what had been expected, a combination of *modern* ape and *modern* human characteristics—a true "missing link." We, of course, now know that no ancestral fossil form is a fifty-fifty com-

promise between modern ones, but represents its own unique adaptation. In addition to mistaken enthusiasm for a missing link, the fossil also represented a "true" man as opposed to the obviously primitive beasts (Java man, Neandertals) found elsewhere. Such a fervently biased desire to find an "ancient modern" in the human lineage has obscured evolutionary studies for decades and still causes confusion in some circles.

While generally accepted in England, experts in France, Germany, and the United States felt uneasy about Piltdown. Many critics, however, were silenced when a second fragmentary find came to light in 1917 (actually found in 1915) in an area two miles away from the original site. The matter stood in limbo for years, with some scientists as enthusiastic supporters of the Piltdown man and others remaining uneasy doubters. The uneasiness continued to fester as more hominid material accumulated in Java, China, and particularly the australopithecines in South Africa. None of these hominids showed the peculiar combination of a human cranium with an apelike jaw seen in Piltdown, but actually indicated the reverse pattern.

The final proof of the true nature of the Dawn Man came in the early 1950s, when British scientists began an intensive reexamination of the Piltdown material. In particular, fluorine analysis (see Chapter 11) performed by Kenneth Oakley showed both the skull and jaw were relatively recent. Later, more extensive tests showed the jaw to be younger than the skull and *very* recent in date. Now a much more critical eye was turned to all the material. The teeth, looking initially as though they had been worn down flat in the typical hominid fashion, were apparently ape teeth filed down deliberately to give that impression. The mixed bag of

Figure 1
The Piltdown skull.

fauna was apparently acquired from all manner of places (a fossil elephant came from Tunisia in North Africa!), and the jaw was deliberately stained with chromate to match the older fossils in color. Finally, some "tools" found at Piltdown also met the hand of a forger, for the bone implements showed modifications that apparently could only have been made by a metal knife.

The "fossil" itself was probably purchased from local dealers. The skull probably came from a moderately ancient grave (a few thousand years old), and the jaw was a specially broken, filed, and stained mandible of a fairly recently deceased adolescent orang! The evidence was indisputable: a deliberate hoax. But who did it?

Just about everyone connected with the "crime" has, at one time or another, been implicated—beginning with Piltdown's discoverer: Charles Dawson. Yet, Dawson was an amateur, and, thus, may have lacked the expertise to carry out the admittedly crafty job of anatomical modification.

In addition, at various times, suspicions have been cast towards neuroanatomist Sir Grafton Elliot Smith, geologist W. J. Sollas, and French philosopher and archaeologist, Father Pierre Teilhard de Chardin. Still, for

Figure 2
The Piltdown committee. The individuals central to the "discovery" and interpretation of the Piltdown "fossil." Back row, standing, left to right: Mr. F. O. Barlow (maker of the casts), Prof. G. Elliot Smith (anatomist), Mr. C. Dawson ("discoverer"), Dr. A. Smith Woodward (zoologist). Front row, seated: Dr. A. S. Underwood (dental expert), Prof. A. Keith (anatomist), Mr. W. P. Pycraft (zoologist), Sir Ray Lankester (zoologist). From the painting by John Cook.

none of these people has a conclusive case been made.

Recently, however, another intriguing possibility has been raised:

. . . there was another interested figure who haunted the Piltdown site during excavation, a doctor who knew human anatomy and chemistry, someone interested in geology and archeology, and an avid collector of fossils. He was a man who loved hoaxes, adventure and danger; a writer gifted at manipulating complex plots; and perhaps most important of all, one who bore a grudge against the British science establishment. He was none other than the creator of Sherlock Holmes, Sir Arthur Conan Doyle (Winslow and Meyer, 1983, p. 34).

Doyle, as a medical doctor, certainly possessed the anatomical know-how to craft the forgery. His other avocations—chemistry, geology, and especially, anthropology—also would have been useful to him, *if* he were the forger.

In a remarkable piece of detective work (worthy of the master sleuth Sherlock Holmes himself), John Winslow has assembled a convincing array of *circumstantial* evidence against Doyle. Doyle, first of all, is the only suspect that can be shown to have had ready access to all the elements of the forgery. He was friendly with collectors or dealers who easily could have provided him with the cranium, the orang jaw, and the stone tools. As far as the animal fossils are concerned, Doyle also could have acquired many of the local (English) fossils from collector friends, but some of the odd bits obviously are from elsewhere (most likely, Malta and Tunisia). And, interestingly enough, Doyle had traveled to Malta a few years before Piltdown came to light, and may have been in Tunisia as well. At the very least, he was closely acquainted with people who had been to this part of North Africa.

But what of motive? As rich and as successful a figure as Doyle would seem an unlikely candidate for such a ruse. Winslow, however, has also found some clues that suggest Sir Arthur *may* indeed have had a motive.

Doyle was a longtime spiritualist who believed firmly in the occult and in extrasensory powers. He bore little patience with scientific critics of such views, whom he regarded as closed-minded. In particular, he had a special rival, Edward Ray Lankester, one of the most renowned evolutionists of the early twentieth century. Perhaps, as Winslow speculates, Doyle invented the whole scheme as farce to embarrass the scientific establishment and, most especially, Lankester.

"So the case against Doyle is made. Besides the necessary skill, contacts, knowledge, and opportunity to qualify as the hoaxer, Doyle also had sufficient motive and an inviting target, Lankester" (Winslow and Meyer, 1983, p. 42).

Fascinating as it all is, we may never know whether the creator of Sherlock Holmes was also the Piltdown forger. Seventy years after the crime, the trail has grown stone cold—the forger covered his tracks very well indeed!

SOURCES:

Weiner, J. W., *The Piltdown Forgery*, London: Oxford University Press, 1955.

Winslow, John Hathaway and Alfred Meyer, "The Perpetrator at Piltdown," *Science '83*, September, 1983, pp. 33–43.

Introduction

We have seen in the last two chapters that hominids can be defined on the basis of dental adaptations and/or toolmaking behavior. In this chapter, we will review a series of remarkable discoveries in East and South Africa that persuaded paleoanthropologists to radically reassess their theories on human evolution.

Early Hominids in the Plio-Pleistocene

The beginnings of hominid differentiation almost certainly have their roots in the late Miocene (*circa* 5–10 m.y.a.). Sometime during the period between 8 and 4 m.y.a., hominids began to adapt more fully to their peculiar ground living niche, and evolutionary evidence from this period would be most illuminating. However, scant information is presently available concerning the course of hominid evolution during this significant 4-million-year gap. But beginning around 4 m.y.a., the fossil record picks up considerably. We now have a wealth of fossil hominid material from the Pliocene and the earliest stages of the Pleistocene (5–1 m.y.a.), and this whole span is usually referred to as the Plio-Pleistocene.

Figure 12-1
East African Plio-Pleistocene hominid sites and the rift system.

The East African Rift Valley

Stretching along a more than 1,200-mile trough extending through Ethiopia, Kenya, and Tanzania from the Red Sea in the north to the Serengeti Plain in the south is the eastern branch of the Great Rift Valley of Africa. This massive geological feature has been associated with active mountain building, faulting, and vulcanism over the last several million years.

Because of these gigantic earth movements, earlier sediments (normally buried under hundreds of feet of earth and rock) are literally thrown to the surface, where they become exposed to the trained eye of the paleoanthropologist. Such earth movements have exposed Miocene beds at sites in Kenya, along the shores of Lake Victoria, where remains of dryopiths and ramapiths have been found. In addition, Plio-Pleistocene sediments are also exposed all along the Rift Valley, and paleoanthropologists in recent years have made the most of this unique opportunity.

More than just exposing normally hidden deposits, rifting has stimulated volcanic activity, which in turn has provided a valuable means of chronometrically dating many sites in East Africa. Unlike the sites in South Africa (see pp. 373–376), those along the Rift Valley are *datable* and have thus yielded much crucial information concerning the precise chronology of early hominid evolution.

East African Hominid Sites

The site that focused attention on East Africa as a potential paleoanthropological gold mine was Olduvai Gorge in northern Tanzania. As discussed in great detail in Chapter 11, this site has offered unique opportunities because of the remarkable preservation of geological, paleontological, and archeological records. Following Mary Leakey's discovery of "Zinj," a robust australopithecine, in 1959 (and the subsequent dating of its find site at 1.75 m.y.a. by the K/Ar method), numerous other areas in East Africa have been surveyed and several intensively explored. We will briefly review the geological and chronological background of these important sites beginning with the earliest.

Earliest Traces

For the period preceding 4 million years ago only very fragmentary remains possibly attributable to the Hominidae have been found. The earliest of these fossils comes from the Lake Baringo region of central Kenya and the Lake Turkana Basin of northernmost Kenya.

In the Lake Baringo region possible hominid fossils have been found within the following geological areas:

1. Ngorora Formation (age approximately 10 m.y.–11 m.y.)—one partial upper molar. Not much can be said about this tooth, except that it is "hominoid-like."
2. Lukeino Formation (age approximately 5.4 m.y.–7 m.y.)—one lower molar. While some authorities believe this tooth has "distinct hominid resemblances" (Howell, 1978), detailed metrical analysis indicates this tooth is clearly primitive as a hominoid and not derived as a hominid (Corruccini and McHenry, 1980).

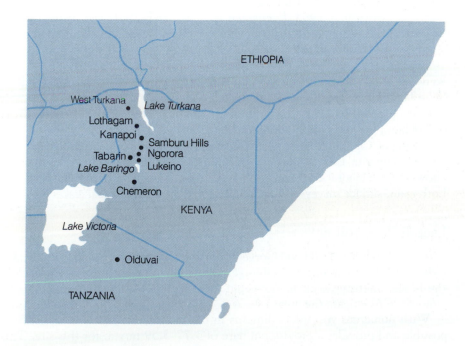

Figure 12-2
Early hominid localities in East Africa: The Baringo and Turkana Basins.

3. Chemeron Formation (age approximately 4 m.y.), but perhaps as late as 1.5 m.y.a.—one isolated temporal bone from the side of a skull (see Appendix A). While not yet completely described, this bone appears quite hominidlike and has been provisionally referred to genus *Australopithecus* (Howell, 1978).

4. Tabarin (4–5? m.y.)—a newly discovered site west of Lake Baringo, where a partial hominid lower jaw was found in February 1984. The find—a small fragment containing two molar teeth—has not yet been described, and the dating for the site also is still quite provisional.

Abundant fossil-bearing beds spanning the period 10–4 m.y.a. are now known in the Lake Baringo area. Further explorations in this region may well contribute to filling that currently vexing gap in hominoid prehistory between 7 m.y.a. and 4 m.y.a.

Samburu Hills   To the north and west of Lake Baringo, some other early and potentially highly productive fossil-bearing beds have recently been explored. In the Samburu Hills of north-central Kenya, a team led by Hidemi Ishida of Osaka University discovered a partial hominoid jaw in August 1982. Consisting of the left half of an upper jaw with five teeth in place, this find has been *very* provisionally estimated as 8 million years old. Detailed descriptions are not yet available, but are eagerly awaited by paleoanthropologists.

Lothagam (Loth'-a-gum)   Located on the southwest side of Lake Turkana in northern Kenya, this site was first explored by a Harvard University team in the middle 1960s. No radiometric dates exist for this site, but faunal correlation suggests a date of around 5.5 m.y.a. While surveying the area in 1967, the Harvard team found one hominoid fossil, the back portion of a mandible with one molar in place. Although this specimen is too fragmentary for any firm decision to be based on it, it is certainly a hominoid and *may* be an early primitive hominid (White, 1986). Caution must be used in making phylogenetic judgments for any of these fragmentary late Miocene discoveries. As we go back ever closer to the hominid—African pongid divergence (see pp. 295–296), the distinguishing characteristics become more difficult to nail down—especially when dental remains are all that we have.

Kanapoi (Kan'-a-poy)   Located close to Lothagam on the southwest side of Lake Turkana, Kanapoi was also surveyed by members of the Harvard University research project. In 1965, they found one hominid bone at this site, the lower end of an upper arm bone, or humerus.

Dating of Kanapoi, also by means of faunal correlation, gives a date of approximately 4 m.y.a. Like Lothagam, the hominid material is too fragmentary to allow much elaboration, except to note that it appears hominid. Also like Lothagam, surface surveys at Kanapoi revealed no archeological traces.

Laetoli (Lye'-toll-ee)

Thirty miles south of Olduvai Gorge in northern Tanzania lie beds considerably older than those exposed at the Gorge. While Laetoli was first surveyed back in the 1930s, intensive work did not begin there until 1974, when Mary Leakey decided to reinvestigate the area.

With numerous volcanic sediments in the vicinity, accurate K/Ar testing is possible and provides a provisional date of 3.77–3.59 m.y.a. for this site. This date must still be considered provisional, since it has been calibrated by only one type of dating technique (K/Ar) and only on one kind of mineral (mica) (Curtis, 1981). As we will see shortly, it is crucial to corroborate dates through use of several different techniques in order to have confidence in the results.

Since systematic fossil recovery began at Laetoli in 1974, twenty-four fossil hominid specimens have been found, consisting almost exclusively of jaws and teeth with fragmentary postcranial remains of one immature individual (Johanson and White, 1979; White, 1980).

In February, 1978 Mary Leakey announced a remarkable discovery at Laetoli: fossilized footprints embossed into an ancient volcanic tuff more than 3.5 m.y.a.! Literally thousands of footprints have been found at this remarkable site, representing more than twenty different taxa (Pliocene elephants, horses, pigs, giraffes, antelopes, hyenas, and an abundance of hares). Several hominid footprints have also been found, including a trail more than 75 feet long, made by at least two—and perhaps three—individuals (Leakey and Hay, 1979) (See Fig. 12-3.)

Figure 12-3
Laetoli hominid footprint trail, northern Tanzania. The trail on the left was made by one individual; the one on the right seems to have been formed by two individuals, the second stepping in the footprints of the first.

Such discoveries of well-preserved hominid footprints are extremely important to furthering our understanding of human evolution. For the first time we can make *definite* statements regarding locomotory pattern and stature of early hominids. Initial analysis of these Pliocene footprints compared to modern humans suggests a stature of about 4 feet, 9 inches for the larger individual and 4 feet, 1 inch for the smaller individual, who made the trail seen in Figure 12-3 (White, 1980). Studies of these impression patterns clearly show that the mode of locomotion of these hominids was fully bipedal, and, further, *very* similar to modern humans (Day and Wickens, 1980). As we will discuss shortly (p. 359), the development of bipedal locomotion is *the* most important defining characteristic of early hominid evolution. Some researchers, however, have concluded that these early hominids were not bipedal in quite the same way that modern humans are (see p. 364). From detailed comparisons with modern humans, estimates of step length, cadence, and speed of walking have been ascertained, indicating that the Laetoli hominids moved in a "strolling" fashion with a rather short stride (Chateris et al., 1981).

Hadar (Ha-dar') (Afar Triangle)

Potentially one of the most exciting areas for future research in East Africa is the Afar Triangle of northeastern Ethiopia, where the Red Sea, Rift Valley, and Gulf of Aden all intersect. A joint American-French team led by Don Johanson and the French geologist Maurice Taieb began intensive field work in this area in 1973. Concentrating on a 42 km² area in the central Afar called the Hadar, paleoanthropologists have found remarkably well-preserved geological beds 400–460 feet thick. Initial K/Ar dating has suggested an age of up to 3.6 m.y.a. for the older hominid fossils and 2.5 m.y.a. for the upper artifactual-bearing beds (Johanson and Edey, 1981). These dates, too, must be considered provisional until systematically corroborated by other laboratories and other dating techniques (Curtis, 1981).

Some of the chronology at the Hadar appears clearcut. For example, there is general agreement that the Lucy skeleton (see below) is about 3 million years old. Analysis of the older beds, however, has led to some ambiguity regarding their precise dating. Study of one of the volcanic tuffs at Hadar has suggested a correlation (i.e., the result of the same volcanic eruption) with well-defined tuffs at Omo in southern Ethiopia and East Lake Turkana in northern Kenya (see below for discussion of these areas). On the basis of this chemical fingerprinting of tuffs (Brown, 1982), the paleomagnetic data, and biostratigraphic interpretations (Boaz et al., 1982), some researchers have concluded the 3.6 m.y. date for the earlier beds at Hadar is too old; accordingly, they suggest a basal date for the hominid-bearing levels of around 3.2–3.3 m.y.a.

However, opinion still varies. The proposed correlation of the volcanic tuffs across northeastern Africa is not accepted by all researchers (e.g., Aronson et al., 1983). Moreover, the biostratigraphy is also subject to differing interpretations (White, 1983).

A 300,000 to 400,000 year discrepancy may not seem all that important, but it is a most significant time period (10% of the total *known* time range of hominids). To form a consistent theory of exactly what was going on in the Plio-Pleistocene, we need precise chronological controls.

The chronologies, however, often take years of study to sort out. Most crucially, cross-correlations between different dating techniques (K/Ar, biostratigraphy, paleomagnetism, fission-track) must be determined. As we will see presently, it took several years of this kind of cross-checking to establish the chronology of the important hominid locality of East Lake Turkana in northern Kenya.

Due to the excellent preservation conditions in the once-lakeside environment at Hadar, an extraordinary collection of fossilized bones has been discovered—6,000 specimens in the first two field seasons alone! Among the fossil remains, at least thirty-six hominid individuals (up to a maximum of as many as sixty-five) have been discovered (Johanson and Taieb, 1980).

Two extraordinary discoveries at Hadar are most noteworthy. In 1974, a partial skeleton called "Lucy" was found eroding out of a hillside. This fossil is scientifically designated as Afar Locality (AL) 288-1, but is usually just called Lucy (after a popular Beatles' song, "Lucy in the Sky with Diamonds"). Representing almost 40% of a skeleton, this is one of the two most complete individuals from anywhere in the world for the entire period before about 100,000 years ago. *

The second find, a phenomenal discovery, came to light in 1975 at AL 333. Johanson and his amazed crew found dozens of hominid bones scattered along a hillside. These bones represented at least thirteen individuals including four infants. Possibly members of one social unit, this group has been argued to have all died at the same time, perhaps during a flash flood. However, the precise deposition of the site has not been completely explained, so this assertion must be viewed as quite tentative. (In geological time, an "instant" could represent many decades or centuries). Considerable cultural material has been found in the Hadar area—mostly washed into stream channels, but some stone tools recently have been reported in context at a ?2.5 m.y.a. site, potentially making it the oldest cultural evidence yet found. Most unfortunately, political unrest and sporadic warfare in Ethiopia forced a halt to further investigations at the Hadar in 1977. As the situation settled somewhat, hopes for further fieldwork were rekindled. In fact, initial survey work in the Afar Triangle (Middle Awash Valley) in 1981 un-

*The other is a newly discovered *H. erectus* skeleton from west of Lake Turkana, Kenya (see p. 422).

Figure 12-4
Hadar deposits, northeastern Ethiopia.

covered fragments of a hominid femur and cranium (dated provisionally, 3.5–4.0 m.y.a.) (Clark et al., 1984). Plans were thus made for full-scale investigations in 1982, but Ethiopian authorities initiated a temporary moratorium on research that, for the moment, has stalled all efforts. As a result, the key researchers (Don Johanson and Tim White) are concentrating their current efforts at Olduvai (from where Mary Leakey has retired).

Omo (Oh'-moh)

The thickest and most continuous Plio-Pleistocene sequence in East Africa comes from the Omo River basin in southern Ethiopia just north of Lake Turkana. This site was also worked jointly by French and American scientists with F. Clark Howell of the University of California, Berkeley, leading the American team.

Total deposits at the Omo are more than one-half mile thick, and the area surveyed extends over more than 200 km². These exceedingly thick sediments are composed largely of lake and river deposits, but more than 100 volcanic ash deposits have also been recognized. These ash deposits provide an excellent basis for accurate K/Ar determinations. This dating technique, supported by paleomagnetic and biostratigraphic results, has placed the hominid-bearing levels at the Omo between 2.9 and 1.0 m.y.a.

A fantastically rich paleontological sample, more than 40,000 mammal specimens alone, has been collected at the Omo. This site, with its well-documented chronology and huge paleontological series, has become the basis for extrapolation to other East African and some South African sites.

Several cultural remains have come to light in the Omo area dating from around 2 m.y.a. Most of this cultural material consists of fragments of flakes struck from stone pebbles and chunks. Only one primary site, where archeological traces retain their original context, has been excavated, and it has revealed a large quantity of these rather crude-looking flakes. What hominids were doing at this location 2 m.y.a. is still somewhat of a mystery. Apparently, it was not a multi-purpose area like those at Olduvai, since no animal bones were found with the tools.

Hominid discoveries at the Omo come from 87 different localities and include more than 200 teeth, 9 lower jaws, 4 partial or fragmentary skulls, and a complete ulna (a lower-arm bone).

East Lake Turkana (Tur-can'-ah)

Richard Leakey, the second oldest son of Louis and Mary Leakey, has greatly benefited from the fossil-hunting training given him by his parents. In fact, in the huge, remote, arid area encompassing more than 400 square miles on the eastern side of Lake Turkana,* he and his field crew have found more than twice as many hominid remains since 1968 as his parents found at Olduvai in more than forty years of searching!

Geologically, the situation at East Lake Turkana is exceedingly complex, with deep sections of lake and river deposits crisscrossed by the effects of **tectonic**

Figure 12-5
"Lucy," a partial hominid skeleton. Discovered at the Hadar in 1974.

*Lake Turkana was formerly called Lake Rudolf, and the naming of specimens reflects the earlier name: KNM-ER 406 = Kenya National Museum—East Rudolf specimen #406.

Discovery of the Hadar "Family," November to December, 1975

On November 1, I set out for the new area with photographer David Brill and a visiting scientist, Dr. Becky Sigmon.

Climbing into my Land Rover, David asked, "When do we find our next hominid?"

"Today," I replied.

In less than an hour, anthropology student John Kolar spotted an arm-bone fragment. From some distance away, Mike Bush, a medical student, shouted that he had found something just breaking the ground surface. It was the very first day on survey for Mike.

"Hominid teeth?" he asked, when we ran to him. There was no doubt.

We called that spot Afar Locality 333 and scheduled full excavation for the next day.

Morning found me at 333, lying on my side so that I could wield a dental pick to excavate the upper-jaw fragment Mike had found. Michèle Cavillon of our motion-picture crew called to me to look at some bones higher up the hill.

Two bone fragments lay side by side—one a partial femur and the other a fragmentary heel bone. Both were hominid.

Carefully, we started scouring the hillside. Two more leg bones—fibulae—showed up, but each from the same side. The same side? That could only indicate two individuals.

Then from high on the slope came a cry, "Look at the proximal femur—it's complete!" Turning I saw, outlined against the blue sky, the top end of a thigh bone. Even from a distance I could tell that it was not Lucy-size; it was much larger. Slowly I groped up the hillside and held the femur.

Mike wanted to come look but was distracted by finding two fragments composing a nearly complete lower jaw. The entire hillside was dotted with the bones of what were evidently at least two individuals.

We held a strategy meeting. Maurice established that the bones we found on the surface had originally been buried several yards up the slope. Mike chose a crew of seven workers to survey carefully every inch of the area and collect all bone material, sifting even the loose soil.

Time was of the essence. Rainstorms during the months of our absence could wash away fragments that would be lost forever down the ravines. I felt I was moving through a dream: Each day produced more remains.

The picture became tangled. Another upper jaw of an adult came to light. The wear pattern on the lower jaw we'd found did not match either of the uppers. At least three individuals had to be represented. More mandible fragments appeared that could not be definitely fitted to either upper jaw. Extraordinary! We had evidence of perhaps as many as five adults of the genus *Homo*.[*]

Apart from teeth and jaws, we recovered scores of hand and foot bones, leg bones, vertebrae, ribs, even a partial adult skull. A baby tooth turned up, suggesting the presence of a sixth hominid at the site. Then a nearly complete lower jaw of a baby appeared, as well as an almost intact palate with baby teeth. Not heavily worn, the teeth suggested that their possessor was only about 3 years old.

So we had evidence of young adults, old adults, and children—an entire assemblage of early hominids. All of them at one place. Nothing like this had ever been found!

SOURCE:

"Ethiopia Yields First 'Family' of Early Man" by Donald C. Johanson, *National Geographic Magazine*, Vol. 150, pp. 790–811, December 1976. Reprinted with permission of the publisher.

[*]Johanson and his colleagues later assigned all this material to *Australopithecus afarensis* (see p. 362).

movements, stream action, and volcanic activity. While the latter is useful in providing material for radiometric dating, the geological complexities have made the precise chronology of the area a matter of dispute.

The latter sediments have been securely dated at 1.3–1.6 m.y.a., and consensus on this part of the chronology has existed for several years. However, there has been considerable dispute regarding the earlier levels, particularly a key volcanic bed called the KBS **tuff**.

Initially, conventional K/Ar was attempted, but frequent contamination of samples made results unreliable. Thus, a modification of this procedure* was performed, giving estimates of about 2.6 m.y.a. Later, on the basis of fission-track results and paleomagnetic interpretations, this date was moved down to 2.4 m.y.a.

Since, as we pointed out in Chapter 11, there are built-in errors in each of these different dating techniques, several methods must be used for cross-checking. Analysis of the faunal components at Turkana associated with the KBS tuff did not correlate with the 2.4 m.y. age when compared to fossil materials from the Omo and Olduvai, but, in fact, suggested a date 600,000 years later. Further radiometric tests (using conventional K/Ar) corroborated these findings, and yet further analyses confirmed them: The lower hominid-bearing levels at Turkana are around 1.8 m.y. old.

Once again, then, as in our example of the dating at Hadar (see p. 346), the cross-correlation of different techniques is crucial to establishing a firm chronology for these ancient fossil sites. The sampling, testing, evaluation, comparison, and reconsideration of the Turkana dating materials took more than ten years before general agreement was reached.

As noted, numerous hominids have been discovered at East Lake Turkana in the last decade. The current total exceeds 150 hominid specimens, probably representing at least 100 individuals, and this fine sample includes several complete skulls, many jaws, and an assortment of post-cranial bones.

Next to Olduvai, Turkana has yielded the most cultural information concerning the behavior of early hominids. More than twenty archeological sites have been discovered, and excavation or testing has been done at ten localities. Two sites are of particular interest and are both directly associated with the KBS tuff

*This technique is called the $^{40}Ar/^{39}Ar$ stepheating method and measures the steady decay of the ^{39}Ar isotope to that of ^{40}Ar.

Table 12-1 *Summary of East African Hominid Discoveries*

Site Name	Location	Age (m.y.a.)	Hominids
Olduvai	N. Tanzania	1.85–1	49 specimens; australopithecines; early *Homo*
Turkana	N. Kenya (eastern side of Lake Turkana)	1.9–1.3	More than 150 specimens; many australopithecines; several early *Homo*
	West side of Lake Turkana	2.5–1.6	1 cranium (australopithecine) 1 nearly complete skeleton (*Homo erectus*)
Omo	S. Ethiopia	2.9–1	215 specimens; several dozen individuals? australopithecines; some early *Homo*
Hadar	N.E. Ethiopia	?3.7–2.6	Minimum of 36 individuals (maximum of 65); early australopithecine (*A. afarensis*)
Laetoli	N. Tanzania	3.77–3.59	24 hominids; early australopithecine (*A. afarensis*)
Kanapoi	N. Kenya (S.W. Lake Turkana	4	1 hominid = australopithecine??
Lothagam	N. Kenya (S.W. Lake Turkana)	5.5	1 hominid = ?

(age, therefore, 1.8 m.y.a.). One is apparently a multi-purpose area, whereas the other is the butchering site of an extinct form of hippopotamus. The stone tools from these earlier sediments at Turkana are in many ways reminiscent of the Oldowan industry in Bed I at Olduvai (with which they are contemporaneous).

West Lake Turkana

Across the lake from the fossil beds discussed above are other deposits that recently have yielded new and very exciting discoveries. In 1984, on the west side of Lake Turkana, a nearly complete skeleton of a 1.6 m.y. *Homo erectus* child was found (see p. 422), and the following year a well-preserved skull, 2.5 m.y. old, was also found. This latter discovery is a most enigmatic fossil that has, to say the least, produced considerable re-evaluation of early hominid evolution (see p. 369).

Olduvai Gorge

The reader should by now be well acquainted with this remarkable site in northern Tanzania, particularly with its clear geological and chronological contributions. Hominid discoveries from Olduvai now total 48 individuals ranging in time from 1.85 m.y.a. to Upper Pleistocene times less than 50,000 years ago.

Hominid Origins

"In each great region of the world the living mammals are closely related to the extinct species of the same region. It is, therefore, probable that Africa was formerly inhabited by extinct apes closely allied to the gorilla and chimpanzee, and as these two species are now man's nearest allies, it is somewhat more probable that our early progenitors lived on the African continent than elsewhere."

S O U R C E :

Charles Darwin. *The Descent of Man,* 1871.

ENDOCAST
An endocast is a solid (in this case, rock) impression of the inside of the skull showing the size, shape, and some details of the surface of the brain.

South Africa: Earliest Discoveries

The first quarter of this century saw the discipline of paleoanthropology in its scientific infancy. Informed opinion considered the likely origins of the human family to be in Asia, where fossil forms of a primitive kind of *Homo* had been found in Indonesia in the 1890s. Europe was also considered a center of hominid evolutionary action, for spectacular discoveries there of early populations of *Homo sapiens* (including the famous Neandertals) and millions of stone tools had come to light, particularly in the early decades of this century.

Few knowledgeable scholars would have given much credence to Darwin's prediction (see Box 12-1) that the most likely place to find early relatives of humans would be on the continent of Africa. It was in such an atmosphere of preconceived biases that the discoveries of a young Australian-born anatomist were to jolt the foundations of the scientific community in the 1920s. **Raymond Dart** arrived in South Africa in 1923 at the age of 30 to take up a teaching position in anatomy at the University of Witwatersrand in Johannesburg. Fresh from his evolution-oriented training in England under some of the leading scholars of the day (especially, Sir Grafton Elliot Smith), Dart had developed a keen interest in human evolution. Consequently, he was well prepared when startling new evidence began to appear at his very doorstep.

The first clue came in 1924 when one of Dart's students saw an interesting baboon skull on the mantelpiece while having dinner at the home of the director of the Northern Lime Company, a commercial quarrying firm. The skull, that of a large baboon, had come from a place called Taung about 200 miles southwest of Johannesburg. When Dart saw the skull, he quickly recognized it as an extinct form and asked that any other interesting fossil material found be sent to him for his inspection.

Soon thereafter he received two boxloads of fossils and immediately recognized something that was quite unusual, a natural **endocast** of the inside of the braincase of a higher primate, but certainly no baboon. The endocast fit into another limestone block containing the fossilized front portion of skull, face, and lower jaw. However, these were difficult to see clearly, for the bone was hardened into a cemented limestone matrix called *breccia.* Dart patiently chiseled away for weeks, later describing the task: "No diamond cutter ever worked more lovingly or with such care on a priceless jewel—nor, I am sure, with such inadequate

Figure 12-7
Dr. Raymond Dart working in his laboratory.

Raymond Dart and the Discovery of the Taung Child, November, 1924

On his return Young told me that at Taungs he had met an old miner, Mr. M. de Bruyn, who for many years had taken a keen interest in preserving fossils. Only the previous week he had brought quite a number of stone blocks containing bone fragments to Mr. Spiers' office. When Young mentioned my interest to Mr. Spiers, Spiers gave instructions for them to be boxed and railed to me.

I waited anxiously for their arrival, reasoning that if fossilized baboon skulls were such a common feature at Taungs many other, more interesting specimens might be found there. Of course, the packages turned up at the most inappropriate time.

I was standing by the window of my dressing room cursing softly while struggling into an unaccustomed stiff-winged collar when I noticed two men wearing the uniform of the South African Railways staggering along the driveway of our home in Johannesburg with two large wooden boxes.

My Virginia-born wife Dora, who was also donning her most formal outfit, had noticed the men with the boxes and rushed in to me in something of a panic.

"I suppose those are the fossils you've been expecting," she said. "Why on earth did they have to arrive today of all days?" She fixed me with a business-like eye. "Now Raymond," she pleaded, "the guests will start arriving shortly and you can't go delving in all that rubble until the wedding's over and everybody has left. I know how important the fossils are to you, but please leave them until tomorrow."

At the time, however, this seemed of little importance when I considered the exciting anthropological bits and pieces that the boxes from Taungs might contain. As soon as my wife had left to complete her dressing I tore the hated collar off and dashed out to take delivery of the boxes which meanwhile obstructed the entrance to the *stoep*. I was too excited to wait until my African servants carried them to the garage, and ordered them to leave the crates under the pergola while I went in search of some tools to open them.

(Later on that momentous day, my wife told me that she had twice remonstrated with me but had been ignored. I had no recollection of any interruptions.)

I wrenched the lid off the first box and my reaction was one of extreme disappointment. In the rocks I could make out traces of fossilized eggshells and turtle shells and a few fragmentary pieces of isolated bone, none of which looked to be of much interest.

Impatiently I wrestled with the lid of the second box, still hopeful but half-expecting it to be a replica of its mate. At most I anticipated baboon skulls, little guessing that from this crate was to emerge a face that would look out on the world after an age-long sleep of nearly a million years.

As soon as I removed the lid a thrill of excitement shot through me. On the very top of the rock heap was what was undoubtedly an endocranial cast or mold of the interior of the skull. Had it been only the fossilized brain cast of any species of ape it would have ranked as a great discovery, for such a thing had never before been reported. But I knew at a glance that what lay in my hands was no ordinary anthropoidal brain. Here in lime-consolidated sand was the replica of a brain three times as large as that of a baboon and considerably bigger than that of any adult chimpanzee. The startling image of the convolutions and furrows of the brain and the blood vessels of the skull was plainly visible.

I stood in the shade holding the brain as greedily as any miser hugs his gold, my mind racing ahead. Here, I was certain, was one of the most significant finds ever made in the history of anthropology.

SOURCE:

Adventures with the Missing Link by Raymond Dart, 1959. Reprinted with permission of the author.

tools. But on the seventy-third day, December 23, the rock parted. I could view the face from the front, although the right side was still imbedded. . . . What emerged was a baby's face, an infant with a full set of milk teeth and its permanent molars just in the process of erupting. I doubt if there was any parent prouder of his offspring than I was of my Taung baby on that Christmas" (Dart, 1959, p. 10).

(a)

(b)

Figure 12-8
(a) *The Taung child discovered in 1924. The endocast is in back with the fossilized bone mandible and face in front; (b) Taung. Location of the initial australopithecine discovery.*

As indicated by the formation and eruption of teeth, the Taung child was probably about 3 to 4 years of age at death. Interestingly, the rate of development of this and many other Plio-Pleistocene hominids, was more like that of apes rather than modern *Homo* (Shipman, 1987; Bromage and Dean, 1985). Dart's initial impression that this form was a hominoid was confirmed when he could observe the face and teeth more clearly. However, as it turned out, it took considerably more effort before the teeth could be seen completely, since Dart worked four years just to separate the upper and lower jaws.

But Dart was convinced long before he had an unimpeded view of the dentition that this discovery was a remarkable one, an early hominoid from South Africa. The question was, what kind of hominoid? Dart realized it was extremely improbable that this specimen could have been a forest ape, for South Africa has had a relatively dry climate for many millions of years. Even though the climate at Taung was not as arid as was previously believed (Butzer, 1974), it was an unlikely place to find an ape!

If not an ape, then, what was it? Features of the skull and teeth of this small child held clues that Dart seized upon almost immediately. The entrance of the spinal column into the brain (the *foramen magnum* at the base of the skull) was further forward in the Taung child than in modern great apes, though not as much as in modern humans. From this fact Dart concluded that the head was balanced *above* the spine, indicating erect posture. In addition, the slant of the forehead was not as receding as in apes, the milk canines were exceedingly small, and the newly erupted first molars were large, broad teeth. In all these respects, the Taung fossil looked more like a hominid than a pongid. There was, however, a disturbing feature that was to confuse and befuddle many scientists for several years: the brain was quite small. Recent studies have estimated the Taung's child brain size at approximately 405 cc. (cubic centimeters), which translates to a fully adult size of only 440 cc., not very large when compared to modern great apes, as the following tabulation (Tobias, 1971; 1983) shows:

	Range	Mean
Chimpanzee	282–500 cc.	394 cm³
Gorilla	340–752 cc.	506 cm³
Orang	276–540 cc.	411 cm³

As the tabulation indicates, the estimated cranial capacity for the Taung fossil falls within the range of all the modern great apes, and gorillas actually *average* about 10% greater. It must, however, be remembered that gorillas are very large animals, whereas the Taung child represents a population whose average adult size may have been less than sixty pounds. Since brain size is partially correlated with body size, comparing such differently sized animals cannot be justified. A more meaningful contrast would be with the pygmy chimpanzee (*Pan paniscus*), whose body weight is more comparable. Pygmy chimps have adult cranial capacities averaging 356 cm³ for males and 329 for females, and thus the Taung child versus a *comparably sized* pongid displays a 25% increase in cranial capacity.

Despite the relatively small size of the brain, Dart saw that it was no pongid. Details preserved on the endocast seemed to indicate that the association areas of the parietal lobes were relatively larger than in any known pongid. However, recent reexamination of the Taung specimen has shown that the sulcal (folding) pattern is actually quite pongidlike (Falk, 1980; 1983).

We must emphasize that attempts to discern the precise position of the "bumps and folds" in ancient endocasts is no easy feat. The science of "paleoneurology" is thus often marked by sharp differences of opinion. Consequently, it is not surprising that the other leading researcher in this field, Ralph Halloway (1981), disagrees with the conclusion by Falk (just cited) and suggests, alternatively, that the Taung endocast has a more hominidlike sulcal pattern.

Realizing the immense importance of his findings, Dart promptly reported them in the British scientific weekly *Nature* on February 7, 1925. A bold venture, since Dart, only 32, was presumptuously proposing a whole new view of human evolution! The small-brained Taung child was christened by Dart **Australopithecus africanus** (southern ape of Africa), which he saw as a kind of halfway "missing-link" between modern apes and humans. The concept of a single "missing link" between modern apes and humans was a fallacious one, but Dart correctly emphasized the hominidlike features of the fossil.

A storm of both popular and scholarly protest greeted Dart's article, for it ran directly counter to prevailing opinion. Despite the numerous hominid fossils already discovered, widespread popular skepticism of evolution still prevailed. The year 1925 was, after all, the year of the Scopes "monkey trial" in Tennessee. The biggest fly in the ointment to the leading human evolutionists of the day—Arthur Keith and Grafton Elliot Smith—was the small size of the brain compared to the relatively large proportions of the face and jaws. At that time, anthropologists generally assumed that the primary functional adaptation distinguishing the human family was an immense increase in brain size, and that dental and locomotory modifications came later. This view was seemingly confirmed by the Piltdown discovery in 1911, which displayed the combination of a large brain (estimated at 1400 cm^3, well within the range of modern man) with an ape-like jaw (see pp. 340–341). Keith even went so far as to postulate a "Cerebral Rubicon" of 750 cm^3 below which—by definition—no hominid could fall. Most scientists in the 1920s thus regarded this little Taung child as an interesting aberrant form of ape.

AUSTRALOPITHECUS
(Os-tral-oh-pith'-e-kus)

AFRICANUS
(af-ra-kan'-us)

Figure 12-9
Pygmy chimpanzee. A modern pongid probably similar in body size to many of the australopithecines.

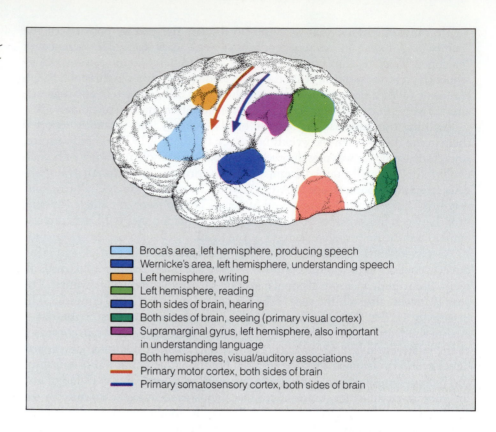

Broca's area, left hemisphere, producing speech
Wernicke's area, left hemisphere, understanding speech
Left hemisphere, writing
Left hemisphere, reading
Both sides of brain, hearing
Both sides of brain, seeing (primary visual cortex)
Supramarginal gyrus, left hemisphere, also important
in understanding language
Both hemispheres, visual/auditory associations
Primary motor cortex, both sides of brain
Primary somatosensory cortex, both sides of brain

AUSTRALOPITHECINE
(os-tral-oh-pith′-e-seen)

Hence, Dart's theories were received with indifference, disbelief, and scorn, often extremely caustic. Dart realized more complete remains were needed. The skeptical world would not accept the evidence of one fragmentary, immature individual no matter how highly suggestive the clues. Clearly, more fossil evidence was required, particularly more complete crania of adults. Not an experienced fossil hunter himself, Dart sought further assistance in the search for more **australopithecines** (the colloquial name referring to the members of genus *Australopithecus*). The designation "*Australopithecus*" will be used repeatedly throughout this chapter to refer to a variety of different species. However, in all contexts we will use it to denote a hominid that is bipedal, small-brained, and large-tooth. In this sense, we use it similarly to Dart's original description and interpretation.

Figure 12-11
Dr. Robert Broom. Shown with one of his paleontological discoveries from South Africa. This photo was taken earlier in Dr. Broom's career; it would be almost thirty years later before he would even begin his search for australopithecines.

South African Hominids Aplenty

Soon after publication of his controversial theories, Dart found a strong ally in **Dr. Robert Broom**. A Scottish physician and part-time paleontologist, Broom's credentials as a fossil hunter had been established earlier with his highly successful paleontological work on early mammallike reptiles in South Africa.

Although interested, Broom was unable to participate actively in the search for additional australopithecines because of prior commitments and did not seriously undertake explorations until 1936. However, soon thereafter he met with incredible success. From two of Dart's students, Broom learned of another commercial limeworks site, called **Sterkfontein**, not far from Johannesburg. Here, as

Dr. Broom and the Discovery of the Kromdraai Ape-Man

On the forenoon of Wednesday, June 8, 1938, when I met Barlow, he said, "I've something nice for you this morning"; and he held out part of a fine palate with the first molar-tooth in position. I said, "Yes, it's quite nice. I'll give you a couple of pounds for it." He was delighted; so I wrote out a cheque, and put the specimen in my pocket. He did not seem quite willing to say where or how he had obtained it; and I did not press the matter. The specimen clearly belonged to a large ape-man, and was apparently different from the Sterkfontein being.

I was again at Sterkfontein on Saturday, when I knew Barlow would be away. I showed the specimen to the native boys in the quarry; but none of them had ever seen it before. I felt sure it had not come from the quarry, as the matrix was different. On Tuesday forenoon I was again at Sterkfontein, when I insisted on Barlow telling me how he had got the specimen. I pointed out that two teeth had been freshly broken off, and that they might be lying where the specimen had been obtained. He apologized for having misled me; and told me it was a school-boy, Gert Terblanche, who acted as a guide in the caves on Sundays, who had picked it up and given it to him. I found where Gert lived, about two miles away; but Barlow said he was sure to be away at school. Still, I set out for his home. There I met Gert's mother and sister. They told me that the place where the specimen was picked up was near the top of a hill about half a mile away, and the sister agreed to take me up to the place. She and her mother also told me that Gert had four beautiful teeth at school with him.

The sister took us up the hill, and I picked up some fragments of the skull, and a couple of teeth; but she said she was sure Gert had some other nice pieces hidden away. Of course, I had to go to school to hunt up Gert.

The road to the school was a very bad one, and we had to leave the car, and walk about a mile over rough ground. When we got there, it was about half-past twelve, and it was play time. I found the headmaster, and told him that I wanted to see Gert Terblanche in connection with some teeth he had picked up. Gert was soon found, and drew from the pocket of his trousers four of the most wonderful teeth ever seen in the world's history. These I promptly purchased from Gert, and transferred to my pocket. I had the palate with me, and I found that two of the teeth were the second pre-molar and second molar, and that they fitted on to the palate. The two others were teeth of the other side. Gert told me about the piece he had hidden away. As the school did not break up till two o'clock, I suggested to the principal that I should give a lecture to the teachers and children about caves, how they were formed, and how bones got into them. He was delighted. So it was arranged; and I lectured to four teachers and about 120 children for over an hour, with blackboard illustrations, till it was nearly two o'clock. When I finished, the principal broke up the school, and Gert came home with me. He took us up to the hill, and brought out from his hiding place a beautiful lower jaw with two teeth in position. All the fragments that I could find at the spot I picked up.

SOURCE:

Finding the Missing Link by Robert Broom (2nd Ed.), 1951. By permission of C. A. Watts/Pitman Publishing Ltd., London.

---

at Taung, the quarrying involved blasting out large sections with dynamite, leaving piles of debris that often contained fossilized remains. Accordingly, Broom asked the quarry manager to keep his eyes open for fossils, and when Broom returned to the site in August 1936, the manager asked, "Is this what you are looking for?" Indeed, it was, for Broom held in his hand the endocast of an adult australopithecine—exactly what he had set out to find! Looking further over the scattered debris, Broom was able to find most of the rest of the skull of the same individual.

Such remarkable success, just a few months after beginning his search, was not the end of Broom's luck, for his magical touch was to continue unabated for several more years. In 1938, he learned from a young schoolboy of another australopithecine site at **Kromdraai** about one mile from Sterkfontein, and, following World War II (1948), he found yet another australopithecine site, **Swartkrans**,

STERKFONTEIN
(Sterk'-fon-tane)

KROMDRAAI
(Kromm'-dry)

SWARTKRANS

Figure 12-12
Australopithecine sites in South Africa.

Figure 12-13
A gracile australopithecine skull from Sterkfontein (Sts. 5). This specimen is the best preserved gracile skull yet found in South Africa. Discovered in 1947.

in the same vicinity. A final australopithecine site, **Makapansgat**, was excavated in 1947 by Raymond Dart, who returned to the fossil-discovering bandwagon after an absence of over twenty years.

Numerous extremely important discoveries came from these five sites, discoveries that would eventually swing the tide of intellectual thought to the views Dart expressed back in 1925. Particularly important was a nearly perfect skull and a nearly complete pelvis, both found at Sterkfontein in 1947. As the number of discoveries accumulated, it became increasingly difficult to simply write them off as aberrant apes.

Although Robert Broom was an absolute wizard at finding fossils, his interpretations of them were clouded by an irresistible urge to give each new discovery a different taxonomic label. Consequently, in addition to Dart's A. *africanus* from Taung, a disconcertingly large number of other names have been used at various times for the South African australopithecines (see Table 12-2). The problem with all this taxonomic splitting was a lack of appreciation for the relevant biological principles underlying such elaborate interpretations (see Chapter 10 for a discussion of the meaning of taxonomic statements).

By 1949, at least thirty individuals were represented from the five South African sites. That year represents an important turning point, since it marks the visit to South Africa and the resulting "conversion" of W. E. Le Gros Clark. As one of the leading human evolutionists of the day, Sir Wilfrid Le Gros Clark's unequivocal support of the australopithecines as small-brained early hominids was to have wide impact. But the tides of wisdom had begun to turn even before this. Writing in 1947, **Sir Arthur Keith** courageously admitted his earlier mistake:

"When Professor Dart of the University of Witwatersrand, Johannesburg, announced in *Nature* the discovery of a juvenile *Australopithecus* and claimed for it human kinship, I was one of those who took the point of view that when the adult was discovered, it would prove to be nearer akin to the living African anthropoids—the gorilla and chimpanzee. . . . I am now convinced of the evidence submitted by Dr. Robert Broom that Professor Dart was right and I was wrong. The Australopithecinae [formal designation of the australopithecines as a subfamily of the hominids] are in or near the line which culminated in the human form" (Keith in Le Gros Clark, 1967, p. 38).

With the exposé of the Piltdown forgery in the early 1950s, the path was completely cleared for the nearly unanimous recognition of the australopithecines as early hominids. With this acceptance also came the necessary recognition that hominid brains had their greatest expansion *after* earlier changes in teeth and

Table 12-2   *Taxonomic Labels Applied to South African Hominids*

	Site	Discovered and Named by
Australopithecus africanus	Taung	Dart
Plesianthropus transvaalensis	Sterkfontein	Broom
Paranthropus robustus	Kromdraai	Broom
Paranthropus crassidens	Swartkrans	Broom
Australopithecus prometheus	Makapansgat	Dart
Telanthropus capensis	Swartkrans	Broom

locomotory systems. In other words, the rates of evolution in one functional system of the body vary from other systems, thus displaying the **mosaic** nature of human **evolution**.

Even today, the evidence from South Africa continues to accumulate. The search continues at Sterkfontein, Swartkrans, and Makapansgat. An important portion of pelvis was found at Swartkrans in 1970, and a partial skull was found at Sterkfontein (west pit) in 1976. Indeed, discoveries are now coming faster than ever. In the last few years alone more than 150 *new* specimens have come to light at Sterkfontein. (See Table 12-3.) A truly remarkable feast of early hominids, the total number of remains from South Africa exceeds 1,500 (counting all teeth as separate items), and the number of individuals is estimated to be close to 190 individuals (Tobias, 1983).

Of all the hominid remains from South Africa, less than 1070 are postcranial (that is, below the head), but this evidence, nevertheless, is crucially significant in revealing the all-important locomotory function of these animals. As of 1972, this extremely informative evidence included twenty-two remains representing the shoulder girdle and upper limb, thirteen from the pelvic girdle and lower limb, and thirty-four from the rib and vertebral areas (Tobias, 1972).

From an evolutionary point of view, the most meaningful remains are those from the australopithecine pelvis, which now includes portions of nine **innominates** (Figs. 12-16, 12-17). Remains of the pelvis are so important because, better than any other area of the body, this structure displays the unique requirements of a bipedal animal, such as modern humans *and* our hominid forebears. (For anatomical comparisons, see Appendix A.)

Hominids on Their Feet

As we discussed in Chapter 7, there is a general tendency in all primates for erect body posture and some bipedalism. However, of all living primates, efficient bipedalism as the primary form of locomotion is seen *only* in hominids. Functionally, the human mode of locomotion is most clearly shown in our striding gait, where weight is alternately placed on a single fully extended hindlimb. This specialized form of locomotion has developed to a point where energy levels are used

MAKAPANSGAT
(Mak-ah-pans'-gat)

MOSAIC EVOLUTION
Rate of evolution in one functional system varies from other systems.

INNOMINATE
The fused half-portion of a pelvis; contains three bones—the ilium, ischium, and pubis.

Figure 12-14
Sir Arthur Keith.

Table 12-3 *Sterkfontein Hominid Specimens, 1936–1984**

	Number in Calendar Year	Cumulative Total
1936–1979	—	145
1979	10	155
1980	5	160
1981	7	167
1982	69	236
1983	44	280
1984 (to 24 August)	164	444

*These are totals for specimens, not individuals. A single individual may be represented by several teeth in a given sample, each tooth of which counts as a different specimen. Data provided courtesy of Professor Phillip Tobias.

Figure 12-15
A partial hominid skull from Sterkfontein (Stw. 53). Discovered during recent excavations (August 1976).

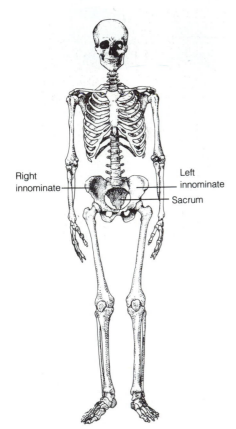

Right innominate

Left innominate

Sacrum

Figure 12-16
The human pelvis. Various elements shown on a modern skeleton.

to near peak efficiency. Such is not the case in nonhuman primates, who move bipedally with hips and knees bent and maintain balance in a clumsy and inefficient manner.

From a survey of our close primate relatives, it is apparent that, while still in the trees, our ancestors were adapted to a fair amount of upper body erectness. Prosimians, monkeys, and apes all spend considerable time sitting erect while feeding, grooming, or sleeping. Presumably, our early ancestors also displayed similar behavior. What caused these forms to come to the ground and embark on the unique way of life that would eventually lead to humans is still a mystery. Perhaps natural selection favored an animal related to *Sivapithecus* coming occasionally to the ground to forage for food on the forest floor and forest fringe. In any case, once it was on the ground and away from the immediate safety offered by trees, bipedal locomotion became a tremendous advantage.

First of all, bipedal locomotion freed the hands for carrying objects and for making and using tools. Such early cultural developments then had an even more positive effect on speeding the development of yet more efficient bipedalism— once again emphasizing the dual role of biocultural evolution. In addition, in the bipedal stance, animals have a wider view of the surrounding countryside, and, in open terrain, early spotting of predators (particularly the large cats, such as lions, leopards, and saber tooths) would be of critical importance. We know that modern ground-living primates, such as the savanna baboon and chimpanzee, will occasionally adopt this posture to "look around" when out in open country. Certainly, bipedal walking is an efficient means of covering long distances, and when large game hunting came into play (several million years after the initial adaptation to ground living), further refinements in the locomotory complex may have been favored. Finally, it has been suggested that bipedalism was initially most adaptive for carrying—particularly food brought by provisioning males to females and young (Lovejoy, 1981). (See pp. 187–188.) Exactly what initiated the process is difficult to say, but all these factors probably played a role in the adaptation of hominids to their special niche through a special form of locomotion.

Our mode of locomotion is indeed extraordinary, involving as it does a unique kind of activity in which "the body, step by step, teeters on the edge of catastrophe" (Napier, 1967, p. 56). The problem is to maintain balance on the "stance" leg while the "swing" leg is off the ground. In fact, during normal walking, both feet are simultaneously on the ground only about 25% of the time, and, as speed of locomotion increases, this figure becomes even smaller.

In order to maintain a stable center of balance in this complex form of locomotion, many drastic structural/functional alterations are demanded in the basic primate quadrupedal pattern. Functionally, the foot must be altered to act as a stable support instead of a grasping limb. When we walk, our foot is used like a prop, landing on the heel and pushing off on the toes, particularly the big toe. In addition, the leg must be elongated to increase the length of the stride and lower the center of gravity. The lower limb must also be remodeled to allow full extension of the knee and to allow the legs to be kept close together during walking, thereby maintaining the center of support directly under the body. Finally, significant changes must occur in the pelvis to permit stable weight transmission from the upper body to the legs and to maintain balance through pelvic rotation and altered proportions and orientations of several key muscles.

The major structural changes that are required for bipedalism are all seen in the australopithecines in East and South Africa. In the pelvis, the blade (ilium—upper bone of the pelvis) is shortened top to bottom, which permits more stable weight support in the erect position by lowering the center of gravity. In addition, the pelvis is bent backwards and downwards, thus altering the position of the muscles that attach along the bone. Most importantly, the gluteus medius (glue-tee'-us meed'-ee-us) now becomes a very large muscle acting to stablize the trunk and keep it from slumping to the unsupported side while the body is supported on one leg. The gluteus maximus (glue-tee'-us max'-a-mus) also becomes important as an extensor—pulls the thigh back—during running, jumping, and climbing. (See Appendix A.)

Other structural changes shown by australopithecine postcranial evidence further confirm the morphological pattern seen in the pelvis. As we just discussed, the remarkable footprints from Laetoli show unequivocally a bipedal adaptation. In addition, the vertebral column, known from beautifully preserved specimens from Sterkfontein, as well as from Lucy, show the same forward curvature as in modern hominids, bringing the center of support forward and allowing rotation of the bottom of the vertebral column (sacrum) below, thereby getting it out of the way of the birth canal. In addition, the lower limb is elongated and is apparently proportionately about as long as in modern man. Fossil evidence of a knee fragment from Sterkfontein and pieces from East Africa also shows that full extension of this joint was possible, thus allowing the leg to be completely straightened, as when a field goal kicker follows through.

Structural evidence for the foot is not abundant in South Africa, but one ankle bone from Kromdraai shows a rather mixed pattern. This particular foot probably belonged to an animal that was a well-adapted biped but still retained considerable climbing ability. More complete evidence for evolutionary changes in the foot skeleton comes from Olduvai Gorge in East Africa, where a nearly

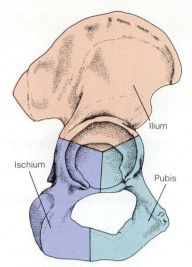

Figure 12-17
The human innominate. Composed of three bones (right side shown).

Figure 12-18
The knee in full extension.

Figure 12-19
Innominates. (a) Homo sapiens; (b) australopithecine (Sts. 14); (c) chimpanzee. Note especially the length and breadth of the iliac blade.

(a)   (b)   (c)

Figure 12-20
*A nearly complete hominid foot (OH 8).
From Olduvai Gorge, East Africa.*

Figure 12-21
*A nearly complete cranium from Swartkrans
(Sk. 48). The best preserved skull of a
robust australopithecine from South Africa.*

complete hominid food is preserved, and from the Hadar in Ethiopia, where numerous foot elements have been recovered. As in the ankle bone from Kromdraai, the East African fossils suggest a well-adapted bipedal gait. The arches are developed and the big toe is pulled in next to the other toes, but some differences in the ankle also imply that considerable flexibility was possible (for climbing?). As we will see below, some researchers have recently concluded that the early forms of australopithecine probably spent considerable time in the trees. Moreover, they may not have been as efficient bipeds as has previously been suggested (see pp. 364–365).

Plio-Pleistocene Hominids

From the time period between 4 and 1 m.y.a., East and South African sites have thus far yielded close to 500 hominid individuals. This huge collection of material (much of it in well-dated contexts) has allowed paleoanthropologists to formulate (and reformulate) their interpretations of human evolution. At present, it appears that at least four groups (which we will refer to as "sets") of hominids are distinguishable in Africa during the Plio-Pleistocene. The first of these sets was distinctly earlier and more primitive, while the others appear somewhat later with at least two lineages surviving beyond 2 m.y.a. and living contemporaneously for 1 million years.

Set I. Early Primitive Australopithecines (A. *afarensis*)

Prior to 4 m.y.a. the fossil hominid (or "hominoid") remains from East Africa (which is all there is anywhere) are extremely scrappy, represented by only two molars, one cranial bone, two fragmentary jaws, and one arm bone (see pp. 343–344). The best that can be said about this material is that it is hominoid, and in some cases, "hominidlike."

It is not until 4–3 m.y.a. that we get the first *definite* collection of hominid fossils. These crucial remains come from two East African sites explored within the last fifteen years: Laetoli in northern Tanzania and Hadar in northeastern Ethiopia. From these two sites together several hundred hominid specimens have been recovered, representing a minimum of 60 individuals and perhaps close to 100. In addition, there are of course those fascinating hominid footprints from Laetoli.

Interpretation of fossil hominids is a laborious and highly technical undertaking. Finding the fossils is only the first step. They then have to be cleaned (often of intractable matrix), measured, described, reconstructed, and then measured again. It is thus not surprising that, although the first hominid specimens were recovered from Hadar and Laetoli in 1973 and 1974 respectively, their taxonomic affinity was not published until 1978 (Johanson et al., 1978); a systematic reappraisal of *all* hominids from the Plio-Pleistocene appeared soon thereafter in early 1979 (Johanson and White, 1979), and comprehensive descriptions were published in April, 1982, in the *American Journal of Physical Anthropology*.

Certainly, the announcement of a new species always raises considerable professional and public interest. The proposal of A. *afarensis* by Johanson and his colleagues was no exception. Predictably, not all the reaction was favorable. In science, this is a healthy attitude; hypotheses *always* need to be scrutinized and tested against further evidence.

What exactly is A. *afarensis*? Without question, it is more primitive than any of the australopithecine material from South Africa or East Africa (discussed subsequently). In fact, A. *afarensis* is the most primitive of any definitely hominid group thus far found anywhere. By "primitive," we mean that A. *afarensis* is less evolved in any particular direction than is seen in later species of *Australopithecus* or *Homo*. That is to say, A. *afarensis* shares more primitive features with other early hominoids (such as *Dryopithecus, Sivapithecus,* etc.) and with living pongids than is true of later hominids, who display more derived characteristics.

For example, the teeth are quite primitive. The canines are often large, pointed teeth that slightly overlap; the first lower premolar is semisectorial, and the tooth rows are parallel or even posteriorly convergent (see Fig. 12-22a).

The pieces of crania that are preserved also display several primitive hominoid characteristics, including a compound sagittal/nuchal crest in the back (see Fig. 12-23), as well as several primitive features of the cranial base (involving the tubular appearance of the external ear canal, as well as an open-appearing articulation for the lower jaw). Cranial capacity estimates for *afarensis* show a mixed pattern when compared to later hominids. A provisional estimate for the one partially complete cranium (see Fig. 12-23b)—apparently a large individual—gives a figure of 500 cm³, but another, even more fragmentary, cranium is apparently quite a bit smaller and has been provisionally estimated at less than 400 cm³ (Holloway, 1983). Thus, for some individuals (males?), *afarensis* is well within the range of other australopithecine species, but others (females?) may be significantly smaller. An overall depiction of cranial size for A. *afarensis* as a species is not possible at this time—this part of the skeleton is unfortunately too poorly represented.

A host of postcranial pieces have been found at Hadar (mostly from the partial skeleton "Lucy," and from individuals at AL 333). Initial impressions suggest that the upper limbs are long relative to the lower ones (also a primitive hominoid condition). In addition, the wrist, hand, and foot bones show several differences from modern humans (Susman *et al.*, 1985). Stature can now be con-

(a)

(b)

Figure 12-22
Jaws of Australopithecus afarensis. (a) Maxilla, AL-200-1a, from Hadar, Ethiopia. (Note the parallel tooth rows and large canines.); (b) mandible, L. H. 4, from Laetoli, Tanzania. This fossil is the type specimen for the new species, Australopithecus afarensis.

Figure 12-23
Comparison of hominoid crania. (a) Chimpanzee; (b) Australopithecus afarensis composite cranium assembled from three individuals—AL 333-45, 200-1a, and 400-1a; (c) human.

fidently estimated: A. *afarensis* was a short hominid. From her partial skeleton, Lucy is figured to be only about 4 feet tall. However, Lucy—as demonstrated by her pelvis—was a female, and at Hadar and Laetoli, there is evidence of larger individuals as well. The most economical hypothesis explaining this variation is that A. *afarensis* was quite sexually dimorphic—the larger individuals are male and the smaller ones such as Lucy are female. Estimates of male stature can be approximated from the larger footprints at Laetoli, inferring a height of about 5 feet.

If we accept this interpretation, A. *afarensis* was a very sexually dimorphic form. In fact, for overall body size, this species may have been as dimorphic as *any* living primate (i.e., as much as gorillas, orangs, or baboons). The elaborate behavioral reconstruction proposed by Lovejoy (1981) (see pp. 187–188), is based upon a *lack* of dimorphism in this species. Lovejoy points particularly to the relatively small degree of canine dimorphism between presumed males and females, but, even here, there are some reasonably good-sized differences apparent. Indeed, in the original description of A. *afarensis* (Johanson et al., 1978), a feature noted to define this form was "strong variation in canine size."

Beyond the claimed lack of canine size dimorphism (which has not been presented as *quantifiable* data compared to known ranges in living primates), there are even more serious problems with the Lovejoy model. In those few nonhuman primates that are monogamous (e.g., marmosets, gibbons) there is clearly little body size dimorphism. Yet, in A. *afarensis*, males may be twice as big as females, and thus rival or even exceed (see below) the amount of dimorphism in the most dimorphic of living primates. Clearly, these highly dimorphic primates are uniformly polygynous, and many less dimorphic species of monkeys also follow mostly polygynous mating strategies.

In conclusion, the evidence presented arguing for sexual dimorphism within A. *afarensis* could hardly be used to infer monogamous mating patterns. Indeed, it could be quite forcefully used to argue against it!

Behavioral debates such as these are certainly stimulating, but what is most interesting about A. *afarensis* is the distinctive physical morphology it displays. In a majority of dental and cranial features A. *afarensis* is clearly more primitive than are later hominids. This should not come as too great a surprise, since *afarensis* is 1 m.y. older than most other East African finds and perhaps .5–.7 m.y. older than the oldest South African hominid. In fact, from the neck up, A. *afarensis* is so primitive, that without any evidence from the limb skeleton, one would be hard-pressed to call it a hominid at all (although the back teeth are large and heavily enameled, unlike pongids). In the teeth particularly, A. *afarensis* is in some ways reminiscent of Miocene hominoids (e.g., *Sivapithecus*) (Greenfield, 1979).

What then makes A. *afarensis* a hominid? The answer is revealed by its manner of locomotion. From the abundant limb bones recovered from Hadar and those beautiful footprints from Laetoli we know unequivocally that *afarensis* walked bipedally when progressing on the ground. Whether Lucy and her contemporaries still spent considerable time in the trees, and just how efficiently they walked, have recently become topics of major dispute.

Locomotion of Australopithecus afarensis   A recent comprehensive analysis of the postcranial anatomy of A. *afarensis* by Jack Stern and Randall Susman of the State University of New York at Stony Brook has challenged the view that this early hominid walked bipedally, much as you or me (Stern and Susman,

1983). Their interpretation is based upon many parts of the skeleton (limbs, hands, feet, pelvis, etc.), which they have compared with other hominids (fossil and modern), as well as with great apes.

Such features as long, curved fingers and toes, long upper limbs but short lower limbs (Jungers, 1982; Susman et al., 1985), the positioning of the hip and knee joints, and pelvic orientation have led these researchers to two conclusions: (1) A. afarensis was capable of efficient climbing and probably spent considerable time in the trees (sleeping, feeding, escaping from predators, etc.); and (2) while on the ground, A. afarensis was a biped, but walked with a much less efficient bent-hip, bent-knee gait than that seen in modern humans.

As might be expected, these conclusions themselves have also been challenged. While pointing out some slight differences from modern humans in post-cranial anatomy, Owen Lovejoy (1983) and his associates (e.g., Latimer, 1984) see nothing that suggests these hominids were arboreal or, conversely, that precluded them from being *very* efficient bipeds. Moreover, Lucy's "little legs" may not really be that small, considering her small body size (although her arms were apparently rather long) (Wolpoff, 1983b).

Other researchers have also noted differences between the postcranium of A. afarensis and later hominids. Interestingly, however, in many respects the hand and pelvis of A. afarensis are extremely similar to some later australopithecines from South Africa (Suzman, 1982; McHenry, 1983).

From all this debate, little has yet emerged in the way of consensus, except that all agree the A. afarensis did exhibit some kind of bipedal locomotion while on the ground. In searching for some middle ground between the opposing viewpoints, several researchers have suggested that A. afarensis could have been quite at home in the trees *as well as* being an efficient terrestrial biped (Wolpoff, 1983; McHenry, 1983). As one physical anthropologist has put it:

> One could imagine these dimirrutive early hominids making maximum use of *both* terrestrial and arboreal resources in spite of their commitment to exclusive bipedalism when on the ground. The contention of a mixed arboreal and terrestrial behavioural repertoire would make adaptive sense of the Hadar australopithecine forelimb, hand, and foot morphology without contradicting the evidence of the pelvis. (Wolpoff, 1983, p. 451).

Challenges to Australopithecus afarensis Following the formal naming of *Australopithecus afarensis* in 1978 (Johanson et al., 1978) and its systematic interpretation a year later (Johanson and White, 1979), some questions have been raised concerning the status of this fossil hominid. In general, these challenges have taken two forms:

1. Is there more than one taxon represented at Hadar and Laetoli?
2. Can *afarensis* simply be included as an earlier member of the later South African hominid A. *africanus* (i.e., the same species as at Taung, Sterkfontein, and Makapansgat)?

Regarding the first question of possible multiple taxa (i.e., more than one species) at Hadar and Laetoli, some of the initial analyses by the primary researchers at Hadar did indeed suggest this possibility (Johanson and Taieb, 1976). Once *all* the Hadar material was evaluated, as well as comparisons made with the Laetoli fossils, this view was rejected (in favor of simply grouping all the fossils into one obviously variable, sexually dimorphic species).

Not all paleoanthropologists, however, are convinced of this latter interpretation. Two French paleoanthropologists, Brigette Senut and Christine Tardieu of the University of Paris, have suggested from analyses of postcranial remains (especially the elbow and knee) that, along with a primitive australopithecine, early members of genus *Homo may* also have been present at Hadar and Laetoli (Senut, 1981; Senut and Tardieu, 1985).

In addition, physical features of the nasal region and cranial base have also led some researchers (Olson, 1985) to suggest more than one species at Hadar (Laetoli fossil material is too scrappy to analyze comparatively for intra-versus inter-specific variation—the essential point here). Indeed, it has been argued that in addition to a possible fairly primitive (generalized) ancestor of *Homo*, there may have been representatives of a robust lineage of australopithecine (see p. 367) also present in the Pliocene. Moreover, an indication of a "robust" morphology present at Hadar (at 3 m.y.a.) is strengthened by its appearance slightly later in the fossil record—as shown by the "black skull" (see p. 369).

Finally, comparisons of joint surfaces between the large and small individuals at Hadar show a tremendous difference, more, in fact, than in any contemporary primate (exceeding that even in the highly dimorphic gorilla and orang) (Zihlman, 1985).

It would seem, then, that there is some good reason to think more than one species has been sampled at Hadar—and perhaps at Laetoli as well. However, these claims have yet to be substantiated. Moreover, on the basis of detailed dental comparisons (White, et al., 1981), there appears to be no reason to "split" the samples into different taxa. Accordingly, A. *afarensis* is seen as a quite variable and most certainly sexually dimorphic form. As we have pointed out in Chapter 10, it is most prudent to assume a minimum number of species to be represented by any given fossil sample, unless *conclusive* evidence can be presented to suggest otherwise. For the present, anyway, most paleoanthropologists are provisionally regarding *all* the Hadar and Laetoli fossils as part of one species.

Equally troublesome, is the second question concerning the status of A. *afarensis*: Is it part of A. *africanus*? Phillip Tobias, the world's leading authority on the morphology of A. *africanus* in South Africa, believes that "the Laetoli and Hadar hominids cannot be distinguished at specific level from A. *africanus*" (Tobias, 1980, p. 1).

This assertion is also entirely possible, and, on the basis of Tobias's familiarity with the South African material, it requires serious consideration. Of all the other hominids to which A. *afarensis* could be compared, it is morphologically and chronologically closest to A. *africanus*. Yet, there are still some important differences in the face, cranial vault, mandible, and teeth, all of which consistently show A. *afarensis* to be more primitive than A. *africanus* (or, for that matter, any other known hominid) (White et al., 1981; Kimbel et al., 1985). More detailed comparisons will have to be done, but, given the overall primitive morphology of at least some of these early fossil hominids from Hadar and Laetoli, they are presently best considered within their own species, A. *afarensis*, and thus separate from A. *africanus*.

Set II. Later Australopithecines—"Robust" Forms (A. *robustus*; A. *boisei*)

After its discovery in 1959, the beautifully preserved cranium and upper dentition of "Zinj" was classified by Louis Leakey into a new and separate genus and species, *Zinjanthropus boisei* (boy'-see-eye). You may well ask, What biological basis was Leakey using to justify such a distinction? As it turned out, there was not much ground for postulating a totally separate genus, and most scientists (later including Leakey himself) have included this specimen in *Australopithecus*.

"Zinj" is a very robust young male australopithecine with enormous back teeth, a large broad face, and a sagittal crest atop the skull. In addition, the skull displays considerable pinching-in behind the orbits and has a cranial capacity of 530 cm³. "Zinj's" third molars are newly erupted and unworn, suggesting his age at death was probably around 18 years. In fact, these robust forms may have had significantly slower maturation rates than *A. afarensis* or other Plio-Pleistocene hominids (even early *Homo*) (Smith, 1985; Shipman, 1987).

There are also numerous specimens of robust australopithecines known from the South African sites of Kromdraai and Swartkrans. When compared with this material from South Africa, "Zinj" does show some differences in detail, but these are apparently due to one functional specialization, the massive increase in cheek tooth size. While sufficient grounds do not exist to justify assigning this East African australopithecine to a genus distinct from those in South Africa, separate specific rank may well be called for. Therefore, "Zinj" is now usually referred to as *Australopithecus boisei*, specifically distinct from *A. robustus*, the name given to the South African robust forms. The direct biological implication is that the East African variety of robust australopithecine, removed by 2,000 miles from South Africa, were reproductively isolated from their contemporaries, *A. robustus*, to the south.

We must, however, remain cautious about unnecessarily splitting these fossil populations into biologically meaningless categories. We have chastised such splitting in the early interpretations of South African australopithecines (for example, Robert Broom's classification, see p. 358), and we should not be guilty of making the same error in East Africa. In fact, many authorities believe there is not a specific difference between *A. robustus* in the south and its robust contemporary in the eastern part of the continent. Since these investigators feel there is

Figure 12-24
Australopithecus afarensis reconstructed cranium—using evidence from several individuals and filling in portions for which no fossil data exist (shown in white).

Figure 12-25
Two mandibles discovered at East Lake Turkana. Note the difference in proportions of jaws and teeth; KNM-ER 818 (right) is one of the largest hominid mandibles ever found. KNM-ER 992 (left) is thought to be an early Homo. (Photographs of casts.)

Figure 12-26

A robust australopithecine mandible from East Lake Turkana (KNM-ER 729). Note the enormous proportions of the molars and premolars.

Figure 12-27

The "demicranium" discovered at East Lake Turkana (KNM-ER 732). A female robust australopithecine?

not sufficient evidence to show that A. *boisei* falls *outside* the range of A. *robustus*, they call *both* A. *robustus* (the earlier name takes precedence).

In our ensuing discussion we will refer to the East African robust group as A. *boisei*, but this reference should not be interpreted as an ironclad biological conclusion. It simply provides, for the moment, a shorthand means of referring to the East African robust australopithecines.

A. *boisei* is a well-defined group in East Africa, not only at Olduvai, but at several other sites as well. From East Turkana, particularly, several fossils have been found that are clearly members of this species, including some mandibles of gigantic proportions. In addition, a few skulls from Turkana also belong to A. *boisei*. One of these, a nearly perfect skull (KNM-ER 406), is very much like "Zinj" and is also apparently a robust male australopithecine. Cranial capacity, estimated at 510 cm^3, is a little smaller for the Turkana male, compared to the 530 cm^3 figure for "Zinj" (the same figure as for the only South African specimen that can be measured).

Postcranial bones at Turkana that are definitely attributable to A. *boisei* are difficult to ascertain exactly, for none has been found directly associated with a skull. However, one upper arm bone (humerus), ER 739, is very robust and quite uniquely shaped. Biomechanical reconstructions show it to be unlike *any* living hominoid. If this arm bone does indeed belong to A. *boisei*, it suggests that, postcranially, they may have been quite unusual compared to other hominids.

Further evidence along the same line comes from the Omo, where several teeth and three mandibles are, because of their size, attributed to A. *boisei*. In addition, an unusual ulna has been found which, like the Turkana humerus, also suggests that the forelimb of A. *boisei* is quite unlike other hominids.

Remains of A. *boisei* are also known from a nearly complete mandible 1 million years old from Peninj, a site near Lake Natron about seventy miles from Olduvai and also from a partial skull of about the same age (1.5–1.2 m.y.a.) from the Chesowanja site in central Kenya (in the Lake Baringo region).

Apparently, A. *boisei* does not appear anywhere in East Africa until about 2 m.y.a., and until about 1 m.y.a. lived basically unchanged. It is interesting to note that South African robust australopithecines (A. *robustus*) at Swartkrans and Kromdraai also do not appear until about this same time. Quite clearly, all varieties of robust australopithecines are later than the more primitive *afarensis*—

up to 1.0 m.y.–1.5 m.y. later. It is thus easier to understand the obviously more *derived* physical characteristics of these robust australopithecines.

Where did the robust forms come from? We mentioned above (p. 366) that some authorities have seen glimmers of robust characteristics in some of the "afarensis" material at Hadar. Further evidence of an early appearance of the robust lineage came to light in 1985 with the discovery on the west side of Lake Turkana of a well-preserved skull (WT-17000) (Walker et al., 1986).

From close correlation with the same volcanic "events" elsewhere in northern Kenya and southern Ethiopia, the date of the skull is well-established at 2.5 m.y. Some paleontologists have suggested that this new fossil be included in yet another species of *Australopithecus*, *A. aethiopicus*, first named at the Omo (Johanson and White, 1986).

This exciting new fossil, called the "black skull," has raised a great deal of scientific as well as popular interest and not a little confusion. Combined with a fairly modern-looking face, the cranial vault is quite primitive—strongly suggestive of *A. afarensis*. Indeed, the cranial capacity (estimated at only 410 cc) is the smallest for any known hominid. As we will discuss in the next chapter, schemes of hominid evolution are currently under major reassessment and revision. However, such is the nature and excitement of science!

It would seem that just about the same time as the black skull was deposited, major environmental changes were afoot in both South and East Africa (Vrba, 1985). It is thus not all that surprising to find new (and, in this case, unexpected) varieties of hominid appearing on the scene. Hominid evolution was not a simple affair, and our interpretations will have to reflect this fact.

Many anthropologists speculate that these robust forms had a specialized vegetarian diet consisting mostly of small, hard objects (seeds, etc.). As a result of the rigorous demands of masticating these kinds of foods, robust forms gradually adopted a large back tooth chewing complex. Accompanying this change, structural modifications also occurred in the jaw and in rearrangements of cranial architecture, eventually producing that highly derived hominid form we recognize as a robust australopithecine.

Set III. Later Australopithecines—"Gracile" Forms (A. *africanus*)

Another variety of australopithecine (also small-brained, but not as large-toothed as the robust varieties) is known from Africa. However, while the robust lineage is represented in both East and South Africa, the smaller and more lightly built (gracile) form is known only from the southern part of the continent.

First named *A. africanus* by Dart for the single individual at Taung (see p. 352), this australopithecine is also found at Makapansgat and, especially, at Sterkfontein.

Traditionally, it has been thought that there was a significant difference in body size between gracile and robust australopithecines. Estimates placed the stature and weight of graciles at 42 to 57 inches and 40 to 60 pounds, with robusts considerably bigger (57 to 65 inches and 70 to 200 pounds). However, recent reanalysis of the relevant postcranial elements has shown that the so-called "gracile" and "robust" may, in fact, not be that different in body size (McHenry, 1987). Most of the differences between the two forms are found in the face and dentition.

The face structure of the graciles is more lightly built and somewhat dish-shaped compared to the more vertical configuration seen in robust specimens. In robust individuals, a raised ridge along the midline of the skull, called a **sagittal crest**, is occasionally observed. This structure provides additional attachment area for the large temporal muscle, which is the primary muscle operating the massive jaw below. Such a structure is also seen in some modern apes, especially male gorillas and orangs; however, in australopithecines, the temporal muscle acts most efficiently on the back of the mouth and is therefore not functionally equivalent to the front tooth emphasis seen in pongids (see Fig. 12-28).

The most distinctive difference observed between gracile and robust australopithecines is in the dentition. Compared to modern humans, they both have relatively large teeth, which are, however, definitely hominid in pattern. In fact, more emphasis is on the typical back-tooth grinding complex among these early forms than the forms of today; therefore, if anything, australopithecines are "hyperhominid"! Robust forms emphasize this trend to an extreme degree, showing deep jaws and much-enlarged back teeth, particularly the molars, severely crowding the front teeth (incisors and canines) together. Conversely, the graciles have proportionately larger front teeth compared to the size of their back teeth. This contrast is seen most clearly in the relative sizes of the canine compared to the first premolar: in robust individuals, the first premolar is clearly a much larger tooth than the small canine (about twice as large) whereas, in gracile specimens, it only averages about 20% larger than the fairly goodsized canine (Howells, 1973).

These differences in the relative proportions of the teeth and jaws best define a gracile, as compared to a robust, form. In fact, most of the differences in skull shape we have discussed can be directly attributed to contrasting jaw function in the two forms. Both the sagittal crest and broad vertical face of the robust form are related to the muscles and biomechanical requirements of the extremely large-tooth chewing adaptation of this animal.

Temporal muscle fibers
oriented towards back
teeth

(a) Hominid
(robust australopithecine)

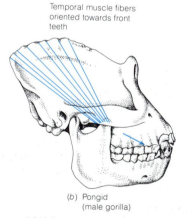

Temporal muscle fibers
oriented towards front
teeth

(b) Pongid
(male gorilla)

Figure 12-28
*Sagittal crests and temporal muscle orienta-
tions. Hominid compared to pongid.*

Set IV. Early *Homo* (also called *Homo habilis*)

The first hint that another hominid was living contemporaneously in Africa with robust australopithecines came at Olduvai Gorge in the early 1960s. Louis Leakey named a new form of hominid *Homo habilis* on the basis of remains, some a little older than "Zinj," others somewhat more recent (Leakey et al., 1964). Unfortunately, the remains at Olduvai attributable to this **taxon** are all either fragmentary or distorted in one way or another. The initial *habilis* material included a fragmentary skull with a distorted juvenile mandible (OH 7) and a partial skull with a complete upper and lower dentition (OH 13), called "Cinderella" by the Leakeys. A third *habilis* specimen, a severely fragmented skull, discovered after being trampled by local Masai cattle (OH 16), is known popularly as "Olduvai George." A final *habilis* skull, found in 1968, is a nearly complete cranium (OH 24) that was severely crushed. It thus required extensive restoration. This fossil, thought to be female, is called "Twiggy."

The *habilis* material at Olduvai ranges in time from 1.85 m.y.a. for the earliest to about 1.6 m.y.a. for the latest. Due to the fragmentary nature of the fossil remains, interpretations have been difficult and much disputed. The most immediately obvious feature distinguishing the *habilis* material from the australo-

Figure 12-29
Two mandibles. Initially assigned to "H. habilis," from Olduvai Gorge. (left) OH 7; (right) OH 13, "Cinderella."

pithecines is cranial size. For all the measurable *habilis* skulls, the estimated average cranial capacity is 646 cm^3 compared to 504 cm^3 for all measurable robust australopithecines and 450 for graciles (Tobias, 1983). *Habilis*, therefore, shows a 26–42% cranial size increase respectively over both forms of australopithecine.

In their initial description of *habilis*, Leakey and his associates also pointed to differences from australopithecines in cranial shape and in tooth proportions (larger front teeth relative to back teeth and narrower premolars).

The naming of this fossil material as *Homo habilis* (handy man) was meaningful from two perspectives. First of all, Leakey inferred that members of this group were the early Olduvai toolmakers. If true, how do we account for a robust australopithecine like "Zinj" lying in the middle of the largest living floor known at Olduvai? What was he doing there? Leakey has suggested he was the remains of a *habilis* meal! Excepting those instances where cutmarks are left behind (see pp. 326–327), we must point out that there is no clear way archeologically to establish the validity of such a claim. However, the debate over this assertion serves to demonstrate that cultural factors as well as physical morphology must be considered in the interpretation of hominids as biocultural organisms. Secondly, and most significantly, by calling this group *Homo*, Leakey was arguing for at least *two separate branches* of hominid evolution in the Plio-Pleistocene. Clearly only one could be on the main branch eventually leading to *Homo sapiens*. Labeling this new group *Homo* in opposition to *Australopithecus*, Leakey was guessing he had found our ancestors.

Since the initial evidence was so fragmentary, most paleoanthropologists were reluctant to accept *habilis* as a valid taxon distinct from *all* australopithecines. Differences from the hyperrobust East African variety (*A. boisei*) were certainly apparent; the difficulties arose in trying to distinguish *habilis* from *A. africanus*, particularly for dental traits that considerably overlap. Moreover, ambiguous

Figure 12-30
A nearly complete skull from Olduvai Gorge. Initially assigned to "H. habilis," OH24, "Twiggy." (Photograph of cast.)

Figure 12-31
Skull profiles (seen from above).

(a)
Robust
australopithecine

(b)
Gracile
australopithecine

(c)
Early Homo

dating of the South African forms made it difficult to interpret the relationship between A. *africanus* and *habilis*.

Recent discoveries, especially from Lake Turkana, of better-preserved fossil material have shed new light on early *Homo* in the Plio-Pleistocene. The most important of this new *habilis* material is a nearly complete cranium (ER 1470) discovered at East Lake Turkana in 1972. With a cranial capacity of 775 cm³, this individual is well outside the known range for australopithecines and actually overlaps the lower boundary for *Homo*. In addition, the shape of the skull vault and face are in many respects unlike that of australopithecines. However, the face is still quite robust (Walker, 1976), and the fragments of tooth crowns that are preserved indicate the back teeth in this individual were quite large.

Additional discoveries at Turkana also strongly suggest the presence of a hominid lineage contemporaneous with and separate from australopithecines. Another skull discovered in 1972 (ER 1590) is similar to 1470 and may even be

Figure 12-32
The Kenyan team at East Lake Turkana. Kamoya Kimeu (driving) is the most successful fossil hunter in East Africa. He is responsible for dozens of important discoveries.

larger! Moreover, several mandibles, including two nearly complete specimens (ER 820 and 992), have tooth proportions (relatively larger front teeth) characteristic of our genus. Finally, several postcranial remains discovered at Turkana show a taller, more gracile group than that inferred for australopithecines. The dating of all this crucial early *Homo* material from Turkana is tied to the dating of the KBS tuff. As we discussed on page 351, the dating of this key bed has recently been established at around 1.8 m.y.a. Thus, the earliest *Homo* materials at Turkana *and* Olduvai are contemporaneous (i.e., 1.8–2.0 m.y.a.).

Other Plio-Pleistocene sites also have revealed possible early members of the genus *Homo*. From the Omo in southern Ethiopia scattered remains of a few teeth and small cranial fragments are similar in pattern to other comparable early *Homo* material.

In addition, early members of the genus *Homo* have also been found in South Africa, there, too, apparently living contemporaneously with australopithecines. At both Sterkfontein (member 5) and Swartkrans, fragmentary remains have been recognized (actually discovered some time ago). In fact, Ron Clarke (1985) has shown that the key fossil of *Homo* from Sterkfontein (Stw-53) is nearly identical to the OH 24 *habilis* skull from Olduvai. Some of the material from Swartkrans may, however, be closer to the later form, *Homo erectus* (see Chapter 14).

If the discussion of *Australopithecus* versus *Homo* seems confusing, do not despair. The distinction is not yet well formulated and causes much confusion even in professional ranks. It is true that the robust group of australopithecines in Africa is quite distinctive, characterized by an enormous back-tooth grinding complex. It is equally true that another whole set of gracile fossil hominids in Africa usually called *Homo habilis* does not fall into this group. The thorny problem comes in trying to distinguish these gracile individuals from the South African gracile variety of australopithecines, *A. africanus*. Since much overlap exists in physical traits (and probably chronology as well) between these two forms, this will never be an easy task. (For a summary of the current perspectives regarding the distinction between *Australopithecus* and *Homo* in the Plio-Pleistocene see Table 12-4.)

On the basis of evidence from Olduvai and particularly from Lake Turkana we can reasonably postulate that *Homo* was present in East Africa by *at least* 2 m.y.a., developing in parallel with at least one line (*A. boisei*) of australopithecines. These two hominid lines lived contemporaneously for a minimum of 1 million years, after which the australopithecine lineage apparently disappears forever. At the same time, the *habilis* line was emerging into a later form, *Homo erectus*, which, in turn, developed into *H. sapiens*.

In the next chapter, we will take up in detail several alternative theories dealing with evolutionary relationships of these fossil hominids in the Plio-Pleistocene.

Geology and Dating Problems in South Africa

While, as we saw in Chapter 11 and the beginning of this chapter, the geological and archeological context in East Africa is oftentimes straightforward, the five South African australopithecine sites are much more complex geologically. All

(a)

(b)

Figure 12-33
A nearly complete "early Homo*" skull from East Lake Turkana (KNM-ER 1470). One of the most important single fossil hominid discovery from East Africa. (a) Frontal view; (b) lateral view.*

Table 12-4 Australopithecus *Compared to Early* Homo

Australopithecus	*Early Homo*
Cranial:	
Face large relative to vault size	Face small relative to vault size
Absolute size of cranium smaller: "gracile" = 450 cm³ (N = 7) "robust" = 504 cm³ (N = 5)	Cranium—larger average = 646 cm³ (N = 6)
Cranial bone thinner	Cranial bone thicker
More postorbital construction	Less postorbital construction
Mandible large, more massive Ramus of mandible, higher	Mandible smaller, not as thick Ramus not as high
Shape of mandible: Narrow in front diverges in back, as:	Mandible more open in front, not as divergent in back; shaped more as:
-shaped	-shaped
Front teeth relatively quite small to very small compared to back teeth	Front teeth are larger relative to size of back teeth—which, in some cases (ER 1470), are still very large
Postcranial:	
Differences not yet well worked out, but some apparent differences in femur: Upper (proximal) end; smaller head, flatter longer neck	Head larger, neck more round in cross-section and not as relatively long

After Leakey et al., 1964; Walker, 1976; Wood, 1976; Tobias, 1976; Howell, 1978; Tobias, 1983.

were discovered by commercial quarrying activity, which greatly disrupted the geological picture and, in the case of Taung, completely destroyed the site.

The australopithecine remains are found with thousands of other fossilized bones embedded in limestone cliffs, caves, fissures, and sinkholes. The limestone was built by millions of generations of shells of marine organisms during the Pre-Cambrian—more than 2 billion years ago—when South Africa was submerged under a shallow sea. Once deposited, the limestones were cut through by percolating ground water from below and rain water from above, forming a maze of caves and fissures often connected to the surface by narrow shafts. Through these vertical shafts and horizontal cave openings, bones either fell or were carried in, where they conglomerated with sand, pebbles, and soil into a cementlike matrix called *breccia*.

As the cave fissures filled in, they were constantly subjected to further erosion forces from above and below, so that caves would be partially filled, then closed to the surface for a considerable time, and reopened again to commence accumulation thousands of years later. All this activity yields an incredibly complex

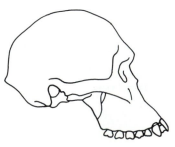

Figure 12-34
A gracile australopithecine.

geological situation that can only be worked out after the most detailed kind of paleoecological analysis.

Since bones accumulated in these caves and fissures largely by accidental processes, it seems likely that none of the South African australopithecine sites are *primary* hominid localities. In other words, unlike East Africa, these are not areas where hominids organized activities, scavenged food, etc.

Just how did all the fossilized bone accumulate and, most particularly, what were the australopithecines doing there? In the case of Swartkrans, Sterkfontein, and Kromdraai, the bones probably accumulated through the combined activities of carnivorous leopards, sabre-toothed cats, and hyenas. However, the unexpectedly high proportion of primate (baboon and hominid) remains suggests that these localities were the location (or very near the location) of primate sleeping sites, thus providing ready prey for the predators (Brain, 1981).

Raymond Dart has argued enthusiastically for an alternative explanation, suggesting the australopithecines camping at Makapansgat regularly used bone, tooth, and horn remains as tools, which he has grandly called the **osteodontokeratic** culture complex. Analogies with modern Hottentot food habits indicate the bone accumulation at Makapansgat may be accounted for simply by hominid and carnivore eating practices. Recent paleoecological work at Makapansgat has thrown Dart's assertions into even greater doubt. Apparently, remains accumulated here primarily in a similar fashion to Sterkfontein and Swartkrans—through a narrow shaft entrance. Therefore, large animals could have entered but not departed the deep subterranean cavern. Makapansgat, like Sterkfontein and Swartkrans, probably also represents the accumulated debris of carnivore activity (perhaps hyenas) outside the cave entrance.

So little is left of the final site, Taung, that accurate paleoanthropological reconstructions are not feasible.

Due to the complex geological picture, as well as lack of appropriate material such as volcanics for chronometric techniques, dating the South African australopithecine sites has posed tremendous problems. Without chronometric dating, the best that can be done is to correlate the faunal sequences in South Africa with areas such as East Africa where dates are better known (this approach is called "biostratigraphy"—see p. 324). Faunal sequencing of this sort on pigs, bovids such as antelopes, and baboons has provided the following tenuous chronology:

Figure 12-35
An "early Homo" mandible from East Lake Turkana (KNM-ER 820). Note the relatively even proportions of back teeth to front teeth.

	1 m.y.	
Kromdraai		
Swartkrans		Taung?
	2 m.y.	
Sterkfontein		
Makapansgat	3 m.y.	

Recent attempts at paleomagnetic dating (see p. 322) suggest an age of 3.3–2.8 m.y.a. for Makapansgat (Brock et al., 1977), thus pushing the estimates to the extreme limits of those provided by biostratigraphy. In fact, some researchers believe the paleomagnetic results are ambiguous and continue to "put their money" on the biostratigraphic data, especially those dates determined by analysis of pig fossils. From such considerations, they place the South African australopithecine sites as much as one-half million years later (i.e., for

Figure 12-36
Swartkrans, geological section. The upper
(reconstructed) part has been removed by
erosion since the accumulation of the fossil-
bearing deposit. (After Brain, 1970).

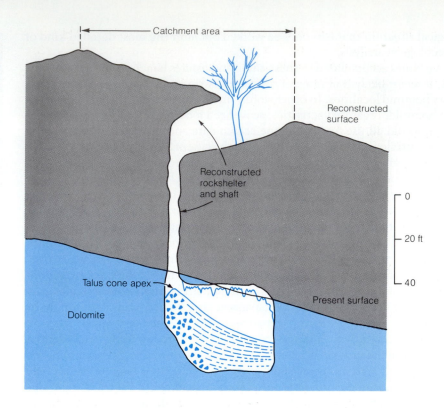

Makapansgat, around 2.5 m.y.a.) (White et al., 1981). This is crucial, since it
places *all* the South African hominids after *Australopithecus afarensis* in East
Africa.

Summary

In East and South Africa during the better part of this century, a vast collection
of early hominids has been gathered, a collection totaling more than 500 individuals (and thousands of fossil specimens). While considerable evolution occurs
during the Plio-Pleistocene (approximately 3 million years are covered in this
chapter), all forms are clearly hominid, as shown by their bipedal adaptation.
The time range for this hominid material extends back to nearly 4 million years
in East Africa, with the earliest and most primitive hominid now recognized—
Australopithecus afarensis.

Later hominids of a robust lineage are known in East Africa (A. *boisei*) and
South Africa (A. *robustus*). These two groups seem to come on the scene about 2
million years ago and disappear around 1 million years ago. However, new evidence from Kenya argues that a probable robust ancestor (the "black skull") is already present 2.5 m.y.a.

In addition, a smaller-toothed (but not necessarily smaller-bodied) "gracile"
form is known exclusively from South Africa, beginning at a time range estimated at around 2.5 m.y.a. However, owing to the geologic complexity, dating
control in South Africa is *much* more tenuous than in East Africa. Thus we cannot be certain of any of these dates for South African hominids.

Finally, best known again in East Africa (but also found in South Africa), a larger-brained and smaller-toothed variety is also present around 2 m.y.a. This species, called *Homo habilis*, is thought by most paleoanthropologists to lie closer to our ancestry than the latter varieties of australopithecines.

Questions for Review

1. In East Africa all the early hominid sites are found along the Rift Valley. Why is this significant?
2. Compare the various East African Plio-Pleistocene sites for the kinds of cultural information uncovered.
3. How does the dating problem of the KBS tuff at Lake Turkana illustrate the necessity for cross-correlation of several dating techniques?
4. Why was Raymond Dart's announcement of a small-brained bipedal hominoid greeted with such skepticism in 1925?
5. What led Dart to suggest the Taung child was *not* an ape?
6. What was Robert Broom's contribution to revealing the hominid nature of the South African australopithecines?
7. (a) Why is postcranial evidence (particularly the lower limb) so crucial in showing the australopithecines as definite hominids? (b) What particular aspects of the australopithecine pelvis and lower limb are hominidlike?
8. What hominid sites have yielded remains of *A. afarensis*? In what ways is the fossil material more primitive than other hominids from South and East Africa?
9. What kinds of robust australopithecines have been found in East Africa? How do they compare with South African australopithecines?
10. Why are some Plio-Pleistocene hominids from East Africa called "early *Homo*" (or *H. habilis*)? What does this imply for the evolutionary relationships of the australopithecines?
11. What did Louis Leakey mean by using the specific name, "habilis" for a fossil hominid from Olduvai?
12. Compare the morphological features of early *Homo* with *Australopithecus*. Is it easier to draw a clear distinction between *Homo* and robust australopithecines (*A. robustus; A. boisei*) or gracile (*A. africanus*) ones? Why?
13. Why are the early hominid sites in East Africa so much better dated than those in South Africa?

CHAPTER 13

Plio-Pleistocene Hominids: Organization and Interpretation

CONTENTS

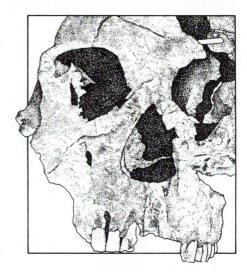

Man, the Hunter; Woman, the Gatherer

Anthropologists have long been concerned with the behavioral evolution of our species. Accompanying changes in anatomy (locomotion, dentition, brain size and shape) were changes in mating patterns, social structure, cultural innovations, and, eventually, language. In fact, changes in these behavioral complexes are what mostly *explain* the concomitant adaptations in human biological structure.

We are, then, vitally interested in the behavioral adaptations of our early hominid ancestors. In seeking to reconstruct the behavioral patterns of these early hominids, anthropologists use inferences drawn from modern primates, social carnivores, and hunting-gathering people (see Chapter 9). In addition, they derive information directly from the paleoanthropological record (see Chapter 11).

Despite numerous detailed and serious attempts at such behavioral reconstructions, the conclusions must largely remain speculative. In point of fact, behavior does not fossilize. Accordingly, researchers must rely considerably upon their imaginations in creating scenarios of early hominid behavioral evolution. In such an atmosphere, biases often emerge; these biased renditions, in turn, stimulate heated debates and alternative scenarios—often as narrow as those being attacked.

Probably no topic has stimulated more controversy (or has been more riddled with implicit biases) than the debate concerning origins of hominid sex-role differences. Did early hominid males have characteristically different behavioral adaptations than their female counterparts? Did one sex dominate the frontier of early hominid cultural innovation? And if one sex did lead the way, which one?

A now well-known rendition of early hominid behavioral development was popularized in the 1960s and 1970s. According to this "man, the hunter" theory, the hunting of large animals by males was the central stimulus of hominid behavioral evolution. According to such widely read works as Desmond Morris' *The Naked Ape* (1967) and several books by Robert Ardrey (including *The Hunting Hypothesis*, 1976), early apish-looking forms *became* hominids as a result of a hunting way of life. As Ardrey states, "Man is man, and not a chimpanzee, because for millions upon millions of evolving years we killed for a living" (1976, p. 10).

In this reconstruction, the hunting of large, dangerous mammals by cooperating groups of males fostered the development of intelligence, language, tools, and bipedalism. Increased intelligence accompanied by the development of weapons is also blamed in this scenario for the roots of human aggressiveness, murder, and warfare.

This "man, the hunter" scenario further suggests that while the males are leading the vanguard in hominid evolution, females remain mostly sedentary, tied to the home base by the burden of dependent young. Females may have contributed some wild plant foods to the group's subsistence, but this is not seen as a particularly challenging (and certainly not a very noble) endeavor. In this situation of marked division of labor, sexual relationships quickly changed. Males, constantly away from the home base (and, thus, away from the females too) could not keep a watchful eye over their mates. In order to better insure fidelity (and to reduce the risk of cuckoldry), monogamy came into being. In this way, a male would be assured that the young in which he invested was his own. This important factor of male-female bonding as a product of differential foraging patterns has recently been forcefully restated by Owen Lovejoy (1981). (See p. 187.)

From the female's point of view, it would be beneficial to maintain a close bond with a provisioning male. Consequently, she would want to appear "attractive," and thus, through time, the female breasts and buttocks would become more conspicuous. Besides rearing their young and being attractive sex objects, females were useful to males in another way. Groups of male hunters living in the same area might occasionally come into potentially dangerous competition for the same resources. As a means of solidifying political ties between groups, the males would thus routinely exchange females (by giving or "selling" their daughters to neighboring bands).

Thus, in a single stroke, this complex of features accounts for human intelligence, sexual practices, and political organization.

As might be expected, such a male-centered scenario did not go unchallenged. Ignoring females or relegating them to a definitely inferior role in human behavioral evolution drew sharp criticism from several quarters. As one anthropologist noted:

> So, while the males were out hunting, developing all their skills, learning to cooperate, inventing language, inventing art, creating tools and weapons, the poor dependent females were sitting back at the home base having one child after another and waiting for the males to bring home the bacon. While this reconstruction is certainly ingenious, it gives one the decided impression that only half the species—the male half—did any evolving. In addition to containing a number of logical gaps, the argument becomes somewhat doubtful in the light of modern knowledge of genetics and primate behavior (Slocum, 1975, p. 42).

In fact, such a rigid rendering of our ancestors' behavior does not stand up to critical examination. Hunting is never defined rigorously. Does it include only large, terrestrial mammals? What of smaller mammals, sea mammals, fish, and birds? In numerous documented human societies, females actively participate in exploiting these latter resources.

Moreover, nonhuman primates do not conform to predictions derived from the "man, the hunter" model. For example, among chimpanzees, females do most of the toolmaking, not the males. Finally, in most nonhuman primates (most mammals, for that matter), it is the females—not the males—who choose with whom to mate.

Granting that the hunting hypothesis does not work, what alternatives have been proposed? As a reaction to male-centered views, Elaine Morgan (1972) advanced the "aquatic hypothesis." In this rendition, females are seen as the pioneers of hominid evolution. But rather than having the dramatic changes of hominid evolution occur on the savanna, Morgan has them take place on the seashore. As females lead the way to bipedal locomotion, cultural innovation, and intellectual development, the poor males are seen as splashing pitifully behind.

Unfortunately, this theory has less to back it up than the hunting hypothesis. Not a shred (even a watery one) of evidence has ever been discovered in the contexts predicted by the aquatic theory. Little is accomplished by such unsubstantiated overzealous speculation. Chauvinism—whether male or female—does not elucidate our origins and only obscures the evolutionary processes that operated on the *whole* species.

Can nothing then be concluded about differential male-female sex roles? While the pattern is not as rigid as the hunting hypothesis advocates would have us believe, in the vast majority of human societies hunting of large, terrestrial mammals is almost always a male activity. In fact, a comprehensive cross-cultural survey shows that of 179 societies, males do the hunting exclusively in 166, both sexes participate in 13, and in *no* group is hunting done exclusively by females (Murdock, 1965).

In addition, as we noted in Chapter 9, there is some incipient division of labor in foraging patterns among chimpanzees. Females tend to concentrate more on termiting, while hunting (though it is only occasional) is done mostly by males. Early hominids, expanding upon such a subsistence base, eventually adapted a greater sexual division of labor than found in any other primate. Two points, however, must be kept in mind. First, both the gathering of wild plant foods and the hunting of animals would have been indispensable components of the diet. Consequently, *both* males and females always played a significant role. Secondly, the strategies must always have been somewhat flexible. With a shifting, usually unpredictable resource base, nothing else would have worked. As a result, males probably always did a considerable amount of gathering and in most foraging societies still do. Moreover, females—while not usually engaged in the stalking and killing of large prey—nonetheless contribute significantly to meat acquisition. Once large animals have been killed, there still remain the arduous tasks of butchering and transport back to the home base. In many societies, women and men participate equally in these activities.

A balanced view of human behavioral evolution must avoid simplistic and overly rigid scenarios. As recently stated by a researcher concerned with reconstructing early hominid behavior:

> *Both* sexes must have been able to care for young, protect themselves from predators, make and use tools, and freely move about the environment in order to exploit available resources widely distributed through space and time. It is this range of behaviors—the overall behavioral flexibility of both sexes—that may have been the *primary* ingredient of early hominids' success in the savanna environment (Zihlman, 1981, p. 97).

SOURCES:

Ardrey, Robert. *The Hunting Hypothesis*. New York: Atheneum, 1976.

Dahlberg, Frances (ed.). *Woman the Gatherer*. New Haven: Yale University Press, 1981.

Lovejoy, C. Owen. "The Origin of Man," *Science*, **211**:341–350, 1981.

Morgan, Elaine. *The Descent of Woman*. New York: Stein and Day, 1972.

Morris, Desmond. *The Naked Ape*. New York: McGraw-Hill, 1967.

Murdock, G. P. *Culture and Society*, Pittsburgh: University of Pittsburgh Press, 1965.

Slocum, Sally. "Woman the Gatherer: Male Bias in Anthropology," In: *Toward an Anthropology of Women*, R. R. Reiter, ed., New York: Monthly Review Press, pp. 36–50, 1975.

Zihlman, Adrienne L. "Women as Shapers of the Human Adaptation," In: *Woman the Gatherer*, op. cit., pp. 75–120, 1981.

Introduction

We have seen in the last chapter that a vast and complex array of early hominid material has been discovered in South and East Africa. In just the past few years, particularly in the eastern part of the continent, a great number of new discoveries have been made. We now have Plio-Pleistocene hominid collections totaling close to 200 individuals from South Africa and probably more than 300 from East Africa. Given the size and often fragmentary nature of the sample, along with the fact that a good deal of it is so recently discovered, we should not be surprised that many complications arise when it comes to interpretation. In addition, both popular enthusiasm and the strong personalities often connected with fossil hominid discoveries have generated even more confusion.

In this chapter, we will look at several *theories* that attempt to organize the huge amount of Plio-Pleistocene hominid material. We ask you to remember that these are only theories and must remain so, given the incomplete nature of the fossil record. Even considering the seemingly very large number of fossils there is a *great* deal of time over which they were distributed. If we estimate about 500 total individuals from all African sites recovered thus far for the period 4–1 m.y.a., we still are sampling just one individual for every 6,000 years! Until much of the new material from East Africa has been properly analyzed and detailed reports published, we cannot form even reasonably secure hypotheses without extreme difficulty. At the present time, only a few East African hominids have been thoroughly studied; all the rest are thus far described in preliminary reports.

It will no doubt appear that many opposing and conflicting theories attempt to describe exactly what is going on in human evolution during the crucial period between 5 and 1 m.y.a. And, indeed, there are many theories. Hominid fossils are intriguing to both scientists and nonscientists, for some of these ancient bones and teeth are probably those of our direct ancestors. Equally intriguing, some of these fossils are representatives of populations of our close relatives that apparently met with extinction. We would like to know how these animals lived, what kinds of adaptations (physical and cultural) they displayed, and why some continued to evolve while others died out.

More Hominids—More Complications

In our review of hominid evolution in the Plio-Pleistocene, we have discussed two varieties of australopithecines in South Africa, probably representing two separate species (A. *africanus* and A. *robustus*). In East Africa, at least three forms are known: an early primitive australopithecine (A. *afarensis*); a later, hyper-robust form (A. *boisei*); and one smaller but brainier than any of the other forms and therefore called an early member of genus *Homo* (H. *habilis*). The vast majority of hominid discoveries from the Plio-Pleistocene can be assigned to one of these groups. However, a few fossils do not fit neatly into this scheme. As noted, most of this material is quite new and conclusions must, therefore, remain highly speculative at this stage. Following are two more considerations drawn

E. Africa

A. robustus   A. africanus   A. boisei   Homo habilis   A. afarensis

Figure 13-1
Plio-Pleistocene hominids.

from this newly discovered fossil material. We will eventually work them into our interpretations of early hominid evolution.

A. *africanus* in East Africa?

We have discussed the gracile form of australopithecine from South Africa called *A. africanus*. This form combines small brain size and relatively small back teeth (premolars and molars, compared to the massive ones seen in the robust forms) and is well known in South Africa at about 3–2 m.y.a. But what about East Africa? From here we have after 2 m.y.a. a very robust form with massive jaws and back teeth (*A. boisei*), and a smaller form with scaled-down tooth proportions and a large brain (*Homo habilis*). Until recently, a hominid with the combination of a small brain and moderately sized teeth (i.e., *africanus*) was not recognized in East Africa. As already noted, it is sometimes extremely difficult to distinguish the individuals assigned to early *H. habilis* from the smaller gracile australopithecines (*A. africanus*).

The major differences most often underscored are in brain size and tooth proportions, but these distinctions are often impossible to define in fragmentary remains. Since both gracile australopithecines and early populations of genus *Homo* have considerable within-group variation (individual, sexual dimorphism, etc.), they may also have considerable overlap of structural traits, such as tooth and brain size. Operationally, then, in East Africa it becomes a tortuous task to distinguish early members of genus *Homo* on one hand and gracile australopithecines on the other. The East African evidence of a third kind of hominid, in addition to robust *A. boisei* and *H. habilis* is tenuous, but some suggestive clues do exist.

A fossil skull found at East Turkana in 1973 (ER 1813) dated 1.6–1.3 m.y.a. led Richard Leakey (1974) to suggest the presence of *A. africanus* in East Africa contemporaneous with *A. boisei* and *Homo*. Additional finds (at the Omo) of mandibular fragments, one upper arm bone, and about twenty teeth (from around 2.5 m.y.a.) may also belong to members of *A. africanus*. Some of the remains from Olduvai initially attributed to "*habilis*," particularly the skull called "Twiggy," may again be a gracile australopithecine.

As yet, this issue is unresolved. Most researchers, for the moment, prefer to keep the evolutionary picture as uncomplicated (parsimonious) as the evidence permits. Consequently, the potential *africanus* individuals noted above are simply regarded as small representatives of *H. habilis*. In fact, within the samples used to estimate cranial capacities for *H. habilis* (cited on p. 371), both ER 1813 (513 cm³) and OH 24 ("Twiggy"—597 cm³) were included (following Tobias, 1983b). It should be noted, however, that if these two specimens were deleted

Figure 13-2
A nearly complete cranium (ER 1813) discovered at east Lake Turkana, 1973. Evidence of A. africanus *in East Africa 1.6–1.3 m.y.a.?*

Figure 13-3
The composite cranium (Sk. 847) from Swartkrans. Evidence of Homo habilis *in South Africa?*

from the *habilis* sample, the average cranial size for the species (using the four other specimens) would be significantly larger.

Homo erectus in the Plio-Pleistocene

Homo habilis in East Africa and probably South Africa appears well on its way in human evolution by 2 m.y.a. Well on its way where? As we shall see in the next chapter, the fossil hominid group that succeeded early *Homo* and preceded *Homo sapiens* is called *Homo erectus*. For several years, *Homo erectus* was thought to have appeared long *after* the australopithecines, coming on the scene as late as 500,000 years ago. However, a fossil skull found at Olduvai by Louis Leakey in 1960 pushed this date back to at least 1 m.y.a., and recent calibration of dates in the upper beds at Olduvai may push this back even further—to about 1.2 m.y.a.

Yet another important fossil hominid discovery from Lake Turkana was uncovered by Richard Leakey's remarkably successful crew in September, 1975. A nearly perfectly preserved skull (ER 3733), looking much like well-known members of Asian *erectus*, was recovered from beds dating 1.6–1.3 m.y.a. What is more, from these same beds come undisputed fossils of robust australopithecines (*A. boisei*) plus perhaps members of *A. africanus*. In addition, on the west side of Lake Turkana an immature *Homo erectus* individual was discovered in 1984. This remarkable find, consisting of a nearly complete skeleton, is thought to represent an individual approximately 12 years of age at the time of death. Most of the skeletal elements are preserved, including the cranium, ribs, and vertebrae. Much detailed analysis is yet to be done on this skeleton, which is by far the most complete *H. erectus* known from anywhere (see p. 422 for a further discussion). Consequently, it appears undeniable that *Homo erectus* was living contemporaneously in East Africa with australopithecines, as much as 1.6 m.y.a.

Hominids in the Plio-Pleistocene outside Africa?

To date, the vast majority of hominid fossils and artifactual material predating 1 million years ago have been found on the African continent. There are, however, some claims (although still unconfirmed) that hominids may have dispersed from Africa earlier than had previously been believed (perhaps well before 1 m.y.a.).

250,000 years — Homo sapiens

1.5 m.y. — Homo erectus

2.0 m.y. — Early *Homo*

Figure 13-4
The "main line" of hominid evolution over the last 2 m.y.

Java

As we will see in the next chapter, there are abundant *Homo erectus* remains known from Java that are almost certainly Middle Pleistocene in date (i.e., after 700,000 B.P.[*]). Some fragmentary finds from earlier beds in Java are also known; their chronological placement, however, is a matter of dispute.

Initial K/Ar dates for these early Javanese hominids place them as far back as 2 million years ago, but these dates still lack confirmation by other techniques and thus are still open to question (see p. 409).

[*]B.P. indicates Before Present.

BOX 13-1

A Visit to the Plio-Pleistocene: East Lake Turkana, Late One Afternoon

If an observer could be transported back through time and climb a tree in the area where the Koobi Fora Formation was accumulating, what would he see?

As the upper branches are reached, the climber would find himself in a ribbon of woodland winding out through open areas. A kilometer or so away to the west would be seen the swampy shores of the lake, teeming with birds, basking crocodiles, and *Euthecodons*. Here and there are schools of hippos. Looking east, in the distance some ten or twelve kilometers away lie low, rolling hills covered with savanna vegetation. From the hills, fingers of trees and bush extend fanwise out into the deltaic plains. These would include groves of large *Acacia*, *Celtis*, and *Ficus* trees along the watercourses, fringed by shrubs and bushes. Troops of colobus move in the tree tops, while lower down are some mangabey. Scattered through the bush, the observer might see small groups of waterbuck, impala, and kudu, while out in the open areas beyond, would be herds of alcelaphine antelope and some gazelle (*Megalotragus* and *Antidorcas*). Among the undergrowth little groups of *Mesochoerus* pigs rootle, munching herbiage.

Peering down through the branches of the tree, the climber would see below the clean sandy bed of a watercourse, dry here, but with a tidemark of grass and twigs caught in the fringing bushes and showing the passage of seasonal floods. Some distance away down the channel is a small residual pool.

Out beyond the bushes can be seen large open floodplains, covered with grasses and rushes, partly dry at those seasons of the year when the lake is low and when the river is not in spate. Far across the plains, a group of four or five men approach; although they are too far off for the perception of detail, the observer feels confident that they are men because they are striding along, fully upright, and in their hands they carry staves.

To continue the reconstruction in a more purely imaginative vein: as the men approach, the observer becomes aware of other primates below him. A group of creatures has been reclining on the sand in the shade of a tree while some youngsters play around them. As the men approach, these creatures rise and it becomes apparent that they too are bipedal. They seem to be female, and they whoop excitedly as some of the young run out to meet the arriving party, which can now be seen to consist mainly of males.

The two groups come together in the shade of the tree, and there is excited calling, gesturing, and greeting contacts. Now the observer can see them better, perhaps he begins to wonder about calling them men; they are upright and formed like men, but they are rather small, and when in groups they do not seem to engage in articulate speech. There are a wealth of vocal and gestural signals in their interaction, but no sustained sequential sound patterns.

The object being carried is the carcass of an impala, and the group congregates around this in high excitement; there is some pushing and shoving and flashes of temper and threat. Then one of the largest males takes two objects from a heap at the foot of the tree. There are sharp clacking sounds as he squats down and bangs these together repeatedly. The other creatures scramble around picking up the small sharp chips that have been detached from the stones. When there is a small scatter of flakes on the ground at his feet, the stone worker drops the two chunks, sorts through the fragments and selects two or three pieces. Turning back to the carcass, this leading male starts to make incisions. First the belly is slit open and the entrails pulled out; the guts are set on one side, but there is excited squabbling over the liver, lungs, and kidneys; these are torn apart, some individuals grab pieces and run to the periphery of the group. Then the creatures return to the carcass; one male severs skin, muscle, and sinew so as to disengage them from the trunk, while some others pull at limbs. Each adult male finishes up with a segment of the carcass and withdraws to a corner of the clearing, with one or two females and juveniles congregating around him. They sit chewing and cutting at the meat, with morsels changing hands at intervals. Two adolescent males sit at the periphery with a part of the intestines. They squeeze out the dung and chew at the entrails. One of the males gets up, stretches his arms, scratches under his armpits and then sits down. He leans against the tree, gives a loud belch and pats his belly. . . . *End of scenario.*

SOURCE:

"The Activities of Early Hominids" by Glynn Ll. Isaac. In *Human Origins. Louis Leakey and the East African Evidence*, G. Isaac and E. R. McCown, eds. The Benjamin/Cummings Publishing Company, Inc. © 1976. Reprinted with permission of the publisher.

Figure 13-5
A *nearly complete* Homo erectus *cranium (ER 3733) from east Lake Turkana. Dated approximately 1.6–1.3 m.y.a.*

Israel

A site on the western side of the Jordan River Valley in Israel, called Ùbeidiya, has been thought for some time to be quite ancient. Little has come from this site in the way of fossil hominids (just some nondiagnostic fragments), but artifacts are abundant. A recent biostratigraphic attempt at aging this site has yielded a provisional date (presumably associated with the ancient artifacts) of 2 million years (or even more!) (Repenning and Fejfar, 1982).

Obviously, the stratigraphic context at Ùbeidiya will have to be completely established, and further cross-correlation of this initial date will have to be performed. At present, it is intriguing to speculate about early hominids (*H. habilis*; very early *H. erectus*??) in southwestern Asia. We can reasonably postulate that *when* hominids first did emigrate from Africa, they passed through this region. Whether they already had done so by 2 m.y.a. remains to be seen.

France

Several sites in France (especially Vallonet Cave) have been suggested as potentially predating 1 m.y.a. No hominid fossils have been found at any of these sites, but stone tools have been discovered in what some researchers thought to be very early contexts. Systematic paleontological and geological work is still going on at several localities in south-central France, and attempts to establish a firm chronology are progressing. The most recent results (from paleomagnetic calibrations) indicate that all the potential hominid localities, in fact, postdate 1 m.y.a., although some of them perhaps not by much (Thouveny and Bonifay, 1984).

Interpretations: What Does It All Mean?

By this time, it may seem anthropologists have an almost perverse fascination in finding small scraps buried in the ground and then assigning them confusing numbers and taxonomic labels impossible to remember. We must realize that the collection of all the basic fossil data is the foundation of human evolutionary research. Without fossils, our speculations would be completely hollow. Several large, ongoing paleoanthropological projects discussed in Chapter 11 are now collecting additional data in an attempt to answer some of the more perplexing questions about our evolutionary history.

The numbering of specimens, which may at times seem somewhat confusing, is an attempt to keep the designations neutral and to make reference to each individual fossil as clear as possible. The formal naming of finds as *Australopithecus*, *Homo habilis*, *Homo erectus*, etc., should come much later, since it involves a lengthy series of complex interpretations. The assigning of generic and specific names to fossil finds is more than just a game, although some paleoanthropologists have acted as if it were just that. When we attach a particular label, such as *A. boisei*, on a particular fossil, we should be fully aware of the biological implications of such an interpretation (see p. 298).

Even more basic to our understanding of human evolution, the use of taxonomic nomenclature involves interpretations of fossil relationships. For

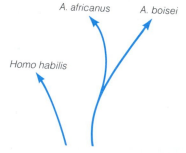

Figure 13-6
Phylogenetic interpretation. Early H. habilis *genetically distinct from australopithecines.*

Glynn Isaac, 1937–1985

In October, 1985, African prehistory and research into the evolution of early human culture was deprived of its acknowledged leader by the untimely and unexpected death of Glynn Isaac.

Born in Cape Town, Glynn was educated at the University there and at Cambridge, England, where he obtained his Ph.D. His training in both the natural sciences (geology and zoology) and archaeology had a profound effect on his subsequent achievements, and enabled him to create a link between disciplines that had a major influence on the remarkable advances in early man studies over the twenty-odd years of his active research.

After leaving Cambridge, he became Warden of Prehistoric Sites in Kenya and, later (1963–1965), Deputy Director of the Centre for Prehistory and Palaeontology at the National Museums of Kenya, where he benefitted greatly from his close association with Louis and Mary Leakey.

In 1966, he joined the Anthropology Faculty at the University of California, Berkeley. He was a moving force in the creation of a highly innovative program in early man studies, and many of his students, black and white, are now in the forefront of early hominid cultural research in Africa. His understanding of Africa's ecology and human behavior led him to initiate a series of field studies using comparable, present-day analogs as clues to past patterns, thereby making it possible to narrow down alternative explanations of the archaeological record. In 1983, he accepted appointment as Professor of Archaeology at Harvard and continued his work on early man research from there.

Glynn wrote or co-edited seven books and sixty-seven scientific papers, many of them advocating revolutionary new methods of investigation and interpretation of very early hominid cultural remains. With a keen intelligence,

he was a highly stimulating teacher with boundless, communicable enthusiasm and essential kindliness, which inspired respect and affection in those who came in contact with him, and many of his students in the field are now actively following his new, wider approach to interpreting the record of human cultural evolution.

Glynn's attitude to his subject was holistic and open, and he showed us clearly that the only possibility for future advance in early man studies is by continued dialogue between the disciplines, a dialogue which, in gratitude, his friends and students must now carry on.

J. Desmond Clark

example, two fossils such as "Zinj" and ER 406 are both usually called A. *boisei*. What we are saying here is they are both members of one *interbreeding* species. These two fossils can now be compared with others, like Sts. 5 from Sterkfontein, which are usually called A. *africanus*. What we are implying now is that "Zinj" and ER 406 are more closely related to each other than *either* is to Sts. 5. Furthermore, that Sts. 5 (*africanus*) populations were incapable of successfully interbreeding with *boisei* populations is a direct biological inference of this nomenclature.

PHYLOGENY
A schematic representation showing
ancestor-descendant relationships, usually
in a chronological framework.

We can carry the level of interpretation even further. For example, fossils such as ER 1470 are called early *Homo* (*Homo habilis*). We are now making a genus-level distinction, and two basic biological implications are involved:

1. *A. africanus* (Sts. 5) and *A. boisei* ("Zinj" and ER 406) are more closely related to each other than either is to ER 1470
2. The distinction between the groups reflects a basic difference in adaptive level (see Chapter 10)

From the time that fossil sites are first located to the eventual interpretation of hominid evolutionary events, several steps are necessary. Ideally, they should follow a logical order, for if interpretations are made too hastily, they confuse important issues for many years. A reasonable sequence is:

1. Selection and surveying of sites
2. Excavation of sites; recovery of fossil hominids
3. Designating individual finds with specimen numbers for clear reference
4. Detailed study and description of fossils
5. Comparison with other fossil material—in chronological framework if possible
6. Comparison of fossil variation with known ranges of variation in closely related groups of living primates
7. Assigning taxonomic names to fossil material

The task of interpretation is still not complete, for what we really want to know in the long run is what happened to the populations represented by the fossil remains. Indeed, in looking at the fossil hominid record, we are looking for our ancestors. In the process of eventually determining those populations that are our most likely antecedents, we may conclude some hominids are on evolutionary side branches. If this conclusion is accurate, they necessarily must have eventually become extinct. It is both interesting and relevant to us as hominids to try to find out what caused some earlier members of our family to continue evolving while others died out.

Putting It All Together

The interpretation of our paleontologic past in terms of which fossils are related to other fossils and how they are all related to us is usually shown diagrammatically in the form of a **phylogeny**. Such a diagram is a family tree of fossil evolution. This kind of interpretation is the eventual goal of evolutionary studies, but it is the final goal, only after adequate data are available to understand what is going on. For example, the phylogeny of horse evolution for the last 60 m.y. is well known (see Fig. 13-7).

Whereas hominid fossil evidence has accumulated in great abundance, the fact that so much of the material has been discovered so recently makes any firm judgments concerning the route of human evolution premature. However, paleoanthropologists are certainly not deterred from making their "best guesses," and thus diverse speculative theories have abounded in recent years. The vast majority of more than 300 fossils from East Africa is still in the descriptive and early analytical stages. At this time, the construction of phylogenies of human evolution is analogous to building a house with only a partial blueprint. We are not even sure how many rooms there are! Until the existing fossil evidence has

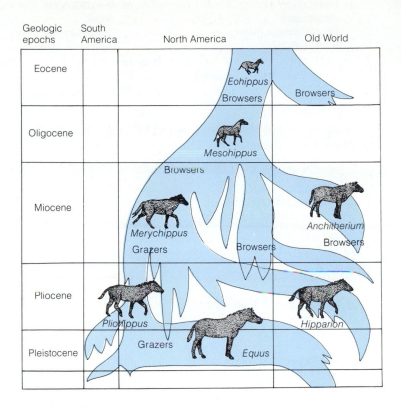

Geologic epochs	South America	North America	Old World

Figure 13-7
Schematic diagram (phylogeny) of horse evolution over the last 60 m.y. (From Heredity, Evolution and Society, *2nd Ed., by I. Michael Lerner and William J. Libby. W. H. Freeman and Company. Copyright © 1976.)*

been adequately studied, to say nothing about possible new finds, speculative theories must be viewed with a critical eye.

In the following pages, we will present several phylogenies representing different and opposing views of hominid evolution. We suggest you do not attempt to memorize them, for they *all* could be out of date by the time you read this book. It will prove more profitable to look at each one and assess the biological implications involved. Also, note which groups are on the main line of human evolution leading to *Homo sapiens* and which are placed on extinct side branches.

Interpreting the Interpretations

While a variety of evolutionary interpretations are depicted in Figure 13-8 (many dating to the 1960s and 1970s), recent interpretations fall into two main schools of thought:

1. A *fairly* simple double lineage hypothesis with *A. afarensis* as the common ancestor of all later hominids. The major split in human evolution is thought by some (Johanson and White, 1979) to occur early, before *A. africanus* (Phylogeny VI), and by others to be later, after *A. africanus* (Skelton et al., 1986) (Phylogeny VII).
2. A more complicated reconstruction, suggesting that what is called "*A. afarensis*" is two different species. Here the split into genus *Homo* may be very early (Senut and Tardieu, 1985). As shown in Phylogeny VIII, the relative positions of the gracile and robust australopithecines are not well worked out, but as many as three (and even four) lineages in the Plio-Pleistocene are thought possible.

(a) PHYLOGENY I
Double Lineage Theory
(LeGros Clark, 1967)

H. sapiens

H. erectus

X
A. robustus

A. africanus

Note: One minor sidebranch. A. africanus on main line

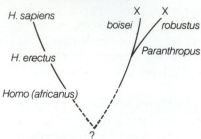

(b) PHYLOGENY II
Paranthropus
Double Lineage Theory
(Robinson, 1972)

H. sapiens

H. erectus

X   X
boisei   robustus

Paranthropus

Homo (africanus)

?

Note: One major sidebranch. Both robust species seen as very distinct. A. africanus seen as same as early Homo.

(c) PHYLOGENY III
Boisei
Double Lineage Theory
(Campbell, 1976)

H. sapiens

X
boisei

H. erectus

X
A. robustus

habilis
phase

A. africanus

?

Note: A. boisei seen as very distinct with very early split—Miocene? Early Homo ("habilis") = transitional.

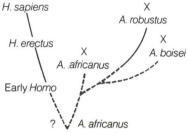

(d) PHYLOGENY IV
Early Homo
Double Lineage Theory
(Leakey, 1974; Pilbeam and Gould, 1974)

H. sapiens

X
A. robustus

H. erectus

X
A. africanus

X
A. boisei

Early Homo

?   A. africanus

Note: A africanus as possible common ancestor in Pliocene? Early Homo already distinct from australopithecines by late Pliocene.

(e) PHYLOGENY V
Nonhominid Double
Lineage Theory
(Oxnard, 1975)

X

Australopithecines
africanus
robustus
boisei
habilis (Olduvai)

H. sapiens

H. erectus

Early Homo
(Lake Turkana)

?

Note: All australopithecines classified as nonhominids comprising long-separate line of hominoid evolution. Extinct sidebranch includes Olduvai "habilis" finds; Turkana early Homo on main line.

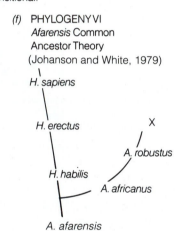

(f) PHYLOGENY VI
Afarensis Common
Ancestor Theory
(Johanson and White, 1979)

H. sapiens

H. erectus

X
A. robustus

H. habilis

A. africanus

A. afarensis

Note: Afarensis postulated as common ancestor to all Plio-Pleistocene hominids.

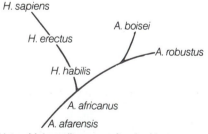

(g) PHYLOGENY VII
Africanus Common
Ancestor Theory
(Skelton, et al. 1986)

H. sapiens

H. erectus

A. boisei

H. habilis

A. robustus

A. africanus

A. afarensis

Note: Major split occurs after A. africanus. Therefore A. africanus is seen as still in our lineage as well as that of more derived australopithecines.

(h) PHYLOGENY VIII
Multiple Lineage/Early
Divergence
(Senut and Tardieu, 1985)

A. africanus

H. sapiens

H. erectus

A. boisei

H. habilis

?

A. afarensis

Homo ?

Note: Major split occurs before A. afarensis. Possible multiple lineages in Plio-Pleistocene.

(i) PHYLOGENY IX
Early Robust Lineage
Theory
(Delson, 1986)

A. robustus

A. boisei

H. sapiens

H. erectus

H. habilis

"A. aethiopicus"
(skull WT 17,000)

A. africanus

A. afarensis

Note: Robust lineage diverges early (as suggested by the "black skull," WT-17000). Africanus potentially on main line.

Figure 13-8 *Phylogenies of hominid evolution.*

More Complications: What to Do with the Black Skull (WT-17000)?

As we discussed in the previous chapter (p. 369), a newly discovered cranium from west of Lake Turkana has caused some major rethinking of hominid evolution. The earlier than previously suspected appearance of robust features can be accommodated by extending this lineage back in time. At the very least, this revised chronology makes the phylogeny (Phylogeny VI) in which robust australopithecines evolved uniquely from already-diverged *africanus* an unlikely reconstruction.

More difficult to explain is the mosaic of very primitive characteristics (like *afarensis*) mixed with highly derived ones (like those in *boisei*). It is possible that these features bespeak of a transitional form; in fact, this is the conclusion we advocate below. Nevertheless, some authorities (e.g., Shipman, 1986) believe that this new find, with its as yet unexplained mix of morphological traits, throws all previous scenarios of hominid evolution into confusion. Moreover, until more fossils are found (particularly those dating 2 to 3 m.y.a.), we are not likely to resolve this muddle.

Conclusions

We feel that present evidence best fits a phylogeny resembling Phylogeny IX. Such an explanation, *for the moment* at least, adequately accounts for variation in the hominid fossil record during the Plio-Pleistocene. The earliest definite hominids of which we have evidence are found in sites dating between 4 and 3 m.y.a. These fossils are also the most primitive of any hominid known, particularly as seen in the conformity of the cranium as well as numerous dental characteristics. Since these early forms combine a small brain with an already completely efficient bipedal adaptation, they are best considered members of the genus *Australopithecus*. However, they are not like the more specialized australopithecines seen later in both South and East Africa. Consequently, we believe the designation of these early australopithecines as a separate species (A. *afarensis*) is justified.

In addition to calling attention to a different morphology, a separate species name also can be used to make phylogenetic inferences. In this case, it appears that *afarensis*—particularly as seen in the dental complex—makes a good *potential* common ancestor for all the later australopithecines and genus *Homo*. In the later australopithecines, the relatively large front teeth are much reduced, while the back teeth become considerably larger. This trend towards a large, grinding tooth specialization is seen most dramatically in the robust australopithecines.

Meanwhile, in the evolutionary line that diverged into genus *Homo*, the front teeth are also reduced, but the back teeth do not undergo the specialized development such as that of the later australopithecines. In addition, as compared to their smaller-brained australopithecine cousins, the *Homo* line displays a progressive increase in cranial capacity. Certainly, by about 2 m.y.a., the early *Homo* line is becoming larger-brained and probably more culture-dependent; these two factors obviously interact with one another as a primary determinant of human biocultural evolution. Evidence such as the 1470 skull from Turkana clearly shows us that such a large-brained lineage was evolving in East Africa in

Table 13-1 *Dates for* Homo habilis

East Lake Turkana	1.8 m.y.a.
Olduvai	1.8 m.y.a.
Omo	1.85 m.y.a.
Sterkfontein	2.0–1.5 m.y.a.
Swartkrans	2.0–1.5 m.y.a.

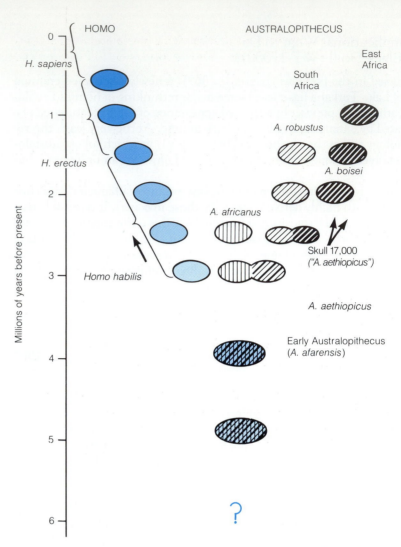

the Plio-Pleistocene. Some fragmentary remains at about the same time from South Africa suggest a similar process, since tantalizing evidence from Swartkrans and Sterkfontein implies a large-brained lineage was evolving there as well.

The other lineage (later *Australopithecus*) seems to have remained in an evolutionary backwater perfecting its already specialized adaptation, probably involving a heavily vegetarian diet with only minimal cultural dependence. By about 1.6 m.y.a., the *Homo* line—in East Africa anyway—had reached the level of *erectus*, the larger-brained, culturally more developed ancestor of our species. (For the story of *erectus*, see Chapter 14.)

A reasonable, though for now still extremely tenuous, hypothesis of the course of hominid evolution in the Plio-Pleistocene is depicted in Figure 13-9.

Summary

The huge amount of fossil hominid material from the Plio-Pleistocene of South and East Africa has generated a great deal of interest. As more evidence is found, more questions rather than answers seem to arise. Some possible additional complexities discussed in this chapter include: (1) evolution of A. *africanus* in East Africa; (2) early appearance by 1.6 m.y.a. in East Africa of *Homo erectus*; (3) Plio-Pleistocene hominids outside Africa?; and (4) what to do with the newly discovered fossil WT-1700.

Attempts to explain all the variation observed in fossil hominid material in the Plio-Pleistocene have yielded many alternative theories. None of these is yet reasonably secure, and new evidence probably will force major reassessments in the next decade. What is significant in all this current debate is the way fossil hominids are utilized to make general biological inferences concerning the mechanics of human evolution.

Questions for Review

1. How secure is the fossil information for hominids outside Africa prior to 1 m.y.a.?
2. What is a phylogeny?
3. Why have so many phylogenies been proposed for hominid evolution covering the last 5 million years?
4. Compare and contrast the biological implications of two of the phylogenies in Figure 13-8. Pay particular attention to the implications of Phylogenies VI, VII, VIII, and IX.
5. Why is it important to be aware of within-species variation (sexual dimorphism, age, individual variation) when assessing the evolutionary relationships of fossil hominid populations?

Homo Erectus

CONTENTS

ISSUE

Seeking the Peking Bones

In the summer of 1941, war between the United States and Japan appeared inevitable to the officials at the Cenozoic Research Laboratory of Peking Union Medical College. To prevent the priceless Peking Man bones from falling into the hands of the Japanese, already in Peking, the officials packed them into boxes and shipped them to a warehouse at Camp Holcomb, a Marine Corps base not far from Peking. The marines, scheduled to leave China on December 8 aboard the S.S. *President Harrison*, were to take the bones with them on their return to the United States.

On December 7, 1941, Pearl Harbor was attacked, and war declared against Japan. Instead of leaving, the marines were arrested by the Japanese and interned for the duration of the war. What happened to the bones has remained a deep mystery ever since.

One account is that in the fall of 1941, Col. Ashurst, Commander of the Marine Corps Headquarters at Camp Holcomb, ordered the boxes of bones sent to Lt. Wm. E. Foley, a Marine Corps physician, who was to take the boxes with him aboard the *President Harrison*. When he received the boxes, Dr. Foley, realizing arrest and internment were imminent, distributed them to institutions and reliable Chinese friends in Tientsin, a city near Camp Holcomb. Dr. Foley has steadfastly refused ever since to divulge the names of these Chinese friends without guarantees for their safety from the Chinese government. Since he did not open the boxes when they arrived,

it is not known for certain whether they even contained the bones.

In 1972, more than twenty-five years after the war ended, another chapter unfolded in the case of the missing bones. Mr. Christopher Janus, an American businessman, became interested in locating the bones after a visit to China and offered a reward of $5,000 for information leading to their recovery. Soon afterward, in New York, Janus received a telephone call from a woman who claimed her husband, a former marine now deceased, had left her a footlocker of what he believed were stolen Peking Man bones. Janus requested a meeting, which the so-called "mystery woman" insisted be held on the observation deck high atop the Empire State Building. At the meeting, the woman, who refused to give her name, showed a photograph of the footlocker's contents to Janus, who later checked the photo with Dr. Harry Shapiro, a physical anthropologist at the American Museum of Natural History. Shapiro, long interested in Peking Man and the missing bones, thought a skull in the photograph resembled that of Peking Man, and with that assurance Janus opened negotiations with the mystery woman's lawyer. The woman wanted $500,000 and guarantees that the United States government would not prosecute for possession of stolen property or confiscate the bones. Later, when these conditions were met, she raised her price to $700,000 and demanded a letter from the Chinese government stating they would not prosecute. The Chinese did not reply to the request for such a letter, and negotiations were never resumed.

Many rumors of the bones' location came to Mr. Janus, who eagerly investigated a number of them. He heard they were in Taiwan; they were not, but while there he increased the reward to

$150,000. He also heard they were in Hong Kong—they were not; in Bangkok—not there, either. He was told they were in Burma, Tokyo, and Manila; but by this time he thought it was a waste of time and money to follow up these leads. Since then, 1975, Janus has not reported any further activity, and in November, 1977, withdrew his offer of reward.

The fate of the Peking bones remains unknown. The New York mystery woman might have a skull; Dr. Foley's friends in China may have all the bones; the bones might have been found in the Camp Holcomb warehouse by Japanese soldiers who, not realizing what they had, destroyed or abandoned them. They may have found their way to Burma, Bangkok, or—though very unlikely—the United States. Whoever has them—if anyone—is not telling.

The New York Times reported (May 11, 1980) that a former marine, Roger Ames, telephoned from his hospital bed in Dallas recently and told Janus the following story:

While on guard duty the night before Pearl Harbor he saw two marine officers, carrying a footlocker and shovels, dig a hole and bury the footlocker.

Urged on by the ex-marine's message, Janus decided to resume his investigation of the missing bones. However, to this point, no further leads have emerged.

SOURCES:

Janus, Christopher G. with William Brashler. *The Search for Peking Man*, New York: Macmillan Publishing Co., Inc., 1975.

The New York Times, Sunday, May 11, 1980.

Shapiro, Harry L. "The Strange, Unfinished Saga of Peking Man," *Natural History*, 80:8 (No. 9), 1971.

———. *Peking Man*, New York: Simon and Schuster, 1974.

Introduction

In the preceding several chapters, we introduced an early grade (see Box 14-1) of hominid evolution, the australopithecines of the Plio-Pleistocene. We discussed at some length the confusion surrounding them, confusion brought about by the various interpretations of the number of australopithecine species or lineages. Furthermore, recent discoveries, such as the "black skull," have added to the complexities of human evolution in the Plio-Pleistocene. These problems, discussed in Chapter 13, become even more complicated with the *H. erectus* (KNM-ER WT 15,000) find at Lake Turkana, discussed in this chapter, a contemporary of both australopithecines and *H. habilis*. It is possible that future discoveries will provide evidence to resolve this phylogenetic puzzle. We certainly hope so.

The next grade of hominid evolution, *H. erectus*, is much clearer, although some aspects remain murky. *H. erectus* inhabited a wider geographic area than australopithecines. We find their remains in Africa, Europe, and Asia, but not in Australia or the New World. They were taller, larger-brained, more culture-dependent, and more skillful toolmakers. Unlike australopithecines, who lived in much of the Pliocene and early Pleistocene, *H. erectus* is mainly a Pleistocene hominid. In our discussion of *H. erectus*, therefore, we must necessarily refer to the Pleistocene—its climate, biosphere, geological events, and dates.

The Pleistocene (1.8 m.y.a.–10,000 y.a.)

During much of the Pleistocene (also known as the Age of Glaciers), large areas of the northern hemisphere were covered with enormous masses of ice, which advanced and retreated as the temperature fell and rose. Until recently, European glaciers were considered to be four in number—Günz, Mindel, Riss, and Würm. In reconstructing the history of the Pleistocene, scholars attempted to work out the dates of these glacial advances. Then they further attempted to develop the hominid history of Europe and Asia by correlating hominid fossil bones and artifacts found in association with animals indicative of the glacial advances or retreats. For example, if human bones were found with those of a warm-weather animal, the researchers assumed that this was an interglacial or **interstadial** period. This procedure may appear straightforward enough, but one of the problems, especially in Europe, was that the Alpine glaciers have not been chronometrically dated.

At one time, the Plio-Pleistocene boundary was defined by the appearance of certain mammals believed to identify the beginning of the Pleistocene. Since the appearance of these mammals—modern cow, modern horse, Indian elephant—occurs at different times on different continents, this criterion could not be used on a worldwide basis. What was needed was an event that occurred everywhere on earth at the same time, and just such an event has been found in the reversal of the earth's magnetic field (Dalrymple, 1972). The study of such reversals is called *paleomagnetism* and is used to cross-check other dating techniques (see p. 322–323).

INTERSTADIAL
Stadial (from stadium): period
The periods of partial retreats during a major glaciation.

BOX 14-1

Grades of Human Evolution

1. *Australopithecus**
2. *Homo erectus*
3. *Homo sapiens* (including transitional forms, Neandertals, and modern populations)

*Contemporaneous with some australopithecines is the hominid, *Homo habilis* (also called "early *Homo*"). We include in Grade 1 (*Australopithecus*) most especially the more primitive form *A. afarensis* and *A. africanus*. *Homo habilis* can be seen as transitional between Grades 1 and 2.

Figure 14-1
A partial listing of Homo erectus *sites.* H. erectus *inhabited areas of Europe, Africa, and Asia, a much wider distribution than australopithecines.*

We have known for a long time that the earth's magnetic field has frequently been reversed. During the reversal period, what we consider to be the North Pole became the South Pole, and a compass needle would have pointed south instead of north as it does now. Earth scientists have now succeeded in dating these reversals, which are worldwide events. The reversals now serve as markers to correlate geophysical activity in different parts of the world.

Although differences of opinion exist concerning the boundary between the Middle and Upper (or Late) Pleistocene, we shall use the widely accepted figure of 125,000 years, correlated with the beginning of the Riss-Würm interglacial. Figure 14-3 correlates Pleistocene, Alpine glacial periods, cultural divisions, and hominid sites.

1. Java
2. Peking, China
3. Lantian, China
4. Hexian, China
5. Yunxi, China
6. Yunxian, China
7. Yuanmou, China
8. Heidelberg, Germany
9. Vérteszöllös, Hungary
10. Petralona, Greece
11. Torralba Ambrona, Spain
12. Terra Amata, France
13. Ternifine, Algeria
14. Sidi Abd er-Raman (Casablanca), Morocco
15. Rabat, Morocco
16. Salé, Morocco
17. Olduvai Hominid 9, Tanzania
18. Olduvai Hominid 13, Tanzania
19. Olduvai Hominid 28, Tanzania
20. KNM-ER 3733, East Turkana
21. Omo, Ethiopia
22. KNM WT 15,000, West Turkana
23. Bodo, Ethiopia
?24. Swartkrans, South Africa
25. Narmada, India

Figure 14-2
Glacial sequence. With the exception of the Würm, dates for glacial and interglacial periods have not been well worked out yet.

TIME (years ago)	GLACIAL AGES (in Europe)	PLEISTOCENE		CULTURAL PERIOD	HOMINIDAE (*H. erectus*)
125,000	RISS	MIDDLE	PALEOLITHIC	ACHELIAN	?Salé
					Terra Amata (arch. site)
265,000	Mindel-Riss (Holstein) Interglacial				Torralba/Ambrona (arch. site)
300,000	MINDEL				Vértesszöllös
					Petralona
					Bodo (date undetermined)
400,000					Peking
430,000	(Cromerian) Günz-Mindel Interglacial				Sangiran 17
					Heidelberg
					Ternifine
500,000					Ndutu
	GÜNZ				Lantian (Chenjiawo)
600,000					Lantian (Gongwangling)
					OH 12
700,000	Sequence and Dates uncertain	LOWER		OLDOWAN	*H. erectus* (Java)
1,000,000					
1,200,000					OH 9
1,500,000					OH 13, KNM-ER 3733
1,600,000					KNM-WT 15,000

Figure 14-3
Lower and Middle Pleistocene (not to scale).
Many dates are best estimates.

NUCHAL
nape
Refers to the nape of the neck area.

ALVEOLAR
(al-vee'-lar)
Tooth-bearing portion of upper or lower jaw.

MASSETER
Chewing

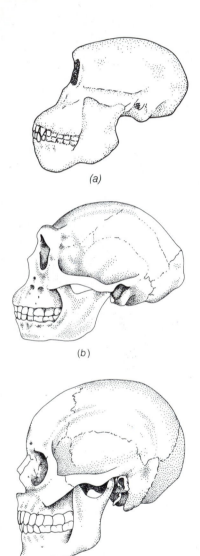

(a)

(b)

(c)

Figure 14-4
(a) Australopithecus (afarensis);
(b) H. erectus (Peking); (c) H. sapiens (anatomically modern). Note the changes in prognathism, ascending ramus, slope of foreheads, vault height, and development of occiput. (Not to scale.)

The Pleistocene, which lasted almost 2 million years, was an important time in hominid evolutionary history. *Homo erectus* appears. From their brain size and tools, we can clearly see that this form, using culture as their strategy of adaptation, should be called human. By the time the Pleistocene terminated, modern humans had already appeared, dependence on culture as the human way of life had dramatically increased, and domestication of plants and animals—one of the great cultural revolutions of human history—was either about to commence or had just been invented. With this background of the time span in which *H. erectus* evolved and developed, let us examine more closely the hominid to whom we owe so much.

Homo erectus

We have already observed that *H. erectus* was taller, larger-brained, and more dependent on culture than australopithecines. These are general statements, and it will therefore be necessary to discuss the characteristics of *H. erectus* in more detail. Since we are dealing with the evolution of hominids from something resembling an australopithecine stage to the modern stage, what we shall see in the modifications of hominids, for the most part, are relative changes. That is, *H. erectus* is taller than australopithecines, but shorter* than *H. sapiens*; larger-brained than australopithecines, but smaller-brained than *H. sapiens*, etc. *Homo erectus*, in many physical and cultural characteristics, is intermediate between the australopithecine and *sapiens* stages.

The cranial capacity of *H. erectus* ranges widely from 775 to 1225 cc, with a mean of 1020 cc. In terms of averages, this would make the skull of *H. erectus* roughly twice the size of australopithecines, 50% larger than early *Homo*, and 75% as large as *H. sapiens*.

When we look at the skull of *H. erectus* in profile (p. 401), several characteristics are immediately apparent. Overhanging the orbits is a pronounced bony ledge, the supraorbital torus, and, just behind it, is a marked depression known as postorbital constriction. The forehead recedes instead of rising sharply as it does in modern humans, and the long, low skull is reminiscent of a deflated football. At the end of the skull is the occiput, a bone forming the back and part of the base of the skull. The occipital bone angles sharply down and forward, unlike the rounded profile of *H. sapiens*. The rear end of the skull profile also points up a ridge of bone—**nuchal** line—for the attachment of neck muscles that hold up the head. Protruding beyond the occiput is an extension of bone called a nuchal torus.

Returning to the front of the profile, we see the **alveolar** prognathism, receding chin, and teeth similar to but slightly larger than modern populations. Such traits reflect heavy chewing, and there is, indeed, a number of indications of well-developed **masseter** muscles. Heavy muscles require bony attachments, and these can be seen in the ridges on the mandible, the "buttresses on the facial skeleton—such as the broad nasal root, the thick supraorbital torus, the thick frontal process of the zygomatic bone—and the well-marked temporal lines" (Jacob, 1975, p. 314).

*A recent find (KNM-WT 15000) of a 12-year-old *H. erectus* boy suggests *erectus* may have been as tall (perhaps taller) than *H. sapiens* (see pp. 422, 423).

Vocabulary

ALVEOLAR PROGNATHISM   Forward projection of the maxilla

ASCENDING RAMUS   Rear upright portion of the mandible

CALLOTE or **CALVA**   Uppermost portion of the braincase

CALVARIUM   The skull minus the face and mandible

CERVICAL   Pertaining to the neck, as in cervical vertebrae

CLAVICLE   Collar bone

CONDYLE   A rounded protuberance of bone which articulates (forms a joint, moves against) with another bone. The ball in a ball and socket joint (humerus and femur)

CORONAL SUTURE   The suture running transversely across the skull joining the frontal and parietal bones

CRANIUM   The complete skull; bones of the head, face, and mandible

FEMUR   Thigh bone

FIBULA   The narrow long bone on the outside of the lower leg (see tibia)

FRONTAL BONE   The front bone of the skull including the forehead

HUMERUS   Upper arm bone

LAMBDOID SUTURE   The transverse suture at the back of the top of the skull joining the parietal and occipital bones

MAGHREB   An area in Northwest Africa

MANDIBLE   Lower jaw

MAXILLA   Upper jaw

OCCIPUT, OCCIPITAL BONE   The rear bone of the skull

PALEOLITHIC   (Paleo: old; lithic: stone) Old Stone Age. The culture period preceding food-producing (farming, herding)

PARIETAL   The right and left side bones on top of the skull; joined by the sagittal suture

PLATYCEPHALY   (platy: flat; cephaly: head) Flatheadedness as opposed to dome shape of anatomically modern human beings

SAGITTAL SUTURE   The suture joining the left and right parietals; bounded by coronal suture in front and lambdoidal suture behind

SCAPULA   Shoulder blade

SUPRAORBITAL TORUS   (supra: above; orbital: eye opening; torus: ridge) Ridge above the orbits on a skull, very pronounced in *H. erectus*, Neandertals, and some australopithecines

TIBIA   The large long bone of the lower leg; the shin (see fibula)

ZYGOMATIC ARCH   The bony arch below the orbit

ZYGOMATIC BONE   Outer portion of orbit forming parts of its floor, and the cheekbone

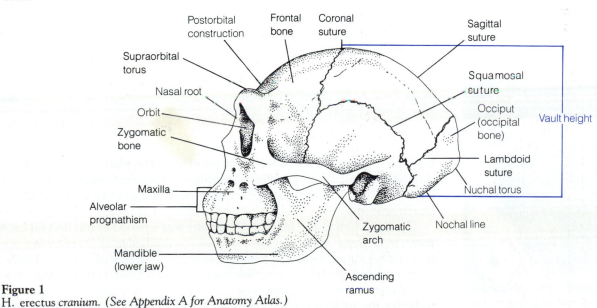

Figure 1
H. erectus *cranium. (See Appendix A for Anatomy Atlas.)*

Figure 14-5
H. erectus (*Peking Man*). *From this view, the supraorbital torus, low vault of the skull, nuchal torus, and angled occiput can be clearly seen.*

Figure 14-6
H. erectus (*Peking Man*). *Note that the widest part of the skull is toward the bottom, giving the skull a pentagonal form.*

Figure 14-7
Shovel-shaped incisors.

From the rear, we can see an important feature that distinguishes an *H. erectus* skull: its pentagonal shape, with maximum breadth at or near the base. In later hominids, maximum breadth is higher up on the skull. (See Fig. 14-6, 14-16, and 14-21.)

Differences in size and structure of teeth occur among the various *H. erectus* forms. In several of the earlier Javanese upper jaws, a surprising **diastema** exists between the lateral incisor and canine, and the canine projects a bit beyond the margin of the other teeth. These are nonhominid primate characteristics that are not found among most australopithecines. What their adaptive function might have been is difficult to know. Characteristic of pongids and many australopithecines, too, is that the molar teeth increase in size from front to back. This sequence varies among *H. erectus*, but in most cases the third molar is *smaller* than the second, a design that is typical of the later hominid pattern.

Two other dental traits may be mentioned. First are **shovel-shaped** incisors (Fig. 14-7). The edges of both sides of the teeth have raised ridges of enamel, and the incisors resemble a tiny scoop or coal shovel. It has been suggested that shovel-shaped incisors are an adaptive response in hunting and gathering societies, such as the Eskimo, in which a great deal of chewing takes place with the front teeth. The additional enamel may serve as structural support that enables the teeth to last longer; it is especially pronounced in Neandertal (see Chapter 15) and some modern populations.

The second trait is known as **taurodontism**, or enlarged pulp cavity (see Fig. 14-8). If roots of the molars (and sometimes premolars) should fail to grow to their adult length, a tendency of the pulp cavity in the center of the tooth to become enlarged occurs. This characteristic is an advantage among hard-chewing humans and such grazing animals as horses and cows that require high crowns on their teeth. In time, the pulp hardens and more wear is possible than in ordinary teeth.

In the past, it was believed that the locomotor skeleton of *H. erectus* was practically indistinguishable from *H. sapiens*. However, more recent analyses suggest that there are a number of morphological differences. "Nonetheless, the functional locomotor capabilities appear to have been generally similar to adaptations in *H. sapiens* for habitual erect posture and efficient striding bipedal gait" (Howell, 1978).

Asia

Java

Scientific discoveries are normally the result of careful planning, hard work, and thorough knowledge of the subject. In addition, they are frequently tales of luck, adventure, and heartbreak, which brings us to the story of Eugene Dubois, a Dutch anatomist.

The latter half of the nineteenth century was a period of intellectual excitement. In England, Darwin's *Origin of Species* (published in 1859) provoked scientists and educated laymen to take opposing sides, often with great emotion. In Germany, for example, the well-known zoologist Ernst Haeckel eagerly supported Darwin's statement that man descended from apes and even suggested the name for the missing transitional link between the two: *Pithecanthropus alalus*, "the ape man without speech." He was criticized by Rudolf Virchow, one of

Europe's most famous scientists and Haeckel's one-time zoology professor, who publicly and scornfully disagreed with these speculations. In 1856, a strange skull had been recovered near Dusseldorf, Germany. This specimen is what we today recognize as a Neandertal skull, but, when a description of it was published, scientific opinion was again divided and feelings ran high. "The opinions and counter-opinions about the Neandertal skull and other odd skulls, jaws, and bones that turned up in Europe kept science and the keenly interested lay public in something of an uproar for many years" (Moore, 1961, p. 235).

This stimulating intellectual climate surrounded the youthful **Eugene Dubois**, born in Holland in 1858, the year before Darwin's *Origin* and two years after the discovery of the Neandertal skull. As a young man, Dubois took up the study of medicine at the University of Amsterdam, and we can imagine how much these debates about human ancestors engaged the interest of an anatomy student. When Dubois graduated, he was appointed lecturer in anatomy at the University in 1886, but his heart was not in it. Visions of finding our fossil ancestors were more exciting than a stodgy academic career, and Dubois made up his mind to resign his university post and search for "Early Man." He was the first person ever to deliberately set out on such a venture. But where did one search in the 1880s?

Haeckel had reasoned that the missing link might be found in the Indonesian Islands under the mistaken notion that gibbons, native to that area, belonged in human ancestry. Virchow had pointed out that tropical habitats of anthropoid apes were still totally unexplored. Indonesia seemed a judicious choice, especially since it was Dutch colonial territory. Dubois secured an appointment as a surgeon in the Royal Dutch Army and sailed for Sumatra in November, 1887, on the beginning leg of his journey to discover the first "apeman."

Dubois started digging in several caves in Sumatra and, except for teeth of extinct orangutan, found nothing of a hominoid nature. Hearing the digging was more favorable on Java, Dubois transferred his operations to that island. While there, he was sent a skull from a rock shelter at Wadjak, Java. Dubois then managed to be transferred to Java and immediately went to Wadjak, where, in 1889, he found a skull known as the Wadjak skull (discussed in Chapter 15).

Moving on, Dubois continued searching, and reached the small village of Trinil in August, 1891. On the banks of the Solo River near the village, he found a molar he thought might belong to a chimpanzee, and this find spurred him to even greater effort. A month later, he discovered what he had come halfway round the world to find. Lodged in the dirt was a dark, bowl-like fossilized bone, which Dubois immediately recognized as the top of a skull. He worked feverishly and carefully to extract the bone "until a fine cranium emerged, a cranium like that of no living creature. Almost the whole skullcap was there, harder than marble and heavy in weight and portentiousness" (Moore, 1961, p. 237). Dubois' dream had become reality!

Or had it? The skullcap was low with a very pronounced supraorbital torus, and Dubois thought it might, like the molar, also belong to a chimpanzee. Digging stopped for the rainy season and, soon after resuming work the following year, Dubois recovered a femur fifteen yards upstream in the same level, the Trinil horizon, as the skullcap. He discerned at once that it resembled a human femur and belonged to an individual with an upright posture. But he was convinced he was dealing with a chimpanzee, or something like it, and that the molar, skullcap, and femur belonged not only to the same kind of creature, but to the same individual.

Taurodont
(Peking Man, Heidelberg, and some modern populations)

Cynodaunt
(modern Europeans)

Pulp cavity

Figure 14-8
Taurodontism.

Figure 14-9
Eugene Dubois.

A Partial Definition of *Homo erectus*

Homo erectus (Dubois) 1894   A species (extinct) of the genus *Homo*, known from Eurasia and Africa, distinguished by very substantial enlargement of the brain size, mean (1,020 cc) nearly twice that of large *Australopithecus* species and substantially above that of antecedent species of genus *Homo*; endocranial cast with essentially (modern) human fissuration pattern; generally low, flattened frontal region and prominent frontal keel; expanded (unilaterally) inferior frontal region, with wide separation from anterior temporal lobe; expanded precentral cortical area; exposed anterior insular area, in whole or part related to substantial development of Sylvian crest; lack of approximation between temporal lobe and cerebellum; absolutely and relatively narrow temporal lobe, tapering anteromedially, with poorly expanded inferior temporal area, salient superior temporal area, and posteriorly expanded posterior part of middle temporal convolution, expanded (unilaterally) inferior parietal region (supramarginal area); cerebellum with ipsilateral asymmetry, and cerebrum largely symmetrical, but with contralateral asymmetry expressed particularly in parieto-occipital and inferior frontal regions.

Cranial length greater than *Australopithecus*; vault bones of substantial to massive thickness, as expressed in outer and inner tables, cranial suture closure apparently earlier than in *H. sapiens*, and with coronal preceding sagittal suture closure; maximum breadth of vault at or toward the cranial base, usually coincident with biauricular breadth, with lesser bitemporal and biparietal dimensions; substantial postorbital constriction; low to more moderately arched vault, with low receding frontal (with or without notable frontal tuberosity), longitudinally flattened parietal, and occipital with marked to substantial angulation between upper (squama) and lower (nuchal) scales; usually distinct sagittal thickening, especially in bregmatic area, often associated with marked parasagittal depression; parietal smaller, more rectangular and transversely more curved than in *H. sapiens*, usually with sub-. . . .

F. Clark Howell, "Hominidae." In: V. J. Maglio and H.B.S. Cooke (eds.). *Evolution of African Mammals*, Cambridge: Harvard University Press, 1978.

After studying his discoveries for a few years, Dubois startled the world in 1894 with a paper sensationally entitled, "*Pithecanthropus erectus*, a Human Transitional Form from Java." In honor of Haeckel, who had already suggested it, the name *Pithecanthropus* "was deliberately adopted by Dubois, who believed he had actually found [the missing] link" between apes and humans (von Koenigswald, 1962, p. 80). A scientific uproar reminiscent of Darwin's time greeted Dubois' publication. Virchow, who did not seem to believe in the existence of fossil humans, rejected Dubois' views; Haeckel, of course, was overjoyed, since he believed his views had been vindicated.

The contrary opinions announced by scientists, and the outrage expressed by the public, especially the clergy, hurt and discouraged Dubois. He locked the bones in strongboxes and steadfastly refused permission to anyone, including scientists and public, to view them. Von Koenigswald, whom we shall meet shortly, gives a painful account of Dubois during this time:

> *Pithecanthropus* became Dubois' destiny. It was his discovery, his creation, his exclusive possession; on this point he was as unaccountable as a jealous lover. Anyone who disagreed with his interpretation of *Pithecanthropus* was his personal enemy. When his ideas failed to win general acceptance he sullenly withdrew, growing mistrustful, unsociable and eccentric. He showed his finds to hardly anyone, and at night he used to hear burglars prowling around the house, bent on stealing his *Pithecanthropus*. If anyone came to his door in whom he scented a colleague, he was simply not at home (von Koenigswald, 1956, p. 32).

Figure 14-10
The Indonesian area.

Dubois was finally persuaded to open the strongboxes, in 1923, to the inspection of Dr. Aleš Hrdlička, an American anthropologist at the Smithsonian Institution. By 1930, the controversy had faded, especially in light of important new discoveries near Beijing,* China, in the late 1920s (discussed subsequently). These finds clearly demonstrated that Peking Man was human, an early form no doubt, but human nevertheless. Resemblances between the Peking skulls and Dubois' *Pithecanthropus* were obvious, and scientists pointed out that the Java form was not an apeman, as Dubois contended, but a true human.

One might expect that Dubois would welcome Peking Man and the support it provided for the human status of *Pithecanthropus*, but the eccentric Dutchman refused to recognize any connection between Peking and Java and described Peking "as a degenerate Neanderthaler" (von Koenigswald, 1956, p. 55). Even more sadly, at about this time, Dubois changed his mind and declared his *Pithecanthropus* was not after all the missing link between ape and human, but a giant gibbon, a position he tenaciously held until his death in 1940.

The story of *Homo erectus* does not, of course, end with the death of the beleaguered Dr. Dubois. Others, notably a younger paleontologist born in Germany, G. H. R. von Koenigswald, took up the search for ancient humans in Java in the 1930s.

Before reviewing the bone material found in Java, we should take note of a problem that paleoanthropologists and other scientists have faced in working out Java prehistoric chronology.

The stratigraphy of Javanese soil presents an especially complex structure. Geologists have attempted to arrange an orderly stratigraphic scheme that would enable paleoanthropologists to attach dates to the hominid fossils they excavate. Unfortunately, this has been a troublesome task, and geologists have given different age ranges for the same stratum. Furthermore, it has been difficult to order the faunal stages, and many scientists believe the old scheme of Djetis (Lower Pleistocene), Trinil (Middle Pleistocene), and Ngandong (Upper Pleistocene) to be inadequate. One of the reasons for this is that the key animals used to identify the Djetis stage are also found in the Trinil. Therefore, we shall use a faunal sequence recently proposed (de Vos, 1985, p. 216) even though it has not yet been widely accepted:

Faunal Stages

Ngandong	Trinil H.K.	Ci Saat
Kedung Brubus	Trinil H.K. (or Ci Saat)	

*Beijing is now the accepted name for Peking; however, when referring to the fossil, we shall continue to use the name Peking.

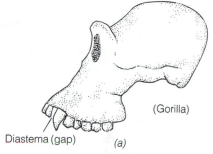

Figure 14-11
Diastema (a) in a male gorilla; (b) in an early Java upper jaw. Diastema occurs between the canine and lateral incisor.

Figure 14-12
Skullcap (Pithecanthropus I, found by Eugene Dubois). Femur, also found by Dubois, led him to name this form Pithecanthropus erectus, now known as H. erectus. The abnormal spur of bone on the femur is known as an exostosis. It has no bearing on the identification of the femur. (Photograph of casts.)

BOX 14-4

Reference List of Scientists Mentioned in Chapter 14

Name	Identification	Associated with
Black, Davidson*	Canadian anatomist	Zhoukoudian, China
Dubois, Eugene*	Dutch anatomist	Java
Haeckel, Ernst*	Nineteenth-century German zoologist	"Pithecanthropus"
Howell, F. Clark	Physical anthropologist, University of California, Berkeley	Torralba/Ambrona, Spain
Isaac, Glynn*	Archeologist, Harvard University	East Turkana, Kenya
Von Koenigswald, G. H. R.*	German paleontologist	Java
Leakey, Louis*	Physical anthropologist	Olduvai Gorge, Tanzania
Leakey, Mary D.	Archeologist	Olduvai Gorge, Tanzania
Leakey, Richard E. F.	Paleoanthropologist	East/West Turkana, Kenya
De Lumley, Henry	French archeologist	Terra Amata, France
Pei, W. C.*	Chinese geologist and archeologist	Zhoukoudian, China
Poulianos, Ari	Greek paleoanthropologist	Petralona, Greece
Virchow, Rudolf*	Nineteenth-century German zoologist and pathologist	
Weidenreich, Franz*	German, later American, anatomist and paleoanthropologist	Zhoukoudian, China; Java
Wu, Rukang	Chinese paleoanthropologist	Zhoukoudian and other sites, China

*Deceased

In Figure 14-13, we have attempted to correlate the faunal sequence with other dating methods; however, the correlations are merely suggestive.

A new set of names have been proposed to replace the well-known Java geologic formations for the Sangiran site. These are listed in the following tabulation.

Old	Proposed	
Nopopuro	Pohjajar	(We shall continue to use the old names.)
Kabuh	Bapang	
Pucangan	Sangiran	

Other dating methods used in Java, such as fission track, potassium-argon, paleomagnetism, and fluorine content, have not always proved reliable. The studies continue, of course, but until the dating situation becomes clearer, we will have to make do with the evidence available. The student is cautioned that

AGE[1] (in millions)	MAGNETO[2] STRATIGRAPHY	PLEISTOCENE[3]	GEOLOGIC[4] FORMATION	FAUNAL[5] STRATA	JAVA[6] HOMINIDS	REMARKS
	BRUNHES (normal)	UPPER	NOTOPURO (Pohjajar)	NGANDONG	H. soloensis	Solo man (usually considered upper Pleistocene)
.51		MIDDLE	Upper KABUH (Bapang)	KEDUNG BRUBUS	H. modjokertensis (Perning 1)	deVos places H. Modiokertensis in either the Kedung Brubus or Ngandong faunal level.
.73			Middle		S12, S17 Sambungmacan	Jacob dates Sambungmacan at 800,000 y.a.
.78 / .83 / .90	MATUYAMA		Lower Formation	TRINIL H.K.	Trinil 2	Trinil 2 (P. erectus found by Dubois.)
1.0					S6, S2	S6 = Meganthropus palaeojavanicus
Jaramillo .90 / .97				TRINIL H.K.	S4	P4 = P. robustus
1.16		LOWER	PUCANGAN (sangiran)	C1 STAAT		
1.4 / 1.5					S5, S9	P dubius — oldest Java hominid
Olduvai 1.69 / 1.81	(reversal)		FORMATION			
2.0						

Figure 14-13

H. erectus *correlations, Java.* *

1. *Dates are tentative. There is much confusion with dates because of Java stratigraphic uncomformities.*

2. *Olduvai and Jaramillo normal events may not necessarily apply to the Java paleomagnetic scheme.*

3. *Some scholars equate Lower, Middle, and Upper Pleistocene with, respectively, Puncangan, Kabuh, and Notopuro Formations.*

4. *A recent report proposes the Sangiran geologic strata be renamed as indicated in parentheses.*

5. *The faunal sequence is taken from de Vos (1985) who follows Sondaar (1984).*

6. *This chart is an attempt to correlate Java hominids with several kinds of dating methods. The chart is intended to give some chronological perspective to the Java hominid finds; more work on the stratigraphy of Java is needed before the problem of Java hominid dates can be resolved.*

*The chart is not to scale; correlations are suggestive.

Figure 14-14
(a) *Sangiran 12. Rear view illustrates pentagonal shape of skull.* (b) *Sangiran 17.*

Figure 14-15
(a) *Lateral view of Solo skull;* (b) *rear view of Solo skull.*

the dates given in the next few pages are estimates—"best-guesses"; nevertheless, they give a probable basis on which to *order* the data.

The Javanese hominids we discuss, listed in Figure 14-13 and Table 14-1, have been found mainly in the areas of Trinil and Sangiran (see map on p. 405).

Dubois recovered his famous skullcap, *Pithecanthropus* (S2) from the geologic formation known as Trinil. Also from the same stratum, but from the nearby remarkably productive Sangiran site, have come many finds. These fossils are considered to be in a possible range of from 1.4 m.y. to about 700 k.y.a.* The range may even be as recent as the Upper Pleistocene if *H. soloensis*, discussed below, is as recent as some researchers suggest.

In addition to Trinil and Sangiran, there are remains from Ngandong, Modjokerto, and a few other sites (see map, Fig. 14-10). Java has been a fruitful source of hominid fossils, so far yielding parts of at least 20 skulls, 4 mandibles, and various isolated teeth and limb bones of more than 40 individuals. The cranial capacity of the skulls range from an estimated 775 cc to 1255 cc, with an average around 900 cc. The lower limb bones of these Java hominids are similar (though not identical) to those of modern *H. sapiens*, and they indicate that the Java population was roughly the same height as (or a few inches shorter than) humans today.

When we compare the skulls of the Lower and Middle Pleistocene of Java, we find a pattern of what Sartono (1975) has called small-brained and large-brained pithecanthropines (see "Cranial Capacity" column in Table 14-1). In the Lower Pleistocene (Pucangan Formation), the evidence from Sangiran 4 suggests characteristic *H. erectus* traits, only more so. The brain is smaller, the bones are thicker, the skull is flatter, the canine projects, and there is that unexpected diastema in the upper jaw.

By the Middle Pleistocene in Java, *H. erectus* had changed. Although these changes were not great, they reflect a trend. There was a slight increase in the height of the vault (see craniograms in Figs. 14-16 and 14-17), and the diastema and projecting canine had disappeared. The small brain—below 1000 cc—continues, but it appears that in the latter Middle Pleistocene there is a significant increase in brain size.

Skulls S12 and S17 from Sangiran and the skull cap from Sambungmacan represent a break from the smaller-brained hominids of the earlier Middle Pleistocene. The cranial capacity of these three skulls are all over 1000 cc, and are quite similar in many respects to the more advanced skulls from Ngandong—*H. soloensis* (see Table 14-1, Figs. 14-15 and 14-16), who may have lived more than a half million years later, in the Upper Pleistocene. The similarities may be seen in the "general size and shape of the skull, the skull contours in all views, the supraorbital torus, the ear region, the occipital torus and the nuchal area, and the cranial base" (Jacob, 1976, p. 86).

Some of Solo's traits reflect a relationship to *H. erectus*, especially Sangiran 17 and Sambungmacan, but there are also affinities to *H. sapiens*. Some students of Java hominids have referred to this Ngandong hominid as a Neandertal, others refer to it as *H. sapiens soloensis*, or a transitional form between *erectus* and *sapiens*, and still others to a late *H. erectus*. If a definite date could be established for Solo, it might help with its classification, but the complex geology of the Ngandong site has made dating the skull problematical.

---

*K represents thousand; k.y.a. therefore indicates one thousand years ago. We shall use this abbreviation from here on.

Table 14-1 *Java Hominidae (H. erectus)**

Pleistocene	Age Years, Geologic Formation, and Faunal Strata	Designation and Other Names	Site	Material	Cranial Capacity (cc)	Discovered by	Year Discovered
Upper ?Middle	Estimated 300,000– 100,000 Notopuro Ngandong	H. soloensis Ngandong Man Solo Man	Ngandong	skull bones, tibia At least 12 individuals	Range: 1035– 1255	C. ter Haar von Koenigswald	1931–1933
Late Middle or Early Upper	Kabuh Ngandong or Kedung Brubus	H. modjokertensis Perning 1	Perning	Infant calvarium	650	von Koenigswald	1936
Middle	800,000 Kabuh Kedung Brubus	S12† P7	Sangiran	skull cap	1004	Sartono	1965
Middle	800,000 Kabuh Kedung Brubus	S17 P8	Sangiran	cranium	Estimated 1059, 1125	Sartono	1969
Middle	Kabuh ?Kedung Brubus	Sambung-macan 1	Sambung-macan	skull cap	1035	Jacob	1973
Middle	800,000– 900,000 Kabuh Trinil H.K.	Tr2	Trinil	skull cap	Estimates: 850–940	Dubois	1891
Middle	900,000 Kabuh Trinil H.K.	S2	Sangiran	skull cap	Estimates: 775–813	von Koenigswald	1937
Middle	900,000+ Kabuh Trinil H.K.	S6 Meganthropus paleojavanicus	Sangiran	partial right mandible		von Koenigswald	1941
Lower	1,000,000 Pucangan Trinil H.K. or Ci Saat	S4 P. robustus	Sangiran	calvarial fragments	900	von Koenings-wald	1938/1939
Lower	1,400,000 Pucangan Trinil H.K. or Ci Saat	S5, S9 P. dubius	Sangiran	right mandibles		S9 Sartono S5 von Koen-igswald	1960 1939

*Lower and Middle Pleistocene (not to scale).

†S=Sangiran; P="Pithecanthropus."

We can say little about the hominid way of life in Java during the Lower and Middle Pleistocene. Except for a few small stone implements associated with the Ngandong bones, along with a few stone balls, there have been no cultural assemblages, and few tools, found in the Java strata. Those that have been found consist mainly of crudely made choppers and chopping tools similar to those found in Burma and northern India.

Figure 14-16
Craniograms.

Craniogram comparing *H. erectus* forms (note change in the cranial height of the later [P. VIII and Solo] forms)

?500,000	....	Pithecanthropus I (Dubois)
2.1–1.9	————	Sangiran 4 (Pithecanthropus IV—von Koenigswald)
?200,000	————	*H. soloensis* (Oppenoorth)
500,000	————	Sangiran 17 (Pithecanthropus VII—Sartono)

Sangiran 17   Craniogram showing outline from an occipital view: note the widest area **in figure on right** is toward base of skull giving a pentagonal form

Figure 14-17
Craniograms.

Peking man
Pithecanthropus I, Sangiran 2, 3, 4, 12
Sangiran 17

Sangiran 4 (robustus)
Sangiran 17

Beijing

The story of Peking Man is another saga filled with excitement, hard work, luck, and misfortune. It began in 1911, when J. Gunnar Andersson, a Swedish geologist, accepted an appointment as adviser to the Chinese government to arrange a survey of its coalfields and ore resources. In his investigations, Andersson became interested in the mammals of Tertiary and Pleistocene deposits, and he and his colleagues collected many specimens. Europeans had known for a long time that the "dragon bones" (like the *Gigantopithecus* teeth mentioned in Chapter 10), so important to the Chinese for their healing and aphrodisiac powers, were actually mammal bones. In 1917, the Geological Survey of China resolved to find the sites where these dragon bones were collected by local inhabitants and sold to apothecary shops. In 1921, Andersson and a few other scientists were investigating a place called Chicken Bone Hill near the village of Zhoukoudian, about thirty miles southwest of Beijing. While laying plans to excavate the hill, they were approached by a local resident who told the scientists that much larger and better dragon's bones could be obtained not far away.

The new discovery lay in an abandoned quarry 500 feet west of the railway station at Zhoukoudian. The villager showed them a fissure in the limestone wall, and in a few minutes they found the jaw of a pig, which indicated that the site was a more important one than Chicken Bone Hill. "That evening we went home with rosy dreams of great discoveries" (Andersson, 1934, pp. 97–98).

Dr. Birgir Bohlin (see Box 14-5) resumed working the site in 1928, and recovered more than a score of teeth, as well as parts of skulls of both young and adult individuals, but a complete skull evaded his efforts. A young Chinese geologist, W. C. Pei, took over the direction of the excavation in 1929, and concentrated in what is called the lower cave. On December 1 of that year, he began digging out the sediment in one branch of the lower cave, and at 4 P.M. of the following day found one of the most remarkable fossil skulls to be recovered up to that time. One of the Chinese workers tells the story:

> We had got down about 30 metres deep. . . . It was there the skull-cap was sighted, half of it embedded in loose earth, the other in hard clay. The sun had almost set. . . . The team debated whether to take it out right away or to wait until the next day when they could see better. The agonizing suspense of a whole day was felt to be too much to bear, so they decided to go on (Jia, 1975, pp. 12–13).

Pei brought the skull to Dr. Davidson Black (see Box 14-5), but because it was embedded in hard limestone, it took Black four months of hard, steady work to free it from its tough matrix. The result was worth the labor since the skull, that of a juvenile, was thick, low, and relatively small, but in Black's mind there was no doubt it belonged to early man. The response to this discovery, quite unlike that which greeted Dubois almost forty years earlier, was immediate and enthusiastically favorable. Peking Man became one of the more famous of fossil human skulls.

Work at Locality 1, as this part of the Zhoukoudian cave is known, continued. Dr. Black maintained a killing schedule, working at night so he would not be interrupted at his desk. His health was not robust, and he probably should not have remained in Beijing's harsh climate. As von Koenigswald related it:

> He tried to stick it out but it was too much for him. When his secretary entered his room on March 15, 1934, she found him slumped over his desk, dead from a heart attack, with the beloved skull of Peking Man in his hand (von Koenigswald, 1956, p. 48).

Finding Peking Man

Working the Zhoukoudian cave site for several summers, Dr. Otto Zdansky took the material he excavated back to Sweden. After carefully cleaning and preparing the material, he wrote, in 1926, to J. Gunnar Andersson, the Swedish geologist in charge back in China. Dr. Zdansky mentioned that he had found a premolar and molar, which he cautiously identified as belonging to a creature resembling *Homo sp.* Andersson, not nearly so cautious, jubilantly exclaimed, "The man I predicted has been found." (Andersson, 1934, p. 103).

With this encouraging news, Dr. Birgir Bohlin of Sweden was appointed to organize a concentrated effort to excavate the Zhoukoudian cave. Work began in April, 1927, two days before the season ended. Dr. Bohlin found a hominid tooth, which he immediately took to Dr. Davidson Black, anatomist at the Peking Union Medical College, and the man responsible for the study of hominid material recovered from the cave.

After carefully examining the tooth, Dr. Black decided it belonged to the same species as the two teeth found by Dr. Zdansky. He thus set up a new genus, *Sinanthropus*, with the species name *pekinensis*. It was an exciting discovery, and *Sinanthropus pekinensis*, which we know today as *H. erectus pekinensis*, immediately acquired worldwide fame. Shortly thereafter, Dr. Black went on leave to visit America and Europe:

> He had a large gold watch chain made for him in Peking with a small receptacle hanging from it, into which the tooth exactly fitted. In this way, he travelled about the world with his precious fossil, showing it to colleagues and asking their opinion (von Koenigswald, 1956, p. 45).

Dr. Franz Weidenreich, distinguished anatomist and well known for his work on European fossil hominids, succeeded Black. Weidenreich left his native Germany because of academic repression and the vicious "racial" policies of the Nazi regime. He was a visiting professor of anatomy at the University of Chicago when he was appointed, in 1935, to be a visiting professor of anatomy at the Peking Union Medical College, and honorary director of the Cenozoic Research Laboratory, Geological Survey of China. Excavations at Zhoukoudian ended in 1937, with Japan's invasion of China, but the Cenozoic Research Laboratory continued.

As relations between the United States and Japan deteriorated, Weidenreich decided he had better remove the fossil material from Beijing to prevent it from falling into the hands of the Japanese. Weidenreich left China in 1941, taking beautifully prepared casts, photographs, and drawings of the Peking material with him. After he left, the bones were packed in November, and arrangements made for the U.S. Marine Corps to take the bones with them when they left Beijing to return to the United States. The bones never reached the United States and have never been found. No one to this day knows what happened to them, and their location remains a mystery (see p. 396).

Zhoukoudian Material   According to a recent account (Wu and Lin, 1983), the total fossil remains of Peking Man unearthed at the Zhoukoudian cave amount to:

  6 complete or almost complete skulls

12 skull fragments

15 pieces of mandibles

157 teeth

  3 humerus fragments

  7 femur fragments

  1 clavicle

  1 tibia fragment

  1 lunate (wrist) bone

(and over 100,000 artifacts)

These belong to upwards of 40 male and female adults and children. This is a respectable amount of evidence, the most and the best of any *H. erectus* specimens, and (with the meticulous work by Dr. Weidenreich) has led to a good overall picture of the northern Chinese *H. erectus*.

Dating caves is not always a simple matter; in some cases, the roof of the cave has fallen in and not only is the stratigraphy disturbed, but fossil bones may have been washed into the cave. After a five-year comprehensive investigation of the Zhoukoudian site by more than 120 Chinese scientists from the Institute of Vertebrate Palaeontology and Palaeoanthropology (IVPP)* the researchers came to the following conclusions about Peking Man dates in the Zhoukoudian caves: There were three cultural stages beginning 460 k.y.a. and ending 230 k.y.a., when the people were forced out as the cave filled with rubble and sediment. These Middle Pleistocene dates place Peking Man considerably later than their conspecifics in Java, a time lapse that probably explains why the Zhoukoudian population had moved a bit further along the hominid trail than most of their Javanese relatives.

That Peking and Java hominids are related is clearly demonstrated by a comparison of the bones. The postcranial material is very similar, except that Peking's leg bones suggest he may have been shorter.

*The Institute (IVPP) was established following the liberation of Beijing in 1949. Several hundred scientists—paleoanthropologists, archeologists, geologists, biologists, botanists, palynologists and others—work at the Institute. Since its inception, there has been an extraordinary amount of paleoanthropological work accomplished throughout China.

Figure 14-19
Dr. Davidson Black.

Subspecies

Populations of a species are often designated by a sub-specific term. Here are three examples of *H. erectus* populations with their subspecific designations.

H. erectus erectus	Java
H. erectus pekinensis	China, Zhoukoudian
H. erectus heidelbergensis	Germany, Mauer

Figure 14-20
Dr. Franz Weidenreich.

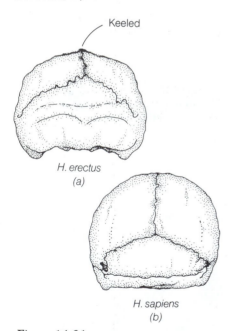

Keeled

H. erectus
(a)

H. sapiens
(b)

Figure 14-21
Keeled skull. (a) H. erectus; (b) H. sa-piens; *(note: does not show keeling).*

Peking, like Java, possesses the typical *erectus* fore and aft bulges—the su-praorbital torus in front and the nuchal torus behind; the skull is **keeled** by a sagittal ridge, the face protrudes in alveolar prognathism, the incisors are shoveled, and molars contain large pulp cavities. Again, like the Java forms, the skull is vintage *H. erectus*, showing its greatest breadth near the bottom. These similarities were recognized long ago by Black and Weidenreich; at one time, in fact, it was suggested that Peking's nomen be changed from *Sinanthropus* to *Pithe-canthropus pekinensis*. However, the similarities of European and African Middle Pleistocene forms to those of Asia, and the resemblance of all these to the genus *Homo*, persuaded taxonomists that the correct name was *Homo erectus*.

What mainly distinguishes Peking from Java is cranial capacity. Java hominids average 900 cc; Chinese average 1088 cc. The difference might be due to the more recent age of the Chinese fossils. As the craniogram illustrates (Fig. 14-16), the larger Peking skull is reflected by a higher vault of the skull, a higher forehead, and a longer and broader cranium. What accounts for the larger brain? Possibly, Peking represents a later period in the evolution of *Homo erectus*. With greater dependence on culture and selective pressures associated with that de-pendence, brain size assuredly increased. It is probably no accident that Peking Man (460–230 k.y.a. in China) and Sangiran 17 (500 k.y.a. in Java), both late in Asiatic *H. erectus* evolution, are relatively "large-brained."

More than 100,000 artifacts were recovered from this site that was occupied for almost 250,000 years, which, according to the Chinese (Wu and Lin, 1983, p. 86), "is one of the sites with the longest history of habitation by man or his an-cestors. . . ." The occupation of the site has been divided into three culture stages:

Earliest stage (460–420 k.y.a.)[*] The tools were large, close to a pound in weight, and made of soft stone, such as sandstone.

Middle Stage (370–350 k.y.a.) Tools become smaller and lighter (under a pound) and these smaller tools comprise 68% of the total; the large tools make up only 12%.

Final Stage (300–230 k.y.a.) Tools are still smaller, and the tool materials were of better quality. The coarse quartz of the earlier periods was replaced by a finer quartz, sandstone tools had almost disappeared, and flint tools in-creased as much as 30%.

[*]These dates should be considered tentative until more precise chronometric techniques are avail-able.

Table 14-2 H. erectus *Fossils of China*

Designation	Site	Age[a] Pleistocene Years	Material	Cranial Capacity (cc)	Year Found	Remarks
Jinniushan	Jinnu Mt., near Yingou	280,000	incomplete skeleton, including calvarium	1400	1984	Lu: most complete *H. erectus* ever found. May be *sapiens*.
Hexian	Longtandong Cave, Anhui	Middle 280–240,000	calvarium, skull frags, mandible frag, isolated teeth	1025	1980/81	First skull found in southern or southwest China.
Peking Man	Zhoukoudian Cave, Beijing	Middle 460–230,000[b]	5 adult crania, skull frags., facial bones, isolated teeth, 40+ individuals	1015–1225; avg: 1088	1927– ongoing	Most famous fossils in China and some of the most famous in the world.
Yunxi	Bailongdong Cave, Hubei	Middle ?500,000	isolated teeth	?	1975	
Yunxian	Longgudong Cave, Hubei	Middle ?500,000	isolated teeth		1976–82	
Yuanmou	Shangnabang	Middle 600–500,000	upper central incisors		1965	Data still in doubt
Lantian	Chenjiawo, Lantian	Middle 650,000	mandible		1963	Old female.
Lantian	Gongwangling, Lantian	Middle 800–750,000 (1.5 m.y.)	calvarium, facial bones	780	1964	Female over 30. Oldest *erectus* found so far in China.

Sources: Wu and Dong (1985); Lisowski (1984); Pope (1984); *Atlas of Primitive Man in China* (1980).
[a]These are best estimates—authorities differ.
[b]In a recent study of dating methods used in China, Aigner (1986) questions the long duration attributed to Zhoukoudian Locality I. She believes it is "mid-middle Pleistocene," can be equated with the Holstein interglacial of Europe, and did not last more than 100,000 years.
[c]Data suggested by An, Z. S. and Ho, C. K. (1989).

The early tools were crude and shapeless but become more refined over time, and, toward the top of Locality 1, there are some finely made tools. Common tools at the site are choppers and chopping tools, but retouched flakes were fashioned into scrapers, points, burins, and awls. Handaxes, found in abundance in Europe and Africa, are absent from Zhoukoudian.

Stone was not the only material selected by Peking hominids; they also utilized bone and horn. Found in the cave were antler fragments, which had been hacked into pieces. Antler roots might have served as hammers and the sharp tines as digging sticks. Many skulls of sika and thick-jaw deer minus facial bones as well as antlers and crania bases leaving only the brain case were also found. Jia suggests that since the skulls show evidence of repeated whittling and over 100 specimens were discovered, all similarly shaped, "it is reasonable to infer they served as 'drinking bowls.' " He goes on to conjecture that the brain cases of Peking Man "retain similar characteristics and probably served the same purpose" (Jia, 1975, p. 31).

Peking Man's way of life at Zhoukoudian has traditionally been described as that of a hunter who killed deer, horses, and other animals, gathered fruits, berries, ostrich eggs, and perhaps killed and ate other Peking individuals, although their practice of cannibalism is doubted by many scholars.

KEEL
The slight ridge where the skull peaks on *H. erectus*—along the sagittal crest (resembling the keel of a boat).

Table 14-3 *Zhoukoudian Material (Middle Pleistocene)*

Material	Discovered		Cultural Material
	Year	*By*	
Premolar, molar	1923	O. Zdansky	Choppers, scrapers, points, hammerstones, anvils, worked deer skulls (?drinking cups), bone "knives," traces of fire—ash layers, charred stone and wood.
Molar	1927	B. Bohlin	
Teeth and skull fragments	1927–28	B. Bohlin	
Skullcap	1929	W. C. Pei	
Portions of skulls, mandibles, teeth, limbs, 6 complete calva, 9 skull fragments, 6 pieces of facial bone, 15 mandibles, 152 teeth, 7 fragmented limb bones; 45 persons represented.	1929–37	W. C. Pei, D. Black, E. Weidenreich	
1 calvarium, 5 teeth, 1 mandible	1960s	Pei and others	
Locality 13 (one-half mile from Peking Cave) older than Locality 1; no human skeletal material; some stone tools and traces of fire.			
Locality 15 (225 feet from Peking Cave) more recent than Locality 1; no human skeletal material, stone implements and traces of fire.			

The evidence for this description comes from the many bones—human and nonhuman—found in the cave. The quantity of nonhuman bones in the cave suggests hunting. Some of the bones appear to have been burned, suggesting cooking skills. Skulls consisting mainly of brain cases and lacking facial and basal bones suggest (a) the use of brain cases as drinking bowls (Jia, 1975, p. 31); or (b) mutilation of the skull, including human skulls, in order to remove the brain for eating; or (c) using the skull as some sort of trophy or possibly in some ritualistic way.

Fragments of charred ostrich eggshells, the copious deposits of hackberry seeds unearthed in the cave, and the flourishing plant growth surrounding the cave, all suggest that the meat diet was supplemented by the gathering of herbs, wild fruits, tubers, and eggs. Layers of ash in the cave, over eighteen feet deep at one point, suggest fire and hearths, but whether Peking Man could actually *make* fire is unknown. Wu and Lin (1983) state that "Peking Man was a cave dweller, a fire user, a deer hunter, a seed gatherer and a maker of specialized tools" (p. 94). This leads them to suggest three social adaptations for the Peking population:

1. Living in a group. Hunting large animals is "complicated, difficult, and hazardous," and cooperation of many individuals would be required; therefore, it is likely that Peking Man lived in a group when he began to hunt deer. (See pp. 380–381 for a discussion of this "hunting hypothesis.")
2. Sexual division of labor. Because of women's physiological constraints, it would be difficult for them to engage in hunting activities, which would then be left to the men. "The pattern of male hunters and female gatherers, which

is common in hunting-and-gathering societies today, may have already been established" (p. 94).

3. Education. Tools during the more than 200,000 years that Peking Man lived in Zhoukoudian became more sophisticated. This "suggests that the earliest practice of education may have taken place in Peking Man's cave" (p. 94). Each generation could not have developed new technological skills without having learned existing ones taught by the older generation.

Could Peking Man speak? Their hunting and technological skills would suggest they possessed some kind of symbolic communication. If the skull was, in fact, used as a symbol as we have speculated, then symbolic communication is even more suggestive. (See Box 14-7 for Wolpoff's neurological evidence.) Did they wear clothing? Perhaps, since they manufactured awls, and one of the bone tools may be a needle. How long did they live? Studies of the fossil remains reveal that almost 40% of the bones belong to individuals under the age of 14, and 2.6% are estimated in the 50 to 60 age group (Jia, 1975, p. 43).

This picture of Peking Man's life has recently been challenged by archeologist Lewis Binford and colleagues (Binford and Ho, 1985; Binford and Stone, 1986a; Binford and Stone, 1986b).*

Binford, et al. reject Peking Man as hunter and believe the evidence clearly points to him as a scavenger. The controversy of early hominids as hunter or scavenger has engaged the attention of paleoanthropologists, taphonomists, archeologists, and other scientists, and the matter is not yet settled. One of the items that persuaded these scientists that early hominids were scavengers, not hunters, is **cutmarks**. (See Chapter 11 for a discussion of scavengers/hunters in the Plio-Pleistocene.)

According to Binford et al., the cutmarks on most of the bones in the Zhoukoudian cave were made by denning animals, indicating that if humans ate meat, they acquired it "second-hand," from the predators. Thus, Peking Man was a scavenger.

Binford and his colleagues also do not believe that Peking Man was associated with fire, except in the later phases of occupation (about 250 k.y.a.). What was defined as ash layers, they claim, "yielded no evidence that these layers were produced by fire" (Binford and Stone, 1986b, p. 467).

In addition, Binford and colleagues deny evidence for cannibalism, another controversial Peking Man topic for the past fifty years. They attribute the lack of facial bones and crania bases to denning animals who brought their prey into the cave. Here they gnawed on the skulls, causing the breakage believed in the past to have been made by humans for cannibalistic purposes.

We might add that many anthropologists agree with these conclusions. But many others disagree (see Bunn and Kroll, 1987, pp. 199–202), criticizing their method, the short time spent examining the specimens at Zhoukoudian, the relatively small (and probably atypical) sample of bones available at the time of their visit to the cave, and their interpretation of the evidence. As the work at Zhoukoudian continues, the life of Peking Man at Zhoukoudian should become clearer.

Peking Man is the best-known hominid fossil from China, and more work has been done at Zhoukoudian than at any other Chinese site—in fact, there is more

---

*Binford and Stone (1986) recently visited a number of hominid sites in China, spending several days at Zhoukoudian.

CUTMARKS
Marks made by predators' teeth as they gnaw on bones, or by humans as they cut into a carcass with a stone tool. It is possible to distinguish between the animal-inflicted cutmarks and tool-inflicted cutmarks.

(a)

(b)

(c)

Figure 14-22
Peking Man (reconstructed cranium).
(a) Frontal view; (b) lateral view; (c) rear view. The widest part of the skull is toward the bottom. The keeled effect can be seen in (a) and (c).

Figure 14-23

Views of: (a) Homo erectus erectus *and (b)* Homo erectus pekinensis; *(c) the Solo XI skull; (d) the Rhodesian skull; (e) the Saccopastore skull; and (f) the skull of La Chapelle-aux-Saints. Note the pentagonal shape of skulls in upper row compared to those of the Neandertal and Rhodesian skulls at widest point in the lower row. (From Weidenreich, 1951.) See Chapter 15 for discussion of (d)–(f).*

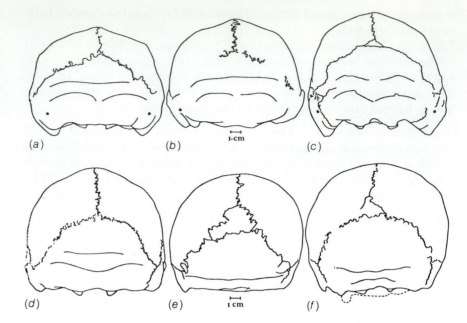

(a)   (b)   (c)

(d)   (e)   (f)

Chopper

Chopper

Pointed tool

Discoidal scraper

Broken bone (note deep incision made in the bone)

Figure 14-24
Tools used by Peking Man.

BOX 14-7

Speech

Human speech capacity is an extremely complicated behavior, involving the development of tracts between the motor and associated speech areas and between the frontal and posterior parietal portions of the brain. The basis for speaking would seem to lie more in neurological structures than in morphological ones. The importance of the frontal–posterior parietal tract is that it allows the frontal area to "make sense" out of the cross-modal associations of the posterior parietal area, while the motor-associational speech area tract provides a pathway for this information to reach the motor–speech area.

The evolution of language ability seems tied to the appearance of hemispheric dominance and asymmetry. The marked bilateral asymmetry in size and morphology in the newly discovered Zhoukoudian cranium 5* provides one of the few direct morphological correlates with the ability to speak in humans. Thus, there is every reason to believe that *Homo erectus* was capable of human vocal language (Wolpoff, 1980a).

*Cranial parts found in 1966 fit the temporal fragments discovered and described by Weidenreich in the 1930s.

material from this cave than from all the other Chinese sites combined. Nevertheless, there are other hominids worth noting. (See Table 14-2.)

Other Fossils in China   Two fossil finds were made near Lantian in Central China. In 1963, investigators found an almost complete mandible, with several teeth, of an old woman. The site has been dated at about 650 k.y.a. The following year the cranium of a female over 30 years of age was found and recently given a date of 1.5 m.y.a. (An and Ho, 1989). The morphology of the cranium bears some resemblance to early Java specimens—bones are thicker, the supraorbital torus is massive, and the cranial capacity is measured at 780 cc, quite a bit less than the Peking Man average of 1088 cc. If Lantian dates are correct, it is the oldest Chinese hominid fossil found to date.

From Longtandong Cave in eastern China come remains of several individuals of *Hexian*. A well-preserved cranium, mandibular fragments, isolated teeth, and other material were found. The cranium, with a capacity of about 1025 cc, and a date of 300 k.y.a., resembles Peking Man in some respects.

According to Professor Lu Zun'e of Beijing University (1987), the "most complete" *H. erectus* ever found in the world (but see WT 1500, p. 435), was discovered in the fall of 1984 on Jinniu Mountain in Liaoning Province, northeast of Beijing. He calls it *Jinniushan Man*—a young male just reaching maturity.

We do not wish to leave the impression that Zhoukoudian Cave provides the only evidence for the way early humans lived in China. There is, in fact, a number of archeological sites considered to be as early as Zhoukoudian, and even earlier.

Early paleolithic stone tools have been found in such widely separated provinces as Hebei, Guizhou, Shanxi, Lantian, Beijing, Yunnan, and Liaoning (see map, Fig. 14-26). At present, there is little reason to believe that *H. erectus* culture in these provinces will differ much from Peking Man.

Traces of fire have been claimed for several of these sites as well as dates of a million or more years. However, serious questions have been raised about the

Figure 14-25
Cannibalism at Zhoukoudian? The area around the foramen magnum appears to have been cut away—in order to remove the brain. Or was the base of the skull gnawed away by hyenas?

Figure 14-26
Fossil and archeological sites of H. erectus *in China.*

dates (Aigner, 1981, 1986), and Binford (p. 427) has expressed doubts about the evidence for fire. With the rate of present research in China, more acceptable statements about the early life of *H. erectus* may be forthcoming in the next few years.

India[*]

On December 5, 1982, Arun Sonakia discovered the first *H. erectus* found on the subcontinent of India. It consisted of a well-preserved partial cranium collected at Hathnora, in the Narmada Valley, central India. No date in years has been assigned, but the geologic evidence points to the later Middle Pleistocene. The skull, estimated between 1155 and 1421 cc, is believed to be a female about 30 years of age.

Like some other *erectus* forms, Narmada Man displays physical traits that are assigned to both *H. erectus* and *H. sapiens*. For example, the supraorbital torus is pronounced, and the greatest width is low on the skull; on the other hand, cranial capacity is quite large for an *erectus*. Because of its *sapiens* characteristics, Narmada Man has been called an "evolved" *H. erectus*.

Associated with the cranium are mammal bones and tools of Acheulian industry, especially handaxes and cleavers.

The first *H. erectus* fossils, as we have seen, were discovered by Dubois near the end of the last century. Almost 40 years later, important *erectus* finds were discovered in the productive Zhoukoudian cave near Beijing. It took another 35 years for the first *H. erectus* fossils to be unearthed in Africa, and these came from the famous site of Olduvai, in East Africa, by the equally famous finder of fossils, Louis Leakey (see p. 314).

Figure 14-27
The Hexian skull (rear view). Similar to Peking Man, but note modified postorbital construction; occipital area does not appear as robust.

[*]For fuller accounts, see H. deLumley and Sonakia, 1985; M-A. deLumley and Sonakia, 1985; Sonakia, 1985a; Sonakia, 1985b.

Figure 14-28
Map of Narmada site.

East Africa

Since 1959, with the discovery of "Zinj," East Africa has become the El Dorado of the search for ancient humans. A prodigious quantity of fossil hominid remains, many of them australopithecines, has been recovered, but an increasing number of *Homo* specimens have been excavated in recent years.

The remains of *H. erectus* have come from three East African areas: Olduvai Gorge, Tanzania; Lake Turkana, Kenya; and Bodo in Ethiopia. (See map, p. 423.)

Olduvai (Tanzania)

As far back as 1960, Dr. Louis Leakey unearthed a skull at Olduvai (OH 9) that he identified as *H. erectus* (and referred to as Chellean Man). The skull of OH 9 from Upper Bed II has a massive cranium; it is faceless, and has the largest cranial capacity (1067 cc) of all the early *H. erectus* specimens. Dated at 1.2–1.1 m.y., this is indeed a large skull for that time period. The browridge is huge, the largest known for any hominid in both thickness and projection, but the vault walls are thin.

Figure 14-29
Outline of Narmada partial cranium.

Figure 14-30
OH 9.

Figure 14-31
OH 13 ("Cinderella" mandible—cast).

Figure 14-32
ER 3733.

Also from Olduvai, from Bed IV of the Middle Pleistocene (dated at 0.83–0.62 m.y.), comes a partial skull, OH 12, probably a female. It resembles OH 9, although the cranial capacity is considerably smaller—700–800 cc. The small size may be due to sexual dimorphism; however, it is puzzling that a skull with similar morphology, and perhaps as much as a million years younger, should have 30% less cranial capacity.

There is another *possible erectus* skull from Olduvai—OH 13—which the Leakeys referred to as "Cinderella" and identified as *H. habilis*. The find consists of the back half of the skull and both upper and lower jaws. The skull walls are thin, an australopithecine trait, but the mandible is believed to resemble early *H. erectus* from Java. The question arises whether "Cinderella" is *A. africanus*, *H. habilis*, or *H. erectus*? It would help if more of Cinderella were available. Perhaps a glass slipper somewhere in the Olduvai volcanic ash may provide the answer.

Lake Turkana (Kenya)

Some 400 miles north of Olduvai Gorge, on the northern boundary of Kenya, is the finger lake—Lake Turkana. Excavated by Richard Leakey and colleagues since 1969, the eastern shore of the lake has been a virtual gold mine for australopithecines, early *Homo*, and a few *H. erectus* fossil remains.

One of the oldest of the *erectus* forms (1.5 m.y.) is a remarkably well-preserved skull, KNM-ER 3733 (Fig. 14-32), found by Bw. Bernard Ngeneo during the 1974/1975 field program in the highly productive Koobi Fora Formation (Leakey and Walker, 1976). Consisting of an almost complete calvarium with a number of *H. erectus* features and resembling OH 9 on a smaller scale, the skull is estimated at about 850 cc, falling toward the lower range of *Homo erectus* cranial measurements.

In August of 1984, Kamoya Kimeu (see Fig. 12-32) with his uncanny knack for finding fossils, lived up to his reputation by discovering a small piece of skull near Richard Leakey's base camp on the west side of Lake Turkana. Leakey and his colleague, Alan Walker of Johns Hopkins University, excavated the site in 1984 and then again in 1985 (see map, Fig. 14-34).

The dig was a smashing success. The workers unearthed the most complete *H. erectus* yet found. Known properly as KNM-WT 15000,[*] the all but complete skeleton includes facial bones and most of the postcranial bones, a rare event indeed for *erectus*, since these bones are scarce at *H. erectus* sites. The completeness of the skeleton (which may become even more complete as the digging continues) should help resolve some of the riddles associated with *H. erectus*.

Another remarkable feature of the find is its age. Its dating is based on the chronometric dates of the geologic formation in which the site is located and is set at about 1.6 million years. The fossil is that of a boy about 12 years of age and 5 feet 5 inches tall. Had he grown to maturity, his height, it is estimated, may have been 6 feet, taller than *H. erectus* was heretofore thought to be. Tentatively, the cranial capacity of WT15k[*] is estimated at 900 cc, intermediate be-

---

[*]WT is the symbol for West Turkana; i.e., the west side of the lake. The east side of the lake is symboled as ER, East Rudolf, the former name of the lake (see p. 348).

[*]k is a symbol often used to indicate one thousand; 15k, therefore, indicates 15000.

Table 14-4 H. erectus, *East Africa*

Site/Age	Designation	Material	Cranial Capacity (cc)	Discovered[a] (Date)	Remarks
Olduvai					
Tanzania					
Bed IV	OH 23	Mandible fragments		1968	
	OH 2	2 vault fragments		1935	
	OH 12	Cranial fragments		1962	
	OH 22	Right half of mandible		1968	
	OH 28	Pelvic bone, femur shaft		1970	
Bed III	OH 51	Left side of mandible		1974	
Bed II 1.5 m.y.	OH 13 Early *Homo* *H. habilis* "Cinderella"	Parts of skull, mandible		1963	Probably *H. habilis* or early *Homo*; has some *erectus*-like traits
1.2 m.y.	OH 9	Calvarium	1067	1960	
Ndutu					
Ngaloba Beds, Tanzania	Ndutu	Cranium	1200	1976	Discovered by Mary Leakey
Lake Turkana[b]					
Koobi Fora, Turkana, Kenya					
1.4 m.y.	KNM-ER 3883	Braincase, some facial bones	800	1974	
1.5–1.4 m.y.	KNM-ER 730	Mandible lacking right side		1970–1980	
1.5–1.4 m.y.	KNM-ER 1808	Skeletal and cranial elements		1973	
1.5 m.y.	KNM-ER 3733	Well-preserved skull	850	1974	Discovered by B. Ngeneo, R. Leakey
West Turkana					
1.6 m.y.	KNM-WT 15000	Almost complete skeleton	1200	1984	Most complete and oldest *erectus* yet found. Discovered by K. Kimieu, R. Leakey, Alan Walker

[a]Louis Leakey and Mary Leakey were directors of excavations at Olduvai when these finds were made.
[b]Richard Leakey is director of excavations at Lake Turkana.

Figure 14-33
H. erectus *sites in East Africa.*

Figure 14-34
Lake Turkana. Site of WT 15000.

Figure 14-35
KNM-WT 15000. The most complete and oldest H. erectus *yet found.*

tween OH 12 and OH 9. The postcranial bones appear to be quite similar, though not identical, to those of modern humans.

African forms considered to be members of *H. erectus* have been undergoing many careful studies in the past few years, and many questions have been raised. There are those who believe the differences between the African forms and those from East Asia are great enough so that both cannot be placed in the same taxon. Others see them as related, and one scholar finds, given the great distance between Africa and East Asia, that it is "surprising . . . that even greater distinctions are not apparent" (Rightmire, 1984, p. 96).

Northwest Africa

Remains of *H. erectus* have also been found in northwest Africa. Fossils come from Algeria and Morocco; all consist of mandibles except for cranial fragments and a partial cranium from Salé. Like several others we have come across, Salé, provisionally dated at about 400 k.y.a., reveals both *erectus* and *sapiens* traits.

H. erectus appears to have lived in northwest Africa from about 600 k.y.a. to about 200 or 300 k.y.a. It is possible the *H. erectus* population of northwest Africa may have played a role in populating Europe.

Finally, from Swartkrans, South Africa, are skeletal fragments now identified as *H. erectus*.

(a)

(b)

Figure 14-37
Ternifine mandible (Tighenif).

Figure 14-36
*The Salé skull. The most complete erectus
skull discovered in Northwest Africa
(a) Lateral view. (b) Rear view. Note that
the greatest width is low on the skull.*

Europe

Although European fossils of this time period may not conform to a strict definition of *H. erectus*, we shall deal with them in this chapter (instead of the next) until their classification is more definitive.

Heidelberg (Mauer)

As its name suggests, this fossil was found near the village of Mauer a few miles from Heidelberg. The entire fossil consists of a massive mandible, including all the teeth. The teeth are more modern than other traits of the jaw, and Mauer's classification remains unclear.[*] Mauer has been dated in the 400 k.y.a. range.

[*]*H. heidelbergensis has been suggested.*

Figure 14-38
Homo erectus in North Africa.

Finding Heidelberg

For a number of years, Professor Otto Schoetensack, a Heidelberg University paleontologist, had been observing the commercial operations at a sandpit near the village of Mauer, six miles southeast of the university town. Because of the Tertiary and Pleistocene strata, Schoetensack had arranged with the owner of the sandpit that all bones uncovered in the ancient strata during the operation be donated to the University. The sandpit had yielded hundreds of mammalian bones, but for twenty years Schoentensack waited in vain for a human fossil. It was not until October 21, 1907, that Herr Rosch, the sandpit owner, sent a thrilling message to the patient professor:

For twenty years you have been making efforts to find traces of primitive men in my sandpit in order to prove human beings lived in this district at the same time as the mammoth. Yesterday we came across this proof. Sixty-five feet below ground level at the bottom of my sandpit the lower jawbone of a prehistoric man was found, in a very good state of preservation (in Wendt, 1963, p. 442).

Schoetensack named the jaw *Homo heidelbergensis*, which raised the hackles of many European scientists who were either still opposed to the idea of evolution or did not believe the Mauer jaw belonged to the genus *Homo*. However, the furor lacked the passionate spirit of Dubois' time and may have helped justify Dubois' views.

Figure 14-39
The Mauer mandible. Note the wide ascending ramus.

Figure 14-40
Map of Heidelberg site.

Bilzingsleben

Bilzingsleben, from East Germany, consists of four skull fragments and a single molar tooth. Although fragments are useful, classification is tricky without more bone material. Expert opinion is divided between *H. erectus* and "pre-Neandertal." The suggested date of 228 k.y.a. is still moot.

Vértesszöllös

From Hungary, near Budapest, there is Vértesszöllös (an occiput and a few fragments of infant teeth), recently dated at 185 k.y.a. The *erectus* and *sapiens* characteristics of the occiput make classification difficult.

Petralona

Just south of the northern Greek capital of Salonika lies Petralona where, in 1959, villagers digging for water fell into a cave that had been sealed and unknown. A year later, a practically complete fossil hominid skull about 1200 cc in size was found, and it has been a problem fossil ever since.

The original excavations were not well done, and precisely where the skull was found is still debated. Because of this confusion, it has been impossible to associate clearly the skull with the strata in the cave, and a reliable date has not yet been determined. Day (1986, p. 94) suggests a consensus date of 400 to 350 k.y.a. Others believe a later date of 200 k.y.a. may be more realistic (Cook et al., 1982).

Also, there is again the question of affiliation—to which subspecies should Petralona be assigned? There is a choice of Neandertals, pre-Neandertals, ar-

Figure 14-41
Sites of European Middle Pleistocene archaic sapiens.

Figure 14-42
Vértesszöllös. The occipital was first described as modern but restudy identifies as H. erectus (more likely) or archaic sapiens.

Figure 14-43
The Petralona skull.

Figure 14-44
Bilzingsleben. The frontal fragment has been identified as archaic sapiens or H. erectus. It is unfortunate that more skull material is unavailable.

Figure 14-45
Partial Arago skull.

chaic *sapiens*, or *H. erectus*. And, we might add, Petralona could be considered transitional between *erectus* and *sapiens*. It is possible to justify, at least to some degree, any of the above.

Arago (Tautavel Man)

Fieldwork at the Arago cave near the village of Tautavel (which is near the Spanish border in southeastern France) began in 1964 under the supervision of the same husband and wife team who excavated Terra Amata—Henry and Marie-Antoinette de Lumley (see below). They were attracted to the site by materials collected over the years by prehistorians and amateurs, and they believed the site to be an early one and well worth excavating (H. de Lumley, and M. A. de Lumley, 1973).

Abundant faunal remains reflect a cold climate, and the third glaciation was originally suggested. A later study gives a much earlier date, the second glaciation (Cook et al., 1982). Several recently developed radiometric measurements have failed to agree on a date, and the dating remains uncertain.

In their excavation of the site, the de Lumleys disclosed more than 20 occupation levels, each separated by 2 to 7 feet of sterile sand. More than 100,000 Acheulian artifacts have been recovered from the site.

Over 50 cranial and postcranial remains of at least four adults and three children have been recovered. Most important of the specimens are a partial cranium, mostly face and frontal bone (Fig. 14-45), two mandibles, a parietal bone, an almost complete innominate, and various other cranial and postcranial fragments.

The cranium is apparently that of a young male, and the face is especially useful because there are so very few available from this period. It gives a pretty good idea of what these Middle Pleistocene Europeans might have looked like. The supraorbital torus is very prominent, the forehead is relatively long, flat, and narrow, and the cranial capacity is estimated to be in the 1050 to 1150 cc range.

The mandibles, neither of which fit the cranium, belong to a young adult male (Arago 13) and a female of around 40 to 55 years of age (Arago 2). These are massive mandibles; the size of the female's teeth fall within the range of Neandertals and anatomically moderns, but those of the male are huge, exceeding those of Heidelberg and matching the largest of Ternifine. The mandibles display *H. erectus*, as well as archaic *sapiens*, characters.

Torralba/Ambrona

One of the best-known sites associated with Middle Pleistocene hominids, dug by F. Clark Howell in the early 1960s and again more recently, is located in central Spain. This site was occupied during a mild recession of the Mindel Glaciation, sometime between 400 and 300 k.y.a., and the archeological evidence reflects hominid occupation. Remains of elephants and other animals, some butchered and some not, and many tools consisting of hand axes, cleavers, and scrapers characteristic of Middle Pleistocene industry known as Acheulian were excavated. Unfortunately, no human bones have so far been discovered.

Terra Amata

Another Middle Pleistocene occupation site lacking human bones, Terra Amata in southern France is described in some detail later in the chapter.

Summary, European Hominids

In Europe, the Middle Pleistocene hominid scene is a complicated story of bits and pieces of skeletons, incomplete skulls, cave strata difficult to interpret, and hominid specimens so situated they are almost impossible to date.

The European fossils we have discussed show a mosaic of features—some archaic, some modern, but very few traits, if any, that are unique to the group. Therefore, dealing with them taxonomically and phylogenetically is a serious problem. To what taxon are they to be assigned? Since they lived contemporaneously with *H. erectus* in Africa and Asia, it would seem reasonable to consider them in the same taxon. But many specialists studying the European group reject this, because the fossils lack certain traits of the African and Asian *erectus* forms and possess others the African and Asian do not.

Also unclear is their phylogenetic relationship. Some paleoanthropologists suggest they are the beginning of modern *sapiens*; others see them as forerunners of Neandertals. Still others believe they are the ancestors of *both* Neandertals and modern *sapiens*.

The central problem in this case, and others similar to it, is how to deal with fossils that show a mosaic of features—a mixture of earlier and later traits. The European fossils display this mosaic of archaic and more modern traits, and paleoanthropologists have not yet settled on a solution that is widely accepted.

The European fossils of the Middle Pleistocene raise another problem. What was going on here evolutionarily? Were these migrants (presumably from Africa) evolving to *H. sapiens*? Do the trait variations simply represent adaptations to local ecological conditions? Or are there other possibilities? Presently, no convincing answers exist.

Evolution of *H. erectus*

Surveying hominid events of the Lower and Middle Pleistocene, we see the disappearance of australopithecines and early *Homo* (?*H. habilis*) and the appearance of *H. erectus* populations, who expand their habitat beyond African boundaries. As we examine *H. erectus*, we find a number of changes that mark human evolution in several directions: *physical, technological, and social.*

Physical From the physical point of view, *H. erectus* is already notably similar to modern populations. The *erectus* femur/pelvis complex may be somewhat different from our own (Day, 1984; Kennedy, 1983), but if it were possible to observe *H. erectus* walking away from us, it is unlikely that we would remark a stride noticeably different from those around us. An *erectus* individual would not slouch forward and walk with bent knees. The stride would compare with ours; the arms would not be especially long, nor would they swing from side to side instead of front to back; and the legs would not be proportionally short. We would also note *erectus*' stature; recall that the recent find of a 12-year-old boy in West

Figure 14-46
H. erectus *archeological sites in Western Europe.*

Figure 14-47
Comparison of H. erectus *(Zhoukoudian) and* H. sapiens *(modern).*

Figure 14-48
Acheulian biface ("handaxe").

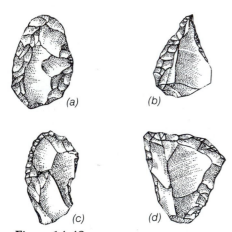

(a)   *(b)*

(c)   *(d)*

Figure 14-49
Small tools of Acheulian industry. (a) Side scraper; (b) point; (c) end scraper; (d) burin.

Figure 14-50
Acheulian cleaver.

Turkana suggests an adult male height of 6 feet. This would have made *H. erectus* a walker far superior to australopithecines and *habilis*.

However, when we examine the skull, obvious differences from us emerge. The vault of the skull is low, not domelike as our own, and the forehead slopes back instead of up. A heavy ridge of bone over the eye is a feature remarkably different, as is the prominent projection in the tooth area of the face, and the receding chin. At the back of the skull, the occipital bone angles sharply forward, and the widest part of the skull is much lower than it is in later hominids.

Changes in the skull, such as the heavy ridges of bone front and back, may have been due to the change in diet that emphasized chewing meat instead of softer plant foods (see Box 14-9). The brain was also evolving into one that was larger and more complex, a most important change in *erectus* evolution. This growth also had an effect on the contours of the skull.

Technological   Growth of the brain enabled *H. erectus* to develop a more sophisticated tool kit. The important change was a core worked on both sides, called a *biface* (known widely as a handaxe, see Fig. 14-48). The biface has a flatter core than, and is a change from, the roundish earlier Oldowan pebble tool. This change enabled the stoneknapper to carefully shape the edges straighter and sharper into a more efficient implement. This Acheulian stone tool became standardized as the basic *erectus* all-purpose tool, with some modification, for more than a million years. It served to cut, scrape, pound, dig, and more—a most useful tool that has been found in Europe, Africa, and Asia.

Like their species elsewhere, *H. erectus* in China manufactured choppers and chopping tools as their core tools, and like other *erectus* toolmakers, fashioned scrapers and other small tools (see Fig. 14-49), but they did not manufacture bifaces (handaxes).

Scholars have noted the remarkable stasis of the physical and cultural characteristics of *Homo erectus* populations, which seemed to change so little in the more than a million years of their existence. However, there were some changes; the brain of later *erectus* was larger, the body not as robust, and there were modifications in their stone technology.

In the early days, toolmakers employed a stone hammer (simply an ovoid-shaped stone about the size of an egg or a bit larger) to percuss flakes from the core, thus leaving deep scars. Later, they put to use other materials such as wood and bone. They learned to use these new materials in the manufacture of softer hammers, which gave them more control over the flaking. These left shallow scars, sharper edges, and a more symmetrical form that appears to us to be esthetically more pleasing. Toward the end of the Acheulian industry, toolmakers blocked out a core with stone hammers, and then switched to wood or bone for refining the edges. This produced more elegant appearing and pear-shaped implements.

Also introduced by *H. erectus* was the cleaver (Fig. 14-50). Instead of coming to a point, like the handaxe, one end of the cleaver was blunted, giving the appearance of a modern axe head. It was probably used in the butchering—chopping and breaking the bones—of large animals.

Evidence of butchering is widespread in *H. erectus* sites and, in the past, has been associated with hunting. However, this assumption has been challenged, especially by archeologists (p. 417) who believe the evidence does not prove the hunting hypothesis, but believe instead that *erectus* was primarily a scavenger.

However, the evidence does not yet prove the scavenger hypothesis either, and the matter is still unresolved.

Social   One of the fascinating qualities of H. erectus was a penchant for travel. From the relatively close confines of East Africa, *erectus* became a world traveler, and by the time *H. sapiens* appears, 1½ million years later, *H. erectus* had trekked to vast points of the earth. Moving north from East Africa, *erectus* could have chosen several directions. One was eastward over the land bridge that joined East Africa at that time to the Arabian Peninsula. Land bridges were exposed in many areas of the world during glacial times, when so much ocean water was locked up in the glacial ice.

The life of hunters/scavengers is nomadic and the woodland and savanna that covered the southern tier of Asia bordering the Indian Ocean, from East Africa to Southeast Asia, would have been an excellent environment for *H. erectus*, similar to the econiche of his African ancestors. As the population grew, small groups budded off the band and moved farther ahead to find their own hunting area. This process, repeated again and again, led *erectus* east to India and, with mountains to the north, through the southern route across the Sunda shelf (Fig. 14-51) to Java, arriving there several hundred thousand years later.

Once in Java, it would have been impossible to take a further step, since there was no land bridge that joined Australia to Java. However, it would have been possible to push north through Malaysia, Thailand, skirt the northern mountains, and travel east to southern China, where Lantian Man lived 700 to 800 k.y.a.

A different route took *H. erectus* to Europe. They could have entered Europe through (what are now) Israel, Turkey, and then to the Balkans. Or *H. erectus* migrants could have turned west from Egypt and crossed the Mediterranean over the land bridge from North Africa to Sicily, then to Italy. There is evidence of fire and Oldowan tools in several caves in southern France with dates of over one

Figure 14-51
Possible H. erectus *routes. The map illustrates several routes* H. erectus *could have taken to reach Java (east through southern Asia and south across the Sunda shelf). Europe could have been reached north via Israel and Turkey, and/or west from Egypt and across the land bridge to Sicily and Italy.*

Figure 14-52
Sunda and Sahul. (The names given to the continental shelves of Southeast Asia and Australia.) (a) The Sunda shelf is a land mass that, during glacial times, formed a bridge joining the Asian continent to what are now separate islands. The map clearly shows that H. erectus could have walked on land from the continent to Java. (b) The Sahul shelf of Australia is separated from Sunda by a group of islands known as Wallacea (named for A. R. Wallace, p. 27), which was not crossed by humans until the time of H. sapiens sapiens.

(a) Sunda

(b) Sahul

million years, but these dates have been questioned. However, by about half a million years ago, archaic *sapiens* (?*H. erectus*) was living in sites across Europe.

Why did *H. erectus* leave home?* We will never know for certain, but there were climatic and geographic changes that may have been responsible. It was a time of heavy precipitation, which fell as snow in the Northern Hemisphere and created the great glaciers of Europe and North America. In tropical areas, heavy rainfall produced rivers, lakes, and new grasslands. With additional food sources

*Sometime around 900 k.y.a. has been suggested.

available, a population increase may have led splinter groups to seek their own areas.

If the new groups succeeded, eventually other small groups may have budded off these, and so the process continued as *erectus* moved farther and farther away from their ancestral home, ultimately reaching Java and China to the east, northwest Africa to the west, and Europe to the north.

Although there is no way of knowing with a high degree of accuracy how *H. erectus* lived, we can make pretty good guesses on the basis of the available evidence. As a hunter of animals often quite larger than they were, *erectus* males hunted in small groups, planning their hunt, organizing themselves and their group on some basis (kinship perhaps?) to cooperate in butchering, distributing (sharing) their catch, and making a variety of decisions.

Since there was no predictable surplus, there was no division of labor except between males and females. All adult men were responsible for the same activities, making their own weapons, collecting their own materials, obtaining food for themselves and the group, and so forth. Similarly, each woman had her individual responsibilities.

Were there chiefs and/or shamans (religious practitioners) or other outstanding individuals of some sort? The evidence does not inform us on this point. Nor is there evidence of ritual or belief in the supernatural, although the distortion of skulls has been interpreted as cannibalism and the cannibalism as ritual (p. 417). This idea has been rejected by many scholars. *

Terra Amata   To illustrate the way *H. erectus* lived, let us observe life at Terra Amata, a Middle Pleistocene site in southern France (for the full account, see de Lumley, 1969; Villa, 1983).

In the heart of the city of Nice, in southern France on the opulent French Riviera, stands the imposing Chateau de Rosemont, once the residence of the king of Yugoslavia and since converted into a museum of paleontology. Scholars had found a few stone tools some years earlier when a shipyard was being constructed a few hundred yards from the Chateau. In October of 1965, during foundation work for the construction of luxury apartments, bulldozers cut into the sloping grounds of the Chateau near an alley named Terra Amata (beloved land). As the bulldozers continued their excavation, closely monitored by de Lumley, a sandy deposit was exposed containing paleolithic implements.

DeLumley, immediately realizing the significance of the discovery, persuaded the builders to halt operations temporarily, and with the assistance of the French Ministry of Culture, mounted a major archeological salvage dig. Collecting a voluntary crew of 300 workers composed of amateurs and archeology students, de Lumley, along with his wife, Marie-Antoinette, and crew, spent 40,000 hours excavating 144 square yards of soil 70 feet deep. They uncovered 21 separate living floors, removed 270 cubic yards of fill using only trowels and brushes and found 35,000 objects, which were recorded on 1,200 charts. Casts were made of 108 square yards of living floor and 9,000 photographs recorded the progress of the work.

Below the surface at Terra Amata is a series of strata indicating advances of Würm, Riss, and Mindel glacial and interglacial periods. The site included three

Figure 14-53
Base of erectus *(Zhoukoudian) skull. Is the lack of skull base evidence of cannibalism? If so, was it ritual or dietary? Many scholars do not believe it was cannibalism.*

*See W. Arens, 1979; Kolata, 1986.

beaches, and it was the most recent beach, about 300,000 years old,* that contained evidence of human habitation. The climate at this time, toward the end of the Mindel, was colder and more humid than it is now. Pine trees covered the hills behind the beach and fresh water was available from a nearby stream. "All things considered, it appears that nothing was lacking even 300 millennia ago to make Terra Amata a beloved land" (deLumley, 1969, p. 43).

H. erectus not only selected a beautiful spot for their brief visits, but also built shelters to protect themselves against the prevailing northwest wind. The shelters were huts, shaped in an elongated oval, ranging from 26 to 49 feet in length and from 13 to nearly 30 feet in width. The evidence comes from a series of stake-holes†—averaging about three inches in diameter, driven into the sand to form the walls of the hut. To brace the walls, there was a line of stones, paralleling the stake imprints, and the sand shows imprints of stones as much as a foot in diameter, with some even stacked one on another.

The living floor inside the huts consisted of a thick bed of organic matter and ash interrupted by imprints of holes left by posts that supported the roof. A basic feature in the center of the hut was a hearth, a foot or two in diameter, scooped out of the sand with a little wall of cobbles or pebbles built up on the northwest side of each hearth as a windscreen. The windscreen suggests that the hut was not draft free, but was a temporary structure to provide some protection against the cold and windy spring weather.

What were the daily activities of the Terra Amata people? They gathered plants, hunted small and large game in the nearby countryside, collected sea food, and manufactured some tools. Animal bones found at the site include remains of birds, turtles, rabbits, and rodents, but the majority of bones are those of larger animals: deer, elephant, wild boar, ibex, rhinoceros, and wild ox. Like

---

*In her recent archeological study, Villa (1983) gives the date as 244 k.y.a.

†Stake holes and post holes are filled with soil, of course, but gentle probing with a trowel can usually distinguish the holes from the surrounding hard-packed soil.

Figure 14-55
Cutaway of Terra Amata hut. Note the hearth, the workspaces where people sat making tools, the poles that supported the roof, and the stones at the base of the hut supporting the sides. (Adapted from de Lumley, 1969.)

other predators, these human hunters selected, not the old, but the young of the species, which would have been much easier to bring down.*

They also visited the beach and gathered shellfish from the Mediterranean, but did not fully exploit the available resources from the sea. Found at the site are shells of oysters, mussels, and limpets; fishbones indicate that they occasionally fished.

Artifacts were mainly stone tools of the Acheulian industry. Interestingly, those found near the sea were an older form of the Acheulian—chopping tools, crude bifaces, cleavers, scrapers, projectile points, and pebble tools flaked only on one side. However, in the huts on the dunes back from the beach, were more advanced tools. While there are choppers and chopping tools present, there are no single-faced pebble tools or cleavers, and more of the tools are made from flakes. The scrapers included the type from the beach in addition to several other kinds, as well as several types of flakes. Some of the flakes were notched and made into perforators.

Inside the huts, evidence of toolmaking can be seen in the bare patches of living floor surrounded by the leftovers of tool manufacture—stone flakes, partially chipped cores, and unworked pebbles. The bare patches are where the toolmakers sat, performing their chipping and flaking chores. Unworked stones were easily available by simply walking along the beach and picking up pebbles of flint, quartzite, limestone, or other rock.

The stone tools tell us quite a bit about *H. erectus* life. Projectile points signify a throwing weapon, probably a spear or lance (bow and arrow came much later). Scrapers are used with meat and chopping tools with butchering. Also, we know that *H. erectus* traveled in southern France, since the stone used for one of the tools could only have come from an area 30 miles away.

---

*We assume here that the bones represent the result of hominid hunting. However, the assumption that bones at a site are necessarily the result of human activity has been seriously challenged. Consequently, archeologists and especially taphonomists now carefully analyze bones for evidence of hunting, scavenging, or natural accumulation.

COPROLITES
copr: excrement
Feces found at an archeological site; if
fossilized, called **coproliths.**

There are other details about their lives. As a raw material for tools, bone was not much utilized, but one end of an elephant's leg bone was hammered into a point. Another bone point looks as if it had been hardened in fire (a technique long used for hardening the tips of spear shafts and digging sticks). Still another bone fragment is smoothed by wear, and there are others that may have served as awls and scrapers. Awls are often used for making holes in hides, and this suggests that *H. erectus* wore some sort of skin clothing.

Besides the stone tools, there are traces of only two other artifacts: a round imprint in the sand, filled with a whitish substance, which might represent a wooden bowl, and some pieces of red ochre with ends smoothed by wear. Red ochre in more recent times has been widely used for painting the body.

What do we know about *H. erectus* visits to Terra Amata, and how do we know it? For one thing, the huts were hardly permanent structures. They probably fell apart after a few days, and were certainly not built to withstand a long, cold glacial winter. **Coprolites** were analyzed, and it was found they contained plants that shed their pollen at the end of spring and beginning of summer. So we know Terra Amata was visited during that period of time. DeLumley describes these brief visits:

> On arrival they set up their huts, built their hearths and windscreens, hunted for a day or two, gathered some seafood, rested by their fires, made a few tools and then departed (1969, p. 49).

That the visits were short is reflected by the dirt living floors, which were not compacted as they would have been after long occupation. The evidence for the early collapse of the huts can be seen from the condition of the pebbles. A freshly chipped stone tool quickly becomes bleached if it is left in the sun, but the underside, concealed from the sun's rays, retains its original coloring. Many of the pebbles found on the living floors show this kind of bleaching, indicating the huts collapsed soon after they were erected and did not protect the pebbles from weathering.

As the summer ended, the winds covered the camp with a layer of sand that the rains then packed down. By the time the hunters returned the following year, evidence of the camp was almost obliterated. The hunters again built their huts in the same place, following the outlines from the previous year, and the entire process was repeated. According to deLumley (1969), this occurred eleven times, since there are eleven living floors, so precisely superimposed that they represent consecutive visits, probably by many of the same individuals. Villa (1983) does not believe the occupation levels are so clearly marked. She states there is some evidence that the site was also occupied during other seasons. These visits suggest that the group was a stable one with complex institutions, perhaps family and band.

Camille Julliard, a French historian, wrote soon after the Terra Amata living floors had been exposed:

> The hearth is a place for gathering together around a fire that warms, that sheds light and gives comfort. The toolmaker's seat is where one man carefully pursues a work that is useful to many. The men here may well be nomadic hunters, but before the chase begins they need periods of preparation and afterward long moments of repose beside the hearth. The family, the tribe will arise from these customs, and I ask myself if they have not already been born.

The Wolpoff Hypothesis

We have covered *H. erectus* in Africa, Asia, and in Europe—if the Middle Pleistocene Europeans do, in fact, belong to the *erectus* taxon. We have described the life at Terra Amata, which probably was not very different from the existence of African and Asian inhabitants of that time. We have also discussed some of the physical changes that occurred in the evolution of *H. erectus* from the preceding hominid species. Can we account for at least some of these physical and cultural changes? Dr. Milford Wolpoff (1980a) of the University of Michigan, offers a suggestive hypothesis. It should be emphasized that Dr. Wolpoff's explanation is hypothetical; direct evidence is often lacking.

The Wolpoff hypothesis is based on the shift from the australopithecine scavenging/gathering adaptation with some small-scale hunting to a hunting/gathering adaptation characteristic of *H. erectus*.

As hunting developed into a more important source of food, it was organized and planned. Meat became a regular and dependable (rather than opportunistic) part of the diet, replacing some of the more difficult-to-chew plant foods that had been dietary staples. Improved technology produced more hunting-efficient and food-processing tools as well as more skillful manufacturing techniques. Archeological evidence shows an increasing number of tool types, such as crudely pointed chopperlike tools and small scraping tools. Spheroids, a round ball-like stone tool—usually showing evidence of battering—greatly increased in frequency, and it is thought the battering resulted from pounding foods to make them easier to chew:

> Every increase in the amount of cutting, chopping, or smashing that took place before food was chewed would have decreased the need to maintain a chewing complex that produced powerful forces (Wolpoff, 1980a, p. 168).

This combination of changes in diet and food preparation probably accounts for the reduction in the postcanine teeth.

The change in diet, from tough foods to meat and softer foods, produced further changes in the skull (Box 14-9). The load on posterior teeth decreased, making for smaller back teeth, and the load on front teeth increased, resulting in their somewhat larger size. However, not only did tooth size change, but the muscles operating the jaw and the forces operating on the skull developed front and back buttressing; i.e., the supraorbital torus and the nuchal torus that provide reinforcement for the chewing and neck muscles. (Although the use of fire came in after hunting had become an important food source, it would also have served to make chewing easier and would have affected the load on posterior and anterior teeth.)

Unlike other carnivores, when primates hunt they depend largely on vision, and early hominids were, therefore, diurnal (daytime) hunters. For diurnal hunting in the tropics it would be a great advantage if the hunter were heat-adapted in order to get rid of excess heat. One of the ways of doing this is by sweating, during which drops of sweat evaporate and cool the skin. Body hair, which makes drop formation and dripping easy, reduces the amount of sweat that evaporates. Adaptation to tropics, therefore, involved reducing the number and size of hair follicles (loss of body hair) and development of sweat glands all over the body.

Water loss through sweating makes for a thirsty hominid, and it is not surpris-

Forces on the Teeth and Skull

(a) Drawing of the later Indonesian *Homo erectus* cranium Sangiran 17 showing the positions of the main jaw-associated muscles that resist a force on the front teeth and the combined horizontal and vertical components that such a force must have (unless the force is completely vertical).

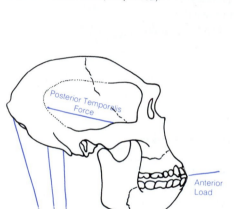

(b) Side view of F. Weidenreich's reconstruction of the Indonesian late Lower Pleistocene cranium Sangiran 4 and the Sangiran 1 mandible. The drawing shows a load between the anterior teeth exerting force in the *horizontal* direction, and indicates the positions of the two main muscles that can resist it. The nuchal (neck) muscles bring the cranium backward, and the posterior temporalis brings the mandible backward. Both of these muscles are well developed in *Homo erectus*.

(c) A simplified model of the reaction of the face to *vertical* anterior loads, based on a drawing of the ER-3733 face. The model is derived from B. Endo's facial stress analysis. In the face below, the upward-pointing arrow represents the force of an object between the teeth. This force is provided by the force of the mandible on the object. Therefore, the muscles closing the mandible also produce forces on the face. These are represented by the arrows on the right, and the main lines of facial resistance to these forces are represented by a simple beam model. The lower (downward-pointing) arrow represents the masseter force, and the upper ones the anterior temporalis force. The actions of these forces meet in the area above the eyes. Their effects in this area can be reduced to a simpler model by representing the region above the eyes by a beam (shown above). On this beam, a central force acts upward, and the forces to the sides act to bend the beam downward and pull it outward. It is the concentration of bending and tensile (producing tension) forces in the beam (supra-orbital region) that creates the necessity of strengthening. In early hominids with low foreheads, the strengthening takes the form of a buttress, or torus, called the *supraorbital torus* or the browridge.

ing that most major early hominid sites are found close to water. But hunting is not always possible near water, so carrying water became very important:

> Carrying water depends on one of the most basic human inventions . . . the container. The innovation of containers was one of the most important human cultural adaptations, and probably one of the critical factors that led to the development of effective organized hunting (Wolpoff, 1980a, p. 169).

It is also possible that the invention of containers may have resulted in increased body size, and to some extent, therefore, brain size. Without sufficient water, a small body is advantageous since skin surface is proportionately greater and heat loss (by sweating) is improved. Carrying containers of water would remove the small-size limitation.

Another possible result of heat adaptation, suggests Wolpoff, is darker skin color as protection against ultraviolet rays of the tropical sun. However, there is currently little concrete evidence to support this.

In addition to these physical and physiological modifications, there were also social innovations. Hunting gives a group more free time, since less meat (compared to plants) is required for the same food value. Also, assuming hunting and gathering activities were planned and cooperatively executed, there was opportunity for more complex social interaction within and between populations.

With a division of labor (males hunting and females gathering), males assumed responsibility for protecting females and young. Not only was food shared within the band, but the sharing was ritualized; strategies were developed requiring cooperation between males, and attempts made at long-range planning.

Table 14-5 Homo erectus *Sites*[*]

Asia	
Java	Trinil, Modjokerto, Sangiran, Sambungmacan
China	Zhoukoudian, Lantian, Hexian, Jinniushan
India	Narmada Valley, Madhya Pradesh
Europe	Heidelberg (Mauer), Germany
	Bilzingsleben
	Vértesszöllös, Hungary
	Petralona, Greece
	Torralba/Ambrona, Spain No fossil hominid bones found
	Terra Amata, France
Africa	
North Africa	Ternifine, Algeria
	Rabat, Morocco
	Salé, Morocco
	Casablanca, Morocco
East Africa	Olduvai Gorge, Tanzania
	East Turkana, Kenya
	West Turkana, Kenya
	Omo, Ethiopia
	Afar, Ethiopia

[*]This is not a complete listing.

Whether or not this scenario proposed by Wolpoff did, in fact, occur, when we look back at the evolution of *H. erectus*, we realize how significant were this early human's achievements toward *hominization*. It was *H. erectus* who increased in body size with more efficient bipedalism; who embraced culture wholeheartedly as a strategy of adaptation; whose brain was reshaped and increased in size to within *sapiens* range; who became a more efficient scavenger and likely hunter with greater dependence on meat (which in turn reduced jaw and posterior teeth size); who apparently established more or less permanent living sites, probably some sort of social organization, such as family and band; and who used fire extensively. We salute *Homo erectus*, the first human beings.

Summary

Homo erectus represents the second grade of human evolution and is usually associated with the Middle Pleistocene, although they appear almost a million years earlier. The beginning of the Middle Pleistocene has been set at the Matuyama-Brunhes paleomagnetic boundary, 700 k.y.a.

Differences from australopithecines are notable in *H. erectus'* larger and reproportioned brain, taller stature, and changes in facial structure and skull buttressing.

Remains of Middle Pleistocene hominids come from three continents. In Asia, there are two locations: Java and China. Africa contains two areas: East Africa and North Africa. There are several sites in Europe with hominid skeletal material: Heidelberg, Vértesszöllös, Petralona, Bilzingsleben, and Arago. Also discussed are two archeological sites lacking human bones: Torralba/Ambrona in Spain and Terra Amata in France, the latter treated in some detail.

Two problems were presented: Were early hominids hunters or scavengers? Binford and colleagues insist they were scavengers, but not everyone agrees. The second problem concerns the taxon of Middle Pleistocene Europeans. Are they *H. erectus*, do they belong to some other known taxon, or are they something else? (*H. heidelbergensis* has been suggested.)

The culture of Middle Pleistocene is reconstructed, and routes *H. erectus* might have taken from East Africa to eastern Asia, northwestern Africa, and Europe are proposed.

A hypothetical reconstruction of evolutionary change from australopithecines to *H. erectus* is presented, suggesting evolution was due to changes in diet, from plant material to greater dependence on meat. Adaptation to tropical diurnal hunting/gathering was perhaps responsible for loss of body hair, sweat glands, and increased body size. Dependence on meat changed chewing habits and, therefore, facial and skull structure. Cultural flexibility required for hunting big game (giving rise to organized and cooperative groups) selected for a larger and reproportioned brain and hastened the process of hominization.

Wolpoff's hypothesis is based on the traditional view that early hominids were hunters. Binford does not believe this view is supported by the evidence; bones, ash, and artifacts, he writes, have not been adequately studied to demonstrate the traditional point of view.

Questions for Review

1. Describe the Pleistocene in terms of (a) temperature and (b) the dating of fossil hominids.
2. Why is paleomagnetism more useful than other methods in dating the earth's history?
3. Describe *H. erectus*. How is *H. erectus* anatomically different from australopithecines? From *H. sapiens*?
4. What are the significant features of *H. erectus*' cultural life?
5. What was the intellectual climate in Europe in the latter half of the nineteeth century, especially concerning human evolution?
6. Why was there so much opposition to Dubois' interpretation of the hominid fossils he found in Java?
7. Why do you think Peking Man was enthusiastically accepted whereas Java Man was not?
8. Describe the life of Peking Man and alternative views.
9. Make a case in favor of *H. erectus* as a valid taxon for the European Middle Pleistocene hominids. Make a case against this.
10. What are the "firsts" in the culture of the Terra Amata inhabitants?
11. What evidence suggests that Terra Amata people were organized in some form of social groups?
12. How do Binford's views differ from the more traditional views?
13. *Homo erectus* is called the first human. Why?
14. What is the *H. erectus* evidence from Africa, and what questions of human evolution does the evidence raise?
15. Summarize the evolutionary events (physical and cultural) of the Middle Pleistocene.
16. What events, according to Wolpoff, led to loss of body hair and increased body size?
17. Why do we "owe so much" to *H. erectus*?

Homo Sapiens

CONTENTS

The Frozen Neandertal

The world is full of wonders! Ivan T. Sanderson, a well-known writer on the subject of primates and a science editor of *Argosy*, wrote an article in the May 1969 issue of that magazine on an adventure he had recently experienced. If we take Sanderson at his word, he was completely serious.

Early in 1969, Sanderson decided to investigate a report concerning a strange-looking corpse encased in a 6,000-pound block of ice that had been placed on display at the annual Stock Fair in Chicago. Accompanying him was Dr. Bernard Heuvelmans of the Belgium Royal Academy of Sciences and a longtime student of matters like the Abominable Snowman and similar singularities.

On a remote Minnesota farm, they met the frozen Neandertal along with a Mr. Frank Hansen who owned it or rented it, or was at least in charge of it. The body was indeed encased in ice (which made examination and measurement difficult), but the two men did their best.

Sanderson described "Bozo," as they nicknamed it, as a very sturdy, approximately six-foot "human" covered with hair over almost the entire body. Its fingers and toes had nails, not claws, and it had practically no neck. Its torso was "barrel-shaped and it tapers down, not to a waist, but to rather narrow hips" (Sanderson, 1969, p. 26). And, although its legs were about the right length, its arms were longer than average. Its most outstanding characteristic was its enormous, spatulate hands, but the thumbs were surprisingly slender and long. The eyeballs were the most bizarre features of Bozo's face—both eyes had been "blown out" of their sockets, and the nose was distinctly pugged, like that of a Pekingese dog. It was also very obviously male.

"Let me say, simply," wrote Sanderson, "that one look was actually enough to convince us that this was—from our point of view, at least—'the genuine article.' This was no phony Chinese trick, or 'art' work" (1969, p. 26).

Whence cometh this Iceman? Several stories purport to explain the presence of the Iceman in the United States and on the carnival circuit. In one tale, Bozo was found floating in a block of sea ice in the Bering Sea by a Soviet whaling ship. When the Soviets put in at a Chinese port, the authorities seized the specimen, which then disappeared into Red China. It finally turned up, no one knows how, in Hong Kong, still in 6,000 pounds of ice, which had apparently not melted even one ounce worth.

An alternate story is that the original discoverers were not Soviet, but Japanese whalers, and that the find occurred somewhere off the coast of Kamchatka, not the Bering Sea. The creature was taken to Japan and then sold to a Hong Kong exporter.

Once in Hong Kong, the ice and the creature were wrapped in a sort of super plastic bag and stored in a deep freeze by an exporter who sold all kinds of curios. An agent for a wealthy American associated with the movie industry heard that the Iceman was for sale and bought it for his client. It was then rented by Mr. Hansen, who took it about, still in the ice block, from carnival to carnival, fair to fair, and sideshow to sideshow, exhibiting it to the public throughout the country.

In his book *Bigfoot* (1973), primatologist Dr. John Napier—who had originally apparently been taken in by all of this—exposed the Iceman for what it really was. After some investigation, Napier concluded that the entire affair was a publicity stunt initiated by Mr. Hansen, who really owned the object, and not the mysterious Hollywood multimillionaire. It also appeared that the "body" was made of latex rubber and hair and had been put together on the West Coast. In 1970, Hansen "confessed" in *Saga* that the story he told Sanderson was simply a showman's spiel. What actually happened, he wrote, was that in 1960, while on a hunting trip in Minnesota, he shot a doe. When he came up to it, three hairy creatures were tearing the animal apart with their bare hands and drinking its blood. One of the creatures sprang screeching at him. Panicked, Hansen fired his rifle point blank, blowing out the creature's eyes and killing it instantly. Terrified, Hansen ran off, but returned a few days later to find the creature frozen stiff. He carried it back to his home, cautioned his wife not to say a word about it, and deposited it in their deep freeze, where it spent the next seven years until Hansen decided to take it on the road.

A different thrilling story was carried in the *National Bulletin* on June 30, 1969, under the heading, "I Was Raped by the Abominable Snowman!" A young woman, Helen Westring by name, alleged that while hunting alone in Minnesota, she met an Abominable Snowman. The monster ripped off her clothes, like peeling a banana, glared at her lustfully, and proceeded to rape her. Luckily, Helen fainted during the action, as a proper maiden should, but when she regained consciousness, she shot the brute through the right eye (which dislocated the left eye). And that was how the Iceman lost his eyes—at the hands of a heroic girl avenging her honor in the Minnesota woods!

Sanderson was convinced Bozo was real and a Neandertal (he—Sanderson—died before Napier completed his investigations). However, Sanderson and Heuvelmans are not the only believers in the presence of Neandertals living in remote areas of the world. Several Soviet paleoanthropologists at the Darwin Museum in Moscow have developed a theory on the origin of *Homo sapiens*, part of which is that "relic hominoids," such as Bigfoot, Yeti, and others of native folklore, are really Neandertals or their descendants (Proshnev, 1974; Bayanov and Bourtsev, 1974, 1976).

The Soviets write persuasively of relic hominoids, but hard, convincing evidence remains surprisingly lacking. Sightings of relic hominoids (much like sightings of UFOs) have been widespread, and the evidence appears to be of about the same caliber. Why all this interest in relic hominoids that propels men to the isolated woods of the Pacific Coast, the mountaintops of the Himalaya, and assorted lonely steppes and deserts? Perhaps Napier's cogent comments may help explain this strange phenomenon:

> Man has an insatiable appetite for ghouls and bogles, and large sections of the entertainment business make it their concern to see that his tastes are well catered for. Horror-films, horror-comics, horror-exhibits are big business. . . . This determination of mankind to frighten itself to death can perhaps be regarded as an endearing trait, an expression of a touching, child-like naiveté in the face of the monstrous Forces of the Unknown. On the other hand, perhaps it is just a cult that owes nothing to nature, religion, philosophy or the mainstream of folklore, but is simply another form of self-indulgence (Napier, 1973, p. 193).

Update

Myra Shackley's archeological research in Mongolia led her to believe ("half sceptically") in the possibility of Neandertal survivals in the Altai ranges of central Asia. Local inhabitants know of people living in the Altai Mountains who are quite different from themselves, and, Shackley says, may be surviving Neandertals.

Until careful studies are made, we withhold judgment.

SOURCES:

Bayanov, Dmitri, and Igor Bourtsev. "Reply [to comments on Proshnev's article]," *Current Anthropology* 15(4):452–456, 1974.

———. "On Neanderthal vs. Paranthropus," *Current Anthropology* 17 (2):312–318, 1976.

Napier, John. *Bigfoot*. New York: E. P. Dutton & Co., Inc., 1973.

Proshnev, B. F. "The Troglodytidae and the Hominidae in the Taxonomy and Evolution of Higher Primates," *Current Anthropology* 15 (4):449–450, 1974.

Sanderson, Ivan T. "The Missing Link," *Argosy*, May, pp. 23–31, 1969.

Shackley, Myra. "The Case for Neanderthal Survival: Fact, Fiction or Faction?" *Antiquity* 56:31–41, 1982.

Introduction

Evolution may proceed by gradual modification, eventually producing a new species or, as a recent theory suggests, it may occur by rapid bursts that punctuate long periods of stability. (See p. 92 for a discussion of punctuated equilibrium.)

In human evolution, there appears to be evidence for gradual modification, since *H. erectus*, for example, did not change significantly (there was some increase in brain size) in more than one million years.

It may also be possible to evidence what may be considered a quick change in human evolution. About 400 kya* or so, there seems to have been a *relatively* sudden appearance, especially in Europe, of forms no longer unambiguously *H. erectus*, as we pointed out in the preceding chapter. About 250 kya, hominid remains reflected an accumulation of neandertal, or neandertal-like traits, which may well have led to the Neandertals of the Upper Pleistocene.

These forms are often referred to as *transitional*, a term that might be applied to the earlier European group as well. The question is: Did these transitional Middle Europeans, in fact, evolve into a later form, and, if so, how shall we classify it? This question is addressed later in the chapter.

In this chapter, then, we shall examine the course of human evolution in the late Middle Pleistocene and Upper Pleistocene. The chapter is divided into three sections: transitional forms of the late Middle Pleistocene, Neandertals,† and anatomically modern (a.m.) human beings (*Homo sapiens sapiens*).‡ This scheme is somewhat simplistic, given the problems of classifying evolving hominids, but it will serve as an adequate device for dealing with the emergence of the *H. sapiens* grade of human evolution.

Transitional Forms

Europe

Although dates for European hominids of the late Middle Pleistocene are still being debated and investigated, we shall assume that the transitional forms we are discussing lived within the period from roughly 250 to 75 kya, the late Riss glacial and the following interglacial. Like their European predecessors, these hominids also displayed mosaic features of older and later traits. During this period, however, there was a definite trend toward neandertal characteristics—and more of them. (See Fossil Background boxes, pp. 571–581).

The neandertal traits found in these pre-Würm hominids have led a number of students of this period to identify them as ancestors of the classic Neandertals**

*Reminder: kya = thousand years ago. The symbol k is commonly used to stand for thousand.

†Neandertals inhabited Eurasia (Europe and the Near East) from about 75 kya to about 30 kya.

‡Included in this chapter are well-known fossils or those that help understand human evolution of the late Middle and Upper Pleistocene. A complete listing is not intended.

**Classic Neandertals lived during the early Würm glacial.

BOX 15-1

Comparison of *Homo sapiens sapiens* and *H. erectus*

Homo sapiens differs from *H. erectus* in a number of characteristics.[*] In *H. sapiens sapiens*:

1. The skull is larger with a 1350 cc mean cranial capacity

2. Muscular ridges in the cranium are not strongly marked

3. The forehead is rounded and vertical

4. The supraorbital ridges are not well developed and do not form a continuous and uninterrupted torus

[*]For a fuller definition see Howell, 1978, pp. 201ff.

5. The occipital region is rounded and the nuchal area is relatively small

6. Mastoid process is prominent and of a pyramidal shape

7. The calvaria is of maximum width, usually in the parietal region

8. Jaws and teeth are relatively small

9. Maxilla has concave surface including a canine fossa

10. The chin is distinct

11. Limb bones are relatively slender and slight

---

of the Upper Pleistocene. That was a time of glacial advances and retreats, very cold weather interrupted by temperate weather, and many animals were available for hunting or scavenging, or both.

Among the best known of this transitional group are Swanscombe, from England, and Steinheim, from Germany. Since they lived at approximately the same time—200 to 250 kya—when Britain was still joined to the continent, it

Figure 15-1
Sites of transitional forms and Neandertals.

Figure 15-2
Early archaic sapiens *sites—Swanscombe and Steinheim.*

(a)

(b)

Figure 15-3
Cast of Steinheim skull. (a) Basal view, showing how the foramen magnum was enlarged, apparently for removal of the brain— for dietary or ritualistic purposes; (b) frontal view showing warped skull.

may not be surprising that these two females share several similar traits, noticeably in the occipital area.

Unfortunately, Swanscombe consists only of parietals and occipital, and lacks frontal bone and face; Steinheim is a more complete—though damaged—skull (it lacks a mandible), so the comparison is obviously limited. Nevertheless, examination by several scientists in recent years has convinced them of the similarity of the two skulls, and that they possess traits associated with Neandertals. It has even been suggested that the Neandertal lineage started with them.

As can be seen from the photograph (Fig. 15-3a), the base of Steinheim's skull has been cut away, apparently to remove the brain. (You will recall Peking Man's skull was similarly multilated). This again raises the question of cannibalism. Present opinion opposes the belief that these early hominids devoured other humans. K. D. Adams, in his study of Steinheim, believes this surgery on the skull "was not a result of hunger or because the brain was regarded as a delicacy. Such a procedure on a dead body may have involved magic or religious activity, and it represents evidence of the degree of intellectual evolution 250,000 years ago" (1985, p. 275). Dr. Adams also believes that the severe damage to Steinheim's skull (Fig. 15-3b) was inflicted during her life by others, obviously with a "blunt instrument."

Several fossil remains of this group have been found in France. One of them, Biache-Saint-Vaast, the only human fossil found in northern France, is represented by the back half of the skull. The occipital and the shape of the skull from a rear view show characteristics of the Neandertal skull.

In the Charente area of southwest France there is a series of cave openings or rock shelters, known as the La Chaise site. One of the rock shelters is L'abri Bourgeois-Delaunay, named after two abbés who published works on its stratigraphy more than a hundred years ago. An interesting point concerning the occipital found here is that its measurements are intermediate between Swanscombe and Neandertal, which provides arguments for placing Swanscombe in the Neandertal line.

Another rockshelter in the La Chaise area is L'abri Suard. Like that of its close neighbor, the bone material reflects archaic and neandertal traits, especially in the occipital and temporal bones.

Two more fossils, of the last interglacial (or possibly late Riss glacial), are worthy of mention: one from Germany—Ehringsdorf; and one from France— Fontechevade. These are well known since they have long played a role in the phylogenetic controversy surrounding Neandertals. Their physical traits were interpreted at one time as being closer to a.m.* humans than to classic Neandertals. Since these fossils are older than the classics, it seemed strange that older fossils would have traits that were more modern.

In recent years, more thorough examination of both Ehringsdorf and Fontechevade has persuaded many paleoanthropologists that these so-called progressive Neandertals are very similar to classic Neandertals. If this is the case, the problem of "progressive" versus classic Neandertals may no longer be a problem.

Ehringsdorf remains have been reconstructed by several scholars, and each reconstruction changes the interpretations. One reconstruction looks more (or less) Neandertal, another more (or less) modern. Recent interpretations stress

*a.m. = anatomically modern.

the Neandertal similarity of the occipital, especially the suprainiac fossa, large anterior teeth, and some taurodontism in one of the mandibles.

The Fontechevade skull fragments have given rise to various interpretations of where it belongs in the phylogenetic scheme. Much of the argument surrounds the frontal area of one fragment, and of the calotte. Is there, or is there not, a supraorbital present? If there is, then the association with classic Neandertal is quite clear; if there is not, then the bones belong to a more modern individual.

The fact that there is no supraorbital torus on either fragment, however, does not settle the matter. The more complete fragment—the calotte—is too incomplete for a final decision. The frontal fragment, comprising the glabellar area, may belong to an immature individual and, therefore, the supraorbital torus may not yet have developed. Consequently, it seems doubtful that Fontechevade can be considered anatomically modern. The date, late Riss or interglacial, suggests a close affinity to the classic Neandertals.

We have now covered the main fossils of this European period and can briefly sum up late Middle Pleistocene (late Riss and third interglacial) evolution by noting the trend from an archaic *sapiens* with a mosaic of earlier and later features to the classic Neandertal form. Evidence for the change comes mainly from cranial bones and teeth (postcranial bones are rather scarce).

Cultural Activities   We also know something of the cultural activities of these preneandertals. They built shelters, although it is not known how common these were. The only shelter that has been described was found in the Lazaret cave, in the city of Nice, southern France, not far from Terra Amata (see Chapter 14), where there is also evidence of shelters. The Lazaret shelter, about 36 by 11 feet,

Figure 15-4
Cast of Swanscombe skull.

Figure 15-5
Fontechevade II fragment. View of left side. The forehead is at the left. (Courtesy of N. Vallois.)

Figure 15-6
Ehringsdorf. Neandertal, probably earlier than Würm glacial. (Courtesy of Fred Smith)

Figure 15-7
Archaic sapiens of France and Germany.

Figure 15-8
African archaic sapiens.

(a)

(b)

Figure 15-9
Broken Hill (Rhodesian Man), Kabwe.
(a) *Note very heavy supraorbital torus;*
(b) *photograph of cast.*

is built against the cave wall, and skins were probably hung over a framework of poles for the shelter walls. The base was supported by rocks and large bones.

Inside the shelter were two hearths. The hearth charcoal indicates they used slow-burning oak and boxwood, with embers easy to rekindle. Very little stone waste was found inside the shelter, suggesting they manufactured tools outside, where there was more light. Also, outside the cave are traces of a series of tents, and just inside the door of each tent was a wolf skull. The exact significance of the wolf skulls may never be known, but they were surely symbolic and possibly indicative of a ritual.

During the Riss, it is possible that geographic differences appeared among human beings as they adapted to different environmental conditions. It was also during this time that humans first began to occupy caves extensively (seasonally in some cases), as well as open sites. Archeological evidence makes it clear that many different food sources were being utilized, such as fruits, vegetables, seeds, nuts, bird eggs, and so forth, each in its own season. Marine life was exploited. From Lazaret and Orgnac, in southern France, comes evidence for freshwater fishing (trout, perch, and carp).

Changes in tool technology also appear. In addition to new styles of stone tools, new materials, such as bone and antler, are utilized. Not many hunting tools have been found, which suggests the possible use of wooden projectile points, or perhaps nets or traps were used. It is also possible that scavenging was important as a source of meat.

From an evolutionary point of view, keep in mind that, in the Middle Pleistocene, there was a great deal of variation in these populations, with differences in many (if not all) features of the skull. Also, as we pointed out at the beginning of this section, some characteristics recall the preceding *H. erectus* forms, and others mark a trend toward *H. sapiens*.

We have seen that after a million years and more of a fairly stable *H. erectus* grade of evolution, there is movement toward a *sapiens* grade. In Europe, the evolutionary course appears to have culminated in Neandertals. Neandertals may, or may not, have continued to evolve to *H. sapiens sapiens*. Recent evidence suggests that a.m. humans may have evolved elsewhere, very likely Africa, and also, perhaps, independently in Asia.

Evolutionary change, of course, was not limited to Europe. In the following sections, we will discuss evolutionary events in Africa and in Asia.

Africa

In Africa, change toward the *sapiens* grade can be seen at several sites. One of the best known is Broken Hill (Kabwe). Found in a shallow Broken Hill mine shaft, at Kabwe, Zambia, South Africa, were a complete cranium and other cranial and postcranial material belonging to several individuals.

Like the Middle Pleistocene Europeans, a mixture of older and later traits can be seen in this fossil material. The skull's massive supraorbital torus (one of the largest of any hominid), low vault, and prominent occipital torus recall those of *H. erectus*. On the other hand, the occipital is less angulated, the vault bones thinner, and the cranial base essentially modern. A cranial capacity of 1280 cc is significantly beyond the *erectus* average of 1000 cc. Characteristics of the parietals and occipital have led Rightmire (1976) to designate this specimen as a separate subspecies, *H. sapiens rhodesiensis.*

(a)

(b)

Figure 15-10
A Middle Pleistocene butchering site at Olorgesaile, Kenya, excavated by Louis Leakey who had the catwalk [(a) and (b)] built for observers. (c) is a closeup view of the Acheulian tools, mainly handaxes, found at the site. Acheulian tools were found at the Bodo site.

(c)

Dating of Broken Hill has ranged throughout the Middle Pleistocene and Upper Pleistocene, but recent estimates have given dates in the neighborhood of 130 kya.

Bodo   Discovered in 1976 in northeast Ethiopia, in the general area where Lucy was found (see Chapter 12), is an incomplete cranium dating from the Middle

(a)

(b)

Figure 15-11
(a) *Bodo. Early archaic* sapiens *of Africa;*
(b) *cutmarks on Bodo—top right and side of orbit.*

Figure 15-12
Sites of Chinese archaic sapiens.

Pleistocene. Like Broken Hill, to which it has been compared, the skull displays a mixture of *H. erectus* and more modern features. Bodo's classification is also murky. It has been called *H. erectus* and also archaic *sapiens*; i.e., transitional between *H. erectus* and a.m. humans.

There are several interesting points associated with Bodo. Some evidence suggests that animals were butchered at the site. Acheulian tools (see Fig. 15-10) are associated with several hippopotamus skeletons, and cutmarks are found on the human skull (Conroy, et al., 1978).

White (1986) examined the skull and counted 17 cutmark areas. These are located in the interorbital area, on the supraorbital torus, and on the posterior parietals. White believes this argues "for a patterned intentional defleshing of this specimen by a hominid(s) with (a) stone tool(s)" (White, 1986, p. 508). That is to say, Bodo was scalped, and this is the earliest solid evidence for deliberate defleshing (see Fig. 15-11, *a* and *b*).

Three other crania, and Elandsfontein (Saldanha), Florisbad from South Africa, and one from Ndutu, near Olduvai Gorge, also show a combination of *erectus* and *sapiens* characteristics, and they are mentioned as being similar to Broken Hill. These similarities may signify a phylogenetic relationship of hominids from East and South Africa. It is also possible that several populations were evolving in a somewhat similar way from *H. erectus* to a.m. humans.

We should point out that the evolutionary path of these hominids did not take a Neandertal turn. It seems there were no Neandertals in Africa. Nor were there any in the Far East.

Eastern Asia

Like their counterparts in Europe and Africa, Chinese archaic *sapiens* also display both older and later characters. Chinese paleoanthropologists believe that archaic *sapiens* traits, such as sagittal keeling, flattened nasal bones, shovel-shaped incisors, and others are shared with *H. erectus*, especially Peking Man. They also point out that some of these features can be found in modern *H. sapiens* in China today, indicating substantial phylogenetic continuity. That is to say, anatomically modern Chinese evolved separately from *H. sapiens* in Europe or Africa.

That such evolution in isolation occurred in China is difficult to demonstrate, one way or the other, in the present state of our knowledge. However, China is

Figure 15-13
Dali. A good example of Chinese archaic sapiens.

Figure 15-14
Maba. Once identified as H. erectus, *but is now considered as archaic* sapiens.

not isolated from the rest of the world. Just south of China is Indonesia, where *H. erectus* evidence is older. Also, during glacial periods, the Sunda shelf (p. 432) joined Indonesia to the mainland, and migrations (and gene mixture) between the two areas would not have been difficult.

Chinese paleoanthropologists note the lack of Neandertal features, such as the occipital bun, prognathic face, and the lack of canine fossae in the archaic *sapiens* of China as evidence of the absence of Neandertals in China. It would appear, then, that Neandertals were a unique development in Europe and western Asia.

Dali, the most complete of the late Pleistocene human fossils in China, displays *erectus* and *sapiens* traits, and is clearly classified as the skull of an archaic *sapiens*. The Maba calotte, because of similarities to Dali, is now considered archaic *sapiens* instead of Neandertal. The Changyang and Ixujiayao fragments also reflect earlier and later traits, and are placed in the same category as Dali and Maba.

Having discussed archaic *sapiens* in Europe, Africa, and China, we return again to Europe to look at that unique and interesting population: Neandertals.

Neandertals (75–30 kya)

Despite their apparent disappearance 40–30 kya, Neandertals continue to haunt the best laid theories of paleoanthropologists. They fit into the general scheme of human evolution, and yet they are misfits. Classified as *H. sapiens*, they are like us and yet different. It is not an easy task to put them in their place.

Figure 15-15
Upper Pleistocene. Correlation approximations. The culture periods of the Upper Paleolithic are not necessarily sequential as shown. This figure is simply meant to assist the student in organizing Upper Pleistocene data.

MOUSTERIAN
(moo-stair'-ee-en)
A cultural tradition of the Upper Pleistocene
associated with Neandertals.

Poor *Homo sapiens neanderthalensis*. Surely no other ethnic group has had so many nasty slurs and insults thrown at itself than our distant cousins of some 40,000 to 50,000 years ago (Holloway, 1985, p. 319).

These troublesome hunters are the cave man of cartoonists, walking about with bent knees, dragging a club in one hand and a woman by her hair in the other. They are described as brutish, dwarfish, apelike, and obviously of little intelligence. This image is more than somewhat exaggerated.

While cartoonists' license is not to be denied, the fact remains that Neandertals walked as upright as any of us, and, if they dragged clubs and women, there is not the slightest evidence of it. Nor are they dwarfish or apelike, and, in the light of twentieth-century human behavior, we should be careful whom we call brutish.

As far as intelligence is concerned, Neandertals produced excellent **Mousterian** implements and, in fact, invented a new technique, the disc-core technique (Campbell, 1976, p. 328). This method is a highly productive one in which a nodule of stone is trimmed around the edges to make it disc-shaped. Then flakes are removed from the core by rapping the edges, knocking off flakes until the core becomes too small and is thrown away. The flakes are then further trimmed to provide the edges necessary for whatever kind of work was needed on wood, carcasses, or hides.

Neandertals were also clever enough to cope with the cold weather of the glacial period. In addition to open sites, they lived in caves, wore clothing, built fires, gathered in settlements (some of which extended right up to the Arctic Ocean), hafted some of their tools, and hunted* with a good deal of skill. They had to be skillful hunters in order to survive by subsisting off herds of reindeer, wooly rhinoceros, and mammoth. There was very little vegetable food available on the cold tundra.

Finally, the brain size of Neandertals is, on the average, at least that of contemporary *H. sapiens sapiens* and probably larger. Estimates for Neandertal skulls range from approximately 1250–1750 cc. Holloway, who has specialized in the study of fossil hominid brains, sums up the case for Neandertals:

> I believe the Neandertal brain was fully *Homo*, with no essential differences in its organization compared to our own. It was simply large, and, for at least two reasons: 1) It was metabolically efficient within periglacial and/or cold tundra habitats, and 2) it was related to a larger amount of lean body mass than our own, and thus the larger size was, in the main, an allometric scaling effect. Two additional speculations are: 1) Neandertals did have language, and 2) they were highly competent, visuospatially (1985, p. 320).

Neandertals lived from about the beginning of the Würm glacial, about 70 kya (or perhaps a bit earlier) until to roughly 30 kya. Although there was, of course, physical variability in the Neandertal population, there is a characteristic morphology that describes them (after Howells, 1973):

> The skull is large, long, low, and bulging at the sides. At the rear of the skull a bun protrudes, but the occiput is rounded without the angulation of *erectus*. There is less spongy bone at the base of the skull, and the greatest breadth is higher up on the skull.

> In front, the forehead rises though not as steeply as in modern *sapiens*, and the brow ridges, not quite as pronounced as *H. erectus*, arch over the orbits in-

---

*Some scholars believe Neandertals were scavengers, not hunters.

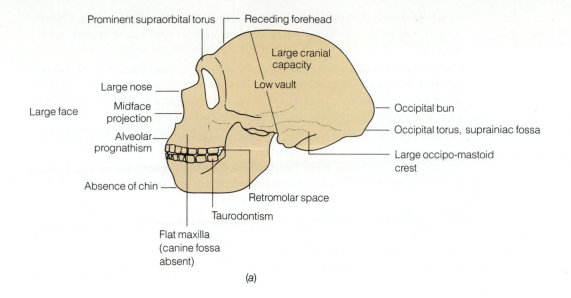

Prominent supraorbital torus
Receding forehead
Large cranial capacity
Low vault
Large nose
Large face
Midface projection
Alveolar prognathism
Absence of chin
Flat maxilla (canine fossa absent)
Taurodontism
Retromolar space
Occipital bun
Occipital torus, suprainiac fossa
Large occipo-mastoid crest

(a)

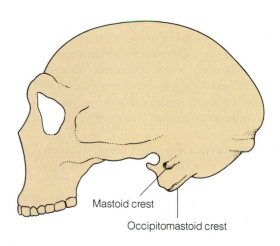

Mastoid crest
Occipitomastoid crest

Figure 15-16
(a) *Neandertal cranial features.* (b) *Several unique (automorphic) Neandertal features mentioned in text. This is not a complete listing; not all features are necessarily unique to Neandertal. Postcranial bones also display some differences from modern sapiens.*

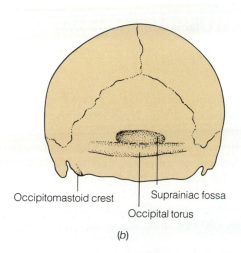

Occipitomastoid crest
Suprainiac fossa
Occipital torus

(b)

AUTAPOMORPH
A new morphological trait unique to a group in an evolutionary lineage.

stead of forming the straight bar of *H. erectus*. Variability found among Neandertals may be seen in the almost complete lack of these ridges in some specimens.

Compared to moderns, the Neandertal face stands out. Facial length is considerably greater for Neandertals than for Upper Paleolithic *sapiens* and even more so compared to ourselves. Alveolar prognathism is noticeable and, in fact, the entire face projects as if it had been pulled forward.

Neandertal's nose was high, angled, and prominent. "Many of the unique features of Neandertal facial morphology center about the nose. A fully fleshed Neandertal nose must have been a phenomenal object" (Wolpoff, 1980a, p. 280). On both sides of the nose the maxillary sinuses expand outward, giving the maxilla a puffy look and convex shape.

The teeth were larger than both Upper Paleolithic and present-day populations, but posterior teeth continued to decrease in size from earlier forms. Anterior teeth in the early Würm increased then reversed growth and began to decrease in size, a process that continued with *H. sapiens sapiens*.

In addition to cranial differences, there were several postcranial differences as well. The bones were considerably more robust, and the scapula, pubic bone, and femur were distinct—at least to some extent—from a.m. humans.

This description of Neandertals stresses the differences between them and those anatomically modern humans who appeared in western Europe about 40 kya. In fact, some scholars would reclassify Neandertals to their original taxon, *H. neanderthalensis*. Actually, many traits are shared by Neandertals and anatomically moderns, and most paleoanthropologists, at least for the present, prefer that Neandertals remain in the taxon *H. sapiens neanderthalensis*. There are probably no Neandertal traits that fall totally outside the variation range of modern humans.

If we now turn to examine the evidence from the early Upper Pleistocene, it may help us understand the Neandertal problem. In the past, the term "Neandertal" included the so-called "progressive" Neandertals of the Riss-Würm interglacial. In this chapter, we shall use the term Neandertal only for European and western Asian populations similar to those (classic) Neandertals from western Europe of the early Würm glacial.

The Würm (Fourth) Glaciation (70–30 kya)

Europe

With the onset of the Würm, about 70 kya, we encounter the complex situation of the Neandertals. For about 40 ky, Neandertals lived in Europe and the Near East, and their coming and going has raised more questions and controversies than perhaps any other hominid group. As William Howells said, "Neandertal man has served to launch, to enhance, and to mar anthropological careers. Perhaps he is like the Tar Baby—each time Brer Rabbit hit him another lick, he got stuck faster" (Howells, 1975, p. 390).

We have traced the beginning of Neandertal traits back to Swanscombe and Steinheim, more than 200 kya, and, as a matter of fact, we could go back even further, to Bilzingsleben, Arago, Petralona, etc. (see Chapter 14) for evidence of these characters. But these were transitional forms, preneandertals, and it is not until we come to the last glaciation, the Würm, or the end of the Riss-Würm Interglacial, that we find the unique populations with the **autapomorphic** features identified as Neandertal.

There are several basic questions to bear in mind as we examine the Neandertal event more closely. Did the anatomically modern humans of Europe evolve from Neandertals? In central Europe, for example, it is the opinion of Dr. Fred Smith, a specialist in this area, that "morphological continuity between Neandertals and the [early modern humans] is clearly documented by the available information" (1984, p. 192). However, he does not insist that the "morphological continuity" is necessarily an evolutionary one. Perhaps the most intriguing questions remain unanswered, and may be unanswerable: Whatever happened to the Neandertals? Are they extinct? Did they merge with their anatomically modern contemporaaries? Or do they still exist in some remote area (Bigfoot? Yeti?) as some writers still insist? In considerating these and other questions, we shall start at the beginning.

Neandertal Beginnings   Neandertal takes its name from the Neander Valley near Düsseldorf, Germany. In 1856, workmen quarrying limestone caves in the valley blew up the entrance to one of the caves and came across fossilized bones. The owner of the quarry believed they belonged to a bear and gave them to Johann Karl Fuhlrott, teacher of natural science in the local high school. Fuhlrott knew his subject, and when he saw the bones he realized they were not the remains of a cave bear. He believed they must be those of an ancient human, something between the gorilla (first discovered a few years earlier) and *Homo sapiens*. Exactly what the bones represented became a *cause célèbre* for many years, and the fate of Neandertal Man, as the bones were named, hung in the balance for years until later finds were made.

What swung the balance in favor of accepting the Neander Valley specimen as a genuine hominid fossil were other nineteenth-century finds similar to it. What is more important, the additional fossil remains brought home the realization that a form of human different from nineteenth-century Europeans had in fact existed.

Some of these nineteenth-century finds include a skull, which no one understood, found at Gibraltar in 1848. A decade later, the Neandertal Valley find placed the Gibraltar skull in a more accurate perspective as a Neandertal. In 1866, in the La Naulette Cave, Belgium, a mandible and a few odd bones were discovered and were attributed to the same species as Neandertal. In 1880, a child's mandible from Sipka, Czechoslovakia, demonstrated that large Neandertal teeth were not pathological, since this young mandible possessed large and normal teeth. Whereas there were cries of pathology and abnormality, voiced especially by Virchow (see Chapter 14), most scientists were impressed by the two skeletons recovered in 1886 from a cave at Spy, near the town of Namur, Belgium. These two skeletons were carefully observed in situ by scientists, and the site and excavation were carefully recorded. Similarities between these remains and those of earlier Neandertals were so extensive there could be no doubt that there really was a Neandertal Man.

In the post-Darwinian period, following the publication of *Origin* in 1859, the evolution controversy continued to rage, as we already have discussed in Chap-

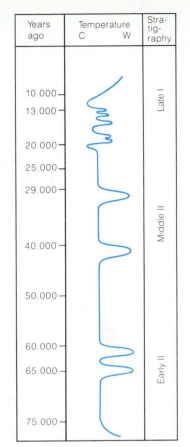

Figure 15-17
The Würm glaciation. During a glacial period, such as the Würm, the temperature—and the presence of ice—varies. The 65,000 years of the Würm were not simply one long cold period.

Figure 15-18
Sites: Gibraltar, Spy, La Naulette, Neandertal.

ters 2, 14, and elsewhere. Not even all scientists were persuaded that evolution was a valid concept; and more to the point, many scientists were very skeptical of the existence of hominid fossils. Cuvier's dictum, "*L'homme fossile n'existe pas*" (free translation: there is no such thing as fossil man), was still accepted by many Europeans, both laypeople and scientists. Virchow, for example, claimed to be a follower of Darwinian evolution, but was apparently unable to accept any of the hominid fossils discovered during his lifetime (he died in 1902) as honest-to-goodness hominid fossils. He described them as moderns, pathological in one way or another, and we have already alluded to the argument between Virchow and Haeckel about the evolution of hominids from pongids.

The discovery, in 1908, of La Chapelle-aux-Saints (discussed in the following section) settled the issue of the existence of fossil hominids once and for all. Unfortunately, by this time Cuvier was long since dead and, we assume, no longer in a position to change his mind. Virchow, too, had died a few years before, although the subsequent description of La Chapelle, written by Professor Marcellin Boule, seems to have been influenced by his predecessors, Cuvier and Virchow.

La Chapelle-aux-Saints One of the most important Neandertal discoveries was made in 1908 at La Chapelle-aux-Saints, near Correze in southwestern France. Found in a Mousterian cultural layer by three French priests, the Abbés A. and J. Bouysonnie and L. Bardon (already known for their archeological researches), was a nearly complete human skeleton. The body had been deliberately buried in a shallow grave and fixed in a ritual position, a bison leg placed on his chest, and the trench filled with flint tools and broken animal bones. This attitude suggests respect toward death, and the tools included with the body may very well indicate a belief in an afterlife where such implements could be used.

The skeleton was turned over for study to a famous French paleontologist, Marcellin Boule, who published his analysis in three volumes from 1911 to 1913. It was his exhaustive, and no doubt biased, publication that set the tone for the description of prehistoric humans that survives to this day.

Why did Boule describe Neandertal as the slouching, brutish, apelike, unintelligent creature that became the staple of the cartoonist's prehistoric man? Professor Brace suggests the reason was that Boule, trained in France in the traditions of Cuvier's catastrophism, did not really believe in evolution. He could not deny, as Cuvier had, the existence of fossil humans, but he could reject the no-

Figure 15-19
(a) *Cast, La Chapelle-aux-Saints. Note the occipital bun, facial and alveolar prognathism, low vault, and lack of chin;* (b) *photo of actual calvarium.*

(a)

(b)

tion that Neandertals were ancestral to anatomical moderns, especially if Neandertal looked noticeably different. "With the over-emphasis of the nonmodern features of the La Chapelle-aux-Saints skeleton it became a much less likely candidate for the forefather of the succeeding Upper Paleolithic forms" (Brace, 1977, p. 219).

The skull of this male, who was at least 40 years of age, is very large, with a cranial capacity of 1620 cc. The vault is low and long, the supraorbital ridges immense, with the typical Neandertal arched shape, and the forehead is low and retreating. Prognathism in the alveolar area is pronounced, and the face is long and projecting. At the rear of the skull, the occiput is protuberant and bun-shaped (see Fig. 15-19).

La Chapelle is not a typical Neandertal, but a very robust male and "evidently represents an extreme in the Neandertal range of variation" (Brace, et al., 1979, p. 117). Unfortunately, this skeleton, which Boule claimed did not even walk completely erect (he walked as erect as any other human with spinal arthritis), has been widely accepted as "Mr. Neandertal." That other Neandertals are not as extreme is shown by examination of several others.

Monte Circeo, from Italy, is one of the most typical of Neandertals, not as robust as La Chapelle, and at least one of the mandibles possesses a chin. Monte Circeo is another skull with the foramen magnum cut away in order (it is assumed) to remove the brain. La Quina is also less robust than La Chapelle, with one of the smallest of Neandertal brains, and, like Monte Circeo, one of the mandibles has a chin.

As a Riss-Würm Neandertal, Saccopastore was one of those believed to be more modern than the Würm Neandertals. However, recent studies confirm that Saccopastore's traits place him among the other Neandertals of western Europe.

La Ferrassie also displays some modification of the typical Neandertal configuration. The supraorbital torus, occipital bunning, and facial bones are less pronounced, and the frontal bone is somewhat more filled out. There is no question that La Ferrassie is a Neandertal—postcranial bones are very much like those of La Chapelle. But it is possible that La Ferrassie's late Würm age (if 38 kya is valid) may be a reason for the less robust appearance of the skull.

St. Cesaire, however, does not support this. St. Cesaire, dated at 31–34 kya, is typically Neandertal and the most recent Neandertal known. The bones were recovered from a bed of discarded chipped blades, hand axes, and other stone tools of a type called "Chatelperronian," a tool industry associated with a.m. humans of the Upper Paleolithic.

That Neandertals were in possession of tools invented and used (it is assumed) by anatomically modern humans immediately informs us of the surprising survival of Neandertals in a region inhabited by a.m. humans. We are also confronted with a number of intriguing questions: How did St. Cesaire acquire those tools—trade for them, steal them, copy them, fight for them? Did they interbreed and become assimilated into the modern population? Did both groups cooperate in hunting, exchange stories over a campfire, wage war, or fear and avoid each other?

Or did a.m. humans annihilate the St. Cesaire population (and thereby terminate Neandertal existence)? From the evidence available at the present time, we may never know. *

*For a fictionalized account of the confrontation of Neandertals and a.m. humans, read Nobelist William Golding's excellent novel *The Inheritors*. Several movies have also been made on this subject. Another novel on the subject is Jean M. Auel's *Clan of the Cave Bear*.

Figure 15-20
Monte Circeo, a more typical Neandertal. Supraorbital torus displays Neandertal traits but the occipital area is more modern.

Figure 15-21
Western European Neandertal sites.

Figure 15-22
St. Cesaire, the "last" Neandertal.

Figure 15-23
La Ferrassie. A more typical Neandertal. Mandible (not shown) has a chin.

Figure 15-24
Spy (spee) 2. A male Neandertal from Belgium. Neandertal characteristics are clearly visible.

Figure 15-25
Neandertal sites. Vindija and Krapina in Yugoslavia.

Although western European Neandertals are the best known and considered the basic measure of Neandertal identification, there are also significant finds in Central Europe.

At Krapina, Yugoslavia, there is an abundance of bones but, unfortunately, they are mostly fragments. It is believed they represent at least 20 individuals—men, women, and children.

At one time, Krapina was considered to be a "progressive" Neandertal of the Riss-Würm Interglacial, and in the lineage leading to modern humans. However, recent studies date the remains to an interstadial of the Würm or the very end of the last interglacial. Furthermore, "while a few features (occipital bunning, midfacial prognathism) may be less markedly expressed or present in lower frequencies in the Krapina hominids than in western European Neandertals, the former do not significantly differ in total morphological pattern from the latter" (Smith, 1984, p. 152).

Krapina is an important site for other reasons. In his study of Krapina bones, Trinkaus (1985) concluded that this was a deliberate burial site, and one of the oldest on record. He was also convinced that bone damage was *not* the result of cannibalism.

This conclusion was confirmed by another examination. By comparing Krapina bones with those made at a known butchering site, Russell (1987) found the cutmarks did not match in kind or frequency. However, she found they did compare with human bones that had been defleshed for secondary burial. Secondary burial is an ancient human custom, practiced in recent times as well. A body that has been buried at the time of death is exhumed, all remaining flesh is removed from the bones, and the bones are washed and ritually reburied.

It is assumed the Krapina bones underwent similar treatment, evidence not only of early Neandertal intentional burial, but also of early Neandertal ritual.

It has been accepted for many years that cannibalism[*] has been an ancient human practice continued until very recent time, with implications that it is still practiced (or was until recently). This assumption has been challenged by Arens (1979) who doubts at least recent practices since, he claims, no one who writes about it has actually seen it. However, a recent excavation in the Fontbréguoa caves of southern France, by Paola Villa of the University of Colorado (Villa, et al., 1986), disclosed what appears to be substantial evidence that it was practiced. Whether this was an isolated incident of survival cannibalism or common practice awaits further evidence.

Another interesting site in Central Europe is Vindija,[†] about 30 miles from Krapina. The site is an excellent source of faunal, cultural, and hominid material in *sequence* throughout much of the Upper Pleistocene. Neandertals were found in level G_3, consisting of some 35 specimens, tentatively dated at about 42 kya. Even though some of their features approach the morphology of early south-central European modern *sapiens*—reduction in size and shape of the supraorbital torus and change in shape, slight mental eminence on the mandibles, narrower nasal breadth, and perhaps the absence of occipital bunning—the overall pattern is definitely Neandertal. However, these modified Neandertal features may also be seen as an evolutionary trend toward modern *sapiens*.

Dr. Fred Smith takes the view that variation in Vindija G_3 skull features points to a trend continuing on to the later anatomically moderns of the upper

[*]We do not include occasional occurrences under catastrophic circumstances.
[†]Vindija is pronounced Vindya; the j is silent.

(a)   (b)

Figure 15-26
(a) *Lateral view of Krapina C showing characteristic Neandertal traits;* (b) *three-quarters view.*

levels. Does Vindija support the proposition that the origin of *H. sapiens sapiens* could have occurred here in Central Europe? As we have already mentioned, Smith does not insist upon it and suggests anatomically moderns could have come from elsewhere. But he does believe there is morphological and genetic continuity between the lower and upper levels of the cave. (For other Central European Neandertal sites, see Table 15-1.)

Table 15-1   *Partial List of European Neandertals**

Site	Year Found	Human Remains	Archeological Period	Date
Sipka, Czechoslovakia	1880	Mandibular symphysis of a child	Mousterian	Podhradem (interstadial, 32–28 kya)
Ochoz, Czechoslovakia	1905 1964	Adult mandible, adult molar, post-cranial fragments	Mousterian	Early Würm
Ganovce, Czechoslovakia	1926 1955	Natural endocast; cranial fragments, natural molds of postcrania	Mousterian	Riss-Würm
Sulbalyuk, Hungary	1932	Adult mandible and postcrania; child's cranium	Mousterian	Early Würm
Sala, Czechoslovakia	1961	Adult frontal	None	Upper Pleistocene
Kulna, Czechoslovakia	1965	Adult right maxilla; teeth, adult parietal fragment	Mousterian	38.6 kya 45.6 kya
Vindija, Yugoslavia	1974	Cranial, mandibular, and postcranial remains from at least 8 individuals	Mousterian	Lower Würm
Taubach, East Germany	1887	Lower first molar; lower first premolar	Middle Paleolithic	None
Wildscheuer, West Germany	1953	Cranial fragments	Mousterian	Early Würm
Salzgitter-Lebenstedt, West Germany	1956	Adult occipital and parietal	Mousterian	55.6 kya
Baco Kiro, Bulgaria	?	Very fragmentary portions	Aurignacian (?)	43.0 kya
(Above portion of table adapted from Smith, 1984, pp. 142–143.)				
Forbes Quarry, Gibraltar	1848 1928	Adult skull, child's skull fragments	Levallois-Mousterian	Early Würm
Spy, Belgium	1886	2 skeletons	Mousterian	Early Würm
Le Moustier, France	1908	Adolescent skeleton	Mousterian	Early Würm

*In addition to those included in text.

Figure 15-27
Tabun. Neandertal from Israel. The supraorbital torus and facial prognathism are similar to Western European Neandertals. Note the lack of occipital bunning.

Western Asia

In addition to European Neandertals are those from sites in southwest Asia, especially Israel and Iraq. In Israel there is Tabun, an almost complete female skeleton, and to the east, near Lake Kinneret (Sea of Galilee) is Amud. Both display some modern features, and they are less robust than western European Neandertals, but the overall pattern is Neandertal.

Shanidar A most remarkable site is Shanidar, in the Zagros Mountains in northeastern Iraq, where partial skeletons of nine male and female individuals—7 adults and 2 infants—were found, 4 of them deliberately buried. These are quite typically neandertal, although the nuchal torus is weak, the occiput is fairly well rounded, and an incipient chin is present on at least one of the jaws. Several skulls look deformed, as if their foreheads had been bound as children (Trinkaus, 1984b). Such cranial deformation is known from several areas of the world in very recent times.

One of the more interesting individuals is Shanidar 1, a male who lived to about 35 years of age, a fairly old age for his time (Trinkaus and Thompson, 1987). His stature is estimated at 5 feet 7 inches, with a cranial capacity of 1600

Figure 15-29
Near Eastern Neandertal sites.

Figure 15-28
Amud. Neandertal from Israel. Less robust than western European Neandertals.

(a)

(b)

Figure 15-30
(a) *The Tabun cave site, located about 15
miles south of Haifa, Israel.* (b) *A closer
view of the Tabun cave.*

Figure 15-31
Shanidar.

cc, quite a bit over the European Neandertal mean of 1415 cc. The right side of his body suffered a crushing injury that affected his right arm, clavicle, scapula, and lower right limb. The injury may have been due to a rockfall, or it is possible that the atrophy of the right arm was the result of nerve injury suffered from severe damage to his left eye. It is also possible that his right arm was amputated at the elbow, which, if true, is the first evidence of deliberate human surgery (see Trinkaus, 1982, 1983; Stringer and Trinkaus, 1981).

Another individual, Shanidar 4, was deliberately buried* on his left side, legs drawn up against his chest in a flexed position. Pollen analysis of the soil associated with the skeleton indicates the presence of a number of spring flowers (hyacinths, daisies, hollyhocks, and bachelor's button) that had apparently been placed on the grave at the time of death.

Neandertals must have lived dangerously, if the Shanidar evidence has been interpreted correctly. An atrophied arm, a crushing eye fracture resulting in blindness in that eye, arm and foot fractures, skull scars, and various rib injuries were found on several of the adult male skeletons. Shanidar 3 suffered a rib injury that may have been caused by a stabbing. One of his ribs was damaged by a sharp instrument that probably caused his death. If this were a deliberate stabbing, it would be the oldest known case of interpersonal violence; however, there is no way of knowing whether it was deliberate or accidental. No matter how it happened, Shanidar 3 was taken care of for at least several weeks and intentionally buried when he died (Trinkaus and Zimmerman, 1982).

Since many of the injuries were serious and the men survived for a time, some for years, it suggests that their social system was organized, that cooperation and care of the sick and disabled were an important value of their culture. Intentional burials and flowers placed on a grave are evidence of a special attitude toward death and perhaps a belief in a future life and the supernatural.

Teshik-Tash   About 1,600 miles east of Shanidar in Soviet Uzbekistan, in a cave at Teshik-Tash, we find another deliberate burial. A 9-year-old boy, with a cranial capacity of 1490 cc, was buried in a shallow grave surrounded by five pairs of wild goat horns, suggesting a burial ritual or perhaps a religious cult. Like many other Neandertals, Teshik-Tash is a mixture of Neandertal traits (heavy brow ridges and occipital bun) and modern traits (high vault and definite signs of a chin).

Neandertals and Evolution

One of the many puzzling questions about human evolution is that of the ancestry of Neandertals and their relationship (if any) to Upper Paleolithic anatomically moderns. Upper Paleolithic humans appear in Europe about 40 kya, at about the time Neandertal physical traits are no longer prevalent in European populations. For decades, paleoanthropologists have been debating whether or not:

1. There are divergent lines leading to Neandertals on the one hand, and Upper Paleolithic *sapiens* on the other.
2. There is only one line of descent, with Neandertals evolving from archaic transitional forms, and anatomically moderns from Neandertals.

*Deliberate burial by Neandertals has been recently questioned.

Figure 15-32
The site of Teskik-Tash, the easternmost Neandertal.

3. Neandertals disappear, to be replaced or absorbed by Upper Paleolithic *sapiens*.
4. Neandertals and modern *sapiens* intermingled, interbred, or remained isolated from each other.

The debate continues, centered around several hypotheses, as follows:

Presapiens Model   According to this view, Swanscombe and Steinheim formed separate lineages back in the Middle Pleistocene. The Swanscombe lineage led to a.m. humans, and Steinheim to Neandertals, who became extinct at the end of the early Würm glaciation.

The Neandertal Phase of Man (or H. erectus-sapiens) Model   This scheme, first advanced by Hrdlička (p. 8) in 1927 (and reintroduced by Brace in 1964), is linear: *H. erectus* to Neandertals to *H. sapiens sapiens*. The hypothesis assumes that Neandertal populations in various parts of the world, including Europe, evolved into a.m. populations in their respective areas.

Preneandertal Model   In this model, the Middle Pleistocene hominids—archaic *sapiens* discussed above in this chapter and in Chapter 14—evolved to Neandertals at the end of the Riss-Würm or the beginning of the Würm glacial. At the end of the Middle Pleistocene, or early in the Upper Pleistocene, the lineage splits: one line leading to Neandertals and the other to a.m. humans.

Primitive sapiens-Neandertal Model   This hypothesis was recently introduced, and is a variation of the preceding model. In this model, the archaic *sapiens* line ends with Neandertals. Anatomically modern humans, it is assumed, entered Europe from elsewhere, probably Africa. (See Stringer, 1985.)

At the present time, the most viable of these models are the last three. One of the problems of the first model is that Swanscombe and Steinheim are seen as two different species or lineages. However, many researchers believe, on the con-

Figure 15-33
Preneandertal model. The hominid line evolves from Homo erectus *to Swanscombe-Steinheim to third interglacial forms. These forms diverge to classic Neandertals, on the one hand, and a.m. humans on the other.*

Figure 15-34
H. erectus-sapiens *model. This is a straight-line evolutionary scheme that considers Neandertals as the ancestors of a.m. humans of the Upper Paleolithic.*

Figure 15-35
Presapiens model. Neandertals evolve from Steinheim. Anatomically modern sapiens originate with Swanscombe.

Figure 15-36
Primitive sapiens-Neandertal *model. This is also a straightline-evolutionary scenario that moves from an early Middle Pleistocene* erectus-*like group to a later Middle Pleistocene early Neandertal group to classic Neandertals. H.* sapiens *enter Europe from elsewhere.*

trary, they are markedly similar and belong to the same species. Also, in order to test this hypothesis, it would be necessary to know the dates hominids appeared in both lineages. Unfortunately, dating is very difficult to determine during this Middle Pleistocene evolutionary period.

The second model proposes a linear scheme from *H. erectus* to Neandertals to anatomically modern humans. One of the objections to this model is the question of evolution from Neandertals to a.m. humans. Some paleoanthropologists believe that a.m. humans evolved *outside* of Europe, entered Europe in the latter part of the Upper Pleistocene, coexisted with Neandertals there, and eventually displaced them. Others fault this scheme because, as we noted in the preceding chapter, they do not agree that the early inhabitants of Middle Pleistocene Europe can be assigned to the *H. erectus* taxon. They may have been *erectus*-like, but not *erectus*.

For many paleoanthropologists the third model has been, for many years, the most acceptable: from *erectus*-like to early (archaic) *sapiens* who diverged, one line evolving to classic Neandertals, and the other line to a.m. humans. Again, there is the problem of the evolution of modern *sapiens* in Europe.

The fourth model, a recent proposal, is essentially similar to the preceding, except there is no mention of a.m. *sapiens* evolving in Europe. To that extent, it may be more acceptable than the preceding.

Culture of Neandertals

Neandertals, who lived in the culture period known as the Middle Paleolithic, are usually associated with the Mousterian industry (although the Mousterian industry is not always associated with Neandertals), which had its roots in the second interglacial, or even the Riss glacial. In the early Würm, Mousterian culture extended from the Atlantic Ocean across Europe and North Africa to the Soviet Union, Israel, Iran, and as far east as Uzbekistan and, perhaps, China.

Technology Mousterian people specialized in the production of flake tools based on the Levallois method, a prepared core technique that originated perhaps as much as 200 kya. A chunk of flint was chipped all the way round and on top, resembling a turtle in form, and then rapped on the side to produce a flake ready for use (Fig. 15-37).

Neandertals improved on the Levallois technique by inventing a variation. They trimmed the flint nodule around the edges to form a disc-shaped core. Each time they struck the edge, they produced a flake until the core became too small and was discarded. Thus, the Neandertals were able to obtain more flakes per core than their predecessors. They then trimmed (retouched) the flake into various forms such as scrapers, points, knives, and so on.

Neandertal craftspeople elaborated and diversified traditional methods, and there is some indication of development in the specialization of tools used in skin and meat preparation, hunting, woodworking, and perhaps hafting (attaching handles to tools). They may have made some use of new materials, such as antler and bone, but their specialization and innovation cannot be compared to the next culture period, the Upper Paleolithic. Nevertheless, the Neandertals advanced their technology, which tended to be similar in typology, over great geographic distances, far beyond that of *H. erectus*. It is quite likely that their modifications in technology laid the basis for the remarkable changes of the Upper Paleolithic.

Settlements People of Mousterian culture lived in a variety of open sites, caves, and rock shelters. Living in the open on the cold tundra suggests the erection of shelters, and there is some evidence of such structures, although the last glaciation must have destroyed many open sites. At the site of Moldova I, in the Ukraine region of the Soviet Union, archeologists found traces of an oval ring of mammoth bones, enclosing an area of about 26 by 16 feet, which may have been used to weigh down the skin walls of a temporary hut or tent. Inside the ring are traces of a number of hearths, hundreds of tools, thousands of waste flakes, and many bone fragments of animals probably brought home for comfortable dining around the fireplace.

Nodule

The nodule is chipped on the parameter.

Flakes are radially removed from top surface.

A final blow at one end removes a large flake.

Figure 15-37
The Levallois method.

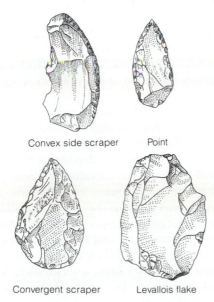

Convex side scraper   Point

Convergent scraper   Levallois flake

Figure 15-38
Mousterian tools (after Bordes).

Evidence for life in caves is abundant, and Mousterians must have occupied them extensively. Windbreaks of poles and skin were probably erected at the cave mouth for protection against the weather. Fire is in general use by this time, of course, and no doubt used for cooking, for warmth, and for keeping dangerous animals at bay.

How large were Neandertal settlements, and were they permanent or temporary? These questions are not yet answered, but Binford (1982) believes the settlements were short-term occupations used over and over again.

Religion   An important innovation of the Middle Paleolithic is deliberate burial, often with indications of funerary ritual. Intentional burials are common, as we have seen, at La Chapelle, La Ferrassie, Shanidar, Teshik-Tash, and there are many other examples. At Teshik-Tash, we find an interesting ring of goat horns surrounding a child's grave, an arrangement that would certainly seem to indicate ritualism of some sort.

Similar practices to this occurred in the Guattari Cave, near Rome, where Monte Circeo was buried. Not only was the foramen magnum cut away, very likely a ritualistic performance, but the skull's right side was crushed and placed in the center of a circle of stones. Near the circle were several piles of deer, cattle, and pig bones. Apparently, the man had been killed (sacrificed?) outside the cave, by a smashing blow to the right side of his head. The head was then taken into the cave and placed within the circle of bones.

Shanidar IV was buried with flowers, an act which may or may not suggest ritual, but which certainly does suggest a special attitude toward death. A remarkable burial occurs at the La Ferrassie rock shelter perhaps 38 kya. It looks like a family cemetery; the presumed parents are buried head to head and four children are interred neatly nearby. A short distance beyond, a small mound contains the bones of a newly born infant, and a bit further under a triangular stone is the grave of a 6-year-old child.

Besides the clearcut evidence of burials and probably secondary burial as well, there has been much speculation about other forms of Neandertal ritual, especially a bear cult. It is reported that a chest containing bear skulls was found in a cave high in the Swiss Alps, with bear skulls placed in niches along the walls. A similar report comes from southern France, where a pit was said to be filled with the bones of more than twenty large bears.

If these reports are accurate, it would not be surprising that bears were the object of special attention. Ceremonial regard for bears has been practiced among some Siberians, the Ainu of northern Japan (who still perform an annual bear dance), and a number of American Indian tribes, among others.

What is the meaning of this remarkable activity? For the first time in human history, we find people who are concerned with more than the material aspects of life. Deliberately burying a corpse and depositing objects that belonged to him alongside his body reflects attitudes and values different from the ordinary. Death had meaning, perhaps mystical, something unknown, and Neandertals recognized that they had to come to terms with what they did not understand.

Similarly with animal cults. Instead of earlier hunting practices of catch-as-catch-can, Neandertals were beginning to single out certain animals for game. Did they believe they could control their game animals? (If so, did these rituals serve as forerunners of Upper Paleolithic cave art that also may have been a form of hunting magic?) Were they attempting to help the animals multiply, improve their own hunting success, or increase the chances of their own safety? Do these rituals signify that Neandertals were becoming aware of their distinctiveness—that they were something more than simply animals? Did the rituals reflect, as they do for many hunting peoples, that killing an animal leaves a void in the universe, and it is necessary to propitiate the animal's spirits to prevent an imbalance in the physical and spiritual universe?

No one, of course, knows the answers to these questions, and we do not even know for certain whether Neandertals believed in spirits, a future life, and the supernatural, but the evidence is suggestive.

Economy Neandertals were successful hunters, as the abundant remains of animal bones at their sites demonstrate. As the evidence from Shanidar suggests, they probably gathered berries, nuts, and other plants. It does not appear that they sought more exotic foods, such as seafood or birds.

It is assumed that, in the freezing weather of the fourth glacial, Neandertals must have worn clothing to survive the winters—and they may have developed methods of curing skins. But since there is no evidence of sewing equipment, the clothing was probably of simple design, like a poncho. Nor is there evidence of

Figure 15-39
La Ferrassie burial.

Figure 15-40

Neandertal ritual and hunt. Neandertals are cutting up a wooly rhinoceros. The men to the left are offering pieces of meat to the rising sun. It is not known for certain whether this ritual was actually performed, but Neandertals did perform burial rituals.

personal ornaments or individual adornment, although these might be difficult to recognize.

Abstract Thought   Neandertal behavior, as deduced from the archeological and osteological evidence, is complex enough to reflect abstract ideas. Braidwood points to the "variety of combinations of the different basic habits or traditions of tool preparation" signifying "mixtures and blends of many of the other ideas and beliefs of these small groups" (Braidwood, 1975, p. 62). Therefore, there was not *one* Neandertal culture but "a great variety of loosely related cultures at about the same stage of advancement." For the first time in hominid history, we can see that humans have the ability to develop a variety of cultural adaptations to a variety of ecological conditions.

With the complexity of Neandertal life comes the question of communication, and scholars are not agreed that Middle Paleolithic people could communicate fluently on a symbolic basis (that is, via language). A controversial paper published some years ago claims that Neandertals were unable to articulate easily because of the anatomical structure of their throats (Lieberman and Crelin, 1971). Given Neandertal brain size, their success in hunting, adaptation to severe weather, their technological improvements, and probably a well-developed social organization, most anthropologists would probably disagree (see Holloway, 1985).

We know much more of European Middle Paleolithic culture than any other because it has been studied longer by more scholars. In recent years, however, Africa has been a target not only of physical anthropologists, as we have seen in preceding chapters, but also of archeologists, who have added considerably to our knowledge of African Pleistocene hominid history.

One of the best-known students of African archeology is Professor J. Desmond Clark, of the University of California. We shall summarize the African Middle Paleolithic (Middle Stone Age) from one of his accounts (1982).

Middle Stone Age (Middle Paleolithic) of Africa

In Africa, the Eurasian Middle Paleolithic is referred to as the Middle Stone Age (MSA) and, in many ways, it is similar to its Eurasian counterpart. The main technological industry of Africa is the Mousterian, the same industry of the Middle Paleolithic. And like its Eurasian contemporary, while the basic industry is Mousterian, regional difference are to be found.

Regional Patterning   At the beginning of the last interglacial, about 120 kya, as the climate became more temperate and sea levels rose, different ecological regions appeared. Populations adapted to drier, warmer, and wetter conditions; the flora and fauna also changed, and people adapted the hunting, gathering, and toolmaking techniques accordingly.

Technology   The most common tool material was stone, and scrapers were the most frequently used tool. In the more humid tropics, where trees were more plentiful, wood and wood products became more important. Also, there was a greater emphasis on woodland food resources. As grains and seeds became more important in the savanna diet, hand grindstones (pestle and grinding stone) were produced.

Food Processing   Hunting strategies varied depending on the kind of game available and on the butchering and processing techniques. Adult males of aggressive species, such as buffalo, were not hunted; instead, young animals and pregnant females were exploited, since they were not as dangerous. Easier to hunt, smaller antelopes of all ages were frequent game.

   Kill sites were generally located close to some natural hazard, such as a swamp, lake, cliff, or sinkhole. Game was driven into these catches, where they would be killed by the fall or drowning, or where hunters could easily dispatch the animals stuck in the muck.

Figure 15-42
Grinding stones, a savanna adaptation (Adapted from Clark, 1982).

Figure 15-43
Site of the Lion Cave quarry, where iron pigment was mined.

It is possible that Africans in the MSA dried meat by heating it over a fire. This is evidenced by thick layers of dispersed ash and carbonized material resulting from meat repeatedly dried in the same spot during rainfalls. According to Clark (1982), it is probable that the drying of meat was one of the major developments in resource processing to take place during the Middle Stone Age.

Art   We do not think of archaic *sapiens*[*] as miners, but in a sense they were. A quarry site in Swaziland was mined for iron pigment about 44 kya. Paint was frequently used by Africans at this time—ochre-stained scrapers, a grindstone with hematite staining, and pieces of ground hematite have been recovered at various sites.

Religion   Like their Neandertal contemporaries in Eurasia, Africans buried their dead. Intentional burials have been excavated at several sites, and, at Border Cave, a burial included adults and infants, recalling the Ferrassie grave in France. We assume, as we did for Neandertals, that this indicates a belief in an afterlife, and that rituals were a part of their culture.

In summary, about 120 kya, the Mousterian industry was widespread in Africa. While there was a general cultural similarity throughout Africa, regional patterns were emerging as populations adapted more efficiently to particular environments. Over thousands of years, tool-and-weapon-manufacturing techniques improved, as did hunting strategies. New materials were utilized, new sources of food exploited, and the nonmaterial aspects of life can be seen in both painting and supernatural beliefs.

Homo sapiens sapiens (Anatomically Modern Humans)

Early Moderns   In the past, anatomically moderns have been associated with the Upper Paleolithic. This notion arose in Europe, where the relationship between humans and technology was first noticed in the archeological record. However, this correlation does not hold in Africa, as we have already noted. Nor is the association in Europe absolute. We may also mention that the line between the Middle Paleolithic and Upper Paleolithic cannot be clearly drawn. Nor is it a simple matter to draw a line between archaic (including Neandertals) *sapiens* and modern humans. This is true wherever we find them, since late archaic *sapiens* may exhibit modern traits, and early moderns may display archaic traits.

Paleoanthropologists make taxonomic decisions by looking at the overall configuration of the fossil find, and the more remains there are, the more valid the conclusion is apt to be. However, there are cases where the skeletal remains (especially the skull) are difficult to read. Then the decision becomes arbitrary, and the fossil may be placed in one or the other group, depending on a particular scientist's interpretation.

Another problem is dating. The proper way to determine the taxon of a fossil is by its morphology. But there are times when what appears to an a.m. human is dated far earlier than the appearance of moderns anywhere else. Then the date may be questioned. Or, conversely, an archaic specimen may appear in what is believed to be a fairly recent date.

[*]If anatomically modern humans were present in Africa during all or much of the Middle Stone Age, it is difficult to know what effect, if any, they may have had on MSA culture.

As an example, we can take the case in Africa where dates of a.m. humans are given as early as 100–120 kya. For scientists accustomed to a 40 kya European or western Asiatic date for the first moderns, 100 kya is completely out of the ball park. Either these specimens are not anatomically modern, they say, or the dates are incorrect. On the other hand, if both morphology and chronology *are* correct, then the only conclusion possible is that a.m. humans evolved in Africa much sooner than elsewhere.

Africa

South Africa   There are several finds in South Africa that "fit the bill" for the situation we just described. In South Africa there are two sites—Klasies River Mouth (KRM) on the southeast coast, and Border Cave, on the border of Kwa-Zula and Swaziland—that are considered to be 100 ky old or more. The skeletal remains in these two sites have been analyzed as *Homo sapiens sapiens*. If the dating and skeletal interpretation are valid, then the earliest anatomically modern human beings evolved in South Africa 100 kya or more.

Paleoanthropologists may be coming around to this conclusion, but not everyone is convinced. The Klasies River Mouth (KRM) remains are quite fragmentary, and their interpretation as a.m. humans would be more enthusiastically supported if there were more bones to encourage the interpretation. At Border Cave, there seems to be little question of their a.m. morphology, but the dating is not as satisfactory as it might be.

Nevertheless, Singer and Wymer, who made an intensive study of the site, stated that a major conclusion is "that in the Middle Stone Age I . . . a very sapient individual was present at KRM" (1982, p. 148). Professor Bräuer (1984) of the University of Hamburg calls the KRM find "astonishingly modern," and Singer and Wymer go on to remark that one of the KRM mandibles represents the earliest *Homo sapiens sapiens* directly associated with a Middle Stone Age culture of southern Africa *or elsewhere* (emphasis added).

East Africa   At Omo, Ethiopia, the remains of a partial skeleton, Omo I, has been recently restudied (Day and Stringer, 1982) and designated as anatomically modern. The mandible, with chin and modern postcranial bones, has persuaded a number of paleoanthropologists that Omo also is a member of the early African anatomically modern select group.

North Africa is the locale for another early *sapiens*, although not of the vintage of the above three. Just south of the earlier *H. erectus* sites in Morocco, between Safi and Marrakech, is the site of Jebel Irhoud. When discovered, it was identified as a Neandertal, and while opinions still differ, it is more likely an early a.m. *sapiens*.

The Jebel Irhoud photograph (Fig. 15-47) displays archaic features in the vault, occiput, and frontal, but facial features, such as the lack of midfacial prognathism and a possible chin, suggest an a.m. human.

If the measurements, statistics, comparisons, observations, analyses, arguments, and interpretations supporting the modern *sapiens* character of these fossils are, in fact, valid, then we must agree that modern humans emerged earlier in Africa than anywhere else in the world.

The notion that Africa may be the single source of all anatomically moderns might be called the "single-source hypothesis." There are others who also believe

Figure 15-44
Early moderns in Africa.

Figure 15-45
Border Cave reconstruction clearly shows modern traits, but dating is unclear.

Figure 15-46
Omo I is considered to be early modern; some believe it to be archaic sapiens.

Figure 15-47
Jebel Irhoud (Djebel Ighoud), an early modern of North Africa with resemblances to Neandertals.

Figure 15-48
Site of Afalou, a later sapiens.

in a single source, but place it elsewhere, such as the Near East, western Asia, eastern Asia and Australia. This hypothesis (which Wolpoff, et al., 1984, call a "punctuation model") denies that gradual evolution in local, separate regions occurred; but holds instead that archaic *sapiens* everywhere in the world were displaced by anatomically modern populations originating in one region.

Opposed to the "single-source" model is a multiple-source model recently advocated as "A Theory of Multiregional Evolution."[*] This model suggests evolutionary continuity occurred in several regions of the world—presumably eastern and southeastern Asia, Africa, and Eurasia—in the Middle Pleistocene, leading from local archaic *sapiens* to modern humans separately in each of those regions. That is, archaic *sapiens* in Europe gradually evolved to Neandertals and then to modern *sapiens*; similarly in East Asia and Africa.

This debate on single source versus multiple sources has a fairly long history in anthropology, and the matter is not yet settled. Many of the fossil discoveries, and refined archeological methods of recent years (as well as recent DNA evidence; see Box 15-2) have added ammunition to both sides. As evidence accumulates, we can look forward to the resolution of the problem.

Later Moderns   Between about 50–40 kya, anatomically modern humans appear in various regions of the world. In general, these humans carried at least some archaic traits; nevertheless, they are more modern looking than the early moderns. We shall briefly review these later moderns in Africa, Eurasia, eastern Asia, Australia, and the New World, from the period of about 50 to 10 kya.

Africa   Later moderns are found in almost all areas of Africa. The table on p. 496 can give only a partial list of what has been discovered, and for whom dates are reliable or fairly reliable. It is clear that a.m. humans continued to evolve in Africa. For example, it is said that Afalou, from Algeria, displays resemblances to archaic *sapiens*, and may be the ancestor of people living in North Africa at the present time. Similar statements have been made about other later moderns in other areas of Africa.

[*]See Wolpoff et al. (1984) for a discussion of this question.

Figure 15-49
Jebel Qafzeh 6, from Israel. A good example of early modern sapiens. Modified archaic traits are clearly visible. (a) Frontal view; (b) lateral view.

(a)

(b)

BOX 15-2

Where Did I Come From, Mommy?

Mitochondrial DNA (mtDNA) is a kind of DNA found in the cell *outside* the nucleus. It is inherited only from the *mother*. The father's sperm (which consists of just a nucleus) does not carry mtDNA; therefore, the father does not transmit this DNA, and genetic recombination of mtDNA does not occur. Consequently, it becomes possible (through mitochondrial DNA) to trace female ancestry back to its source.

In their study of this DNA, several molecular biologists accumulated samples from 133 children from Africa, Europe, Asia, Australia, and New Guinea. Comparing the mtDNA of the samples, they discovered that 126 carried mtDNA from all five regions, but 7 samples carried mtDNA only from Africa. That is, whereas 126 samples had at least one African ancestor, 7 samples had *only* African ancestors.

Having found that the mutation rate of mtDNA is 2 to 4% every million years, and because mtDNA is inherited only from the mother, the scientists concluded that the origin of all humans living today could be traced to one woman ("Eve"), who nursed her children in Africa somewhere between 285–143 kya, or, on average, about 200,000 years ago. (This estimate has recently been reduced to 140,000 years ago.)

This evidence supports a single-source model for the origin of *H. sapiens sapiens* and, furthermore, points to Africa as the site of the origin of anatomically modern humans.

These interpretations and conclusions, however, are not acceptable to all paleoanthropologists or molecular biologists. It has been suggested, for example, that the mutation rate may have been misinterpreted; the study is presently being examined by other scientists.[*]

SOURCES:

Cann, Rebecca L. "In Search of Eve," *The Sciences*, Sept./Oct., pp. 199–202, 1987.

Lewin, Roger. "Africa: Cradle of Modern Humans," *Science* 37:1292–1295, 11 Sept. 1987.

[*]See Roger Lewin, "The Unmasking of Mitochondrial Eve," *Science* 238:24–26, 2 Oct. 1987.

See also Stephen Jay Gould, "Bushes All the Way Down," *Natural History*, June 1987.

There is much more work to be done in Africa, both in continuing the search for fossil remains and restudying carefully many that have already been discovered.

Eurasia

The Near East   There is no fossil evidence of a.m. humans in Eurasia that is as old as that in Africa, assuming the dates to be valid. It appears that the oldest Eurasian moderns come from Israel: Jebel Qafzeh[*] and Mugharet es-Skhūl. These are modern *sapiens* who possess a number of archaic traits, but whose overall configuration places them in the a.m. category. Although quite robust, their skulls and postcranial bones are more gracile than archaic *sapiens*. The occiput is rounded, the vault is higher, the supraorbital torus is reduced, the chin has a definite eminence, midfacial and facial prognathism is reduced (although alveolar prognathism is accented), anterior teeth are smaller, canine fossae are present, and leg bones are more gracile.

These changes suggest an increase in human adaptive efficiency made possible by major improvements in human sociocultural abilities. And when we consider the traits of archaic forms, such as Tabun, those of earlier moderns, such as Qafzeh and Skhūl, and later moderns, such as Ein Gev, the process of gracilization is very clear. The evolution from archaic to later modern in the Near East, within

*Recently, a thermoluminescence date of 92 kya was assigned to Jebel Qafzeh (see Valladas et al., in *Nature*, 331: 614–616, 2 Feb. 1988).

Figure 15-50
Skhūl V, an early modern from Israel.

Table 15-2 *African Moderns**

Name/Country	Date (kya)	Material
Dar-es-Soltan, Morocco	Uncertain	Adult young; adult calotte; teeth, limb bones, phalanges
Afalou, Algeria	12–8	Over 50 individuals; skeletons, male, female, children; blades, scrapers, burins
Kom Ombo, Egypt	13	Calvaria, adult male frontal and other cranial parts
Elmenteita, Kenya	10	Adults and juveniles: crania and cranial bones; skeletons
Lukenya Hill, Kenya	17	Adult frontal and parietal, probably male
Naivasha, Kenya	11	Adult female, over 50, cranium mandibles, long bones
Lothagam Hill, Kenya	9–6	Remains of nearly 30 individuals, skeletons and various skeletal bones
Gamble's Cave, Kenya	8	Cranium; cranial bones, mandibles, limb bones; skeleton
Asselar, Mali	7	Adult male and postcranial skeleton
Taforalt, Morocco	11	Skeleton; cranium; skeleton fragments; remains of 180 adults, 6 adolescents, 97–100 children
Hmatjes River, South Africa	10.5	18 individuals of both sexes and varying ages
Wadi Halfa, Sudan	15	Mandible
Ishango, Zaire	9	Many cranial and postcranial bones
Kalemba, Zambia	15	Several crania; mandibles; vertebrae; postcranial fragments; both sexes, varying ages
Leopard's Hill, Zambia	16.7	Occipital and parietal
Mumbwa, Zambia	20	Several calvaria; cranium, mandible, limb bones

*In addition to those included in text.

Figure 15-51
The Skhūl cave.

a narrow geographic area, supports the notion of local and gradual evolution of the multiple-source model. We should point out that changes in this area could also be due to gene flow; i.e., the migration of African moderns, who apparently evolved earlier. This possibility is denied by Trinkaus (1984b).

Central Europe Central Europe has been a source of many fossil finds, including Neandertals and anatomically moderns. Like the Near East, it is an interesting area because it has been suggested as a locality where evolution from archaic *sapiens* (Neandertal) to moderns may have occurred.

In Yugoslavia is the Velika Pečina site, consisting of a portion of a frontal bone, probably female, in the 33 kya range. Morphologically, the reduced form of the supraorbital torus suggests it is modern or transitional from archaic to modern.

Figure 15-52
Modern sapiens *sites in Czechoslovakia.*

(a)

(b)

Figure 15-53
(a) *Mladeč 5, an early a.m. human. Supraorbital torus slight; occiput somewhat archaic; (b) Mladeč 1. Female. An early a.m.*

Vindija₁, in the upper level, contains a small sample of fragmentary remains, which may be considered as archaic or Upper Paleolithic. The artifacts may be Aurignacian, usually thought of as an Upper Paleolithic industry. Although it is not possible to clearly place these upper-level remains as archaic or modern, they tend in the modern direction, and may be viewed as transitional.

Definitely *H. sapiens sapiens* is Mladeč of Czechoslovakia. One of the earlier European moderns, at about 33 kya, the Mladeč 5 skulls (2 female, 3 male), like Skhūl, display a great deal of variation, partly due to sexual dimorphism. Although the skulls (except one of the females) possess a prominent supraorbital torus, they are reduced from the Neandertal type, and show a division at the approximate position of the middle of the orbit, a modern trait. Also modern is the reduction of the occipital projection, which has been called a *hemibun*. Reduced midfacial projection, a higher forehead, and postcranial elements "are clearly modern *H. sapiens* in morphology and not specifically Neandertal-like in a single feature" (Smith, 1984, p. 174).

A recent analysis of Mladeč/Neandertal cranial capacity raises an interesting point, i.e., the widespread belief that Neandertals possessed larger cranial capacities than Upper Paleolithic moderns is not supported by the Mladeč evidence. Eight Würm male Neandertals cranial measurements averaged 1530 cc and four females averaged 1300 cc, with a combined average of 1415 cc. The Mladeč moderns—two Mladeč females (1540 cc and 1390 cc) averaged 1465 cc; and one male, 1650 cc—averaged 1557 cc. The Aurignacian Mladeč moderns averaged over 100 cc larger than the Würm Neandertals (Wolpoff, personal comment).

(a)

(b)

Figure 15-54
Cro-Magnon 1. Modern traits are quite clear. (a) Lateral view; (b) frontal view.

There are a number of other rather early moderns in Central Europe (Czechoslovakia, Bulgaria, Rumania, Yugoslavia, and Germany). Among the best known of these are intentional burials from Předmostí and Dolní Věstonice of Czechoslovakia. These are dated at, respectively, about 26 kya and 29 kya. Both sites reflect the robust development of early moderns in Central Europe, with an overall morphology of modern *sapiens*.

In Central Europe, we find a situation rather similar to Israel. The older modern *sapiens* are more robust and display more archaic characteristics. Later *sapiens* continue with archaic traits, but there is a definite trend toward gracilization, as in Předmosti. This trend also offers support for local continued evolution from archaic to modern *sapiens*; however, there remains opposition to this model by paleoanthropologists who do not agree that the late *sapiens* traits in Europe were derived from Neandertals (see Stringer et al., 1984, and Stringer, 1985).

Western Europe   This area and its fossils have received the greatest paleoanthropological attention for several reasons, one of which is probably serendipity. Many of the scholars interested in this kind of research happened to live in western Europe, and the southern region of France happened to be a fossil gold mine; at least it seemed so for many years. Also, the idea of discovering and learning about ancient human ancestors caught the attention of the native population more so than it did peoples in other regions.

Because of this scholarly interest, a great deal of data were gathered, with little reliable information from elsewhere in the world. Consequently, theories of human evolution were based upon the western European situation. It has only been in recent years, with the advent of overwhelming evidence from other areas of the world by archeologists, paleontologists, paleobotanists, with new dating techniques, and with a great deal more money available for field research that human evolutionary theory has been seriously considered on a worldwide basis.

Unlike the two previous Eurasian evolutionary sequences, the evidence for earlier moderns is ambiguous. Combe Capelle from France and Grimaldi (Grotte des Enfants) from Italy are often mentioned, but there are serious dating problems involved with these. Combe Capelle looks archaic and could be an earlier modern, but there is much controversy about the date. The Grimaldi material suffers from a faulty reconstruction of the skulls and from questions about the date of the layer in which they were found.

Best known of western European *sapiens* is unquestionably Cro-Magnon of southern France. Associated with an evolved Aurignacian industry, which is not the earliest Upper Paleolithic industry in France, Cro-Magnon cannot be considered among the earliest of France's a.m. humans. The date for Cro-Magnon is usually given as Würm III, around 25 kya. The so-called "Old Man" (Cro-Magnon 1) became the type specimen for what was known as the Cro-Magnon, or Upper Paleolithic, race of Europe. Actually, of course, there is no such race, and the old man is really not typical even of the other two male skulls that were found at the site.

The three male skulls reflect a mixture of modern and archaic traits. The old man is the most gracile of the three; one of the males has a Neandertal-like bun, and the forehead is lower and browridge more developed than the old man's. The third male has an even heavier browridge development, but the occipital lacks a bun. Most gracile, and most modern-looking is the female skull (which may be a factor of sexual dimorphism).

Later *sapiens* in western Europe are found throughout the area. Physical traits did not undergo very much change from the earlier form, perhaps due, at least in part, to the onset of the last phase of the Würm glaciation, which was extremely cold.

The question of continuing, local evolution from Neandertals to anatomically moderns throughout Eurasia is far from settled. It seems unlikely that the area was divided into these isolated regions without gene flow. However, tracing such movements—considering the ever-present problems of dating, lack of fossils, fragmented condition of fossil finds, and many fossils that remain unstudied—is going to take some time.

With the retreat of the glacier and the introduction of farming and more efficient technology about 10 kya, anatomically moderns in Europe were on their way to their present physical characteristics.

East Asia and Australia

China   Most Late Pleistocene sites in China are not well dated, and it is assumed that faunal association and human morphology suggest the Late Pleistocene.

The early moderns (it is difficult to know how early) of the Late Pleistocene display a mixture of archaic and modern features (see Fossil Background Boxes). Archaic traits include the supraorbital torus and the occipital area, but the lack of facial prognathism is modern. However, the archaic traits are more gracile than the same traits of earlier *sapiens*. Also, the archaic traits are less robust than the Europeans of the same period.

Chinese paleoanthropologists see continuing evolution from archaic *sapiens* to anatomically moderns within China. In fact, they believe that a.m. humans are the end of a long evolutionary process from Chinese *H. erectus* to the present Chinese population. Wolpoff points out that the Late Pleistocene specimens

> provide a reasonable basis for the evolution [of present-day Chinese from early moderns]. The required changes would be a shortening and broadening of the cranium, an increase in cranial height . . . a reduction in browridges, a forward expansion and size increase for the zygomatics, and a significant reduction in skeletal robustness and limb thickness (Wolpoff, 1980a, p. 322).

Australia   Indonesian islands, during glacial times, were joined to the Asian mainland, but Australia was not (see p. 432). In order for humans to enter Australia, they must have developed water transport before 32 kya.

The oldest Australian fossils are from Lake Mungo, where the remains of two burials (one of them was first cremated) date to 25 kya and at least 30 kya, respectively. Their crania are rather gracile with, for example, only moderate development of the supraorbital torus. The Keilor find, more recent than these (about 15 kya) is another gracile cranium that fits in well with the Mungo forms. Dubois, who found the first *H. erectus*, also found a modern *sapiens* in Java, known as Wadjak. Similarities between Wadjak and Lake Mungo and especially Keilor have been noted by a number of researchers. These gracile specimens are quite different from the more robust Australian aborigines today.

More similar to the present aborigines are the relatively recent remains from Kow Swamp. Believed to have lived 10 kya, Kow Swamp fossils are noted for

Figure 15-55
Early modern sites in Israel.

Figure 15-56
Chinese Upper Paleolithic H. sapiens sapiens *sites.*

Figure 15-57
Map of several Australian H. sapiens sapiens *sites, and one from Java.*

Figure 15-58
Mungo I, lateral view. The frontal bone reflects the gracile character of the skull. Less robust.

Figure 15-59
Kow Swamp 5. Note the greater robusticity of this skull compared with Mungo.

Figure 15-60
Wadjak. A fully modern sapiens from Java with resemblances to Lake Mungo. Found by Dubois.

their robustness: sloping forehead, thick bones, heavy supraorbital torus, and so on. It is strange that humans living 30 kya should be more gracile than those living 20 ky later. However, the Kow Swamp sample consists of over 40 burials, and Lake Mungo only 2. There is much variation (gracile and robust) in the Kow sample and, as a matter of fact, several Kow Swamp crania resemble the Mungo crania. Perhaps if the Mungo sample were as large as the Kow, there might be a similar intrapopulation variation of robust and gracile forms.

It has been suggested that some Kow Swamp features are reminiscent of Solo (Ngandong, p. 408, or Sangiran 17, p. 408), and we have mentioned the similarity of Wadjak and Lake Mungo/Keilor. This has led paleoanthropologists to postulate an evolutionary relationship between Indonesia and Australia; that is to say, Australia was occupied by immigrants from Indonesia. Routes have been suggested (Birdsell, 1977) that took the immigrants across the islands from Java to New Guinea and south on the Sahul shelf to what is now Australia. From southern Australia, early *sapiens* moved across the Bass Strait to settle in Tasmania, the island just to the south.

The Upper Pleistocene populations of Australia, Indonesia, and southern China share similarities that suggest connections not yet sorted out. There are a number of scientists who are studying the situation in Australia and Indonesia to unravel this web of relationships.

Human Achievement in the Upper Paleolithic

About 30 kya, a warming trend of several thousand years partially melted the glacial ice. The result was that much of Eurasia consisted of tundra and steppe. It was a vast area of treeless country covered with lakes and marshes and a permafrost that prevented the growth of trees but permitted the growth, in the short summers, of flowering plants, mosses, and other kinds of vegetation. The vegetation served as an enormous pasture for herbivorous animals, huge and small, and carnivorous animals that fed off the herbivores.

It was a hunter's paradise, with hundreds of thousands of animals stretched across miles of tundra, from Spain through Europe and into the Russian steppes.

New tools for coping with large, and possibly dangerous, animals appeared. The last stage of the Upper Paleolithic, known as the Magdalenean, was a spectacular period of technological innovation. The spear thrower (Fig. 15-64), a wooden or bone hooked rod, extended the hunter's arm, thus enabling him to throw a spear with greater penetrating force. For catching salmon and other fish in rivers, the barbed harpoon was a clever example of the craftsperson's skill. There is also some evidence that the bow and arrow may have been used during this period. The introduction of the punch technique provided blank cores that could be fashioned into burins, for working wood, bone, and antler; into borers, for drilling holes in skins, bones, and shells; and into blades with serrated or notched edges for scraping wooden shafts for a variety of tools.

Large herds of reindeer roamed the tundra along with mammoths, bisons, horses, and a host of smaller animals that served as a bountiful source of food. It was a time of affluence, and the Magdaleneans spread out over Europe, living in caves and open-air camps, and building large shelters. Mammoth bone dwellings with storage pits have been excavated in the Soviet Union, with evidence of social status distinctions (Soffer, 1985). It was during this period that western Europe achieved the highest density of population in human history up to that time.

Hunters in Europe continued an older practice of driving animals into bogs and swamps, where they could easily be dispatched and butchered. They also used the method of stampeding horses and caribou over cliffs or into canyon cul-de-sacs. Food was so abundant that it has been suggested that the extinction of some of these Pleistocene prey animals was due to overkill. It is also possible that the change of climate, as the glaciers retreated, affected vegetation and created generally unfavorable ecological conditions for those animals.

The **Upper Paleolithic** was a technological age and, in its way, can be compared to the past several hundred years, in our own time, of amazing invention and technology after centuries of relative quiet. It appears those living then not only invented new and specialized tools, but the increased use of, and probable experiment with, new materials and new tools, indicating an involvement in technology unknown up to that time.

In addition to their reputation as hunters, western Europeans of the Upper Paleolithic are even better known for their art. There is little evidence of art before this time. Neandertals may have spent additional time on some tools, making them more symmetrical and balanced, but we can see the development of intense artistic interest among a.m. humans everywhere.

Solutrean tools may be an example of this. No one is quite sure who made them or where they came from, but stoneknapping developed to the finest degree ever known. Using a pressure-flaking technique, they made beautiful parallel-sided lance-heads, sensitively flaked on both surfaces, with such delicate points they can be considered works of art that never served a utilitarian purpose.

UPPER PALEOLITHIC
Culture period noted for technological, artistic, and behavioral innovations. Also known for appearance of anatomically modern human beings. (See p. 453.)

Figure 15-61
The punch blade technique.

Burin

Figure 15-62
Burin, a kind of chisel.

Figure 15-63
Upper Paleolithic economy. A common method of hunting used in recent times in North America. This method involves driving a herd over a cliff where they could be easily killed by the hunters. (Courtesy California Academy of Sciences.)

Human Achievement in the Upper Paleolithic   **481**

Interest in art can be seen throughout the Upper Paleolithic. Fine sculpture has been excavated in western, central, and eastern Europe, but it is in western Europe during the Upper Paleolithic's final stage that European art surpassed itself. The Magdalenean, in southern France and northern Spain, climaxed years of Upper Paleolithic fine art achievement.

Tools and tool handles often engraved with beautiful and realistic animal carvings and sculptured figurines can be found in many areas of Europe. In the Aurignacian/Perigordian stage, preceding the Magdalenean, cave wall art (see Fig. 15-66) is already in full display, and sculpture in the round is achieved with surprising grace and style. In the Lascaux Cave of southern France, immense wild bulls dominate what is called the Great Hall of Bulls, and horses, deer, and other animals adorn the walls in black, red, and yellow, drawn with remarkable skill.

Female figurines, known as Venuses, were sculpted not only in western Europe, but in central and eastern Europe, and Siberia as well. Some of these figures were realistically carved, and the faces appear to be modeled after actual women. Other figurines may seem grotesque (Fig. 15-67) with sexual characteristics exaggerated, perhaps for fertility or ritual purposes.

The age of art continues and, arguably, reaches its pinnacle in the last Upper Paleolithic stage, the Magdalenean. Although their artwork is also found in France, it is a cave at Altamira in northern Spain that is the most famous. Superb portrayals of bison in red and black, painted on walls and ceilings, taking advantage of natural bulges to give a sense of relief, fill the cave. It is a cornucopia of beautiful art whose meaning has never been satisfactorily explained. It could have been ritualistic, religious, magical, a form of visual communication, or art

Figure 15-66
Cave painting. A fine painting of a bison bellowing.

for the sake of its beauty. Volumes have been written in explanation, but no one really knows.

Most of our knowledge of the Upper Paleolithic stems from European studies. There were similar changes in other parts of the world, but they have yet to be as thoroughly examined. In Africa, microliths (thumbnail-sized stone flakes hafted to make knives, saws, etc.) and blades characterize Late Stone Age technology.

Open-air settlements, probably temporary camps for a particular purpose, such as butchering, are well known. Also common, and continuing from the Middle Stone Age, are settlements at springs, caves, and rock shelters. These constructed shelters continue to be simple windbreaks, however. Personal adornment items come into use in the Late Stone Age. Bone beads and shell and stone pendants have a wide distribution, and ochre and other coloring materials may have been used for painting the body or decorating clothing. Rock art of the Late Stone Age is known from many areas of sub-Sahara Africa.

In Australia, the coast, river, and lake areas were already inhabited. Core tools were used for procuring wood and shaping such implements as throwing sticks. More than 20 kya, Australians had begun grinding stone ax heads, the first ever made anywhere, and a few thousand years later ground stone mortars, pestles, grinders, and grinding slabs had become established. These stone tools suggest the gathering of seeds, roots, and, vegetables, and at least made possible a semisedentary lifestyle.

The early Australians buried their dead, and some were ceremoniously cremated and then buried, a practice maintained by aborigines through the last century. They also produced a rock art—red ochre was used to decorate artifacts, walls, and bodies of the living. Bone beads were another decorative, and perhaps, ceremonial item.

As we look back at the Late Pleistocene (or Upper Paleolithic), we can see it as the culmination of several million years of cultural development. Change was slow at first, but as cultural traditions and materials accumulated and the brain (and, we assume, intelligence) expanded, the rate of change quickened.

Cultural evolution continued with the appearance of early archaic *sapiens* and

Figure 15-67
Venus of Willendorf.

moved a bit faster with later archaic *sapiens*. Neandertals in Eurasia, and their contemporaries elsewhere, added ceremonial burials, rituals, technological innovations, and much more.

Building on the existing culture, Late Pleistocene populations attained sophisticated cultural and material heights in a seemingly short burst of exciting activity.

In Europe

> Everything seems to have exploded during the upper paleolithic, which saw the appearance of big-game hunting on a regular mass-killing basis; of potent new weapons, including harpoons, spear-throwers, and possibly the bow and arrow; of necklaces and other body ornaments; long-distance trade; needles and "tailored" clothing; burials with grave goods, indicating people of status; and very probably basic changes in the nature of language itself. (Pfeiffer, 1987, p. 88)

Upper Paleolithic changes also occurred on other continents, but it is in the caves of western Europe where its display is most spectacular.

This dynamic age was doomed, or so it appears, with the climatic changes of about 10 kya. As the temperature slowly rose and the glaciers retreated, animal and plant species were seriously affected, and humans were thus affected as well. As traditional prey animals and easy-to-process food were depleted or disappeared altogether, other means of obtaining food were sought.

Grinding hard seeds or roots became important, and as familiarity with vegetation increased, domestication of plants and animals developed. Dependence on domestication became critical; permanent settlements, new technology, and more complex social organization appeared.

With the advent of the Upper Paleolithic, the long period of *sapiens* evolution, beginning in the latter half of the Middle Pleistocene, reaches *H. sapiens sapiens*. Starting with transitional forms between *H. erectus* and *sapiens*, (Petralona, Vérteszöllös, Bilzingsleben, Arago—see Chapter 14), this mosaic of earlier and later forms continues with later archaic *sapiens* in the latter portion of the Middle Pleistocene.

It has been suggested that since the more modern traits resemble those of Neandertals rather than fully anatomical moderns, these individuals (La Chaise, Biache, etc.) are more properly called preneandertal. That is, they were the ancestors of the Würm populations of Eurasia.

Human evolution was also proceeding in Africa and the Far East, including Indonesia and Australia. Australia has no record of *H. erectus*, and it is clear, at the present time, that it was settled by *sapiens* migrants from Indonesia (and perhaps other nearby islands), who evolved to the present aborigines.

Chinese human evolution begins with *H. erectus*, then to archaic *sapiens*, and finally to modern *sapiens*. This may have occurred without gene flow (as Chinese and other paleoanthropologists believe), or there may have been migrations from southeast Asia.

Africa's hominid history is much older than China's and, according to present evidence, the oldest hominids (australopithecines) are found here. Also, the oldest *H. erectus* was recently discovered in Africa and, if the dates and fossil designations are correct, the oldest fully moderns as well.

Finally, we would emphasize that Neandertals and all humans on earth today belong to the same species: *H. sapiens*.* There are physical differences between us, of course, and for that reason Neandertals are assigned to the subspecies

*Not all paleoanthropologists agree that Neandertals belong to the species *H. sapiens*.

H. sapiens neanderthalensis, and we to the subspecies *H. sapiens sapiens*. Neandertals have received a bad press for the past seventy-five years and are often portrayed as pathological creatures of little skill, grace, or intelligence. Actually, the differences between "us" and "them" are minor, but the overhanging brow, facial prognathism, and the absence of a chin influence our judgment. If we prefer the modern face, it is pertinent to recall the suggestion that our present face became modern because our ancestors were compelled for a variety of reasons to change the food they chewed.

The New World

Anthropologists generally agree that modern *H. sapiens* entered the New World across the Bering Strait *sometime* in the past 40 kya. Most likely, this movement would have occurred during the last glaciation (Wisconsin in New World terminology), when a land bridge some 1,300 miles from north to south joined Asia to North America. The newcomers settled in central Alaska, which was free from ice, and later made their way east into presentday Canada, and later into what is now the United States (an alternative route might have been down the Pacific coast) on to Mesoamerica, and South America.

There are (at least) two schools of thought on the matter: (1) those who believe that these hunters came across the Bering Strait more than 12.5 kya and (2) others who claim there is no *solid* evidence beyond about 12.5 kya. Archeological evidence is abundant for the more recent date, and this evidence is quite common in the western United States, where the early projectile points known as Folsom and Clovis were found. However, there are a number of sites that may be considerably older than 12 kya, and it is possible that human occupation in the New World may prove to be more, perhaps far more, than 12,500 years old.

Figure 15-68
H. sapiens sapiens sites. Note that anatomically moderns inhabit all continents. Only better known fossils are listed.

1 Cro-Magnon, Combe Capelle, Chancelade	4 Skhūl, Qafza	9 Gambles Cave, Lukenya Hill, Olduvai	14 Laibin	21 Devils Lair
2 Oberkassel	5 Afalou	10 Border Cave	15 Niah	22 Tepexpan
3 Prědmosti, Brno, Mladeč Dolní Věstonice	6 Jebel Irhoud	11 Klasies River	16 Wadjak	23 Marmes
	7 Asselar	12 Hotu	17 Talgai	24 Los Angeles, Laguna, San Diego
	8 Omo 1	13 Liujing	18 Keilor	25 Guitameo Cave
			19 Kow Swamp	
			20 Mungo	

The earliest people of the New World are known as big game hunters, the big game being mammoths and other large animals, which they hunted with spears or lances and also by driving them into a surround or over a cliff.

All of the excavated bone material (which is scarce) indicates these early inhabitants were anatomically modern humans. As a matter of fact, there is little acceptable osteological evidence that can be dated from much more than 12 kya or so. Tepexpan in Mexico and Marmes in Washington State are dated at 11 kya, and Guitarrero Cave in Peru at 12.5 kya. California specimens from Laguna, Los Angeles, and San Diego are sometimes given older dates, but these are debatable.

A controversial archeological site, allegedly *200,000 years old* is Calico, in the Mohave Desert of southern California. Digging began more than twenty years ago under the direction of Dr. Ruth Simpson. Many of the lithics that have been identified as artifacts have been challenged. Dr. Simpson believed these were artifacts, and were made by an "early form" of *Homo sapiens*. If both artifacts and makers are verified, it will revolutionize American archeology and paleoanthropology.

At the present time, there is no *indisputable* evidence for artifacts more than 12,500 years old nor for any type of human in the New World except anatomically modern *Homo sapiens*—no Neandertals, no archaic *sapiens*, no Bigfoot.

Summary

Archaic *sapiens* continue to evolve, as transitional forms gradually develop more modern traits. This leads to the appearance of Neandertals about 75 kya in Europe and western Asia. Archaic *sapiens* were also present in China and Africa, and in both cases led to a.m. humans without a Neandertal phase. In Africa, there is a possibility of anatomically moderns evolving long before their appearance in China or Eurasia; however, questions have been raised concerning both their modern morphology and dates.

Neandertals introduced technological innovations, new settlement patterns, and methods of obtaining food. They also practiced some forms of religious ceremonies. Similar innovations occurred in Africa and China, although it is not known whether these inventions and practices developed through independent invention or diffusion.

In the Late Pleistocene (Upper Paleolithic in Eurasia and China; Late Stone Age in Africa), new technological, ritual, and artistic developments appeared at a more rapid rate. The most artistic achievements are seen in the caves of western Europe.

Several questions are raised in this chapter. What is the phylogenetic line from *H. erectus* to *H. sapiens sapiens*? Was this transition rapid (punctuated) or gradual? Did anatomically modern humans evolve from a single source and spread throughout the world, or was this evolution local? What is the role of Neandertals in the evolution of moderns in Eurasia? Did anatomically moderns migrate to Eurasia and displace—by assimilation, absorption, or aggression—Neandertal populations?

Possible solutions to most of these questions have been suggested. Unfortunately, however, entirely satisfactory answers are still unavailable.

Questions for Review

1. Support the argument for and against gradual human evolution.
2. What role have Steinheim and Swanscombe played in the history of human phylogenetic theory?
3. Why is the concept of "progressive Neandertal" no longer useful?
4. Is the concept of archaic *sapiens* a useful one? Can you think of a more appropriate term? Try.
5. What evidence supports the early emergence of anatomical moderns in Africa?
6. Discuss the pros and cons of the four models of Middle Pleistocene human evolution in Europe.
7. Why are the Neandertals so well known to the general public as well as to paleoanthropologists?
8. What technological innovations did Neandertals introduce? Does this impress you? Why?
9. Account for Neandertal autapomorphs.
10. It has been said that La Chapelle was one of the most important Neandertal discoveries. Explain why La Chapelle does, or does not, deserve this attention.
11. Discuss the case of St. Cesaire. What problems does this fossil raise? What problems does it resolve?
12. Were Neandertals cannibals? Defend your answer.
13. Discuss the question of single source vs. multiple sources of *H. sapiens sapiens*. Give examples to support your choice.
14. Describe the Neandertal lifestyle. Why do you believe it was a (good) (poor) time to live?
15. Do you see basic differences between Neandertal and African Middle Stone Age cultures? Explain.
16. Of what theoretic significance is it if anatomical moderns *did* evolve in Africa more than 100 kya.
17. Why is Australia significant in a.m. human history?
18. How does the New World fit into the history of a.m. humans?
19. In what way(s) was Upper Paleolithic inferior/superior to Middle Paleolithic culture.
20. Discuss the following statement from the text: "If we prefer the modern face, it is pertinent to recall the suggestion that our present face became modern because our ancestors were compelled for a variety of reasons to change the food they chewed."

CHAPTER 16

Post-Pleistocene Adaptations in the Old World

CONTENTS

Why Was Stonehenge Built?

Stonehenge is probably the best-known archeological site in the world. As a British tourist attraction, it ranks second only to the Tower of London. Yet, the only thing about Stonehenge that people can agree on is its location on the Salisbury Plain, Wiltshire, in southcentral England.

Stonehenge is the most elaborate of the surviving prehistoric stone circle sites. Stone circles, in turn, are the most complex form of ancient megalithic (or large stone) construction, the others being single-standing stones, stone alignments, and burial chambers. Stone circles are confined to Great Britain, whereas the other styles are common throughout western Europe.

There is more to Stonehenge than simply a ring of large stones. Jacquetta Hawkes has characterized it as a "composite structure," built in three phases between 2800 and 1100 B.C. The monument comprises a circular earth-

en embankment of 320 feet in diameter, within which a circle of 56 small pits encloses 2 semicircular arrangements of larger pits. The dominant central features of the site are its two circles of large standing stones and two horseshoe-shaped stone arrangements. The larger stone circle and horseshoe are formed of immense sandstone blocks having an average weight of 28 tons and a length of up to 30 feet. These stones were obtained from Marlborough Downs, at a distance of 15 to 20 miles. Though smaller in scale, the inner circle and horseshoe are even more intriguing. Their stones, weighing about 8000 pounds apiece, were derived from the Presely Mountains in Wales, at a distance of some 300 miles by the shortest practical land and water route. One estimate places the cost of building Stonehenge at 30 million work-hours.

How were these stones quarried, transported, and set into place without benefit of metal tools? What people designed and erected the monument? And, the greatest mystery of all: *Why* was Stonehenge built?

Stonehenge today guards her secrets closely. One might almost say there is a "stony silence" about the place. Not that there has been any lack of specula-

tion applied to all these questions. Even in medieval times, Stonehenge was an object of fascination. Geoffrey of Monmouth, a twelfth-century chronicler, maintained that the monument was built by Merlin the Magician as a tomb for the father of King Arthur. Through the ages, alternate views have favored giants, dwarfs, Atlanteans, and extra-terrestrials as the architects of Stonehenge. In his book *Megalithomania*, John Michell cites some of the other groups who have at various times received credit: Phoenicians, Romans, Danes, Saxons, Celts, aboriginal Britons, Brahmins, Egyptians, Chaldeans, and even American Indians.

The most persistent association, however, is the Druid connection. More than 2000 years ago, Julius Caesar described Druid priests in Britain and noted their interest in astronomy and divination. While Caesar's account does not mention Stonehenge, the temptation to view the monument as a Druidical observatory has proven irresistible to some. John Aubrey, a seventeenth-century Stonehenge researcher, was the first modern writer to make the case, and the idea gained currency in the subsequent 200 years. In the late nineteenth century, the Druid hypothesis temporarily lost ground as scientific excavations at monuments like Stonehenge seemed to promise the ultimate answers. But, to quote John Michell's assessment of decades of archeological work on the megalithic sites, "the sum total of all their labours has contributed scarcely at all to resolving the problem obviously presented by the substantial presence of the megalithic monuments, the problem of why they were built."

Since the mid-1960s, a different approach to solving the riddle has gained followers. Researchers calling themselves "archeoastronomers" are endeavoring to prove that prehistoric societies in many parts of the world had the interest and capacity to make careful observations of major heavenly bodies. The information these ancients gathered was then applied to practical purposes that ranged from planting to prophecy. Stonehenge seemed to be a fruitful site for archeoastronomers, since it has long been accepted that its builders aligned it with the position of the midsummer sunrise.

The astronomer Gerald Hawkins, whose book *Stonehenge Decoded* helped launch the study of archeoastronomy, believes that the site is literally a Stone Age computer. He argues that the stones provided sight lines for precisely calculating important solar, lunar, and planetary events. Alexander Thom, a retired Oxford engineering professor, was likewise convinced that many of the megalithic constructions found throughout the British Isles were used for similar purposes. His careful surveys suggest that distant uprights were often linked by lines of sight to form a network of astronomical observation posts.

Some archeologists, such as Glyn Daniel, an eminent authority on megaliths, are not so sure. Daniel found archeoastronomy "an all too clear demonstration of the imagination, wishful thinking and credulousness of many authors, and the abysmal ignorance of many alleged archeologists who can only be described, if uncharitably, as fantasy buffs." The case for ancient astronomers, he maintains, "has never been proved." Christopher Chippindale considers recent enthusiasm for the idea of Stonehenge as a computer/observatory to be merely another "scientific myth devised in a scientific age."

While he is unsympathetic to the hard-line position taken by these archeologists, John Michell cautions that the archeoastronomers have not found all the answers. "Anyone who pretends to have 'decoded' Stonehenge has seriously underestimated the magnitude of that task and the quality of learning, imagination and understanding that would be required to accomplish it." Stonehenge and other megalithic sites may "touch on such fundamental matters as the origins of human culture and the first principles behind the development of modern civilization and science."

SOURCES:

Chippindale, Christopher. "Stonehenge Astronomy: Anatomy of a Modern Myth," *Archaeology*, **39:1**, 48–52, January, 1986.

Daniel, Glyn. "Megalithic Monuments," *Scientific American*, **243:15**, 78–81, July, 1980.

Hawkes, Jacquetta. "Stonehenge," *Scientific American*, **188:14**, 25–31, June, 1953.

Hawkins, Gerald. *Stonehenge Decoded*, New York: Souvenir Press, 1966.

Michell, John. *Megalithomania*, Ithaca, N.Y.: Cornell University Press, 1982.

Renfrew, Colin. "The Social Archaeology of Megalithic Monuments," *Scientific American*, **249:5**, 152–163, May, 1983.

Thom, Alexander. *Megalithic Sites in Britain*, Oxford: Oxford University Press, 1967.

Introduction

AUROCHS
European wild ox.

MESOLITHIC
meso: middle
lith: stone
Middle Stone Age, period of foragers.

NEOLITHIC
neo: new
New Stone Age, period of farmers.

Scientists date the end of the Pleistocene or Ice Age period to around 10,000 years ago. Although few climatologists or geologists are really convinced that large-scale glaciation will never again occur, they generally apply the term *Holocene* to designate the Recent, or postglacial, period. During initial phases of the Holocene, the climate continued to slowly warm until only the polar regions and Greenland today have permanent ice sheets. Glacial meltwater returning to the seas inundated some coastlines to a depth of 100 meters or more (over 300 feet). In other areas, flooding was offset by the uplift of land that had been compressed under the ice masses. The exposed areas were soon colonized by plants, animals, and *Homo sapiens sapiens*.

These transformations most directly affected the middle latitudes, including northern and central Europe and North America. The climatic and topographic shifts were sufficient to alter conditions of life for flora and fauna, presenting new opportunities for some species while driving others to extinction. In northwestern Europe, for example, as forests expanded across the open landscape, red deer, elk, and **aurochs** replaced the reindeer, horse, and bison of Pleistocene times. Anatomically modern people, armed with highly efficient tools and weapons, also contributed to the success or decline of various species as they ranged into new regions.

A combination of plant food collecting and broad-based hunting (often supplemented by fish and shellfish) replaced specialized hunting as the primary subsistence economy. This pattern formed the basis of the **Mesolithic** way of life, which persisted well into the Holocene, especially in marginal areas. In more temperate zones to the south, post-Pleistocene human adaptations came to include some preliminary farming activities, which ultimately led to the domestication of selected plant and animal species. In these areas, and later in adjoining regions as well, Mesolithic foraging gradually yielded to a **Neolithic** lifeway based on food-producing strategies and other technological innovations. This new economic base frequently promoted further cultural expansion and elaboration, giving rise to civilizations in Mesopotamia, Egypt, the Indus valley, northern China, and the Mediterranean world.

Mesolithic Hunter-Fisher-Gatherers

Much of northern Europe underwent radical environmental change during the Pleistocene/Holocene transition around 10 kya. Climatic fluctuation, the redistribution or even extinction of many plant and animal species, and the reshaping of coastlines as glaciers contributed their meltwater—each entailed further consequences, many of which affected the region's human inhabitants. The archeological record reveals new economic patterns and technologies that aided people in adjusting to their changing world.

Mesolithic is the term used to characterize those Old World cultures that turned to an intensive hunting, fishing, and gathering routine in response to post-Pleistocene conditions. The relative importance of each activity varied from region to region, and even from season to season within a given area. Of importance here is the fact that people extracted their subsistence from a wider variety of localized resources, rather than from a small number of wide-ranging species. Following the Ice Age, the Mesolithic focus on exploitation of new food sources, particularly more plants, fish, and shellfish, corresponded to a de-emphasis on large game. What accounts for this shift? First, many former prey animals were by now extinct. Additionally, one way to accommodate human population growth would be to broaden the definition of "food" by exploiting more species. Foraging held high prospects for good returns, especially since anyone—young or old, male or female, experienced or not—might participate and so contribute to the general food supply.

New habitats and unfamiliar species presented both opportunities and challenges. The invention and use of an array of tools and weapons promoted efficiency in exploiting varied resources. Mesolithic people commonly crafted not only stone, but also bone and antler, leather, bark, and other plant materials. With the spread of forests in the mid-latitudes, wood became more generally

Figure 16-1
Mesolithic tool kit. (a) Barbed bone harpoon head; (b) bone needle; (c) stone mortar, showing section; (d) two views of flint knife; (e) stone ax in antler sleeve; (f) horn reaping knife with inset flint blades.

Figure 16-2
A Mesolithic forager uses baskets or bags to collect honey from a nest of wild bees in this painting on a rockshelter wall in southeastern Spain.

available. It replaced bone and tallow and dung as the primary fuel, and served also as a useful raw material for making dugout canoes, house posts, javelins, bowls, and smaller items. The tough antlers of the red deer or elk were used as picks in quarrying flint for production of chipped or polished stone tools. Many **composite** weapons, made up of several elements, were in wide use by early Mesolithic times. The bow and arrow and the harpoon are examples: Each is comprised of a blade or point, a foreshaft, main shaft, bindings, and other parts expertly combined into a sophisticated weapon system. Nets, woven basketry traps, and cleverly constructed stone or brushwood **weirs** (or fish dams), placed across the mouths of small tidal streams, enabled people to obtain large quantities of fish. The honey of wild bees was a prize extracted from hollow trees with the aid of axes and containers.

Given the environmental complexity of the mid-latitudes in the Holocene, including a diversity of potentially exploitable plants and animals, Mesolithic foragers made use of a broader spectrum of species than did their Paleolithic predecessors. In addition to more specific-purpose tools, they also required an intimate knowledge of their local environment and its assets to predict when each resource should reach its peak productivity or desirability. By making well-informed decisions, people scheduled their movements so as to arrive on the scene at the optimum time. This concept of "seasonality and scheduling," or **transhumance**, is a key to understanding Mesolithic lifeways. (The often misused term **nomadism**—a more or less random wandering existence—cannot properly be applied to most hunting-gathering groups.) It is estimated that hunters-gatherers using this approach could have maintained a stable population density of about one person per 10 km^2 (Jochim, 1976).

Variety of Mesolithic Adaptations

Northern Europe People colonized Europe's northern reaches within centuries after the glacial ice sheets withdrew (Dennell, 1983). Rising waters had already reclaimed the continental shelf and filled its shallow basins to create the North and Baltic seas. Temperate plant and animal species succeeded their Pleistocene counterparts. Grasses and then forests covered the broad shores of the shallow seas, and several kinds of deer, wild cattle, and pigs displaced reindeer, Irish elk, and horse as the climate warmed. Sites such as Star Carr, near Scarborough in Yorkshire, England, and Maglemose and Ertebølle, near Copenhagen, Denmark, document early Mesolithic settlement in this region (Clark, 1972, 1979).

Star Carr provides many clues to the habitat and economy of northern Mesolithic peoples. Excavated some 40 years ago by the British prehistorian Grahame Clark and collaborators, the site still represents a milestone of archeological technique and interpretation (Clark, 1972). The site's occupied area accommodated perhaps fifteen to twenty individuals. Hunting was the primary activity, with red deer, elk, aurochs, and roe deer serving as the major prey. Hazelnut shells suggest another food source. Hunters used long wooden arrows tipped by *microliths*—small flint blades of geometric shape—set into slots along the end of the shaft and held in place by resin. An extremely effective weapon, the bow had been in use by the end of the Ice Age. The domesticated dog found at Star Carr may have aided in the hunt as well. Sophisticated toolmaking was practiced here, too. People were using stone axes and adzes to fell trees and make useful objects from wood. Barbed bone and antler spear points, butchering implements,

Figure 16-3
Skeleton of extinct Irish elk.

and stone **burin** blades for working antler were common artifacts. Deer grow and shed their antlers annually, on a species-specific cycle; the several stages of antler development on deer killed at Star Carr indicates the site was probably in use through much of the year (Pitts, 1979).

Along the coasts of northern Europe, the British Isles, and even the Mediterranean, some people eventually turned to shellfish collecting as a productive food source. The later Mesolithic Ertebølle culture of northern Denmark is well known for its huge shellheaps, called **middens**. Although the site's favorable location permitted year-round occupation, its inhabitants probably turned to shellfish only in the spring, when their normal fare of fish, sea mammals, and birds was at low ebb (Rowley-Conwy, 1983). The countless shells piled along these shores should not disguise the fact that one red deer carcass may represent the *caloric* equivalent of 50,000 oysters (Bailey, 1975). Still, for at least some Mesolithic groups, shellfish were a ready alternative source of *protein*, at least seasonally (Erlandson, 1988).

Southwest Asia Star Carr and the Maglemosian sites of northern Europe represent the classic expression of the Mesolithic, since people in those areas had to devise new lifeways as they adjusted to dramatic postglacial changes. Farther south, in central and southern Europe and Asia Minor, peoples in less marginal circumstances developed a Mesolithic subsistence strategy based more firmly on plant resources. The residents of Franchthi cave on the southern tip of Greece exploited a rich assortment of species ranging from large mammals (wild horses, deer, pigs, and goats), to fish and shellfish, and a number of prominent plant resources (among them wild barley and oats, three kinds of legumes or peas, and two species of nuts). Several of the cereals and legumes may already have been coming under human control before 8 kya at this site (Dennell, 1983).

Likewise, the Natufian culture of southwestern Asia, roughly contemporary with the northern European foragers of about 10 kya, exploited a wealth of local products that included herds of goats and gazelle and lush stands of wild seed-grasses (Redman, 1978; Bar-Yosef, 1987). There was intensive interaction be-

COMPOSITE
Made of several parts.

WEIR
(weer)
A brush or stone obstruction for trapping fish.

TRANSHUMANCE
Seasonal migration from one resource zone to another.

NOMADISM
Lifeway of wandering in search of food.

BURIN
A chisel-ended stone blade used for working bone and antler.

MIDDEN
A refuse heap marking a Mesolithic campsite.

Figure 16-4
Mesolithic sites of northern Europe.

Figure 16-5
Mesolithic stone ax with antler sleeve.

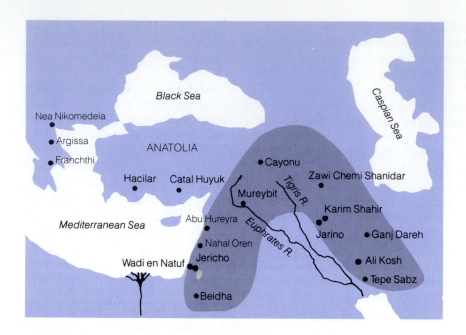

tween Natufians and their resources. Bone and stone points and bone hooks suggest the role of game and fish. Close study of the animal bones revealed that selective hunting or other herd management practices preserved breeding females and young animals at the expense of adult males. Horn sickles with inset flint blades and an abundance of grinding stones and mortars, as well as an increase in dental caries, all testify to the prominence of starchy cereal grains in the Natufian diet. Their residence in small clusters of semipermanent pit houses with stone foundations and the size of their cemeteries (such as those excavated at Nahal Oren in Israel and Abu Hureyra in Syria), indicate that they relied upon local species without moving from place to place.

In essence, the lifestyle of some foragers anticipated many of the developments usually associated with sedentary farmers, yet they did not (strictly speaking) make use of domesticates. Did they adopt this mode of life because of its perceived benefits or simply because they were forced to do so by overcrowding? At this point it is impossible to say. It is clear that the Mesolithic was a time of economic and cultural transformation. While we may consider Mesolithic foragers to be transitional between Paleolithic hunters and Neolithic farmers, we must also indicate that only the more southerly of the Mesolithic cultures fully effected this transition to food production. Those in the northern latitudes long remained marginal to the process; they are of interest to us because their specialized adaptation to a difficult environment enabled them to put off agriculture for thousands of years (Zvelebil, 1986).

The "Neolithic Revolution" and Its Consequences

A famous European archeologist, V. Gordon Childe, proposed the term "Neolithic Revolution" to express the fundamental importance of food production in human history. Besides domestication and food production, the Neolithic involved new settlement patterns and new technology. Thus, while we now recognize that Neolithic lifeways did not suddenly spring forth and radiate from a single Near Eastern center as Childe surmised, we must acknowledge that the Neolithic was truly revolutionary in a broader sense. The emergence of food production eventually transformed most human societies, and, in the process, prompted changes in the natural world as well.

Why Did Domestication Occur?

Domestication implies an interdependency between humans and one or more selected plant or animal species. Scholars once vainly hoped to pin down the very place where some genius had first planted a seed or harnessed an animal. However, we may safely assume that people recognized the role of the seed in plant reproduction long before they turned to farming as a way of life. From the perspective of our modern cultivated world, some find it hard to accept the notion that earlier peoples did not aspire to be farmers and, in fact, resisted the opportunity for as long as possible. Today we understand that domestication is really a *process*, not an *event*. But just why and how the process started is a matter for some debate.

Environmental Explanation Childe himself conjectured that a radical climatic shift at the end of the Ice Age increased Europe's rainfall while bringing widespread dessication to southwestern Asia and North Africa (Childe, 1952). Humans, animals, and vegetation in the drought zones congregated in the decreasingly small areas around permanent water sources. In these oases, intensive interaction among humans and certain other plant and animal species resulted in the domestication of some, including wheat, barley, sheep, and goats. Today, the "oasis theory" of domestication, along with environmental determinism in general, finds little support. Moreover, pollen and sediment profiles indicate that the climatic changes hypothesized by Childe did not actually occur before Neolithic times.

Marginal Zone Hypothesis The role of population pressure as the prime stimulus for agriculture comprises the core of another model. Contemplating the situation in the ancient Near East, Binford (1968) concluded that (a) humans had moved into every prime ecological niche, and (b) the population had reached a state of equilibrium with the environment. Expansion of the population was possible only in the marginal zones on the frontiers of the optimal areas. Since even these domains were already occupied (usually by semisedentary hunter-gatherers), a zone of tension was established. In order to compete, according to Flannery (1973), the incoming population attempted to artifically reproduce the stands of wild cereal grasses they knew from their previous home. The original inhabitants, now compelled to seek new ways of obtaining sufficient food to feed themselves once their foraging was restricted, likewise turned to farming.

Demographic Explanation A related concept maintains that societies finally committed themselves to farming only when no other alternatives remained sufficient to feed a human population that had outgrown the capacity of its environment (Boserup, 1965). For example, the concentration of people in a re-

SYMBIOSIS
syn: together
bios: life
Mutually advantageous association of two
different organisms.

RACHIS
The stalk of a plant, to which individual
seeds attach.

stricted territory or, perhaps, the sudden failure of a once-reliable natural resource might stimulate foragers to take up farming or herding to enhance the natural distribution of species and productivity of their environment.

This idea is extended in Binford's (1983) "packing model," which holds that, as modern climatic and biotic conditions became established at the end of the Pleistocene, people came to permanently occupy the temperate middle latitudes. Binford sees this broad zone as an optimal breeding ground and suggests a rapid increase in human population density. Foraging patterns became more confined as territories filled, leading to "packing" and overexploitation of primary resources. Forced to make more intensive use of smaller segments of habitat, people soon applied their Mesolithic technology to exploit a wider range of species, including smaller animals and plants encountered in their local econiches. Gathering seeds became a more efficient and intensive activity than ever before, given the use of special sickles, basketry containers, and substantial processing tools. Under these circumstances, people began to make a greater impact on the species they were exploiting, so that significant changes of the kind outlined below soon developed.

Symbiosis and Domestication   It is difficult to separate the issue of why people turned to farming from the question of how domestication came about. Domestication denotes a changing relationship between humans and selected plant and/or animal species. This relationship may be characterized as **symbiosis**, a mutually beneficial association between individuals of different species. For example, we now know that the domestication of many plants involved genetically based biological changes that ultimately made the species more useful to people, while often and at the same time resulting in the plant's increased dependency on human intervention in dispersing its seeds (Rindos, 1984). In the case of wheat, the domesticated varieties average more grains per head than their wild relatives. Also, the **rachis**, or short stem connecting seed to stalk, is less brittle in the domesticated forms, making it easier for people to harvest the grain with less loss because the plant is unable to scatter its own seed. At the same time, individual seed coats or husks become less tough. Gradually, as they were transported and nurtured by humans, the domesticates became adapted to new environments well beyond their ancestral range. Such changes probably resulted from long-term pressure by human gatherers, who consistently selected for those traits that improved the plant's productivity and quality (Flannery, 1973).

Archeological Evidence for Domestication

Charles A. Reed has noted that "the first postglacial period of environmental change following the evolution of anatomically modern man (*Homo sapiens sapiens*) was accompanied by, or followed shortly by, the appearance of agriculture in several areas on several continents" (1977, p. 941). The accumulated data reveal that plant domestication got underway in Southwest Asia, Southeast Asia, and Mexico and Peru in the New World, all around the same time. Jumping to the conclusion that the idea diffused from a single source is as dramatic as it is easy, but the evidence offers no support. On the contrary, most domesticated species are unique to a given area and reflect relatively long-term evolutionary development from local wild ancestors. It is more appropriate to consider the issue of concurrent domestication from a cultural and ecological standpoint. It then comes as no surprise that broadly parallel developments occurred in several geographic regions, given the favorable conditions for human population growth in each of these areas by about 10 kya and the resulting need to respond to critical resource shortages.

Although ancient plant remains are uncommon on archeological sites, evidence of domestic grains is occasionally available. Generally, domesticated specimens average larger in size than their wild progenitors, and may exhibit other morphological variations as well. Archeologists sometimes recover actual kernels preserved by charring or carbonization. More often, seeds are represented only by the impressions of individual grains that once adhered to wet plaster, mud brick, or pottery surfaces.

The precise course of plant domestication may never be fully traced, given the scarcity of ancient botanical specimens. Most likely, the process was not only lengthy but somewhat casual as well. Since at least the last ice age, people were utilizing a number of plant and animal resources that eventually emerged as domesticates. In the case of cereal grains, for instance, it would be difficult to decide when harvesting activities may have expanded to include the deliberate scattering of selected wild seeds in new environments. Such manipulation must have favored certain genetic variables, resulting from careful human selection and isolation from other plants of the same species. From there, the steps to full domestication would have been small ones.

The process of animal domestication differed from plant domestication to a certain extent, and probably varied even from one species to another. The dog appears to have been our first domesticated animal and may have accompanied hunters even during the Ice Age. Its relationship with humans differed (and still does) from that of most subsequently domesticated species. Valued less for its meat or hide, the dog's oldest role was as a ferocious hunting weapon under at least a modicum of human control and direction. Early hunting dogs undoubtedly extracted substantial payments of fresh meat before finally relinquishing a carcass to their human allies. As other animals were domesticated, the dog's behavior had to be further curbed for service as a herder, and later even as an occasional mode of transportation among such people as the American Plains Indians. In return, the tamer canids of later times were granted the privilege of scavenging for scraps and other camp waste.

Of course, animals are more mobile than plants, and may have been no less so than the early people who exploited them. Therefore, it is unlikely that hunters could have promoted useful genetic changes in wild animals merely by stocking them in new environments or by selective hunting alone. Animals such as gazelle or reindeer might be managed to a degree even in the wild state, perhaps by establishing a "rapport" with the herds and encouraging them to graze in harvested areas in the winter, or perhaps by restricting hunting activities to a few quick raids, during which the herd might be selectively harvested or thinned. We have noted evidence in the Near East that wild sheep, goats, and gazelle were being managed in this manner by Mesolithic Natufians some 10 kya. The gazelle never attained complete domestication. Nor are reindeer herds in Lapland even today comprised of truly domesticated or even fully "tame" animals. Herds and herders exist in a state of mutual toleration and interdependency.

Full domestication, involving dramatic genetic changes, might be reached only by more direct steps. To attain this degree of domestication in animals such as cattle, sheep, goats, pigs, horses, or camels, people had to first restrain the ani-

Against the Grain

Archeologists have long acknowledged that several areas of the Near East exhibit some of the earliest evidence for agriculture. But few were prepared for the announcement of *Late Paleolithic* plant domestication in the Nile valley! Fred Wendorf and Romuald Schild, excavating prehistoric fishing camps in Wadi Kubbaniya (not far from Aswan, Egypt) in 1978 discovered a buried hearth containing several carbonized grains of barley and einkorn wheat. When numerous charcoal samples from the hearth were radiocarbon dated to between 17,000 and 18,500 y.a., the associated grains suddenly took on great significance. Another kernel found on the living floor, and still more barley discovered on a comparable site nearby in 1981, increased the researchers' confidence. The barley was a six-row variety, apparently a domesticate. An abundance of milling stones further supported the idea that the site's ancient inhabitants had made use of domesticated cereals more than 9000 years earlier than their first known appearance elsewhere.

People probably had been attracted to Wadi Kubbaniya because it was an area where huge Nile catfish might become stranded in low water adjacent to the river after each year's inundation. The excavators reasoned that grain seeds were deliberately planted in the wet mud at the conclusion of the fishing season, as the pools began to dry up. Months later, the people would return to the same camps to hunt waterfowl and harvest their crops.

To put their theories to the test, the archeologists made use of recent advances in radiocarbon-dating techniques, which require only minute samples for analysis. Now, the tiny cereal grains themselves could be submitted for direct dating. If their ages matched that of the hearth from which they were recovered, then the idea of early Nile valley fisher-farmers would be difficult to dismiss.

But the outcome did not favor this scenario. On the contrary, the application of improved dating methods brought results favorable to the more conservative and gen-

Figure 1
Location of Wadi Kubbaniya.

Figure 2
Carbonized barley from Wadi Kubbaniya, Egypt.

erally accepted view of a post-Pleistocene Neolithic adaptation in the region. Though varied (presumably because of contamination from substances applied to the kernels in earlier laboratory studies), the carbon dates for the Wadi Kubbaniya grains suggest an age of less than 5000 years. In other words, the seeds must have gotten into the older levels of the site long after its abandonment by the mobile fishing people who had lived there some 18 kya. What about the milling stones? The researchers now assume they were used to process starchy wild tubers that grew plentifully along the banks of the Nile.

S O U R C E S:

Wendorf, Fred, and Romuald Schild. "The Earliest Food Producers," *Archaeology*, **34**(5): 30–36, 1981.

——— et al. "New Radiocarbon Dates on the Cereals from Wadi Kubbaniya," *Science*, **225**: 645–646, 1984.

mals somewhat or maintain them in captivity and then selectively breed for those traits deemed most useful or desirable, such as meat, fat, milk or wool production, strength, and speed. This process might begin with young animals spared by hunters for that purpose. Captive animals not suitable for breeding represent meat on the hoof, a convenient method of storing food against spoilage or future want.

Archeological evidence of animal domestication is difficult to assess. For most species no significant increase in body size seems to have accompanied domestication. Attempts have been made to compare the bone structure and allometric proportions of wild and domestic members of the same species, with some apparent success (Herre, 1969). Other persuasive arguments have been based on observed changes in herd demography. For example, a notable increase in the number of skeletal elements of young rams may indicate that humans had an opportunity to deliberately select these animals for slaughter, while reserving most females and young for breeding purposes (Bökönyi, 1969). The population curve for animals hunted from a wild herd would more likely reflect a normal distribution, with more equal age and sexual representation. None of these indicators is definitive, however, and large samples of faunal remains must be studied to verify domestication.

Animal domestication in the Old World involved many economically and technologically important species. The cultures of Asia, Europe, and Africa domesticated, and came to rely heavily upon, a large number of animals. Some domesticates were maintained solely for meat at first. Richard J. Harrison's (1985) insightful analysis of faunal collections from Neolithic sites in Spain and Portugal concludes that meat remained the primary product only until about 4 kya, when subsequent changes in herd composition (age and sex ratios), slaughter patterns, and popularity of certain breeds all point to new uses for some livestock. Oxen pulled plows, horses provided transport, cattle and goats contributed milk products, and sheep were bred for wool. Animal waste, too, became a valued fertilizer in agricultural areas. Leather, horn, and bone (and even social status for their owners) were additional by-products of value. Oddly, the few animal species domesticated by the New World's native inhabitants—llama, guinea pigs, and fowls—were small and of relatively minor importance beyond their localized distribution.

Again, we should emphasize that domestication is not an event, but a process. As such, it is nearly impossible to say precisely when a species has become domesticated, for the process involves much more than an indication of "tameness" in the presence of humans. Of much greater significance are the changes in allele frequencies that result from selective breeding and long isolation from wild relatives. Once people consistently select seed or breeding stock according to some desirable trait (size, hardiness, fecundity, etc.) and succeed in perpetuating those characteristics through succeeding generations, then domestication has clearly occurred. These "artificial" (as opposed to "natural") selection pressures constitute an evolutionary force in their own right. The rate of divergent evolution from the wild ancestral forms of the species accelerates as humans continue to exercise control. Moreover, we should acknowledge that, because of the interdependent relationship inherent in domestication, humans also sustained major changes in their culture and behavior—and even in their biology—as a result of resource domestication. Those consequences are what the term "Neolithic Revolution" should connote.

QUERN
A grinding slab or mortar for processing grain.

Consequences of Food Production

Domestication and food production were the driving forces of the Neolithic revolution, but the impact of Neolithic lifeways went far beyond subsistence. While accepting the advantages of a more or less reliable food supply, we tend to take little notice of some of its drawbacks. As an adaptive mechanism, the Neolithic way of life has been a mixed blessing for humankind, one that promoted a dramatic worldwide population explosion at the cost of many social, environmental, and health-related problems. One writer has aptly referred to agriculture as "the worst mistake in the history of the human race" (Diamond, 1987).

Increased Population Density and Permanent Settlements   Population size and density both tended to increase as farming activities produced larger and more predictable yields. People clustered in more permanent villages and towns, surrounded by their fields and pastures. Sedentary living permitted closer birth spacing since mothers no longer lugged infants from site to site, and a woman was therefore likely to bear more children. It is not surprising that many early Neolithic settlements, such as Jericho in the Jordan river valley and Çatal Hüyük in Turkey, so quickly attained considerable size.

New Technologies   Changes in material culture accompanied food production and the development of permanent settlements. For example, Neolithic people soon replaced most of their basketry and skin containers with bulkier but more versatile ceramic vessels. They used looms to weave cloth from wool and plant fibers. Some items, such as grinding **querns** and axeheads, were still being made of stone, but with greater care and crafting. (Early archeologists considered polished stone tools to be the hallmark of this era, hence the term *Neolithic*— "new stone.") The use of copper increased as people found ways to refine and process the ore into a variety of metallic implements and ornaments. Specialized tasks of this type required the attention of full-time craftsworkers, who exchanged the products of their skill for food produced by others.

New Economic and Social Relations   Food surplus in the form of stored grain or herds of animals served as a kind of capital that fostered new economic transactions. Barter and exchange flourished, as did credit, or lending against future productivity. The desire to keep accurate accounts inspired some of the earliest forms of writing, which was occasionally preserved on baked clay tablets. Because land itself was the source of potential capital, its possession became the basis for a new social order that distinguished between landowners and tenants. In many early societies, all or much of the arable land was reserved for the king or royal family. It was worked by the peasants, but the produce was collected, to be later redistributed to all elements of the society, although usually in proportions that varied according to social rank rather than need. As agricultural techniques and resulting harvests continued to improve, a few more segments of the population were relieved of the obligation of producing food and enabled to fill roles as priests, merchants, administrators, and the like. A social and economic hierarchy of productive peasants, nonfarming specialists of many kinds, and an elite class frequently emerged.

Destruction of Environment   Unlike hunters and gatherers, who extract their livelihood from the available natural resources, Neolithic farmers found it expedient to alter their environment by removing natural species and substituting their own domesticated plants and animals. Plowing, terracing, clear-cutting forests, draining wetlands, and other Neolithic activities contributed to deforestation, erosion, and the decline of many native species. Some areas associated with early farming societies were so damaged that they remain unproductive thousands of years later. One example is the lower Tigris-Euphrates valley, where high levels of soluble salts carried by irrigation waters poisoned the soil. In North Africa, Neolithic herders allowed their animals to overgraze the Sahara grasslands and so furthered the development of the world's largest desert. Unfortunately, these processes continue at an accelerated pace into our present day, hastening environmental degradation on a catastrophic scale.

Diminished Diversity   Mesolithic foragers utilized hundreds of wild species as they moved from camp to camp throughout the year. The strategy of Neolithic societies differed in that they emphasized only a small number of domesticated crops and animal species and had little interest in maintaining native flora and fauna. Through selective breeding, Neolithic people sought to further enhance the traits they valued in their domesticates (thicker wool or body fat, more and larger seeds, greater milk production, etc.) while limiting random variability. These experiments produced genetically homogeneous strains. Today the earth's five billion people rely primarily on the seeds of just a half dozen grasses (wheat, corn, barley, oats, rice, millet) and a few root crops (potatoes, yams, cassava) and several birds and mammals (in addition to fish) for their nutrition. The relative homogeneity of most domesticated species renders them highly susceptible to disease, drought, or insect pests.

Development of Science and Religion   Prescribed rites, sanctions, and shrines insured bountiful harvests and other supernatural blessings for Neolithic farmers. Disciplines such as botany, zoology, astronomy, meteorology, and mathematics trace their origins back to ancient attempts to improve agricultural techniques, to predict or ameliorate the weather, and to divide land. Most of these early "sciences" were understood and practiced by a select group of priestly scholars.

Cultural Competition and Change   Neolithic societies made a tremendous impact on their nonfarming neighbors. Hunter-gatherers often were displaced or altogether eradicated as a result of habitat changes or direct competition from farmers. Agriculturalists involved other societies in exchange networks, trading surplus products of agriculture, animal husbandry, or new technology for raw materials, wild produce, and even slaves.

Health Factors   Clearly, not all consequences of food production were beneficial. People experienced negative biological effects as well. Neolithic diets tended to be starchy and lacking in protein. Reliance on easily stored and processed carbohydrates brought on long-term malnutrition, manifested in dental disease, decreased stature, and susceptibility to other serious disorders. Outright starvation was the not infrequent result of crop failures due to drought, blight, or insects. Long-term settlement in one location produced overcrowding, poor sanitation, and a host of epidemic diseases. And, agricultural activities required long periods of grinding toil!

Examples of Early Neolithic Cultures

Since Childe's day, archeologists have become increasingly convinced that farming has been "invented" any number of times in various parts of the Old World. Independent invention best accounts for the diversity of domesticates and the distinctiveness of Neolithic lifeways in the Far East, Southeast Asia, India, sub-Saharan Africa, and the Near East. Moreover, we now recognize that wild species such as wheat or sheep probably shared more extensive natural ranges in early Holocene times and were, in fact, locally domesticated in more cases than previously acknowledged (Dennell, 1983). However, the *diffusion* of Neolithic lifeways cannot be discounted entirely. In a very few cases—central Europe may be one—colonizing farmers apparently brought their domesticates and their culture with them as they migrated into new territories. The Neolithic complex also spread to people on the margins of Neolithic societies as they acquired certain traits and passed them along to cultures yet farther removed. Seeds and animals too must have become commodities in prehistoric exchange networks. The explanation that best fits the facts in any given archeological setting is not always apparent, for the end results were usually much the same—the expansion of Neolithic lifeways.

Near Eastern Farmers   The transition to agriculture in the Near East was accomplished slowly, even reluctantly, by hunting-gathering cultures such as the Natufians, whom we met previously. Their use of stone-bladed sickles by some 10 kya aided them in harvesting wild grasses, among them the ancestral forms of wheat and barley native to the region (Henry, 1989). This efficient technique may have netted greater yields, encouraging dependency on grain supplies that could be conveniently stored for weeks or months after the short harvest period. Stone- or clay-lined pits or "silos" appear on Natufian sites such as Ain Mallaha, Jericho, and Nahal Oren in Israel by about 10 kya, within round stone or mud-brick houses that indicate long residence in one area (Moore, 1985; Bar-Yosef, 1987). The process of genetic selection that we considered as a possible basis for plant domestication must have been underway by this time.

According to the cumulative evidence from southwest Asia, wheat and barley were first domesticated, while sheep and goats were the earliest herd animals brought under human control, probably followed by pigs, then cattle and camels (Reed, 1977). Still, the seeds of wild cereals, fruits, nuts, and the meat of wild game long remained an important component of the diet. Although pottery would not be made for another thousand years, most other important Neolithic traits were now in place. By some 9 kya, sedentary villages engaged in agriculture and herding were well established across a broad arc from the Red Sea to western Iran, known as the "Fertile Crescent." Among them were Abu Hureyra in Syria and Ali Kosh on the Deh Luran plain of Iran (Hole, et al., 1969; Moore, 1985). Families at these later villages resided in adjacent multiroom rectangular houses, in contrast to the compounds of small round shelters seen previously. Flannery (1972) believes this change signals a shift from traditional group society in favor of individual family economic and production units.

Asian and African Farmers   A growing corpus of archeological data bears on the antiquity of Neolithic lifeways in several other regions. One Southeast Asian site, Spirit Cave in Thailand, yielded tantalizing but inconclusive evidence for cultivation of bottle gourds, cucumbers, water chestnuts, and various legumes as early as 14 kya (Solheim, 1972)! Most archeologists remain skeptical about the status of these plants. More persuasive finds pertaining to the initial stages of rice agriculture derive from two other northern Thailand localities, Ban Chiang and Non Nok Tha, where domesticated plant remains date back to 6 kya (Reed, 1977).

China's earliest farming phase, in the Huang Ho (or Yellow) river valley, dates to about the same period (Chang, 1977). Farmers there selected well-drained locations for planting **millet**, a small-seeded but productive cereal grass native to the region. Domestic dogs and pigs are also represented at these **Yangshao** or earliest Chinese Neolithic sites. Pottery production and possibly even silk weaving occupied the residents as well. Subsequently, rice agriculture spread into China's major river systems from the south. Since all the early domesticates were native to Asia, there seems, at least initially, to have been no stimulation from Near Eastern centers.

During the past decade, the nature of Neolithic beginnings on the Indian subcontinent have at last been illuminated by excavations at **Mehrgarh** in central Pakistan (Jarrige and Meadow, 1980; Allchin and Allchin, 1982). Located at the edge of a high plain overlooking the broad Indus valley, the site's lower levels, dating between 8 to 6 kya yielded both wild and domesticated forms of barley and wheat as well as some domesticated cattle and goat bones (although the latter were outnumbered by wild gazelle, sheep, goats, cattle, and deer). Here again, local domestication of local resources is indicated. Researchers believe this early Neolithic phase represents the transition from seminomadic herding to a more sedentary agricultural emphasis that became the basis for later urban development in the Indus valley. By the end of this initial period, planned settlements of multiroom mud-brick dwellings and granaries appeared, as well as prominent graves containing materials acquired through trade.

Tracing sub-Saharan Africa's Neolithic past is a challenge, given the vastness of the region and its shifting climate and vegetation zones. Mobile foragers and semisedentary fishers may have practiced yam **horticulture** along river margins or in tropical forest clearings as early as 5 kya (Clark, 1976). Somewhat later experiments with cattle herding and indigenous cereals, including local millet and **sorghum**, achieved success along the margins of the rainforest and the savanna grasslands. About 2 kya, now armed with iron weapons and tools with which to create slash-and-burn garden plots, agriculturalists brought their animals and crops into the tropical forest itself. Their produce was supplemented by bananas and coconuts, both of which somehow had reached Africa from Southeast Asia (Murdock, 1959).

European Farmers Having noted so many areas where Neolithic lifeways emerged independently, we now turn to southeastern Europe. Farmers there already were tilling the Balkan peninsula by about 8 kya at sites such as Argissa and Nea Nikomedeia. The interpretation of the European data remains open, but most archeologists conclude that the initial farming cultures actually derived from Asia Minor and the Near East. Such a relationship would account for the apparently sudden appearance of fully domesticated sheep, goats, wheat, and barley in the Balkans, along with a host of specific Near Eastern cultural traits, including burial practices, clay figurines, painted pottery, and chipped stone

MILLET
Small-grained cereal grass native to Asia and Africa.

YANGSHAO
First phase of Chinese Neolithic period.

MEHRGARH
(mare-gar′)

HORTICULTURE
Farming method in which only hand tools are used.

SORGHUM
Cereal grass with sweet juicy stalk.

Figure 16-7
Asian pearl millet.

WATTLE AND DAUB
A framework of woven sticks plastered with clay.

CIVILIZATION
Large-scale, complexly organized society.

forms (Tringham, 1971). Adjustment to European climatic conditions required some modifications, such as the use of **wattle and daub** and pitched roofs for houses in the wetter and well-forested temperate regions, but otherwise the cultures seem to be an extension of the Near Eastern Neolithic. Still, not everyone agrees. Dennell (1983) believes the indigenous domestication of local plant and animal species, supplemented later by more productive strains of wheat obtained through exchange, transformed native societies in southeastern Europe with no influx of colonists. In either case, minor variations in settlements, pottery, and subsistence activities define several developing subcultures in the region: Karanovo I in southern Bulgaria and Starcevo in eastern Yugoslavia are two of the earliest.

During another expansive phase beginning around 6500 y.a., village farmers rapidly planted themselves across southern and central regions of the continent, some archeologists even calculating an expansion rate of about 1.6 kilometers (km) or 1 mile (mi) per year (Ammerman and Cavalli-Sforza, 1973). As farming spread ever deeper into Europe's heartland along the Danube and the Rhine and their tributaries, distinctive pottery sherds became mixed with other debris on settlement sites. Decorated with incised lines, these wares are the most familiar hallmark of the so-called Linear Pottery or Danubian people. The locations and narrow dating of their many settlements suggest they may have been shifting

Figure 16-8
Stonehenge.

slash-and-burn cultivators who sought out the light well-drained **loess** soils neglected by earlier hunter-gatherers and farmers (Piggott, 1965). They sheltered their extended families and their harvests within sturdy timber longhouse/barns up to 36.5 meters (m) or 120 feet (ft) in length. As their crops depleted the soil's nutrients, they moved on to new locations. In this way, most archeologists surmise, the Danubians quickly spread through central Europe and onto the northern plains. However, Dennell (1983) doubts that shifting cultivation was really practiced here, suggesting instead that a ready acceptance of Neolithic resources and techniques by Mesolithic Europeans best accounts for the swift diffusion of farming through the area. Others, too, find indications of material and economic continuities between Mesolithic and Neolithic cultures in central and western Europe (Geddes, 1986; Gregg, 1988). As is often the case in archeology, either interpretation is supportable by the evidence now available, so more focused investigations will be required to test conflicting hypotheses.

Prehistoric farmers along the western and northern margins of Europe, including Spain, France, the British Isles, and Denmark, were responsible for an even more intriguing archeological enigma! We have no reason to suppose that there was anything particularly advantageous about the prospects for agriculture in this area, yet communities of Neolithic farmers found the wherewithal to erect thousands of puzzling prehistoric structures known collectively as **megaliths**. (See Issue this chapter.) Megaliths include such famous and complex formations as Stonehenge and Avebury in England, and Carnac in France, as well as numerous unnamed single-stone sites throughout the British Isles and northwestern Europe. Burial chambers or tombs, constructed of large stones and sometimes covered by earth, appeared during the earliest phases of the megalith-building era, beginning some 6 kya and continuing through the next two millennia. While the purpose of the tombs seems obvious, there is considerable debate about the significance of the individual standing stones, stone circles, and alignments. Some monuments, like Stonehenge, were built with great effort over the course of centuries, many of the enormous stones having been moved substantial distances by land and sea. Researchers have proposed that megalithic constructions served as astronomical observatories, enabling ancient priests to predict solstices and eclipses with accuracy. Many archeologists, however, remain skeptical of these explanations, while nevertheless agreeing that the monuments must have been inspired by some type of religious fervor (Daniel, 1980; Renfrew, 1983).

Ancient Civilizations of the Old World

By about 5500 y.a. in the Old World, a number of Neolithic cultures were in the process of becoming **civilizations**. These societies underwent a subtle yet profound metamorphosis nearly as mysterious as a butterfly's. Their emergence signalled the climax of Old World prehistory and laid the foundations of our modern historic era.

Considering Civilization

Conceptualizing "civilization" has proven to be a challenge to archeologists and philosophers of history. The list of cultures in both hemispheres that might be

LOESS
(luss)
Fine-grained soil composed of glacially pulverized rock.

MEGALITH
mega: large
lith: stone

ranked as prehistoric civilizations is long and varied. Accounting for how or why such societies developed is a frustrating task. Archeologists realize that the material artifacts they work with are but imperfect reflections of complex social systems. And yet, because the objects were once part of those systems, they may serve as tangible clues to the nature of early civilizations.

Some three decades ago, V. Gordon Childe enumerated the traits that he believed contributed to the evolution of early urban societies and civilizations by increasing productivity, social complexity, and economic advantage. The use of writing, animal traction, wheeled carts, plows, metallurgy, standard units of weight and measure, sailing boats, surplus production, craft specialization, irrigation, and mathematics all had a stimulating effect, according to Childe (1951, 1957). Although these traits characterized the Near Eastern societies with which Childe was most familiar, his list was not universally applicable. For example, American Indian societies such as the Maya and the Inca lacked a number of traits cited by Childe; yet, they clearly were civilizations, too.

Prehistorians sought to overcome these difficulties by singling out the several most essential qualities shared by every civilization. Harvard anthropologist Clyde Kluckhohn proposed that civilizations are societies having (1) towns with at least 5000 residents, (2) writing, and (3) monumental ceremonial architecture (Kraeling and Adams, 1960). Each of these criteria is an outward indicator of the society's complex nature. Thus, if a culture is able to maintain thousands of

Figure 16-9
Mesopotamia, showing extent of Sumerian civilization, and Upper and Lower Egypt.

people in a permanent settlement, then it clearly is exercising some form of non-kin-based governance or administrative control, as well as redistribution of goods and services. Writing manifests a need to keep accurate records and accounts, ranging from economic reports and tax tallies to law codes, histories, and literature. Large-scale construction activities that set up temples, pyramids, or other ceremonial architecture represent a society's surplus production, since such projects do not contribute directly to immediate and basic needs, such as food, in the same way that digging an irrigation canal might. A culture that can afford monumental ceremonial architecture shows it has attained a measure of success in supplying the needs of its population and in maintaining some control over it.

Definitions such as those of Childe and Kluckhohn are considered naive and inadequate today because they do not really address the question of how or why civilizations emerged. Most archeologists now view civilization as one of humankind's primary adaptive mechanisms. Through their culture, people may devise some appropriate response to a challenging situation and thereby extend their society's chances of survival and success. In this sense, the formation of a large-scale and complexly organized society may have been an accommodation to rapid population increases brought about by agricultural prosperity. Or, conversely, perhaps a concentrated and hungry population might prompt the building of irrigation works in an attempt to increase crop yields. Will the effort to control the water supply require the entire society to abide by the decisions of a dominant organizer and leader? Have warfare and the need for common defense sometimes played a stimulating role? Perhaps religion or the vision of a theocratic leader gave rise to civilization in some cases. Or, possibly, the new order served primarily to legitimize and protect the differential access to resources and wealth initiated by increased production. These and other hypotheses have been tested against data from individual prehistoric societies, though with few broadly applicable conclusions.

We must accept that no single or prime factor invariably propels a society along the path to civilization. Instead, anthropologists favor multidimensional explanations that recognize the complex structure of all societies. Even the simplest human cultural system is comprised of the same interrelated components: technology, subsistence economy, social organization, beliefs and symbolic expression, communication and exchange with other groups. Each of these elements is part of the culture's adaptive mechanism. Moreover, any change in the *status quo*, whether internally or externally derived, requires a response from one or more of these components and thus stimulates a dynamic adjustment in their interrelationships.

As an illustration of how this systemic approach to culture change may be used to explain the development of a civilization, consider the following hypothetical example.

Intensive agricultural practices, often including irrigation, occasionally produced harvests that exceeded the requirements of the local population. Sustained surplus food production could, in turn, eventually stimulate a variety of further responses: population growth, trade or exchange with other societies, or possibly disproportionate accumulations of wealth leading to social stratification. Technological innovations, in part fostered by increased prosperity and greater demand, would at the same time precipitate additional consequences. An invention as simple as the potter's wheel, for example, might revolutionize the craft of

TELL
A mound of accumulated rubble on the site of an ancient city.

producing ceramic vessels. Fulfilling the wheel's mass production capabilities required the participation of many specialists (mixers, potters, glazers, kiln masters, merchants, accountants, and so on). So long as the society's food supplies remained adequate, these specialists were exempted from the obligation of producing food and engaged in their respective tasks on a full-time basis. Thus, pottery making contributed to a new order of social and economic relationships within the society. Each development might prompt yet other transformations that would together move the society closer to what we recognize as civilization.

As with any other complex adaptive mechanism, civilization's effect on individuals was not uniformly beneficial. Robert J. Wenke aptly observes:

> We might suspect that the transition to social complexity was made in spite of its effect on the quality of life, and that its causes are not to be found in the choices of individuals or groups about how they want to live, but in the material factors of ecology, economics and technology (Wenke, 1984, p. 200).

Cities and Civilization   The most dramatic and dynamic invention associated with civilizations is the city. Civilizations are closely linked with the rise of city life, although not every civilization produced true cities. Archeologist Charles Redman has found that most early cities shared several major characteristics (Redman, 1978, p. 216). These include:

1. large and dense population
2. complexity and interdependence
3. formal and impersonal organization
4. many nonagricultural activities
5. a diversity of central services for inhabitants as well as for nearby communities

No one is certain when city life really began, but a number of early citylike communities have been excavated in the Near East. It is significant that the oldest of these sites clearly predate any Neolithic farming activities. Lewis Binford (1983) has pointed out that agriculture *follows* the first signs of sedentism in the Fertile Crescent area, while farming *preceded* settled life in most of the New World except in Peru.

Surely, one of the first towns anywhere in the world is the Near Eastern site known as Jericho, near the present city of that name in the lower Jordan river valley. A flowing spring in an otherwise arid region was the principal attraction for the Natufians, who first settled here around 11,500 y.a. A thousand years later, they were just beginning their transition to Neolithic ways, but they took time from their hunting and gathering to obtain salt, sulphur, shells, obsidian, and turquoise for trade with other groups. They also constructed early Jericho's remarkable architectural features. A massive stone wall 800 m (.5 mi) in circumference and 1.8 m (6 ft) thick enclosed the modest settlement of dome-shaped mud and stone houses. A deep trench cut into the bedrock beyond the wall afforded even greater security to Jericho's first citizens. Just inside the wall was an 8 m (26 ft) stone tower with interior stairs (Kenyon, 1957). Although originally viewed as fortifications against unknown human enemies, Jericho's wall and ditch have been reinterpreted as an attempt by the early inhabitants to combat the effects of mudflows brought on by severe erosion upslope of the site, while the tower is now seen as a community shrine (Bar-Yosef, 1986).

In time, early towns and cities of the Near East, like Jericho, became **tells**. Tells are mounds of archeological rubble, built up of mud brick, ash, stone, and other accumulated debris from successive settlements. Some of these features attained the size of small hills and are prominent local landmarks. Others, such as Jerusalem, continue to be occupied to this day. As one might expect, the older components of the site are generally found closer to the base of the tell, nearer the original ground surface. But neat layer-cake structures are the exception, since most tells accumulated in a sporadic way as individual buildings or sections were erected or demolished.

Another notable early settlement is marked by a 13 hectare (32 acre) tell in south-central Turkey. Both larger and later than Jericho, Çatal Hüyük was a trade and religious center of importance some 8 kya (Mellaart, 1967). Its densely packed houses of timber and mud brick had only rooftop entrances; their painted plaster interiors included living and storage space, sleeping platforms, and hearths. The city's several thousand inhabitants farmed outside its walls or engaged in craft production. Some exploited nearby sources of obsidian or volcanic glass to make beads, mirrors, and blades to export in exchange for raw materials and finished goods. The wealth this trade generated apparently went in part to support religious activities in the more than 40 elaborately decorated shrines uncovered in the excavated portion of the city. Many of these places held representations of cattle, then only recently domesticated, as focal points for the worshippers.

Jericho and Çatal Hüyük may be somewhat exceptional in that specialized trade or religious activities promoted their development. In size and sophistication, they surpassed contemporary settlements at Jarmo (Iraq), Çayönü (Turkey), and Hacilar (Turkey), which remained modest peasant villages. But, though the larger centers attained considerable size and local importance, even they did not evolve into the kind of true city that characterized the first civilization.

Mesopotamia

During the centuries before 7 kya, pioneer farmers settled the vast alluvial plains bordering the lower Tigris and Euphrates rivers, an area known as **Mesopotamia**. These agriculturalists shared the heritage of such Neolithic communities as Jarmo in the Zagros foothills to the east and Çayönü at the edge of the Anatolian plateau. Indeed, they were most likely descendants of the Samarran farmers of the upper Tigris valley, who practiced small-scale irrigation agriculture and obtained painted pottery and obsidian through their wide trade connections with highlands communities. Now entering the lowlands, perhaps in search of vacant or more productive lands, they encountered great flood-prone streams bound only by immense mud flats and marshes. But the deep stone-free silt that had accumulated along these rivers held tremendous potential for the future. Their cereal grains adapted well to this place.

The earliest farmers in the delta apparently did little to modify their new environment, choosing initially to plant in naturally irrigated plots along the river. Barley was their primary grain, but wheat, millet, and emmer also grew well, along with the date palm and a variety of vegetables. Animals included pigs and several kinds of sheep. Domesticated donkeys and oxen performed heavy tasks. Abundant harvests more than kept pace with the rapidly growing floodplain communities.

The **Ubaid** villagers, as archeologists know them, flourished during the fifth and fourth millennia B.C. (7300–5500 y.a.). A degree of cultural uniformity

MESOPOTAMIA
meso: middle
potamos: river
Land between the Tigris and Euphrates rivers; also known as the Fertile Crescent.

UBAID
(oo-bide')

Table 16-1 *Early Cereal Production and Animal Husbandry**

		Barley	Einkorn	Emmer	Bread-wheat	Sheep	Goats	Cattle	Pigs
The Aegean									
Argissa	8500 y.a.	+	+	+		+	+	+	+
Knossos	8100 y.a.	+		+	+			+	
Anatolia									
Hacilar	9000–7000 y.a.	+	+	+	+				
Levant									
Tell Ramad	9000 y.a.	+	+	+	+				
Jericho	9000–7500 y.a.	+	+	+					
Deh Luran									
Ali Kosh	8750–8000 y.a.	+	+	+		+	+	+	
Tepe Sabz	7500–7000 y.a.	+			+	+	+	+	
Kurdistan									
Karim Shahir	10,900 y.a.					+			
Jarmo	8750–8500 y.a.		+	+		+	+		+
									(also dogs)

*Blank spaces indicate that the grain or animal in question was not present.

Source: Personal communication, Robert Redden.

marked their settlements along the Tigris and Euphrates. Each centered around a platform-based stepped temple. Ubaidians maintained contact with their own and more distant Neolithic peoples through trade in decorated pottery, obsidian, lapis (a valued blue stone), copper, and possibly grain. These exchanges have been traced as far to the west as the Semitic cultures of Syria through chemical analyses of distinctive trace elements found in their raw materials and artifacts (Adams, 1972).

Unusual developments distinguished the latter Ubaid period. The population of some communities swelled to as many as 50,000, as people from outlying districts massed together behind protective walls. What might these events signify? Robert McC. Adams (1981) postulates that we are witnessing the birth of the true city, stimulated perhaps by intensified economic and even military rivalries among the population centers of the area. Extensive irrigation projects initiated around many cities at this time were intended to increase food for the concentrated populace. Altering the riverine environment by digging drainage and irrigation channels was a daunting enterprise, one that could be accomplished only through organized communal effort, including a high degree of cooperation and direction. The activity unquestionably transformed not only the landscape but also the agricultural societies themselves. The cities and their expanded irrigation systems, along with plow agriculture, wheeled carts, draught animals, advanced copper metallurgy, massive architecture, and increasing social and religious complexity all contributed to a new order in southern Mesopotamia after 5 kya. Archeologists recognize this stage as the inception of Sumerian civilization.

In many senses, the Sumerians lived in the world's first modern society (Kramer, 1963). Theirs was an urbanized and technologically accomplished culture, economically dependent on large scale irrigation agriculture. Their many practical innovations included the use of wheeled carts, the plow, and possibly sailing boats. They were among the first to refine metals such as gold, silver, and copper and to make bronze alloys. They had an advanced system of numeration and mathematics, including even the concept of zero. Their sophisticated architecture incorporated the true arch and the dome. An accurate calendar reflected a knowledge of astronomy. Their system of law became a basis for later legal codes, and their contributions to literature included many of the traditions subsequently recorded in the Old Testament. Numerous skilled craftsworkers produced fine jewelry and textiles, while artists created sculpture and music.

Much like city dwellers everywhere, Sumerians experienced social problems and pollution in their urban environment. Sumer comprised about a dozen largely autonomous political units, called city-states, in the southern Tigris-Euphrates valley. Each city-state included a major population center—Ur, Lagash, Kish, Nippur, Eridu, and Uruk are examples—as well as some smaller satellite communities and, of course, a great deal of irrigated cropland. Perhaps governed at first by its citizens, the later city-state was controlled by hereditary kings, who contested for dominance over their counterparts in neighboring cities.

The focal point of the city-state was its central sacred district, called the *tenemos*. Here rose the massive **ziggurat**, an impressive stepped temple built of millions of molded and baked mud bricks. Sumerians worshipped scores of major and minor deities who exhibited remarkably human characteristics. Chief among them was En-lil, the air god, who had a fatherly concern for mortals and their daily affairs, but who also meted out punishment and misfortune. Ringing the great civic center were palaces of the priests and ruling elite. Beyond them, narrow unpaved alleyways twisted through crowded residential areas. The size and complexity of individual homes correlated with family wealth and position. The populace comprised three general classes: nobility, commoners, and slaves. Numbered among the latter were former free citizens who had fallen on hard

ZIGGURAT
Sumerian mud-brick temple-pyramid.

Figure 16-10
Ziggurat at Ur.

times and sold themselves into bondage, as well as other Sumerians taken in conflicts with neighboring city-states. Many of the commoners engaged in craft or merchant activities, but most were farmers with fields and herds beyond the surrounding walls. The houses of all but the nobility were generally one-story, with several rooms opening onto a central courtyard. Wall and floor coverings brightened the interiors, which were furnished with wooden tables, chairs, and beds, and an assortment of household equipment for cooking and storage.

From our perspective, their writing system was perhaps the Sumerians' most significant invention, for it has enabled us to discover much more about them than their other artifacts and monuments could ever disclose. Using a wedge-shaped, or **cuneiform**, script, formed by pressing a reed stylus into a damp clay tablet (later baked for preservation), specially trained scribes recorded everything from recipes and love poems to the great events and traditions of their times. Literacy was a hard-won accomplishment, limited to those who undertook years of formal study and practice. Over time, the original pictographic form of written Sumerian evolved into a phonetic system of some 2000 symbols. Nine-tenths of their writing concerned economic, legal, and administrative matters; like us, Sumerians belonged to a complex and bureaucratized society. But about 4500 y.a., scribes began recording more literary works, including several poetic accounts featuring the adventures of Gilgamesh, a culture hero who performed many brave deeds in the face of overwhelming odds.

Unfortunately, much of the energy of Sumerian society was dissipated in fruitless competition. Clustered together in an area about the size of Vermont, the city-states of Sumer were all too often vying with one another for supremacy in commerce, prestige, or religion. At the same time, their overreliance on irrigation agriculture was slowly poisoning the fields that supported the large populations. Soluble salts carried in the irrigation water accumulated in the soil, destroying its fertility. Eroding silt threatened to choke the canals themselves. The rise of a number of powerful Semitic city-states in the central Tigris-Euphrates valley boded more ill for the Sumerians. Finally, around 2370 B.C. (*circa* 4400 y.a.), Sargon, the king of Akkad, led armies from the north into one after another of the Sumerian lands. The process was repeated several centuries later by King Hammurabi of Babylon. After that episode, the ancient cities and culture of Sumer were absorbed into the powerful empire of the Babylonians.

Other civilizations differed greatly in detail from the Sumerian example we have just considered. But, pointing to this cultural diversity is not to deny that there were some basic similarities shared by many ancient societies at this level. We have already indicated that civilizations generally included focal points of production, trade, religion, and administration. Often these central places took form as cities, although some civilizations—Egypt and the New World's Inca, for examples—did not develop true cities of large size. The economies of even the most advanced societies continued to be based primarily on domesticated plants and animals, of course. But increased social complexity, along with the development of technological innovations, stimulated the production of new kinds of products that contributed to the growth of a nonsubsistence economy. These new economic factors often fostered further societal changes. Thus, specialized production, utilizing trained craftpersons who were not obliged to grow their own food, created goods that could be consumed within the culture itself or, as was frequently the case, exchanged with other societies for comparable goods or desirable raw materials. One's access to these products usually depended upon social or economic status. Nowhere was this more true than in ancient Egypt.

Figure 16-11
Mesopotamian clay tablet with cuneiform writing.

Egypt

The pyramids of Egypt are unrivalled as the ancient world's most imposing monuments. They have adorned the Nile's banks for so long that it is hard to imagine there was a time when they had not yet taken form. Yet, of course, Egyptian culture took root in the Nile valley well before the pyramids.

Geologists and paleoecologists assert that over the past 10,000 years or more the Nile behaved essentially as it did until the construction of the Aswan High Dam in the 1960s. Extended cycles of increased rainfall broadened the river and its valley, while intervening drier periods saw a contraction of the life-giving flow. The Nile retained its seasonal rhythm, responding to the summer runoff by overtopping its banks in mid-July and flooding the lowlying basins for about three months annually. Desiccation followed flood, but fertile new silt grew lush with grasses through the dry season, long before farmers made the river's rhythm their own.

Remnants of the earliest Nile cultures are elusive and rarely encountered by archeologists digging in the much-disturbed river floodplain. However, recent efforts to trace the beginnings of Egyptian civilization have been rewarded (Trigger, 1983). The Mesolithic foragers who occupied the Nile valley some 8 kya and before were equipped with bone-tipped harpoons for fishing. They gathered wild produce, and probably ground starchy tubers on their milling stones. Simple pottery vessels and clay-daubed reed huts reveal their willingness to stay in one spot for at least a while. By some 1500 years later, the descendants of these collecting and fishing people exhibited a Neolithic farming adaptation, one that already was familiar in southwest Asia. Although some local Nile species may have been domesticated initially, these soon were supplanted by crops and animals first brought under human control in the Fertile Crescent: barley and wheat, sheep

Figure 16-12
Egyptian Old Kingdom pyramids at Giza.

HIEROGLYPHICS
hiero: sacred
glyphein: carving
The picture-writing of ancient Egypt.

FAIENCE
(fay-ahnz')
Glassy-surfaced pottery.

and goats. Cattle, pigs, and donkeys were added later and may, in fact, represent locally domesticated varieties. Agricultural settlements scattered along the river's high banks consisted of reed-mat or skin-covered huts, with basket-lined storage pits or granaries. Pottery vessels of Nile clay, linen woven from flax fibers, flint work, and occasional hammered copper items were produced locally.

In the section of the Nile valley just north of present-day Aswan (the "First Cataract" of ancient times), some of these Neolithic villages, collectively known to archeologists as the Gerzean culture, contrast with those of the delta region. Gerzean sites yield more evidence of Mesopotamian influence, introduced perhaps through direct contact or by way of Palestinian traders. Mineral resources, including gold, may have first attracted the notice of outsiders. By a little more than 5 kya, this part of the Nile valley, called Upper Egypt, was using carved stone cylinder seals, vessel forms, artistic influences, and architectural techniques derived ultimately from the east. Other important innovations, apparently from the same source, transformed this basic Nile culture most profoundly (Hoffman, 1979).

Ancient Egyptians rather suddenly began using a complex pictographic script called **hieroglyphics**, a writing system that is Egyptian in form but probably Mesopotamian in inspiration. Advanced methods of copper working came into use as well, including refining of ores and alloying, casting, and hammering techniques. An important by-product of copper metallurgy was **faience**, an Egyptian invention produced by fusing powdered quartz and copper ore. The blue-green glassy substance that resulted was molded into beads or statuettes. At the same time, archeologists find evidence for increasing political and social cohesion, as though the Gerzean settlements may be forming into small city-states under the leadership of a king. Again, these changes may have been stimulated by contact with the eastern Mediterranean. No evidence of comparable Egyptian influence in the other direction has been recognized.

Figure 16-13
A royal Egyptian hunting marsh birds from a papyrus boat.

Historical tradition and contemporary textual fragments record that one of Upper Egypt's early kings, named Narmer, dominated the other towns of that region and succeeded also in extending his control over the delta villages to the north. This unification of Upper and Lower Egypt under Narmer, the traditional beginning of the First Dynasty of Egyptian civilization, dates to around 3100–2900 B.C. (5100–4900 y.a.). The merger of the Nile valley societies under one king marked an important step in the development of ancient Egypt.

The following centuries, known as Old Kingdom times (4700–4400 y.a.), represent the fullest flowering of Nile valley civilization. The ruler, or Pharaoh, was during this period the supreme power of the society, and under his direction Egypt became a wonder of the ancient world and a source of endless fascination for millennia to follow. The pharaoh was a godlike king who ruled with divine authority through a bureaucracy of priests and public officials. Memphis, about 15 miles southeast of present-day Cairo, was the royal center through most of this period. Local administrators, or *nomarchs*, governed about 40 individual districts, or *nomes*, each with its principal town. There were few large cities or urban centers in the ancient Nile valley. It is well to remember that Egypt remained basically a Neolithic culture, with the vast majority of its citizenry comprised of peasants and tradesmen carrying out their timeless routines (Aldred, 1961).

The great pyramids constructed during the Old Kingdom period best exemplify the pharaoh's absolute authority over the people and resources of his domain. In one sense, these monuments were immense public-works projects that undoubtedly served to solidify the power of the state while at the same time glorifying the memory of individual rulers. The familiar pyramids at Giza evolved out of a tradition of royal tomb-building that began by 5 kya with a brick-lined burial pit and adjoining chambers stocked with offerings for the deceased king's afterlife, the whole of which was then capped by a low rectangular brick superstructure (Emery, 1957). The first stepped pyramids were raised a few centuries later, and after 4600 y.a., the massive tombs of Khufu and Khafra, Fourth Dynasty rulers, were built in true pyramid form. Khufu's Great Pyramid is 232 m (765 ft) square at its base and 147 m (485 ft) in height, with well over 2 million enormous stone blocks required in its construction (Mendelssohn, 1974). Khafra's tomb is about 20 percent smaller, but he compensated by having his likeness carved from a nearby outcrop, known today as the Great Sphinx.

The stark structures that remain were once adjoined by extensive complexes of connecting causeways, shrines, altars, and storerooms filled with statuary and furnishings and ornamented with colorful friezes and carved stonework. These monumental tombs represent a remarkable engineering triumph and an enormous cultural achievement. We can also readily recognize that the mortuary cult of the pharaohs absorbed a great proportion of the work and wealth of Egyptian society. But pyramid building climaxed quickly; later rulers apparently channeled some of the energies that would have been used in erecting additional monuments into other kinds of projects. Subsequent kings contented themselves with burial in smaller but nonetheless lavishly furnished tombs. Discovered in the 1920s, the treasure-choked sepulcher of the young pharaoh **Tutankhamen**, who had died in 1346 B.C. (about 2450 y.a.) during New Kingdom times, is convincing evidence that dead royalty was not neglected after the era of the pyramids had passed (Carter and Mace, 1923).

Much of what we know of ancient Egypt derives from the translation of countless hieroglyphic inscriptions. The 1799 discovery at Rosetta, a small Nile delta

TUTANKHAMEN
(toot-en-cahm′-en)
Informally referred to as King Tut.

BOX 16-2

Opening the Innermost Coffin of King Tutankhamen

"The lid was fastened to the shell by means of eight gold tenons (four on each side), which were held in their corresponding sockets by nails. Thus, if the nails could be extracted the lid could be raised. In the narrow space between the two coffins ordinary implements for extracting metal pins were useless, and others had to be devised. With long screwdrivers converted to meet the conditions, the nails or pins of solid gold, that unfortunately had to be sacrificed, were removed piecemeal. The lid was raised by its golden handles and the mummy of the king disclosed.

"At such moments the emotions evade verbal expression, complex and stirring as they are. Three thousand years and more had elapsed since men's eyes had gazed into that golden coffin. Time, measured by the brevity of human life, seemed to lose its common perspectives before a spectacle so vividly recalling the solemn religious rites of a vanished civilization. But it is useless to dwell on such sentiments, based as they are on feelings of awe and human pity. The emotional side is no part of archaeological research. Here at last lay all that was left of the youthful Pharaoh, hitherto little more to us than the shadow of a name.

"Before us, occupying the whole of the interior of the golden coffin, was an impressive, neat and carefully made mummy, over which had been poured anointing unguents as in the case of the outside of its coffin—again in great quantity—consolidated and blackened by age. In contradistinction to the general dark and sombre effect, due to these unguents, was a brilliant, one might say magnificent, burnished gold mask, or similitude of the king, covering his head and shoulders, which, like the feet, had been intentionally avoided when using the unguents. . . . The beaten gold mask, a beautiful and unique specimen of ancient portraiture, bears a sad but calm expression suggestive of youth overtaken prematurely by death. Upon its forehead, wrought in massive gold, were the royal insignia—the Nekhevet vulture and Buto serpent—emblems of the Two Kingdoms over which he had reigned."

SOURCE:

Carter, Howard, and A. C. Mace. *The Tomb of Tutankhamen*, London: Cassell and Co., Ltd., 1923, pp. 82–84.

Figure 16-14
The Rosetta Stone, as displayed in the British Museum in the nineteenth century.

town, of a stone bearing an identical decree engraved in three different languages, including Greek and hieroglyphics, enabled the French linguist Jean-François Champollion to first decipher the mysterious writing. Egyptian hieroglyphics comprise a complex system that combines symbols representing ideas with those that indicate sounds. Because hieroglyphics were used primarily in formal contexts (in much the same way Latin has been used in more recent times), their translation tells us much about pharaohs and their deeds, but reveals little of the commonplace events and people of the day. In fact, archeologists have been able to learn frustratingly little about daily life in Egypt's Old Kingdom period outside the major administrative and mortuary centers. Fortunately, somewhat more is known about the later periods of Egyptian civilization (Ruffle, 1977; Montet, 1981).

Egypt proved remarkably resilient through the centuries, surviving foreign invaders like the Hyksos and Hittites of southwest Asia, as well as occasional episodes of internal misrule and rebellion. It enjoyed periods of resurgence and revival, although nothing equalled the original glory of the Old Kingdom period. Eventually, in a state of decline, and defeated by the Persians, Egypt was absorbed into the Greek sphere under Alexander the Great and eventually came under the rule of Rome.

The Indus Valley

As the last great pyramids along the Nile were being erected in the mid-third millennium B.C., a less flamboyant civilization was coming to maturation in another valley far to the east, along the Indus river of Pakistan. People there had gained a tentative control over the flood-prone stream, repelling its silted water with mud-brick walls and channeling part of its flow through irrigation sluices. They laid out fields for their vegetables and cotton and cereals on its alluvial plains. They rode the great river itself as a commercial highway.

These people were relative newcomers to the floodplains. Their ancestors had farmed the highland valleys to the west for thousands of years at sites like Mehrgarh, herding cattle and harvesting a variety of local grains and rice. What drew them into the lowlands about 5 kya is not known. But for a time they prospered at the edge of the great river. The locations of nearly a thousand Indus valley agricultural and pastoral villages have now been plotted by archeologists.

The largest Indus sites so far excavated are Mohenjo-Daro and Harappa, which flourished between about 4200 and 3700 y.a. (Wheeler, 1968; Fairservis, 1976; Allchin and Allchin, 1982). Built according to precise plans, these major riverport cities were laid out in neatly gridded rectangles of approximately 400 by 200 meters. The windowless walls of standardized brick residence units bordered their broad streets. What was probably the world's first efficient sewage system conveyed waste away from thousands of densely packed dwellings. In other sections of the larger cities, roomier houses with interior courtyards sheltered members of a privileged social class. A "great bath," or pool, lies near what has been interpreted as Mohenjo-Daro's government center, a complex that also included elite residences and a large assembly hall. Close by was a capacious granary, serving perhaps as a state storehouse. Harappa, too, had such granaries, as well as rows of furnaces that probably were used for smelting ore.

Though its impressively large sites hint at some sort of central control and social complexity, the Indus valley civilization remained a relatively simple **Bronze Age** culture. Nowhere, for example, is there evidence of a genuine palace or a monumental religious structure. Nor are there indications of international trade or warfare. In these regards, the culture stands in stark contrast to both Egypt and Sumer. Perhaps there was wider participation in economic and social aspects of Indus society than in these other civilizations. What might the culture have to say for itself? Unfortunately, the writing system, consisting of brief pictographic notations on seal stones and pottery, is not yet fully translated, although there has been some recent headway on this front (Fairservis, 1983).

The river that spawned the principal urban centers may have played a role in their final chapter, gradually reclaiming the surrounding fields and eventually the cities themselves. But hundreds of other towns and villages outlasted them, some even persisting into the modern era as peasant villages of western India and Pakistan.

Northern China

The roots of China's first civilization were nurtured in the Neolithic villages on the great alluvial plains of the north. We have seen that farmers along the Huang Ho river cultivated millet, a small-grained cereal grass, by 5500 y.a. Fertile de-

BRONZE AGE
Period of early Old World civilizations, beginning with widespread use of metal tools after 5500 y.a.

Figure 16-15
Location of the Indus valley civilization.

DIVINATION
A method of foretelling the future.

posits of deep loess soil helped ensure large yields and undoubtedly contributed to the growth of populous settlements during this Yangshao, or initial farming, period. Even at this stage, some elements of later Chinese culture already were anticipated, including jade carving, painted ceramics, and possibly even silkworm cultivation. A shift to rice farming and the herding of domesticated cattle, horses, and water buffalo initiated the later Neolithic, or Lung-shan period, along China's central valleys, beginning around 4700 y.a. (Chang, 1977).

Perhaps due to their success in directing water control projects along the major rivers, local leaders who emerged in northern China over the next few centuries commanded the allegiance of ever-larger regions. These areas functioned much like feudal states, supporting a rising noble class that took a prominent role in the subsequent era of Chinese civilization. Beginning with the Shang dynasty in the sixteenth century B.C. (3500 y.a.), material culture, architecture, art styles, and writing had attained a level of refinement that emanated from a highly structured society. The large population of peasant farmers lived and labored as they always had, but now an elite ruling class, supported by slaves, craftspersons, scribes, and other functionaries, had been added to the top of the social hierarchy.

The power and actions of the Shang rulers were apparently justified in many cases through the practice of **divination**, or prophecy. Divination was performed by first writing a question on certain specially prepared bones, such as turtle shells or ox and deer scapulae. Applying heat to the bone caused cracks to appear, whereupon the answer to the question could be "read." Divination was a vital activity in Shang society, and thousands of the marked bones still survive (Fitzgerald, 1978).

One of the early capitals of the Shang dynasty was located at the present-day city of Zhengzhou (Cheng-chou), along the Huang Ho river. Here, archeologists located remains of a large rectangular precinct comprising the residences of nobles and rulers as well as their temples and other ceremonial structures. A massive

Figure 16-16
Centers of early Chinese civilization.

Figure 16-17
Bronze ritual vessel of Shang dynasty.

wall of packed earth nearly 10 m (30 ft) in height separated the royal compound from surrounding clusters of huts and workshops. Among the latter were several bronze foundries. Shang artisans produced remarkable bronze work, especially their elaborate footed cauldrons, cast in sectional molds. Decorated with stylized animal motifs and dedicatory inscriptions, these vessels were used by the nobility in making ritual offerings of wine and food to ancestors and deities. They also appear as prominent funerary items in royal tombs, including those in the vicinity of the later Shang capital at Anyang. In addition to their bronzes, the rulers were accompanied in death by lavish offerings of carved jade, horse-drawn chariots, and scores of human sacrificial victims (Chang, 1980). In later times, life-size clay sculptures of horses and soldiers were sometimes substituted.

Although limited in area, the Shang civilization influenced the future course of Chinese culture. The social and cultural innovations introduced by the Shang were adopted and extended by succeeding rulers, until much of China was apportioned among competitive Bronze Age warlords. Not until the Han dynasty (206 B.C. to A.D. 220) was this huge region at last politically unified into a cohesive Chinese empire, protected within its Great Wall.

The Mediterranean World

By comparison with the ancient cultures of Egypt and Mesopotamia and Asia, the Mediterranean societies of the second millennium B.C. were relatively late and unimpressive in scale and achievement. Their real significance for us is that they were the bridges between the old civilizations of the East and the formative societies of barbarian Europe. The Bronze Age Minoans had a maritime orientation that kept them in contact with peoples of the Aegean. Their contemporaries and successors, the Mycenaeans, created the first civilization on the European mainland itself.

Minoans Neolithic farmers were the first occupants of Crete, the large caterpillar-shaped island in the eastern Mediterranean. Arriving by boat, they introduced domesticated sheep, olives, grapes, and lentils, all of which adapted well to the island's rough semi-arid terrain. A desire to exchange their surplus products for others that were locally unavailable soon prompted the island's inhabitants to look seaward. First using oar-propelled galleys, then sailing vessels, the Minoans of Crete mastered the sea lanes of the eastern Mediterranean. They plied among neighboring islands and on to the mainland of Egypt, **Anatolia**, and the Levant, exchanging their foodstuffs, woolen cloth, pottery, and timber primarily for raw materials that they could convert into luxury goods. Attractively colored stones such as carnelian, agate, sard, and jasper became carved seals for impressing clay and other substances with an owner's personal mark. Copper and tin ores were smelted, alloyed, and cast into weapons, armor, tools, and ornaments. Minoans also gained fame as skilled artisans in gold and silver. Some of these finished goods reentered the exchange network, while others remained on Crete to supply the wants of the growing Minoan elite.

The rapid transformation of Minoan society after 4500 y.a. reflects successful maritime trading (Hood, 1973). A number of communities formed around the multistoried palaces and spacious homes that sheltered wealthy merchant-kings and others of privileged status. Crete's coastal towns dominated the Mediterranean trade for several centuries prior to about 3450 y.a. (1450 B.C.). Knossos, on

ANATOLIA
Asia Minor; present-day Turkey.

Figure 16-18
Minoan and Mycenaean civilizations.

the island's northern side, had been one of the earliest settlements on the island. Now it boasted a rambling palace of more than a thousand rooms. These local palaces were the focus of Minoan life, the centers of its economy, arts, crafts, and social hierarchy. The balconies of the Knossos palace overlooked tiled courtyards where religious celebrations took place. Within, brightly frescoed walls revealed the Minoan love of art. Painted scenes of commerce and exotic ports were combined with views of lush gardens, dancers and daring athletes, mythological landscapes, and imaginary creatures to capture the visitor's attention. Within palace workshops, artisans created delicate jewelry and elegant metal drinking vessels. Some rooms held ranks of gaily decorated ceramic jars filled with olive oil and awaiting shipment. In others, scribes carefully impressed clay tablets with symbols that remain to this day an untranslatable script known simply as *Linear* A. Finally, one approached the colonnaded chamber that was the heart of the great palace—the royal court with its carved gypsum throne.

The civilization of Crete was highly distinctive. Despite long contact with the Nile valley and Near East, Minoans retained their cultural identity in every sphere, from art and architecture to statecraft and religion. Unlike many contemporary societies, the Minoans apparently were content to worship at modest local shrines, sometimes tenanted by small figurines in the form of a buxom young woman holding a serpent on each arm. This so-called "snake goddess" may have been a fertility figure or mother goddess. Another prominent character in the Minoan pantheon was the bull, who probably signified virility. In one ritual, Minoan female athletes performed somersaults over the back of a raging bull. The familiar myth of the fierce half-man, half-bull Minotaur is likewise associated with the Minoans of Crete.

This intriguing and colorful island civilization was relatively peaceful, yet it ended amid great devastation. There is some disagreement as to the cause of its demise, but natural catastrophe almost surely played a key role. Geologically recent, the island of Crete is earthquake prone. A number of Minoan centers already had been damaged and reconstructed periodically. Then, about 3450 y.a. (1470 B.C.), according to most estimates, one-third of the nearby island of Thera, a Minoan outpost 120 km (75 mi) off Crete's north coast, exploded into the sky, propelling lava and volcanic ash into the atmosphere. Seawater surged into the volcano's gaping submarine crater. For weeks after, severe tremors shook apart the great palaces and houses on Crete itself, and tidal waves may have swept the island's north shore (Sparks and Sigurdsson, 1978; but also see Chen, 1989). Damage was so extensive everywhere that, while rebuilding took place at a few sites, the Minoans were unable to retain control of the Mediterranean trade routes.

Mycenaeans   Even as Minoan civilization reached its zenith, other Mediterranean societies were responding to the stimuli of contact and trade. One of these emergent cultures was the Mycenaean. They brought their basic Bronze Age culture and proto-Greek language into southeastern Europe about 4200 y.a., when they left their Anatolian homeland. Inspired by the Minoans, they soon secured a share of the lucrative sea trade by successfully establishing an exchange network that included Cyprus, Egypt, Anatolia, and the central Mediterranean. By 3600 y.a. they already could afford to richly stock the graves of their dead kings within their principal hilltop fortress-city of Mycenae. The massive stonework protecting this citadel recalls the militarism that pervaded Mycenaean society. Likewise, scenes engraved on finger rings, seal stones, and gold-inlaid weapons characteristically exhibit combat themes. Much Mycenaean bronze work (their primary commercial product) took the form of daggers, swords, helmets, and other armaments. Mycenaean militarism flavors the epics of Homer, whose *Iliad* and *Odyssey* recount the long struggle with the rival city of Troy, across the Aegean.

Figure 16-19
Minoan bull-jumping ceremony, depicted on the palace wall at Knossos.

AMBER
Fossil pine pitch or resin.

Figure 16-20
Winged palstave or ax, Bronze Age.

The extent to which Minoans and Mycenaeans competed or coexisted is not clear. But only when disaster weakened the culture of Crete did the Mycenaeans dominate. Over the two centuries following the decline of Knossos and other Minoan centers, Mycenaeans gained full control of the Mediterranean trade and of Crete itself. They incorporated the Minoan palace-based economic system, written recordkeeping, and artistic and technical achievements into their own culture (Warren, 1975). Now Mycenaean ships plowed the waves unchallenged. Wealthy merchant-kings enjoyed the highest stations in their society. At home, their colonnaded palaces were virtual warehouses bulging with trade goods and imported luxuries. The elite, local administrators, landholders, craftsworkers, peasants, and slaves participated in descending degree in the social and economic benefits of this stratified society. Their insatiable need of raw materials for art objects and armaments drew the Mycenaeans to distant Mediterranean and Near Eastern ports. One crucial resource was metal. The key to bronze making is the alloy added in small amounts to harden the copper. Arsenic may be used, but smiths who worked that substance rapidly experienced its lethal side-effects. Tin, the preferred alloy, was very scarce. Mycenaean demand for it stimulated mining activities as far away as western and central Europe and the Near East. Other northern European resources also attracted them. **Amber**, or fossil pine resin, a translucent yellow-brown substance that may have fascinated the ancients because of its static electrical properties, arrived from the far-off shores of the Baltic Sea. Mycenaean ships visited the Mediterranean seaports at the terminus of overland supply and exchange routes, dispensing articles of commerce that filtered into the tribal societies of the European hinterlands (Harding, 1984; Bouzek, 1985). Their own exposure to Minoan trade and culture had earlier transformed the Mycenaeans, and now the Mycenaeans themselves were making a similar, though indirect, impact on barbarian Europe. Mycenaean supply routes were cultural arteries, infusing the Europeans with new technologies and other far-reaching innovations (Piggott, 1965).

While we cannot yet precisely delineate the later relationship between western Europe and the Mediterranean world, we can observe that the Mycenaean sphere began to contract before collapsing altogether. Had these Europeans so quickly reached the point of seriously challenging Mycenaean trade and access to strategic resources? It seems doubtful. On the other hand, there were the tribal peoples of the eastern Mediterranean, including some of Mycenae's near neighbors, who appear to have become aggressive raiders. Early texts make cryptic references to "sea people" and to "people of the north" who began to close in on the civilized world, armed with cutting-and-slashing swords. Thus began an unsettled era, a time of troubles for many of the ancient societies that rimmed the Mediterranean. About 3200 y.a., the principal Mycenaean cities were destroyed, their populations dispersed, and their trade routes abandoned. From the Nile delta to Anatolia, invaders swept through the old kingdoms, creating chaos. In the wake of this destruction came a dark age, a period that is but sketchily known to prehistorians. When the dust settled, centuries later, we find an Iron Age Europe peopled by Greeks, Etruscans, and Celts—the principals of a new era.

Summary

About 10 kya, significant climatic adjustments brought about changes in geography and in the configuration of animal and plant communities in the northern hemisphere. There were some important consequences for humans as well, particularly in their subsistence economy. Post-Pleistocene cultural adaptations in the Old World were expressed through new technologies and a more intensive utilization of local resources, a way of life we call Mesolithic. Mesolithic cultures of northern Europe continued to develop specializations in their hunting-gathering-fishing economies for many centuries. Contemporary cultures of the Near East, such as the Natufian, were already taking steps toward food production, and the success of such experimentation led ultimately toward a more self-sufficient and sedentary existence in the Neolithic period.

The rise of ancient civilization is a further manifestation of post-Pleistocene adaptations following the technological achievement of agricultural food production. Appearing in scattered parts of the globe, early civilizations flourished particularly on the alluvial plains of some of the Old World's major river systems: the Tigris-Euphrates, the Nile, the Indus, the Huang Ho. Cities, monumental architecture, writing, trade, social stratification, development of art and science, all aided in constructing the foundations on which much of our cultural heritage is based.

Questions for Review

1. Cite some of the significant changes associated with the end of the Pleistocene. Explain how Europe's natural environment was altered.
2. Why and in what ways did the Mesolithic adaptations of northern Europe and southwest Asia differ? What long-term consequences resulted?
3. Evaluate several of the major theories that account for plant and animal domestication.
4. What kinds of archeological evidence may be used to indicate plant and animal domestication?
5. Cite several important positive and negative consequences of food production.
6. Devise an hypothesis to test whether farming in central Europe may have been indigenous or imported. Why is it so difficult to prove the case?
7. Compare the typical Sumerian city-state with the ancient Egyptian state. Cite some similarities and contrasts. What role was played by ordinary individuals in each?
8. Suggest why river valleys were the primary setting for so many early Old World civilizations.
9. Why was writing so closely associated with the rise of civilizations?
10. Explain how bronze technology stimulated cultural expansion and trade throughout the Mediterranean basin and Europe.

Prehistory of the Americas

CONTENTS

In Pursuit of the Earliest Americans

A surefire way to enliven any gathering of American archeologists is to ask for, or express an opinion on, the earliest evidence of people in the New World. There is a wide spectrum of positions on this issue. One extreme view even holds that modern humanity originated in the American Southwest and spread from there to the Old World! But most archeologists agree upon the Old World origin of American Indians, yet express varied opinions about the date of the first arrivals.

Most of the debate about the New World's first inhabitants focuses on the span between 30 and 12 kya. The former represents the period by which anatomically modern people were occupying the part of Asia that lies closest to North America. By the latter date, unquestionable sites associated with Paleo-Indians were already established in many parts of the Western Hemisphere. The scanty evidence submitted as proof of a very early human presence is of dubious quality. In some cases, crude artifacts retrieved from erosion channels, blowouts, lake beds, or even plowed fields could be of considerable antiquity, but their disturbed contexts generally preclude a realistic assessment of age. Other stone or bone fragments, some found within datable contexts, simply are not accepted by most archeologists as humanly produced artifacts.

Typical of these disputed claims is the Calico site near Barstow, California. The late Louis Leakey, Ruth D. Simpson, and others contend that certain chert fragments recovered from alluvial gravel deposits at depths of up to 8 m (26 ft) constitute artifacts dating to perhaps 200 kya. Many archeologists discount a human origin for these specimens altogether, noting that their flaking angles indicate natural breakage due to soil movement and compaction. The uranium-thorium date on calcium carbonate encrusting the flakes and gravels is inconclusive until it can be confirmed by other methods.

All too often, preliminary results of experimental dating techniques have been rashly accepted and allowed to fuel unwarranted assertions about the age of the earliest Americans. The dating of bones by amino acid racemization, a technique that measures postmortem changes in the body's protein components, initially produced estimates of 30,000 to 50,000 years for several human skeletons found near San Diego, California. Most researchers, guided by the bones' unremarkable modern morphology, remained skeptical of these findings, reserving judgment on the dating technique itself. But a few seized the dates to boldly challenge long-held conservative views. They uncritically accepted dates of extreme antiquity for other human remains, as well: more than 40,000 years for the bones of an infant found at Taber in southern Alberta, Canada, and as much as 24,000 years for an adult skeleton found under a rock in the Yuha Desert of southern California. Fortunately, recent refinements in the radiocarbon dating technique now allow direct counting of the carbon-14 isotope in a specimen, thus producing much more reliable dates for even tiny samples of bone and other organics. Each of the controversial finds just cited has now been redated, using the improved procedure. The results in all cases are consistent with an age of between 4000 and 6000 years.

Simple stone tools, in the form of crude choppers and large flakes or scrapers, have been found widely throughout the Americas. Some archeologists consider them evidence of a period predating the use of bifacial projectile points (which were used in North America by 12 kya). Unfortunately, many of these typologically "primitive" tools cannot be readily or securely dated. Some are merely surface finds, while others are from disturbed contexts. The lowest levels of Pikimachay (Flea Cave) in Peru's Ayacucho Valley contained bones of giant sloth and what the excavator, Richard S. MacNeish, interpreted as crude stone butchering tools of 15 to 20 kya. But, here again, the nature and dating of the artifacts are disputed by many.

Purported bone artifacts have claimed considerable attention in recent years. Archeologist Robson Bonnichsen and others have shown that bone may have been of greater technological importance than archeologists previously recognized. Fresh bone could be worked into useful forms by controlled flaking and breaking techniques, which produce distinctive spiral fracture patterns not normally duplicated by natural processes. Thousands of Pleistocene animal bones lie scattered through the gravel bars and in the banks of the meandering Porcupine River and its tributaries in the Old Crow region of Alaska. Among the bones found here are some that may show signs of human activity, including flakes, cuts, and even injuries induced by bone spearpoints (Fig. 1). One notable implement is a caribou tibia fleshing tool, or scraper, with finely serrated teeth cut into its working edge. At first dated to more than 27 kya by conventional radiocarbon

Figure 1
Flaked bone from the upper reaches of the Old Crow River, Alaska. The wavy lines are weathering caused by small roots.

Figure 2
Knifelike implement from Stratum IIa at Meadowcroft Rockshelter, Pennsylvania.

methods, this artifact has now been re-dated to approximately only 1350 y.a. However, mammoth bones showing green-bone fractures and flaking continue to indicate ages of 25 to 45 kya, though few archeologists are willing to identify these specimens as tools.

In eastern North America, the Meadowcroft rockshelter near Pittsburgh, Pennsylvania, is a deeply stratified site containing cultural levels that have been dated to more than 19 kya by standard radiocarbon methods. Stratum IIa, from which this date derives, contained several prismatic blades, a retouched flake, a chipped biface, and a crude knifelike implement (Fig. 2). Unfortunately, none of the tools from this deep stratum is particularly distinctive, so it is difficult to assess technological relationships with other assemblages. The unexpectedly early radiocarbon results for this site have not escaped challenge, either.

One of the most intriguing sites under scrutiny at present is a Paleo-Indian settlement at Monte Verde, Chile. Tom Dillehay's evidence of wood and skin structures, along with wood and stone tools, plant remains, and mastodon bones, has been dated to about 13 kya. The early presence of Paleo-Indians in South America, and especially the nature of this site, do not completely square with current notions. Archeologists are viewing this find with interest and some justifiable caution. After all, the casualty rate for earlier claims has increased alarmingly in recent years, largely due to carbon-dating advances. There presently are no *indisputable* sites, artifacts, or human remains in the New World earlier than about 12,000 years. Older American sites may exist, but the burden of proving great antiquity is considerable and must be borne by those who make the claim.

SOURCES:

Bryan, Alan L. *New Evidence for the Pleistocene Peopling of the Americas.* Orono: University of Maine Center for Study of Early Man, 1986.

Dincauze, Dena F. "An Archaeological Evaluation of the Case for Pre-Clovis Occupations." In *Advances in World Archaeology,* Fred Wendorf and Andrea Close, eds., 3:275–323. New York: Academic Press, 1984.

Fagan, Brian M. *The Great Journey.* London: Thames and Hudson, 1987.

Irving, William N. "Context and Chronology of Early Man in the Americas," *Annual Review of Anthropology,* **14**:529–555, 1985.

Taylor, R. E., L. A. Payen, C. A. Prior et al. "Major Revisions in the Pleistocene Age Assignments for North American Human Skeletons by C-14 Accelerator Mass Spectrometry: None Older than 11,000 C-14 Years B.P.," *American Antiquity,* **50**(1):136–139, 1985.

Introduction

The preceding chapter highlighted the major trends in Old World prehistory for the post-Pleistocene era. In this chapter, we shall consider the somewhat parallel developments in the New World that occurred during approximately the same time span. The first problem we must deal with, however, is the matter of human arrival in the Western Hemisphere. Since evolution of Old World anthropoids took place only in Africa and Eurasia, the anatomically modern humans who occupied the Americas before the coming of the Europeans were clearly immigrants themselves. Archeologists are actively seeking to determine where and when the first people arrived in the New World.

As was the case in Europe, the inhabitants of the Americas made some major adjustments to rapidly changing environmental conditions in the period following the retreat of continental glaciers. Generally speaking, these cultural responses contributed to a way of life that was based upon a pattern of intensive and mobile foraging for a wide variety of plant and animal foods. In some cases, a reliance upon selected wild resources led to experimentation that altered the natural species. Cultivated crops, and even a handful of animal domesticates, became locally significant in a few areas. Meanwhile, in Mesoamerica and the Andean region, these productive resources served as a primary economic base for several flourishing civilizations after about 5 kya. These complex and highly sophisticated cultures in turn had an impact upon even wider areas of the New World through the diffusion of domesticates, trade, and even invasion.

While there seem to have been some fundamental regularities in the major features of Old and New World development, the distinctions cannot be overlooked. Transoceanic contact appears to have been minimal. The effect of this isolation was a divergence between the populations of the two hemispheres, particularly in the cultural dimension. With the recombination of Old and New World peoples that took place during the age of exploration, the long isolation came to an end; so, very nearly, did the New World societies themselves.

Old World Origins of New World Peoples

Scientists generally agree that the original New World population was drawn from northeastern Asia. But questions such as "How long ago?" and "What kind of people were they?" are still being debated. Was there more than one migration? What kinds of cultural equipment did the newcomers bring with them? Unfortunately, there is very little archeological material or undisputed skeletal evidence with which to document the earliest arrival of people in the New World.

The spread of people into the Western Hemisphere represents a rapid and most significant expansion of the range of an Old World species. Aided by improved technology, and perhaps prodded by a growing population, *Homo sapiens* had reached the farthest limits of Eurasia by the late Pleistocene or Ice Age period. By some 30 kya, Siberia and the northeast Asian mainland were home to

Homo sapiens of a primary and generalized "Caucasoid type," having long heads and short but slender body builds (Birdsell, 1981), and a set of distinctive dental features including shovel-shaped incisors (Turner, 1984). Generalities regarding human variation must, given the nature of genetic recombination, be taken simply as that—"generalities" (see Chapter 3). Moreover, there are, of course, really no "types" of human beings in the sense once used by traditional classifiers of race (see Chapter 5).

The cultural adaptation of these people focused upon the hunting of large herbivores with stone- and bone-tipped weapons and probably also with the aid of domesticated dogs. Their use of fire, tailored skin clothing, and shelters made from the hides of butchered animals contributed to their survival in these bleak northern regions (Klein, 1969). Culturally, and probably genetically, these north Asian people comprised the ancestral stock of the American Indians.

During the latest period of continental glaciation, known as the **Wisconsin** stage by New World geologists, massive ice sheets blanketed much of the higher latitudes. For periods of thousands of years at a time, northeastern Asia and Alaska remained linked by a "land bridge" (Hopkins, 1982). This connection was in reality the dry floor of the shallow Bering Sea, exposed while water locked in the glacial ice reduced worldwide sea levels by as much as 100 m (330 ft) during maximum glaciation. At these times, **Beringia**, as it is known, comprised a broad plain up to 2000 km (1300 mi) wide from north to south. Ironically, its

WISCONSIN
The period of the last major glacial advance in North America; analogous to Weichsel in the Old World.

BERINGIA
(bare-in'-jya)
The dry-land connection between Asia and America that existed periodically during the Ice Age.

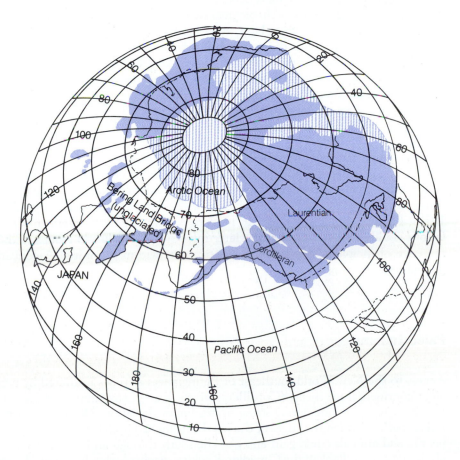

Figure 17-1
Cordilleran and Laurentian ice sheets during the late Pleistocene, about 18 kya. (Adapted from David M. Hopkins, "Landscape and Climate of Beringia during Late Pleistocene and Holocene Time," in The First Americans: Origins, Affinities, and Adaptations, *William S. Laughlin and Albert B. Harper (eds.), figure 1.2, New York: Gustav Fischer, 1979. Copyright © The Wenner-Gren Foundation for Anthropological Research, Inc.)*

cold, dry Arctic climate kept Beringia itself an ice-free refuge, an area of low relief covered with vegetation of mosses, lichens, and sedges. Despite its treeless and barren appearance, Beringia's steppes and tundra supported at least some herds of grazing animals, as well as the hunters who preyed on them. It was, in fact, pretty much an extension of the familiar landscape of Asia. Moreover, Beringia's south coastal margin was a rich marine environment (Fladmark, 1986).

It is not really surprising, then, that one or more groups of people might have ventured well across Beringia during the millennia when it bridged the continents. Perhaps they followed game, or maybe they purposefully sought new hunting grounds. No matter what brought them here, they became the first Americans.

Geologists have determined that, except for short spans, the passage was dry land between 23 kya and 13 kya, and for other extended periods even before that time. The New World received its first human inhabitants during one of these episodes. Precise dating of this entry is especially significant, but it remains one of the nagging unsolved problems of American prehistory. If, as a few suggest, the date was much before about 35 kya, we would have to conclude that the first Americans were either of an archaic physical type (such as Neandertal) or else were among the earliest anatomically modern humans found beyond Africa or southwest Asia. Up to now, no skeletal remains have been accepted in support of this position. Conceivably, the descendants of the initial arrivals may have died out during later stages of the Pleistocene, leaving few skeletons and no surviving progeny. In that case, most archeological sites and all of the more recent Amerind peoples would derive from later, fully modern *Homo sapiens sapiens* immigrants. In any event, with the exception of Eskimo-Aleuts and Athabaskans, who migrated separately, the American natives generally share a number of distinctive physical traits that seem to indicate one small founding population.

The "founder effect" would explain the high incidence of shovel-shaped incisors and a score of other dental diagnostics (Turner, 1987), presence of rare blood types in relatively high frequencies, and absence of blood groups A^2, B, D, and r among Amerinds. This mosaic of traits reflects the limited variability of the small founding gene pool. On the other hand, some observable variation among modern native American populations in body build, skin color, and the like may be credited to more recent genetic drift or microevolution due to natural selection pressures affecting isolated populations within local environments (Spuhler, 1979). Physical similarities shared by modern Asian and native American populations could be the result of either later infusions of Old World groups or the presence of incipient "Mongoloid" genetic traits within the initial American population.

Paleo-Indians

Access to the New World southeast of Beringia was at times restricted by two great continental ice sheets (**Cordilleran** to the west, **Laurentian** to the east), which coalesced as one during stages of maximum glaciation. However, during milder periods, when the edges of the ice sheets melted back from one another, people and animals could gain entry to the south through an ice-free corridor along the eastern flank of the Canadian Rockies. Archeologists have found very

Figure 17-2
North American archeological sites mentioned in the text.

few sites that they can confidently attribute to the earliest Americans. Many ancient camp locations undoubtedly were inundated when rising seas once more submerged Beringia at the end of the Pleistocene. In other areas, silt and gravels borne by glacial meltwaters must have deeply buried the sites.

Evidence of people in the New World prior to about 12 kya is very controversial (see this chapter's Issue). Crudely flaked flints and weathered bone recovered from surface locations and other undatable contexts are regarded with justifiable caution by most scientists. But archeologists generally acknowledge a great many sites formed after about 12 kya. These components are well dated and contain recognizable tools. The latter most often consist of bifacially flaked projectile points, scrapers, and knives, many of which apparently were used in securing and processing large game animals. The wide distribution of very similar sites throughout North America and into Central and South America suggests that early Americans made a rapid cultural adaptation to the varied environments of the New World during the late Pleistocene.

Specialists refer to this era of mobile hunters and gatherers with a big-game orientation as the Paleo-Indian period. Evidence of their way of life comes from widely scattered sites, including many in the western United States. The most spectacular of these sites are kill locations, where large herbivores, such as mammoth and giant bison, were hunted and butchered. Here, stone artifacts often are found in association with the massed bones of these huge animals. But the dramatic nature of such sites should not lead us to overemphasize this big-game hunting aspect of Paleo-Indian life and economy. The same people exploited a diverse range of plants and animal foods within their environments. Still, their association with the preserved bones of the large herbivores is undeniable. At most of these sites, butchered remains are accompanied by distinctive and finely flaked **fluted** projectile points of **lanceolate** shape. Each face typically displays a groove (or flute) that represents the removal of a channel flake to facilitate the special hafting technique.

Figure 17-3
Paleo-Indian mammoth-butchering spot, Colby site, Wyoming.

Figure 17-4
Major types of North American Paleo-Indian projectile points: (a) Clovis, (b) Folsom, (c) Plano, (d) Dalton.

(a)   (b)   (c)   (d)

On the basis of tool technology, chronology, and the primary prey species of each Paleo group, archeologists conclude that the period between about 12 kya and 11 kya was a time of hunters who employed **Clovis** type fluted points. At many sites in the West, these points are associated with mammoth remains. Although there has been less in the way of preserved animal bone found at sites in eastern North America, the same style of projectile point was in use in that area at about the same time. At the Vail site in northern Maine, Clovis points were recovered in numbers from a caribou-hunting camp (Gramly, 1982), and in eastern Pennsylvania a mixed subsistence of smaller game and plant products supplied the Paleo-Indians at the Shawnee-Minisink site (McNett, 1985). Evidently, the Paleo-Indians' adaptation was flexible enough to accommodate the climatic and geographic diversity encountered throughout North America near the end of the Pleistocene.

The mammoth hunters who used Clovis points were succeeded in the West by people who concentrated their efforts on herds of giant long-horned bison. Around 10 kya, some of these hunters in the Southwest adopted another style of fluted point, called **Folsom**. These specialized weapons, however, were soon replaced by unfluted but finely parallel-flaked lanceolate projectile heads of the **Plano** type, which came into wide use throughout the West just as the ancient Pleistocene bison was being supplanted by its smaller cousin, the modern-day *Bison bison occidentalis*.

A number of sites on the Great Plains demonstrate that the natives' favorite technique of hunting bison was to stampede them into arroyos or over cliffs, then to quickly dispatch those that survived the fall (Wheat, 1972; Frison, 1978). Remember, the domesticated horse had not yet been introduced onto the Plains, so these early hunters were strictly pedestrians. In the East, the later Paleo-Indians employed different types of projectile points, such as the Dalton variety, but poor bone preservation again leaves us with little information about their hunting techniques or favored prey.

CLOVIS
Phase of North American prehistory, 12 kya to 11 kya in the West, during which short-fluted projectile points were used in hunting mammoths.

FOLSOM
Phase of southern Great Plains prehistory, 10 kya to 8 kya, during which long-fluted projectile points were used for bison hunting.

PLANO
Great Plains bison-hunting culture of 8 kya to 7 kya, which employed narrow unfluted points.

Figure 17-5
Clovis fluted point with reconstructed mounting. (Courtesy, Royal Ontario Museum, Toronto.)

Figure 17-6
Molar teeth of mammoth (left) and mastodon (right). Mammoth grazed on low vegetation; mastodon browsed on evergreen branches. The New World's earliest hunters preyed on both animals and may have contributed to their extinction.

Figure 17-7
Giant Pleistocene bison. Width of horn cores is 83 cm.

Circumstantial evidence like that found mainly in the West has led some researchers to ponder the question of human involvement in the extinction of major North American Pleistocene fauna, including the mammoth, mastodon, giant bison, horse, camel, ground sloth, and many others. Paul S. Martin (1967, 1982) is fervent in his assertion that the overhunting of these animals by Paleo-Indians resulted in their rapid extermination throughout the New World about 11 kya. But the issue is complicated by the fact that some of the species may have been extinct by the time humans came to the New World. Others, like the gigantic ground sloth of the southwestern United States, seem not to have been hunted at all. Biologists point out that species extinction is an ongoing phenomenon that can result even today from a variety or even a combination of circumstances, ranging from climate change to human involvement. The matter of the human role in New World extinctions remains unresolved.

Distinctive Paleo-Indian artifacts appear through Central America and all the way along western South America to Tierra del Fuego (southern tip of Argentina) by 11 kya. The South American hunters concentrated their efforts along the Pacific slopes of the Andes, where horses and sloths comprised an important part of the diet, along with deer, camelids, and undoubtedly a wide variety of tuberous plants. An important part of Paleo-Indian adaptation to the Andean region may have been the seasonal utilization of varied resource zones in that mountainous environment (Lynch, 1983).

Just how advanced might these early societies have been? Recent excavations at Monte Verde in southern Chile have revealed a unique and surprising site of apparent Paleo-Indian age (Dillehay, 1984). Remnants of the wooden foundations of a dozen rectangular huts were arranged back to back in a parallel row. The structures measured between 3 m and 4.5 m on a side, and their sapling frameworks were once draped with hides. Apart from the main cluster a separate "wishbone" shaped building contained distinctive stone tools and faunal remains. Numerous spheroids (possibly sling stones), a wooden lance, digging sticks, mortars, fire pits, mastodon and camelid bones, along with nuts, fruits, berries, wild tubers, and firewood testify to subsistence activities. Dillehay believes this site to have been a "planned settlement that was integrated both spatially and functionally," to a degree unsuspected up to now for other contemporary sites in the Americas. If the age of Monte Verde is substantiated, the insights it offers will be widely applied and should lead to a fuller appreciation of Paleo-Indian lifeways.

New World Hunters and Gatherers

As in the Old World, in both North and South America, the end of the Pleistocene or Ice Age some 10 kya was accompanied by major changes in climate, landscape, flora, and fauna. The great continental ice sheets left behind thick mantles of pulverized rock and till. This debris subsequently was sorted by wind and by streams that flowed in newly defined drainage systems. Midlatitude coastlines were drowned by rising sea levels, while the land in some northern areas rebounded once the earth's crust was no longer compressed by the tremendous weight of the glacial mass. As deglaciation proceeded, the major biotic zones expanded northward, so that areas once covered by ice were clothed successively in tundra, grassland, fir and spruce forests, pine and mixed deciduous forests—each with its distinctive complement of fauna (Bryson et al., 1970). The annual mean summer temperatures continued to climb until local climatic maxima were reached between 6 kya and 8 kya in many areas. Lakes that had formed during the Ice Age with increased precipitation in nonglaciated areas of the American West evaporated under modern arid conditions.

The changes associated with the end of the Pleistocene occurred slowly over many human generations, but their impact was cumulative. Cultures responded by making major adjustments in their ways of coping with the environment. For example, the disappearance of so many Pleistocene herbivores required people to devise new subsistence strategies. In general, the period following the Pleistocene seems to be characterized by the intensified hunting and gathering of a wider spectrum of natural resources. American archeologists refer to this time as the **Archaic** period. It is approximately equivalent to the Mesolithic stage in the Old World. Here, as there, people utilized a greater variety of plant species and both large and small animal species, including significant amounts of fish and shellfish where available. To make possible the effective exploitation of these food sources, hunters and gatherers developed a number of new technologies involving composite weapons (such as harpoons, the spear, and the throwing board, or **atlatl**), fishing gear, traps and snares, baskets and other containers, canoes, and many more as well.

ARCHAIC
Cultural stage of hunting and gathering after the end of the Wisconsin ice age; equivalent to "Mesolithic" in the Old World.

ATLATL
A throwing board, or spearthrower.

Figure 17-8
Use of the atlatl, or spearthrower, with a stone weight for balance.

Figure 17-9
Yahgan hunter of Cape Horn, South America, late nineteenth century.

In most areas of the New World, hunter and gatherer bands adapted with remarkable precision to their local environments and resources. Most groups scheduled seasonal movements through the diverse ecological zones of their regions. This transhumance, or seasonal migration, was linked to the availability of resources at different locations during successive seasons of the year. Culturally, and even biologically, societies of Archaic hunters and gatherers became more diversified and distinctive from one another as they adjusted to conditions within their own territories. Despite some common themes, the Archaic period is a time of increasing regional variation.

As we shall see shortly, this tradition of intensive foraging led in some cases to the domestication of selected plant species and the subsequent development of New World farming cultures. But for most of the native societies in the Americas, hunting and gathering remained the standard subsistence approach for thousands of years. In a few areas where they were not eventually replaced by horticulturalists (as in regions of too little water or too few frost-free days to promote crop development), hunters and gatherers persisted down to modern times.

The **Great Basin** of the American West, now a largely dry expanse between the Rockies and the Sierra Nevada mountains, was home to hunters and gatherers for at least 10,000 years. Evidence of their way of life has been preserved in dry caves and rock-shelters in the vicinity of the Great Salt Lake (Jennings, 1957; Heizer and Napton, 1970; Aikens, 1970). Excavations at Danger, Lovelock, and Hogup caves in Nevada and Utah have produced thousands of preserved weapons, milling stones, baskets, nets, fur-cloth blanket fragments, sandals and moccasins, bone tools, gaming items, animal bones, and even coprolites, or dried human feces. The latter often contain seeds, insect exoskeletons, and often the bones of fish, small rodents, and amphibians, which provide direct dietary evidence (Bryant and Williams-Dean, 1975). Although large game animals were hunted whenever possible, it was the seasonal variety of seed-bearing plants and small animals, such as jackrabbits and waterfowl, that provided the greatest proportion of food for these hunters and gatherers.

Some coastal tribes of the northwestern United States and Canada exploited a combination of unusually rich and diverse resources through their elaborate redistribution system (known in historic times as the **potlatch**), which enabled the **Kwakiutl**, Haida, and others to prosper without domesticated crops (Piddocke, 1965). In the eastern United States, major river valleys, such as the Mississippi, Tennessee, and Savannah, provided ample resources to permit hunters and gatherers in those regions to establish fairly complex societies without relying upon the products of agriculture. Nuts of many kinds provided an important staple for the forest groups. Acorn, chestnut, black walnut, butternut, hickory, and beechnut represent high quality and palatable foods. Some nuts were prepared by parching or roasting, others by crushing and boiling into soups; leaching neutralized the toxic tannic acids in acorns. Intensive and efficient exploitation of these edible nuts, deer, shellfish, forest, and riverine products (Caldwell, 1962), and the participation in regional exchange networks (Ford, 1974), enabled these Southeastern Archaic societies to develop a degree of social organization, religious ceremonialism, and economic interdependence not usually observed among nonfarming peoples.

Evidence of this sophistication is demonstrated by long-term residence at selected sites dating between 2 kya and 6 kya. These include the Eva hunting, gathering, and fishing site on the Tennessee River (Lewis and Lewis, 1961), which probably was permanently occupied for generations. More than a thousand burials at Indian Knoll, Kentucky (Webb, 1946), many accompanied by tools and other grave goods, also testify to a successful long-term residence. And an impressive 3200-year-old complex of concentric earthwork mounds at Poverty Point, Louisiana (Ford and Webb, 1956), hints at Archaic social organization and ritualism. As these examples signify, food production was not a necessary prerequisite for a satisfactory existence.

Development of Agriculture in the New World

In both the Old and New Worlds, the initial steps toward a way of life that was based upon food production rather than hunting and gathering were taken by about 9 kya. There is little question today that these trends toward domestication occurred independently in the two hemispheres. Nevertheless, although different domesticates were involved, the process appears to have been broadly similar in both cases.

We considered the transition from food collecting to food production in the preceding chapter, emphasizing Old World examples. While that general consideration applies as well to the New World, there are some specific additional points worth noting. In contrast to the situation in the Old World, for example, the number of animal species brought under domestication in the Americas was minor, as was their economic importance outside a few areas. It is also apparent that domesticated plant resources in this hemisphere underwent longer periods of selection and evolutionary change, most likely as a result of human interference. Thus, it is more difficult to determine the precise ancestry of major New World domesticates. Nor did the products of agriculture so quickly replace wild produce as the primary components of the prehistoric American diet. The social consequences of farming, including the rise of complex urbanized societies, were not so immediately and dramatically obvious as in the Old World, either.

The best archeological data on the transition to food production in the New World come once more from arid regions, not unlike the Near East setting, in which we encountered Old World agriculture. It is fair to raise the question, Did the first steps to farming really take place in such situations, or do deserts themselves merely provide a better environment for preservation? As we shall see, some of the primary New World domesticates derived from species native to such areas, but still others were introduced from more humid tropical environments. Thus, in general, the developed Neolithic phase in the New World represents a

GREAT BASIN
Rugged, dry plateau between the mountains of California and Utah, comprising Nevada, western Utah, and southern Oregon and Idaho.

POTLATCH
Ceremonial feasting and gift-giving among the Northwest Coast Indians.

KWAKIUTL
(quah-cue'-tul)
Northwest Coast Indian tribe.

mosaic of plants brought together to meet many specific requirements: nutrition, palatability, hardiness, yield, processing, storage.

Since our clearest view of the domestication process in the Americas is revealed in the dry highlands of Mexico and western South America, we must give these regions our primary attention. In such areas, naturally occurring food resources were sparse and widely scattered. To take optimal advantage of them, a hunter and gatherer band required a large territory. The foragers planned their yearly movements throughout the varied biotic zones of their territory so as to best exploit the most productive, nutritious, or reliable products at the appropriate seasons. Thus, each band devised a well-defined set of subsistence strategies in order to cope with its own local environment.

From here, there is disagreement about the exact route to domestication. The first view holds domestication to be the natural consequence of intensive foraging activities in a marginal environment (Flannery, 1968, 1973). Their exploitation of specific productive localities (or microenvironments) within their overall territory led hunters and gatherers to an increasing reliance upon selected plant resources, especially those preferred because of their concentrated growth pattern, ease of harvest, greater productivity, or food value. People sometimes sought to make more intensive and efficient use of these resources through the development of new foraging strategies, new technological equipment, or even through tampering with the plants themselves. Intensive human interaction with these plants readily could have favored significant genetic alterations in some species. Whenever more desirable traits might have resulted, people could be expected to respond to these "improvements" by quickly adapting their collecting behavior to take fullest advantage. As they intensified their focus on such species as maize or runner beans, the foragers eventually abandoned the rhythm of their traditional food-collecting schedule and committed themselves to further increasing the productivity of the chosen plant foods through horticulture.

An alternative explanation explored at length (Cohen, 1977) is that plant domestication was an outgrowth of human overpopulation. Since population growth reached critical levels more quickly in marginal environments, it was here that domesticated plants first developed. In a conscious effort to encourage certain "weedy" plants that had been used customarily as secondary or even emergency food sources, people began to propagate maize, beans, and others. As one researcher (Yudkin, 1969) notes, given their choice people everywhere generally prefer fruit and meat, but will turn to root crops and grain when more desirable foods are in short supply. Yet, these low-priority foods share some important qualities as potential domesticates: (1) they grow in disturbed ground; (2) do well in dense concentrations; (3) respond to human manipulation and selection; and (4) are storable forms of protein or carbohydrate (Flannery, 1973). From this viewpoint, horticulture may be seen as an adaptation of a growing population to the natural poverty of its environment.

In either case, the role of wild plants eventually declined, while an increased interdependence, or symbiotic relationship, developed between the horticulturalists and their crops. In this partnership, humans obtained food, while the plant species were nurtured, genetically "improved," and often given an extended range by having their seeds traded, transported, or dispersed in feces. One consequence of food production is that it may support a larger number of people within a given territory. That is, population density and overall numbers may increase without the need to exploit a larger area. Stated another way, if the natural food supply is no longer adequate to feed its numbers, a society must maintain itself either by extending its **catchment area** or by turning to a more intensive use of its environment.

Initial domestication of plants in the Americas did not take place within one restricted locale, nor did it occur at the same time in scattered locations. Native peoples of many regions engaged in incipient domestication activities involving local plant resources that were essential to their foodways. Most species retained only local significance: seed-bearing marshelder, **amaranths**, and **chenopods** in the eastern United States and the breadnut (*ramón*) in **Mesoamerica** are examples of locally important **cultivars**. These and many other selected plants never attained full domestication, but hunters and gatherers encouraged them by collecting and propagating their seeds or by reducing species competition through selective weeding and burning. Such steps promoted abundance and growth, but did not necessarily involve the kind of permanent genetic changes associated with domestication.

Of the more than 100 New World plant species fully domesticated by the Amerinds, maize (a grass), beans (legumes), and squashes (curcurbits) were among those of widest significance in prehistoric America. Early stages in the development of these important foods are most thoroughly documented in parts of highland Mexico. Sites pertaining to the history of maize, beans, and squash in the millennia after 9 kya have been encountered in the states of **Oaxaca** and **Tamaulipas**, and especially in the **Tehuacán Valley** southeast of Mexico City. Archeologist Richard MacNeish led an exemplary interdisciplinary research effort to this arid highland valley in the 1960s, where archeology, botany, and paleoecology have shed much light on early agriculture in the New World (MacNeish, 1964, 1978).

Researchers acknowledge that the local microenvironments—valley floor, canyons, limestone slopes, and cactus forests—initially provided small bands of human foragers with scattered and seasonally varied seeds, fruits, and game. Some of the Tehuacán food collectors may have begun experimenting with certain of their plant resources, including wild maize, or the grass *teosinte*, in order to encourage a higher level of productivity. These methods could have involved eliminating competition by "weeding," transplanting young stalks to more favorable locations, scattering seeds, or even altering the genetic makeup of some plants by cross-pollinating them with other varieties. Such manipulation produced new traits appreciated by humans. Further such "artificial" selection brought about permanent genetic changes and created the first in a series of domesticated forms of maize, a **cultigen** having much larger, more numerous, and more easily processed kernels. Today's many varieties of maize or corn make it one of the world's primary staples.

Other plants probably were coming under cultivation around the same time throughout highland Mexico, including several varieties of beans and squash, gourds, chili peppers, avocados, and cactus fruit (Schoenwetter, 1974; Flannery, 1986). Several of these—squash, gourds, and chilies—were perhaps introduced from the lowlands. We should note that agricultural products in the Tehuacán Valley still contributed less than one-third of the diet before about 4300 y.a. (MacNeish, 1964). Until then, people were reluctant to fully commit themselves to farming, and continued to move about and collect many wild foods. In time, though, the demands of caring for valuable gardens and meeting the needs

CATCHMENT AREA
Zone within which a group exploits its resources.

AMARANTH
(am'-ar-anth)

CHENOPOD
(keen'-o-pod)

MESOAMERICA
meso: middle
The region from southern Mexico through Panama.

CULTIVAR
A wild plant encouraged by humans.

OAXACA
(wah-ha'-kah)

TAMAULIPAS
(tah-mah-leep'-ahs)

TEHUACÁN VALLEY
(tay-wah-kahn')
A dry highland region on the boundary of the states of Puebla and Oaxaca in southern Mexico.

CULTIGEN
A plant that is wholly dependent on humans; a domesticate.

Figure 17-10
Development and use of prehistoric maize in the Tehuacán Valley, Mexico. (Adapted from Richard S. MacNeish, The Science of Archaeology?, figure 5.10, North Scituate, MA: Duxbury Press, 1978.)

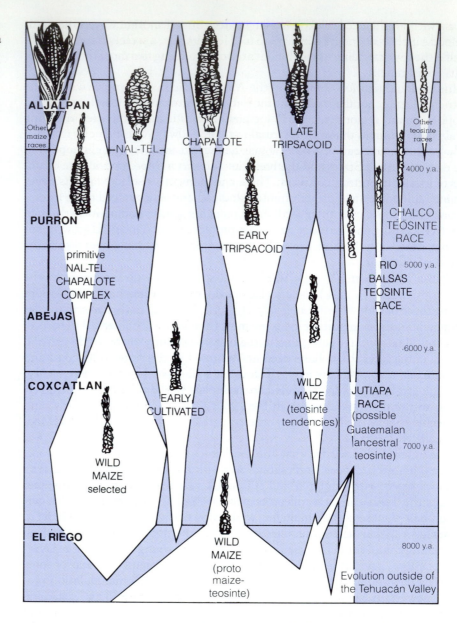

of a growing population forced the issue. Soon the Tehuacán Valley was divided into permanent villages and fields.

Even as the ancient Mexicans were experimenting with maize and slowly adding other domesticates to their subsistence economy, people in the Andean highlands of western South America likewise were cultivating species such as beans and chilies by between 10,500 and 9000 y.a. (Lynch, 1980, 1983). These foods added essential proteins and vitamins to the local diet of starchy roots and tubers. The reported presence of maize in South America by as early as 8 kya (Stothert, 1985) is more surprising and, if verified, would require a reevaluation of the presumed Mexican origin of the grain. There is less question of its widespread appearance through highland South America. from Ecuador to Argentina, at least after about 5 kya (Lynch, 1983). Vessel decorations and even the impression of a kernel on a clay pot in Ecuador (Zevallos et al., 1977), as well as an increase in grinding stones and human dental caries, offer indirect evidence of the presence of maize. The probability of exchange of cultigens between the Americas is being pursued, but so far there is no substantial evidence bearing upon this question.

Wherever maize was used, its storability and nutritional value assured its popularity. Additional cultigens of importance in South America derived both from the uplands and Amazon basin. Examples include the white potato, sweet potato, manioc or cassava, lima beans, peanuts, and **quinoa**.

Tracing the ancestry and spread of perishable plant products involves challenging research. After all, most vegetables produce no durable remains; unconsumed grain or seeds usually sprout or rot. Dry environments, such as the southwestern United States, offer some of the best opportunities for study. Maize, beans, and squash seeds as old as 3000 years are preserved on Archaic sites in New Mexico (Simmons, 1986). These plants ultimately derived from central Mexican domestication centers, including Tehuacán.

In turning to farming, Southwest hunters and gatherers at first probably reaped no significant increase in *productivity*, yet may have benefitted from greater *predictability*, with their domesticated crops aiding them in minimizing environmental and seasonal variability (Wills, 1988). The new species were fostered by small-scale horticultural efforts and added to the wild food diet. Nutritionists now recognize that maize and beans contain complementary amino acids, which, when consumed together, form a "complete" protein that can be synthesized by the human body. Squash and similar vegetables add other essentials to a reasonable diet.

Population growth and development of settled village life were long-run consequences in centuries to follow, as farming gained precedence over hunting and gathering in the American Southwest. Between about 2300 y.a. and 1300 y.a., the greater reliance upon domesticated products, increased population density, and a general cultural elaboration resulted in the emergence of several distinctive cultural traditions in the Southwest (Lipe, 1983). These included **Hohokam** (an archeological culture that is probably ancestral to modern Piman-speaking peoples of southern Arizona); **Anasazi** (builders of the largest prehistoric pueblo villages and cliff dwellings and the forerunners of more recent Puebloan peoples); and **Mogollon** (a culture of pit-house dwellers that had dispersed before the arrival of Europeans).

These regional traditions can be distinguished on the basis of their cultural traits, including pottery styles, architecture, religious ideas, and sociopolitical organization. Some Southwestern societies may have been sustained in part by maintaining contact with Mesoamerica. The Casas Grandes district of northern Chihuahua, Mexico, served as a major exchange corridor between Mesoamerica and the Southwest (DiPeso, 1974). Classic-period Hohokam sites of *circa* 1000 y.a. in the vicinity of Phoenix, Arizona, such as Las Colinas and Snaketown, include Mesoamerican-type ball courts and platform mounds, as well as shell jewelry, copper bells, parrot feathers, mirrors, anthropomorphic figurines, irrigation canals, and other artifacts of Mesoamerican style (Haury, 1976).

Anasazi sites are among the most well-known archeological locations in the United States due to their scale, picturesque setting, and often excellent preservation. Many ancient village ruins are protected as popular national parks today.

QUINOA
(keen-oh'-ah)
Seed-bearing member of the genus *Chenopodium*, cultivated by early Peruvians.

HOHOKAM
(ho-ho-kahm')

ANASAZI
(an-ah-saw'-zee)

MOGOLLON
(mo-go-yohn')

Figure 17-11
Village farming cultures of the American Southwest, showing trade routes and major sites.

The cliff dwellings of Mesa Verde, Colorado, and the structures of Chaco Canyon, New Mexico, represent the apex of this prehistoric farming culture. Pueblo Bonito, the primary town in Chaco Canyon, was a five-tiered, D-shaped building of some 800 rooms that housed perhaps 2000 people 750 y.a. With 200,000 wooden beams and rafters, it was the largest building in America until the first skyscraper of the nineteenth century. Chaco served as a marketplace and religious center connected by radiating foot-roads to as many as 80 far-flung villages in an area of 800 square kilometers, or about 300 square miles (Lister and Lister, 1981).

Most societies, including Indians of eastern North America and others living beyond the periphery of the nuclear zone of agricultural development, only gradually abandoned their hunter and gatherer lifeways. Some added to their diets a few cultivars (sunflowers and chenopodium are examples) and perhaps a cultigen, such as squash, selected to complement rather than curtail their foraging (B. Smith, 1985; Wills, 1988). As we have seen, the productive river valleys of the Southeast and the rich forests covering much of the Northeast, as well as the broken prairies of the Midwest, provided adequate returns to support a degree of Archaic cultural elaboration even without maize agriculture.

Indeed, some of the most noteworthy phases of eastern North American prehistory preceded any reliance upon maize. For example, the widespread practice of moundbuilding and associated rituals pertaining to death and burial persisted from Archaic times in this region and culminated about 2300 y.a. in the **Hopewell** Interaction Sphere (Struever, 1964). Well-organized groups throughout the Southeast and midcontinent areas constructed earthen burial mounds of impressive size and participated in exchanges of ritual goods and ideological concepts that found expression in elaborate burials and their exotic furnishings. We have only recently recognized that, while these Indians were not yet growing maize, they may have adopted nonlocal species of squash and were already cultivating a number of indigenous domesticates (such as marshelder, *Iva annua*) by about 3 kya (Conard et al., 1984).

Only after 1000 y.a. in the Southeast and somewhat later in the Northeast, did new varieties of maize and the introduction of domesticated beans make agriculture more practical in those areas. Even then, wild nuts, seeds, fish, and game retained their primary place in the diet of many groups. But in the broad

HOPEWELL
A culture centered in southern Ohio between 2100 and 1700 y.a., but influencing a much wider region through trade and the spread of a religious cult.

Figure 17-12
Anasazi "cliff palace" at Mesa Verde, Colorado, was built by early Southwestern farmers.

Figure 17-13
Plan view of Pueblo Bonito, New Mexico, showing living and storage rooms and round ceremonial chambers.

MISSISSIPPIAN
A Southeastern moundbuilding culture that
flourished from 1100 to 500 y.a.

MANIOC
Cassava; a starchy edible root crop of the
tropics.

OLMEC
Culture in the Gulf Coast lowlands of Veracruz and Tabasco, Mexico, with a highly developed art style and social complexity;
flourished from 3500 to 2500 y.a.

river valleys of the Southeast, maize farming may have stimulated the remarkable cultural expression known as **Mississippian**. Reaching its apex about 800 y.a., the Mississippian was a structured society, probably ruled by powerful chiefs. Its population and ceremonial centers throughout the region were linked by their common focus on construction of impressive flat-topped earthen mounds. These structures, the largest in prehistoric America north of Mexico, served the living as temple and residence platforms, while the elite dead and their elaborate offerings were sometimes interred within.

Among other New World societies, farming had not yet attained much importance even by the time Europeans were arriving with their new way of life and their Old World domesticates. In fact, throughout much of the far West, the far North, and most of South America, hunting and gathering remained the principal way of making a living. What is more, the products of agriculture were not always superior in terms of nutritional value to the mixed diet obtained through foraging. Peoples of the Amazon basin in South America domesticated yams, bitter **manioc**, and other starchy root crops before 1500 y.a. These foods supplied bulk and carbohydrates, but relatively little protein—a deficiency overcome only with continued reliance upon hunting and gathering.

New World Civilizations

In many of the places where farming prevailed, the combination of maize, beans, and plants such as squash came to serve as a suitable substitute for a diet containing animal protein. The major American domesticates formed the nutritional subsistence base for a series of prehistoric New World civilizations. Thus, the story of ancient America's most highly advanced cultures is closely intertwined with the progress of New World agriculture.

In overview, the high cultures of the New World offer an interesting comparison with those of the Old World. They share a great many basic similarities: establishment of state economies based on agriculture and long-distance trade; emergence of powerful leaders and social stratification; investment of organized human labor in large-scale constructions; creation of public art styles; invention of record keeping; role of warfare. Yet there are small but significant points of contrast as well. For example, as previously mentioned, we will find that domesticated animals had relatively little impact in the New World; the technological role of metal was limited; the wheel played no important function, nor did water-

Figure 17-14
An early view of Monks Mound, part of the Cahokia group of Mississippian mounds near East St. Louis, Illinois. Built in late prehistoric times, it is 300 m (1000 ft) long and 30 m (100 ft) high.

Figure 17-15
Mesoamerican archeological sites mentioned in the text.

craft. How might the later history of the New World be written if both (or neither) the Europeans and the Amerinds had the advantage of these inventions?

Lowland Mesoamerica

Archeologists believe that by 4 kya more productive varieties of maize at last made it feasible for people in Mesoamerica to maintain permanent villages close to their fields (Flannery, 1973). One clue used by archeologists to denote this change is the presence of pottery sherds. Mobile foragers had no use for heavy, fragile vessels, but farmers needed them for cooking and storage. The distribution of pottery, then, may be used as a guide to the spread of farming.

By some 3500 y.a., sedentary farming villages spread into the Mesoamerican lowlands. Maize without doubt grew exceptionally well in this environment, and an increased yield might have been responsible for initiating some of the cultural changes we see in the following centuries. Archeologists have long been especially interested in one of these formative cultures found along the southern and eastern Gulf Coast of Mexico. This culture, known as **Olmec**, dates from about 3200 to 2000 y.a. The Olmec anticipated, and may have been the inspiration for, a number of features encountered in later Mesoamerican civilizations. For example, a highly distinctive art style and large-scale ceremonial constructions clearly set the Olmec apart from their neighbors. Later Olmec employed hieroglyphic writing and a calendar that would be adopted by the Maya and others. So far, the stimulus for these developments remains undiscovered.

The two best-known Olmec sites are the important ceremonial centers at San Lorenzo and La Venta (Coe, 1968; Coe and Diehl, 1980). Each site challenges the imagination with its large-scale constructions accomplished without the aid of modern machinery. Alignments of earthen mounds enclose wide courtyards, plazas, and even artificial ponds. Many large-scale features incorporated tons of rock imported from the highlands 100 km (60 mi) away. Within and close to the sites themselves are hundreds of small platforms that once supported homes and workshops. Aside from their ceremonial architecture, the Olmecs produced remarkable monumental sculptures and other distinctive art objects. **Anthropomorphic** forms predominate, including figurines and *bas-reliefs* that combine the features of humans with those of jaguars and caymans (alligator-like reptiles). Most notable are the characteristic Olmec heads, each carved from a massive boulder of basalt weighing as much as 18 tons. Olmec art and iconography are fascinating but poorly understood. What did these monstrous figures represent? Why did the Olmec intentionally bury caches of beads, figurines, and implements of their highly valued jade? One offering at La Venta consisted of an assemblage of small jade figures set into position so that all confronted one individual. Then, still in position, the group had been buried.

Just as inexplicably, San Lorenzo's demise, about 2850 y.a., is indicated by the startling destruction of most of its artwork and architecture. Although there is some evidence of outside interference at this time, the Olmec apparently inflicted the damage themselves, perhaps to save their gods from dishonor (Weaver, 1981), or to mark the passing of some esteemed leader (Grove, 1984). Olmec culture persisted at La Venta down to about 2550 y.a. Its latest phase is represented by the little-known site of Tres Zapotes, where a carved calendar stone yielded a date equivalent to 31 B.C. (Coe, 1977).

Olmec influence extended east through Guatemala and west as far as central Mexico, where carvings and paintings in the familiar Olmec style appear in graves, caves, and open sites. Although scholars have invoked models of empire and conquest to explain it, the Olmec presence in these areas is most likely the result of trade. Their own culture required quantities of raw materials such as basalt, obsidian, and jade, available only in the adjacent highlands. In ex-

Figure 17-16
Olmec head being excavated at San Lorenzo, Mexico.

Figure 17-17
Buried cache of Olmec jade figurines found at La Venta, Mexico.

change, Olmec artists and craftsworkers supplied clay figurines, ceramic vessels, stone masks and sculptures, and many other items, especially those of ritual nature, to neighboring peoples (Stocker et al., 1980). These interchanges may have stimulated the further growth of regional sociopolitical units that already were verging on civilization.

One of these emergent societies was the **Maya**. What stirred that small-village farming culture into a civilization has been long debated. It is probable that the stimulation came in part from the Olmec, whose art and architecture are recalled in early Maya sites (Coe, 1980). But it is as likely that Maya civilization resulted from an internal reorganization of Maya society itself. Most areas occupied by Preclassic Maya, notably the scrublands of Yucatan and the Peten jungles farther south, were incapable of supporting an ever-increasing population that relied solely upon simple slash-and-burn farming. Moreover, some essential materials, among them suitable stone for making tools and milling slabs, were lacking altogether in this region. To increase their food supply and to obtain important products, the Maya resorted to more intensive farming techniques. They set up redistribution networks among their communities and they opened trade with more distant societies. But establishing and maintaining the new agricultural system and commercial connections could be accomplished only under the authority and oversight of a strong leadership. Thus, the transformation from small-scale villages to a more integrated and centralized society seems to have begun as an adaptive strategy for supporting a growing population in an area of scarce resources (Carneiro, 1970; Rathje, 1971; Adams, 1977).

By some 1800 y.a., after centuries of development, the elements of Maya civilization were coming into place. Control of waterways or trade routes promoted the early growth of sites, such as El Mirador, **Uaxactún**, and **Tikal** in northern Guatemala, and contributed to the emergence of an elite social class. Powerful rulers, claiming descent through royal lineages back to the gods them-

MAYA
Prehistoric Mesoamerican culture that represented the climax of pre-European cultural development between 1700 and 1100 y.a.

UAXACTÚN
(wash-akh-toon')

TIKAL
(tee-kal')

Figure 17-18
View of ceremonial center complex, Tikal, Guatemala.

How to Count Like the Maya

The Maya number system was closely linked to their elaborate calendar, which was comprised of 20-day months. The numbers from 1 to 19 were represented by a simple bar-and-dot notation, wherein a dot equalled 1 and a bar had a value of 5. Note the use of the 0, a device not recognized in Europe until the Middle Ages.

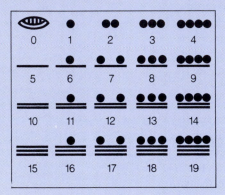

Numbers larger than 19 may be expressed as multiples of 20. The value of the number was determined by its position in a vertical column (much as the value of our numbers is indicated by their position relative to a decimal point). Thus, numbers in the first-place (lowest) position were multiplied by 1; those in the next higher position by 20; in the third, by 400 (that is, 20 × 20); in the fourth by 8000 (20 × 400), etc. The number for 1992 may be written as follows:

selves, held sway over modest regional kingdoms or city-states. Writing, fine arts, and architecture flourished in the Maya lowlands. For six centuries, from 300 to 900 A.D. (1700 to 1100 y.a.), the Maya experienced their own golden age, or Classic Period (Henderson, 1981; Hammond, 1982).

The Maya are best known for their impressive ceremonial centers: Tikal, Copán (Honduras), and Palenque (Mexico) among them. Archeologists historically have devoted much of their attention to these most spectacular sites. But their importance can be overemphasized. The more holistic approach of modern anthropological archeology demands a fuller understanding of Maya culture than might be derived from their monumental constructions alone.

We should recognize that the Maya remained fundamentally agrarian, or farming-based. Most of the population lived in rural hamlets clustered within sight of a ceremonial center. As archeologists have focused more attention on individual households and villages, they have been forced to re-examine the issue of Maya subsistence. Estimates of overall Maya population in the lowlands during the late Classic period have ranged widely, but it may have been about three million (Coe et al., 1986). As many as 15,000 people could have been associated with the medium-sized center of Uaxactún (Adams, 1977). Most of this number resided in small hamlets outside the central core itself. Their house platforms appear throughout the nearby jungle, wherever maize might have been grown by the slash-and-burn, or **milpa**, technique. According to one estimate (U. Cowgill, 1962), shifting cultivation in this region could provide for up to 200 people per square mile (2.6 km^2). We now recognize the Maya employed more intensive farming techniques as well: raised and ridged fields in swampy zones; hillside terracing; irrigation and drainage canals; fertilizing and multiple-cropping for maximum production (Flannery, 1982). In addition, the Maya diet included possible cultivars such as *ramón* or breadnut, and probably other systematically collected foods (Puleston, 1971).

These approaches sustained the fairly large Maya population without much nucleation in urban settings. Even the largest of the sites did not serve primarily as urban residence areas, although a few did house thousands of people, including the ruling elite and their retainers, craftsworkers and other specialists, and farmers. Local centers, having a couple of carved stela or a small temple maintained by nearby hamlets, were subsidiary to regional centers, which were themselves under the domain of the major centers (such as Tikal) at the top of the hierarchy. Yet, despite their somewhat dispersed constituencies, the major centers did function essentially as cities in that they provided a focus for sociopolitical activity, religious ceremonies, and commerce.

Formal, large-scale architecture dominated the great ceremonial centers. Most obvious were the stepped limestone-sided pyramids capped with their crested temples. Facing the broad stuccoed plazas were multiroomed "palaces," generally a ritual ball court or two, and always a number of elaborately carved monuments. Other features might include graded causeways leading into the complex, and masonry reservoirs for storing runoff from tropical rainfalls. Of smaller scale, but of great interest to archeologists, are the **stelae** or carved stone columns. Scholars have made much progress in interpreting the complex hieroglyphic inscriptions on stelae, temples, and other monuments. They have found that many of the texts proclaim the ancestry and noble deeds of Maya rulers, while others record dates of important events. These inscriptions provide an insight into Classic Maya sociopolitical organization, including the sometimes uneasy relationships among the leading ceremonial centers and rival aristocracies

MILPA
Slash-and-burn or swidden farming.

STELA
(stee'-la) (plural: stelae)
An upright post or stone, often bearing inscriptions.

Figure 17-19
Maya Temple of the Inscriptions, at the site of Palenque, Chiapas, Mexico.

(Proskouriakoff, 1960; Graham, 1976; Marcus, 1976; Schele and Miller, 1986). Detailed studies of the calendrical notations on Maya sculptures provide a precise chronology of major events in lowland Mesoamerica. For example, when the Maya calendar system is correlated with our own, the beginning of the Classic period can be set in the year 292 A.D.

Religion entranced the Maya. Most of their architecture and their art pertained to the worship of perhaps hundreds of major and minor deities. The Maya hierarchy included a priestly caste who carefully observed the stars, predicted the rains, prescribed the rituals, and performed the sacrifices. Most of the priestly lore and learning recorded in the Maya **codices** was lost when the Spanish burned the books during the conquest. The recently discovered sacred cave of **Naj Tunich** in Guatemala reveals new dimensions of Maya religion (Brady and Stone, 1986). Within its dusky chambers archeologists came upon offerings, paintings that graphically depict ritual intercourse and self-mutilation, and the remains of young sacrificial victims.

For two and a half centuries, lowland Maya culture developed at an unabated pace, and ceremonial centers grew larger and more impressive. Then for sixty years, until 593 A.D., construction and expansion stalled dramatically. Most archeologists believe a breakdown in relations with Teotihuacán in highland Mexico was the cause. From the end of this episode to about 790 A.D., Maya civilization at first seemed reinvigorated as it underwent unparalleled population

Figure 17-20
Early drawing of an elaborate Maya stela at Copán, Honduras.

Figure 17-21
Maya hieroglyphics on a stela at Copán, Honduras.

BOX 17-2

The Classic Maya Collapse

The decline of Classic Maya culture rapidly encompassed all of southern lowland Mesoamerica during the course of the ninth century A.D. Everywhere in this region, archeologists have found that Maya artisans no longer turned out polychrome-decorated ceramics, nor did they carve and erect inscribed stelae. In fact, ceremonial center construction ceased altogether, and nearly all were abandoned before long. Maya culture never revived here.

There has been much speculation in accounting for the Maya collapse. Archeologists have sometimes invoked single-cause explanations, among them devastation by hurricanes or earthquakes, extreme climatic fluctuations, insect infestations, epidemic diseases, malnutrition, overpopulation, an unbalanced male/female sex ratio, peasant revolts against the elite, competition and warfare between individual centers, and mass migrations. Other scholars have cited external factors, such as the breakdown of trade relations with the areas that supplied the resource-poor Maya, or invasion by people from highland Mexico.

Archeologists today are convinced that a tangle of ecological and social stresses brought on the rapid demise. To produce enough food for their own growing population and surplus for trade, the Maya had overextended their agricultural capacity by cutting more forest and intensifying their use of farmland through irrigation, multicropping, and perhaps by shortening the critical fallow period when fields are given a rest. Such procedures inevitably led to soil infertility, erosion, grass invasion, and poor harvests. Facing a degraded environment and reduced crop yields in the southern lowlands, the Maya elite demanded more temples to appease the gods, thus further burdening the farmers and provoking an abandonment of the region's centers.

Ecological problems may also have sparked internal conflict and even civil war among the late Classic Maya.

Arthur Demarest's discovery of the first fortified Mayan centers during his summer 1989 fieldwork points to just such a scenario. The strongly built site of Punta de Chimino, Guatemala, was compact and completely protected by water. But the hastily erected walls thrown up around the older nearby site of Dos Pilas apparently failed to fend off an aggressive conqueror known only as Ruler 2. Demarest believes Ruler 2's exploits temporarily brought an area about half the size of Rhode Island under his control and precipitated even more widespread warfare.

While acknowledging that a collapse did occur, archeologists note that its effects were restricted primarily to the southern Maya. Even here, sizable populations of peasants remained in the vicinity of the silent centers. Moreover, some *northern* lowland sites actually expanded and continued to flourish for centuries. New cities, like Mayapán, emerged in late post-Contact times. The character of these sites was profoundly different, their architecture and achievements unspectacular. Recent research portrays these late-period Maya as merchants engaged in an active coastal trade until the Spanish arrival brought their enterprise to an end.

SOURCES:

Culbert, T. Patrick. "The Collapse of Classic Maya Civilization." In *The Collapse of Ancient States and Civilizations*, Norman Yoffee and George Cowgill, eds., pp. 69–101. Tucson: University of Arizona Press, 1988.

———, ed. *The Classic Maya Collapse*. Albuquerque: University of New Mexico Press, 1973.

Sabloff, Jeremy A., and William L. Rathje. "The Rise of a Maya Merchant Class," *Scientific American*, 233(4): 72–82, 1975.

growth and monumental development, but the rapid decline that followed was essentially complete by 909 A.D., the terminal date for the Classic Period. After that, only a modest and much-modified Postclassic Maya culture persisted in northern Yucatan (Friedel and Sabloff, 1984). The remarkable Maya collapse has intrigued scholars for years. Explanations have been offered ranging from theories of peasant revolt, widespread disease or famine, invasion by the militaristic Toltecs from the Valley of Mexico, to others that are marvelously imaginative (for review, see Box 17-2). The most likely scenario involves long-term environmental degradation of the fragile lowland ecology (Culbert, 1988).

Highland Mexico

The Valley of Mexico, in the central highlands, supported large urban centers beginning about 2150 y.a. with the rise of Teotihuacán. Several lakes and springs at the southern end of the valley attracted farmers, and nearby deposits of obsidian fostered stone toolmaking and trade. With its water brought under control through a system of irrigation canals, Teotihuacán experienced rapid growth. Already by 1900 y.a. it had become the paramount urban center in the Americas, and probably the sixth largest city in the world at the time (G. Cowgill, 1974; Millon, 1988).

Teotihuacán bustled with the activity of 200,000 residents, buyers and sellers at the markets, and visitors to its monumental shrines. This city was carefully planned and organized, somewhat in contrast to those of the Maya. Built on a grid pattern with a primary north-south axis, its avenues, plazas, major monuments and homes alike—and even the San Juan River—were aligned with the master plan. The people of Teotihuacán lived in some 2000 large apartment compounds arranged into neighborhoods or **barrios** that denoted occupation or social class, ranging from tradesworkers to merchants, military officers, and foreigners. Civic and religious leaders enjoyed more luxurious facilities in the central district (Millon, 1988). Artisans labored in one or another of some 500 specialized workshops making ceramic vessels, obsidian blades, shell and jade carvings, fabrics, leather goods, and other practical or luxury items.

Imaginative Europeans applied the name "Avenue of the Dead" to the main street extending northward 2.5 km (1.5 mi) to a massive structure they called "Pyramid of the Moon." An even greater "Pyramid of the Sun," its base equal to that of Khufu's pyramid in Egypt, occupied a central position along the same avenue. At the very heart of the city, the "Citadel" was the major temple complex, and the "Great Compound" served as Teotihuacán's central marketplace.

Teotihuacán's influence extended throughout Mexico's great central valley and well beyond. Its fine orange-slipped ceramics, architectural and artistic styles, and other elements appear at contemporary centers, such as Monte Alban

Figure 17-22
Feathered-serpent figure on temple façade, Teotihuacán, Mexico.

in Oaxaca; the Maya site of **Kaminaljuyú** in the Guatemalan highlands; and at Tikal, Uaxactún, and Becán in the Maya lowlands (Adams, 1977). Although trade or military conquest are possibilities, the real nature of these contacts is not yet clear. An enclave of Oaxacans maintained long-term residence at Teotihuacán (Millon, 1988), and at least a few Teotihuacanos were present in some prominent capacity at Tikal during the reign of the Maya ruler Stormy Sky (Culbert, 1985). Certainly it seems that the fortunes of the Maya were somehow linked to Teotihuacán: the Maya Classic period opened as Teotihuacán's expansion began; the Maya's sixty years of stagnation coincided with disrupted relations with the Mexican city; and the pinnacle of Maya achievement came only after the fall of Teotihuacán and the probable dispersal of its population and artisans.

Teotihuacán's brutal demise remains an archeological mystery. After five remarkable centuries, the city's hegemony beyond the Valley of Mexico clearly was waning. Internally, not all was well either. Physical anthropologists have noted common skeletal indicators of nutritional stress and disease, as well as high infant mortality rates. Still, population levels remained stable for another century or so before declining rapidly. Then, just about 1250 y.a., the end came in flame and havoc (Millon, 1988). The entire ceremonial precinct blazed as temples were thrown down and idols smashed. In the frenzy, some of the nobility were seized and dismembered, apparently by their own people. The destruction signalled the end of Teotihuacán as a political and religious power, but the factors that brought about the dissolution of this first large urban center of the New World are not yet understood (Davies, 1983).

Teotihuacán's collapse left highland Mesoamerica devoid of its primary sociopolitical and religious center. Of several smaller communities contending for control of the region, **Tula** eventually emerged as the most powerful. Located on the northern periphery of the Valley of Mexico some 65 km (40 mi) northwest of Teotihuacán, Tula swelled with the arrival of immigrants after the old city's fall (Adams, 1977). By the tenth century A.D. (1050 y.a.), the people known historically as the **Toltecs** had built a city about half the size of Teotihuacán, with several pyramids, a ball court, and central altar.

Although its modest ceremonial center did not rival those built during Classic times, Tula did fulfill its role as the successor to Teotihuacán in another way: For a brief period, the Toltecs guided a commercial and military enterprise that expanded through trade networks, colonization efforts, and possible conquest (Coe, 1977; Davies, 1983).

The Toltecs reached in several directions. We recognize their influence in the presence of copper bells, ball courts, and other exotic goods on Hohokam Pueblo sites in the southwest United States, from which the Toltecs acquired their valued blue turquoise stone. Their association with the late Maya site of **Chichén Itzá** in far-off northern Yucatan is most intriguing. Tula and Chichén Itzá share details of art style as well as strikingly similar ball courts, temple pyramids, and other major public buildings. A cult of militarism and sacrifice to the rain god Tlaloc permeated both sites. Archeologists are still debating the nature of the relationship. Some who once interpreted the evidence as an indication of Toltec domination have now reassessed their opinions to suggest that Mexican and Mayan cultures may have interacted more or less amiably during a period of extensive trade contact between Yucatan and the Valley of Mexico (Weaver, 1981). But others still view the Toltecs as masters of a small empire lording over

BARRIO
District or neighborhood.

KAMINALJUYÚ
(cam-en-awl-hoo'-yoo)

TULA
(too'-la)

TOLTECS
A central Mexican highlands people who created a pre-Aztec empire with its capital at Tula in the Valley of Mexico.

CHICHÉN ITZÁ
(chee-chen' eet-zah')

CENOTE
(sen-o'tay)
A sinkhole or collapsed cavern filled with water.

AZTECS
A militaristic people who dominated the Valley of Mexico and surrounding area at the time of European conquest.

CHINAMPA
(cheen-ahm'-pah)
Aztec garden plots made by dredging muck from the lake bottom and canals.

TENOCHTITLÁN
(tay-nosh-teet-lahn')

Figure 17-23
Toltec serpentine columns and votive figure, Temple of the Warriors, Chichén Itzá, Yucatan, Mexico.

the Maya from their second capital at Chichén Itzá (Coe et al., 1986). Despite research at some of Chichén's more interesting features, including the Sacred **Cenote** or sacrificial pool, no definitive clue to this puzzle has surfaced.

As Toltec power declined around 750 y.a., Chichén Itzá yielded its preeminence to Mayapán, an unspectacular city to the west (Sabloff and Rathje, 1975). Back home in the central highlands, the Toltecs countered internal dissension and pressure on their frontiers before finally abandoning Tula and leaving its temples and palaces in rubble. A prolonged drought that withered many of the farming communities in northern Mexico and the American Southwest brought streams of refugees into the Valley of Mexico, throwing all into chaos. One new group to appear was the Mexica, better known as the **Aztecs**.

Impoverished but ruthlessly ambitious, the Aztecs were eager to temporarily ally themselves with anyone who could further their own interests (Fagan, 1984). Pushed from place to place, they finally were able to take over an easily defended group of small islands near shallow Lake Texcoco's western shore, in the very heart of the Valley of Mexico. With great industry they created causeways, canals, and **chinampas**, rich agricultural plots formed by dredging up muck from the lake bottom. They constructed a great central plaza that included palaces, administrative buildings, and huge twin pyramid-based temples for their gods.

The Aztecs incorporated and built on many of the accomplishments of earlier Mesoamerican cultures. Their calendar, for example, is a modification of that employed by the Maya a thousand years earlier. Aztec religion, with its emphasis on the sun and on war and human sacrifice, seems to be derived from Toltec practices and, ultimately perhaps, from ancient Teotihuacán. Without doubt, the Aztecs also learned a great deal about social and political organization, warfare, and economic enterprise from their predecessors. They recognized an hereditary nobility, including a royal lineage from which emperors were drawn. The commoners, comprising the majority of Aztec society, were organized into about 20 large kin-based groups and worked their own lands, while slaves labored for the nobles.

Through their well-trained military and an aggressive state-sponsored corps of professional merchants, the Aztecs dominated neighboring peoples and otherwise extended their influence well beyond the Valley of Mexico. Tribute in the form of maize, cloth, and slaves flowed into the capital, and many of the war captives seized by the Aztec army were reserved for the periodic bloody sacrifices to the Aztec gods.

Until the arrival of the Spanish, **Tenochtitlán**, the Aztec capital, was a large and lively urban and religious center, the capital of an empire of 10 million souls. With its magnificent public buildings, the houses built on the water, and canoes crowding its canals, the Aztec city reminded the Spanish conquistadors of Venice. One of the soldiers recalled that "so large a market place and so full of people, and so well regulated and arranged, (we) had never beheld before" (Diaz del Castillo, 1956, pp. 218–19). Some of its impressive ruins recently have been excavated beneath the streets of modern Mexico City (Moctezuma, 1984).

Peru

The great Inca Empire encountered by Europeans in the sixteenth century extended over most of highland and coastal South America from Colombia to Argentina and Chile. In many respects this Inca civilization was the culmination

Figure 17-24
Peruvian archeological sites mentioned in the text.

Map labels: COLOMBIA, ECUADOR, PERU, BRAZIL, Chan Chan, Moche, Chavín de Huántar, Cerro Sechín, Kotosh, Las Haldas, Guitarrero Cave, El Paraiso, Pachacamac, Huari, Chilca, Pikimachay, Ayacucho, Cuzco, BOLIVIA, Nazca, Tihuanaco, CHILE

of much that had preceded it. Its foundations were rooted in the earlier prehistory of western South America, especially in Peru, where sociopolitical complexity developed together with an increasing proficiency in food production.

On first view, Peru seems an unlikely region for nurturing agricultural civilizations. Its Pacific shore forms a coastal desert averaging only a few miles in width, a dry fringe of land broken at intervals by deeply entrenched valleys cutting laterally from the Andes to the ocean. The mountains rise abruptly and dramatically behind this narrow coastal plain to create a rugged and snow-capped continental spine extending along the whole Pacific flank of South America. These geographical contrasts figured prominently in Peru's prehistory. Indeed, the dynamic tension between coast and highlands, fishers and farmers, provides a key to understanding the region's past.

In the beginning, the zone between the sea and the mountains served as a primary thoroughfare for the continent's earliest humans and for the late Pleistocene herbivores and edible plants that sustained them. The menagerie of South American fauna hunted by Paleo-Indians ranged from mammoth and mastodon to giant ground sloths, horses, deer, camelids, and even the ostrichlike rhea (Lynch, 1983). Preserved food materials on the early site of Monte Verde, Chile (see p. 537), show that generalized hunters and gatherers quickly adapted to this resource zone by practicing transhumance or carefully scheduled movements between coastal and upland microenvironments where various plants, animals, or seafoods were available at different times of the year.

Even before 5 kya, a few groups modified this Archaic exploitation pattern significantly. For example, at Chilca on Peru's coast a short distance south of Lima, people extended their summer fishing into a year-round reliance on sea mammals, fish, shellfish, turtles, and sea birds. Then, about 4500 y.a., some of these central coast fishing villagers began to grow and weave cotton into nets and cloth. Small-scale agriculture in nearby river valleys also furnished chilies, squash, and beans as supplements to the primarily seafood diet. These additions were indicators of more important changes to come.

Farming was already well underway in a few highland areas even before this time. The complex of crops grown there included some, like lima beans and chili peppers, believed to derive from the tropical forests east of the Andes, and others, including maize, thought to have been introduced *via* Mesoamerica. Native highland crops of importance were starchy tubers, such as oca and potatoes of many varieties (Moseley, 1983).

The relative role of farming *versus* fishing in the development of Peruvian civilization has generated intense discussion (see Moseley, 1975b), since most advanced societies elsewhere were agriculture-based. The scale and complexity of some pre-agricultural coastal sites, such as El Paraiso, which boasts a complex of large masonry constructions arranged around an open square, is surprising (Moseley, 1983). The site of Kotosh in the central Andes represents a highlands counterpart, except that here agriculture was primary (Lumbreras, 1974). Because the few permanent residents could not have built these sites on their own, archeologists believe villagers from a wider area worked together under the direction of a chief to create the combined ceremonial and market centers, early examples of the "corporate construction" projects used so often in Peru (Moseley, 1975a, 1983). Most likely, farmers and fishers alike travelled to one another's centers to exchange products (Coe et al., 1986).

Whether spurred by a growing population or by environmental failure, or both, even coastal peoples wholeheartedly committed themselves to subsistence agriculture after about 3800 y.a. This new emphasis correlates with a population shift out of coastal fishing villages and up into river valleys, such as the Casma, Moche, and Rimac. Here, organized communities excavated irrigation canals into the adjacent desert to bring water to maize and peanut crops. The success of this initial farming period in the lowlands is measured by the terraced brick plazas studded with ceremonial structures and art at sites such as Las Haldas and Cerro Sechín on the plateau between the Casma and Culebra valleys of northern Peru. Skilled specialists created loom-woven fabric of cotton and llama or **alpaca** wool, molded ceramic vessels, and formed small objects from precious metals. The step toward civilization accelerated.

What inspired the collective efforts that produced the civic architecture and defined styles of art? Archeologists believe these developments indicate greater centralization of authority in the hands of civil and/or religious leaders. Under their direction, the public energies were applied to large-scale projects. But pyramids and canals are just the outward signs of underlying social processes. What motivated individuals to participate in these collective enterprises? What considerations guided the leaders, and from where did they derive their persuasive powers? Must military coercion serve as the midwife to civilization? Does religious fervor leaven the rising state? Will a people crawl toward higher social complexity on an empty stomach? In Peru, as elsewhere, archeologists have considered militarism, religion, and control of resources among other motivating forces in the rise of civilizations, but have come to few conclusions (e.g., Haas et al., 1987).

Settlements encountered in a number of Peruvian valleys during the period from 3750 y.a. to 2850 y.a. share some similarities (Moseley, 1975b). Most apparent are the distinctive elements of a common art style represented in their sculpture and architecture. The rendering of rather sinister anthropomorphic figures that combine human characteristics with the features of jaguars, snakes, **raptorial** birds, and mythological beings is one hallmark of the widespread Chavín art style. **Chavín de Huantar**, an impressive ceremonial complex high in the Andes, embodied this iconography in its most classic phase. Raised stone platforms overlooked a sunken courtyard where ceremonies took place in the shadow of the Castillo, an elaborate temple or mausoleum riddled by underground chambers and labyrinthine passageways (Burger, 1984). While Chavín de Huantar itself may have served as a religious retreat or perhaps as the seat of an **oracle**, the Chavín art style was disseminated widely throughout Peru. Its symbolism and artifacts conveyed prestige upon those who were privileged to acquire them. Thus Chavín, much like the Olmec art of Mesoamerica, constituted an agent of cultural unification, at least on a stylistic and ideological level. By about 2100 y.a., the appeal of Chavín had faded somewhat.

The next few centuries saw the founding and somewhat parallel growth of influential urban centers in the Moche Valley on the north coast and the Nazca in the south. The construction of numerous pyramids, canals, and public buildings, as well as production of specialized crafts, implies complex societies under effective management.

Elaborate high-status burials and military symbolism, combined with elements derived from the Chavín cult, hint at the nature of that control. Monumental constructions marking the ceremonial precincts of each city represent an impressive expenditure of the society's energy and resources. Moche's **Huaca del Sol** (Pyramid of the Sun) incorporated 100,000,000 hand-made **adobe** bricks! Artists in both cities created fabulous objects that adhered to formally defined local styles. Unique **polychrome** ceramic vessels modelled to represent portrait heads, buildings, everyday scenes, or imaginative fantasies were a Moche speciality. Nazca pottery had an appeal of its own, with brightly painted symbolic motifs. Metalsmiths hammered, alloyed, and cast breathtaking adornments, ceremonial weapons, and religious objects of precious gold, silver, and copper. Most of these creations served the elite as status symbols, especially as grave furnishings. The newly found tomb of a Moche warrior-priest rivals those of the rulers of Egypt or Mesopotamia (Alva, 1988). Surrounded by several dead retainers and a dog, the man's coffin yielded a trove of precious ornaments and ceremonial attire indicative of his elevated status. Prominent Nazca dead customarily were

ALPACA
A South American camelid related to the llama, but having longer wool.

RAPTOR
A hunting bird with talons and hooked beak, such as an eagle or hawk.

CHAVÍN DE HUANTAR
(cha-veen' day wahn'-tar)

ORACLE
A person believed to be in touch with the deities.

HUACA DEL SOL
(wah'-ka dell soul)

ADOBE
Sun-baked mud or clay.

POLYCHROME
Many-colored.

Figure 17-25
Nazca ceramic vessel, southern Peru.

Figure 17-26
*Detail of Paracas textile, Nazca culture,
Peru.*

HUARI
(wah'-ree)

TIAHUANACO
(tee-eh-wahn-ah'-ko)

CHIMU
A powerful culture that dominated the
northern Peruvian coast between about
1000 and 500 y.a.

INCA
The people whose sophisticated culture
dominated Peru at the time of the European
arrival; also, the term for that people's highest ruler.

CUZCO
(coos'-co)

wrapped in yards of brilliant textiles richly embroidered with stylized animal and
human figures and trophy heads reminiscent of the Chavín style.

The most mystifying feature of Nazca culture may be the radiating lines,
geometric figures, and animal outlines "drawn" in gigantic scale on the flat desert
tableland of the south coast. Fully visible only from the air, the patterns were laid
out, then swept to expose lighter soil beneath the surface. Interpreted by some as
appeals to gods for water, many of the motifs are seen also on Nazca burial wrap-
pings and decorated ceramic vessels (Kosok and Reiche, 1949; Isbell, 1978;
Aveni, 1986).

Archeologists have noted that the prehistory of western South America reflects a theme of increasing sociopolitical integration (Moseley, 1983). This process may be examined most clearly in the northern coastal areas and the southern
highlands. Highland peoples tended to push "downward," toward the lowlands;
those along the coast spread laterally, incorporating adjacent coastal valleys. In
either case, the object was to gain access to additional resource zones through
what has been described as "vertical control" and "horizontal control" (Murra,
1972; Moseley, 1983). Overpopulation, resource depletion, and/or environmental degradation may have stimulated the aggressive expansionism observed
periodically in Peru's prehistory.

Although Moche and Nazca influences remained localized within their respective coastal regions, the southern highlands witnessed a renewed period of
expansionism around 1400 y.a. **Huari** and **Tiahuanaco** were well-organized
highland cities that used religion, trade, control of food and labor, and military
conquest to further their interests from the Andes to the coast (Kolata, 1987).
Neither of these kingdoms endured for long, but the impetus toward unification
of ever larger regions did not end with them. In fact, Peru's north coast was involved in a parallel development about 1000 y.a.

This **Chimu** Empire had its roots in the earlier Moche Valley culture (Moseley, 1975a). The eroded mud-brick architecture of its capital, Chan Chan, still blankets several square miles of coastal desert. Near its center, ten walled compounds each in turn served as a grand and secluded palace, storehouse, and tomb for the successive monarchs of the ruling dynasty. At the end of each reign, the ruler was interred in a burial platform amidst prodigious wealth, and the compound was sealed. By contrast, the adobe quarters of thousands of urban peasants crammed the space below the massive walls. The Chimu state extended control along the north coast by establishing regional administrative centers to watch over local populations and coordinate canal construction and agricultural terracing (Kus, 1984).

Lessons learned and taught by the Chimu were not lost on their rivals and successors, the **Inca**, the final native empire builders of ancient Peru. Their minor highland society, centered around present-day **Cuzco**, gained rapid ascendancy over the southern highlands through some bold military enterprises in the mid-fifteenth century (650 y.a.). The aging Chimu Empire itself offered little resistance in the north, and by 1476 the Inca consolidated an imperial domain over all of modern Peru and the adjacent region. The Inca army had taken a major role in the enterprise, but equally important in maintaining it was an efficient administration that established communication and supply systems to hold the empire together. The absolute rule of the divine emperor, or *Inca*, was effectively carried out by subordinates who oversaw the collection of taxes, allotment of communal lands, dispersal of malcontents, and selection of the "Chosen Women" destined for marriage to the nobles or sacrifice to the gods.

Cuzco served as capital of an empire of six million (Lanning, 1967), but in contrast to the principal cities of other earlier American civilizations, the highland town retained its modest rural character. Cuzco's center comprised a simple

Figure 17-27
Nazca ground drawings as seen from the air include zoomorphic and linear motifs. The monkey is longer than a football field.

Figure 17-28
Aerial view of one of the royal enclosures at Chan Chan, the Chimu capital.

ceremonial district amid surrounding residential areas. On an overlooking hill rose **Sacsahuamán** fortress, its massive mortarless walls formed by gargantuan stone blocks expertly dressed and fitted together. This distinctive architectural style was found throughout the Inca realm in religious shrines, state warehouses, and administrative centers.

Figure 17-29
Inca stone walls at Sacsahuamán, near Cuzco, Peru.

Well-maintained roads led out of Cuzco to the four quarters of the Inca Empire, crossing mountains, valleys, and deserts to tie the far-flung domain together (Morris, 1988). Beyond Cuzco, the only sizable settlements were Pachacamac, the seat of a respected oracle on Peru's north coast, and Quito, in Equador, established as a second capital by the Inca leader **Huayna Capac**. The Inca deliberately countered the development of major urban centers, fearing the possibility that large numbers of city dwellers might be a potential source of unrest. Resettlement programs broke up established population clusters in newly conquered areas so that the populace consisted almost entirely of rural peasants. Most grew maize, potatoes, quinoa, and other crops in irrigated alluvial valleys or hillside terraces prepared by state-directed labor. Herders in the highlands drove flocks of domesticated llama and alpaca, which supplied transport, dung for fuel, wool, objects for religious sacrifices, and food (although the only meat consumed by most people was the domesticated guinea pig, a small tailless rodent). Perhaps two-thirds of the produce was claimed by the state, although most of it was redistributed back to the citizens as they labored on roads and other civic projects. Despite its precautions and organization, the Inca Empire lasted only about sixty years.

European Conquest of the New World

By the first quarter of the sixteenth century, many Europeans were well aware that what Columbus had come upon was truly a new world, rather than the new route to the East Indies he and his sponsors had sought. Most people having any interest at all in the episode expressed only disappointment. But after disillusionment came a determination to make something of the situation. Spanish, Portuguese, English, Dutch, and French parties set off, each to see what might be wrung from this "newe found land" that lay across the path to the exotic wealth of the Orient. In the meantime, all would be searching for any possible way over, around, or past America.

Perhaps it is unfortunate that there were no anthropologists in the 1500s to alert their fellow citizens to the unique circumstances that were coming to a climax not only in America but in Africa and Asia as well. Never before and never again would there be such a large-scale confrontation between peoples and cultures who had evolved in isolation over hundreds of generations. On the other hand, it is doubtful that the painful course of events that was to follow could have been altogether avoided even if the situation had been fully appreciated.

The Western Hemisphere was populated by perhaps 100 million people (Dobyns, 1966) who shared a remarkable range and richness of genetic, cultural, and linguistic variation. Small bands of hunters and fishers peopled the northernmost and southernmost extremes of the continents. Foragers and tribes of horticulturalists occupied most of the middle latitudes. A few large agricultural chiefdoms maintained sway in the southeast United States, the Caribbean islands, and northern South America. But as many as a third of all the New World's peoples were subjects of one or the other of the great societies that prevailed in highland Mexico and Peru in the early 1500s.

Aztec and Inca were the nuclear civilizations of America. Each represented the culmination of many centuries of cultural tradition and development in its respective area. Both had reached an apex of achievement in every dimension—art, social organization, commerce, technology, learning, government, and religion. The Aztec and Inca states commanded the resources, talents, and vigor of vast territories. At the same time, their influence radiated into even larger regions of the two continents. These centers of wealth and power attracted the armored Europeans like a magnet.

Their end came with shocking swiftness. The two decades following the year 1520 saw both the Aztec and the Inca and their domains thoroughly enslaved by Spanish conquerors (Prescott, 1906). Leaving Cuba in 1519, Hernán Cortés and his fellow adventurers pressed through the swampy lowlands of Veracruz and into the central highlands of Mexico, where, in 1521, they were received with some justifiable suspicion by the Aztec emperor Moctezuma II. Cortés' arrival coincided remarkably with the predicted return of the Aztec god **Quetzalcoatl**. But the Spaniards' obsession with gold and plunder seemed all too earthly. As Cortés and his 400 soldiers entered Tenochtitlán, they were reminded of the principal cities of Europe, which hardly surpassed the Aztec capital in size or grandeur. Their admiration notwithstanding, the newcomers resolved to seize Tenochtitlán. Almost immediately Moctezuma found himself imprisoned and the Spanish in control. An uprising against the European invaders was quelled with the willing assistance of thousands of the Aztec's disenchanted former subjects. By 1524, the Spanish were the uncontested successors to the great empire in the heartland of Mesoamerica.

The conquest of Peru took much the same course. An expeditionary force of 180 men led by Francisco Pizarro entered the Inca domain in 1527, just as **Atahuallpa** claimed victory in a bitter five-year struggle for succession to the throne of his father, Huayna Capac. Pizarro found many disappointed followers of Huascar, Atahuallpa's half-brother and rival for the throne, eager to assist in deposing the new Inca. Through treachery, the Spanish eliminated both contenders, but not until they had first amassed a fabulous ransom in gold and silver from the unfortunate Atahuallpa, who was then put to death. Despite some resistance following these episodes, the Spanish had firm control of Peru by 1538.

In one brief and tragic, yet remarkable, moment of history, the crowning achievements of half a world had been undone. Successive decades would witness the wholesale devastation of peoples and cultures that had represented tens of thousands of years of development and adaptation. The Spanish conquest proceeded outward from the Mexican and Peruvian centers while other Europeans began the process anew in the more peripheral areas occupied by tribal peoples and bands. The cost of the confrontation, in human and cultural terms, was enormous; the foregone potential will be forever incalculable. The loss, if not the shame, is borne by all humankind.

Summary

In this chapter, we have considered the long prehistory of the New World's inhabitants. We began by tracing the original American cultural and genetic stock back to northeastern Asia. While the date of human entry into the New World via a now-submerged Bering land bridge cannot presently be determined with precision, it undoubtedly occurred at least by 12 kya, when sites of big game hunters appeared in many parts of the Americas.

After the end of the Pleistocene, groups in most regions were engaged in the intensive hunting and gathering of a wide variety of plant and animal resources. In a few areas, such as highland Mexico and Peru, some of these foragers gradually increased their reliance on a few favored species, then eventually began to produce a significant portion of their food from fully domesticated crops. The impact of agriculture spread well beyond these initial zones and in some cases stimulated further cultural elaboration.

The development of highly complex societies in Mesoamerica and the west coast and Andean areas of South America after about 4 kya set the trend for the later stages of prehistory. The alternate flourishing and waning of successive civilizations affected the larger regions that were linked to these centers through military, political, religious, and/or economic ties. The shocking dissolution of America's native cultures was a tragic consequence of the Old World's rediscovery of the New.

Questions for Review

1. What kinds of biological and cultural clues reveal the Asian ancestry of the Amerinds?
2. Indicate several factors that make it difficult to address the question of whether people were living in the New World before the last glaciation.
3. How does the nature of the archeological evidence pertaining to the Paleo-Indians bias our view of them as big-game hunters?
4. What alternative explanations may account for evidence of early food production in such marginal environments as the Tehuacán Valley, rather than in more temperate regions, such as the woodlands of the eastern United States?
5. What are some qualities of maize that contributed to its great importance as a New World domesticate?
6. What functions did ceremonial centers serve in the cultures of Mesoamerica?
7. In what ways does it appear that Olmec and Chavín had a similar impact on their respective culture areas?
8. Describe the relationship between the lowland Maya and the early civilizations of the Valley of Mexico.
9. What are some of the historical parallels between the Aztec and Inca cultures?
10. Contrast the earliest civilizations of the New World with those of the Old World. Might some of these differences have ultimately contributed to the European conquest of the Americas?

Human Evolution: A Biocultural Process

What does it mean to be human? Certainly, part of the answer is understandable in terms of organic evolution—as it applies to any animal. Indeed, we are animals, and the evolutionary process acts similarly on humans through the combined action of the major evolutionary factors: mutation, genetic drift, migration, and natural selection. Human populations have evolved and continue to do so as allele frequencies shift in response to these factors.

Thus, our origins are ultimately traceable to the roots of life on this planet, close to 3.5 billion years ago (Gurin, 1980). The last 500 million years of evolution, as told by the fossil vertebrate record, informs us more directly of our immediate precursors. Even more specifically, we can trace our roots to the placental mammal radiation and from here to the beginnings of the primate order more than 60 m.y.a.

Through comparative studies of modern primates, prosimians, monkeys, apes, and ourselves, we are able to flesh out the bits and pieces of bones and teeth that comprise the fossil record of our primate ancestors. From such comparisons we know that early anthropoids began diverging in the Old World by probably 40 m.y.a. and the first hominoid was already on the scene by 20 m.y.a.

When, however, did the unique evolutionary radiation occur that produced the first hominid? The exact timing of this evolutionary event is still disputed, but evidence suggests a date somewhere between 10–5 m.y.a. for the appearance of the first member of the human family.

The first half of hominid evolutionary history is still clouded in mystery, but ongoing research by Richard Leakey, Donald Johanson, David Pilbeam, and others is aimed at filling in this gap. We now know considerably more about the last 5 million years. Abundant evidence from the Plio-Pleistocene of South and East Africa tells of a variety of early hominid forms. The earliest definite hominid—*Australopithecus afarensis*—is an extremely small-brained, but completely bipedal, hominid. It remains to be seen if this primitive hominid consistently made tools, but to date no stone artifacts have been found in association with this fossil form. Despite its relative primitiveness, *A. afarensis* may indeed be our ancestor.

A more definitive biocultural interaction among our ancestors is indicated by 2 m.y.a. At this time, early members of our genus (*Homo*) are emerging in Africa (also possibly Asia), and they are associated with stone tool remains at several localities. Not surprisingly, then, early members of the genus *Homo* show significantly larger brains than their australopithecine cousins—whom they eventually outcompeted.

The fossil record of our ancestors continues its saga with *Homo erectus*, transitional forms, a variety of *sapiens* forms (among them, Neandertal), and finally the wide geographic expansion of fully modern humans (*Homo sapiens sapiens*) around 40,000 years ago (and, in Africa, probably already on the scene as early as 100,000 years ago).

This then, briefly, is the human evolutionary journey. But it is told to us in more than just morphological details of tooth and bone, for we *and* our ancestors are more than just physical organisms blindly following the dictates of organic evolution. Several million years ago our early hominid ancestors began culturally to modify their environments, thus drastically altering their ecological niche and henceforth setting a new direction for human evolution.

What we are and how we came to be that way can only be answered in terms of biocultural processes. Whether we are talking about the first crude attempts to knock a flake off a lava cobble or the landing of human beings on the moon, the process is a unified one. It may well be true that "man makyth tools" but it is equally true that "tools makyth man."

The results of our unique evolutionary history are recounted in the size and the structure of our brain, our dental apparatus, and our bipedal gait (with its manifold physical requirements). We, however, can also see the imprint of our special hominid origins in our behavior: our cultural abilities to make and use tools, our symbolic language, our passion to be social.

Indeed, as we have emphasized repeatedly, the physical structure of our body has been molded by evolutionary factors relating to concomitant development of *all* these behavioral characteristics. Does our evolution, then, *explain* our behavior? Today, there are those in biology and anthropology who believe that it does.

A new emphasis in behavioral biology developed over the last decade has been given the name "sociobiology" (Wilson, 1975; Barash, 1982). In its more restrained pragmatic applications, this approach attempts to understand social behavior among insects and birds in terms of natural selection models. In other words, sociobiology assumes that social behavior among these animals can be best understood by relating such behavior to reproductive success of individuals. In some cases, such as sterile "altruistic" worker castes among social insects, such a perspective is most helpful (Hamilton, 1964).

What, however, can we say about human behavior? Many popular writers have argued that humankind's current behavior involving territorial nation-states, organized warfare, etc., is merely an extension of hominid behavioral propensities developed during the last several million years. Often emphasized as a primary determinant in shaping human behavior is the role of hunting (Ardrey, 1976), creating a "killer-ape" (Morris, 1967).

We have seen that some hunting or at least consistent exploitation of big game did become an important factor in *erectus* times around 1 m.y.a. The behavioral demands of such social hunting *may* have selected for more cohesive social organization, more effective means of communication, and more specialized tools. These demands in turn *may* have placed a higher selection benefit on larger brains. It makes a neat model, but even at this level it is highly speculative. Neither the fossil record nor archeological traces inform us directly concerning the exact circumstances that caused increases in hominid brain size.

Even more speculative are the postulations concerning the determining influence of hunting on human aggression, territoriality, male/female differences, and so on. Given the nature of the evidence, such wanton speculation—no matter how intellectually appealing—is to be avoided.

What then can we say about the evolution of human behavior? The development of culture most assuredly has shaped our behavioral *capacities*. The facts, that *Homo sapiens* characteristically has such a complex neurological foundation and that we are all capable of symbolic language reveal our biocultural evolutionary heritage. However, the development of culture also created an entirely new realm of behavioral possibilities. Our hominid ancestors, like us, were symbol-making, cognitively complex animals. Their behavior, and ours, thus has a large element of choice built in. The capacity for language and culture is inherited, but the form it will take is *learned*. As such, our behavior is subject to considerable modification even during one individual's lifetime.

Humans are not blind gene-machines simply pursuing the ultimate end of greater individual reproductive success. *Unlike any other animal on earth* we have the possibility of almost infinite behavioral creativity; what is more, we have the self-awareness that such flexibility exists. By means of cognitive devices that Richard Dawkins calls "memes," humans have forever departed from the course of gene-determined biological evolution into the sphere of a culturally and symbolically mediated development (Dawkins, 1976).

While cultural norms (as applied to the group) and biological success (as applied to the individuals within the group) may occasionally come into conflict, over the long run they should harmonize to some degree (Cavalli-Sforza and Feldman, 1981). Without a viable interaction of biocultural elements, neither human beings—nor the human groups upon which we depend for survival—could be expected to long endure.

Hominid evolutionary development has created *Homo sapiens*, an animal with behavioral flexibility. In a sense, we are products of our evolution. But unlike any other organism on this planet we can infinitely mold our own behavior through exercise of our own uniquely human creativity.

Homo sapiens groups increased the pace of cultural modification around 10,000 years ago. We have traced how—in the span of just a few millennia—a number of societies in the Old World turned to plant and animal domestication. At about the same time, human groups began to experiment with agriculture in the New World. The control of these resources supported ever-increasing populations but also altered profoundly the relationship between people and their environments. Human interactions intensified as well. We have noted the emergence of advanced and complex societies—civilizations—in both hemispheres. The dynamic ferment of these structured populations resulted in the first cities, monumental constructions, and writing—as well as class divisions, poverty, and warfare.

These cultural developments did not render our species immune to evolutionary forces. As environments change, evolution does not stop—it changes direction. With the establishment of agriculture and dense permanent settlements came new selection pressures, including infectious disease. For example, the spread of the sickle-cell trait in response to pressure from malaria demonstrates how the natural selection process continues to act on human populations within their cultural environments.

Many cultural anthropologists/archeologists find it intriguing that such broadly parallel developments as agriculture and civilization occurred *independently* (barring unlikely transoceanic contacts) in both areas of the globe. Some argue for regular patterns—even "laws"—governing the direction of culture change. A few have gone so far as to postulate models explaining how culture *evolves*. Thus, given a defined set of circumstances—environmental, social, technical, economic, and so on—cultures might be expected to react and develop in predictable ways. We must bear in mind, however, that the processes underlying cultural evolution differ fundamentally from those of biological evolution: There are no discrete units of cultural transmission (analogous to genes) nor does cultural selection (measured by the success of groups) parallel natural selection (measured by the success of individuals).

Given these considerations, it still cannot be denied that cultures do change, that these changes have direction, and that some cultures survive and grow while others perish. In fact, if we are meaningfully to understand anything of the last few thousand years of human history, it is only through studying these *cultural* factors.

Does this mean we have at last left the realm of biological evolution completely? By no means. Mutation still occurs, and the potential mutagenic effects of artificial radiation and chemicals pose the danger of still further increasing the frequency of genetic "mistakes." Natural selection is also still operating in a very powerful way; perhaps as many as 85% of all the zygotes conceived never reproduce. Moreover, results of the accelerated pace of migration in the last five centuries are visible all around us.

What we are saying is that our profound ability to modify our environments has outdistanced our biological capacity to respond. As slowly maturing mammals, our generation span is considerably longer than that of most other animals. Unlike the mosquitoes that have biologically (adaptively) responded to massive environmental changes such as DDT, we cannot adapt so quickly. If mosquitoes had sprayed us continually with equal amounts of pesticides, we almost certainly would have been completely wiped out.

How then can we be expected to cope with the new biological pressures of the modern technological world? Clearly, the biggest dangers are the cultural ones we have created for ourselves: overcrowding, pollution, radiation, and so forth.

What does the future hold for the planet earth and for us, *H. sapiens sapiens*? We are not seers and cannot predict what will happen. However, the future may not all be gloom and doom. Already, beginning steps are being taken to preserve the rainforests of the world. Also, the industrialized nations are becoming more aware of the warming effect of the chemicals we use so profusely and which are causing holes in the ozone layer that protects us from the sun's burning ultraviolet rays.

Above all, biotechnology—especially genetic engineering—may neutralize and even reverse the effects of the cultural modifications of the environment that are so potentially dangerous to us and all the earth's inhabitants. Genetic engineering has only begun but it has already made remarkable progress.

Just possibly, with increased awareness of environmental dangers, with a strong will to preserve our environment, and with new biological techniques that can rectify mutations, natural and humanmade, the future may be more promising than we had reason to believe just a few years ago. As human beings, we possess the capability to remake our world—for better or for worse. The choice is ours.

Atlas of Primate Skeletal Anatomy

Parietal

Temporal

Zygomatic

Occipital

Cervical
vertebrae (7)

Frontal

Maxilla

Mandible

Clavicle

Scapula

Sternum

Ribs

Thoracic vertebrae (12)

Humerus

Lumbar
vertebrae (5)

Ilium

Sacrum

Pubis

Ulna

Radius

Carpals (8)

Metacarpals (5)

Phalanges (14)

Ischium

Femur

Patella

Tibia

Fibula

Tarsals (7)

Metatarsals (5)

Phalanges (14)

Figure A-1
*Human skeleton (Homo sapiens)—bipedal
hominid.*

Figure A-2
Chimpanzee skeleton (Pan troglodytes) A
knuckle-walking pongid.

Frontal

Parietal

Temporal

Maxilla

Cervical
vertebrae

Mandible

Clavicle

Thoracic vertebrae

Sternum

Humerus

Lumbar vertebrae

Sacrum

Ilium

Radius

Ulna

Pubis

Ischium

Femur

Carpals

Patella

Metacarpals

Tibia

Fibula

Phalanges

Tarsals

Metatarsals

CHIMPANZEE SKELETON

MONKEY SKELETON

Figure A-3
Monkey skeleton (rhesus macaque; Macaca mulatta)—A typical quadrupedal primate.

Glabella

Nasion

Nasal bone

Parietal

Frontal process
of maxilla

Frontal

Coronal
suture

Temporal

Greater wing
of sphenoid

Lacrimal

Zygomatic

Ethmoid

Maxilla

Infraorbital
foramen

Vomer
(nasal septum)

Anterior
nasal spine

Alveolar process
of maxilla

Ascending ramus
of mandible

Mental foramen

Body of mandible

(a) Frontal (anterior) view

Coronal suture

Parietal bone

Superior
temporal line

Frontal bone

Inferior
temporal
line

Sphenoid

Squamosal
suture

Ethmoid

Temporal
bone

Nasal

Occipital
bone

Lacrimal

Lambdoidal
suture

Maxilla

Zygomatic

Mandibular condyle

Anterior
nasal spine

Occipitomastoidal suture

Incisors

Mastoid process

Canine

External auditory meatus

Styloid process

Mental
foramen

Ascending ramus
of mandible

(b) Lateral view

Body of mandible

Premolars   Molars

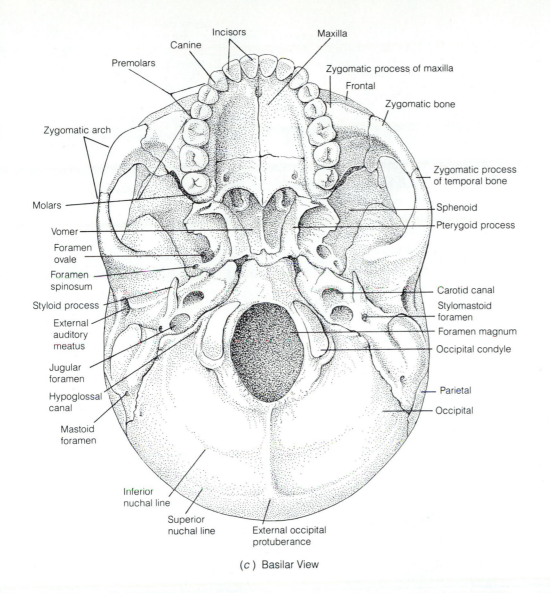

Incisors

Canine

Premolars

Maxilla

Zygomatic process of maxilla

Frontal

Zygomatic bone

Zygomatic arch

Molars

Vomer

Foramen ovale

Foramen spinosum

Styloid process

External auditory meatus

Jugular foramen

Hypoglossal canal

Mastoid foramen

Zygomatic process of temporal bone

Sphenoid

Pterygoid process

Carotid canal

Stylomastoid foramen

Foramen magnum

Occipital condyle

Parietal

Occipital

Inferior nuchal line

Superior nuchal line

External occipital protuberance

(c) Basilar View

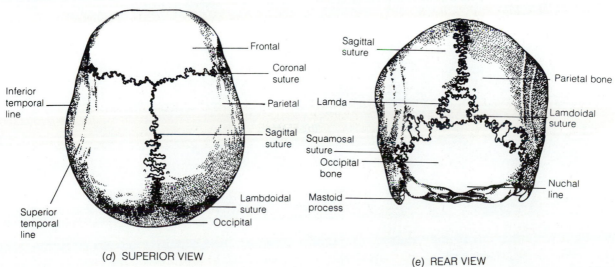

Frontal

Coronal suture

Parietal

Sagittal suture

Lambdoidal suture

Occipital

Inferior temporal line

Superior temporal line

(d) SUPERIOR VIEW

Sagittal suture

Lamda

Squamosal suture

Occipital bone

Mastoid process

Parietal bone

Lamdoidal suture

Nuchal line

(e) REAR VIEW

(a) MALE

(b) FEMALE

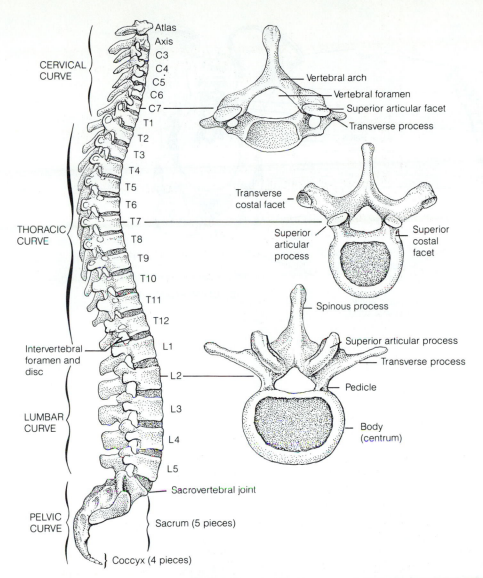

CERVICAL CURVE

Atlas
Axis
C3
C4
C5
C6
C7

Vertebral arch
Vertebral foramen
Superior articular facet
Transverse process

T1
T2
T3
T4
T5
T6
T7
T8
T9
T10
T11
T12

THORACIC CURVE

Transverse costal facet

Superior articular process

Superior costal facet

Spinous process

Intervertebral foramen and disc

L1
L2
L3
L4
L5

Superior articular process
Transverse process
Pedicle

Body (centrum)

LUMBAR CURVE

Sacrovertebral joint

Sacrum (5 pieces)

PELVIC CURVE

Coccyx (4 pieces)

Human vertebral column (lateral view) and representative views of selected cervical, thoracic, and lumbar vertebrae (superior views).

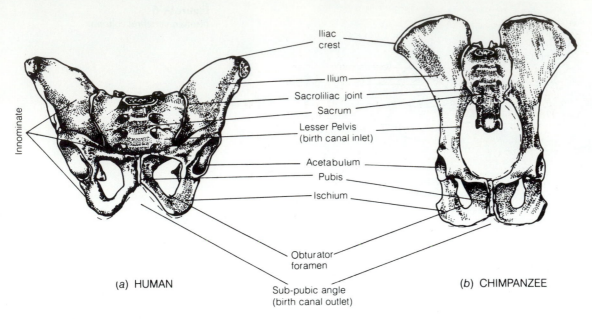

Iliac crest
Ilium
Sacroiliac joint
Sacrum
Lesser Pelvis (birth canal inlet)
Acetabulum
Pubis
Ischium
Obturator foramen
Sub-pubic angle (birth canal outlet)
Innominate

(a) HUMAN

(b) CHIMPANZEE

Figure A-7 Pelvic girdles.

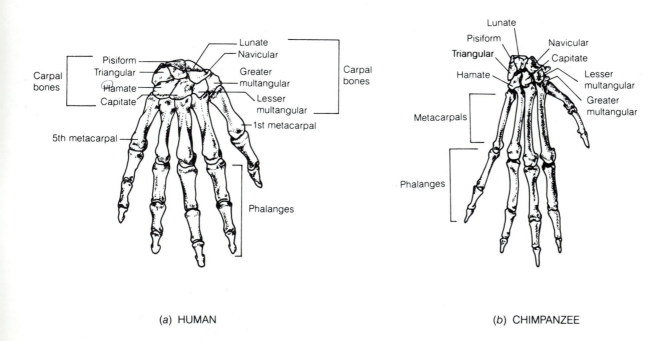

Carpal bones
Pisiform
Triangular
Hamate
Capitate
Lunate
Navicular
Greater multangular
Lesser multangular
1st metacarpal
Carpal bones
5th metacarpal
Phalanges

(a) HUMAN

Lunate
Pisiform
Triangular
Hamate
Navicular
Capitate
Lesser multangular
Greater multangular
Metacarpals
Phalanges

(b) CHIMPANZEE

Figure A-8
Hand anatomy.

(a) Human (dorsal view)

(c) Chimpanzee

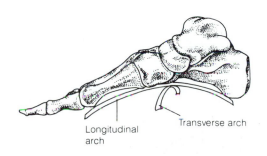

(b) Human (medial view)

Forensic Anthropology*

It is a fascinating and startling fact that there are hundreds of millions of humans buried around this planet, and often their bones come to light for one reason or another. Indeed, thousands of skeletons have been excavated and are now curated in various natural history and anthropology museums. Skeletal biologists (also called *human osteologists*) are often asked to assist in unearthing these human remains and to perform various specialized analyses on them when prehistoric or, occasionally, historic burial sites are excavated.

Many situations occur in which forensic anthropologists are called upon by the police and other law enforcement agencies to assist in identification by using their knowledge of skeletal biology. Usually, the anthropologist is called upon to provide clues as to the personal identity of a deceased individual or individuals (through analysis of partially skeletalized remains), but is also occasionally asked to perform other tasks. Some examples of these tasks are: to identify skeletal trauma, match remains from a suspected scene of a crime with the corpus delecti, sort human from nonhuman remains, and, sometimes, to either compare a photograph to a living person, or to compare two photographs to determine the identity of the persons pictured. A few case reports will better illustrate the types of problems encountered by a forensic anthropologist. These are based on actual cases, and will be resolved for you at the end of this section.

Case 1: An old plane crash was discovered in the remote mountains of Colorado, and skeletal material was still inside. How many people are represented by this skeletal material, and who were they?

Case 2: A skeleton was discovered by a farmer while plowing his fields before planting. He contacted the local sheriff, who wondered if a past homicide victim could have been buried there.

Case 3: A building has exploded because of a natural gas leak, and five people are thought to have been inside at the time of the explosion and fire. These individuals were: a 23-year-old female and a 24-year-old female, both with no children, a 32-year-old female with three children, a 53-year-old male and a 54-year-old male. As these remains were almost completely skeletonized, how could they be identified?

*This appendix was written by Diane France and Robert Jurmain, with special thanks to George Gill for his contributions.

Case 4: A very old photograph that bore a striking resemblance to Abraham Lincoln was discovered in the attic of an old house. Tests could be performed by other forensic specialists (questioned documents examiners, for example) to determine the age of the photographic paper, etc., and, of course, these would aid in discounting a fraudulent claim; but the photograph could still be of the correct age and be of a person other than Lincoln.

The first three cases must begin with a determination of the species represented by the remains. If the bones are not human, the forensic anthropologist's role is usually over, but if they are human, the work has just begun. Even if the police have an idea of who is represented by these remains, the specialist usually begins the investigation with a determination of the basic features: sex, age, race, stature, skeletal pathology, and notation of idiosyncrasies that could aid in final identification (such as healed fractures, prosthetic devices, and so on).

Sexing the Skeleton

Several evolutionary factors have helped us to be able to identify sex in the human skeleton. The pelvic girdles in quadrupeds do not differ greatly between males and females of a species, but in humans the birth canal had a tendency to become smaller with bipedalism. This problem was compounded by the human newborn, whose head was relatively larger than the newborns of other animals, so throughout our evolution modifications were selected for in the female pelvic girdle relating to proportionately larger birth outlets, and these modifications aid in the determination of sex today. This sexual dimorphism (difference in morphology between the sexes) is most reliably diagnosed in the pelvic girdle, as shown below (see Figures B-1 and B-2).

Figure B-1
Male pelvic girdle.

Figure B-2
Female pelvic girdle.

Pelvic Girdle	Typical Male	Typical Female
Subpubic angle	Less than 90 degrees	More than 90 degrees
Pubic shape	Triangular	Rectangular
Subpubic angle shape (see also Phenice, 1969)	Convex	Concave
Greater sciatic notch	Less than 68 degrees	More than 68 degrees
Sacrum	Smaller and more curved	Larger and straighter

In addition, humans display types of sexual dimorphism also common to most other animals: Males are usually larger and have more rugged areas for muscle attachments than do females of the same species. However, in order to utilize this size difference in sex determination, the researcher must be able to identify the population from which the skeleton was taken, as whole populations differ in skeletal size and robusticity. For instance, Asian Indians are much smaller and more gracile than Australian Aborigines.

After the pelvis, the cranium is the area of the skeleton most commonly used for sex determination. Some of these traits are listed below (see Figure B-3).

Cranium	Typical Male	Typical Female
Muscle attachment areas (mastoid process, etc.)	More pronounced	Less pronounced
Supraorbital torus (brow ridges)	More pronounced	Less pronounced
Frontal bone	Slanting	Globular
Supraorbital rim (in eye orbit)	Rounded	Sharp
Palate	Deep	Shallow

Figure B-3
Cranium and mandible: female (top); male (bottom).

(a) Birth: The crowns for all the deciduous (milk) teeth (shown in color) are present; no roots, however, have yet formed.

First permanent molar

(b) 2 years: All deciduous teeth (shown in color) are erupted; the first permanent molar and permanent incisors have crowns (unerupted) formed, but no roots.

Third molar

(c) 12 years: All permanent teeth are erupted except the third molar (wisdom tooth).

Figure B-4
Skeletal age: dental development.

Other bones of the body also show secondary sex characteristics, but are often less reliable than those of the cranium, as heavy muscle use affects the size and ruggedness of the muscle attachments, which can then sometimes change the diagnosis of sex. Areas probably not as affected by muscle use are:

Suprascapular notch on scapula	Often present	Often absent
Femur: angle of neck to shaft	Smaller angle	Greater angle

The standards discussed here are for adult skeletons; sexing techniques for pre-adolescents are not as yet widely used.

Determination of Age

During growth, the skeleton and dentition undergo regular changes that allow the determination of age at death. The age determination in individuals under about 20 years centers on deciduous (baby) and permanent dentition eruption times, on the appearance of ossification centers, and on the fusion of the separate ends of long bones to bone shafts.

Dental Eruption

The determination of the ages at which the deciduous and permanent dentition erupts is useful in identifying age to approximately 15 years. The third molar (wisdom tooth) erupts after this time, but is so variable in age of eruption (if it erupts at all) that it is not a very reliable age indicator. (See Fig. B-4.)

Bone Growth

Postcranial bones are preceded by a cartilage model that is gradually replaced by bone, both in the primary growth centers (the diaphyses) and in the secondary centers (the ends of the bones, or epiphyses). The initial ossification centers are, of course, very small, and are only rarely encountered by a forensic anthropologist. The bone continues to grow until the epiphyses fuse to the diaphyses. Because this fusion occurs at different times in different bones, the age of an individual can be determined by which epiphyses have fused and which have not (see Figs. B-5 and B-6). The characteristic undulating appearance of the unfused surfaces of bone helps differentiate it from the mature long bond (smooth) or merely a broken end of a bone (sharp and jagged).

Females mature more quickly than males, so usually 1 to 2 years must be subtracted from the previous ages for female skeletons.

Once a person has reached physiological maturity (by the early 20s), the determination of age becomes more difficult. Several techniques are used, including the progressive, regular changes in the pubic symphyseal face (the most common technique), in the sternal ends of the ribs, in the auricular surface of the ilium, in ectocranial (outside the cranium) and endocranial (inside the cranium)

Greater tubercle fuses
to head at 2 to 4 years.

Head fuses to shaft:
males aged 16 to 18
females aged 15 to 17

(a) Birth

(b) 5 years

(c) 10 years

(d) 15 years

(e) 16+ years

Trochlea fuses to lower shaft:
males aged 14 to 16
females aged 13 to 15

Medial epicondyle fuses:
males aged 16 to 18
females aged 15 to 17

Figure B-5
Skeletal age: epiphyseal union in the humerus. Some regions of the humerus exhibit some of the earliest fusion centers in the body, while others are among the latest to complete fusion (not until late adolescence).

suture closures, and in cellular changes determined by microscopic examination of the cross section of various long bones. In addition, degenerative changes, including arthritis and osteoporosis, can aid in the determination of relative age, but should not be used by themselves to determine age, as injury and certain diseases can cause changes that mimic old age in bones.

Pubic Symphyseal Face: The pubic symphyseal face in the young (Fig. B-8) is characterized by a billowing surface (with ridges and furrows), such as seen on a normal epiphysis, but undergoes regular metamorphosis from age 18 onwards. Figure B-9 shows a symphyseal face typical of an age in the mid-30s, with a more finely grained face and perhaps still containing remnants of the ridge and furrow system. Figure B-10 is typical of an age in the early 60s, with bony outgrowths often developing on the outer rims of the symphyseal face. The first technique for dating the pubic symphyseal face was developed by T. W. Todd (1920, 1921) utilizing dissection room cadavers. McKern and Stewart (1957) developed a technique using American males killed in the Korean War. Both of these samples have limitations in that the dissection room sample used by Todd is based on individuals of uncertain age (Brooks, 1985, 1986) and the Korean War dead sample is predominantly young Caucasoid males, with few individuals over age 35.

Figure B-6
Distal femur. (The knee articulation is shown at the top, and is still unfused.)

Pubic Symphysis

Position of the public symphysis. This area of the pelvis shows systematic changes progressively throughout adult life. Three of these stages are shown in B-8, B-9, and B-10.

Figure B-8
Pubic symphyseal face typical of an age in the late teens or early twenties.

Figure B-9
Pubic symphyseal face typical of an age in the mid-thirties.

Recently a system has been developed by J. M. Suchey, D. Katz, and S. T. Brooks based on a large sample ($n = 739$) of males for whom legal documentation of age is provided by death certificates. This autopsy room sample should be more representative of the general population than past samples. The majority of the males were born either in the United States or Mexico. This sample was taken at autopsies involving homicides, suicides, accidents, or unexpected natural deaths.

Determination of Race

When an anthropologist is asked to help in the identification of a parcel of bones, part of that identification must include a statement as to probable race, because society includes race as a part of the personal identity. Racial identification is often difficult, however, as most of the morphological characteristics we use to distinguish race follow a continuum; that is, one trait is more often, but not exclusively, associated with one race. Even skin color, the most noticeable of characteristics, cannot adequately categorize all individuals, for there are dark-skinned Caucasoids and Mongoloids (disregarding the effects of tanning), and light-skinned Negroids. In fact, it can be said that for many traits, there is more variation *within* races than *between* races. (See Chapter 5.)

The races of the world have been divided in different ways in history, but many anthropologists today identify five or six basic groups: Mongoloids (including Japanese, Chinese, and North, Central, and South American Indians), Negroids (including African and American Blacks), Caucasoids (including Europeans, and other people with European ancestry, West Asians, Asian Indians, and some North American peoples), Australoids (Australian Aborigines), and Polynesians. This is not by any means a complete classification scheme, nor is it the only classification scheme used by physical anthropologists today.

The chart lists some of the differences we usually see in the skulls of three races common to the Western Hemisphere (most of the currently important differences used in the identification of race occur in the skulls). (See also Brues, 1977; Krogman, 1962; Stewart, 1979; Bass, 1987; and Gill, 1986).

Feature	Negroid	Caucasoid	Mongoloid
Central incisors (cross section) (Dahlberg, 1951)	Blade	Rarely shoveled	Shoveled
Cranial shape[a]	Dolicocranic (long)	Mesocranic (medium)	Brachycranic (round)
Nasal root (top of nasal bridge)	Wide, rounded	Narrow, pinched	Medium tented
Nasal aperture[b]	Platyrrhiny (wide)	Leptorrhiny (narrow)	Mesorrhiny (medium)
Zygomatic bone	Medium	Retreating	Projecting
External auditory meatus (ear opening)	Round	Round	Oval
Facial shape	Prognathic (lower face projects forward)	Orthognathic (lower face nonprojecting)	Medium

Figure B-10
Pubic symphysed face typical of an age in the early sixties.

In addition to the standard measurements, indices, and observations discussed here, further methods using skull and face measurements have been developed to aid in race determination. The most widely used of these is a *discriminant function* method (using a set of formulae), and was developed by Giles and Elliot (1962) for distinguishing Blacks, Caucasoids, and American Indians. Measurements are taken on the cranium of each adult, plugged into the formulae, and the final values plotted on a graph. It must be pointed out that, first, sex must be established (the formulae vary for males and females) and, secondly, the method is devised to answer only a limited question ("Is the cranium from a Black, from a Caucasoid, or from an American Indian?"). The discriminant function method itself helps address the first point (sex) since the technique has also been used to devise a formula for sex determination (from a few of the same measurements). The problem with this method is not so much the need to determine sex first, or the fact that it answers a limited question (since most skulls on this continent come from Blacks, Caucasoids, or American Indians), but rather it relates to its accuracy. Particularly regarding American Indian specimens from the western United States, the percentage of correct ascertainment is quite low (Birkby, 1966; Gill, 1986). The sexing formula has proven quite accurate, however.

[a] The cranial shape is obtained from the Cranial Index, calculated from:

$$\frac{\text{Cranial breadth}}{\text{Cranial length}} \times 100$$

Up to 75	= Dolicocrany
75–79.9	= Mesocrany
80–84.9	= Brachycrany
85 and up	= Hyperbrachycrany

(Bass, 1987)

[b] The nasal aperture shape is obtained from the Nasal Index:

$$\frac{\text{Nasal breadth}}{\text{Nasal height}} \times 100$$

Up to 47.9	= Leptorrhiny
48–52.9	= Mesorrhiny
53 and up	= Platyrrhiny

(Bass, 1987)

A new metric method developed by Gill and Hughes (Gill et al., 1988) appears to be much more accurate in race determination than the widely used Giles-Elliot approach. With six measurements (and three indices from them), it defines the amount of projection of the mid-face (which is extreme among the sharp-featured Caucasoids). The method does require a specialized (and rather rare) caliper, but is quite reliable in sorting Caucasoids from members of all other populations (in approximately 90 percent of cases). This method is also mathematically simple, and can be performed quickly in an autopsy setting. However, it cannot address the problem of sorting Mongoloids from Blacks, since their mid-facial projections are similar.

So, even today, with many new techniques and extensive use of the computer, race determination remains a challenging and somewhat subjective area. It requires the simultaneous use of many approaches rather than any single "foolproof" method. "By definition, race is quantitative [no sharp boundaries]. Perfection can never be attained in defining or diagnosing a condition that does not even exist in absolute form" (Gill, 1986: 156).

Estimation of Stature

Formulae for stature reconstruction in unidentified individuals have been developed by measuring the long bones of deceased individuals of known stature (Trotter and Glese, 1952; Genoves, 1967). As is true of any statistical approxi-

Figure B-11
Estimating stature: measuring the length of the femur.

Femur length (mm)[*]	Stature	
	cm	inches
452	169	66
456	170	66
461	171	67
465	172	67
469	173	68

[*]Note: Data drawn from White males with known statures at time of death.

mation of a population, these formulae are applied most reliably to the samples from which they are derived, though they may also be used on wider populations represented by these samples. Because these formulae were derived for each sex of various racial groups, the sex and race of the unknown individual must be known before these formulae can be reliably applied.

Resolution of the Case Studies

Case 1: Even though the remains were burned, at least two individuals were identified as the pilot and friend who had filed the initial flight plan. It had been suspected at the time of the crash that at least one more person had been aboard, but there was no evidence to support that claim.

Case 2: The skeleton was human, and was determined to be that of an American Indian male. Although often remains of this kind in these circumstances are automatically diagnosed as an archeological burial, the rapid decay rates of flesh and bone in many areas of the United States and other countries will cause the remains to look ancient in a very short time; thus, a forensic anthropologist must be alert to this possibility. In this case, however, further circumstantial evidence suggested that this was archeological, in that a projectile point was found in the tibia at the knee.

   Cases of this kind are useful in disputes between American Indian groups in land and resource ownership, for, in increasing numbers, the tribal affinity of remains can be determined. Human identification in these circumstances has far-reaching ramifications.

Case 3: As noted in the introduction, the ages of two of the females and two of the males were very similar to each other, so that even with the determination of sex and age, the identity of these very fragmentary remains was not easily determined. The 32-year-old female was identified by age determination of the pubic symphysis, and by the evidence on the pelvis that she had had children. There was evidence of at least two other women aside from the 32-year-old female, but because the stature of these other women was very similar, the identification was only tentative. Completely reliable identification was not possible, and it was noted only that there was no evidence that those women were *not* present in the building. The identification of the men was similarly difficult, as they again were about the same age. In addition, though one of the men had a surgical staple in his right knee, which would ordinarily have been evidence for identification, that area of the body was not recovered for either individual. One of the men, however, was over 6 feet tall, while the other was around 5 feet 8 inches tall. Stature reconstruction using the femur, and premortem and postmortem x-rays of the pelvic region of the men were ultimately used for the identification.

Case 4: Dr. Ellis Kerley (1984) determined, by comparing many features of a known Lincoln photograph to this photograph, that this was of a person other than our sixteenth president.

Photo Superimposition

Employed when a probable identification has been made, the technique of photo superimposition has been used in many cases lately, including the famous case of the identification of the Nazi war-criminal Josef Mengele (presented at the Annual Meeting of the American Academy of Forensic Sciences in New Orleans in 1986). In this and other cases, the skull (or large portions of the skull) are superimposed onto photographs of the known individual. If enough landmarks fall on the same position on the skull *and* on the photograph, the researcher is satisfied that he has made the correct identification. (Note: this technique could also have been used to reinforce the decision made in some of the cases outlined above.)

Facial Reconstruction in Human Identification*

Facial reconstruction (also termed *facial reproduction*) is a process used when other identification procedures (including fingerprints and dental matches) have been unsuccessful. Two different methods of producing a face on the skull are employed: a portrait of the individual using clues from the bones of the face; and a more direct, three-dimensional method of applying clay to the skull (or to a plaster cast of the skull). These techniques employ both science and art: The physical anthropologist discovers the age, sex, and race of the skull, but there is no direct evidence from bone that indicates the eye color, hair color and style, lip form, or degree of wrinkling or fleshiness in the individual. Therefore, there is a great deal of subjectivity in the rendering of the finished product; an exact reproduction is not expected, only a general likeness.

The following photographs show a facial reproduction taking shape. Erasers or blocks of clay marking tissue depths (arrived at experimentally from cadavers) are commonly glued to the skull. Clay strips, graduated to the various tissue depths, then "fill in the dots" between erasers, and the face is "fleshed out." The eyes, nose, lips, and sometimes ears are then fashioned according to various guidelines, and a wig is usually added.

Figures i and j show the reproduction of a Caucasoid female, over 60 years old. The first figure shows a nearly complete reproduction, but without the effects of aging, while Figure j is the finished product, including the features characteristic of a woman of that age.

*Contributed by Diane France and Sandra C. Mays, Supervisor, Crime Laboratory Section, Wyoming State Crime Laboratory. Stages of reconstruction are from both authors; finished reconstruction by Sandra Mays.

Figure B-12
Facial reconstruction from a skull.

Figure a
Erasers precut to experimentally determined tissue depths are glued to skull.

Figure b
Sandra Mays applies strips of clay between erasers, graduated to eraser depths.

Figure c
Strips of clay connect erasers.

Figure d
Clay is added to "flesh out" the face.

Figure e and f
A nose and lips are added and refined.

Figure g and h
Glass (or plastic) eyes are placed into orbits and eyelids are fashioned.

Figure i and j
Completed reproduction. (i) Before adding aging features. (j) After "aging" the face to correspond with aging indicators ascertained from other parts of the skeleton.

The Archeological Research Project

To the uninitiated, archeology probably appears to be a field of endeavor whose principal reason for existence is to discover interesting and valuable objects that once were associated with ancient and exotic cultures. There were times when archeology may have seemed, in fact, to be little more than a glorified treasure hunt. Modern archeology, however, is a method of scientific investigation with the goal of learning something about humans and their behavior. Archeologists may focus on one people or time period or site, but ideally each individual project should contribute to a broader understanding of what it means to be human.

1. Formulating a Research Program

Modern research archeology is problem-oriented, meaning that today's archeologists are seeking answers to specific questions. Depending on the extent of previous work in an area, it usually should be possible to go beyond basic matters of *where* or *when*: "Where did people settle in this valley?" "When was this site occupied?" Archeologists are most interested in seeking explanations about the past: "*Why* did farming develop in the Tehuacán Valley at such an early date?" "*How* did the impact of European exploration affect the balance of power among West African societies in the sixteenth century?"

To address topics such as these, archeologists have adopted the general scientific method of hypothesis-testing. Considerable background research is necessary even before the archeologist steps onto a site. Familiarity with all previous archeological study of the problem or the region, examination of ethnographic accounts covering the more recent cultures that could provide clues to ancient lifeways, and a consideration of nonanthropological topics that may have a bearing on the issue at hand—all may assist the archeologist in framing a reasonable hypothesis that can be examined archeologically; for example: "Overexploitation of their environment forced the people of Mesa Verde to abandon their sites in the thirteenth century A.D."

Once the problem has been defined and a hypothesis proposed, the archeologist must devise a research design, a specific strategy to test the hypothesis by collecting new data. Where might appropriate sites be sought? How can the essential resources—money, labor, equipment—be obtained? What permissions are needed? What specialists from other disciplines must be contacted for their assistance?

A site is a location of past human activity. The archeologist seeks to find the right site (or portion of a site) that will yield some pertinent information about the research question or hypothesis. To delimit the area of investigation, archeologists choose from several survey and sampling techniques:

■ Walkover Survey. Team members walk across the surface of potential sites, usually in a series of parallel transects, marking locations of all finds. Any concentration of appropriate artifacts or features may merit further investigation.

Figure C-1
Survey and sampling techniques of the archeologist.

(a) Walkover Survey

(b) Simple Random Sampling

(c) Systematic Sampling

(d) Stratified Random Sampling

- Simple Random Sampling. A map of the study area is gridded into sampling units of standard size (10 m², 100 m²), and a predetermined percentage of these units (perhaps 10% or 20%) is selected randomly for collection or testing.
- Systematic Sampling. The grid of the proposed study area is again used to guide the on-the-ground surveyors. This time, units are selected for examination in some systematic way—every tenth unit (for a 10% sample), every fifth unit (for a 20% sample), and so on.
- Stratified Random Sampling. If the archeologist has some basis for differentiating the study area into distinct zones, he or she may then wish to randomly sample each zone separately, to insure that all are represented and examined for sites.

The use of standardized survey and sampling techniques makes it possible to use statistics and apply probability predictions with confidence. Nonprobabilistic techniques, such as intuition, informants, or incantations sometimes have been used successfully to locate sites, but they do not permit the researcher to make any statistically valid statements about the representativeness of the site.

Excavation is, of course, the activity most closely associated with archeology by the general public. At one time, archeologists routinely excavated entire sites, sometimes employing enormous numbers of untrained diggers. Excavation is a labor-intensive activity, so as techniques have become more refined and costs have risen, large-scale excavation is less common. Fortunately, probabilistic sampling and the use of innovative analytical techniques and interdisciplinary research efforts have largely eliminated the need for total site excavation. In fact, archeologists prefer to preserve untouched portions of their sites for the benefit of future scientists, who may develop even better ways of extracting archeological information. Thus, much excavation today is a sampling procedure.

Sites may be classified on the basis of their culture histories. Was the site occupied for a long time, or only briefly? The answer to this question often determines the techniques required to excavate the site. Single-component sites were occupied by only one culture and usually for a relatively short period. Therefore they generally produce only one cultural "layer," or stratum, in the otherwise natural stratigraphy of the site. On the other hand, multicomponent sites are those that preserve evidence of several cultures, or perhaps a long-term occupation by one culture, and so produce successive layers or strata of cultural debris or overlapping features.

On multicomponent sites, it is especially important that each stratum be recognized and individually excavated in order to keep the cultural materials from each component separate. At times, such a site may be comprised of a vertical stack of stratigraphic layers, all easily distinguishable from the others. More often, though, the strata may be undulating, or may disappear intermittently, or may have been thoroughly mixed by later activities, such as laying foundations or digging ditches. Archeologists use any and all characteristics to distinguish between strata: color, texture, artifact contents, degree of disturbance by earthworms or rodents, or even the variable sound of a trowel scraping across them!

Excavation is a meticulous process, and the most useful hand tools of the archeologist reflect the delicacy of the operation: trowel, brushes, dental picks. Keeping records is as important (and equally time-consuming) as digging itself. The archeologist carefully notes the nature of each stratum, photographs artifacts and features as they are uncovered, and records the exact provenience or

Figure C-2
Stratigraphy.

Depth
in cm.

Key

	fine yellow sand		red-orange sandy clay
	coarse yellow sand		stained sand
	coarse gray sand		charcoal-bearing soil
	humic soil		fire-altered cobbles

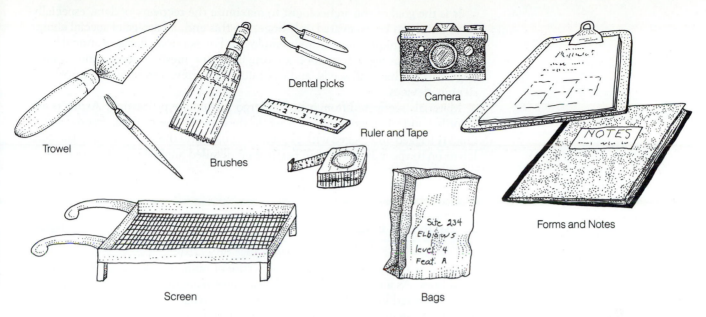

Trowel

Brushes

Dental picks

Ruler and Tape

Camera

NOTES

Forms and Notes

Screen

Site 234
Elbows
level 4
Feat. A

Bags

Tools of the Archeologist

Figure C-3
Tools of the archeologist.

location of each find. Archeologists lay out their sites in a gridwork of squares, or excavation units, usually 1 or 2 meters on a side. These units are keyed to a central datum point, or permanent marker. In this way, excavators can precisely locate the horizontal position of anything they find. By carefully noting the depth of the find as well, they can pinpoint its location in three dimensions. This locational information is the artifact's provenience. It is faithfully recorded and mapped and will enable the archeologist to reconstruct the context of the artifact after the fieldwork has ended.

Naturally, the kinds of data recovered from a site will depend upon several factors: past and recent site environment, earlier disturbance by people or animals, original nature of the site and its contents. During its period of occupation, a site represents an interplay between additive and subtractive processes: building vs. destruction, growth vs. decay. When a site is finally abandoned, the subtractive processes are seldom interrupted. Organic matter decays, structures and other features become disarranged, weathering and breakdown proceed unchecked. Depending upon when the archeologist breaks into this process, and what recovery and conservation techniques are used, the site may yield much or little pertaining to the research topic.

Figure C-4
The excavation unit.

It is the goal of the archeologist to maximize the recovery of data, especially since a site can be excavated only once. To this end, a barrage of special equipment and techniques are routinely employed. For example, flecks of animal bone and microflakes from stone tools are caught in fine-mesh screens, while minute fragments of charcoal, seeds, and nut hulls are retrieved from flotation, or wet-sieving, devices.

Materials recovered from a site undergo immediate processing. Artifacts are recorded and photographed even while they are in the ground. Everything is quickly bagged and tagged with provenience data and then forwarded to the field lab or on to specialists who will begin their detailed analyses.

3. Analyzing Data

Archeology today makes use of the expertise of numerous specialists from many disciplines. As a result, field archeologists must recognize and collect many previously ignored kinds of data from their sites. Artifacts, the products of human behavior, remain a primary focus of interest and study. In addition, a site may yield identifiable faunal remains ranging from large prey species to tiny snails. Plants may be represented by carbonized wood, preserved seeds, pollen, or even leaf impressions on a clay floor. Soil samples yield evidence of past environments and human activity through analysis of composition and chemistry. And, of course, some materials may be collected for dating purposes. Few archeologists can claim competence in working with more than one or two of these categories of material, which is why interdisciplinary research is so essential in the modern study of the past.

Artifacts themselves are cleaned, numbered, and sorted into major categories: ceramics, lithics, organics. The archeologist may then turn some of these materials over to colleagues who specialize in ceramic studies or lithic technology, for example. These experts will then attempt to extract relevant cultural information from a systematic study of other people's garbage.

Artifacts of all kinds may be organized and classified into significant groups for study and interpretation. Archeologists create "types," categories of artifacts that share selected characteristics:

- Morphological Types. Herein the common attributes of size, shape, color, etc., are recognized. This classification is descriptive, and does not presume a specific purpose for the objects. Example: "bifacially flaked lanceolate object."
- Functional Types. This category focuses on artifacts wherein evidence of use is preserved, such as food residue in cooking vessels or edge wear on lithic blades. If function can be determined by objective means, it is proper to assign the artifact in question to a specific functional category. Example: "arrowhead," "hide scraper."
- Temporal Types. Many categories of cultural artifacts undergo stylistic changes through time, making it possible to assign an example of a given type to a specific position in the stylistic sequence. (A modern example would be the yearly models turned out by automobile manufacturers.) In the same way,

a prehistoric artifact may be placed in its proper relative position in a series from one site, and perhaps even dated by comparison with artifacts of the same style from another site of known age.

Archeologists use these classification techniques to enable them to deal with a few groupings of related artifacts rather than countless individual specimens. Typology allows one to note significant trends and associations that might otherwise be obscured by minor stylistic details and individual variations.

With the advent of radiocarbon and other physico-chemical dating methods, the age of archeological materials often can be established with some precision. Carbon 14, potassium-argon, and dendrochronology analyses produce chronometric (or "absolute") dates, expressed in terms of years. Other dating techniques provide only "relative" ages, indicating merely that an object or site is older/younger than another. Relative dating techniques include stratigraphy and fluorine analysis. Most dating techniques (and all of those mentioned here, except stratigraphy) require the use of specialized laboratory equipment and procedures. Each method also has its own limitations and shortcomings, among them the kinds of materials that can be dated, upper and lower age limits, sources of error, and degree of precision.

Much of the remaining data collected in the field can be examined for clues about past environments. Some residual categories are considered *ecofacts* (as opposed to artifacts, which are cultural products). Plant and animal remains aid archeologists in identifying probable foods and reconstructing the native ecology of the site and its vicinity. There may also be further clues about how humans interacted with their environments: what kinds of wood they collected for fires, where they planted their fields, how they processed acorns, and when they hunted deer or gathered shellfish.

Figure C-5
Ecofacts.

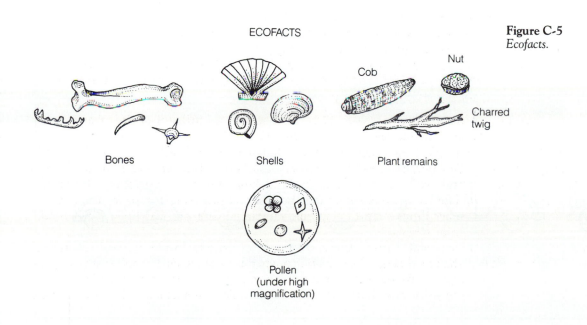

ECOFACTS

Bones

Shells

Cob   Nut

Plant remains

Charred twig

Pollen (under high magnification)

TYPOLOGY OF MODERN ARTIFACTS

Morphological types

| Swirly | Agate | Cat's eye | Steely | Clay |

CHILD'S MARBLES

Functional Types

CONTAINERS

Temporal Types

| Model T Ford | 1940s Chevrolet | Late 1950s Cadillac | 1960s Volkswagon |

AUTOMOBILES

Figure C-6 *Typology of artifacts.*

TYPOLOGY OF PREHISTORIC ARTIFACTS

Morphological types

| Side-notched | Corner-notched | Straight-stemmed | Contracting-stemmed | Expanding-stemmed | Triangular | Lanceolate |

FLAKED BIFACES

Functional Types

| Axe | Drill | Spearhead | Knife | Pipe |

IMPLEMENTS

Temporal Types

Type 1
Tenth century A.D.

Type 2
Eleventh century A.D.

Type 3
Late eleventh century A.D.

Type 4
Late eleventh century A.D.

McElmo
Early twelfth century A.D.

STONE MASONRY TYPES AT CHACO CANYON, NEW MEXICO

Many seasons of fieldwork are sometimes necessary to produce enough data to address the investigator's research questions. Each hour that each person spends digging on a site may later require at least several more hours away from the site devoted to processing artifacts or records or to analyzing nonartifactual samples. The increasingly sophisticated laboratory techniques employed by archeologists often are available from only a small number of specialists or labs, so the time needed to process these samples may run into many months. When, at last, everything has been examined, considered, re-examined, and argued about, the time has come to synthesize the data into a comprehensive final report. Doing so obviously demands that the archeologist be thoroughly conversant with the results of any specialist studies commissioned for the project.

Documenting a project and making its results available to colleagues, funding agencies, and the interested public is an important obligation. Although a "final report" may eventually be published for a project or a site, it probably will contain very few final answers. A fruitful archeological project is one that has tested a hypothesis or two and shown it to be reasonable or not. Very likely, though, new questions will have arisen out of the work, which may in turn lead to new or more refined hypotheses to be tested on yet another site.

Glossary

Acheulian The culture period, or stone tool industry, of the Middle and part of the Lower Pleistocene; characterized by the handaxe.

Acquired characteristics The notion developed by Lamarck that traits acquired during the lifetime of an organism could be passed on to offspring. Known as the theory of acquired characteristics.

Acrocentric chromosome A chromosome with its centromere towards one end.

Adaptation Genetic changes within populations in response to selection (environmental) pressure; usually takes many generations.

Adaptive niche The whole way of life of an organism: where it lives, what it eats, how it gets food, and so forth.

Adaptive radiation The rapid increase and spread of an evolving group of organisms which diversify and adapt to new niches.

Adenine One of the chemical bases (purines) found in both DNA and RNA.

Adobe Sun-baked mud or clay used as a building material.

Advanced In evolutionary terms, an organism further removed from an evolutionary divergence than a more primitive one; usually now termed "derived." *See* Primitive.

Aegyptopithecus An early hominoid form from the Oligocene; Fayum, Egypt.

Agonistic behavior Behavior actively related to fighting—aggression, conciliation, or retreat.

Allele An alternative form of a gene at the same locus (position) on a chromosome.

Allo Combining form indicating different or other.

Allometric growth Differential patterns of growth whereby some parts of the body are disproportionately related to other parts.

Alpaca A South American camelid related to the llama, but having longer wool.

Altruism Helping others without direct benefit to oneself. In natural selection terms: sacrificing your own reproductive success to help another.

Alveolar Tooth-bearing portion of the upper jaw.

Alveolar prognathism Forward projection of the maxilla (much reduced in anatomically modern humans).

Amber Fossil resin or pine pitch, often prized by ancient cultures because of its static electrical properties.

Ameslan American sign language. AMESLAN is used among deaf humans and also for teaching language to some apes.

Amino acids Small molecules that are the building blocks of protein.

Amniote egg The developing reptilian embryo is surrounded by three sacs: one for food, one for waste matter, and one filled with liquid—amniotic fluid—for protection. This egg evolved with reptiles.

Analogous structures Similarities in parts of the anatomy not based on descent from a common ancestor (the bird wing and butterfly wing, for example), but based on common function.

Analogy Similarities between organisms based on common function, not due to evolutionary relationship. *See* Homology.

Anatolia Asia Minor; present-day Turkey.

Anatomically modern (a.m.) *H. sapiens* **(or human beings)** Populations of the Upper Paleolithic who physically resemble populations of today.

Anomaly Different, irregular deviation.

Anthropoidea The suborder (of Primates) of anthropoids, including New World monkeys, Old World monkeys, and hominoids (apes and hominids).

Anthropology The study (or science) of humankind.

Anthropometry Measurement of the human body.

Anthropomorphic Having or being given a humanlike appearance; usually applies to art.

Anticodon A triplet of bases in tRNA which complements the triplet of bases in mRNA. The anticodon corresponds to a particular amino acid.

Arboreal Tree-living. Many prosimians and monkeys, as well as the gibbon and the orangutan, are arboreal.

Archaic New World cultural stage of hunting and gathering, equivalent to the term *Mesolithic* in the Old World.

Archeology The study of prehistoric culture through remains left by ancient humans.

Artifacts (archeological traces) Traces of hominid behavior. Very old artifacts are usually made of stone.

Artiodactyl Even-toed hoof (e.g., cows, pigs, camels).

Ascending ramus Rear upright portion of the mandible.

Association What an archeological trace is found with (other archeological traces, bone refuse, etc.).

Atlatl A throwing board or spearthrower, used in both the Old and New Worlds.

Aurignacian A culture period (*circa* 30,000 y.a.) of the Upper Paleolithic; probable beginning of Upper Paleolithic art.

Aurochs European wild ox, ancestral to modern cattle.

Australopithecine The common term for members of the genus *Australopithecus*.

Australopithecus The extinct genus of Plio-Pleistocene hominids found in South and East Africa; usually divided into: *A. africanus* and *A. robustus* (S. Africa), and *A. boisei* and an early primitive representative, *A. afarensis* (E. Africa).

Autapomorph (-ous, -ic [adj.]) A new morphological trait unique to a group in an evolutionary lineage.

Autosome Any chromosome except a sex chromosome.

Aztecs A militaristic people who dominated the Valley of Mexico and surrounding area at the time of the European conquest.

Barrio A district or neighborhood in a Mesoamerican or South American town site.

Base One of the four chemicals attached to a sugar molecule and a phosphate to make up a nucleotide. In DNA, a base is always paired with another base.

Behavior, social The behavior of animals that live together as a group; gregariousness, sociability.

Beringia The dry-land connection between Asia and America that existed periodically during the Ice Age.

Binomial The binomial (two-term) system of classification developed by Linnaeus. Every organism is identified by two Latin names: The first word is the generic term; the second, the specific.

Biocultural An approach to the study of human beings, their evolution and behavior. The biocultural approach considers both human biology and culture.

Biological adaptation Genetic changes within populations in response to selection (environmental) pressure; usually takes many generations.

Biosphere The entire area inhabited by organisms.

Biostratigraphy Dating method based on evolutionary changes within an evolving lineage.

Bipedalism Walking on two legs as the natural means of locomotion.

Blade A parallel-sided flake at least twice as long as it is wide.

Brachiation Arm-over-arm suspensory locomotion beneath branches.

Brachycephalic Broad-headed. A skull in which the width of the skull is 80% or more of the length.

Breccia Cemented conglomerate containing limestone, sand, and bone.

Breeding isolate A population geographically and/or socially separate and, therefore, relatively easy to define.

Bronze Age Period of early Old World civilizations, beginning with the widespread use of metal tools and weapons after 5500 y.a.

Burin A chisellike stone tool used for engraving on horn, wood, and ivory; characteristic of the Upper Paleolithic.

Calva (or callote) Uppermost portion of the braincase.

Calvaria The skull minus the face and mandible.

Calvarium The skull minus the mandible.

Cambrian The first period of the Paleozoic.

Canine Usually a long and pointed (conical) tooth in front of the mouth, lateral to incisors; used for piercing and grasping.

Carbon 14 (^{14}C) dating A method of determining the age in years of an organic specimen by measuring the loss of the radioactive isotope, ^{14}C.

Carboniferous Fifth period of the Paleozoic. The first reptiles appear during this period.

Carnivore A meat-eating animal. Also the common name for a member of the mammalian order, Carnivora (for example, dogs, cats, bears).

Catarrhine The group (infraorder) comprising all Old World anthropoids, living and extinct.

Catastrophism The idea that there was a series of violent and sudden catastrophes which destroyed most living things. This would explain the extinction of many species. Also part of catastrophism was the belief that after each catastrophe, a new set of creations established new species. Associated with Cuvier.

Catchment area Zone within which a group exploits its resources.

Ceboidea The anthropoid superfamily of New World monkeys, including marmosets and cebids.

Cenozoic Era (65 m.y.a.–present) The present era; the era following the Mesozoic.

Centromere The constricted part of the chromosome to which spindle fibers are attached during mitosis and meiosis.

Cercopithecoidea The anthropoid superfamily of Old World monkeys including colobines and cercopithecines.

Cerebellum Hind portion of brain. The cerebellum is the center of unconscious control of skeletal muscles.

Cerebrum The front portion of the brain; the largest portion of the brain in placental mammals.

Cervical Pertaining to the neck, as in cervical vertebrae.

Chatelperronian An early culture period (circa 32,000 y.a.) of the Upper Paleolithic; perhaps transitional between Mousterian and later Upper Paleolithic culture.

Cheek teeth Premolars and molars.

Chimu A powerful culture that dominated the northern Peruvian coast between about 1000 and 500 y.a. Chan Chan was its capital city.

Chinampa Aztec garden plots built up and fertilized by dredging organic muck from adjacent canals and lake beds.

Chromatid One of the two strands of a chromosome joined by a centromere.

Chromosomal mutation A rearrangement of large sections of DNA (whole pieces of chromosomes) such as deletions, translocations, inversions, and duplications.

Chromosome Threadlike, gene-carrying body, consisting of 1 or 2 DNA molecules.

Chronometric dating Determining the age of a specimen in number of years. Potassium-argon, ^{14}C, ^{238}U, dendrochronology (and others) are used to obtain chronometric dates.

Civilization Large-scale, complexly organized society.

Cladistics The school of evolutionary biology that seeks to make evolutionary hypotheses through interpreting patterns of primitive/derived characteristics.

Class A category of classification in the Animal (or Plant) Kingdom; a subdivision of subphylum. A class includes those animals (or plants) that have adapted to a similar way of life. Vertebrate classes are Pisces, Amphibia, Reptilia, Aves, and Mammalia.

Clavicle Collar bone.

Clovis Phase of North American prehistory, 12,000 to 11,000 y.a. in the West, during which short-fluted projectile points were used in hunting mammoths.

Codex An illustrated book.

Codon A triplet of bases in mRNA that codes for a specific amino acid. The triplet is matched by another triplet of bases in tRNA.

Composite Made of several parts; a harpoon or a bow and arrow are examples of composite implements made in prehistoric times.

Condyle A rounded protuberance of bone which articulates with another bone (that is, forms a joint with or moves against another bone).

Context The environmental setting where an archeological trace is found.

Convergence (convergent evolution) Evolution of similar adaptive traits in unrelated forms; for example, the wings of birds and wings of butterflies. *See* Parallelism.

Coprolite Feces found at an archeological site; if fossilized, called *coprolith*.

Core Stone reduced by flake removal.

Core area Area, within the home range, of greatest regular use.

Coronal suture The suture running transversely across the skull joining the frontal and parietal bones.

Cosmology The study of the creation of the universe and the laws that govern it.

Cranium The complete skull; bone of the head, face, and mandible.

Crepuscular Active at twilight or dawn.

Cretaceous Final (third) period of Mesozoic. Dinosaurs become extinct. Probable appearance of first primates.

Crossing-over The exchange of genetic material between homologous chromosomes during meiosis.

Crossopterygians Lobe-finned fish; probably gave rise to amphibians.

Cultigen A plant that is wholly dependent on humans; a domesticate.

Cultivar A wild plant encouraged by humans.

Culture The ways humans discover, invent, and develop in order to survive. Culture is the human strategy of adaptation.

Cuneiform Wedge-shaped writing, usually associated with Mesopotamia.

Cytoplasm That portion of the cell lying outside the nucleus.

Cytosine One of the chemical bases (pyrimidines) found in both DNA and RNA.

Dental arcade The shape of the tooth row: posteriorly divergent, parallel, parabolic, etc.

Dental formula The number of each kind of tooth present. Shown usually for one-quarter of the mouth as: Incisors; Canine; Premolars; Molars.

Devonian Fourth period of the Paleozoic. Age of Fish. Appearance of amphibians.

Diastema Gap, space, especially between the upper lateral incisor and canine (also seen in the lower jaw between the canine and first premolar); found in many monkeys and pongids.

Diploid number (2n) The full complement of chromosomes—46 in humans—in a somatic cell or in a sex cell before meiosis.

Direct percussion Striking core or flake with a hammerstone.

Display Stereotyped behavior that serves to communicate emotional states between individuals. Display is most often associated with reproductive or agonistic behavior.

Diurnal Active during daylight hours.

Divination A method of foretelling the future.

Division of labor Activities performed only by members of a particular status, such as age or sex.

DNA (deoxyribonucleic acid) A large molecule composed of adenine, guanine, cytosine, and thymine plus phosphate and sugar; DNA carries the genetic code.

Dolichocephalic Narrow or long-headed. A skull in which the width is less than 75% of the length.

Dominance (dominance hierarchy) The physical domination of some members of a group by other members. A hierarchy of ranked statuses sustained by hostile, or threat of hostile, behavior which results in greater access to resources such as food, sleeping sites, and mates.

Dominant A trait determined by a dominant allele. A trait that is visible or measurable and that prevents the appearance of the recessive.

Dorsal Pertaining to the back (toward the backbone) of an animal.

Double helix The structure of DNA composed of a pair of matching helixes.

Dryopith The common term for *Dryopithecus* and *Proconsul*; distributed mostly in Africa, but with some representatives in Europe.

Dryopithecus The genus name referring to a diverse group of extinct hominoids from the Miocene.

East Lake Turkana A Plio-Pleistocene locality in northern Kenya which has yielded dozens of fossil hominids. Hominid-bearing levels date 1.8–1.0 m.y.a.

Ecological niche (econiche) Environment to which a species is adapted.

Eemian "Third" interglacial; between the Riss and Würm glaciations.

Effective breeding population Those individuals in a population actually producing offspring; usually about one-third total population size.

Empirical Derived from or depending on experience or experiment.

Endocast An impression of the inside of the skull showing the size, shape, and some details of the surface of the brain.

Endogamy Mating within the social unit (that is, the population). *See* Exogamy.

Endoskeleton An internal bony skeleton, characteristic of vertebrates. *See* Exoskeleton.

Eocene Second epoch of Cenozoic. Radiation of prosimians. Possible appearance of anthropoids.

Estrous cycle An hormonally initiated cycle in female mammals correlated with ovulation. Estrus may involve observable physical and behavioral changes.

Ethnography The study of surviving, nonliterate societies.

Eutheria The most numerous subclass of Mammalia. Embryo and fetus of these (placental) mammals are nourished by a placenta.

Evolution A change in allele frequency in a population from one generation to the next.

Evolutionary reversal The reacquisition of a structure previously lost in the evolution of a life form—an extremely unlikely event.

Evolutionary trend A set of anatomical and/or behavior traits which tend to characterize a group of evolutionarily related organisms. For example: pentadactyly, retention of complete clavicle, and stereoscopic vision among the primates.

Exogamy Mating outside the social unit (that is, the population).

Exoskeleton A hard, supporting external covering, characteristic of many invertebrates such as ants and lobsters. *See* Endoskeleton.

F_1 First filial generation; offspring resulting from a cross of homozygous dominants and homozygous recessives. All individuals resulting from such a cross are heterozygous.

F_2 Second filial generation; offspring of a cross of F_1 individuals—a mating of two heterozygous individuals (or selfing in a species where this is possible, as in the case of Mendel's peas).

Faience Pottery with a glassy glazed surface, developed by Egyptians.

Family Members of a family usually inhabit a similar environment; a category that includes genera and species.

Fayum An Oligocene fossil primate site in Egypt yielding several early anthropoid forms.

Femur Thigh bone.

Fibula The narrow long bone of the lower leg. *See* Tibia.

Fixity of species The belief that species, once created, never changed but remained fixed. This belief was firmly held by most scholars in the eighteenth century.

Flake Thin-edged fragment removed from a core.

Fluorine dating A method of relative dating by measuring the amount of fluorine in a specimen. More fluorine indicates a greater age.

Fluting Technique of removing large flakes in order to prepare projectile points for hafting; popular during the Paleo-Indian period in the New World.

Folsom Phase of southern Great Plains prehistory, 10,000 to 8000 y.a., during which long-fluted projectile points were used for killing bison.

Foramen magnum Opening in the base of the skull through which the spinal cord passes.

Forensic Pertaining to courts of law. In anthropology, the use of anthropology in questions of law.

Founder effect A type of genetic drift resulting from the isolation of a small nonrandom population drawn from a larger gene pool; also called the Sewall-Wright effect.

Frontal bone The front bone of the skull including the forehead and the brow region over the eyes.

Gamete A haploid cell (sperm or ovum) that may combine with a haploid cell of the other sex to form a fertilized cell.

Gene That section of DNA responsible for the ultimate synthesis of a specific polypeptide chain of amino acids; that portion of DNA with a detectable function.

Gene frequency (allele frequency) A numerical indicator of the proportion of genes (alleles) in a population. *See* Hardy-Weinberg Equilibrium.

Gene pool The total complement of genes in a population.

Generalized Pertains to a trait capable of several functions. The human hand is generalized because it is used for a number of functions; the human foot is specialized and is used in a very limited way. *See* Specialized.

Genetic drift (random genetic drift) The evolutionary factor which accounts for evolutionary changes (shifts in allele frequency) due to random events. A function of population size.

Genotype The genetic makeup of a particular organism; an individual's "genetic formula"; the genes at one or more loci.

Genotypic proportion The relative frequency of the genotypes in a population. For a two-allele system (such as A, a), there will be three genotypes (AA, Aa, aa). Hardy-Weinberg Equilibrium makes idealized predictions of these genotypes according to the formula: $p^2 + 2pq + q^2 = 1$. *See* Hardy-Weinberg Equilibrium.

Genus (pl. genera) A category of classification in the Animal (or Plant) Kingdom. Genus groups together closely related species usually inhabiting similar ecological niches; for example, *Homo, Pan, Felis, Canis*.

Geochemistry The study of the chemical composition of the earth's crust.

Geology The study of the history and structure of the earth as recorded in rocks.

Gracile Small, lightly built; used to refer to smaller australopithecines. *See* Robust.

Gravettian A culture period (*circa* 25,000 y.a.) of the Upper Paleolithic; associated with Lascaux Cave art.

Great Basin Rugged, dry plateau between the mountains of California and Colorado, and southern Oregon and Idaho.

Grooming Cleaning the body of another by picking through the hair and fur with the fingers or teeth. Grooming is common among primates.

Guanine One of the chemical bases (purines) found both in DNA and RNA.

Günz First glacial of the Pleistocene.

Habilis A species of genus *Homo*, first applied by Louis Leakey to Plio-Pleistocene hominids from East Africa.

Hadar A Plio-Pleistocene hominid locality in northeastern Ethiopia. Hominid-bearing levels dated ?3.7–2.6 m.y.a.

Haploid number (n) The number of chromosomes in the gamete after meiosis (23 in humans).

Haplorhini The classificatory term used to group tarsiers with monkeys, apes, and humans (either suborder or semiorder).

Hardy-Weinberg Equilibrium The mathematical relationship expressing—under ideal conditions—the predicted distribution of genes in populations; the central theorem of population genetics.

Helix A spiral or anything with a spiral form.

Helix, double The structure of DNA resembles a double helix (spiral).

Herbivore A plant-eating animal.

Heritability The relative amount of variation in a trait due to genetic causes as part of total phenotypic variation.

Heterodontism Having different teeth. Characteristic of mammals whose teeth consist of incisors, canines, premolars, and molars.

Heterozygote A cell or individual that is heterozygous. (A hybrid is heterozygous for a particular trait.)

Heterozygous Having different alleles at a given locus on a pair of homologous chromosomes.

Hieroglyphics Sacred "picture-writing" used in ancient Egypt; term used in other areas, too.

Holistic Viewing the whole as an integrated and interdependent system. Anthropology includes as its concern all aspects of human beings—physical and behavioral.

Holocene Second (present) epoch of Quaternary; begins with end of Pleistocene glaciation.

Holstein Second interglacial between the Mindel and Riss glaciations.

Home range The area utilized by an animal; the area the group is most familiar with and which provides the group with food.

Hominid Popular form of Hominidae, the family to which humans belong. Hominids include bipedal primates such as *Australopithecus* and *Homo*.

Hominidae The family, of the order Primates, to which humans belong.

Hominization Process of becoming more human.

Hominoid Abbreviated or popular form of Hominoidea, the superfamily to which hominids, pongids, and gibbons belong.

Homo The genus to which humans belong, including *habilis, erectus*, and *sapiens*.

Homodontism Having the same teeth. Refers to the situation wherein all teeth of the mouth are similar, as in fish and reptiles.

Homoiothermy Pertains to an organism that maintains the same temperature (mammals and birds, for example). Warm-blooded.

Homologous chromosomes Paired chromosomes. Chromosomes that are paired during meiosis and participate in cross-over. Homologous chromosomes contain the same loci.

Homologous structures Similarities in parts of the anatomy based upon common descent.

Homologue Occurs in meiosis when a chromosome duplicates itself. The double-stranded chromosome is a homologue.

Homology Similarities of organisms based on common evolutionary descent.

Homo sapiens The species which appeared 200,000 to 300,000 years ago; includes Neandertals and anatomically modern humans.

Homo sapiens sapiens The subspecies to which modern humans belong; anatomically modern human beings.

Homozygote A cell or individual that is homozygous. (A purebred is homozygous for a particular trait.)

Homozygous Having the same allele at a given locus on a pair of homologous chromosomes.

Hopewell A culture centered in southern Ohio between 2100 and 1700 y.a., but influencing a much wider region through trade and the spread of a religious cult.

Horticulture Farming method in which only human energy and hand tools are used for cultivation.

Human A term now generally applied to *H. erectus* and *H. sapiens*.

Human evolution Biological changes over time leading to anatomically modern human beings.

Human variation Physical differences among humans.

Humerus Upper arm bone.

Hybrid   Offspring of parents of mixed ancestry. A heterozygote.

Hypothesis   Unproved theory. A theory is a statement with some confirmation.

Immune response system   The production of specific antibodies in response to the introduction of specific foreign antigens into the body.

Inca   The people whose sophisticated culture dominated Peru at the time of the Europeans' arrival; also, the term for that people's highest ruler.

Incisors   Front teeth, usually spatulate in primates; used for cutting and nipping.

Independent assortment   Where gene pairs on one set of homologous chromosomes do not influence the distribution of gene pairs on other chromosomes—they separate independently from one another during meiosis and are randomly assorted in the gametes. Known as Mendel's second law.

Innominate   The fused half-portion of a pelvis; contains three bones—the ilium, ischium, and pubis.

In situ   In its original or natural position.

Interspecific variation   Variation between two separate species.

Interstadial   The period of partial retreat during a major glaciation.

Intraspecific variation   Variation within a species due to age, sexual dimorphism, individual genetic differences, or geographic separation.

Intron   Within a genetic locus, a section of DNA that is not translated.

Ischial callosities   Hardened sitting pads found on the rear ends of Old World monkeys. Also seen to some degree in chimpanzees.

Jurassic   Second period of Mesozoic. Great age of dinosaurs. First appearance of birds.

Kabuh   Middle Pleistocene geologic formation.

Kanapoi   A Plio-Pleistocene hominid site in northern Kenya. Estimated age approximately 4 m.y.a.

Karyotype   The chromosome complement contained in a cell, especially the diagram of chromosomes arranged according to size and banding patterns of each chromosome.

KNM-ER   Kenya National Museum—East Rudolf (the former name for Lake Turkana). The prefix preceding paleontological discoveries from East Lake Turkana.

Kromdraai   A Plio-Pleistocene hominid site in South Africa yielding remains of robust australopithecines.

Laetoli   A Plio-Pleistocene hominid site in northern Tanzania. Dated 3.77–3.59 m.y.a.

Lamarckism   Lamarck's ideas about evolution. *See* Acquired characteristics.

Lambdoidal suture   The horizontal or transverse suture at the back of the top of the skull joining the parietal and occipital bones.

Lanceolate   Narrow and tapering form, used to describe American projectile points.

Lemuroidea   The prosimian superfamily of lemurs, today confined to Madagascar.

Levant   Countries bordering the eastern Mediterranean.

Lineage   An evolutionary line of related forms distinct from other such lines.

Linguistics   In anthropology, the description and study of the structure and history of language and its relationship to culture.

Living floor   A narrow horizon of archeological remains. Corresponds to brief period of hominid occupation.

Locus (pl. loci)   The position of a gene on a chromosome.

Loess   Fine-grained, well-drained soil composed of glacially pulverized rock; preferred by early Neolithic farmers.

Lorisoidea   The prosimian superfamily of lorises. Today all are nocturnal forms, found in Africa and southern Asia.

Lothagam   A Plio-Pleistocene hominid site in northern Kenya. Estimated age, approximately 5.5 m.y.a.

Macroevolution   Large evolutionary changes (result of long-term major shifts in allele frequencies) produced only after many generations. *See* Microevolution.

Magdalenean   Final period of the Upper Paleolithic (*circa* 15,000 y.a.) (in Europe) and a time of spectacular technological growth; associated with art from Altamira Cave in Spain.

Makapansgat   A Plio-Pleistocene hominid site in South Africa yielding remains of gracile australopithecines.

Mammals   The class of animals that nurse their young from mammary glands. Primates belong to this class.

Mandible   Lower jaw.

Manioc   Cassava; a starchy edible root crop of the tropics.

Marsupials   A subclass of mammals—Metatheria—that bear live young; infants are nursed in the mother's pouch, Marsupium pouch.

Masseter   Chewing; refers to muscles used in the operation of the jaw—originating on the zygomatic (cheek) bones and inserting on the mandible.

Mastoid process   A triangular bone behind the ear hole on a human skull; usually more pronounced in males than females.

Matriline   Individuals related through the mother.

Maxilla   Upper jaw.

Maya   Prehistoric Mesoamerican culture that represented the climax of pre-European cultural development between 1700 and 1100 y.a.

Megalith   A large-stone construction erected by early Neolithic farmers of western Europe and elsewhere; Stonehenge is an elaborate example, but single-stone monuments and tombs were common.

Meiosis   Cell division, consisting of two divisions, in which the total complement (diploid number) of chromosomes is reduced by half (haploid number) in the gametes (sperm in males; ova in females). Also known as reduction division.

Melanin   The biochemical compound produced by specialized cells in the basal layers of the epidermis. Melanin is very important in influencing skin pigmentation.

Mendelian trait (simple trait)   An inherited trait with a straightforward pattern, controlled by one genetic locus.

Mesoamerica   The region from southern Mexico through Panama.

Mesolithic   A cultural phase dominated by a foraging and fishing economy in the Old World, where it also is referred to as the Middle Stone Age; equivalent to *Archaic* in the New World.

Mesopotamia   Land between the Tigris and Euphrates rivers; known also as the Fertile Crescent.

Mesozoic Era (225–65 m.y.a.)   The era following the Paleozoic. Known as the Age of Reptiles.

Metacentric chromosome   A chromosome with its centromere near the center.

Metatheria   A subclass of mammals (marsupials); infants are nursed in the mother's pouch.

Metazoa   Multicellular animals. A major division of the Animal Kingdom.

Microevolution The small-scale evolutionary changes occurring over just a few generations and involving relatively small changes in allele frequencies. What the Hardy-Weinberg formula measures. *See* Macroevolution.

Microlith Small (minute) stone tools.

Microwear Polishes, striations and other diagnostic microscopic changes on the edges of stone tools produced during use.

Midden A refuse heap marking a Mesolithic campsite; often composed of discarded shells, bones, ash and other organic material.

Migration Movement of individuals (and, necessarily, genes) between populations. An evolutionary factor that may cause changes in allele frequencies.

Millet Small-grained cereal grass native to Asia and Africa and domesticated there by early farmers.

Milpa Slash-and-burn or swidden farming; this term is usually associated with Mesoamerica.

Mindel Second glacial of the Pleistocene.

Miocene Fourth epoch of Cenozoic. Radiation of hominoids. Possible appearance of hominids.

Mississippian A Southeastern U.S. moundbuilding culture which flourished from 1100 to 500 y.a.

Mitosis Cell division into two daughter cells in which the chromosome complement is identical to the mother cell and to each other.

Molars Cheek teeth, following the premolars. In anthropoids these are the last three teeth of the tooth row; used for grinding and chewing.

Molecule Smallest portion of a substance that acts like that substance and is capable of existing independently. Several to many atoms constitute a molecule.

Mongrelization Racial mixture.

Monogenists Term applied to those who believe that all races derived from a single pair (Adam and Eve).

Monotreme A subclass of mammals—prototheria—that lay eggs.

Mosaic evolution Term applied when the rate of evolution in one functional system varies from other systems.

Mousterian A culture period, or stone tool industry, of the Middle Paleolithic; usually associated with Neandertals. Characterized mainly by stone flakes.

Multivariate Pattern for several variables assessed simultaneously.

Mutagen An agent that mutates (alters the DNA of a cell).

Mutation An alteration in the genetic material (DNA). The true "creative" factor in evolution. Mutation is the only way to produce new variation and the starting point of all evolutionary change.

Natural selection The evolutionary factor, first articulated by Charles Darwin, that causes changes in allele frequencies in populations due to differential net reproductive success of individuals. *See* Net reproductive success.

Neandertals *H. sapiens* form that preceded anatomically modern human beings (*H. sapiens sapiens*); usually associated with Mousterian culture and the Middle Paleolithic.

Neolithic Literally, "new stone" age; associated with the development of domesticated resources and farming practices.

Neopallium or Neocortex A covering of the cerebral hemispheres begun in reptiles, expanded in mammals, and reaching its greatest expansion in humans. Higher mental activity is concentrated in this area.

Net reproductive success The number of offspring successfully raised; the bottom line of natural selection.

Nocturnal Active during nighttime. *See* Diurnal and Crepuscular.

Nomadism Lifeway of wandering in search of food; often associated with herders.

Nuchal Pertaining to the neck.

Nucleotide A purine or pyrimidine base attached to a sugar and a phosphate group: a subunit of DNA and RNA.

Nucleus A body, present in most types of cells (i.e., eukaryotes), containing chromosomes.

Nulliparous Never having given birth.

Occiput (occipital bone) The rear bone of the skull. The occiput also forms most of the base, including the occipital condyles and foramen magnum.

OH Olduvai Hominid. The prefix preceding hominid discoveries (numbered sequentially) from Olduvai Gorge.

Olduvai Gorge A paleoanthropological site in northern Tanzania yielding remains of Plio-Pleistocene hominids and a wealth of biocultural data.

Olfactory Smell.

Oligocene Third epoch of Cenozoic. Radiation of anthropoids.

Olmec Culture in the Gulf Coast Lowlands of Veracruz and Tabasco, Mexico, with a highly developed art style and high degree of sociopolitical complexity; flourished from 3500 to 2500 y.a.

Omnivore An animal that will eat both plants and meat.

Omo A Plio-Pleistocene hominid locality in southern Ethiopia. Hominid-bearing levels dated 2.9–1.0 m.y.a.

Oöcyte Female sex cell; a cell that undergoes meiosis and produces an egg (ovum).

Oögenesis Division process of the female sex cell that produces ova.

Oötid A haploid cell produced by meiosis and differentiating into an ovum.

Oracle A person believed capable of communicating with the deities on behalf of others.

Order A category of classification in the Animal (or Plant) Kingdom. A subdivision of Class. Members of an order usually inhabit a similar environment; for example, Carnivora, Rodentia, Primates.

Ordovician The second period of the Paleozoic. First fishes appear.

Osteology The study of bones.

Ostracoderm Shell-skin or armored.

Oviparity Egg birth, characteristic of most animals.

Ovum Female sex cell.

P_1 The parental generation in which homozygous dominants and recessives are crossed. Parents homozygous (pure) for round seeds and parents homozygous for wrinkled represent such a parental cross.

Paleo "Ancient"; in the Americas, refers to the early period of big-game hunting cultures, from about 12,000 to 8000 y.a.

Paleoanthropology The multidisciplinary approach to the study of human biocultural evolution. Includes physical anthropology, archeology, geology, ecology, and many other disciplines.

Paleocene First epoch of Tertiary. Prosimians present.

Paleolithic Old Stone Age. The culture period that includes the beginning of culture up to approximately the end of the Pleistocene glaciation. Usually divided into Lower, Middle, and Upper.

Paleolithic, Lower The earliest period of the Paleolithic, characterized by Oldowan (pebble tools) and Acheulian (handaxe) industries.

Paleolithic, Middle A stone flake industry associated with the Mousterian culture period and Neandertals.

Paleolithic, Upper The final stage of the Paleolithic, associated with more sophisticated culture such as cave painting, sculpting, engraving, and stone tools made from blades. Appearance of anatomically modern humans.

Paleomagnetism Dating method based on the shifting nature of the earth's geomagnetic field.

Paleontology The study of the fossils of ancient animals.

Paleopathology The study of ancient diseases.

Paleospecies A group of organisms found in paleontological contexts and usually separated by large amounts of time, thus adding to the amount of variation seen in extant groups.

Paleozoic Era (570–225 m.y.a.) The era following the Proterozoic, beginning 570 m.y.a. The first era in which fossils are relatively abundant.

Palynology The analysis of pollen found in the soil of archeological excavations to determine the kinds of plants present at the ancient site.

Parallelism (parallel evolution) Evolution of similar adaptive traits in forms that were once related but then diverged, developing along similar lines. *See* Convergence.

Paranthropus The genus name sometimes used to refer to robust australopithecines and, therefore, making a generic distinction between them and gracile australopithecines (*Australopithecus*).

Parietal The right and left side bones on top of the skull, joined by the sagittal suture.

Pentadactyly Having five digits. A generalized trait of mammals and primates.

Penultimate Last but one; next to last.

Peptide A compound of two or more amino acids joined by peptide bonds. Linked peptides form polypeptides which, in turn, join to form proteins.

Perineum The area between the anus and genitalia.

Periodontal Gum and jaw.

Perissodactyl Odd-toed hoof (e.g., horse).

Permian Final period of the Paleozoic. Appearance of mammallike reptiles.

Phenotype The observable or measurable characteristic of an organism. Roundness in a seed is an observable phenotype. In blood groups, A, B, and O and AB are measurable phenotypes.

Phenotypic ratio The ratio of phenotypes, especially from a hybrid cross. Mendel's famous F_1 hybrid cross of peas produced a 3:1 phenotypic ratio.

Phylogeny The study of evolutionary lines of descent. A "family tree."

Phylum (pl. phyla) A primary division of the Animal (or Plant) Kingdom; for example, Arthropoda, Chordata.

Piltdown A forged "fossil" hominid from England, "discovered" in 1911. Combining a fully *sapiens* cranium with a modern pongid jaw, it served to confuse anthropologists for four decades.

Pithecanthropus Name originally given to *H. erectus* by Eugene Dubois.

Placenta Tissue connected to the uterus that nourishes the fetus and absorbs its waste. This structure is characteristic of most mammals and has given its name to that form—placental mammals.

Placental mammals (Eutheria) Mammals whose embryonic development is associated with a placenta.

Plano A Great Plains bison-hunting culture of 8000 to 7000 y.a. that used narrow unfluted lanceolate points.

Platycephaly Flatheadedness, as opposed to the dome shape of the skull of anatomically modern humans.

Pleistocene Sixth epoch of the Cenozoic. *H. sapiens* becomes widespread throughout Old World. *H. sapiens sapiens* evolves toward end of Pleistocene. Ice Age.

Plesiomorph (-ous, -ic [adj.]) A character of common inheritance found in an evolving lineage; primitive traits.

Pliocene Fifth epoch of Cenozoic. Hominids definitely present.

Point mutation Change in just one base in the DNA sequence. Probably the most common kind of mutation with evolutionary impact.

Polychrome Multicolored.

Polygenists Term applied to those who believe in a multiple origin of races.

Polygyny One male and two or more females in a mating relationship.

Polymorphism The situation when two or more alleles at a given genetic locus occur with frequencies greater than 1% in a population.

Polypeptide A group of peptides linked together. One or more polypeptide chains make a protein.

Population Within a species, a community of individuals where mates are usually found.

Population genetics Studies in contemporary populations through measurement of allele frequencies. *See* Hardy-Weinberg Equilibrium.

Postcranial The skeleton behind (below) the skull.

Postorbital bar The bony element that closes in the outside of the eye orbit—a characteristic of primates.

Potassium-argon (K/Ar) dating Determining absolute age (in years) by measuring the amounts of potassium-40 (^{40}K) and argon-40 (^{40}Ar). The greater the amount of argon that has built up, the older the specimen. Used only on rocks once heated to a very high temperature, such as that generated by volcanic activity.

Potlatch Ceremonial feast and gift-exchange among the Northwest Coast Indians.

Prehensility Adaptation for grasping.

Premolars Cheek teeth similar in form to the molars; situated between canines and molars. Old World anthropoids possess two premolars and New World forms normally three in each quadrant. Human premolars have two cusps, compared to four or more in molars, and are known as bicuspids.

Presenting A behavior, often indicating subordination or appeasement, in which an animal places itself on all fours and elevates its rear end toward another. During estrus a female may present for purposes of copulation.

Pressure flaking A stoneworking technique in which flakes are removed from the edges by pressure rather than percussion.

Primates The order of mammals to which humans, apes, monkeys, and prosimians belong.

Primitive In evolutionary terms, an organism that is closer to an evolutionary divergence than a later (more derived) one. *Also see* Plesiomorph.

Principle of independent assortment The distribution of one pair of genes does not influence the distribution of other pairs of genes.

Principle of segregation Genes occur in pairs. In the production of a gamete, the pair is separated so that each gamete contains only one of the pair.

Prosimian Common form for Prosimii; the suborder of primates, including lemurs, lorises, and tarsiers.

Protein A macromolecule, composed of one or more polypeptide chains of amino acids. Proteins are responsible for carrying out most of the cell's metabolic activities, and are thus the basic structural and functional compounds of the cell.

Protein synthesis The manufacture of a protein from the DNA to the final product. The process by which amino acids are linked (by a peptide bond) to form a polypeptide chain. The completed chain or chains form a protein.

Proterozoic A geologic era immediately preceding the Paleozoic. Not much evidence of life.

Prototheria A subclass of mammals (monotremes) that lay eggs and nurse their young.

Punctuated equilibrium The view that evolutionary rates are not constant, but proceed slowly (equilibria) until "punctuated" by rather sudden spurts.

Purines   A class of chemical bases—adenine and guanine—found in DNA and RNA.

Pyrimidines   A class of chemical bases—cytosine, thymine, uracil—found in nucleic acids.

Quadrumanual   Using all four limbs for grasping during locomotion, as in the orang.

Quadrupedal (quadrupedalism)   Using all four limbs as weight supports while moving. Trunk typically horizontal. The basic mammalian, and primate, form of locomotion.

Quaternary   Second (present) period of Cenozoic. Period of *Homo erectus* and *Homo sapiens*.

Quern   A grinding slab or mortar used for processing grain.

Quinoa   Seed-bearing member of the genus *Chenopodium*, cultivated by early Peruvians.

Race   Currently defined by anthropologists as a breeding population; formerly applied to a group of people who resembled each other in physical appearance. Many anthropologists do not believe the term to be a useful one when applied to humans.

Rachis   On a plant, the short stem by which individual seeds are attached to the main stalk.

Ramapithecus   An extinct hominoid from the Miocene (13–9 m.y.a.) thought by some to be an early hominid. Now usually included within *Sivapithecus*. See *Sivapithecus*.

Raptor   A hunting bird with talons and hooked beak, such as an eagle or hawk.

Recessive   A trait that is not phenotypically expressed in heterozygotes. A trait that is phenotypically expressed only in the homozygous state.

Recombination   The reshuffling of genetic material every generation as the result of sexual reproduction. Recombination occurs during meiosis (through crossing-over and random assortment) and provides variation for natural selection to act upon.

Ribosomes   Small, spherical particles, composed of rRNA and proteins, found in the cytoplasm. The ribosome is the site of protein synthesis.

Rift Valley (Great Rift Valley)   A massive (1200 mile long) geological feature in East Africa associated with mountain building, volcanoes, faulting, etc. The results of "rifting" have provided preservation and access to several superb Plio-Pleistocene sites (Olduvai, East Lake Turkana, Hadar, etc.).

RNA (ribonucleic acid)   A nucleic acid found both in the nucleus and the cytoplasm. RNA differs from DNA in that its sugar component is ribose.

  mRNA   Messenger RNA. This RNA carries genetic information from DNA in the nucleus to the ribosomes in the cytoplasm.

  rRNA   Ribosomal RNA; a major constituent of ribosomes.

  tRNA   Transfer RNA. This RNA brings amino acids together to form a polypeptide chain.

Riss   The third major glaciation of the Alpine system.

Robust   Larger, more heavily built; used to refer to the larger australopithecines. See Gracile.

Sagittal crest   Raised ridge along the midline of the skull where the temporal muscle (used to move the jaw) attaches.

Sagittal suture   The suture joining the left and right parietals; extending the length of the skull from the coronal suture in front to lambdoidal suture behind.

Savanna   A grassland with a scattering of trees, usually in the tropics or subtropics.

Scapula   Shoulder blade.

Sectorial   Compressed single-cusped tooth (1st lower premolar) seen in pongids (and many extinct hominoids); compared to the bicuspid form found in most hominids.

Segregation   Genes exist on paired chromosomes. At meiosis, the pairs are segregated so that a gamete has only one of the pair. Mendel's first law.

Sex cells   Cells that divide by meiosis and become gametes.

Sexual dimorphism   Marked physical differences between adult males and females of a species. Examples: greater size of gorilla and baboon males; sagittal and occipital crest of male gorilla.

Shovel-shaped incisors (shoveling)   Incisors with raised ridges of enamel on both sides of the teeth.

Sickle-cell anemia (sicklemia)   A severe, usually lethal disease caused by an alteration (point mutation) in adult hemoglobin. The disease is only expressed when the mutant allele is inherited in double dose.

Sickle-cell trait   An alteration (point mutation) in adult hemoglobin. This term usually refers to carrying the mutant allele in single dose (that is, a carrier).

Silurian   Third period of the Paleozoic. Jawed fishes appear. First air-breathing animals.

Sinanthropus   The name originally given by Davidson Black to hominid specimens from Zhoukoudian; now known as *H. erectus pekinensis*.

Sivapithecus   An extinct hominoid from the Miocene (*circa* 13–7 m.y.a.) found mostly in Eurasia. Some species are probably closely related to orangs.

Sociobiology   An evolutionary approach to the explanation of behavior—largely in terms of natural selection (individual reproductive success).

Solutrean   A culture period (*circa* 20,000 y.a.) of Europe; known for its magnificent flintwork.

Somatic cells   Cells that do not divide by meiosis and do not become gametes. Body cells.

Sorghum   An African cereal grass favored for its sweet juicy stem as well as its head of small edible seeds.

Specialized   A trait that evolved for a specific function is said to be specialized. The human foot is specialized, the hand generalized. See Generalized.

Speciation   The evolutionary process that produces new species from previous ones.

Species   A category of classification of the Animal (or Plant) Kingdom. A population or group of populations living in the same econiche that can, or actually do, interbreed and produce fertile offspring.

Sperm   Male fertilizing fluid; semen.

Spermatid   A haploid cell produced by meiosis and differentiating into a sperm cell.

Spermatocyte   A cell that undergoes meiosis and produces a spermatid. A male sex cell.

Stela   An upright stone or post, often bearing inscriptions or carvings.

Sterkfontein   A Plio-Pleistocene hominid site in South Africa yielding remains of gracile australopithecines and, perhaps, early *Homo*.

Stratigraphy   Sequential layering of deposits. The sequence of layers is used as a means of dating, relatively, the layers as well as the materials in the layers.

Strepsirhini   The classificatory term used to group lemurs and lorises (either suborder or semiorder).

Subphylum   A major division of a phylum—such as Vertebrata.

Substrate   The physical surface on which an animal moves or rests.

Superfamily   A group of closely related families.

Supraorbital torus   Ridge above the orbits on a skull. The supraorbital torus is very pronounced in *erectus*, Neandertals, and some australopithecines.

Swartkrans   A Plio-Pleistocene hominid site in South Africa yielding remains of robust australopithecines and, perhaps, early *Homo*.

Symbiosis   Mutually advantageous association of two different organisms.

Sympatric   Two or more species living in the same area.

Synapomorph   (-ous, -ic [adj.]) A new morphological feature, shared between two or more groups in an evolving lineage, that signifies their close and unique relationship; restricted to characters.

Taphonomy   Study of how bones come to be buried in the earth and preserved as fossils.

Tarsiioidea   The prosimian superfamily of tarsiers, a nocturnal form found in southern Asia.

Taung   A South African Plio-Pleistocene australopithecine site. The location of the first australopithecine discovery (1924).

Taurodontism   Bulltoothedness.

Taxon   A population (or group of populations) judged to be sufficiently distinct to be assigned to a separate category (such as genus or species).

Taxonomy   The science of the classification of organisms, including the principles, procedures, and rules of classification.

Tectonic movement   Movements of the earth (along fault lines, during mountain building, and so forth).

Tehuacán Valley   A dry highland region on the boundary of the states of Puebla and Oaxaca in southern Mexico; location of early New World domestication and farming activities.

Tektite   A round, glassy body of unknown origin.

Tell   A mound of accumulated rubble on the site of an ancient city.

Terrestrial   Living on the ground. Humans, gorillas, and some monkeys are terrestrial.

Territoriality   Behavior in defense of the territory of a group; establishment of exclusive right to the use of a territory. Some primates are much more territorial than others.

Territory   The area a group defends. That part of the home range used exclusively by one group. Neighbors of the same species do not enter or else enter only on a brief foray.

Tertiary   First period of the Cenozoic. Period of primate radiation. (Includes: Paleocene, Eocene, Oligocene, Miocene, and Pliocene.)

Tetrad   A structure of four chromatids of a pair of homologous chromosomes. Seen during meiosis.

Thymine   One of the chemical bases (pyrimidines) found in DNA, but not in RNA.

Tibia   The large long bone of the lower leg; the shin. *See* Fibula.

Toltecs   A central Mexican highlands people who created a pre-Aztec empire with its capital at Tula in the Valley of Mexico.

Tool   A natural object deliberately modified for utilitarian purposes.

Transhumance   Seasonal population movement from one resource zone to another; compare with *nomadism*.

Triassic   First period of Mesozoic. First dinosaurs.

Trinil fauna   Animal remains associated with the Middle Pleistocene Trinil period in Java.

Triplet   A sequence of three bases; found in mRNA and tRNA. Codes for a specific amino acid. A codon or anticodon.

Tuff   A solidified sediment of volcanic ash.

Typology, racial   Dividing humans into discrete racial types.

Uniformitarianism   A concept maintaining that the ancient changes in the earth's surface were caused by the same physical principles acting today. The earth's crust was formed slowly and gradually. Mountains, rivers, valleys, etc., were the result of purely natural forces such as erosion by wind, water, frost, ice, and rain. Although not originated by Charles Lyell, uniformitarianism is associated with him because he popularized it.

Upper Paleolithic   A culture period noted for technological, artistic, and behavioral innovations. Also known for the appearance of anatomically modern human beings.

Uracil   One of the chemical bases (pyrimidines) found in RNA, but not in DNA.

Variation (genetic)   Inherited differences between individuals. The basis of all evolutionary change.

Ventral   Toward the belly; the front of an organism (as in humans) or the undersurface of an animal that does not stand erect (as a dog).

Vertebra (pl. vertebrae)   A single bone of the spinal or vertebral column (backbone).

Viviparity   Live birth; characteristic mainly of mammals.

Wattle and daub   A building technique, using a framework of interwoven branches or sticks plastered over with clay.

Weichsel   The fourth glacial period (correlated with Würm in the Old World).

Weir   A brush or stone obstruction placed across a stream or inlet for the purpose of trapping fish.

Wisconsin   The period of the last major glacial advance in North America; analogous to "Weichsel" or Würm in the Old World.

World view   A literal translation from the German, *Weltanschauung*. A personal or group philosophy explaining history; a way of looking at the world.

Würm   The fourth glacial in the Old World.

Xenophobic   Fear of foreigners.

Y-5 pattern (Dryopithecine Y-5)   A pattern of cusps on the molar teeth characteristic of hominoids.

Yangshao   First phase of the Chinese Neolithic period, centered along Huang Ho river.

Ziggurat   Sumerian mud-brick temple-pyramid.

Zygomatic (or zygomatic bone)   Malar or cheek bone.

Zygomatic arch   The bone along the side of the skull connecting the zygomatic and temporal bones.

Zygote   A fertilized cell formed by the union of a male gamete and a female gamete.

Bibliography

Adam, Karl Dietrich
1985 "The Chronological and Systematic Position of the Steinheim Skull." *In* Delson, q.v., 272–276.

Adams, Richard E. W.
1977 *Prehistoric Mesoamerica.* Boston: Little, Brown.

Adams, Robert McC.
1972 "Patterns of Urbanization in Early Southern Mesopotamia." *In: Man, Settlement, and Urbanism*, Peter J. Ucko, Ruth Tringham, and G. W. Dimbleby (eds.), London: Duckworth, pp. 735–749.

———
1981 *Heartland of Cities.* Chicago: University of Chicago Press.

Aigner, Jean S.
1981 *Archaeological Remains in Pleistocene China.* Munich: C. H. Beck.

———
1986 "The Age of Zhoukoudian Locality 1." *Anthropos* (Brno), **23**: 157–173.

Aigner, Jean S. and Wm. S. Laughlin
1973 "The Dating of Lantian Man and His Significance for Analyzing Trends in Human Evolution." *American Journal of Physical Anthropology*, **39**:97–110.

Aikens, C. Melvin
1970 *Hogup Cave.* University of Utah Anthropoligical Papers, 93.

Aldred, Cyril
1961 *The Egyptians.* New York: Frederick A. Praeger.

Alland Jr., Alexander
1971 *Human Diversity.* New York: Anchor Press/Doubleday.

Allchin, Briget and Raymond Allchin
1982 *The Rise of Civilization in India and Pakistan.* Cambridge: Cambridge University Press.

Allen, J., J. Golson and R. Jones
1977 *Sunda and Sahul.* New York: Academic Press.

Altmann, Jeanne
1981 *Baboon Mothers and Infants.* Cambridge: Harvard University Press.

Altmann, Stuart A. and Jeanne Altmann
1970 *Baboon Ecology.* Chicago: University of Chicago Press.

Alva, Walter
1988 "Discovering the New World's Richest Unlooted Tomb." *National Geographic*, **174**(4):510–555.

Ammerman, A. J. and L. L. Cavalli-Sforza
1973 "A Population Model for the Diffusion of Early Farming in Europe." *In: The Explanation of Culture Change*, Colin Renfrew (ed.), London: Duckworth, pp. 343–357.

Andersson, J. Gunnar
1934 *Children of the Yellow Earth.* New York: Macmillan.

Andrews, P. J.
1983 "The Natural History of *Sivapithecus*." *In*: R. Ciochon and R. Corruccini (eds.), q.v., pp. 441–463.

Andrews, Lauline
1985 "Family Group Systematics and Evolution Among Catarrhine Primates." *In*: E. Delson (ed.), q.v., pp. 14–22.

Andrews, Peter and Elizabeth Evans
1979 "The Environment of *Ramapithecus* in Africa." *Paleobiology* **5**(1):22–30.

Andrews, Peter and Jens Lorenz Franzen (eds.)
1984 *The Early Evolution of Man.* Frankfurt A.M.: Cour. Forsch.-Inst. Seckenberg, 69.

Ardrey, Robert
1976 *The Hunting Hypothesis.* New York: Atheneum.

Arens, W.
1979 *The Man-Eating Myth.* New York: Oxford University Press.

Aronson, J. L., R. C. Walter, and M. Taieb
1983 "Correlation of Tulu Boi Tuff at Koobi Fora with the Sidi Hakoma Tuff at Hadar." *Nature*, **306**:209–210.

Aveni, Anthony F.
1986 "The Nazca Lines: Patterns in the Desert." *Archaeology*, **39**(4):32–39.

Baba, M. L., L. L. Darga and M. Goodman
1981 "Maximum Parsimony Test of the Clock Model of the Molecular Change Using Amino Acid Sequence Data." Paper presented at the Annual Meetings, American Association of Physical Anthropologists, April 1981.

Badrian, Alison and Noel Badrian
1984 "Social Organization of *Pan paniscus* in the Lomako Forest, Zaire." *In:* Randall L. Susman, *The Pygmy Chimpanzee*, New York: Plenum Press, 325–346.

Bailey, G.
1975 "The Role of Molluscs in Coastal Economies." *Journal of Archaeological Science*, 2:45–62.

Baker, Paul T.
1966 "Human Biological Variation as an Adaptive Response to the Environment." *Eugenics Quarterly*, 13:81–91.

Baker, Paul T. and Michael A. Little
1976 "Environmental Adaptations and Perspectives." *In: Man in the Andes*, P. T. Baker and M. A. Little (eds.), Stroudsburg, Penn.: Dowden, Hutchinson, and Ross, Inc., pp. 405–428.

Barash, David
1982 *Sociobiology and Behavior*. 2nd Ed. New York: Elsevier.

Bar-Yosef, Ofer
1986 "The Walls of Jericho; An Alternative Explanation." *Current Anthropology*, 27:157–162.

——— 1987 "Late Pleistocene Adaptations in the Levant." *In: The Pleistocene in the Old World: Regional Perspectives*, Olga Soffer (ed.), New York: Plenum, pp. 219–236.

Bartholomew, C. A. and J. B. Birdsell
1953 "Ecology and the Protohominids." *American Anthropologist*, 55:481–498.

Barzun, Jacques
1965 *Race: A Study in Superstition*. New York: Harper and Row.

Bass, W. M.
1987 *Human Osteology: A Laboratory and Field Manual* (3rd Ed.). Columbia, Mo.: Missouri Archaeological Society Special Publication No. 2.

Bayanov, Dmitri and Igor Bourtsev
1974 "Reply (to comments on Proshner's article)." *Current Anthropology*, 15(4):452–456.

——— 1976 "On Neanderthal vs. Paranthropus." *Current Anthropology*, 17(2):312–318.

Beck, Benjamin B.
1980 *Animal Tool Behavior*. New York: Garland Publishing, Inc.

Behrensmeyer, A. K., D. Western, and D. E. Dechant Boaz
1979 "New Perspectives in Vertebrate Paleoecology from a Recent Bone Assemblage." *Paleobiology*, 5(1):12–21.

Behrensmeyer, Anna K. and Andrew P. Hill
1980 *Fossils in the Making: Vertebrate Taphonomy and Paleoecology*. Chicago: The University of Chicago Press.

Bennett, Kenneth A.
1979 *Fundamentals of Biological Anthropology*. Dubuque: Wm. C. Brown Co. Publishers.

Biddiss, Michael D.
1970 *Father of Racist Ideology: The Social and Political Thought of Count Gobineau*. New York: Weybright and Talley.

Binford, Lewis R.
1968 "Post-Pleistocene Adaptations." *In:* Sally R. Binford and Lewis R. Binford (eds.), q.v., pp. 421–449.

——— 1981 *Bones. Ancient Men and Modern Myths*. New York: Academic Press.

——— 1982 Comment on White's article, "Rethinking the Middle/Upper Paleolithic Transition." (*See* White, 1982a)

——— 1983 *In Pursuit of the Past*. New York: Thames and Hudson.

——— 1985 "Ancestral Lifeways: The Faunal Record." *AnthroQuest*. Pasadena: The L.S.B. Leakey Foundation News, 32, Summer, 1985.

Binford, Lewis R. and Chuan Kun Ho
1985 "Taphonomy at a Distance: Zhoukoudian, 'The Cave Home of Beijing Man'?" *Current Anthropology*, 26:413–442.

Binford, Lewis R. and Nancy M. Stone.
1986a "The Chinese Paleolithic: An Outsider's View." *AnthroQuest*, Fall 1986(1):14–20.

——— 1986b "Zhoukoudian: A Closer Look." *Current Anthropology*, 27(5):453–475.

Binford, Sally R. and Lewis R. Binford (eds.)
1968 *New Perspectives in Archaeology*. Chicago: Aldine.

Birdsell, Joseph B.
1981 *Human Evolution*. (3d Ed.), Boston: Houghton Mifflin Co.

Birkby, W. H.
1966 "An Evaluation of Race and Sex Identification from Cranial Measurements," *American Journal of Physical Anthropology*, 24:21–28.

Black, Francis L.
1975 "Infectious Diseases in Primitive Societies." *Science*, 187:515–518.

Boas, Franz
1938 *General Anthropology*. New York: D. C. Heath and Co.

——— 1940 "New Evidence in Regard to the Instability of Human Types." *Reprinted In*: F. Boas (ed.), *Race, Language and Culture*. New York: The Free Press, pp. 76–81.

Boaz, N. T.
1977 "Paleoecology of Early Hominidae in Africa." *Kroeber Anthropological Society Papers*, 50:37–62.

Boaz, N. T. and A. K. Behrensmeyer
1976 "Hominid Taphonomy: Transport of Human Skeletal Parts in an Artificial Fluviatile Environment." *American Journal of Physical Anthropology*, 45:53–60.

Boaz, N. T., F. C. Howell, and M. L. McCrossin
1982 "Faunal Age of the Usno, Shungura B and Hadar Formation, Ethiopia." *Nature*, 300:633–635.

Bodmer, Walter F.
1972 "Race and IQ: The Genetic Background." *In: Race and Intelligence*, Ken Richardson and David Speers (eds.), Baltimore: Penguin Books, Inc., pp. 83–113.

Bodmer, W. F. and L. L. Cavalli-Sforza
1976 *Genetics, Evolution, and Man*. San Francisco: W. H. Freeman and Company.

Bogaarts, John
1980 "Does Malnutrition Affect Fecundity? A Summary of Evidence." *Science*, 208:564–569.

Boggess, Jane
1984 "Infant Killing and Male Reproductive Strategies in Langurs (*Presbytis entellus*)." *In: Infanticide*, G. Hausfater and S. Blaffer Hrdy (eds.), Hawthorne, N.Y.: Aldine de Gruyter, pp. 280–310.

Bökönyi, S.
1969 "Archaeological Problems and Methods of Recognizing Animal Domestication." *In:* Peter J. Ecko and G. W. Dimbleby (eds.), q.v., pp. 207–218.

Bonner, T. I., R. Heinemann and G. J. Todardo
1980 "Evolution of DNA Sequences Has Been Retarded in Malagasy Primates." *Nature*, **286**:420–423.

Bordes, François
1968 *The Old Stone Age*. New York: McGraw-Hill Book Co.

Boserup, Ester
1965 *The Conditions of Agricultural Growth*. Chicago: Aldine.

Bouzek, Jan
1985 "Relations between Barbarian Europe and the Aegean Civilizations." *Advances in World Archaeology*, **4**:71–114.

Bowler, J. M. and A. G. Thorne (eds.)
1976 "Human Remains from Lake Mungo: Discovery and Excavation of Lake Mungo III." *In: The Origin of the Australians*, R. L. Kirk and A. G. Thorne (eds.), Canberra: Australian Institute of Aboriginal Studies (Humanities Press Inc., New Jersey), pp. 127–138.

Boyd, Wm. C.
1950 *Genetics and the Races of Man*. Boston: Little, Brown.

Brace, C. Loring
1964 "The Fate of the 'Classic' Neanderthals: A Consideration of Hominid Catastrophism." *Current Anthropology*, **5**:3–43.

———
1967 *The Stages of Human Evolution*. Englewood Cliffs, N.J.: Prentice-Hall, Inc.

———
1973 "Sexual Dimorphism in Human Evolution." *In: Man in Evolutionary Perspective*, C. L. Brace and J. Metress (eds.), New York: Wiley Publishing Co., pp. 238–254.

———
1979 "Biological Parameters and Pleistocene Hominid Lifeways." *In: Primate Ecology and Human Origins*, Irwin S. Bernstein and E. O. Smith (eds.), New York: Garland Publishing Co., pp. 263–289.

Brace, C. Loring and Frank B. Livingstone
1971 "On Creeping Jensenism," *In: Race and Intelligence*, C. L. Brace, G. R. Gamble and J. T. Bond (eds.), Anthropological Studies, No. 8, American Anthropological Association, Washington, D.C.

Brace, C. Loring, Harry Nelson and Noel Korn
1971 *Atlas of Human Evolution*. New York: Holt, Rinehart and Winston. (2nd Ed. 1979)

Brady, James E. and Andrea Stone
1986 "Naj Tunich: Entrance to the Maya Underworld." *Archaeology*, **39**(6):18–25.

Braidwood, Robert J.
1975 *Prehistoric Men* (8th Ed.). Glenview, Ill.: Scott, Foresman.

Brain, C. K.
1970 "New Finds at the Swartkrans Australopithecine Site." *Nature*, **225**:1112–1119.

———
1975 "The Bone Assemblage from the Kromdraai Australopithecine Site." *In: Paleoanthropology: Morphology and Paleoecology*, R. Tuttle (ed.), World Anthropology Series, Chicago: Aldine, pp. 225–243.

———
1981 *The Hunters or the Hunted? An Introduction to African Cave Taphonomy*. Chicago: University of Chicago Press.

Bramblett, Claud A.
1976 *Patterns of Primate Behavior*. Palo Alto, Ca.: Mayfield Publishing Co.

Brauer, Gunter
1984 "A Craniological Approach to the Origin of Anatomically Modern *Homo sapiens* in Africa and Implications for the Appearance of Modern Europeans." *In: Smith and Spencer, q.v.*, 327–410.

Brock, A., P. L. McFadden and T. C. Partridge
1977 "Preliminary Paleomagnetic Results from Makapansgat and Swartkrans." *Nature*, **266**:249–250.

Bromage, Timothy G. and Christopher Dean
1985 "Re-evaluation of the Age at Death of Immature Fossil Hominids." *Nature*, **317**:525–527.

Brooks, S. T.
1985 Personal Communication.

———
1986 "Comments on 'Known' Age at Death Series." Presented in conjunction with "Skeletal Age Standards Derived from an Extensive Multi-Racial Sample of Modern Americans," by J. Suchey and D. Katz, at the Fifty-Fifth Annual Meeting of the American Association of Physical Anthropologists, Albuquerque, New Mexico.

Brose, David and Milford H. Wolpoff
1971 "Early Upper Paleolithic Man and Late Middle Paleolithic Tools." *American Anthropologist*, **73**:1156–1194.

Brues, A. M.
1977 *People and Races*. New York: MacMillan Publishing Company.

Bryant, Vaughan M., Jr. and Glenna Williams-Dean
1975 "The Coprolites of Man." *Scientific American*, **232**:100–109.

Bryson, Reid A., David A. Baerreis, and Wayne M. Wendland
1970 "The Character of Late Glacial and Post-Glacial Climatic Changes." *In: Pleistocene and Recent Environments of the Central Great Plains*, Wakefield Dort, Jr., and J. Knox Jones, Jr. (eds.), pp. 53–74. Lawrence: Department of Geology, University of Kansas.

Buettner-Janusch, John
1973 *Physical Anthropology: A Perspective*. New York: John Wiley and Sons.

Buffon, George Louis Leclerc, Compte de
1860 "*Histoire Naturelle Generale et Particuliere*." Translated by Wm. Smellie, London. *In: Louis L. Snyder, q.v.*, pp. 102–103.

Bunn, Henry T.
1981 "Archaeological Evidence for Meat-eating by Plio-Pleistocene Hominids from Koobi Fora and Olduvai Gorge." *Nature*, **291**:574–577.

Bunn, Henry T. and Ellen M. Kroll.
1987 "On Inferences from the Zhoukoudian Fauna." *Current Anthropology*, **28**(2):199–202.

Burger, Richard L.
1984 *The Prehistoric Occupation of Chavin de Huantar*. Berkeley: University of California Press.

Busse, Curt D.
1978 "Do Chimpanzees Hunt Cooperatively?" *American Naturalist*, **112**:767–770.

Butynski, Thomas M.
1982 "Vertebrate Predation by Primates: A Review of Hunting Patterns." *Journal of Human Evolution*, **11**:421–430.

Butzer, Karl W.
1974 "Paleoecology of South African Australopithecines: Taung Revisited." *Current Anthropology*, **15**:367–382.

Butzer, Karl W. and Glynn L. Isaac, (eds.)
1975 *After the Australopithecines*. The Hague: Mouton Publishers and Chicago: Aldine Publishing Co.

Bygott, J. David

1979   "Agonistic Behavior, Dominance, and Social Structure in Wild Chimpanzees of the Gombe National Park." *In*: Hamburg and McCown (eds.), q.v., pp. 405–427.

Caldwell, Joseph R.
1962   "Eastern North America." *In*: *Courses Toward Urban Life*, Robert J. Braidwood and Grodon R. Wiley (eds.), Wenner-Gren Foundation for Anthropological Research, Publications in Anthropology, 32:288–308.
Campbell, Bernard
1974   *Human Evolution*. Chicago: Aldine Publishing Co. (2nd Ed., 1985).

——   1976   *Humankind Emerging*. Boston: Little, Brown and Co. (4th Ed., 1984).
Cann, Rebecca L.
1987   "In Search of Eve." *The Sciences*, Sept./Oct.:30–37.
Carneiro, R.
1970   "A Theory of the Origin of the State." *Science*, **169**:733–738.
Carpenter, C. R.
1965   "The Howlers of Barro Colorado Island." *In*: I. DeVore, (ed.), q.v., pp. 250–291.
Carter, Howard and A. C. Mace
1923   *The Tomb of Tutankhamen*. London: Cassell and Co., Ltd.
Cartmill, Matt
1972   "Arboreal Adaptations and the Origin of the Order Primates." *In*: *The Functional and Evolutionary Biology of Primates*, R. H. Tuttle (ed.), Chicago: Aldine-Atherton, pp. 97–122.

——   1974   "Rethinking Primate Origins." *Science*, **184**:436–443.
Cavalieri, Liebe F.
1976   "New Strains of Life—or Death." *New York Times Magazine*, **22**:8, August.
Cavalli-Sforza, L. L. and M. W. Feldman
1981   *Cultural Transmission and Evolution: A Quantitative Approach*. Princeton, N.J.: Princeton University Press.
Chalmers, Neil
1980   *Social Behaviour in Primates*. Baltimore: University Park Press.
Chang, Kwang-chih
1977   *The Archaeology of Ancient China (3rd Ed.)*. New Haven: Yale University Press.

——   1980   *Shang Civilization*. New Haven: Yale University Press.
Charteris, J., J. C. Wali, and J. W. Nottrodt
1981   "Functional Reconstruction of Gait from Pliocene Hominid Footprints at Laetoli, Northern Tanzania." *Nature*, **290**:496–498.
Chen, Allan
1989   "The Thera Theory." *Discover*, **10**(2):76–83.
Chia, Lan-Po
1975   *The Cave Home of Peking Man*. Peking: Foreign Language Press.
Childe, V. Gordon
1951   *Man Makes Himself*. New York: Mentor Books.

——   1952   *New Light on the Ancient Near East*. New York: Frederick A. Praeger.

——   1957   *What Happened in History*. Baltimore: Pelican Books.

China Pictorial
1981   "A Complete Ape-Man's Skull Unearthed at Longtan Cave." *China Pictorial*, 3:20–21, Beijing, China, March 1981 (no author).
Chivers, David J., Bernard A. Wood and Alan Bilsborough
1984   *Food Acquisition and Processing in Primates*. New York: Plenum.
Chopra, S.R.K.
1983   "Significance of Recent Hominoid Discoveries from the Siwalik Hills of India." *In*: R. Ciochon and R. Corruccini (eds.), q.v., pp. 539–557.
Ciochon, Russel L.
1983   "Hominoid Cladistics and the Ancestry of Modern Apes and Humans. A Summary." *In*: R. Ciochon and R. Corruccini (eds.), q.v., pp. 783–843.
Ciochon, R. L. and A. B. Chiarelli (eds.)
1980   *Evolutionary Biology of the New World Monkeys and Continental Drift*. New York: Plenum Publishing Co.
Ciochon, Russel L. and Robert S. Corruccini
1983   *New Interpretations of Ape and Human Ancestry*. New York: Plenum.
Clark, J. Desmond
1976   "Prehistoric Populations and Resources Favoring Plant Domestication in Africa." *In*: *Origins of African Plant Domestication*, Jack R. Harlan, John DeWet and Ann Stemler (eds.), The Hague: Mouton, pp. 69–84.

——   1981   "The Cultures of the Middle Palaeolithic/Middle Stone Age." *In*: J. Desmond Clark (ed.), *The Cambridge History of Africa* I:248–341.
Clark, J. Grahame D.
1972   *Star Carr: A Case Study of Bioarchaeology*. Reading, MA: Addison-Wesley.

——   1979   *Mesolithic Prelude*. Edinburgh: Edinburgh University Press.
Clark, W. E. LeGros
1967   *Man-apes or Ape-men?* New York: Holt, Rinehart and Winston.

——   1959,   *The Antecedents of Man*. New York:Quadrangle/
       1971   The New York Times Books (3rd Ed.).
Clarke, R. J.
1976   "New Cranium of *Homo erectus* from Lake Ndutu, Tanzania." *Nature*, **262**:485–487.

——   1985   "*Australopithecus* and Early *Homo* in Southern Africa." *In*: Eric Delson, q.v., pp. 171–177.
Clarke, R. J. and F. Clark Howell
1972   "Affinities of the Swartkrans 847 Hominid Cranium." *American Journal of Physical Anthropology*, 37:319–336.
Clodd, Edward
1897   *Pioneers of Evolution from Thales to Huxley*. New York: Freeport (Reprinted 1972).
Clutton-Brock, T. H., S. D. Albon, and F. E. Guinness
1984   "Maternal Dominance, Breeding Success, and Birth Sex Ratios in Red Deer." *Nature* **308**:358–360.
Clutton-Brock, T. H., F. E. Guiness, and S. D. Albon
1982   *Red Deer Behavior and Ecology of Two Sexes*. Chicago: University of Chicago Press.
Clutton-Brock, T. H. and Paul H. Harvey

1977 "Primate Ecology and Social Organization." *Journal of Zoological Society of London*, **183**:1–39.

Coe, Michael D.
1968 *America's First Civilization*. New York: American Heritage.

———
1977 *Mexico*. London: Thames and Hudson.

Coe, Michael D. and Richard A. Diehl
1980 *The Maya*. New York: Thames and Hudson.

Coe, Michael, Dean Snow and Elizabeth Benson
1986 *Atlas of Ancient America*. New York: Facts on File Publications.

Cohen, Mark N.
1977 *The Food Crisis in Prehistory*. New Haven: Yale University Press.

Conrad, Nicholas, David L. Asch, Nancy B. Asch, David Elmore, Harry Gove, Meyer Rubin, James A. Brown, Michael D. Wiant, Kenneth B. Farnsworth, Thomas G. Cook
1984 "Acceleration Radioactive Dating of Evidence for Prehistoric Horticulture in Illinois." *Nature*, **308**:443–446.

Conroy, G., C. J. Jolly, D. Cramer and J. E. Kalb
1978 "Newly Discovered Fossil Hominid Skull from the Afar Depression." *Nature*, **276**:67–70.

Constable, George
1973 *The Neanderthals* (Emergence of Man Series, Time-Life Books). Waltham, Mass.: Little, Brown and Co.

Cook, J., C. B. Stringer, A. P. Currant, H. P. Schwarcz and A. G. Wintle
1982 "A Review of the Chronology of the European Middle Pleistocene Hominid Record." *Yearbook of Physical Anthropology*, **25**:19–64.

Cooke, H.B.S.
1978 "Faunal Evidence for the Biotic Setting of the Early African Hominids." *In: Early Hominids of Africa*, C. Jolly (ed.), New York: St. Martin's Press.

Corruccini, R. S.
1975a "Multivariate Analysis of *Gigantopithecus* Mandibles." *American Journal of Physical Anthropology*, **42**:167–170.

———
1975b "The Interaction Between Neurocranial and Facial Shape in Hominid Evolution." *Homo*, **26**:136–139.

Corruccini, R. S. and H. M. McHenry
1980 "Cladometric Analysis of Pliocene Hominids." *Journal of Human Evolution*, **9**:209–221.

Corruccini, R. S., M. Baba, M. Goodman, R. L. Ciochon and J. E. Cronin
1980 "Non-Linear Macromolecular Evolution and the Molecular Clock." *Evolution*, **34**:1216–1219.

Count, Earl W. (ed.)
1950 *This Is Race*. New York: Henry Schuman.

Cowgill, George L.
1974 "Quantitative Studies of Urbanization at Teotihuacán." *In: Mesoamerican Archaeology: New Approaches*, Norman Hammond (ed.), Austin: University of Texas Press, pp. 363–396.

Cowgill, Ursula M.
1962 "An Agricultural Study of the Southern Maya Lowlands." *American Anthropologist*, **64**: 273–286.

Cronin, J. E.
1983 "Apes, Humans, and Molecular Clocks. A Reappraisal." *In:* R. Ciochon and R. Corruccini (eds.), q.v., pp. 115–150.

Cronin, J. E. and V. M. Sarich

1980 "Tupaiid and Archonta Phylogeny: The Macromolecular Evidence." *In:* W. P. Luckett (ed.), q.v., pp. 293–312.

Crook, J. H.
1970 "Social Organization and Environment: Aspects of Contemporary Social Ethology." *Animal Behavior*, **18**:197–209.

Culbert, T. Patrick
1985 "The Maya Enter History." *Natural History*, **94**(4):41–49.

———
1988 "The Collapse of Classic Maya Civilization." *In: The Collapse of Ancient States and Civilizations*, Norman Yoffee and George Cowgill (eds.), Tucson: University of Arizona Press, pp. 69–101.

Curtis, Garniss
1981 "A Matter of Time: Dating Techniques and Geology of Hominid Sites." Paper delivered at the symposium, "Our Ancestors, Ourselves," Davis, Ca., May 10, 1981.

Curtis, G. H., T. Drake, R. Cerling and A. Hampel
1975 "Age of KBS Tuff in Koobi Fora Formation, East Rudolf, Kenya." *Nature*, **258**:395.

Dahlberg, A. A.
1951 "The Dentition of the American Indian." *In: The Physical Anthropology of the American Indian*. Viking Fund, Inc., **5**:138–176.

Dalrymple, G. B.
1972 "Geomagnetic Reversals and North American Glaciations." *In:* Calibration of Hominoid Evolution, W. W. Bishop and J. A. Miller (eds.), Edinburgh: Scottish Academic Press, pp. 303–329.

Daniel, Glyn
1980 "Megalithic Monuments." *Scientific American*, **243**(7):15, 78–81.

Dart, Raymond
1959 *Adventures with the Missing Link*. New York: Harper and Brothers.

Darwin, Charles
1859 *On the Origin of Species*. A Facsimile of the First Edition, Cambridge, Mass.: Harvard University Press (1964).

Darwin, Francis (ed.)
1950 *The Life and Letters of Charles Darwin*. New York: Henry Schuman.

Davies, Nigel
1983 *The Ancient Kingdoms of Mexico*. New York: Penguin.

Dawkins, Richard
1976 *The Selfish Gene*. New York: Oxford University Press.

Day, Michael
1986 *Guide to Fossil Man*. Chicago: The University of Chicago Press, 4th ed.

Day, M. H., M. D. Leakey and C. Magori
1980 "A New Fossil Hominid Skull from Nu Ngaloba Beds, Laetoli, Northern Tanzania." *Nature*, **289**:55–56.

Day, M. H. and E. H. Wickens
1980 "Laetoli Pliocene Hominid Footprints and Bipedalism." *Nature*, **286**:385–387.

DeBonis, L.
1983 "Phyletic Relationships of Miocene Hominoids and Higher Primate Classification." *In:* R. Ciochon and R. Corruccini (eds.), q.v., pp. 625–649.

Delson, Eric (ed.)
1985   *Ancestors: The Hard Evidence.* New York: Alan R. Liss, Inc.

─────

1986   "Human Phylogeny Revised Again." *Nature,* **322**:496–497.
De Luce, Judith and Hugh T. Wilder
1983   *Language in Primates.* New York: Springer-Verlag New York Inc.
De Lumley, Henry
1969   "A Paleolithic Camp at Nice." *Scientific American,* May, **220**:42–50.
De Lumley, Henry and Marie-Antoinette
1973   "Pre-Neanderthal Human Remains from Arago Cave in Southeastern France." *In: Yearbook of Physical Anthropology 1973,* **16**:162–168.
De Lumley, Henry and Arun Sonakia
1985   "Contexte Stratigraphique et Archeologique de L'Homme de la Narmada, Hathnora, Madhya Pradesh, Inde." *L'Anthropologie* (Paris), **89**(1):3–12.
De Lumley, Marie-Antoinette
1975   "Ante-Neanderthals of Western Europe." *In: Paleoanthropology: Morphology and Paleoecology,* Russel H. Tuttle (ed.), The Hague: Mouton Publishers, pp. 381–387.
De Lumley, Marie-Antoinette and Arun Sonakia
1985   "Premiere Decouverte d'un *H. erectus* sur le Continent Indien a Hathnore dans la Moyenne Vallee de la Narmada." *Anthropologie* (Paris), **89**(1):13–61.
Dene, H. T., M. Goodman and W. Prychodko
1976   "Immunodiffusion Evidence on the Phylogeny of the Primates." *In: Molecular Anthropology,* M. Goodman, R. E. Tashian and J. H. Tashian (eds.), New York: Plenum Press, pp. 171–195.
Dene, H., M. Goodman, W. Prychodko and G. Matsuda
1980   "Molecular Evidence for the Affinities of Tupaiidae." *In:* W. P. Luckett (ed.), q.v., pp. 269–291.
Dennell, Robin
1983   *European Economic Prehistory: A New Approach.* New York: Academic Press.
De Vos, J.
1985   "Faunal Stratigraphy and Correlation of the Indonesian Hominid Sites." *In:* Delson, q.v., pp. 215–220.
Diamond, Jared
1987   "The Worst Mistake in the History of the Human Race." *Discover,* **8**(5):64–66.
Diaz del Castillo, Bernal
1956   *The Discovery and Conquest of Mexico.* New York: Farrar, Straus and Cudahy.
Dillehay, Tom D.
1984   "A Late Ice-Age Settlement in Southern Chile." *Scientific American,* **251**(4):106–117.
Dingle, Herbert
1959   "Copernicus and the Planets." *In: A Short History of Science,* Jean Lindsay (ed.), New York: Doubleday & Co., pp. 18–26.
DiPeso, Charles C.
1974   *Casas Grandes, A Fallen Trading Center of the Gran Chichimeca, I, II, III.* Flagstaff: Northland Press.
Dobyns, Henry F.
1966   "Estimating Aboriginal American Population: An Appraisal of Techniques with a New Hemisphere Estimate." *Current Anthropology,* **7**:395–449.

Dobzhansky, Theodosius
1970   *Genetics of the Evolutionary Process.* New York: Columbia University Press.

─────

1971   "Race Equality." *In: The Biological and Social Meaning of Race,* Richard H. Osborne (ed.), San Francisco: W. H. Freeman Co., pp. 13–24.
Drake, R. E., et al.
1980   "KBS Tuff Dating and Geochronology of Tuffaceous Sediments in the Koobi Fora and Shungura Formations, East Africa." *Nature,* **283**:368–372.
Dunn, Frederick L.
1968   "Epidemiological Factors: Health and Disease in Hunter-Gatherers." *In: Man the Hunter,* R. B. Lee and I. DeVore (eds.), Chicago: Aldine, pp. 221–228.
Dunn, L. C.
1951   *Race and Biology. The Race Question in Modern Science.* UNESCO.

─────

1965   "Mendel, His Work, and His Place in History." *In: Proceedings of the American Philosophical Society,* Vol. 109, No. 4 (Commemoration of the publication of Gregor Mendel's pioneer experiments in genetics), August 18, Philadelphia: American Philosophical Society.

Eiseley, Loren
1961   *Darwin's Century.* New York: Anchor Books.
Ekberg, Douglas R.
1979   *Intelligence and Race.* New York: Praeger.
Eldredge, Niles and Joel Cracraft
1980   *Phylogenetic Patterns and the Evolutionary Process.* New York: Columbia University Press.
Emery, Walter B.
1957   "The Tombs of the First Pharaohs." *Scientific American,* **197**(7):36, 106–112.
Erison, Harry J.
1973   *Evolution of the Brain and Intelligence.* London: Academic Press.
Erlandson, Jon M.
1988   "The Role of Shellfish in Prehistoric Economies: A Protein Perspective." *American Antiquity,* **53**(1):102–109.

Fagan, Brian M.
1984   *The Aztecs.* San Francisco: W. H. Freeman.
Falk, Dean
1980   "A Reanalysis of the South African Australopithecine Natural Endocasts." *American Journal of Physical Anthropology,* **53**:525–539.

─────

1983   "The Taung Endocast: A Reply to Holloway." *American Journal of Physical Anthropology,* **60**:479–489.
Fairservis Jr., Walter A.
1976   *The Roots of Ancient India* (2nd Ed.). New York: MacMillan.

─────

1983   "The Script of the Indus Valley Civilization." *Scientific American,* **248**(3):58–66.
Fedigan, Linda M.
1982   *Primate Paradigms.* Montreal: Eden Press.

1983 "Dominance and Reproductive Success in Primates." *Yearbook of Physical Anthropology*, **26**:91–129.

Fisher, R. A.
1930 *The Genetical Theory of Natural Selection*. Oxford: Clarendon.

Fladmark, Knut R.
1986 "Getting One's Berings." *Natural History*, **95**(11):8–19.

Flannery, Kent V.
1968 "Archaeological Systems Theory and Early Mesoamerica." *In: Anthropological Archaeology in the Americas*, Betty J. Meggers (ed.), Washington, D.C.: Anthropological Society of Washington, pp. 67–87.

1972 "The Origins of the Village As a Settlement Type in Mesoamerica and the Near East: A Comparative Study." *In: Man, Settlement and Urbanism*, Peter J. Ucko, Ruth Tringham and George W. Dimbleby (eds.), London: Duckworth, pp. 23–53.

1973 "The Origins of Agriculture." *Annual Review of Anthropology*, **2**:217–310.

1986 *Guila Naquitz: Archaic Foraging and Early Agriculture in Oaxaca, Mexico*. New York: Academic Press.

Flannery, Kent V. (ed.)
1982 *Maya Subsistence: Studies in Memory of Dennis E. Puleston*. New York: Academic Press.

Fleagle, J. G.
1983 "Locomotor Adaptations of Oligocene and Miocene Hominoids and their Phyletic Implications." *In:* R. Ciochon and R. Corruccini (eds.), q.v., pp. 301–324.

Fleagle, J. G. and R. F. Kay
1983 "New Interpretations of the Phyletic Position of Oligocene Hominoids." *In:* R. Ciochon and R. Corruccini (eds.), q.v., pp. 181–210.

1985 "The Paleobiology of Catarrhines." *In:* E. Delson (ed.), q.v., pp. 23–36.

Fleischer, R. C. and H. R. Hart, Jr.
1972 "Fission Track Dating, Techniques and Problems." *In: Calibration of Hominoid Evolution*, W. W. Bishop and J. A. Miller (eds.), Edinburgh: Scottish Academic Press, pp. 135–170.

Flynn, L. J. and G. Qi
1982 "Age of the Lufeng, China Hominoid Locality." *Nature*, **298**:746–747.

Fobes, James L. and James E. King (eds.)
1982 *Primate Behavior*. New York: Academic Press.

Ford, James A. and Clarence H. Webb
1956 *Poverty Point: A Late Archaic Site in Louisiana*. Anthropology Papers of the American Museum of Natural History, **46**.

Ford, Richard I.
1974 "Northeastern Archaeology: Past and Future Directions." *Annual Review of Anthropology*, **3**:385–413.

Fossey, Dian
1981 "The Imperiled Mountain Gorilla." *National Geographic*, **159**(4):501–523.

1983 *Gorillas in the Mist*. Boston: Houghton-Mifflin.

Fouts, D. H.
1985 *Friends of Washoe*. Central Washington University, Winter.

Fouts, Roger S.
1982 *Friends of Washoe*. Central Washington University, Spring.

1983 "Chimpanzee Language and Elephant Tails: A Theoretical Synthesis." *In:* Judith DeLuce and Hugh T. Wilder (eds.), q.v., pp. 63–75.

Fouts, Roger S. and Richard L. Budd
1979 "Artificial and Human Language Acquisition in the Chimpanzees." *In:* D. Hamburg and E. McCown (eds.), q.v., pp. 375–392.

Fox, Michael W.
1978 "Man, Wolf, and Dog." *In: Wolf and Man*, R. L. Halland and H. S. Sharp (eds.), New York: Academic Press, pp. 19–30.

Fox, Robin (ed.)
1971 "The Cultural Animal." *In: Man and Beast*, John F. Eisenberg and Wm. S. Dillon (eds.), The Smithsonian Institution Press (reprinted in Yehudi A. Cohen, *Man in Adaptation, The Biosocial Background*, 2d Ed., Chicago: Aldine Publishing Co., 1974).

1975 *Biosocial Anthropology*. New York: John Wiley & Sons.

Francoeuer, Robert T.
1965 *Perspectives in Evolution*. Baltimore: Helicon.

Frayer, David
1973 "*Gigantopithecus* and Its Relationship to *Australopithecus*." *American Journal of Physical Anthropology*, **39**:413–426.

1984 "Biological and Cultural Change in the European Late Pleistocene and Early Holocene." *In:* Smith and Spencer, q.v., 211–250.

Freedman, Jonathan L.
1975 *Crowding and Behavior*. New York: The Viking Press.

Freeman, L. G.
1975 "Acheulian Sites and Stratigraphy in Iberia and the Maghreb." *In:* K. W. Butzer and G. L. Isaac (eds.), q.v., pp. 661–743.

Friedel, David A. and Jeremy A. Sabloff
1984 *Cozumel: Late Maya Settlement Patterns*. New York: Academic Press.

Frison, George C.
1978 *Prehistoric Hunters of the High Plains*. New York: Academic Press.

Galdikas, Birute M.
1979 "Orangutan Adaptation at Tanjung Puting Reserve: Mating and Ecology." *In: The Great Apes*, D. A. Hamburg and E. R. McCown (eds.), Menlo Park, Ca.: The Benjamin/Cummings Publishing Co., pp. 195–233.

Galdikas, B.M.F. and G. Telecki
1981 "Variation in Subsistence Activities of Male and Female Pongids: New Perspectives on the Origins of Hominid Labor Division." *Current Anthropology*, **22**:241–256.

Gantt, D. G.
1983 "The Enamel of Neogene Hominoids. Structural and Phyletic Implications." *In:* R. Ciochon and R. Corruccini (eds.), q.v., pp. 249–298.

Gardner, Beatrice T. and R. Allen Gardner
1975 "Evidence for Sentence Constituents in the Early Utterances of Child and Chimpanzee." *Journal of Experimental Psychology: General*, **104**:244–267.

Gardner, Eldon
1965 *History of Biology.* Minneapolis: Burgess Publishing Co.
Garn, Stanley M.
1969 *Human Races.* Springfield, Ill.: Charles C. Thomas.
Gavan, James
1977 *Paleoanthropology and Primate Evolution.* Dubuque, Iowa: Wm. C. Brown Co.
Geddes, David S.
1986 "Neolithic, Chalcolithic, and Early Bronze in Western Mediterranean Europe." *American Antiquity,* **51**(4):763–778.
Gelvin, Bruce R.
1980 "Morphometric Affinities of *Gigantopithecus.*" *American Journal of Physical Anthropology,* **53**:541–568.
Gighlieri, Michael P.
1984 *The Chimpanzees of Kibale Forest.* New York: Columbia University Press.
Giles, E. and O. Elliot
1962 "Race Identification from Cranial Measurements," *Journal of Forensic Sciences,* **7**:147–157.
Gill, G. W.
1986 "Craniofacial Criteria in Forensic Race Identification." *In: Forensic Osteology: Advances in the Identification of Human Remains,* K. J. Reichs (Ed.), Springfield: Charles C Thomas.
Gill, G. W., S. S. Hughes, S. M. Bennett, and B. M. Gilbert
1988 "Racial Identification from the Mid-facial Skeleton with Special Reference to American Indians and Whites," *Journal of Forensic Sciences,* **33**(1).
Gingerich, Phillip D.
1986 "Early Eocene *Cantius torresi*—Oldest Primate of Modern Aspect from North America." *Nature* **319**:319–321.
Gingerich, P. D. and A. Sahni
1979 "*Indraloris* and *Sivaladapis.* Miocene Adapid Primates from the Siwaliks of India and Pakistan." *Nature,* **279**:415–416.
Ginger, Ray
1958 *Six Days or Forever?* Boston: Beacon Press.
Glass, Bently (ed.)
1959 *Forerunners of Darwin, 1745–1859.* Baltimore: Johns Hopkins Press.
Goodall, Jane
1965 "Chimpanzees of the Gombe Stream Reserve." *In: Primate Behavior,* I. DeVore (ed.), New York: Holt, Rinehart and Winston, Inc., pp. 425–473.

———— 1968a "A Preliminary Report on Expressions, Movements and Communications in the Gombe Stream Chimpanzees." *In: Primates,* P. C. Jay (ed.), New York: Holt, Rinehart and Winston, pp. 313–374.

———— 1968b "The Behavior of Free Living Chimpanzees in the Gombe Stream Reserve." *Animal Behavior Monographs,* **1**:(3).

———— 1971 *In the Shadow of Man.* Boston: Houghton Mifflin Co.

———— 1978 Public Lecture at San Jose State University. April 26.

———— 1979 "Life and Death at Gombe." *National Geographic,* **155**(5):597–620.

———— 1986 *The Chimpanzees of Gombe.* Cambridge: The Bellknap Press of Harvard University Press.

Goodall, Jane, A. Bandora, E. Bergmann, C. Busse, H. Matama, E. Mpongo, A. Pierce and D. Riss
1979 "Intercommunity Interactions in the Chimpanzee Population of the Gombe National Park." *In:* D. A. Hamburg and E. R. McCown (eds.), q.v., pp. 11–53.
Goodman, M., M. L. Baba and L. L. Darga
1983 "The Bearing of Molecular Data on the Cladogenesis and Times of Divergence of Hominoid Lineages." *In:* R. Ciochon and R. Corruccini (eds.), q.v., pp. 67–86.
Goodman, Morris and Gabriel W. Lasker
1975 "Molecular Evidence as to Man's Place in Nature." *In: Primate Functional Morphology and Evolution,* R. H. Tuttle (ed.), The Hague: Mouton Publishers, pp. 71–101.
Gorcyca, Diane A., Patrick Garner and Roger Fouts
1975 "Deaf Children and Chimpanzees." Paper presented at the Speech Communication Association Convention, Houston, Texas, December.
Gossett, Thomas F.
1963 *Race, the History of an Idea in America.* Dallas: Southern Methodist University Press.
Gould, Stephen Jay
1976 "Darwin and the Captain." *Natural History,* January, **85**:32–34.
Gould, S. J. and N. Eldredge
1977 "Punctuated Equilibria: the Tempo and Mode of Evolution Reconsidered." *Paleobiology,* **3**:115–151.
Gould, S. J. and R. Lewontin
1979 "The Spandrels of San Marco and the Panglossian Paradigm: A Critique of the Adaptionist Programme." *Proceedings of the Royal Society of London,,* **205**:581–598.
Graham, Ian
1976 *Corpus of Maya Hieroglyphic Inscriptions* (Vol. I, Introduction). Cambridge, Mass.: Peabody Museum of Archaeology and Ethnology.
Gramly, Richard Michael
1982 "*The Vail Site: A Palaeo-Indian Encampment in Maine.*" Bulletin of the Buffalo Society of Natural Sciences, **30**.
Greenberg, Joel
1977 "Who Loves You?" *Science News,* **112**:139–141, August 27.
Greene, John C.
1959 *The Death of Adam.* Ames, Iowa: The Iowa State University Press (Mentor Book).
Greenfield, L. O.
1979 "On the Adaptive Pattern of *Ramapithecus.*" *American Journal of Physical Anthropology,* **50**:527–548.

———— 1980 "A Late Divergence Hypothesis." *American Journal of Physical Anthropology,* **52**:351–365.

———— 1983 "Toward the Resolution of Discrepancies between Phenetic and Paleontological Data Bearing on the Question of Human Origins." *In:* R. Ciochon and R. Corruccini (eds.), q.v., pp. 695–703.
Gregg, Susan Alling
1988 *Foragers and Farmers: Population Interaction and Agricultural Expansion in Prehistoric Europe.* Chicago: University of Chicago Press.
Grobstein, Clifford
1977 "The Recombinant DNA Debate." *Scientific American,* **237**:22–31, July.

Grootes, P. M.
1978 "Carbon-14 Time Scale Extended: Comparison of Chronologies." *Science*, **200**:11–15.

Grove, David C.
1984 *Chalcatzingo: Excavations on the Olmec Frontier*. New York: Thames and Hudson.

Gurin, Joel
1980 "In the Beginning." *Science 80*, **1**(5):44–51.

Haas, Jonathan, Sheila Pozorski and Thomas Pozorski (eds.)
1987 *The Origins and Development of the Andean State*. New York: Cambridge University Press.

Haldane, J.B.S.
1932 *The Causes of Evolution*. London: Longmans, Green (reprinted as paperback, Cornell University Press, 1966).

Halstead, L. B.
1968 *The Pattern of Vertebrate Evolution*. San Francisco: W. H. Freeman & Co.

Hamburg, David A. and E. R. McCown (eds.)
1979 *The Great Apes*. Menlo Park, Ca.: The Benjamin/Cummings Publishing Co.

Hamilton, W. D.
1964 "The Genetical Theory of Social Behavior: I and II." *Journal of Theoretical Biology*, **7**:1–52.

Hammond, Norman
1982 *Ancient Maya Civilization*. New Brunswick, N.J.: Rutgers University Press.

Harding, A. F.
1984 *The Mycenaeans and Europe*. New York: Academic Press.

Harding, Robert and Shirley C. Strum
1976 "The Predatory Baboons of Kekopey." *Natural History Magazine*, **85**(3):46–53.

Harlow, Harry F.
1959 "Love in Infant Monkeys." *Scientific American*, **200**:68–74.

Harlow, Harry F. and Margaret K. Harlow
1961 "A Study of Animal Affection." *Natural History*, **70**:48–55.

Harrison, Richard J.
1985 "The 'Policultivo Ganadero,' or Secondary Products Revolution in Spanish Agriculture, 5000–1000 B.C." *Proceedings of the Prehistoric Society*, **51**:75–102.

Hatley, T. and J. Kappelman
1981 "Bears, Pigs, and Pliopleistocene Hominids: A Case for the Exploitation of Belowground Food Resources." *Human Ecology*, **8**:371–387.

Haury, Emil W.
1976 *The Hohokam. Desert Farmers and Craftsmen: Excavations at Snaketown, 1964–1965*. Tucson: University of Arizona Press.

Hausfater, Glenn
1976 "Predatory Behavior of Yellow Baboons." *Behaviour*, **56**:44–68.

——
1984 "Infanticide in Langurs: Strategies, Counter Strategies, and Parameter Values." *In: Infanticide*, G. Hausfater and S. Blaffer Hrdy, (eds.), pp. 257–281.

Hausfater, Glenn and Sarah Blaffer Hrdy (eds.)
1984 *Infanticide. Comparative and Evolutionary Perspectives*. Hawthorne, New York: Aldine de Gruyter.

Heizer, Robert F. and I. K. Napton
1970 *Archaeology and the Prehistoric Great Basin Subsistence Regime as Seen from Lovelock Cave, Nevada*. University of California Archaeological Research Facility Contribution, **10**.

Henderson, John S.
1981 *The World of the Ancient Maya*. Ithaca, N.Y.: Cornell University Press.

Henry, David O.
1989 *From Foraging to Agriculture: The Levant at the End of the Ice Age*. Philadelphia: University of Pennsylvania Press.

Herre, Wolf
1969 "The Science and History of Domestic Animals." *In: Science in Archaeology*, D. Brothwall and E. Higgs (eds.), New York: Frederick A. Praeger, 257–272.

Hiatt, H. H., J. D. Watson and J. A. Winsten (eds.)
1977 *Origins of Human Cancer* (3 volumes). Cold Spring Harbor Laboratory, Cold Spring Harbor, New York.

Hiernaux, Jean
1964 "The Concept of Race and the Taxonomy of Mankind." *In: The Concept of Race*, Ashley Montagu (ed.), New York: The Free Press, pp. 29–45.

Hoffman, Michael A.
1979 *Egypt Before the Pharaohs*. New York: Alfred A. Knopf.

Hoffstetter, R.
1972 "Relationships, Origins, and History of the Ceboid Monkeys and the Caviomorph Rodents: A Modern Reinterpretation." *In: Evolutionary Biology*, Th. Dobzhansky, T.M.K. Hecht and W. C. Steere (eds.), Vol. 6, New York: Appleton-Century-Crofts, pp. 323–347.

Hole, Frank, Kent V. Flannery and James A. Neely (eds.)
1969 *The Prehistory and Human Ecology of the Deh Luran Plain*. Ann Arbor: University of Michigan Museum of Anthropology.

Holloway, Ralph L.
1969 "Culture: A Human Domain." *Current Anthropology*, **10**:395–407.

——
1981 "Revisiting the South African Taung Australopithecine Endocast: The Position of the Lunate Sulcus as Determined by the Stereoplotting Technque." *American Journal of Physical Anthropology*, **56**:43–58.

——
1983 "Cerebral Brain Endocast Pattern of *Australopithecus afarensis* Hominid." *Nature*, **303**:420–422.

——
1985 "The Poor Brain of *Homo sapiens neanderthalensis*: See What You Please." *In: Delson, q.v., pp. 319–324.

Hood, Sinclair
1973 *The Minoans*. London: Thames and Hudson.

Hooton, E. A.
1926 "Methods of Racial Analysis." *Science*, **63**:75–81.

Hopkins, David
1982 "Aspects of the Paleogeography of Beringia During the Late Pleistocene." *In: The Paleoecology of Beringia*, D. Hopkins, J. Matthews, C. Schweger, and S. Young (eds.), New York: Academic Press, pp. 3–28.

Howell, F. Clark
1966 "Observations on the Earlier Phases of the European Lower Paleolithic." *American Anthropologist*, **68**(2):88–201.

——
1978 "Hominidae." *In: Evolution of African Mammals*, V. J. Maglio and H.B.S. Cooke (eds.), Cambridge: Harvard University Press, pp. 154–248.

1982 "Ambrona." *Leakey Foundation News*, Spring.

Howells, W. W.

1971 "The Meaning of Race." *In: The Biological and Social Meaning of Race*, Richard H. Osborne (ed.), San Francisco: W. H. Freeman and Co., pp. 3–10.

———

1973 *Evolution of the Genus* Homo. Reading, Mass.: Addison-Wesley.

———

1974 "Neanderthals: Names, Hypotheses, and Scientific Method." *American Anthropologist*, **76**:24–38.

———

1975 "Neanderthal Man: Facts and Figures." *In: Paleoanthropology: Morphology and Paleoecology*, R. H. Tuttle (ed.), The Hague: Mouton Publishers, pp. 389–407.

———

1980 "*Homo erectus*—Who, When, Where: A Survey." *Yearbook of Physical Anthropology* 1980, **23**:1–23.

Hrdy, Sarah Blaffer

1977 *The Langurs of Abu*. Cambridge, Mass.: Harvard University Press.

———

1984a "Female Reproductive Strategies." *In: Female Primates*, M. Small (ed.), New York: Alan R. Liss, pp. 103–109.

———

1984b "Assumptions and Evidence Regarding the Sexual Selection Hypothesis: A Reply to Boggess." *In: Infanticide*, G. Hausfater and S. Blaffer Hrdy (eds.), q.v., pp. 315–319.

Hublin, J. J.

1985 "Human Fossils from the North African Middle Pleistocene and the Origin of *Homo sapiens. In*: Delson, q.v., pp. 283–288.

Hudson, Liam

1972 "The Context of the Debate." *In: Race and Intelligence*, K. Richardson and D. Spears (eds.), Baltimore: Penguin Books, Inc., pp. 10–16.

Iltis, Hugo

1966 *Life of Mendel*. New York: Hafner Publishing Co. (first published in Germany, 1924).

The Institute of Vertebrate Palaeontology and Paleoanthropology, Chinese Academy of Sciences

1980 *Atlas of Primitive Man in China*. Beijing: Science Press (Distributed by van Nostrand, New York).

Isaac, G.

1971 "The Diet of Early Man." *World Archaeology*, **2**:278–299.

———

1975 "Stratigraphy and Cultural Patterns in East Africa During the Middle Ranges of Pleistocene Time." *In*: K. W. Butzer and G. L. Isaac (eds.), q.v., pp. 495–542.

———

1976 "Early Hominids in Action: A Commentary on the Contribution of Archeology to Understanding the Fossil Record in East Africa." *Yearbook of Physical Anthropology* 1975, **19**:19–35.

Isbell, William H.

1978 "The Prehistoric Ground Drawings of Peru." *Scientific American*, **239**(10):20, 140–142.

Jacob, François

1975 "Morphology and Paleoecology of Early Man in Java." *In*:

Paleoanthropology: Morphology and Paleoecology, R. H. Tuttle (ed.), Chicago: Aldine Publishing Co., pp. 312–325.

Jacob, Teuku

1976 "Early Populations in the Indonesian Region." *In*: R. L. Kirk and A. G. Thorne (eds.), q.v., pp. 81–93.

Jacobs, Louis L. and David Pilbeam

1980 "Of Mice and Men: Fossil-Based Divergence Dates and Molecular 'Clocks.' " *Journal of Human Evolution*, **9**:551–555.

Jarrige, Jean-François and Richard H. Meadow

1980 "The Antecedents of Civilization in the Indus Valley." *Scientific American*, **243**(2):122–133.

Jarvis, J.V.M.

1981 "Eusociality in a Mammal: Cooperative Breeding in Naked Mole-Rat Colonies." *Science*, **212**:571–573.

Jaeger, Jean-Jacques

1975 "The Mammalian Faunas and Hominid Fossils of the Middle Pleistocene of the Maghreb." *In*: K. W. Butzer and G. L. Isaac (eds.), q.v., pp. 399–418.

Jelinek, Arthur J.

1982 "The Tabun Cave and Paleolithic Man in the Levant." *Science*, **216**:1369–1375.

Jennings, Jesse D.

1957 *Danger Cave*. Society for American Archaeology Memoir, **14**.

———

1983a *Ancient North Americans*. San Francisco: W. H. Freeman.

———

1983b *Ancient South Americans*. San Francisco: W. H. Freeman.

Jensen, Arthur

1969 *Environment, Heredity, and Intelligence*. Cambridge, Mass.: Harvard Educational Review.

———

1974 "Kinship Correlations Reported by Sir Cyril Burt." *Behavior Genetics*, **4**:1–28.

———

1980 *Bias in Mental Testing*. New York: The Free Press.

Jerison, H. J.

1973 *Evolution of the Brain and Behavior*. New York: Academic Press.

Jochim, Michael

1976 *Hunting-Gathering Subsistence and Settlement: A Predictive Model*. New York: Academic Press.

Johanson, Donald and Maitland Edey

1981 *Lucy: The Beginnings of Humankind*. New York: Simon and Schuster.

Johanson, Donald C. and Maurice Taieb

1976 "Plio-Pleistocene Hominid Discoveries in Hadar, Ethiopia." *Nature*, **260**:293–297.

———

1980 "New Discoveries of Pliocene Hominids and Artifacts in Hadar." International Afar Research Expedition to Ethiopia (Fourth and Fifth Field Seasons, 1975–77). *Journal of Human Evolution*, 9:582.

Johanson, D. C. and T. D. White

1979 "A Systematic Assessment of Early African Hominids." *Science*, **203**:321–330.

———

1986 Fossil Debate. Letter, *Discover* 7:116.

Johanson, D. C., T. D. White and Yves Coppens

1978 "A New Species of the Genus *Australopithecus* (Primates: Hominidae) from the Pliocene of Eastern Africa. *Kirtlandia*," No. 28, pp. 1–14.

Johnson, A. E., Jr.
1979 "Skeletal Estimates of *Gigantopithecus* Based on a Gorilla Analogy." *Journal of Human Evolution*, 8:585–587.

Jolly, Alison
1984 "The Puzzle of Female Feeding Priority." *In*: Meredith F. Small, q.v., pp. 197–215.

———
1985 *The Evolution of Primate Behavior*. (2nd Ed.), New York: Macmillan.

Jolly, C. J.
1970 "The Seed Eaters: A New Model of Hominid Differentiation Based on a Baboon Analogy." *Man*, 5:5–26.

Jungers, W. L.
1982 "Lucy's Limbs: Skeletal Allometry and Locomotion in *Australopithecus afarensis*." *Nature*, 297:676–678.

Kamin, Leon
1974 *The Science and Politics of IQ*. New York: John Wiley & Sons.

Katz, D., and J. M. Suchey
1986 "Age Determination of the Male Os Pubis," *American Journal of Physical Anthropology*, 69:427–435.

Kawamura, Syunzo
1959 "The Process of Sub-culture Propagation among Japanese Macaques." *In: Primate Social Behavior*, C. H. Southwick (ed.), Princeton: D. Van Nostrand Co. Inc., pp. 82–90 (originally published in the *Journal of Primatology*, 2(1):43–60).

Kawanaka, Kanji
1982 "A Case of Inter-Unit-Group Encounter in Chimpanzees of the Mahale Mts." *Primates*, 23(4):558–562.

Kay, John P., et al.
1981 "Normalization of Low-Density Lipoproteins Levels in Heterozygous Familial Hypercholesterolemia with a Combined Drug Regimen." *New England Journal of Medicine*, 304:251–258.

Kay, Richard F.
1981 "The Nut-Crackers—A New Theory of the Adaptations of the Ramapithecinae." *American Journal of Physical Anthropology*, 55:151–156.

Kay, R. F., J. G. Fleagle and E. L. Simons
1981 "A Revision of the Oligocene Apes of the Fayum Province, Egypt." *American Journal of Physical Anthropology*, 55:293–322.

Kay, R. F. and E. L. Simons
1983 "A Reassessment of the Relationship Between Late Miocene and Subsequent Hominoidea." *In*: R. Ciochon and R. Corruccini (eds.), q.v., pp. 577–624.

Keeley, Lawrence H.
1980 *Experimental Determination of Stone Tool Uses: A Microwear Analysis*. Chicago: University of Chicago Press.

Kelso, A. J.
1974 *Physical Anthropology* (2nd Ed.). New York: J. B. Lippincott Co.

Kennedy, G. E.
1980a *Paleoanthropology*. New York: McGraw-Hill Book Co.

———
1980b "The Emergence of Modern Man." *Nature*, 284:11–12.

———
1984 "The Emergence of *Homo sapiens*: The Post Cranial Evidence." *Man* (N.S.), 19:94–110.

Kenyon, Kathleen M.
1957 *Digging Up Jericho*. New York: Frederick A. Praeger.

Kimbel, William H., Tim D. White and Donald C. Johanson
1985 "Craniodental Morphology of the Hominids from Hadar and Laetoli: Evidence of 'Paranthropus' and *Homo* in the Mid-Pliocene of Eastern Africa?" *In*: E. Delson (ed.), q.v., pp. 120–137.

King, J. L. and T. H. Jukes
1969 "Non-Darwinian Evolution." *Science*, 164:788–798.

Kirk, R. L. and A. G. Thorne
1976 *The Origin of the Australians*. Human Biology Series, N.Y. Australian Institute of Aboriginal Studies, Canberra. New Jersey: Humanities Press Inc.

Klein, R. G.
1969 *Man and Culture in the Late Pleistocene*. San Francisco: Chandler.

———
1977 "The Ecology of Early Man in Southern Africa." *Science*, 197:115–126.

Kolata, Alan L.
1987 "Tiwanaku and Its Hinterland." *Archaeology*, 40(1):36–41.

Kolata, Gina
1986 "Anthropologists Suggest Cannibalism is a Myth." *Science*, 282:1497–2000.

Konigsson, Lars-Konig (ed.)
1980 *Current Argument on Early Men*. Oxford: Pergamon Press.

Kortland, Adriaan
1965 "A comment on 'On the Essential Morphological Basis for Human Culture.'" *Current Anthropology*, 6:320–326.

Kosok, Paul and Maria Reiche
1949 "Ancient Drawings on the Desert of Peru." *Archaeology*, 2:206–215.

Kraatz, Reinhart
1985 "A Review of Recent Research on Heidelberg Man, *Homo erectus heidelbergensis*." *In*: Delson, q.v., pp. 268–271.

Kraeling, Carl H. and Robert M. Adams (eds.)
1960 *City Invincible*. Chicago: University of Chicago Press.

Kramer, Samuel N.
1963 *The Sumerians*. Chicago: University of Chicago Press.

Krogman, W. M.
1962 *The Human Skeleton in Forensic Medicine*. Springfield: C. C. Thomas.

Kummer, Hans
1971 *Primate Societies*. Chicago: Aldine-Atherton, Inc.

Kus, James S.
1984 "The Chicama-Moche Canal: Failure or Success? An Alternative Explanation for an Incomplete Canal. *American Antiquity*, 49(2):408–415.

Lack, David
1966 *Population Studies of Birds*. Oxford: Clarendon.

Lancaster, Jane B.
1975 *Primate Behavior and the Emergence of Human Culture*. New York: Holt, Rinehart and Winston, Inc.

———
1984 "Introduction." *In*: Small, q.v., pp. 1–10.

Lanning, Edward P.
1967 *Peru Before the Incas*. Englewood Cliffs, N.J.: Prentice-Hall.

Latimer, Bruce
1984 "The Pedal Skeleton of *Australopithecus afarensis*." *American Journal of Physical Anthropology*, 63:182.

Leakey, L.S.B.
1966   "*Homo habilis, Homo erectus*, and the Australopithecinae." *Nature*, 209:1279–1281.
Leakey, L.S.B., J. F. Everden and G. H. Curtis
1961   "Age of Bed I, Olduvai Gorge, Tanganyika." *Nature*, 191:478–479.
Leakey, L.S.B., P. V. Tobias and J. R. Napier
1964   "A New Species of the Genus *Homo* from Olduvai Gorge." *Nature*, 202:7–10.
Leakey, Mary D.
1971   "Remains of *Homo erectus* and Associated Artifacts in Bed IV at Olduvai Gorge, Tanzania." *Nature*, 232:380–383.
Leakey, M. D. and R. L. Hay
1979   "Pliocene Footprints in Laetolil Beds at Laetoli, Northern Tanzania." *Nature*, 278:317–323.
Leakey, R.E.F.
1974   "Further Evidence of Lower Pleistocene Hominids from East Rudolf, Kenya, 1973." *Nature*, 248:653–656.

1976   "New Hominid Fossils from the Koobi Fora Formation in Northern Kenya." *Nature*, 261:572–574.
Leakey, R.E.F. and Alan C. Walker
1976   "*Australopithecus, Homo erectus* and the Single Species Hypothesis." *Nature*, 261:572–574.

1985   "New Higher Primates from the Early Miocene of Buluk, Kenya." *Nature* 318:173–175.
Lee, Richard B.
1984   *The Dobe !Kung.* New York: Holt, Rinehart and Winston.
Lerner, I. M. and W. J. Libby
1976   *Heredity, Evolution, and Society.* San Francisco: W. H. Freeman and Company.
Lewin, Roger
1981   "Biggest Challenge Since the Double Helix." Research News, *Science*, 212:28–32.

1983   "Is the Orangutan A Living Fossil?" *Science*, 222:1222–1223.

1987   "Africa: Cradle of Modern Humans." *Science*, 237:1292–1295.
Lewis, Thomas M. N. and Madeline Kneberg Lewis
1961   *Eva, an Archaic Site.* Knoxville: University of Tennessee Press.
Lewontin, R. C.
1972   "The Apportionment of Human Diversity." *In: Evolutionary Biology* (Vol. 6), Th. Dobzhansky et al. (eds.), New York: Plenum, pp. 381–398.
Li, Wen-Hsiung and Masako Tanimura
1987   "The Molecular Clock Runs More Slowly in Man than in Apes and Monkeys." *Nature* 326:93–96.
Lieberman, P. and E. S. Crelin
1971   "On the Speech of Neanderthal." *Linguistic Inquiry*, 2:203–222.
Lindroth, Sten
1983   "The Two Faces of Linnaeus." *In:* Tore Frangsmyr (ed.), *Linnaeus: The Man and His Work.* Berkeley: University of California Press.
Lindsay, Jean
1959   *A Short History of Science.* New York: Doubleday & Co.
Lipe, William D.
1983   "The Southwest." *In:* Jesse D. Jennings (ed.), q.v., pp. 421–493.

Lisowski, F. P.
1984   "Introduction." *In:* Whyte, q.v., pp. 777–786.
Lister, Robert and Florence C. Lister
1981   *Chaco Canyon: Archaeology and Archaeologists.* Albuquerque: University of New Mexico Press.
Little, M. A., R. Brooke Thomas, Richard B. Mazess and Paul T. Baker
1971   "Populational Differences and Developmental Changes in Extremity Temperature Responses to Cold Among Andean Indians." *Human Biology*, 43:70–91.
Livingstone, Frank B.
1964   "On the Nonexistence of Human Races." *In: Concept of Race*, A. Montagu (ed.), New York: The Free Press, pp. 46–60.

1969   "Polygenic Models for the Evolution of Human Skin Color Differences." *Human Biology*, 41:480–493.

1980   "Natural Selection and the Origin and Maintenance of Standard Genetic Marker Systems." *Yearbook of Physical Anthropology*, 1980, 23:25–42.
Lovejoy, Arthur L.
1959   "Buffon and the Problem of Species." *In: Forerunners of Darwin, 1745–1859*, Bentley Glass (ed.), Baltimore: Johns Hopkins Press, pp. 84–113.
Lovejoy, C. Owen
1981   "The Origin of Man." *Science*, 211:341–350.

1983   Paper presented at the Institute of Human Origins Conference on the Evolution of Human Locomotion (Berkeley).
Lovejoy, C. O., G. Kingsbury, G. Heiple and A. H. Burstein
1973   "The Gait of *Australopithecus*." *American Journal of Physical Anthropology*, 38:757–780.
Lovejoy, Thomas E.
1982   "The Tropical Forest—Greatest Expression of Life on Earth." *In: Primates and the Tropical Forest*, Proceedings, California Institute of Technology, World Wildlife Fund—U.S., pp. 45–48.
Löwenberg, Bert James
1959   *Darwin, Wallace, and the Theory of Natural Selection.* Cambridge, Mass.: Arlington Books.
Lu, Zun'e
1987   "Cracking the Evolutionary Puzzle—Jinniushan Man." *China Pictorial*, 1987/4 [April].
Luckett, W. Patrick
1980   "The Suggested Evolutionary Relationships and Classification of Tree Shrews." *In: Comparative Biology and Evolutionary Relationships of Tree Shrews*, W. P. Luckett (ed.), New York: Plenum Press, pp. 3–31.
Lumbreras, Luis G.
1974   *The Peoples and Cultures of Ancient Peru.* Washington: Smithsonian Institution Press.
Lynch, Thomas F.
1983   "The Paleo-Indians." *In:* Jesse D. Jennings (ed.), San Francisco: W. H. Freeman, q.v., pp. 87–137.
Lynch, Thomas F. (Ed.)
1980   *Guitarrero Cave.* New York: Academic Press.

MacNeish, Richard S.
1964   "Ancient Mesoamerican Civilization." *Science*, 143:531–537.

1978   *The Science of Archaeology?* North Scituate, Mass.: Duxbury Press.

Mai, L. L.
1983   "A Model of Chromosome Evolution and Its Bearing on Cladogenesis in the Hominoidea." *In:* R. Ciochon and R. Corruccini (eds.), q.v., pp. 87–114.

Maier, W.
1977   "Chronology and Biology of the South African Australopithecines." *Journal of Human Evolution* 8:89–93.

Mann, Alan
1975   "Some Paleodemographic Aspects of the South African Australopithecines." *University of Pennsylvania Publications in Anthropology* (No. 1), Philadelphia.

Marcus, Joyce
1976   *Emblem and State in the Classic Maya Lowland: An Epigraphic Approach to Territorial Organization.* Washington: Dumbarton Oaks Foundation.

Marschack, A.
1972   *The Roots of Civilization.* New York: McGraw-Hill Publishing Co.

Martin, Paul S.
1967   "Prehistoric Overkill." *In: Pleistocene Extinctions: The Search for a Cause,* Paul S. Martin and Herbert E. Wright, Jr. (eds.), New Haven: Yale University Press, pp. 75–120.

1982   "The Pattern of Meaning of Holarctic Mammoth Extinction." *In: Paleoecology of Beringia,* D. Hopkins, J. Matthews, C. Schweger, and S. Young (eds.), New York: Academic Press, pp. 399–408.

Maw, B., R. L. Ciochon, and D. E. Savage
1979   "Late Eocene of Burma Yields Earliest Anthropoid Primate, *Pondaungia cotteri.*" *Nature,* **282**:65–67.

Mayr, Ernst
1962   "Taxonomic Categories in Fossil Hominids." *In: Ideas on Human Evolution,* W. W. Howells (ed.), New York: Atheneum, pp. 242–256.

1970   *Population, Species, and Evolution.* Cambridge: Harvard University Press.

1982   *The Growth of Biological Thought.* Cambridge: Belknap Press.

McGrew, Wm. C.
1979   "Evolutionary Implications of Sex Differences in Chimpanzee Predation and Tool Use." *In:* Hamburg and McCown (eds.), q.v., pp. 441–463.

McHenry, Henry
1975   "Fossils and the Mosaic Nature of Human Evolution." *Science,* **190**:425–431.

1982   "The Pattern of Human Evolution: Studies on Behavior, Mastication, and Encephalization." *Annual Reviews of Anthropology,* **11**:151–173.

1983   "The Capitate of *Australopithecus afarensis* and *A. africanus.*" *American Journal of Physical Anthropology,* **62**:187–198.

1985   "Implications of Postcanine Megadontia for the Origin of *Homo.*" *In:* E. Delson, ed., q.v., pp. 178–183.

McKern, T. W., and T. D. Stewart
1957   "Skeletal Age Changes in Young American Males, Technical Report EP-45." Natick, MA: U.S. Army Quartermaster Research and Development Center.

McKusick, Victor
1980   "Anatomy of the Human Genome." *Journal of Heredity,* **71**:370–391.

1983   *Mendelian Inheritance in Man* (6th Ed.). Baltimore: Johns Hopkins Press.

McNett, Jr., Charles W. (Ed.)
1985   *Shawnee-Minisink: A Stratified Paleoindian-Archaic Site in the Upper Delaware Valley.* Orlando: Academic Press.

Mech, L. David
1966   *The Wolves of Isle Royale.* Washington, D.C.: U.S. Government Printing Office.

Mellaart, James
1967   *Çatal Hüyük: A Neolithic Town in Anatolia.* New York: McGraw-Hill.

Mendel, Gregor
1965   "Experiments in Plant Hybridisation" (A paper read before the Natural History Society of Brünn in 1865). Cambridge: Harvard University Press.

Mendelssohn, Kurt
1974   *The Riddle of the Pyramids.* New York: Frederick A. Praeger.

Merrick, H. V. and J. P. S. Merrick
1976   "Archeological Occurrences of Earlier Pleistocene Age from the Shungura Formation." *In: Earliest Man and Environments in the Lake Rudolf Basin,* Y. Coppens et al. (eds.), Chicago: University of Chicago Press, pp. 574–584.

Miles, H. Lyn
1983   "Apes and Language: The Search for Communicative Competence." *In:* J. de Luce and H. T. Wilder (eds.), q.v., pp. 43–62.

Millon, René
1988   "The Last Years of Teotihuacán Dominance." *In: The Collapse of Ancient States and Civilizations,* Norman Yoffee and George Cowgill (eds.), Tucson: University of Arizona Press, pp. 102–164.

Mittermeir, Russel A.
1982   "The World's Endangered Primates: An Introduction and a Case Study—The Monkeys of Brazil's Atlantic Forests." *In: Primates and the Tropical Rain Forest,* Proceedings, California Institute of Technology, World Wildlife Fund—U.S., pp. 11–22.

Moctezuma, Eduardo Matos
1984   "The Great Temple of Tenochtitlan." *Scientific American,* **251**(2):80–89.

Montagu, Ashley (ed.)
1980   *Sociobiology Examined.* New York: Oxford University Press.

Montet, Pierre
1981   *Everyday Life in Egypt in the Days of Ramesses the Great.* Philadelphia: University of Pennsylvania Press.

Moore, Andrew M. T.
1988   "The Development of Neolithic Societies in the Near East." *Advances in World Archaeology,* **4**:1–70.

Moore, Lorna G. and Judith G. Regensteiner
1983   "Adaptation to High Altitude." *Annual Reviews of Anthropology,* **12**:285–304.

Moore, R. V.
1987   "Variation in *Homo erectus* and Its Effect on Our Understand-

ing of the Distribution of this Hominid Species." (Abstract of above paper in *American Journal of Physical Anthropology*, **72**(2):234, 1987.)

Moore, Ruth
1961 *Man, Time and Fossils*. New York: Alfred A. Knopf.
Morbeck, M. E.
1975 "*Dryopithecus africanus* Forelimb." *Journal of Human Evolution*, 4:39–46.

——
1983 "Miocene Hominoid Discoveries from Rudabánya. Implications from the Postcranial Skeleton." *In*: R. Ciochon and R. Corruccini (eds.), q.v., pp. 369–404.
Morgan, Elaine
1972 *The Descent of Women*. New York: Stein and Day.
Morris, Craig
1988 "A City Fit for an Inka." *Archaeology*, **41**(5):43–49.
Morris, Desmond
1967 *The Naked Ape*. New York: McGraw-Hill.
Moseley, Michael E.
1975a "Chan Chan: Andean Alternative to the Preindustrial City." *Science*, **187**:219–225.

——
1975b *The Maritime Foundations of Andean Civilization*. Menlo Park, Calif.: Cummings Publishing Company.

——
1983 "Central Andean Civilization." *In*: Jesse D. Jennings (ed.), q.v., pp. 179–239.
Mturi, A. A.
1976 "New Hominid from Lake Ndutu, Tanzania." *Nature*, **262**:484–485.
Murdock, George Peter
1959 *Africa: Its Peoples and Their Culture History*. New York: McGraw-Hill.
Murra, John V.
1972 "El 'control vertical' de una maximo de pisos ecologicos en la economia de los sociedades andines." *In*: *Vista de la Provincia de Leon de Huanaco (1562)*, J. V. Murra (ed.), Huanaco, Peru, Universidad Nacional Hermilio Valdizen, Vol. 2, pp. 427–476.
Myerowitz, Rachel and Norman D. Hogikyan
1986 "Different Mutations in Ashkenazi Jewish and Non-Jewish French Canadians with Tay-Sachs Disease." *Science*, **232**:1646–1648.

Napier, John
1967 "The Antiquity of Human Walking." *Scientific American*, **216**:56–66.

——
1973 *Bigfoot*. New York: E. P. Dutton & Co., Inc.
Napier, J. R. and P. H. Napier
1985 *The Natural History of the Primates*. London: British Museum (Natural History).
Napier, Prue
1977 *Chimpanzees*. New York: McGraw-Hill Book Co.
Ninkovich, D. and L. H. Burcle
1978 "Absolute Age of the Base of the Hominid Bearing Beds in Eastern Java." *Nature*, **275**:306–308.
Nishida, Toshisada
1979 "The Social Structure of Chimpanzees of the Mahale Mountains." *In*: *The Great Apes*, David A. Hamburg and E. R. McCown (eds.), q.v., pp. 73–121.

——
1983 "Alloparental Behavior in Wild Chimpanzees of the Mahale Mts., Tanzania." *Folia Primatologica*, **41**:1–33.
Nishida, Toshisada and M. Hiraiwa-Hasegawa
1985 "Response to a Stranger Mother-Son Pair in the Wild Chimpanzee: A Case Report." *Primates*, **6**:1–13.
Nishida, Toshisada and Kenji Kawanaka
1985 "Within-Group Cannibalism by Adult Male Chimpanzees." *Primates*, **26**(3):274–284.
Nishida, Toshisada, S. Uehara, and R. Nyundo
1979 "Predatory Behavior among Wild Chimpanzees of the Mahale Mts." *Primates*, **20**(1):1–20.
Norikashi, Kohshi
1982 "One Observed Case of Cannibalism Among Wild Chimpanzees of the Mahale Mountains." *Primates*, **23**(1):66–74.

Oakley, Kenneth
1963 "Analytical Methods of Dating Bones." *In*: *Science in Archaeology*, D. Brothwell and E. Higgs (eds.), New York: Basic Books, Inc.
Oakley, Kenneth Page, Bernard G. Campbell and Theya I. Mulleson
1977 *Catalogue of Fossil Hominids*. Part I: Africa; Part II: Europe (1971); Part III: Americas, Asia, Australia (1975). London: The British Museum (Natural History).
Olby, Robert O.
1985 *Origins of Mendelism*. (2nd Ed.), Chicago: University of Chicago Press.
Oldroyd, D. R.
1980 *Darwinian Impacts: An Introduction to the Darwinian Revolution*. Atlantic Highlands: Humanities Press.
Olson, Everett C.
1980 "Taphonomy: Its History and Role in Community Evolution." *In*: *Fossils in the Making*, K. Behrensmeyer and A. Hill (eds.), Chicago: University of Chicago Press, pp. 5–19.
Olson, Todd R.
1985 "Cranial Morphology and Systematics of the Hadar Formation Hominids and *Australopithecus africanus*." *In*: E. Delson (ed.), q.v., pp. 102–119.
Osborne, Richard (ed.)
1971 *The Biological and Social Meaning of Race*. San Francisco: W. H. Freeman Co.
Ovey, C. D. (ed.)
1964 "The Swanscombe Skull." Royal Anthropological Institute, Occasional Paper 20.
Oxnard, C. E.
1975 "The Place of the Australopithecines in Human Evolution: Grounds for Doubt?" *Nature*, **258**:389–395.

Park, Edwards
1978 "The Ginsberg Caper: Hacking It As in Stone Age." *Smithsonian*, **9**:85–96.
Parks, Michael
1981 "Skulls Found in China Important in the Puzzle of Man's Evolution." *San Jose Mercury News*, Sunday, May 17, 1981.
Passingham, R. E.
1982 *The Human Primate*. San Francisco: W. H. Freeman and Co.
Patterson, Francine
1983 "Why Koko (and Michael) **Can** Talk." *Gorilla*, **6**(2), June.
Pauling, Linus
1974 "The Molecular Basis of Biological Specificity." *Nature*, **248**:769–771.

Petit, Charles
1981 "Ancient Skull Raises New Storm." *San Francisco Chronicle*, September 26, 1981.
Pfeiffer, John E.
1985 *The Emergence of Man* (4th Ed.). New York: Harper and Row, Publishers.

——— 1987 "Underground Bestiary." *Natural History*, October: 84–88.
Phenice, T. W.
1969 "A Newly Developed Visual Method of Sexing the Os Pubis," *American Journal of Physical Anthropology*, 30:297–302.
Pickford, M.
1983 "Sequence and Environments of the Lower and Middle Miocene Hominoids of Western Kenya." *In*: R. Ciochon and R. Corruccini (eds.), q.v., pp. 421–439.
Piddocke, Stuart
1965 "The Potlatch System of the Southern Kwakiutl: A New Perspective." *Southwestern Journal of Anthropology*, 21:244–264.
Piggott, Stuart
1965 *Ancient Europe*. Chicago: Aldine.
Pilbeam, David
1972 *The Ascent of Man*. New York: Macmillan.

——— 1975 "Middle Pleistocene Hominids." *In*: K. W. Butzer and G. L. Isaac (eds.), q.v., pp. 809–856.

——— 1977 "Beyond the Apes: Pre-*Homo* Hominids: The Ramapithecines of Africa, Asia, and Europe." Symposium Lecture, March 5, Davis, Calif.

——— 1979 "Recent Finds and Interpretations of Miocene Hominoids." *Annual Reviews of Anthropology*, 8:333–352.

——— 1981 "New Fossil Hominoid from Pakistan." Paper presented at the Annual Meeting, American Association of Physical Anthropologists, April, 1981.

——— 1982 "New Hominoid Skull Material From the Miocene of Pakistan." *Nature*, 295:232–234.

——— 1986 "Distinguished Lecture: Hominoid Evolution and Hominoid Origins." *American Anthropologist*, 88:295–312.
Pilbeam, David, G. E. Meyer, C. Badgley, et al.
1977 "New Hominoid Primates from the Siwaliks of Pakistan and Their Bearing on Hominoid Evolution." *Nature*, 270:689–695.
Pitts, M. W.
1979 "Hides and Antlers: A New Look at the Gatherer-Hunter Site at Star Carr, North Yorkshire, England." *World Archaeology*, 11(1):32–42.
Pope, G. G.
1984 "The Antiquity and Paleoenvironment of the Asian Hominidae." *In*: Whyte (ed.), q.v., pp. 822–847.
Pope, G. G. and J. E. Cronin
1984 "The Asian Hominidae." *Journal of Human Evolution*, 13:377–396.
Popp, Joseph L. and Irven DeVore
1979 "Aggressive Competition and Social Dominance Theory." *In*: *The Great Apes*, David A. Hamburg and E. R. McCown (eds.), q.v., pp. 317–318.
Potts, Richard and Pat Shipman

1981 "Cutmarks Made by Stone Tools from Olduvai Gorge, Tanzania." *Nature*, 291:577–580.
Poulianos, Aris N.
1981 "Pre-*sapiens* Man in Greece." *Current Anthropology*, 22(3):287–288.
Premack, David
1971 "Language in Chimpanzee?" *Science*, 172:808–822.
Premack, David and Ann J. Premack
1983 *The Mind of an Ape*. New York: W. W. Norton & Co.
Prescott, William H.
1906 *History of the Conquest of Peru*. New York: Everyman's Library.
Proshnev, B. F.
1974 "The Troglodytidae and the Hominidae in the Taxonomy and Evolution of Higher Primates." *Current Anthropology*, 15(4):449–450.
Proskouriakoff, Tatiana
1960 "Historical Implications of a Pattern of Dates at Piedras Negras, Guatemala." *American Antiquity*, 25:454–475.
Puleston, David E.
1971 "An Experimental Approach to the Function of Maya Chultuns." *American Antiquity*, 36:322–335.

Radinsky, Leonard
1973 "*Aegyptopithecus* Endocasts: Oldest Record of a Pongid Brain." *American Journal of Physical Anthropology*, 39:239–248.
Rak, Y.
1983 *The Australopithecine Face*. New York: Academic Press.
Ransom, Timothy W.
1981 *Beach Troop of the Gombe*. Lewisburg: Bucknell University Press.
Rathje, William
1971 "The Origin and Development of Lowland Classic Maya Civilization." *American Antiquity*, 36(3):275–285.

——— 1979 "Modern Material Culture Studies." *Advances in Archaeological Method and Theory*, 2, pp. 1–37.
Rathje, William L. and Michael McCarthy
1977 "Regularity and Variability in Contemporary Garbage." *In*: *Research Strategies in Historic Archaeology*, Stanley South (ed.), New York: Academic Press, pp. 261–286.
Raza, S. Mahmoud, et al.
1983 "New Hominoid Primates from the Middle Miocene Chinji Formation, Potwar Plateau, Pakistan." *Nature*, 306:52–54.
Redman, Charles L.
1978 *The Rise of Civilization*. San Francisco: W. H. Freeman and Co.
Reed, Charles A. (Ed.)
1977 *Origins of Agriculture*. The Hague: Mouton Publishers.
Renfrew, Colin
1983 "The Social Archaeology of Megalithic Monuments." *Scientific American*, 249(5):152–163.
Repenning, Charles A. and Oldrich Fejfar
1982 "Evidence for Earlier Date of Ubeidya, Israel, Hominid Site." *Nature*, 299:344–347.
Richard, Alison F.
1985 *Primates in Nature*. New York: W. H. Freeman and Co.
Richard, A. F. and S. R. Schulman
1982 "Sociobiology: Primate Field Studies." *Annual Reviews of Anthropology*, 11:231–255.
Rightmire, G. P.
1976 "Relationships of Middle and Upper Pleistocene Hominids from Sub-Saharan Africa." *Nature*, 269:238–240.

1979 "Cranial Remains of *Homo erectus* from Beds II and IV, Olduvai Gorge, Tanzania." *American Journal of Physical Anthropology*, **51**:99–116.

1983 "Lake Ndutu Cranium and Early *Homo sapiens* in Africa." *American Journal of Physical Anthropology*, **61**:245–254.

1985 "The Tempo of Change in the Evolution of Mid-Pleistocene *Homo*." *In*: Delson (ed.), q.v., pp. 255–264.

Rindos, David
1984 *The Origins of Agriculture: An Evolutionary Perspective*. Orlando: Academic Press.

Robinson, J. T.
1953 "Telanthropus and Its Phylogenetic Significance." *American Journal of Physical Anthropology*, **11**:445–501.

1972 *Early Hominid Posture and Locomotion*. Chicago: University of Chicago Press.

Rodman, Peter S. and John G. H. Canat (eds.)
1984 *Adaptations for Foraging in Nonhuman Primates*. New York: Columbia University Press.

Romer, Alfred S.
1959 *The Vertebrate Story*. Chicago: University of Chicago Press.

Rose, M. D.
1983 "Miocene Hominoid Postcranial Morphology. Monkey-like, Ape-like, Neither, or Both?" *In*: R. Ciochon and R. Corruccini (eds.), q.v., pp. 405–417.

1984 "Food Acquisition and the Evolution of Positional Behaviour: The Case of Bipedalism." *In*: David J. Chivers, et al., q.v., pp. 509–524.

Rose, Noel R.
1981 "Autoimmune Diseases." *Scientific American*, **244**(2):80–103.

Rose, Steven
1972 "Environmental Effects on Brain and Behavior." *In*: *Race and Intelligence*, Ken Richardson and David Speers (eds.), Baltimore: Penguin Books, Inc., pp. 128–144.

Rovner, Irwin
1983 "Plant Opal Phytolith Analysis." *Advances in Archaeological Method and Theory*, **6**:225–266.

Rowell, Thelma E.
1972 *The Social Behaviour of Monkeys*. Baltimore: Penguin Books.

1984 "Introduction." *In*: Small, q.v., pp. 13–16.

Rowley-Conwy, Peter
1983 "Sedentary Hunters: The Ertebölle Example." *In*: *Hunter-Gatherer Economy in Prehistory; A European Perspective*, Geoff Bailey (ed.), Cambridge: Cambridge University Press, pp. 111–126.

Rudnai, Judith
1973 *The Social Life of Lions*. Wallingford, Pa.: Washington Square East.

Ruffle, John
1977 *The Egyptians*. Ithaca: Cornell University Press.

Rumbaugh, D. M.
1977 *Language Learning by a Chimpanzee: The Lana Project*. New York: Academic Press.

Rumbaugh, Duane M., E. Sue Savage-Rumbaugh and John L. Scanlon
1982 "The Relationship Between Language in Apes and Human Beings." *In*: James E. King and James L. Fobes (eds.), q.v., pp. 361–385.

Russell, Mary D.
1987 "Mortuary Practices at the Krapina Neandertal Site." *American Journal of Physical Anthropology*, **72**:381–397.

Sabloff, Jeremy A. and William L. Rathje
1975 "The Rise of a Maya Merchant Class." *Scientific American*, **233**(4):72–82.

Sanders, Richard J.
1986 "Teaching Apes to Ape Language: Explaining the Imitative and Nonimitative Signing of a Chimpanzee (*Pan troglodytes*)." *Journal of Comparative Psychology*, **99**(2):197–210.

Sanderson, Ivan T.
1969 "The Missing Link." *Argosy*, May, pp. 23–31.

Sarich, Vincent
1971 "A Molecular Approach to the Question of Human Origins." *In*: *Background for Man*, P. Dolhinow and V. Sarich (eds.), Boston: Little, Brown & Co., pp. 60–81.

Sarich, V. M. and A. C. Wilson
1967 "Rates of Albumen Evolution in Primates." *Proceedings, National Academy of Sciences*, **58**:142–148.

Sartono, S.
1975 "Implications Arising from *Pithecanthropus* VIII." *In*: *Paleoanthropology: Morphology and Paleoecology*, R. H. Tuttle (ed.), Chicago: Aldine Publishing Co., pp. 327–360.

Savage-Rumbaugh, E. Sue et al.
1983 "Can a Chimpanzee Make a Statement?" *The Journal of Experimental Psychology: General*, **112**(4):457–492.

Scarr, Sandra
1981 "The Effects of Family Background: A Study of Cognitive Differences among Black and White Twins." *In*: *Race, Social Class, and Individual Differences in I.Q.*, S. Scarr (ed.), Hillsdale, N.J.: Lawrence Erlbaum Associates, Inc., pp. **261–315.**

Scarr, Sandra and R. A. Weinberg
1976 "IQ Test Performances of Black Children Adopted by White Families." *In*: S. Scarr (ed.), q.v., pp. 109–159.

Schaller, George B.
1963 *The Mountain Gorilla*. Chicago: University of Chicago Press.

1972 *The Serengeti Lion*. Chicago: University of Chicago Press.

Scheidt, Walter
1924 "The Concept of Race in Anthropology and the Divisions into Human Races from Linnaeus to Deniker." *In*: *This Is Race*, E. W. Count (ed.), New York: Henry Schuman, pp. 354–391.

Schele, Linda, and Mary Miller
1986 *The Blood of Kings*. Austin: University of Texas Press.

Scheller, Richard H. and Richard Axel
1984 "How Genes Control Innate Behavior." *Scientific American*, **250**:54–63.

Schiffer, Michael B., Theodore E. Downing, and Michael McCarthy
1981 "Waste Not, Want Not: An Ethnoarchaeological Study of Reuse in Tucson, Arizona." *In*: *Modern Material Culture: The Archaeology of Us*, Richard A. Gould and Michael B. Schiffer (eds.), New York: Academic Press, pp. 67–86.

Schoenwetter, James
1974 "Pollen Records of Guila Naquitz Cave." *American Antiquity*, **39**(2):292–303.

Scopes, John T. and James Presley
1967 *Center of the Storm*. New York: Holt, Rinehart and Winston.

Sebeok, Thomas A.
1980 *Speaking of Apes*. New York: Plenum Press.

Senut, Brigette
1981   "Humeral Outlines in Some Hominoid Primates and in Plio-pleistocene Hominids." *American Journal of Physical Anthropology*, **56**:275–283.

Senut, Brigette and Christine Tardieu
1985   "Functional Aspects of Plio-Pleistocene Hominid Limb Bones: Implications for Taxonomy and Phylogeny." *In*: E. Delson (ed.), q.v., pp. 193–201.

Service, Elman R.
1966   *The Hunters*. Englewood Cliffs, N.J.: Prentice-Hall, Inc.

Seyfarth, Robert M., Dorothy L. Cheney and Peter Marler
1980a   "Monkey Responses to Three Different Alarm Calls." *Science*, **210**:801–803.

——   1980b   "Ververt Monkey Alarm Calls." *Animal Behavior*, **28**:1070–1094.

Shipman, P. L.
1983   "Early Hominid Lifestyle. Hunting and Gathering or Foraging and Scavenging?" Paper presented at 52nd Annual Meeting, American Association of Physical Anthropologists, Indianapolis, April, 1983.

——   1985   "The Ancestor That Wasn't." *The Sciences*, March/April:42–48.

——   1986   "Baffling Limb on the Family Tree." *Discover*, **7**:87–93.

——   1987   "An Age-Old Question: Why Did the Human Lineage Survive?" *Discover*, **8**:60–64.

Sibley, Charles and Jon E. Ahlquist
1984   "The Phylogeny of the Hominoid Primates as Indicated by DNA-DNA Hybridization." *Journal of Molecular Evolution*, **20**:2–15.

Simmons, Alan H.
1986   "New Evidence for the Use of Cultigens in the American Southwest." *American Antiquity*, **51**(1):73–89.

Simons, E. L.
1969   "The Origin and Radiation of the Primates." *Annals of the New York Academy of Sciences*, **167**:319–331.

——   1972   *Primate Evolution*. New York: Macmillan.

——   1985   "African Origin, Characteristics and Context of Earliest Higher Primates." *In*: *Hominid Evolution: Past, Present, and Future*. P. Tobias (ed.), New York: Alan R. Liss, pp. 101–106.

Simons, E. L. and P. C. Ettel
1970   "Gigantopithecus." *Scientific American*, **222**:76–85.

Simpson, G. G.
1945   "The Principles of Classification and a Classification of Mammals." *Bulletin of the American Museum of Natural History*, **85**:1–350.

——   1961   *Principles of Animal Taxonomy*. New York: Columbia University Press.

Simpson, G. G., C. S. Pittendright and L. H. Tiffany
1957   *Life*. New York: Harcourt, Brace and Co., Inc.

Singer, Charles
1959   *A Short History of Scientific Ideas to 1900*. London: Oxford University Press.

Singer, R. and Wymer, J. J.
1982   *The Middle Stone Age at Klasies River Mouth in South Africa*. Chicago: The University of Chicago Press.

Skelton, R. R., H. M. McHenry and G. M. Drawhorn
1986   "Phylogenetic Analysis of Early Hominids." *Current Anthropology*, **27**:1–43; **27**:361–365.

Small, Meredith F. (ed.)
1984   *Female Primates. Studies by Women Primatologists*. Monographs in Primatology, Volume 4. New York: Alan R. Liss.

Smith, Bruce D.
1985   "The Role of *Chenopodium* As a Domesticate in Pre-maize Garden Systems of the Eastern United States." *Southeastern Archaeology*, **4**:51–72.

Smith, B. Holly
1986   "Dental Development in *Australopithecus* and Early *Homo*." *Nature*, **323**:327–330.

Smith, Fred H.
1982   "Upper Pleistocene Hominid Evolution in South-Central Europe." *Current Anthropology*, **23**:667–703.

——   1984   "Fossil Hominids from the Upper Pleistocene of Central Europe and the Origin of Modern Europeans." *In*: Smith and Spencer, q.v., pp. 187–209.

Smith, Fred H. and Frank Spencer (eds.)
1984   *The Origins of Modern Humans*. New York: Alan R. Liss, Inc.

Smuts, Barbara
1985   *Sex and Friendship in Baboons*. Hawthorne, N.Y.: Aldine de Gruyter.

Snyder, Louis L.
1962   *The Idea of Racialism*. New York: Van Nostrand Reinhold Co.

Soffer, Olga
1985   *The Upper Paleolithic of the Central Russian Plain*. New York: Academic Press.

Solecki, Ralph
1971   *Shanidar, The First Flower People*. New York: Alfred A. Knopf.

Solheim II, Wilhelm G.
1972   "An Earlier Agricultural Revolution." *Scientific American*, **226**(4):10, 34–41.

Sonakia, Arun
1985a   "Skull Cap of an Early Man from the Narmada Valley Alluvium (Pleistocene) of Central India." *American Anthropologist*, **87**(3):612–616.

——   1985b   "Early *Homo* from Narmada Valley, India." *In*: E. Delson, (ed.), q.v., pp. 334–338.

Sondaar, Paul Y.
1984   "Faunal Evolution and the Mammalian Biostratigraphy of Java." *In*: Andrews and Franzen (eds.), q.v., pp. 219–235.

Sparks, Stephen and Haraldur Sigurdsson
1978   "The Big Blast at Santorini." *Natural History*, **87**(4):70–78.

Speth, J. D. and D. D. Davis
1976   "Seasonal Variability in Early Hominid Predation." *Science*, **192**:441–445.

Spuhler, James N.
1979   "Genetic Distances, Trees, and Maps of North American Indians." *In*: *The First Americans: Origins, Affinities, and Adaptations*, William S. Laughlin and A. B. Harper (eds.), New York: Gustav Fischer, pp. 135–183.

Stanyon, Roscoe and Brunetto Chiarelli
1982   "Phylogeny of the Hominoidea: The Chromosome Evidence." *Journal of Human Evolution*, **11**:493–504.

Stern, Curt
1973   *Principles of Human Genetics* (3rd Ed.). San Francisco: W. H. Freeman and Company.

Stern, Jack T. and Randall L. Susman

1983 "The Locomotor Anatomy of *Australopithecus afarensis.*" *American Journal of Physical Anthropology*, 60:279–317.

Stewart, T. D.
1979 *Essentials of Forensic Anthropology: Especially as Developed in the United States.* Springfield: C. C. Thomas.

Stocker, Terry, Sarah Meltzoff and Steve Armsey
1980 "Crocodilians and Olmecs: Further Interpretations in Formative Period Iconography." *American Antiquity*, 45(4):740–758.

Stocking, George W. Jr.
1968 *Race, Culture, and Evolution.* New York: The Free Press.

Stothert, Karen E.
1985 "The Preceramic Las Vegas Culture of Coastal Ecuador." *American Antiquity*, 50(3):613–637.

Streuver, Stuart
1964 "The Hopewell Interaction Sphere in Riverine-Western Great Lakes Culture History." *In: Hopewellian Studies*, Joseph Caldwell and Robert Hall (eds.), Springfield: Illinois State Museum Scientific Papers, 12:87–106.

Stringer, C. B. (ed.)
1981 *Aspects of Human Evolution.* London: Taylor & Francis Ltd. (Symposia of the Society for the Study of Human Biology, Vol. XXI).

———
1982 "Towards a Solution to the Neanderthal Problem." *Journal of Human Evolution*, 11(5):431–438.

———
1984 "Fate of Neandertal." *Natural History.* Vol. 93, 12:6–12.

———
1985 "Middle Pleistocene Hominid Variability and the Origin of Late Pleistocene Humans." *In:* Delson (ed.), q.v., pp. 289–295.

Stringer, Christopher B., F. Clark Howell and John K. Melentis
1979 "The Significance of the Fossil Hominid Skull from Petralona, Greece." *Journal of Archaeological Science*, 6:235–253.

Stringer, C. B., J. J. Hublin and B. Vandermeersch
1984 "The Origin of Anatomically Modern Humans in Western Europe." *In:* Smith and Spencer, q.v., pp. 51–135.

Stringer, C. B. and E. Trinkaus
1981 "The Shanidar Neanderthal Crania." *In: Aspects of Human Evolution*, C. B. Stringer (ed.), London: Taylor & Francis Ltd., pp. 129–165.

Struhsaker, Thomas T. and Lysa Leland
1979 "Socioecology of Five Sympatric Monkey Species in the Kibale Forest, Uganda." *Advances in the Study of Behavior*, Vol. 9. New York: Academic Press, pp. 159–229.

Struhsaker, Thomas T. and John F. Oates
1975 "Comparison of the Behavior and Ecology of Red Colobus and Black-and-White Colobus Monkeys in Uganda: A Summary." *In: Socioecology and Psychology of Primates*, R. H. Tuttle (ed.), Chicago: Aldine Publishing Co.

Strum, Shirley C.
1981 "Processes and Products of Change at Gilgil, Kenya." *In: Omnivorous Primates*, R.S.O. Harding and Geza Teleki (eds.), New York: Columbia University Press.

———
1983 "Baboon Cues for Eating Meat." *Journal of Human Evolution*, 12:327–336.

———
1987 "The 'Gang' Moves to a Strange New Land." *National Geographic* (Nov.):pp. 677–690.

Sugiyama, Yukimaru and Jeremy Koman
1979 "Tool-Using and -Making Behavior in Wild Chimpanzees at Bossou, Guinea." *Primates*, 20:513–524.

Sumner, D. R., M. E. Morbeck and J. Lobick
1987 "Age-Related Bone Loss in Female Gombe Chimpanzees." *American Journal of Physical Anthropology*, 72:259.

Suomi, Stephen J., Susan Mineka and Roberta D. DeLizio
1983 "Short- and Long-Term Effects of Repetitive Mother-Infant Separation on Social Development in Rhesus Monkeys." *Developmental Psychology*, 19(5):710–786.

Susman, Randall L., Jack T. Stern and William L. Jungers
1985 "Locomotor Adaptations in the Hadar Hominids." *In:* E. Delson (ed.), q.v., pp. 184–192.

Suzman, I. M.
1982 "A Comparative Study of the Hadar and Sterkfontein Australopithecine Innominates." *American Journal of Physical Anthropology*, 57:235.

Szalay, Frederick S.
1968 "The Beginnings of Primates." *Evolution*, 22:19–36.

Szalay, Frederick S. and Eric Delson
1979 *Evolutionary History of the Primates.* New York: Academic Press.

Tanner, J. M.
1977 "Human Growth and Constitution." *In: Human Biology*, G. A. Harrison, et al. (eds.), New York: Oxford University Press, pp. 299–385.

Tanner, Nancy M.
1981 *On Becoming Human.* New York: Cambridge University Press.

Tattersall, Ian
1986 "Species Recognition in Human Paleontology." *Journal of Human Evolution*," 15(3):165–175.

Tattersall, Ian and Niles Eldredge
1977 "Fact, Theory and Fantasy in Human Paleontology." *American Scientist*, 65:204–211.

Tauxe, Lisa
1979 "A New Date for *Ramapithecus.*" *Nature*, 282:399–401.

Teleki, G.
1973 *The Predatory Behavior of Wild Chimpanzees.* Cranbrook, N.J.: Bucknell University Press.

———
1986 "Chimpanzee Conservation in Sierra Leone—A Case Study of a Continent-wide Problem." Paper presented at "Understanding Chimpanzees" Symposium, Chicago Academy of Sciences, Chicago, Nov. 7–10, 1987.

Terrace, Herbert S.
1979 *Nim.* New York: Alfred A. Knopf.

———
1982 "Why Koko Can't Talk." *The Sciences*, 22(9):8–10, Columbia University.

———
1983 "Apes Who 'Talk': Language or Projection of Language by Their Teachers" *In:* deLuce and Wilder, q.v., pp. 19–42.

Thomsen, Dietrick E.
1978 "Radioisotope Dating with Accelerators." *Science News*, 113:29–30, January 14.

Thorne, A. and P. Macumber
1971 "Discoveries of Late Pleistocene Man at Kow Swamp, Australia." *Nature*, 238:316–319.

Thouveny, N. and E. Bonifay
1984   "New Chronological Data on European Plio-Pleistocene Faunas and Hominid Occupation Sites." *Nature,* 308:355–358.

Tiger, Lionel and Robin Fox
1971   *The Imperial Animal.* New York: Holt, Rinehart and Winston.

Tobias, Phillip
1967   *Olduvai Gorge* (Vol. 2). *The Cranial and Maxillary Dentition of Australopithecus (Zinjanthropus) boisei.* Cambridge: Cambridge University Press.

——   1971   *The Brain in Hominid Evolution.* New York: Columbia University Press.

——   1972   "Early Man in Sub-Saharan Africa." *In: The Functional and Evolutionary Biology of the Primates,* R. Tuttle (ed.), Chicago: Aldine-Atherton, pp. 63–93.

——   1976   "African Hominids: Dating and Phylogeny." *In:* G. L. Isaac and E. R. McCown (eds.), q.v., pp. 377–422.

——   1980   "*Australopithecus afarensis* and *A. africanus.* Critique and an Alternative Hypothesis." *Palaeontologica Africana,* 23:1–17.

——   1983a   "Hominid Evolution in Africa." *Canadian Journal of Anthropology,* 3:163–185.

——   1983b   "Recent Advances in the Evolution of the Hominids with Especial Reference to Brain and Speech." Pontifical Academy of Sciences, *Scrita Varia,* 50:85–140.

Tobias, P. V. and G.H.R. von Koenigswald
1964   "A Comparison between the Olduvai Hominines and Those of Java and Some Implications for Hominid Phylogeny." *Nature,* 204:515–518.

Todd, T. W.
1920–21   "Age Changes in the Pubic Bone," *American Journal of Physical Anthropology,* 3:285–334; 4:1–70.

Tomkins, Jerry R. (ed.)
1965   *D-Days at Dayton.* Baton Rouge: Louisiana State University Press.

Trigg, Roger
1982   *The Shaping of Man. Philosophical Aspects of Sociobiology.* New York: Shocken Books.

Trigger, Bruce G., Barry J. Kemp, David O'Connor, and Alan B. Lloyd
1983   *Ancient Egypt: A Social History.* Cambridge: Cambridge University Press.

Tringham, Ruth
1971   *Hunters, Fishers, and Farmers of Eastern Europe, 6000–3000 B.C.* London: Hutchinson University Library.

Trinkaus, Eric
1982   "The Shanidar 3 Neandertal." *American Journal of Physical Anthropology,* 57:37–60.

——   1983   *The Shanidar Neandertals.* New York: Academic Press.

——   1984a   "Neandertal Pubic Morphology and Gestation Length." *Current Anthropology,* 25(4):509–514.

——   1984b   "Western Asia." *In:* Smith and Spencer, q.v., pp. 251–293.

Trinkaus, E. and W. W. Howells
1979   "The Neandertals." *Scientific American,* 241(6):118–133.

Trinkaus, Eric and Marjorie LeMay
1982   "Occipital Bunning Among Later Pleistocene Hominids." *American Journal of Physical Anthropology,* 57:27–35.

Trinkaus, Eric and Fred H. Smith
1985   "The Fate of the Neandertals." *In:* Delson, q.v., pp. 325–333.

Trinkaus, Eric and David D. Thompson
1987   "Femoral Diaphyseal Histomorphometric Age Determinations for the Shanidar 3, 4, 5, and 6 Neandertals and Neandertal Longevity." *American Journal of Physical Anthropology,* 72:123–129.

Trinkaus, Eric and M. R. Zimmerman
1982   "Trauma Among the Shanidar Neandertals." *Ibid,* pp. 61–76.

Trivers, R. L.
1971   "The Evolution of Reciprocal Altruism." *Quarterly Review of Biology,* 46:35–57.

——   1972   "Parental Investment and Sexual Selection." *In: Sexual Selection and the Descent of Man,* B. Campbell (ed.), Chicago: Aldine, pp. 136–179.

Turner, C.
1975   "The Correlation and Duration of Middle Pleistocene Interglacial Periods in Northwest Europe." *In:* K. W. Butzer and G. L. Isaac (eds.), q.v., pp. 259–308.

Turner, Christy G., II
1984   "Advances in the Dental Search for Native American Origins." *Acta Anthropogenetica,* 8:23–78.

——   1987   "Telltale Teeth." *Natural History,* 96(1):6–10.

Tuttle, Russell H.
1985   "Ape Footprints and Laetoli Impressions: A Response to the SUNY Claims." *In:* P. Tobias (ed.), q.v., pp. 129–133.

Ucko, Peter J. and G. W. Dimbleby (Eds.)
1969   *The Domestication and Exploitation of Plants and Animals.* Chicago: Aldine.

Van Couvering, A. H. and J. A. Van Couvering
1976   "Early Miocene Mammal Fossils From East Africa." *In: Human Origins,* G. Isaac and E. R. McCown (eds.), Menlo Park, Ca.: W. A. Benjamin, pp. 155–207.

Vandermeersch, B.
1981   "A Neandertal Skeleton from a Chatelperronian Level at St. Cesaire (France)." *American Journal of Physical Anthropology,* 54:286.

——   1985   "The Origin of the Neandertals." *In:* Delson, q.v., pp. 306–309.

Van Lawick, Hugo and Jane van Lawick-Goodall
1970   *Innocent Killers.* Boston: Houghton Mifflin.

Van Lawick-Goodall, Jane
1971   *In the Shadow of Man.* Boston: Houghton Mifflin Co.

Van Valen, L. and R. E. Sloan
1965   "The Earliest Primates." *Science,* 150:743–745.

Vaughan, Patrick C.
1985   *Use-Wear Analysis of Flaked Stone Tools.* Tucson: University of Arizona Press.

Villa, Paola
1983   *Terra Amata and the Middle Pleistocene Archaeological Record of*

Southern France. University of California Publications in Anthropology, Vol. 13. Berkeley: University of California Press.

Vleck, F.
1978 "New Discovery of *Homo erectus* in Central Europe." *Journal of Human Evolution,* **7**:239–252.

Vogel, F., M. Kopun and R. Rathenberg
1976 "Mutation and Molecular Evolution." *In: Molecular Anthropology,* M. Goodman, et al. (eds.), New York: Plenum Press, pp. 13–33.

Von Koenigswald, G.H.R.
1956 *Meeting Prehistoric Man.* New York: Harper & Brothers.

Vrba, E. S.
1985 "Ecological and Adaptive Changes Associated with Early Hominid Evolution." *In:* E. Delson (ed.), q.v., pp. 63–71.

Walker, A.
1976 "Remains Attributable to *Australopithecus* from East Rudolf." *In: Earliest Man and Environments in the Lake Rudolf Basin,* Y. Coppens, et al. (eds.), Chicago: University of Chicago Press, pp. 484–489.

——— 1981 Presentation of New Miocene Hominoid Material from East Africa. Annual Meeting, American Association of Physical Anthropologists, April, 1981.

Walker, Alan, Dean Falk, Richard Smith and M. Pickford
1983 "The Skull of *Proconsul africanus:* Reconstruction and Cranial Capacity." *Nature,* **305**:525–527.

Walker, Alan and Richard E. F. Leakey
1978 "The Hominids of East Turkana." *Scientific American,* **239**:54–66.

Walker, A., R. E. Leakey, J. M. Harris and F. H. Brown
1986 "2.5 Myr *Australopithecus boisei* from West of Lake Turkana, Kenya." *Nature,* **322**:517–522.

Walker, A. C. and M. Pickford
1983 "New Postcranial Fossils of *Proconsul africanus* and *Proconsul nyanzae.*" *In:* R. Ciochon and R. Corruccini (eds.), q.v., pp. 325–351.

Walker, A., D. Pilbeam, and M. Cartmill
1981 "Changing Views and Interpretations of Primate Evolution." Paper presented to the Annual Meetings, American Association of Physical Anthropologists, April, 1981.

Ward, Steven and William H. Kimbel
1983 "Subnasal Alveolar Morphology and the Systematic Position of *Sivapithecus.*" *American Journal of Physical Anthropology,* **61**:157–171.

Ward, S. C. and D. R. Pilbeam
1983 "Maxillofacial Morphology of Miocene Hominoids From Africa and Indo-Pakistan." *In:* R. Ciochon and R. Corruccini (eds.), q.v., pp. 211–238.

Warren, Peter
1975 *The Aegean Civilizations.* Oxford: Elsevier/Phaidon.

Washburn, S. L.
1963 "The Study of Race." *American Anthropologist,* **65**:521–531.

Watson, J. B.
1924 *Behaviorism.* New York: W. W. Norton.

Watson, James D.
1968 *The Double Helix.* New York: Atheneum.

Weaver, Muriel Porter
1981 *The Aztecs, Maya, and Their Predecessors.* (Second edition.) New York: Academic Press.

Webb, William S.
1946 "The Indian Knoll, Site Oh 2, Ohio County, Kentucky." *University of Kentucky Reports in Anthropology and Archaeology,* **4**:111–365.

Weidenreich, Franz
1946 *Apes, Giants, and Man.* Chicago: University of Chicago Press.

——— 1951 "Morphology of Solo Man." *Anthropological Papers of the American Museum of Natural History,* Vol. 43, No. 3.

Weiner, J. S.
1955 *The Piltdown Forgery.* London: Oxford University Press.

Weiner, J. S. and B. G. Campbell
1964 "The Taxonomic Status of the Swanscombe Skull." *In: Royal Anthropological Institute of Great Britain and Ireland,* Occ. Paper 20, D. Ovey (ed.), pp. 175–215.

Weiss, Mark L. and Alan E. Mann
1981 *Human Biology and Behavior* (3rd Ed.). Boston: Little, Brown, and Co.

Wendt, Herbert
1963 *In Search of Adam.* New York: Collier Books.

Wenke, Robert J.
1984 *Patterns in Prehistory* (2nd Ed.). New York: Oxford University Press.

Wheat, Joe Ben
1972 "The Olsen-Chubbuck Site: A Paleo-Indian Bison Kill." Memoirs of the Society for American Archaeology, **26**.

Wheeler, Mortimer
1968 *The Indus Civilization* (3rd Ed.). Cambridge: Cambridge University Press.

White, Randall
1982a "Rethinking the Middle/Upper Paleolithic Transition." *Current Anthropology,* **23**:169–192.

——— 1982b "On the Middle/Upper Paleolithic Transition: A Response to Mellars." *Current Anthropology,* **23**:358–359.

White, T. D.
1980 "Evolutionary Implications of Pliocene Hominid Footprints." *Science,* **208**:175–176.

——— 1983 Comment Made at Institute of Human Origins Conference on the Evolution of Human Locomotion (Berkeley, Ca.).

——— 1986a "*Australopithecus afarensis* and the Lothagam Mandible." *Anthropos,* **23**:79–90.

——— 1986b "Cut Marks on the Bodo Cranium: A Case of Prehistoric Defleshing." *American Journal of Physical Anthropology,* **69**(4):503–509.

White, T. D. and J. M. Harris
1977 "Suid Evolution and Correlation of African Hominid Localities." *Science,* **198**:13–21.

White, T. D., D. C. Johanson and W. H. Kimbel
1981 "*Australopithecus Africanus:* Its Phyletic Position Reconsidered." *South African Journal of Science,* **77**:445–470.

Whyte, Robert Orr (ed.)
1984 *The Evolution of the East Asian Environment.* Centre of Asian Studies Occasional Papers and Monographs, No. 59. Hong Kong: Centre of Asian Studies, University of Hong Kong.

Willerman, L., A. F. Naylor, and N. C. Myrianthopoulos
1970 "Intellectual Development of Children from Interracial Matings." *Science,* **170**:1329–1331.

Williams, G. C.
1966 *Adaptation and Natural Selection: A Critique of Some Current Evolutionary Thought.* Princeton: Princeton University Press.

Wills, W. H.
1988   *Early Prehistoric Agriculture in the American Southwest.* Santa Fe: School of American Research Press.

Wilson, E. O.
1975   *Sociobiology, The New Synthesis.* Cambridge: Harvard University Press.

Wolbarsht, M. L.
1975   "Letter to the editor." *Science,* **187**:600.

Wolpoff, Milford H.
1980a   *Paleoanthropology.* New York: Alfred A. Knopf.

———
1980b   "Cranial Remains of Middle Pleistocene European Hominids." *Journal of Human Evolution,* **9**:339–358.

———
1983a   "*Ramapithecus* and Human Origins. An Anthropologist's Perspective of Changing Interpretations." *In:* R. Ciochon and R. Corruccini (eds.), q.v., pp. 651–676.

———
1983b   "Lucy's Little Legs." *Journal of Human Evolution,* **12**:443–453.

Wolpoff, Milford H. et al.
1981   "Upper Pleistocene Human Remains from Vindija Cave, Croatia, Yugoslavia." *American Journal of Physical Anthropology,* **54**:499–545.

Wolpoff, Milford, Wu Xin Chi, and Alan G. Thorne
1984   "Modern *Homo sapiens* Origins." *In:* Smith and Spencer (eds.), q.v., pp. 411–483.

Wood, B.
1976   "Remains Attributable to *Homo* in the East Rudolf Succession." *In: Earliest Man and Environments in the Lake Rudolf Basin,* Y. Coppens et al. (eds.), Chicago: University of Chicago Press, pp. 490–506.

Wood, Bernard
1985   "Early *Homo* in Kenya, and its Systematic Relationships." *In:* E. Delson (ed.), q.v., pp. 206–214.

Wrangham, Richard
1980   "An Ecological Model of Female-Bonded Primate Groups." *Behavior,* **75**:262–300.

Wu, Rukang
1981   "Where Did Humankind Originate?" *China Pictoral,* No. 7, pp. 16–18.

———
1982   "Paleoanthropology in China, 1949–79." *Current Anthropology,* **23**:473–477.

Wu, Rukang and S. Lin
1983   "Peking Man." *Scientific American,* **248**(6):86–94.

Wu, Rukang and John W. Olsen (eds.)
1985   *Palaeoanthropology and Palaeolithic Archaeology in the People's Republic of China.* New York: Academic Press, Inc.

Wu, Rukang and C. E. Oxnard
1983   "Ramapithecines from China: Evidence from Tooth Dimensions." *Nature,* **306**:258–260.

Wu, Rukang and Xingren Dong
1985   "*Homo erectus* in China. *In:* Wu and Olsen, q.v., pp. 79–89.

Yellen, John E.
1977   *Archaeological Approaches to the Present.* New York: Academic Press.

Yudkin, J.
1969   "Archaeology and the Nutritionist." *In:* Peter J. Ucko and G. W. Dimbleby (eds.), q.v., pp. 547–554.

Yunis, Jorge J. and Om Prakesh
1982   "The Origin of Man: A Chromosomal Pictorial Legacy." *Science,* **215**:1525–1530.

Zevallos, Carlos, et al.
1977   "The San Pablo Corn Kernel and Its Friends." *Science,* **196**(4288):385–389.

Zihlman, Adrienne L.
1985   "*Australopithecus afarensis*: Two Sexes or Two Species?" *In:* P. Tobias (ed.), q.v., pp. 213–220.

Zvelebil, M.
1986   "Postglacial Foraging in the Forests of Europe." *Scientific American,* **254**:104–115.

Index

1 semester ACCESS CODE for

NATIONAL GEOGRAPHIC LEARNING | WADSWORTH CENGAGE Learning

Includes access to the eBook for National Geographic Learning Reader *Green*

This access code is valid for **6 months** from the date of registration. You will only enter it once to register. After that, you will log in to the eBook with the username and password that you created during the registration process.

Access Code

PP40WCDP5Q0P3W

ISBN-13: 978-1-133-94179-8
ISBN-10: 1-133-94179-6

9 0 0 0 0

9 781133 941798